Houghton Mifflin
California
Math

 HOUGHTON MIFFLIN

BOSTON

ISBN-13: 978-0-618-82741-1

ISBN-10: 0-618-82741-2

3 4 5 6 7 8 9 - VH - 15 14 13 12 11 10 09 08

Houghton Mifflin
California Math

Authors & Consultants

Authors

Renee Hill
Mathematics Specialist
Riverside Unified School District
Riverside, CA

Matt Larson
Curriculum Specialist for
Mathematics
Lincoln Public Schools
Lincoln, NE

Miriam A. Leiva
Bonnie E. Cone Distinguished
Professor Emerita
Professor of Mathematics Emerita
University of North Carolina
Charlotte, NC

Jean M. Shaw
Professor Emerita of Curriculum
and Instruction
University of Mississippi
Oxford, MS

Dr. Lee Stiff
Professor of Mathematics
Education
North Carolina State University
Raleigh, NC

Dr. Bruce Vogeli
Clifford Brewster Upton Professor
of Mathematics
Teachers College, Columbia
University
New York, NY

Consultants

Mental Math Strategies

Greg Tang
Author and Mathematics
Consultant
Belmont, MA

English Learners

Dr. Russell M. Gersten
Executive Director, Institutional
Research Group & Professor
Emeritus
College of Education, University of
Oregon
Long Beach, CA

Lisette Estrella-Henderson
Director of District and School
Support
Solano County Office of Education
Fairfield, CA

Language and Vocabulary

Dr. Shane Templeton
Foundation Professor, Department
of Educational Specialties
University of Nevada at Reno
Reno, NV

Strategic Consultant

Dr. Liping Ma
Senior Scholar
Carnegie Foundation for the
Advancement of Technology
Palo Alto, CA

Special Projects

Catherine Valentino
Author-in-Residence
Houghton Mifflin
West Kingston, RI

Content Reviewers

Dr. W. Stephen Wilson
(Grades K–2)
Professor of Mathematics
Johns Hopkins University
Baltimore, MD

Dr. Kurt Kreith
(Grades 3–4)
Emeritus Professor of Mathematics
University of California at Davis
Davis, CA

Dr. Solomon Friedberg
(Grade 5)
Professor of Mathematics
Boston College
Chestnut Hill, MA

Dr. Bert Fristedt
(Grade 6)
Professor of Mathematics
University of Minnesota
Minneapolis, MN

California Reviewers

Grade K

Cynthia Dominguez
Highlands Elementary School
Saugus, CA

Dana Hight
Royal Oaks Elementary School
Visalia, CA

Patricia Mahoney
John Adams Elementary School
Madera, CA

Teresa Rogers
Skyline North Elementary
School
Barstow, CA

Schelly Solko
Roy W. Loudon Elementary
School
Bakersfield, CA

Julie Towne
Jurupa Vista Elementary School
Fontana, CA

Grade 1

Kirsten Marsh
Edgemont Elementary School
Moreno Valley, CA

Jill McCarthy
Edgemont Elementary
School
Moreno Valley, CA

Brandee Ramirez
Myford Elementary
School
Tustin, CA

Rebecca Solares
Cerritos Elementary School
Glendale, CA

Leanne Thomas
Scott Lane Elementary School
Santa Clara, CA

Sheila Vann
Folsom Hills Elementary School
Folsom, CA

Grade 2

Deborah Nelson
North Park Elementary School
Valencia, CA

Kathryn Smith
Quail Run Elementary School
San Ramon, CA

Angelica Yates
Allen at Steinbeck
Elementary School
San José, CA

Grade 3

Pamela Aurangzeb
Grapeland Elementary School
Etiwanda, CA

Veronica Fowler
Challenger School of Sports &
Fitness
Victorville, CA

Nancy Hayes
Toro Park School
Salinas, CA

Megan Heavens
North Park Elementary School
Valencia, CA

Caryl Lyons
Manuel L. Real Elementary
School
Perris, CA

Stacey McKay
Glenn E. Murdock Elementary
School
La Mesa, CA

Peggy Morrill
Grapeland Elementary School
Etiwanda, CA

Kristine Salomonson
Freedom Elementary School
Clovis, CA

Susan Steubing
Folsom Hills Elementary School
Folsom, CA

The reviewers work with the authors, consultants, and publisher to be sure that problems are correct, instructions work, and this book is the best it can be.

California Reviewers

Grade 4

Cheryl Robertson
McPherson Magnet School
Orange, CA

JoAnna Trafecanty
North Park Elementary School
Valencia, CA

Grade 5

Karen Clarke
Manuel L. Real Elementary
School
Perris, CA

Bonita DeAmicis
Highlands Elementary School
Saugus, CA

Gretchen Oberg
Ralph Dailard Elementary
School
San Diego, CA

Grade 6

Judy Denenny
McPherson Magnet School
Orange, CA

Terri Parker
Leo B. Hart Elementary School
Bakersfield, CA

George Ratcliff
Joseph Casillas Elementary
School
Chula Vista, CA

Patricia Wenzel
Cloverly Elementary School
Temple City, CA

These reviewers are math teachers, principals, and other people who are really committed to helping kids learn math.

California Reviewers

Across Grade

Gina Chavez
California State University, Los Angeles
Los Angeles, CA

Catherine De Leon
Washington Elementary School
Madera, CA

Cindy Ellis
Madera Unified School District
Madera, CA

Jenny Maguire
Orinda Union School District
Orinda, CA

Ernest Minelli
Selby Lane School
Redwood City, CA

Barbara Page
Modesto City Schools
Modesto, CA

Ian Tablit
Delano Union Elementary School District
Delano, CA

Jeannie Tavolazzi
Grapeland Elementary School
Etiwanda, CA

Dina Tews
John J. Pershing Elementary School
Madera, CA

California Mathematics
Content Standards

What are Key Standards?

- The California math standards are goals for what you will learn in math this year.

- The standards have five strands: Number Sense; Algebra and Functions; Measurement and Geometry; Statistics, Data Analysis, and Probability; Mathematical Reasoning.

- The symbol ⬭ means a standard is a KEY to success this year.

- Knowing and understanding the content standards means you can do well on tests.

How will this book help you succeed?
It's easy as one, two, three.

Doing well feels terrific!

① Look for **Key Standards** in this book.

② Do your best work. Ask questions.

③ Use the Key Standards Handbook on pages KSHI–KSH34.

Number Sense

	Standards You Will Learn	Some Places to Look
1.0	Students compute with very large and very small numbers, positive integers, decimals, and fractions and understand the relationship between decimals, fractions, and percents. They understand the relative magnitudes of numbers:	Lessons 3.1, 3.2, 3.3, 3.4, 4.5, 8.2, 8.3, 9.2, 9.3, 9.4, 10.4, 11.1, 12.1, 12.3, 13.2, 13.4, 13.5, 13.6, 14.1, 14.2, 14.4, 14.5, 15.1, 17.5, 18.4, 21.5, 23.1, 23.2, 23.3, 24.1, 24.3 Unit 2 Reading and Writing Math
1.1	Estimate, round, and manipulate very large (e.g., millions) and very small (e.g., thousandths) numbers.	Lessons 3.1, 3.2, 3.5, 3.6, 12.2, 12.3, 13.3, 13.6
KEY 1.2	Interpret percents as a part of a hundred; find decimal and percent equivalents for common fractions and explain why they represent the same value; compute a given percent of a whole number.	Lessons 23.1, 23.2, 23.3, 23.4, 23.5, 24.1, 24.2, 24.3, 24.4, 25.5, 27.5 Key Standards Handbook, pp. KSH2–KSH3; Chapters 23, 24 Challenge; Chapter 26 Key Standards Review
1.3	Understand and compute positive integer powers of nonnegative integers; compute examples as repeated multiplication.	Lessons 1.4, 1.5, 3.2, 4.5, 5.2, 5.3, 20.3, 20.4, 22.3, 22.4, 22.5
KEY 1.4	Determine the prime factors of all numbers through 50 and write the numbers as the product of their prime factors by using exponents to show multiples of a factor (e.g., $24 = 2 \times 2 \times 2 \times 3 = 2^3 \times 3$).	Lessons 1.1, 1.2, 1.3, 1.4, 1.5, 1.6, 10.2 Key Standards Handbook, pp. KSH4–KSH5; Chapters 2, 3, 4, 5, 9, 11 Key Standards Review
KEY 1.5	Identify and represent on a number line decimals, fractions, mixed numbers, and positive and negative integers.	Lessons 2.1, 2.2, 2.3, 2.4, 3.4, 4.1, 4.2, 4.3, 4.4, 4.5, 8.4, 23.3, 25.1, 25.2, 25.4, 25.5, 26.2, 26.4 Key Standards Handbook, pp. KSH6–KSH7; Chapters 3, 4, 5, 6, 7, 10, 11, 12, 27 Key Standards Review; Unit 11 Reading and Writing Math; Chapter 26 Challenge
2.0	Students perform calculations and solve problems involving addition, subtraction, and simple multiplication and division of fractions and decimals:	Lessons 7.1, 7.2, 7.3, 7.4, 9.1, 9.2, 9.3, 9.4, 10.2, 11.1, 11.2, 11.3, 13.1, 13.2, 13.3, 13.4, 13.5, 13.6, 14.1 Unit 4 Reading and Writing Math
KEY 2.1	Add, subtract, multiply, and divide with decimals; add with negative integers; subtract positive integers from negative integers; and verify the reasonableness of the results.	Lessons 12.1, 12.2, 12.3, 12.4, 13.1, 13.2, 13.4, 13.5, 14.1, 14.2, 14.4, 14.5, 14.6, 15.4, 18.4, 20.3, 21.5, 23.4, 23.5, 24.1, 25.3, 25.4, 25.5, 26.1, 26.3, 27.5 Key Standards Handbook, pp. KSH8–KSH9; Unit 6 Reading and Writing Math; Chapters 13, 14, 15, 18 Key Standards Review
KEY 2.2	Demonstrate proficiency with division, including division with positive decimals and long division with multidigit divisors.	Lessons 14.1, 14.2, 14.3, 14.4, 14.5, 14.6, 15.1, 15.2, 15.3, 15.4, 15.5, 15.6, 16.2 Key Standards Handbook, pp. KSH10–KSH11; Chapters 17, 19 Key Standards Review

Number Sense (continued)

	Standards You Will Learn	Some Places to Look
KEY 2.3	Solve simple problems, including ones arising in concrete situations, involving the addition and subtraction of fractions and mixed numbers (like and unlike denominators of 20 or less), and express answers in the simplest form.	Lessons 7.1, 7.2, 7.3, 7.4, 7.5, 8.1, 8.2, 8.3, 8.4, 9.1, 9.2, 9.3, 9.4, 9.5, 20.4 Key Standards Handbook, pp. KSH12–KSH13; Chapter 7 Challenge; Chapters 8, 9, 10, 13, 14, 18 Key Standards Review
2.4	Understand the concept of multiplication and division of fractions.	Lessons 10.1, 10.2, 10.3, 11.1, 11.2, 11.3, 11.4, 14.4, 14.5, 21.5, 23.4, 24.3
2.5	Compute and perform simple multiplication and division of fractions and apply these procedures to solving problems.	Lessons 10.2, 10.3, 11.1, 11.2, 11.3, 11.4, 11.5, 14.4, 14.5, 20.4, 24.3

Algebra and Functions

	Standards You Will Learn	Some Places to Look
1.0	Students use variables in simple expressions, compute the value of the expression for specific values of the variable, and plot and interpret the results:	Lessons 5.3, 5.5, 9.5, 13.2, 17.3, 17.4, 20.3, 26.3, 27.3, 27.4, 28.1, 28.2, 28.3
1.1	Use information taken from a graph or equation to answer questions about a problem situation.	Lessons 1.2, 5.5, 16.3, 16.4, 16.5, 17.1, 17.2, 17.4, 23.5, 27.2, 28.2, 28.5 Unit 7 Reading and Writing Math
KEY 1.2	Use a letter to represent an unknown number; write and evaluate simple algebraic expressions in one variable by substitution.	Lessons 5.3, 5.4, 5.6, 6.5, 8.3, 9.5, 17.3, 22.5, 23.5, 26.3, 28.2, 28.3 Key Standards Handbook, pp. KSH14–KSH15; Chapter 5 Challenge; Chapters 6, 8, 12, 15, 19, 22, 24 Key Standards Review
1.3	Know and use the distributive property in equations and expressions with variables.	Lessons 6.1, 6.2, 6.5, 13.4
KEY 1.4	Identify and graph ordered pairs in the four quadrants of the coordinate plane.	Lessons 17.3, 17.4, 27.1, 27.2, 27.5, 28.1, 28.3, 28.4, 28.5 Key Standards Handbook, pp. KSH16–KSH17; Chapters 27, 28 Challenge
KEY 1.5	Solve problems involving linear functions with integer values; write the equation; and graph the resulting ordered pairs of integers on a grid.	Lessons 5.5, 11.2, 17.3, 17.4, 27.3, 27.4, 28.1, 28.3, 28.4, 28.5 Key Standards Handbook, pp. KSH18–KSH19; Chapter 28 Challenge

Measurement and Geometry

	Standards You Will Learn	Some Places to Look
1.0	Students understand and compute the volumes and areas of simple objects:	Lessons 20.3, 20.4, 21.1, 21.2, 21.3, 21.4, 22.3, 22.4, 23.4 Unit 9 Reading and Writing Math; Chapter 21 Challenge
KEY 1.1	Derive and use the formula for the area of a triangle and of a parallelogram by comparing each with the formula for the area of a rectangle (i.e., two of the same triangles make a parallelogram with twice the area; a parallelogram is compared with a rectangle of the same area by pasting and cutting a right triangle on the parallelogram).	Lessons 21.1, 21.2, 21.3, 21.4, 21.5 Key Standards Handbook, pp. KSH20–KSH21; Chapter 21 Challenge; Chapters 22, 24 Key Standards Review
KEY 1.2	Construct a cube and rectangular box from two-dimensional patterns and use these patterns to compute the surface area for these objects.	Lessons 22.1, 22.3, 22.5 Key Standards Handbook, pp. KSH22–KSH23; Chapter 25 Key Standards Review
KEY 1.3	Understand the concept of volume and use the appropriate units in common measuring systems (i.e., cubic centimeter [cm^3], cubic meter [m^3], cubic inch [$in.^3$], cubic yard [$yd.^3$]) to compute the volume of rectangular solids.	Lessons 22.4, 22.5 Key Standards Handbook, pp. KSH24–KSH25; Chapter 26 Key Standards Review
1.4	Differentiate between, and use appropriate units of measures for, two- and three-dimensional objects (i.e., find the perimeter, area, volume).	Lessons 20.3, 20.4, 21.1, 21.2, 21.3, 22.4, 22.5, 21.4
2.0	Students identify, describe, and classify the properties of, and the relationships between, plane and solid geometric figures:	Lessons 18.1, 18.2, 18.3, 19.1, 19.2, 19.3, 19.4, 19.5, 20.1, 20.2, 22.1, 22.2, 27.5
KEY 2.1	Measure, identify, and draw angles, perpendicular and parallel lines, rectangles, and triangles by using appropriate tools (e.g., straightedge, ruler, compass, protractor, drawing software).	Lessons 18.1, 18.2, 18.3, 18.4, 19.1, 19.2, 19.3, 19.4, 19.5, 20.1, 20.2, 24.1, 24.4 Key Standards Handbook, pp. KSH26–KSH27; Chapters 20, 23 Key Standards Review
KEY 2.2	Know that the sum of the angles of any triangle is 180° and the sum of the angles of any quadrilateral is 360° and use this information to solve problems.	Lessons 19.1, 19.2, 19.3, 19.5 Key Standards Handbook, pp. KSH28–KSH29; Chapter 19 Challenge; Chapter 21 Key Standards Review
2.3	Visualize and draw two-dimensional views of three-dimensional objects made from rectangular solids.	Lessons 20.2, 22.1, 22.2 Chapter 22 Challenge

Statistics, Data Analysis, and Probability

	Standards You Will Learn	Some Places to Look
1.0	Students display, analyze, compare, and interpret different data sets, including data sets of different sizes:	Lessons 1.2, 2.5, 10.4, 16.2, 16.3, 24.1, 24.2, 28.5 Chapters 16, 17 Challenge
1.1	Know the concepts of mean, median, and mode; compute and compare simple examples to show that they may differ.	Lessons 16.1, 16.2, 16.5, 17.5 Chapter 16 Vocabulary
1.2	Organize and display single-variable data in appropriate graphs and representations (e.g., histogram, circle graphs) and explain which types of graphs are appropriate for various data sets.	Lessons 16.4, 16.5, 16.6, 24.1, 24.4
1.3	Use fractions and percentages to compare data sets of different sizes.	Lessons 2.5, 24.2 Chapter 24 Challenge
KEY 1.4	Identify ordered pairs of data from a graph and interpret the meaning of the data in terms of the situation depicted by the graph.	Lessons 16.3, 17.1, 17.2, 17.4, 24.3, 27.2, 28.2, 28.3, 28.5 Key Standards Handbook, pp. KSH30–KSH32
KEY 1.5	Know how to write ordered pairs correctly; for example, (x, y).	Lessons 5.5, 17.1, 17.2, 17.3, 17.5, 24.3, 27.1, 27.2, 27.3, 28.1, 28.2, 28.5 Key Standards Handbook, pp. KSH33–KSH34

Mathematical Reasoning

	Standards You Will Learn	Some Places to Look
1.0	Students make decisions about how to approach problems:	Lessons 1.6, 2.3, 3.5, 3.6, 4.5, 6.5, 10.4, 11.3, 12.4, 13.6, 18.4, 21.5, 24.3, 24.4, 25.5, 27.5
1.1	Analyze problems by identifying relationships, distinguishing relevant from irrelevant information, sequencing and prioritizing information, and observing patterns.	Lessons 1.6, 2.5, 5.1, 5.6, 6.5, 7.5, 8.2, 8.4, 9.5, 15.6, 16.6, 19.5, 20.4, 26.4, 28.5
1.2	Determine when and how to break a problem into simpler parts.	Lessons 2.5, 7.5, 9.3, 9.4, 9.5, 10.4, 12.4, 14.4, 15.6, 18.4, 20.4, 21.2, 21.5, 24.3, 24.4, 27.5
2.0	Students use strategies, skills, and concepts in finding solutions:	Lessons 1.6, 2.5, 3.4, 3.6, 5.3, 5.6, 7.5, 8.4, 9.5, 10.2, 10.4, 11.2, 11.4, 11.5, 12.4, 13.6, 14.6, 15.6, 16.6, 17.5, 19.5, 20.4, 21.5, 22.5, 23.2, 24.1, 24.2, 24.4, 25.5, 26.4, 27.5, 28.5
2.1	Use estimation to verify the reasonableness of calculated results.	Lessons 12.3, 13.3, 13.4, 14.2, 14.5, 17.5, 18.4, 21.5
2.2	Apply strategies and results from simpler problems to more complex problems.	Lessons 8.2, 8.3, 14.6, 15.1, 15.2, 19.1
2.3	Use a variety of methods, such as words, numbers, symbols, charts, graphs, tables, diagrams, and models, to explain mathematical reasoning.	Lessons 1.1, 1.3, 1.6, 2.1, 2.5, 3.6, 4.1, 4.2, 4.5, 5.6, 7.5, 8.1, 10.4, 11.5, 12.1, 13.1, 15.6, 16.6, 17.1, 19.2, 19.5, 21.5, 22.5, 24.1, 24.4, 25.5, 26.1, 26.4, 27.5, 28.5
2.4	Express the solution clearly and logically by using the appropriate mathematical notation and terms and clear language; support solutions with evidence in both verbal and symbolic work.	Lessons 1.2, 1.5, 2.5, 3.6, 5.6, 7.5, 9.4, 9.5, 11.5, 14.6, 15.6, 16.6, 17.1, 19.5, 20.4, 21.5, 22.5, 24.4, 25.5
2.5	Indicate the relative advantages of exact and approximate solutions to problems and give answers to a specified degree of accuracy.	Lessons 3.6, 12.2, 12.3, 13.6
2.6	Make precise calculations and check the validity of the results from the context of the problem.	Lessons 2.2, 7.5, 8.2, 10.1, 11.2, 11.5, 15.6, 19.3, 21.2, 21.5, 23.5, 27.5

Mathematical Reasoning (continued)

	Standards You Will Learn	Some Places to Look
3.0	Students move beyond a particular problem by generalizing to other situations:	Lessons 2.5, 3.2, 3.6, 5.3, 5.6, 7.1, 7.5, 9.5, 10.1, 11.5, 13.5, 13.6, 14.6, 15.6, 16.5, 16.6, 17.3, 19.1, 19.2, 19.5, 20.4, 22.5, 24.1, 24.2, 25.3, 28.5
3.1	Evaluate the reasonableness of the solution in the context of the original situation.	Lessons 2.5, 3.2, 5.3, 5.6, 7.5, 8.4, 9.5, 11.5, 13.5, 14.6, 15.6, 16.6, 20.4, 22.5, 28.5
3.2	Note the method of deriving the solution and demonstrate a conceptual understanding of the derivation by solving similar problems.	Lessons 2.5, 3.6, 5.6, 7.1, 7.5, 9.5, 11.5, 13.5, 13.6, 14.6, 15.6, 16.6, 19.5, 20.4, 22.5, 24.2, 28.5
3.3	Develop generalizations of the results obtained and apply them in other circumstances.	Lessons 2.5, 3.6, 5.3, 6.2, 7.2, 9.5, 11.5, 13.5, 13.6, 14.6, 15.6, 16.5, 16.6, 19.1, 20.4, 24.1, 24.2

Key Standards
Handbook

It's important to be a great problem solver in mathematics.

This is what problem solving means to me.

I use the correct operations when solving a problem.

Buffalo	34
Albany	312
New York	460

I know that different strands of math are related.

Math is important to me and everyone around me!

I share mathematical ideas with others.

I can think logically about a problem and analyze ideas.

I always find math in everyday life.

NS 1.2 What is a percent?

▶ **Connect It**

Percent means "out of one hundred" or "per hundred." The symbol for percent is %. A number out of 100 is written with the percent symbol after the number. For example, 60 out of 100 is written as 60%.

Read More
See Unit 10, pages 500–501, on modeling percent.

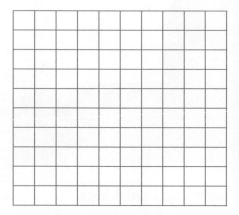

The whole grid is 100 out of 100 or 100%.

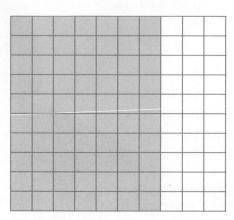

70 out of 100 squares are shaded, so 70% of the squares are shaded.

USE YOUR SKILLS

Write the percent of the squares that are shaded for each.

1.

2.

3. Of the 100 vehicles in a parking lot, 34 are silver. What percent of the vehicles are silver?

4. **Relate** How is 1 *cent* related to 1 *percent*?

KEY NS 1.2 Interpret percents as a part of a hundred; find decimal and percent equivalents for common fractions and explain why they represent the same value; compute a given percent of a whole number.

NS 1.2 How can percents and decimals show the same relationship as fractions?

Read More
See Unit 10, pages 502–504, on relating percents to fractions and decimals.

▶ **Connect It**

A **fraction** , **decimal** , and **percent** can be used to show the same part of a whole.

The grid shows 25 shaded squares out of 100. The shaded amount can be written as follows:

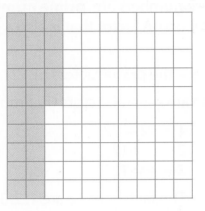

25%   0.25 $\frac{25}{100}$ or $\frac{1}{4}$

To write a fraction as a percent or decimal, first change the fraction to an equivalent fraction out of 100:

$\frac{3}{4} = \frac{75}{100}$

75 out of 100 is 75%, or 0.75.

USE YOUR SKILLS

Write percent and decimal equivalents for each fraction.

1. $\frac{1}{2}$
2. $\frac{1}{5}$
3. $\frac{1}{10}$

4. **Use** How can you use equivalent fractions to find percent?

NS 1.2 How do you find a percent of a whole number?

Read More
See Unit 10, pages 508–510, on percent of a number.

▶ **Connect It**

A percent of a number is a part, or fraction, of the number. To find the percent of a number, change the percent to a fraction, and then find the fraction of the number.

Example: What is 50% of 6?

50% is the same as $\frac{1}{2}$. $\frac{1}{2}$ of 6 is 3. So 50% of 6 is 3.

USE YOUR SKILLS

5. What is 50% of 12?   6. What is 25% of 8?

7. **Explain** How can you use a fraction to find the percent of a group of items?

KEY **NS 1.2** Interpret percents as a part of a hundred; find decimal and percent equivalents for common fractions and explain why they represent the same value; compute a given percent of a whole number

NS 1.4 What are prime factors?

▶ Connect It

Read More
See Unit 1, pages 6–13, on finding prime numbers and factors.

A **factor** is one of the numbers that are multiplied together to get a product. In $2 \times 3 = 6$, both 2 and 3 are factors. Some numbers, like 2, 5, and 7, have only two factors—1 and the number itself. These numbers are **prime numbers**. (Zero and 1 are not prime numbers). A factor that is also a prime number is a prime factor.

Example: What are the prime factors of 12?

There are several factors that multiply to make 12.

$$1 \times 12 = 12$$
$$2 \times 6 = 12$$
$$3 \times 4 = 12$$

The factors of 12 are 1, 2, 3, 4, 6, and 12.

Pick out the factors that are prime.
Prime factors are 2 and 3.

USE YOUR SKILLS

State the prime factors of each number.

1. 20   **2.** 27

3. 42   **4.** 30

5. Verify How do you know if you have written all the factors of a number?

KEY **NS 1.4** Determine the prime factors of all numbers through 50 and write the numbers as the product of their prime factors by using exponents to show multiples of a factor (e.g., $24 = 2 \times 2 \times 2 \times 3 = 2^3 \times 3$).

NS 1.4 How is a number written as the product of its prime factors?

Read More
See Unit 1, pages 6–13, on prime factorization.

▶ **Connect It**

Prime factorization is a way to show a number using two or more prime numbers. For example, $12 = 2 \times 2 \times 3$ is a way to write 12 as the product of prime factors. A **factor tree** is a way to break down a number into the product of its prime factors.

Write the number. ⟶ 12

Break the number down into two factors. ⟶ 4 × 3

Break each factor down into two other factors until the factors are prime. ⟶ 2 × 2

USE YOUR SKILLS

Write each number as a product of prime factors.

1. 8   **2.** 40   **3.** 18   **4.** 48

5. Verify How do you know if your prime factorization is correct?

NS 1.4 How else can you express a number as a product of prime factors?

Read More
See Unit 1, pages 14–15, on exponents and prime factorization.

▶ **Connect It**

A factor that repeats itself can be written with **exponents**. The multiplication $2 \times 2 \times 2$ can be written as 2^3—the **base** 2 is the factor that repeats, and the exponent 3 is the number of times the factor repeats itself.

$36 = 2 \times 2 \times 3 \times 3 = 2^2 \times 3^2$ Both factors repeat twice, so both have an exponent of 2.

USE YOUR SKILLS

Write each number as a product of prime factors.

6. 24   **7.** 50   **8.** 28   **9.** 44

10. Examine If you had a number written as the product of prime factors with exponents, how would you know the number of prime factors the number has?

KEY **NS 1.4** Determine the prime factors of all numbers through 50 and write the numbers as the product of their prime factors by using exponents to show multiples of a factor (e.g., $24 = 2 \times 2 \times 2 \times 3 = 2^3 \times 3$).

NS 1.5 How are integers represented on a number line?

Read More
See Unit 11, pages 542–547, on integers.

▶ **Connect It**

Numbers on a number line are greater as you move to the right. Numbers to the left of zero on a number line are **negative numbers**, and numbers to the right of zero are **positive numbers**. Zero is neither positive nor negative.

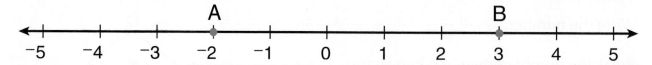

Point A is at ⁻2, and point B is at 3.

USE YOUR SKILLS
Write the number that represents each letter.

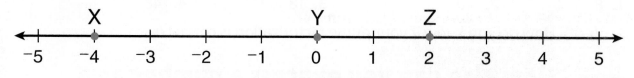

1. X   **2.** Y   **3.** Z

4. Place point W at ⁻1 on the number line above.

5. Locate Is ⁻9 or ⁻10 closer to zero on the number line?

KEY NS 1.5 Identify and represent on a number line decimals, fractions, mixed numbers, and positive and negative integers

NS 1.5 How are numbers in different forms represented on a number line?

Read More
See Unit 2, pages 76–80, on relating fractions and decimals.

▶ Connect It

Decimals and **fractions** represent part of a whole. The distance between two **integers** on a number line can be divided into parts to show decimal and fraction amounts.

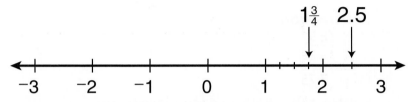

$1\frac{3}{4}$ is three-fourths of the way between 1 and 2.

2.5 is halfway between 2 and 3.

USE YOUR SKILLS

Write the letter that represents each number.

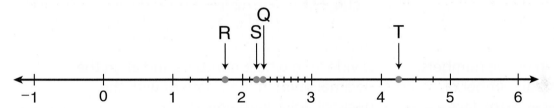

1. Q   **2.** R   **3.** S   **4.** T

5. Place Point U at 2.9 on the number line above.

6. **Explain** How would you place 0.6 on the number line?

KEY NS 1.5 Identify and represent on a number line decimals, fractions, mixed numbers, and positive and negative integers.

Key Standards Handbook **7**

NS 2.1 How are operations performed with decimals?

Read More
See Unit 6, pages 254–261, 270–275, 278–285, and 294–305, on adding, subtracting, multiplying, and dividing decimals.

▶ Connect It

Operations with decimals are performed similarly to operations with **whole numbers**. You can check your answer by performing the operation with whole numbers.

Follow the rules to place the decimal point.

Addition

```
  112.6
+   3.45
-------
 116.05
```

Add the digits in each **place**, regrouping as needed. Then align the decimal point in the sum with the decimal point in the addends.

Subtraction

```
  15.3
-  7.55
------
  7.75
```

Subtract the digits in each place value, regrouping as needed. (Use zero place holders if needed.) Then align the decimal point in the difference with the decimal point in the problem.

Multiplication

```
  12.2
×  0.5
------
  6.10
```

Multiply as in whole numbers. Count the total number of decimal places in the factors. Put the same number of decimal places in the product.

Division

$21.6 \div 3$

```
        7.2
   3 )21.6
```

Divide as in whole numbers and align the decimal point in the quotient with the decimal point in the dividend.

USE YOUR SKILLS

Find each answer. Check to make sure the answer is reasonable.

1.
```
  14.62
+  7.9
```

2.
```
  81.2
-  7.32
```

3.
```
  35.1
×  0.16
```

4. $41.55 \div 5$

5. Compare How are operations with whole numbers similar to and different from operations with decimals?

KEY NS 2.1 Add, subtract, multiply, and divide with decimals; add with negative integers; subtract positive integers from negative integers; and verify the reasonableness of the results.

NS 2.1 How are operations performed with integers?

Read More

See Unit 11, pages 548–552 and 562–570, on adding and subtracting integers.

▶ **Connect It**

To add **negative integers**, add the digits as in positive numbers. The sign will be negative.

$^-6 + {^-8} = {^-14}$

The answer is reasonable because, if you are 6 units below zero and you move down 8 more units below zero, you are 14 units below zero.

To subtract integers, add the **opposite**. Since addition and subtraction are inverse operations, you can add the opposite when subtracting.

$^-6 - 8 = {^-6} + (^-8) = {^-14}$

Change the subtraction sign to an addition sign, and change the next integer to its opposite: the opposite of 8 is $^-8$.

USE YOUR SKILLS

Find each sum or difference. Check to make sure your answer is reasonable.

1. $^-9 + {^-7} =$ **2.** $^-15 + {^-3} =$

4. $^-10 - 6 =$ **5.** $^-4 - 9 =$

5. Determine Does adding the opposite always work for subtraction? Explain why or why not.

KEY NS 2.1 Add, subtract, multiply, and divide with decimals; add with negative integers; subtract positive integers from negative integers; and verify the reasonableness of the results.

Key Standards Handbook **9**

NS 2.2 How is long division performed?

▶ **Connect It**

Read More
See Unit 6, pages 320–321, on dividing by 2-digit divisors.

Long division is performed by dividing each place value in the dividend by the divisor (from left to right).

Divide 19 by 16. Put 1 in the quotient.⟶

Multiply 16 × 1, and subtract from 19.⟶

$$16\overline{)192}$$
quotient 12
$-16↓$
32 ⟵ Bring down the 2.

Divide 32 by 16. Put 2 in the quotient. ⟶ -32
Multiply 16 × 2, and subtract from 32. $\quad 0$

USE YOUR SKILLS

Find each quotient.

1. 264 ÷ 12

2. 275 ÷ 25

3. 1,480 ÷ 20

4. 5,775 ÷ 275

5. **Verify** If you divided and had a remainder, how would you check to make sure your answer was correct?

KEY **NS 2.2** Demonstrate proficiency with division, including division with positive decimals and long division with multidigit divisors.

NS 2.2 # How do you divide with decimals?

Read More
See Unit 6, pages 294–305, on dividing decimals.

▶ **Connect It**

When there is a decimal divisor in a division problem, move the decimal point to the right of the last digit in the divisor. Then move the decimal point in the dividend the same number of places to the right.

Example: $6.09 \div 0.3$ is equivalent to $60.9 \div 3$.

The decimal point moved one place in 0.3 to become 3, so the decimal point is moved one place in 6.09 to become 60.9.

$$\begin{array}{r} 20.3 \\ 3\overline{)60.9} \end{array}$$

Divide as in whole numbers and align the decimal point in the quotient with the decimal point in the dividend.

An infinite number of zeros can be placed after the last digit after the decimal point without changing the value of the number. As you divide, if necessary, bring down the zeros to continue dividing.

Example: $2.8 \div 0.16$ can be written as $2.800 \div 0.16$.

Move the decimal point two places to the right in the divisor, 0.16, to get 16. Then move the decimal point the same number of places in 2.800 to get 280.0.

$$\begin{array}{r} 17.5 \\ 16\overline{)280.0} \\ -16 \\ \hline 120 \\ -112 \\ \hline 80 \\ -80 \\ \hline 0 \end{array}$$

Bring down the zero.

USE YOUR SKILLS

Find each quotient.

1. $17.5 \div 0.5$ **2.** $2.79 \div 0.3$ **3.** $75 \div 0.12$ **4.** $0.075 \div 0.15$

5. Explain Why does the quotient for $2.4 \div 0.3$ have the same value as the quotient for $24 \div 3$?

KEY **NS 2.2** Demonstrate proficiency with division, including division with positive decimals and long division with multidigit divisors.

Key Standards Handbook **11**

NS 2.3 How are fractions added and subtracted when denominators are alike?

Read More
See Unit 4, pages 146–150, on adding and subtracting fractions with like denominators.

▶ **Connect It**

Like fractions have the same **denominators**, such as $\frac{3}{5}$ and $\frac{1}{5}$.
To add or subtract like fractions, add or subtract the numerators.

Erin ate $\frac{3}{5}$ of a pizza for lunch. She had $\frac{1}{5}$ of the pizza for a snack after dinner.
How much of the pizza did Erin eat altogether?
  The clue word *altogether* suggests addition. Add $\frac{3}{5}$ and $\frac{1}{5}$.

$\frac{3}{5} + \frac{1}{5} = \frac{4}{5}$ Add the numerators. The denominator does not change.

So Erin ate $\frac{4}{5}$ of the pizza altogether.

How much more of the pizza did Erin have for lunch than for a snack?
The clue words *how much more* suggest subtraction. Subtract $\frac{1}{5}$ from $\frac{3}{5}$.
$\frac{3}{5} - \frac{1}{5} = \frac{2}{5}$ Subtract the numerators. The denominator does not change.
So Erin ate $\frac{2}{5}$ more pizza for lunch than for a snack.

USE YOUR SKILLS

Solve each problem.

1. Jake used $\frac{5}{8}$ cup of nuts and $\frac{2}{8}$ cup of raisins in a trail mix. How many more nuts than raisins did Jake use?

2. Of the books on a shelf, $\frac{3}{10}$ are autobiographies and $\frac{4}{10}$ are fiction. What fraction of the books on the shelf do autobiographies and fiction make up altogether?

3. Carlos rode his bike $1\frac{1}{4}$ miles to the library and then rode $1\frac{2}{4}$ miles to his friend's house. How many miles did Carlos ride in all?

4. **Show** How can you use a model to show the result of $\frac{5}{6} - \frac{1}{6}$?

 KEY NS 2.3 Solve simple problems, including ones arising in concrete situations, involving the addition and subtraction of fractions and mixed numbers (like and unlike denominators of 20 or less), and express answers in simplest form.

NS 2.3 How are fractions added and subtracted when denominators are not alike?

Read More
See Unit 4, pages 152–156, on adding and subtracting fractions and mixed numbers.

▶ Connect It

Unlike fractions have **unlike denominators**, such as $\frac{1}{4}$ and $\frac{1}{2}$.

To add or subtract any fractions, the denominators must be the same.

You can make the denominators the same by finding equivalent fractions.

Example: Briante is using $2\frac{1}{2}$ cups of almonds and $1\frac{1}{4}$ cups of walnuts in a recipe. How many cups of nuts does she need?

Add $2\frac{1}{2}$ and $1\frac{1}{4}$. $2\frac{1}{2} + 1\frac{1}{4}$

1 **Find a common denominator.**

Find the least common multiple of the denominators.

Multiples of 2 = 2, **4**, 6, 8…   Multiples of 4 = **4**, 8, 12…

The least common multiple is 4, so the common denominator is 4.

2 **Change each fraction to an equivalent fraction with the common denominator.**

$2\frac{1}{2} = 2\frac{2}{4}$ $1\frac{1}{4} = 1\frac{1}{4}$

$2\frac{1}{2} + 1\frac{1}{4} = 2\frac{2}{4} + 1\frac{1}{4} = 3\frac{3}{4}$

Add the numerators.
Add the whole numbers.

So Briante needs $3\frac{3}{4}$ cups of nuts.

USE YOUR SKILLS

Solve each problem. Write your answer in simplest form.

1. Julie bought $2\frac{2}{3}$ apple pies at a bake sale. She bought $1\frac{1}{5}$ blueberry pies at the bakery. How many more apple pies did she buy than blueberry?

2. Ben spent $1\frac{1}{2}$ hours doing his homework. Charro spent $1\frac{3}{10}$ hours doing her homework. How much more time did Ben spend doing homework than Charro? (Write your answer in simplest form.)

3. **Analyze** If you used a common multiple other than the least common multiple to add or subtract unlike fractions, would the answer be correct? Explain.

KEY NS 2.3 Solve simple problems, including ones arising in concrete situations, involving the addition and subtraction of fractions and mixed numbers (like and unlike denominators of 20 or less), and express answers in the simplest form.

AF 1.2 How can an unknown number be represented?

Read More
See Unit 3, pages 100–115, on expressions and equations.

▶ Connect It

A **variable** is a symbol that represents an unknown quantity. A variable is usually a letter that stands for a number. The two **equations** below have the same meaning—one uses an underline to represent the unknown number and the other uses a letter.

$3 + \underline{\quad} = 5$ Instead of using the underline for the unknown number, a letter such as p can be used.

$3 + p = 5$ Both equations have the same meaning.

USE YOUR SKILLS

Use a variable to represent each unknown.

1. $\underline{\quad} + 3$ **2.** $2 \times \underline{\quad} = 6$

3. John read a number of pages in his book. How many pages did he read?

4. **Decide** Does it matter which letter is used to represent an unknown number? Explain.

▶ Connect It

When you have an **expression** in words, you can translate it to math symbols. You use variables in expressions to represent the unknown quantity.

"three more than a number" $n + 3$ "a number times four" $a \times 4$ or $4a$

"two less than a number" $b - 2$ "a number divided by 5" $x \div 5$

USE YOUR SKILLS

Write each expression using symbols.

5. the sum of 2 and a number   **6.** twice a number

7. Toni read 6 less pages today than she did yesterday. How many pages did she read today?

8. **Explain** How do you know which operation to use when translating from a verbal expression to one with math symbols?

KEY **AF 1.2** Use a letter to represent an unknown number; write and evaluate simple algebraic expressions in one variable by substitution.

AF 1.2 How do you find the value of an algebraic expression?

Read More
See Unit 3, pages 104–106, on evaluating expressions.

▶ Connect It

If you know the value of the variable in an **algebraic expression**, you can find the value of the **expression**. Substitute the value of the variable into the expression, and perform the operation(s).

Example: The value of $3 + p$, when $p = 5$, is evaluated as follows:

$3 + 5$ Replace the variable, p, with its value, 5.

$= 8$ Perform the operation.

Example: There are 3 chairs at each table. How many chairs are there at 8 tables? How many chairs at 10 tables?

$3 \times t$ The expression represents the number of chairs at an unknown number of tables, t.

$3 \times \mathbf{8} = 24$ Replace t with 8 (the number of tables) to find the value of the expression. Solve. There are 24 chairs when there are 8 tables.

$3 \times \mathbf{10} = 30$ Replace t with 10 (the number of tables) to find the value of the expression. Solve. There are 30 chairs when there are 10 tables.

USE YOUR SKILLS

Find the value of each expression.

1. $12 - j$, when $j = 5$

2. $6c$, when $c = 8$

3. There are 4 more girls than boys in each class. How many girls are in a class when there are 15 boys?

4. **Interpret** Why can an algebraic expression have different values?

KEY AF 1.2 Use a letter to represent an unknown number; write and evaluate simple algebraic expressions in one variable by substitution.

Key Standards Handbook **15**

AF 1.4 How are locations shown on a grid?

Read More
See Unit 12, pages 586–587, on plotting points.

▶ Connect It

Ordered pairs describe where a point is located on a **coordinate grid**. In an ordered pair such as (1, 4), the first number is the **x-coordinate**. The x-coordinate describes the horizontal position. The second number is the **y-coordinate**. The y-coordinate describes the vertical position.

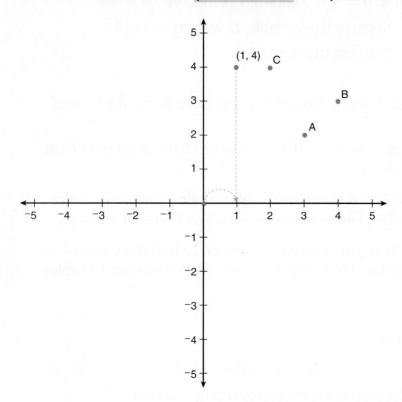

The point (1, 4) is 1 unit to the right of zero along the **horizontal axis**, and 4 units up from zero along the **vertical axis**.

USE YOUR SKILLS

1. Which number describes the horizontal position of point *A*?

2. What are the coordinates of point *B*?

3. What are the coordinates of point *C*?

4. Plot point *D* at (3, 0) on the graph.

5. **Investigate** Does (1, 2) show the same location as (2, 1)? Explain.

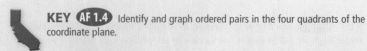

KEY AF 1.4 Identify and graph ordered pairs in the four quadrants of the coordinate plane.

KSH**16**

AF 1.4 How are negative numbers shown on a grid?

Read More
See Unit 12, pages 586–595, on integers and the coordinate plane.

▶ Connect It

On a grid, *x*-coordinates with a negative value are to the left of zero on the horizontal axis. *Y*-coordinates with a negative value are down from zero on the vertical axis.

The point ($^-1$, $^-4$) is 1 unit to the left of zero along the horizontal axis, and 4 units down from zero along the vertical axis.

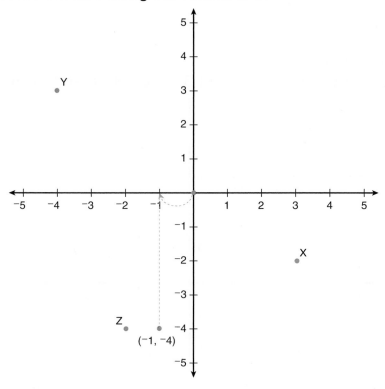

USE YOUR SKILLS

1. Which number describes the vertical position of point *X*?

2. What are the coordinates of point *Y*?

3. What are the coordinates of point *Z*?

4. Plot point *W* at (0, $^-2$) on the graph.

5. **Explain** How would you plot (4, $^-5$) on a coordinate grid?

KEY **AF 1.4** Identify and graph ordered pairs in the four quadrants of the coordinate plane.

AF 1.5 **How are a table of values, an equation, and a graph related?**

Read More
See Unit 12, pages 606–615, on graphing equations and writing equations from graphs.

▶ Connect It

When you use functions, you input a number to get the output. The value of the output depends on the input. You can use the pattern in a **function table** to write a rule in the form of an equation for the function. You can also create a graph from the table of values.

x	⁻1	0	1	2
y	2	3	4	5

The values ⁻1, 0, 1, and 2 are the input values.
When ⁻1 is the input, 2 is the output. When 0 is the input, 3 is the output, and so on.

The x- and y-values can be graphed. The ordered pairs for the table of values are (⁻1, 2), (0, 3), (1, 4), and (2, 5).

The pattern in the table and graph shows that each output value is 3 more than the input value. This equation shows the relationship.

$y = x + 3$

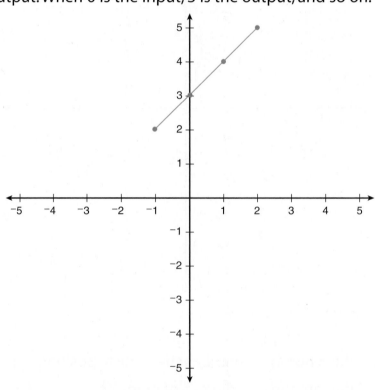

USE YOUR SKILLS

Write the equation for each table of values.

1.

x	⁻1	0	1	2
y	⁻2	⁻1	0	1

2.

x	⁻1	0	1	2
y	⁻4	0	4	8

3. Explain How do you know which operation to use to write the equation for a table of values?

 KEY **AF 1.5** Solve problems involving linear functions with integer values; write the equation; and graph the resulting ordered pairs of integers on a grid.

AF 1.5 How do you solve problems involving linear functions?

Read More
See Unit 12, pages 606–615, on functions, and equations for function tables and graphs.

▶ Connect It

You can solve problems involving linear functions using a table of values, an equation, and/or a graph.

Example: Kenneth earns $7 for each hour he babysits. How much does he earn for babysitting 3 hours? The table, equation, and graph below show that when the number of babysitting hours (x) is 3, the amount earned (y) is $21.

Number of Babysitting Hours (x)	1	2	**3**	4
Amount Earned (y)	7	14	**21**	28

The table shows that the output is 21 when the input is 3.

The equation $y = 7x$ describes the relationship. By substituting $x = 3$ into the equation, you can find the value of y. $y = 7 \times 3 = 21$

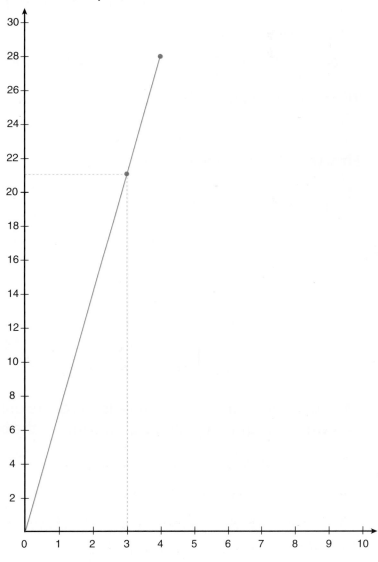

USE YOUR SKILLS

Solve each problem.

1. There are 2 fewer rats, r, than mice, m. Which equation represents this situation?

2. There are 3 more cows than horses. Write three ordered pairs that can be graphed to show this relationship.

3. **Decide** When might it be easier to use an equation rather than a graph or table of values to solve a problem involving linear functions? Explain why.

KEY **AF 1.5** Solve problems involving linear functions with integer values; write the equation; and graph the resulting ordered pairs of integers on a grid.

MG 1.1 **How does the area of a triangle compare to the area of a rectangle?**

Read More
See Unit 9, pages 458–462, on area of triangles.

▶ **Connect It**

The area of a rectangle is *length × width*. You can use the formula for the area of a rectangle to find a formula for the area of a triangle.

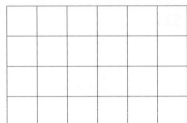

width = 4

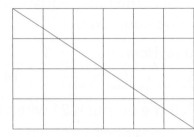

width (height) = 4

length = 6

length (base) = 6

The area of one triangle is one half the area of the rectangle, or $\frac{1}{2} l \times w$.

The formula for area of a triangle is $\frac{1}{2}$ *base × height*.

USE YOUR SKILLS

Find the area of each triangle.

1.

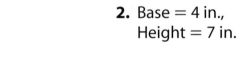

3

8

2. Base = 4 in., Height = 7 in.

3.

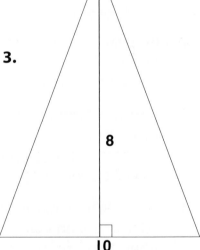

8

10

4. Solve If the area of a triangle is 53 square units, what is the area of a rectangle whose length and width are the same as the base and the height of the triangle?

KEY **MG1.1** Derive and use the formula for the area of a triangle and of a parallelogram by comparing each with the formula for the area of a rectangle.

MG 1.1 # How does the area of a parallelogram compare to the area of a rectangle?

Read More
See Unit 9, pages 452–456, on area of parallelograms.

▶ **Connect It**

The area of a rectangle is *length × width*. Use the formula for the area of a rectangle to find a formula for the area of a parallelogram.

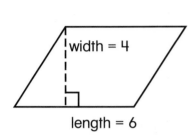

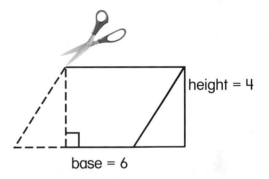

The area is $l \times w = 6 \times 4 = 24$ square units.

The area of the parallelogram is the same as the area of a rectangle. You can call the length of the parallelogram its *base* and the width its *height*.

The formula for area of a parallelogram is *base × height*.

USE YOUR SKILLS

Find the area of each parallelogram.

1.

height = 3 in.

base = 5 in.

2.

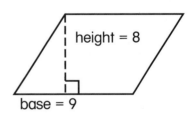

height = 8

base = 9

3. base = 7 m, height = 5 m

4. **Solve** If the area of a rectangle is *x* square units, what is the area of a parallelogram and a triangle whose base and height are the same as the length and the width of the rectangle?

MG 1.2 How are nets and solids related?

▶ Connect It

A **net** is a two-dimensional pattern that can be folded to form a solid. Imagine that you have a box and you open it to lay it flat. The flat pattern is its net.

Read More
See Unit 9, pages 472–473, on making solids using nets.

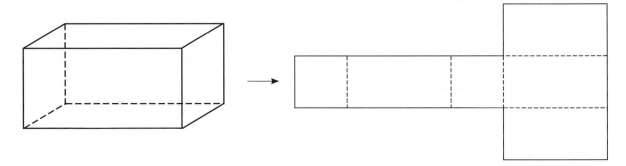

There are 6 **faces** on this rectangular box.

The faces on the net form the faces on the box.

USE YOUR SKILLS

State whether the net forms a *rectangular box*, a *cube*, or *neither*.

1.

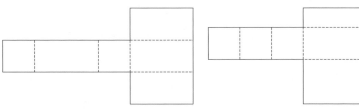

2.

3.

4. Explain Why will the net of a cube always have six squares?

KEY MG 1.2 Construct a cube and rectangular box from two-dimensional patterns and use these patterns to compute the surface area for these objects.

MG 1.2 **How can the net of a solid be used to find its surface area?**

Read More
See Unit 9, pages 478–481, on surface area.

▶ **Connect It**

The **surface area** of a solid is the sum of the areas of its faces. Add the area of each face in the net of a solid to find its surface area.

The area of each rectangular face that makes up the net is found using length × width.

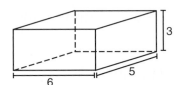

There are two faces, each with area
6 × 5 = 30 square units.

There are two faces, each with area
6 × 3 = 18 square units.

There are two faces, each with area
5 × 3 = 15 square units.

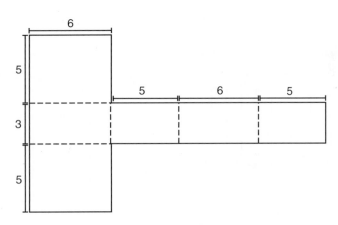

The surface area of the box is 30 + 30 + 18 + 18 + 15 + 15 = 126 square units, or 126 units^2.

USE YOUR SKILLS

Find the surface area of each object.

1.

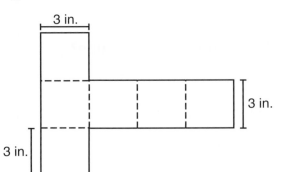

3 in.

3 in.

3 in.

2.

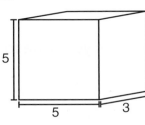

5

5

5

3

3. Decide What formula can you write to find the surface area of a cube?

MG 1.3 **What is volume?**

▶ **Connect It**

The amount of space a solid figure contains is the **volume** .
Volume is measured in **cubic units** .

Read More
See Unit 9, pages 482–484, on volume.

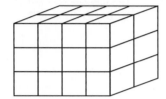

Each cube is 1 unit.

The figure is 4 units by 3 units by 2 units.

There are 24 units in all.

The volume is 24 cubic units, or 24 units^3.

USE YOUR SKILLS

Find the volume of each object.

1.

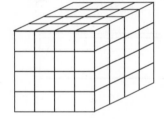

2.

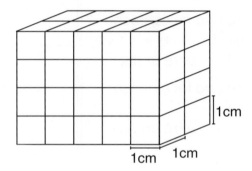

1cm

1cm   1cm

3.

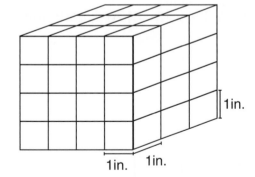

1in.

1in.   1in.

4. **Decide** What formula can you write to find the surface area of a cube?

KEY **MG1.3** Understand the concept of volume and use the appropriate units in common measuring systems (i.e., cubic centimeter [cm^3], cubic meter [m^3], cubic inch [in.^{3}], cubic yard [yd^3]) to compute the volume of rectangular solids

MG 1.3 How is volume computed?

▶ Connect It

Read More
See Unit 9, pages 482–484, on volume.

You can use the formula *length × width × height* to compute the volume of a **rectangular prism**.

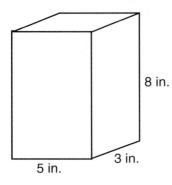

8 in.

5 in.   3 in.

Volume = 5 in. × 3 in. × 8 in. = 120 in.³

USE YOUR SKILLS

Find the volume of each object.

1.

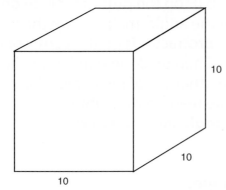

10

10

10

2.

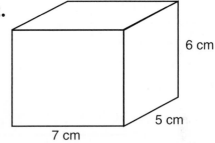

6 cm

5 cm

7 cm

3.

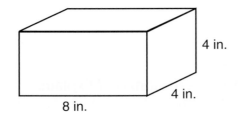

4 in.

4 in.

8 in.

4. Solve How many smaller boxes measuring 1 ft³ would fit into a larger box that is 4 feet × 4 feet × 2 feet?

KEY MG1.3 Understand the concept of volume and use the appropriate units in common measuring systems (i.e., cubic centimeter [cm³], cubic meter [m³], cubic inch [in.³], cubic yard [yd³]) to compute the volume of rectangular solids.

Key Standards Handbook **25**

MG 2.1 How do you name different kinds of angles?

Read More
See Unit 8, pages 390–396, on measuring, drawing, and classifying angles.

▶ Connect It

An angle is formed by two **rays** with a common **endpoint**. **Angles** are measured in degrees. An angle is named by its measure.

A **right angle** has a square corner and measures 90°.

An **acute angle** measures less than 90° but greater than 0°.

An **obtuse angle** measures greater than 90° but less than 180°.

A **straight angle** measures 180°.

  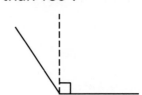

You can use a **protractor** to get the exact measure of an angle or to help draw the angle.

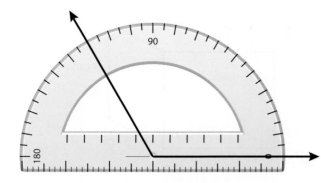

Line up 0° on the protractor with one ray of the angle, making sure the center of the protractor is on the vertex of the angle. Then read the number of degrees at the other ray of the angle. Make sure you are reading the right scale.
This angle measures 120°.

USE YOUR SKILLS **Find the measure of each angle.**

1.

2.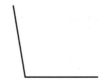

3. **Verify** How can you know if your angle measure is reasonable? Explain.

KEY **MG2.1** Measure, identify, and draw angles, perpendicular and parallel lines, rectangles, and triangles by using appropriate tools.

MG 2.1 How do you construct lines and figures?

Read More
See Unit 8, pages 430–435, on constructing parallel and perpendicular lines, and triangles and rectangles.

▶ **Connect It**

Perpendicular lines meet at a right angle.
Parallel lines will never meet. You can use perpendicular and parallel lines to construct rectangles and triangles.

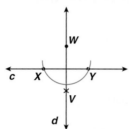

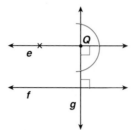

To construct **perpendicular lines**, draw a line. Use a point above the line to draw an arc.

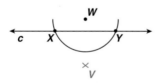

Draw two new arcs by placing the point of the compass on the points where the first arc intersect the line. The new arcs intersect at a point below the line.

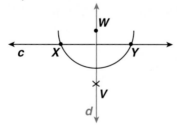

Connect the points above and below the line.

To construct **parallel lines**, draw perpendicular lines.

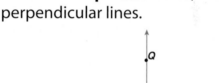

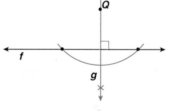

Construct a line perpendicular to the vertical line. This line is parallel to the horizontal line.

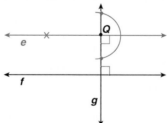

USE YOUR SKILLS

Construct the figures below.

1. a pair of parallel lines

2. a pair of perpendicular lines

3. **Solve** Use parallel and perpendicular lines to construct a rectangle.

KEY MG2.1 Measure, identify, and draw angles, perpendicular and parallel lines, rectangles, and triangles by using appropriate tools.

 **How does the angle sum of a triangle help to solve problems?**

Read More
See Unit 8, pages 412–414, on the sum of the angles of a triangle.

▶ **Connect It**

The sum of the angles of any triangle is 180°.
You can use this information to find other information about the triangle.

Example: A picture frame in the shape of a triangle has a right angle and a 30° angle. What is the measure of the third angle of the triangle?

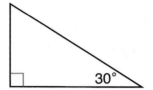
30°

The sum of the angles must equal 180°. The right angle measures 90°.
$90° + 30° + \underline{\quad} = 180°$
$180 - (90 + 30) = 60$
The measure of the third angle is 60°.

USE YOUR SKILLS

Solve each problem.

1. What is the measure of the angle marked x?

x
60° 60°

2. A tile is cut in the shape of a triangle.
   Two of the angles of the triangle measure 80° and 70°.
   What is the measure of the third angle?

3. Larry cut a triangle out of construction paper. One angle measured 70°, and the other two angles had equal measure. What is the measure of each of the other two angles?

4. **Investigate** Can a triangle have two right angles? Explain.

KEY MG2.2 Know that the sum of the angles of any triangle is 180° and the sum of the angles of any quadrilateral is 360° and use this information to solve problems.

MG 2.2 How does the angle sum of a quadrilateral help to solve problems?

Read More
See Unit 8, pages 416–418, on the sum of the angles of a quadrilateral.

▶ Connect It

A **quadrilateral** is any closed four-sided figure. The sum of the angles of a quadrilateral is 360°. You can use this information to find other information about the quadrilateral.

Example: A mirror in the shape of a quadrilateral has a right angle and two other angles each measuring 70°. What is the measure of the fourth angle of the quadrilateral?

The sum of the angles must equal 360°. The right angle measures 90°.

So $90° + 70° + 70° + \underline{\quad} = 360°$
$360 - (90 + 70 + 70) = 130$

The measure of the fourth angle is 130°.

USE YOUR SKILLS

Solve each problem.

1. A pool is made in the shape of a quadrilateral. What is the measure of the angle marked x?

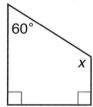

2. A piece of cardboard is cut in the shape of a quadrilateral. Three of the angles of the quadrilateral measure 150°, 70°, and 80°. What is the measure of the fourth angle?

3. A garden is made in the shape of a quadrilateral. The opposite angles of the quadrilateral have the same measure. One angle measures 70°. What are the measures of the other three angles?

4. **Solve** If all the angles of a quadrilateral have the same measure, what is the measure of each angle? Explain.

KEY MG2.2 Know that the sum of the angles of any triangle is 180° and the sum of the angles of any quadrilateral is 360° and use this information to solve problems.

Read More

See Unit 7, pages 364–365, on integers and the coordinate plane and reading a graph.

SDAP 1.4 How do you read ordered pairs of data from a graph?

▶ **Connect It**

You can read data from the points and lines on a graph.

Example:

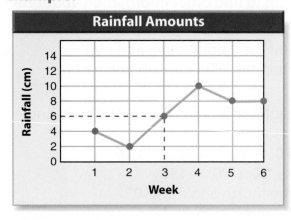

You can get the data for a point by reading the number on the horizontal axis and the corresponding number along the vertical axis. For example, the point for week 3 corresponds with 6 centimeters. The **ordered pair** is written as (3, 6)—the number along the horizontal axis followed by the number along the vertical axis.

USE YOUR SKILLS

Use the graph to answer the questions.

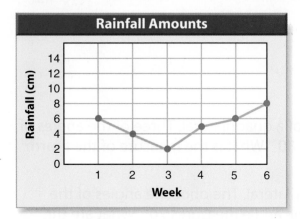

1. Which week represents (3, 2)?

2. Which amount of rainfall is shown for the point (2, 4)?

3. What is the ordered pair for the last week shown on the graph?

4. **Decide** Would the ordered pairs change if the vertical axis was labeled in increments of 1 (0, 1, 2, 3, and so on)? Explain.

KEY SDAP 1.4 Identify ordered pairs of data from a graph and interpret the meaning of the data in terms of the situation depicted in the graph.

SDAP 1.4 How do you interpret data in a graph?

Read More
See Unit 7, pages 366–368, on reading and using a graph.

▶ Connect It

A graph organizes information and presents a picture of the information. You can interpret the information shown on a graph.

Example: How much rain fell in six weeks?

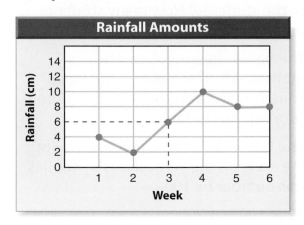

1. Find the value for the rainfall each week.
    Week 1, 4 cm
    Week 2, 2 cm
    Week 3, 6 cm
    Week 4, 10 cm
    Week 5, 8 cm
    Week 6, 8 cm

2. Find the total.

$4 + 2 + 6 + 10 + 8 + 8 = 38$

So 38 cm of rain fell during the six weeks.

USE YOUR SKILLS

Use the graph below to answer each question.

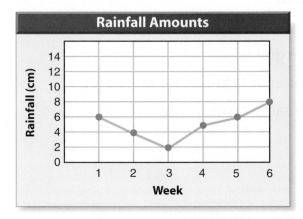

1. During which weeks did the same amount of rain fall?

2. **Interpret** How much more rain fell during Week 4 than during Week 3?

KEY **SDAP 1.4** Identify ordered pairs of data from a graph and interpret the meaning of the data in terms of the situation depicted in the graph.

SDAP 1.4 **How do you interpret data in a bar graph?**

Read More
See Unit 12, pages 616–617, on reading and using a graph.

▶ **Connect It**

You can interpret the information shown on a bar graph.

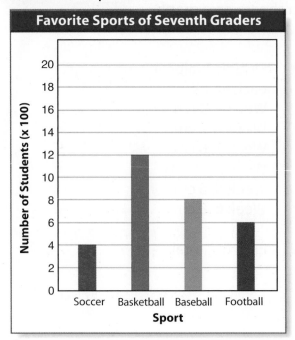

Favorite Sports of Seventh Graders

Number of Students (x 100)

Sport: Soccer, Basketball, Baseball, Football

Example: What is the favorite sport of the students? How many students prefer this sport?

The bar for basketball reaches the highest, which represents the most students. So basketball is the favorite sport of the students.

The bar for basketball reaches 12. But the scale on the vertical axis multiplies this number by 100.

$12 \times 100 = 1,200$

1,200 students prefer basketball.

USE YOUR SKILLS

Use the graph above to answer each question.

1. How many students prefer football?

2. How many students are represented in the graph?

3. Which sport is preferred by twice the number of those that prefer soccer?

4. **Interpret** If two bars on a graph have the same height, what does that mean?

KEY SDAP 1.4 Identify ordered pairs of data from a graph and interpret the meaning of the data in terms of the situation depicted in the graph.

SDAP 1.5 How do you write ordered pairs?

Read More
See Unit 12, pages 594–595, on graphing.

▶ **Connect It**

Ordered pairs are used to describe a certain location on a graph. The first number in an ordered pair describes the horizontal position. The second number describes the vertical position. You can write an ordered pair to describe a point on the graph.

Example: The graph below shows the profit Jill plans to earn during each year of business.

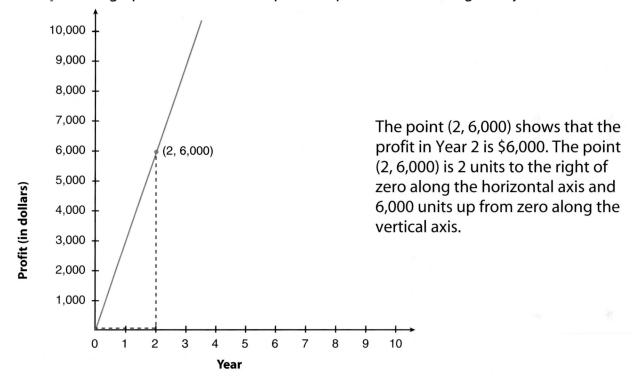

The point (2, 6,000) shows that the profit in Year 2 is $6,000. The point (2, 6,000) is 2 units to the right of zero along the horizontal axis and 6,000 units up from zero along the vertical axis.

USE YOUR SKILLS

Use the graph in the example above to write each ordered pair.

1. Which ordered pair describes the amount Jill earns in Year 4?

2. Which ordered pair describes the year Jill earns $9,000?

3. Which ordered pair represents the time when Jill first started the business?

4. **Locate** On which axis is the ordered pair (0, 4) located—the horizontal or the vertical? Explain.

KEY SDAP 1.5 Know how to write ordered pairs correctly; for example (x, y).

SDAP 1.5 **How do you write ordered pairs with negative numbers?**

Read More
See Unit 12, pages 594–595, on graphing and integers on the coordinate plane.

▶ Connect It

On a grid, x-coordinates with a negative value are to the left of zero in the horizontal position. Y-coordinates with a negative value are down from zero in the vertical position.

Example: The graph below shows the temperatures a scientist recorded at different elevations. The elevation at sea level is zero, elevations below zero have negative values, and those above sea level have positive values.

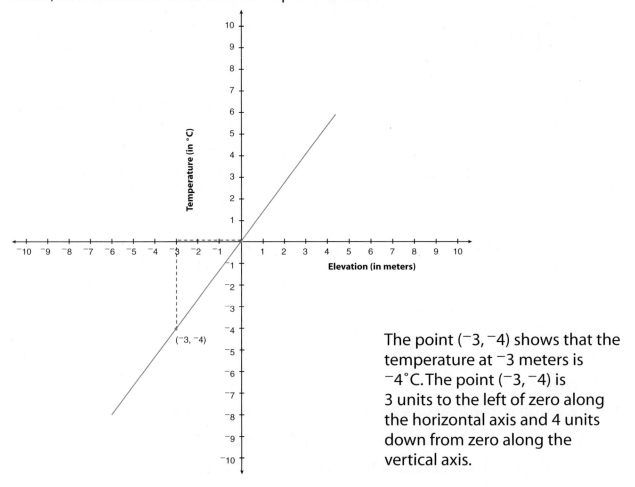

The point ($^-3$, $^-4$) shows that the temperature at $^-3$ meters is $^-4$°C. The point ($^-3$, $^-4$) is 3 units to the left of zero along the horizontal axis and 4 units down from zero along the vertical axis.

USE YOUR SKILLS

Use the graph in the example above to write each ordered pair.

1. Which ordered pair describes the temperature at $^-6$ meters?

2. Which ordered pair describes the elevation when the temperature is 4°C?

3. **Locate** Which ordered pair describes the temperature at sea level?

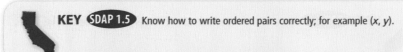

KEY **SDAP 1.5** Know how to write ordered pairs correctly; for example (x, y).

Using the Table of Contents

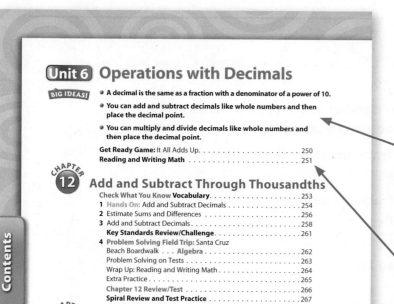

A table of contents helps you find special features in your math book.

Each unit teaches big ideas in 2–4 chapters. You get ready for the unit with a game.

Reading and writing can help you learn math.

All chapters have hands on and problem solving lessons.

Field Trips let you do math in special places in California.

Table of Contents

Unit 1 ## Number Theory and Fractions

BIG IDEAS!

● You can write any number as the product of its prime factors, using exponents to show multiples of a factor.

● You can identify fractions and mixed numbers as points on a number line.

● You can rename fractions as mixed numbers to show the simplest form.

CHAPTER 1

Prime Factorization and Exponents

CHAPTER 2 Fractions and Mixed Numbers

Maintaining California Standards	**Reading & Writing Math**	**Science, History-Social Science, and Data**
Key Standards Review, pages 11, 33 **Problem Solving on Tests,** page 21 **Spiral Review and Test Practice,** pages 25, 45	**Reading and Writing Math,** pages 3, 22, 42 **Vocabulary,** pages 5, 27	**Problem Solving Field Trip,** page 20 **Science Link,** pages 18, 36 **History-Social Science Link,** page 32 **Real World Data,** page 10

Contents

Unit 2 Equivalence: Fractions and Decimals

BIG IDEAS!

● Each place value to the left of another is ten times greater than the one to the right.

● A decimal is another name for a fraction, and both can be represented on a number line.

CHAPTER 3 Place Value Through Thousandths

Contents

Relate Fractions and Decimals

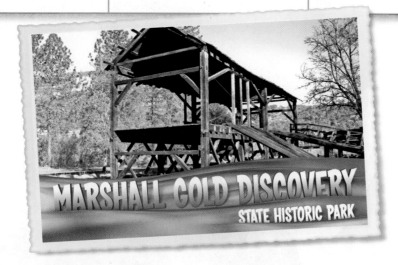

MARSHALL GOLD DISCOVERY
STATE HISTORIC PARK

Contents

Unit 3 **Algebra**

 BIG IDEAS!

- You can solve problems by finding the value of variables in an equation.

- You can use the Distributive, Commutative, Associative, Identity, and Equality Properties to solve equations.

Contents

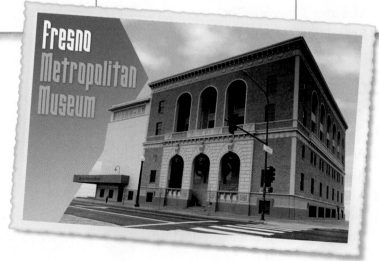

Unit 4 # Add and Subtract Fractions and Mixed Numbers

BIG IDEAS!

● You can add fractions by using equivalency to make a common denominator.

● When adding or subtracting mixed numbers you sometimes regroup as you do for whole numbers.

CHAPTER 7

Add and Subtract Fractions

CHAPTER 8

Add with Mixed Numbers

CHAPTER 9

Subtract with Mixed Numbers

Unit 4 Review/Test

Unit 5 **Multiply and Divide Fractions**

BIG IDEAS!
- When you multiply two fractions, the product is less than either fraction.
- Since division is another way of writing multiplication, you can rewrite division with fractions as multiplication with fractions.

 CHAPTER 10

Multiply Fractions

Contents

CHAPTER 11 Divide Fractions

Contents

Unit 6 Operations with Decimals

BIG IDEAS!

- A decimal is the same as a fraction with a denominator of a power of 10.
- You can add and subtract decimals like whole numbers and then place the decimal point.
- You can multiply and divide decimals like whole numbers and then place the decimal point.

CHAPTER **12** Add and Subtract Through Thousandths

CHAPTER **13** Multiply Decimals

Contents

Unit 7 # Data and Graphs

 BIG IDEAS!

- *Mean*, *median*, and *mode* are three ways to interpret the same set of data.
- Each type of graph is suited to display a different type of data.
- Ordered pairs locate and describe specific points on a coordinate grid.

CHAPTER 16

Graphs and Statistics

CHAPTER 17 Graphs on a Coordinate Grid

Maintaining California Standards	Reading & Writing Math	Science, History-Social Science, and Data
Key Standards Review, pages 355, 369 **Problem Solving on Tests,** page 377 **Spiral Review and Test Practice,** pages 361, 381	**Reading and Writing Math,** pages 339, 358, 378 **Vocabulary,** pages 341, 363	**Problem Solving Field Trip,** page 376 **Science Link,** pages 354, 368 **History-Social Science Link,** pages 348, 372

Contents

Unit 8 **Geometry**

 BIG IDEAS!

- Angles are measured and compared by the number of degrees of their openings.

- The sum of the angles in any triangle is 180 degrees and the sum of the angles of any quadrilateral is 360 degrees.

- Perpendicular lines intersect at right angles and parallel lines never intersect.

CHAPTER 18 **Angles and Lines**

Unit 9 Geometry and Measurement

BIG IDEAS!

- The formulas for the area of parallelograms, rectangles, and triangles are related to one another.

- Surface area and volume are two ways to describe solid objects.

CHAPTER 21 Area

Maintaining California Standards	Reading & Writing Math	Science, History-Social Science, and Data
Key Standards Review, pages 457, 477	**Reading and Writing Math,** pages 449, 466, 488	**Problem Solving Field Trip,** page 464
Problem Solving on Tests, page 465	**Vocabulary,** pages 451, 471	**Science Link,** pages 456, 484
Spiral Review and Test Practice, pages 469, 491		**History-Social Science Link,** page 462
		Real World Data, page 481

Percent

Unit 11 # Integers

 BIG IDEAS!

- You can identify, compare, and order negative numbers on a number line.

- You can model addition and subtraction with negative numbers on a number line.

- There is a set of rules to follow when adding and subtracting integers.

CHAPTER 25

Understand and Add Integers

Contents

CHAPTER 26 Add and Subtract Integers

Maintaining California Standards	Reading & Writing Math	Science, History-Social Science, and Data
Key Standards Review, pages 547, 567 **Problem Solving on Tests,** page 555 **Spiral Review and Test Practice,** pages 559, 577	**Reading and Writing Math,** pages 539, 556, 574 **Vocabulary,** pages 541, 561	**Problem Solving Field Trip,** page 554 **Science Link,** pages 546, 566 **Real World Data,** pages 552, 570

Contents

Unit 12 Coordinate Plane

BIG IDEAS!

- Using integers, you can plot points in the coordinate plane.
- Rules about sets of numbers can be written as equations, used to complete function tables, and plotted on graphs as lines.

CHAPTER 27 Plot Points

Contents

Graph Linear Equations

Contents

Maintaining California Standards	Reading & Writing Math	Science, History-Social Science, and Data
Key Standards Review, pages 593, 609	**Reading and Writing Math,** pages 583, 598, 618	**Problem Solving Field Trip,** page 596
Problem Solving on Tests, page 597	**Vocabulary,** pages 585, 603	**Science Link,** page 608
Spiral Review and Test Practice, pages 601, 621		**Real World Data,** page 592

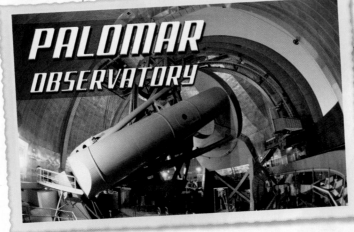

PALOMAR OBSERVATORY

Back to School

Welcome!

Scientists, athletes, artists, and health-care workers all use math every day—and you will too. This year in math you'll learn about numbers, patterns, shapes, and different ways to measure. You'll use the mathematics you know to solve problems and describe objects and patterns you see. You can get started by finding out about yourself as a mathematician and about the other students in your class.

Real Life Connection
Collecting Data

About Me

Write your math autobiography by answering these questions. You can write about other experiences as well, as long as they tell about you as a math student.

- What do you like best about math class?
- What are you good at in math class?
- How do you use math outside of math class?
- How do you think you might use mathematics in the future?

About My Class

Many of your classmates may like the same things in math that you like. Other classmates may like totally different things.

- Think of one topic you'd like to know your classmates' opinions about.
- Write a survey question for your topic.
- Conduct your survey among your classmates.
- Make a line or bar graph to show your results.
- Write a paragraph, using words and numbers to describe your results. Include predictions about your survey results if you surveyed 100 students.

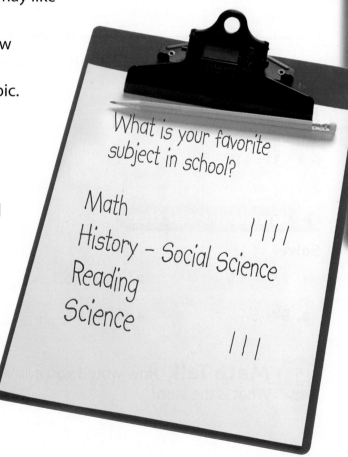

Back to School

Problem Solving and Numbers

Objective Review basic number and problem-solving skills

▶ Review and Remember

You have worked before with whole numbers and decimals. You can use the math you already know to find information about a lot of things.

Josh, Micki, and Jana walked in a walkathon for charity. To raise money, they asked friends and family to pledge an amount of money for each mile they walked. Josh's uncle pledged $3 per mile.

Josh recorded each distance as he completed the walkathon. How far has he walked? How much did Josh's uncle give?

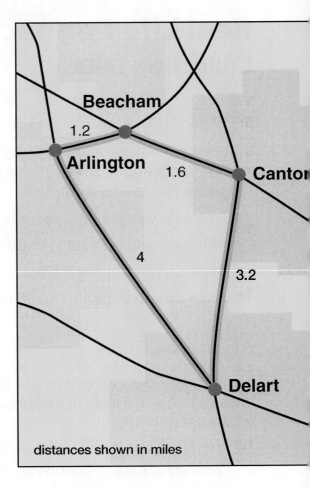

distances shown in miles

Arlington to Beacham	1.2 miles
Beacham to Canton	1.6 miles
Canton to Delart	3.2 miles

You can add and multiply to find the answers.

Distance
$1.2 + 1.6 + 3.2 = 6.0$ miles

Amount
$6 \times \$3 = \$18$

▶ Guided Practice

Solve.

1. $2.5 + 5.9$

2. $14.5 - 6.3$

3. 9×5

4. 17×4

Ask Yourself

- Did I align the decimal points?
- Are my answers reasonable?

 Math Talk How would you add 4.7 and 5.68? What is the sum?

Solve.

5. 9.45 − 3.46

6. 5.25 + 4.53 + 2.4 + 0.32

7. 100.3 − 17.67

8. 18 × 6

9. 7 × 70

10. 38 × 9

11. 46 × 76

You have learned many problem-solving strategies. Solve each problem. Explain which strategy you used.

12. Look at the map on the previous page. What is the distance of the entire walkathon? How much farther does Josh have to walk?

13. Micki and Jana ran for part of the route. Micki ran $\frac{3}{8}$ mile and Jana ran $\frac{5}{8}$ mile. Who ran farther?

14. Josh and Jana completed the entire walkathon. Micki had time to walk only 4.8 miles. Which sections of the route did she walk?

15. Multistep Josh's mother pledged $2.00 a mile. Jana's uncle pledged $1.50 a mile. How much did they give for Jana's and Josh's walk?

16. Create and Solve Write and solve a word problem using the information from the map on page B2. Exchange with a partner.

 Spiral Review and Test Practice

Open Response

Multiply or divide. (Grade 4)

17. 14 × 3

18. 27 × 200

19. 168 ÷ 3

20. 2,064 ÷ 2

Multiple Choice

21. Robert ate $\frac{1}{4}$ of the pizza and his brother ate $\frac{1}{4}$. How much was left for their mother?

A $\frac{1}{4}$ **B** $\frac{1}{2}$ **C** 0 **D** $\frac{2}{8}$

Measurement

Objective Review basic measurement skills needed to start fifth grade.

▶ Explore

You can use math to describe the size of your classroom. (With your teacher, you may decide to describe the size of a smaller, rectangular section of the room.) First, review how to measure length to the nearest foot.

Materials
12-inch ruler yardstick

inches

0 1 2 3 4 5 6 7 8 9 10 11 12 13 14 15 16 17 18 19 20 21 22 23 24 25 26 27 28 29 30 31 32 33 34 35 36
yardstick

Work with a partner. First, make a chart like this one to record your work.

		My Estimate	Measurement
1.	Length		
2.	Width		
3.	Area		

1 Estimate the length and width of your classroom in feet. Record your estimate.

2 Decide whether you will use a yardstick or ruler to measure your classroom. Measure and record the length and width of the room. Round each measurement to the nearest foot.

• How close are your measurements to your estimates?

3 Estimate the area of your classroom. Then use your measurements to find the area of the classroom.

• How do you find the area of a rectangle?

• How do you label area?

• How close was your estimate to the actual area of your classroom?

4. Draw a sketch of your classroom. Use the measurements in your chart to label each side of your sketch.

5. Use your sketch and measurements to find the perimeter of your classroom.

Use centimeter grid paper to answer these questions.

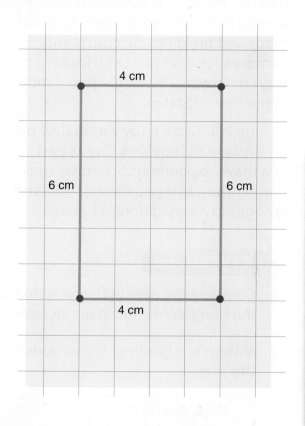

6. Copy this rectangle on your paper. Find the perimeter and area of the rectangle.

7. Draw another rectangle with the same area but different length and width. Label the length, width, and perimeter.

8. What is the area of a rectangle that has twice the length and twice the width of the rectangle at the right?

9. What is the perimeter of a rectangle with the same length and width as the rectangle in Problem 8?

Writing Math

10. You are explaining to a younger student how to choose the best measuring instrument for a project. For which types of projects would you use a ruler? A yardstick?

11. Suppose the rectangles you drew for Problems 6 and 7 were models for the floors of two classrooms. Which rectangle do you think is a better shape for a classroom? Tell why you think so. Use the words *length*, *width*, *perimeter*, and *area* in your explanation.

Science Connection
Meet the Eagles

Eagles are large birds that usually build their nests near the tops of tall trees. Many eagle habitats have been destroyed, though, as people have cut down forests to build roads and buildings. Scientists and conservationists have been looking for ways to increase the eagle population in the United States.

In June 2002, four baby eagles flew on an airplane to New York City as part of a brave experiment. Scientists were hoping the eagle pairs would nest and lay eggs in a very different habitat!

▶ **Try These**

1. Compare the data in the table. In the 1990s, did the number of eagle pairs increase or decrease?

2. Make a line graph of the data, using a grid like this one.

Eagle Pairs in the United States	
Year	Number of Eagle Pairs
1990	3,035
1993	4,015
1996	5,094
1999	6,104

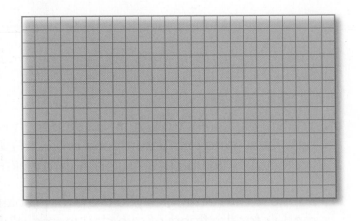

3. When did the number of eagle pairs increase the most? The least?

4. Would you say that the efforts of scientists and conservationists to increase the eagle population have been successful? Why or why not?

Unit 1

Number Theory and Fractions

BIG IDEAS!

- You can write any number as the product of its prime factors, using exponents to show multiples of a factor.
- You can identify fractions and mixed numbers as points on a number line.
- You can rename fractions as mixed numbers to show the simplest form.

Chapter 1
Prime Factorization and Exponents

Chapter 2
Fractions and Mixed Numbers

Songs and Games

Math Music Track 1:
Composite or Prime?

eGames at
www.eduplace.com/camap/

Math Readers

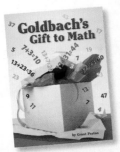

California is the second largest producer in the United States of oranges, lemons, and other citrus fruits.

Game

Roll the Factors

Object of the Game Find the product of four digits using a number cube.

Materials
Number cube (labeled 1–6)

Number of Players 2–3

How to Play

1 Player 1 rolls a number cube four times. He or she writes each number down and then multiplies all the digits. This number is the player's beginning number of points.

2 The other players take turns rolling the number cube and multiplying the digits to calculate their points.

3 The players continue taking turns rolling the number cube 4 times and finding the product of the digits. After each set of rolls, players add the new product to their points total.

4 Play continues until one player gets 1,000 points or above. That player wins the game.

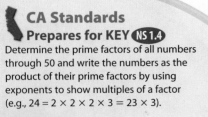

CA Standards
Prepares for KEY NS 1.4
Determine the prime factors of all numbers through 50 and write the numbers as the product of their prime factors by using exponents to show multiples of a factor (e.g., 24 = 2 × 2 × 2 × 3 = 23 × 3).

Also MR 2.3

Education Place
Visit www.eduplace.com/camap/ for **Brain Teasers** and **eGames** to play.

Reading Before reading a story or article, you can preview it to get an idea of what it's about and how it's organized. You can also preview a math lesson.

Preview Lesson 1 on pages 6–7.
This is what you'll find.

<u>Lesson 1 Preview</u>

✓ Lesson title: Find Prime Numbers

✓ Special kind of lesson: Hands On

✓ Objective (what you will learn): Identify prime numbers.

✓ Vocabulary (highlighted words): counting number, prime number, factor

✓ Main headings: Explore, Extend

✓ Special sections: Writing Math

✓ Special features: arrays, numbered steps, chart

This is a hands-on lesson. I'll follow the numbered steps to learn how to tell if a number is a prime number.

Writing Use the checklist to preview another lesson. See if the lesson includes the items listed in **red type**. Then write a sentence or two telling what you think the lesson is about or what you expect to do or to learn.

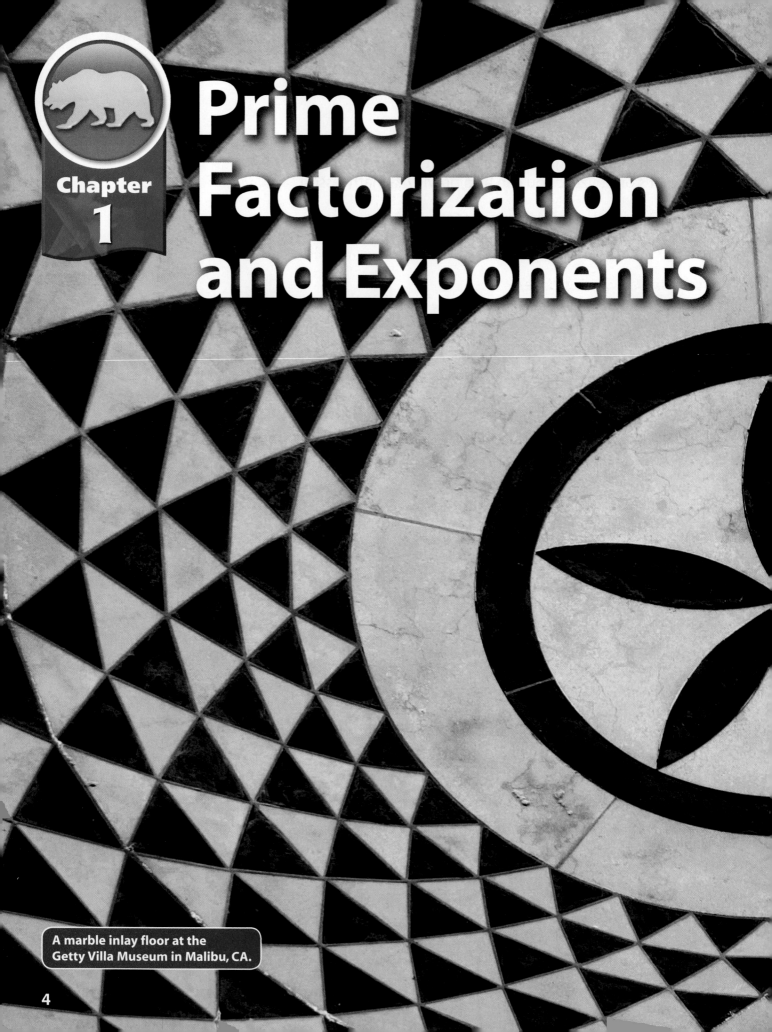

Prime Factorization and Exponents

A marble inlay floor at the
Getty Villa Museum in Malibu, CA.

Vocabulary and Concepts   GRADE 4 KEY NS 4.2 , MR 2.3

Match each word with a definition.

1. factor

2. prime number

3. composite number

a. A whole number that has more than two factors.

b. One of two or more numbers that are multiplied to give a product.

c. A whole number greater than 1 that has exactly two factors 1 and itself.

Which number is prime?

4. 2, 9, 13, 21

5. 4, 16, 25, 37

6. 33, 39, 41, 45

Skills   GRADE 4 AF 1.1

Add. Grade 4

7. $4 + 4 + 4 + \blacksquare = 17$

8. $7 + 7 + \blacksquare + 7 = 26$

9. $5 + 5 + 5 + 5 + \blacksquare = 31$

Problem Solving and Reasoning   GRADE 4 KEY NS 3.0

10. Emily had 48 muffins to sell. She wanted to sell the muffins in equal groups. What are four different ways she can group the muffins?

Vocabulary

Visualize It!

A **factor tree** is a diagram used to find the prime factors that make up a number.

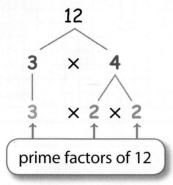

prime factors of 12

Language Tips

In everyday language, the word *common* means "usual or ordinary." In mathematics, *common* means "shared." The numbers 6 and 9 have 3 as a common factor.

Math words that look alike in English and Spanish often have the same meaning.

English	Spanish
number	**número**
factor	**factor**

See **English-Spanish Glossary** pages 628–642.

 Education Place Visit eduplace.com/camap for the **eGlossary** and vocabulary **eGames**.

CA Standards MR 2.3 Use a variety of methods, such as words, numbers, symbols, charts, graphs, tables, diagrams, and models, to explain mathematical reasoning. **Also KEY NS 1.4**

Chapter 1   5

CA Standards
KEY NS 1.4 Determine the prime factors of all numbers through 50 and write the numbers as the product of their prime factors by using exponents to show multiple factors (e.g., $24 = 2 \times 2 \times 2 \times 3 = 2^3 \times 3$).
Also MR 2.3, MR 2.4

Vocabulary

counting number

prime number

factor

Materials
- Learning Tool 9 (Inch Grid)
- Learning Tool 10 (Centimeter Grid)
- Crayons

Hands On
Find Prime Numbers

Objective Identify prime numbers.

▶ **Explore**

The numbers 1, 2, 3, 4, and so on are called **counting numbers**.

Numbers that have exactly two counting numbers as **factors** are called **prime numbers**. 2, 3, 5, 7, and 11 are examples of prime numbers.

1 is *not* a prime number because it has only 1 factor.

Henry has 24 tiles to make a table top. He can find the factors of 24 to find out how he can arrange 24 tiles into a rectangle for the table top.

Question How many ways can Henry arrange 24 tiles in equal rows to make a rectangular table top?

1 Cut out 24 squares from inch grid paper. Arrange them in equal rows.

2 Draw and shade the array on centimeter grid paper.

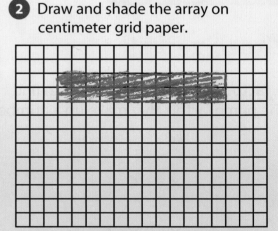

3 Record the array as a product of the rows × the number in each row.

$$2 \times 12$$

4 Repeat steps 1–3 until you have found all the possible arrangements.

How many different arrays can you make with 19 tiles?

1 Use 19 squares. Arrange them in equal rows.

2 Draw the array on grid paper.

3 Record the array.

4 Model and record all the possible arrays.

▶ **Extend**

Work with a partner. Choose 5 more numbers between 2 and 50. Copy and complete the table for each of your numbers.

	Number	Arrangements Possible	Factors
1.	24	1×24, 2×12, 3×8, 4×6, 6×4, 8×3, 12×2, 24×1	1, 2, 3, 4, 6, 8 12, 24
2.	19		1, 19
3.			
4.			
5.			
6.			
7.			

Compare tables as a class.

8. Which numbers between 1 and 50 are prime numbers?

9. What do you notice about the even numbers?

10. What do you notice about the odd numbers?

11. True or False? The greater the number, the more factors it has. Use your table to prove your answer.

Writing Math

Why is an even number greater than 2 never prime?

CA Standards

KEY NS 1.4 Determine the prime factors of all numbers through 50 and write the numbers as the product of their prime factors by using exponents to show multiple factors (e.g., $24 = 2 \times 2 \times 2 \times 3 = 2^3 \times 3$).

MR 2.4 Express the solution clearly and logically by using the appropriate mathematical notation and terms and clear language; support solutions with evidence in both verbal and symbolic work.

Also AF 1.1, SDAP 1.0

Vocabulary

composite number

Hint
The array for 2×6 and the array for 6×2 show the same pair of factors. So you do not need to draw both of them.

Find Factors of a Number

Objective Identify the factors of a number and write whether the number is prime or composite.

▶ **Learn by Example**

In Lesson 1, you learned some ways to identify prime numbers. In this lesson, you will find all the factors of a number and use the factors to decide if the number is prime or composite.

A prime number is a counting number greater than 1 with exactly two different factors—1 and itself.

A **composite number** is a number that has more than two different factors that are counting numbers.

The number 1 is neither prime nor composite.

Different Ways to Find Factors of 12

Way 1 **Draw rectangular arrays.**

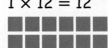

$1 \times 12 = 12$

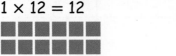

$2 \times 6 = 12$

$3 \times 4 = 12$

Way 2 **Use division.**

1 Divide by 1. $12 \div 1 = 12$
There is no remainder, so 1 and 12 are factors of 12. Other factors of 12 will be between 1 and 12.

2 Divide by 2. $12 \div 2 = 6$
2 and 6 are factors of 12. Other factors of 12 will be between 2 and 6.

3 Divide by 3. $12 \div 3 = 4$
3 and 4 are factors of 12.

4 There are no counting numbers between 3 and 4. So you know you have found all the factors.

Solution: The factors of 12 are 1, 2, 3, 4, 6 and 12. So, 12 is a composite number.

Ask Yourself
Can I use a different method to check my work?

Draw arrays to find the factors of the number. Then write if the number is *prime* or *composite*.

1. 7   **2.** 9   **3.** 11   **4.** 15

Use division to find the factors of the number. Then write if the number is *prime* or *composite*.

5. 12   **6.** 19   **7.** 21   **8.** 27

9. 43   **10.** 50   **11.** 4   **12.** 6

Guided Problem Solving

Use the questions to help you solve this problem.

13. Pedro has 16 tiles. He wants to arrange them in an array. How many different arrays can Pedro make using the tiles?

   a. Understand How many tiles does Pedro have?

   b. Plan How can drawing pictures help you find the number of arrays Pedro can make?

   c. Solve Draw pictures that show possible arrays. Pedro can make ◯ arrays.

   d. Look Back How can you use division to check your answer?

 Math Talk Is any odd number composite?

Hint
The arrays for 1×16 and 16×1 look different. Count them both to find the total number of arrays.

▶ **Practice and Problem Solving**

Draw arrays to find the factors of the number. Then write if the number is *prime* or *composite*.

14. 13   **15.** 22   **16.** 26   **17.** 34   **18.** 39

Use division to find the factors of the number. Then write if the number is *prime* or *composite*.

19. 11   **20.** 14   **21.** 17   **22.** 33   **23.** 48   **24.** 49

Solve.

25. At a science museum, visitors were handed numbered tickets. Tickets with prime numbers won free posters. Which tickets at the right would win posters?

26. Zach has 12 photos. Tara has 17 photos. Who can make more arrays with their photos? Explain.

27. Right or Wrong? Rosa says that 12, 18, and 20 all have the same number of possible arrays. Is she right or wrong? Explain.

 Real World Data

Use the pictograph to solve Problems 28–31.

28. How many students voted for Zeum?

29. How many students voted in all?

30. How many more students voted for Zeum than for the Palm Springs Air Museum?

31. Suppose you want to redo the pictograph but you want to be sure you can use only whole symbols, not just parts of symbols.

   a. Could you use a symbol to stand for 2 votes?

   b. Could you use a symbol to stand for 5 votes?

   c. Challenge What is the greatest number of votes a symbol could stand for?

Which Museum Would You Like to Visit?

Ms. Ramos asked students to choose a museum they would like to visit. The votes are shown in the pictograph.

Zeum	웃 웃 웃 웃 웃 웃 웃 웃 웃 웃
Palm Springs Air Museum	웃 웃 웃 웃 웃 웃
Golden Gate Railroad Museum	웃 웃 웃 웃 웃 웃 웃 웃

Key: 1 웃 stands for 3 votes.

Spiral Review and Test Practice

Simplify. GRADE 4 KEY **AF 1.2**

32. $2 + (3 \times 1)$ **33.** $(38 - 4) - 6$ **34.** $6 \times (4 - 3)$ **35.** $38 - (4 \div 2)$

Write the letter of the correct answer. KEY **NS 1.4**

36. Which number has only two different factors?

   A 10   **B** 9   **C** 6   **D** 3

Key Standards Review

Multiply or divide. GRADE 4 KEY **NS 3.3** , GRADE 4 KEY **NS 3.4**

1. 16×22

2. $7\overline{)175}$

3. $128 \div 4$

4. $\begin{array}{r} 32 \\ \times\ 15 \\ \hline \end{array}$

5. $387 \div 9$

6. $\begin{array}{r} 82 \\ \times\ 14 \\ \hline \end{array}$

7. $3\overline{)546}$

8. 49×11

9. $432 \div 8$

10. $\begin{array}{r} 18 \\ \times\ 21 \\ \hline \end{array}$

11. $945 \div 9$

12. $\begin{array}{r} 24 \\ \times\ 11 \\ \hline \end{array}$

Write the value of each expression below. GRADE 4 KEY **AF 1.2**

13. $17 - (6 + 4)$

14. $(13 + 5) - (9 - 1)$

15. $(11 + 5) \div 4$

16. $(14 \div 2) \times (4 - 1)$

17. $(8 \times 7) \div (4 - 2)$

18. $(16 \div 4) \times (8 - 4)$

19. $(18 + 12) \div (3 \times 2)$

20. $(21 \div 7) \times (9 + 4)$

21. $(6 \times 3) \div (14 - 5)$

22. $(4 \times 3) \times (7 + 5)$

23. $(10 \times 10) \div (4 \div 2)$

24. $(16 + 9) \times (5 + 2)$

Challenge

Number Sense

Twin Primes KEY AF 1.4

Prime numbers with a difference of 2 are called twin primes. The numbers 3 and 5 are twin primes. List all pairs of twin primes between 1 and 99.

Consecutive Factors

A three-digit number greater than 500 has five consecutive whole numbers among its factors. What could the three-digit number be?

Vocabulary Tip

Consecutive whole numbers are whole numbers that increase by one at each step.

CA Standards

KEY NS 1.4 Determine the prime factors of all numbers through 50 and write the numbers as the product of their prime factors by using exponents to show multiple factors (e.g., $24 = 2 \times 2 \times 2 \times 3 = 2^3 \times 3$).

MR 2.3 Use a variety of methods, such as words, numbers, symbols, charts, graphs, tables, diagrams, and models to explain mathematical reasoning.

Vocabulary

prime factorization

$20 = 2 \times 2 \times 5$

factor tree

Prime Factorization

Objective Write the prime factorization of a composite number.

▶ **Learn by Example**

In Lesson 2, you learned that a *composite number* has more than two factors. Any composite number can be written as the product of prime factors. An expression written as a product of prime numbers is called the **prime factorization** of the number.

You can use a **factor tree** to find the prime factorization of a number.

Write the prime factorization of 24.

---

1 Write 24 as the product of two factors that are either prime or composite.

24
$4 \quad \times \quad 6$

2 Write each composite factor as a product of numbers until only prime numbers are obtained.

24
$4 \quad \times \quad 6$
$2 \times 2 \times 2 \times 3$

3 Write the prime factors from the bottom row of the factor tree.

$2 \times 2 \times 2 \times 3$

Solution: The prime factorization of 24 is $2 \times 2 \times 2 \times 3$.

▶ **Guided Practice**

Ask Yourself

· Are all my factors prime numbers, or can some be factored further?

· Does the product of all the prime factors give the original number?

Make a factor tree. Then write the prime factorization. If the number is prime, write *prime*.

1. 27   **2.** 29   **3.** 33   **4.** 45

 Math Talk Look back at Exercise 1. If you used a different first factor pair, would the prime factorization be the same? Explain.

**Make a factor tree. Then write the prime factorization.
If the number is prime, write *prime*.**

5. 2   **6.** 3   **7.** 4   **8.** 5   **9.** 6

10. 7   **11.** 8   **12.** 9   **13.** 10   **14.** 11

15. 14   **16.** 28   **17.** 35   **18.** 42   **19.** 49

Solve.

20. The director of the art museum has between 45 and 55 paintings to display. She wishes to display an equal number on each of two walls. How many paintings could the museum display? Give all possible answers.

21. Challenge Each of two composite numbers has 2, 3, and 5 in its prime factorization, but one number is twice as large as the other. What might the numbers be?

 Real World Data

Solve.

22. In 1848, a star for Wisconsin was added to the flag. The number of stars was between 25 and 40 and had three different prime factors. Write the number and its prime factorization.

23. After the California star was added in 1851, the flag had a prime number of stars. This had last happened when the flag had 29 stars. How many stars were on the flag?

Stars and Stripes

- Since 1818, the United States flag has had 13 stripes (one for each of the 13 original states), and one star for each state.

- New stars are added on the 4th of July following the admission of each new state.

- Until 1912, the arrangement of the stars on the flag could vary. So all flags did not look the same.

✓ **Spiral Review and Test Practice**

Multiply. GRADE 4 KEY **NS 3.2**

24. 345 × 22   **25.** 451 × 30   **26.** 405 × 28   **27.** 500 × 23

Write the letter of the correct answer. KEY **NS 1.4**

28. What is the prime factorization of 48?

   A 3 × 4 × 4   **B** 2 × 2 × 2 × 2 × 3   **C** 2 × 2 × 2 × 3   **D** 2 × 2 × 2 × 6

Vocabulary

base

exponent

The base is the repeated factor.

$$2^3$$

The exponent tells how many times the base is a factor.

Exponents and Prime Factorization

Objective Use exponents to show repeated multiplication of a number and to write the prime factorization of a number.

▶ **Learn by Example**

In this lesson, you will learn how to use exponents and to write the prime factorization of a number using exponents.

A short way to write the expression $2 \times 2 \times 2$ is 2^3. Read as "2 to the third power."

The 2 is the **base**, or repeated factor. The 3 is the **exponent**.

$$2^3 = 2 \times 2 \times 2 = 8$$

Use exponents to write the prime factorization of 36.

---

1 Find the prime factors of 36.

$$2 \times 2 \times 3 \times 3$$

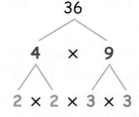

2 Write the expression using prime factors and exponents.

$$36 = 2^2 \times 3^2$$

$$36 = \underbrace{2 \times 2}_{2^2} \times \underbrace{3 \times 3}_{3^2}$$

Ask Yourself

• Did I use exponents?

• Does the exponent show the correct number of factors?

▶ **Guided Practice**

Write the expression using exponents.

1. $4 \times 4 \times 4$ **2.** $3 \times 3 \times 3 \times 3 \times 3 \times 3$

Write the expression as a product of the factors. Find the value.

3. 7^2 **4.** 2^6 **5.** 8^1 **6.** 4^4

Write the prime factorization. Use exponents if possible. If the number is prime, write *prime*.

7. 15   **8.** 37   **9.** 48   **10.** 32

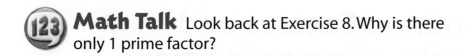 **Math Talk** Look back at Exercise 8. Why is there only 1 prime factor?

▶ Practice and Problem Solving

Write the expression using exponents.

11. $3 \times 3 \times 3 \times 3$

12. 4×4

13. $10 \times 10 \times 10 \times 10 \times 10$

14. $11 \times 11 \times 11 \times 11 \times 11 \times 11$

Write the expression as a product of the factors. Find the value.

15. 6^2

16. 9^3

17. 5^4

18. 10^5

19. 3^4

20. 2^4

21. 4^3

22. 1^5

Write the prime factorization. Use exponents if possible. If the number is prime, write *prime*.

23. 9   **24.** 21   **25.** 40   **26.** 41   **27.** 45   **28.** 47

Solve.

29. Light travels at a speed of 3×10^8 meters per second. Write the speed of light as a product of the factors.

30. Jing's mother has a habit of telling her age as a prime factorization. Her age now is $2^2 \times 3^2$. How old is Jing's mother?

31. Write the prime factorization of your age and the date of your birthday. Use exponents if possible.

32. Challenge Write the expression using exponents.
$a \times a \times a \times b \times b$

 Spiral Review and Test Practice

Add. KEY NS 2.3

33. $\frac{1}{4} + \frac{2}{4}$

34. $\frac{2}{5} + \frac{2}{5}$

35. $\frac{1}{3} + \frac{2}{3}$

36. $\frac{3}{6} + \frac{2}{6}$

Write the letter of the correct answer. KEY NS 1.4 page 14

37. What is the prime factorization of 18?

   A $2^2 \times 3$ **B** 2×3^2 **C** $2^2 \times 3^2$ **D** 2×9

Extra Practice See page 23, Set C.

CA Standards

KEY **NS 1.4** Determine the prime factors of all numbers through 50 and write the numbers as the product of their prime factors by using exponents to show multiple factors (e.g., $24 = 2 \times 2 \times 2 \times 3 = 2^3 \times 3$).

MR 2.4 Express the solution clearly and logically by using the appropriate mathematical notation and terms and clear language; support solutions with evidence in both verbal and symbolic work.

Also NS 1.3, MR 2.3

Vocabulary

common factor

greatest common factor (GCF)

Common Factors and Greatest Common Factor

Objective Find common factors of two numbers. Find the greatest common factor of two numbers.

▶ **Learn by Example**

You know how to find the factors of a number. Two numbers may have some of the same factors. These are called **common factors**. In this lesson you will learn how to find the **greatest common factor (GCF)** of two numbers.

Nam has 32 red chairs and 40 blue chairs to set up. The chairs must be in equal rows. All chairs in a row must be the same color. What is the longest possible row of chairs he can make?

Ways to Find the Greatest Common Factor of 32 and 40

Way 1   **You can use prime factorization.**

1 Make factor trees for 32 and 40.

$$
\begin{array}{cc}
32 & 40 \\
4 \times 8 & 2 \times 20 \\
2 \times 2 \times 4 \times 2 & 2 \times 2 \times 10 \\
2 \times 2 \times 2 \times 2 \times 2 & 2 \times 2 \times 2 \times 5
\end{array}
$$

2 Identify all the common prime factors.

$32 = 2 \times 2 \times 2 \times 2 \times 2$
$40 = 2 \times 2 \times 2 \times 5$

3 The greatest common factor (GCF) is the product of the common prime factors.

$2 \times 2 \times 2 = 2^3$
Greatest Common Factor

Way 2 You can make a list.

1 List all the factors of each number.

32: 1, 2, 4, 8, 16, 32
40: 1, 2, 4, 5, 8, 10, 20, 40

2 Identify common factors.

The common factors are 1, 2, 4, and 8.

3 Compare to find the greatest common factor.

The greatest common factor of 32 and 40 is 8.

Solution: The longest possible row Nam can make has 8 chairs.

▶ **Guided Practice**

Find the greatest common factor (GCF) of the numbers.

1. 9, 12   **2.** 2, 13   **3.** 4, 6

4. 8, 16   **5.** 3, 7   **6.** 16, 20

7. 9, 36   **8.** 18, 48   **9.** 17, 51

Ask Yourself
• What are all the factors of each number?
• Did I find all the common factors?
• Which is the greatest factor common to both numbers?

 **Math Talk** Is the GCF of two different prime numbers always 1? Explain.

▶ **Practice and Problem Solving**

Find the greatest common factor (GCF) of the numbers.

10. 14, 22   **11.** 10, 15   **12.** 9, 25   **13.** 15, 17

14. 20, 38   **15.** 4, 12   **16.** 13, 19   **17.** 3, 9

18. 6, 15   **19.** 8, 32   **20.** 10, 14   **21.** 12, 42

22. 9, 21   **23.** 20, 25   **24.** 7, 11   **25.** 12, 24

True of false?

26. The GCF of 126 and 45 is 9.

27. The GCF of 126 and 70 is 7.

28. The GCF of 357 and 102 is 3.

29. The GCF of 260 and 308 is 4.

Hint
Divide both numbers by the GCF. The statement is true if the two new numbers have no common factors.

 Science Link

Solve. Use the Fun Facts to help you solve problems 30–32.

30. What fraction of the atoms in a molecule of sugar are carbon atoms? What fraction are hydrogen atoms?

31. The students making models are using balls of clay to represent the atoms in a sugar molecule. If each student makes one sugar molecule, how many balls of clay are needed for 18 students?

32. A class is learning how different atoms combine to form molecules. Students are divided into equal groups. There are 18 students making models and 12 students making posters.

   a. Could the students be working in equal groups of 2? equal groups of 3? equal groups of 4?

   b. What are the largest equal-size groups the class could be divided into?

Food Chemistry

• Table sugar is a compound made of 3 elements: carbon, hydrogen, and oxygen.

• Each molecule of table sugar has 6 carbon atoms, 12 hydrogen atoms, and 6 oxygen atoms. The formula is $C_6H_{12}O_6$.

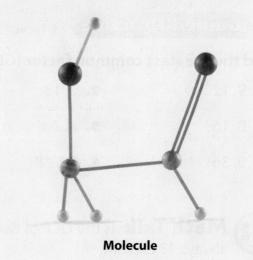

Molecule

Science PS 1.b, PS 1.g

 Spiral Review and Test Practice

Divide. GRADE 4 KEY NS 3.2

33. $264 \div 3$ **34.** $4\overline{)456}$ **35.** $754 \div 5$ **36.** $6\overline{)247}$ **37.** $897 \div 6$

Write the letter of the correct answer. Prepares for KEY NS 1.4

38. What is the greatest common factor (GCF) of 36 and 48?

   A 1   **B** 3   **C** 6   **D** 12

Extra Practice See page 23, Set D.

Use the Clues

Use the clues to solve.

1. I'm less than 50. I have factors of 3, 5, and 9. Who am I?

2. I am a common factor in 12, 24, 36, and 48. I am greater than 5 but less than 10. Who am I?

3. We both have a zero in the ones place. We both have a factor of 15. We are both less than 75. Who are we?

4. I am a common factor in 14, 21, and 42. Who am I?

5. We have a product less than 60. Our product has two odd, prime factors and one is 13. Who are we?

6. We both have a common factor of 3. We are both two-digit numbers between 60 and 100. We have the same digits but they have different place values. Who are we?

7. Add all of the answers from Exercises 1–6. Did you get more than the number of days in a year?

8. What if, in Problem 4, 14 was 9? Who am I?

9. Design your own puzzle with 2 prime factors and a product which is greater than 100.

CA Standards
Prepares for KEY **NS 1.4**,
MR 1.1, MR 3.1

LESSON **6**

Field Trip...

Palm Springs, CA

CA Standards
MR 1.0, MR 1.1,
MR 2.0, MR 2.3,
MR 3.1

KEY **NS 1.4**
Prepares for
KEY **AF 1.5**

Problem Solving

Objective Use skills and strategies to solve word problems.

The Agua Caliente Cultural Museum teaches people about the Agua Caliente Band of Cahuilla Indians.

Solve. Tell which strategy or method you used.

1. The museum's southern California basket collection contains over 200 baskets. The staff wants to display 50 coil baskets on shelves. Each shelf will hold the same number of baskets.

   a. How many different ways can they arrange the baskets?

   b. Justify Which arrangements will the staff most likely consider? Explain why this is reasonable.

2. The baskets in the museum were crafted by Cahuilla women. Designs on the baskets include people, plants, and animals. Suppose three baskets had 15, 24, and 29 symbols. Write each number as a product of prime factors. Is one of them a prime number?

3. The museum is having a meeting and needs to set up 48 chairs in equal rows. What are all of the possible arrays the chairs can be arranged? Use a drawing to help you.

4. A basket was purchased for $300 one year. The next year the same basket was valued at $325. In the third year, the value was $350. If the pattern continues, predict how much the basket will be worth in six years.

Rabbit basket from the Agua Caliente Cultural Museum

Problem Solving On Tests

Select a Strategy
- Draw a Picture
- Write an Equation
- Guess and Check
- Choose the Operation
- Make a Table

1. The table shows the population of four U.S. cities in 2004. Which city had the greatest population?

Population in 2004	
City	**Population**
San Diego, CA	1,263,756
Phoenix, AZ	1,418,041
Philadelphia, PA	1,470,151
San Antonio, TX	1,236,249

A San Diego, CA

B Phoenix, AZ

C Philadelphia, PA

D San Antonio, TX

Test Tip
Use place value to help eliminate answer choices.

GRADE 4 KEY NS 1.2

2. In a close election for mayor Mrs. Callahan received 2,687 votes and Miss Devlin received 2,459 votes. What was the total number of votes cast for these two candidates?

A 4,136   **C** 5,136

B 4,146   **D** 5,146

GRADE 4 KEY NS 3.1

3. A total of 36,452 tickets were sold for the county fair this year. Last year, 28,385 tickets were sold. How many more tickets were sold this year than last year?

A 8,067   **C** 12,133

B 12,063   **D** 18,067

GRADE 4 KEY NS 3.1

4. At 6:00 A.M., the temperature was ⁻9°F. By 10:00 A.M., the temperature was 5 degrees higher. What was the temperature at 10:00 A.M.?

A ⁻14°F

B ⁻4°F

C 4°F

D 14°F

Test Tip
Draw a thermometer or a number line to check your answer.

GRADE 4 KEY NS 1.8

5. Maureen bought a rectangular picture frame. Which equation represents the perimeter (*P*) of the picture frame in centimeters?

8 cm ▭ 24 cm

A $P = 24 \text{ cm} \times 8 \text{ cm}$

B $24 \text{ cm} = P \times 8 \text{ cm}$

C $P = (8 \text{ cm} \times 24 \text{ cm}) + (2 \text{ cm} \times 8 \text{ cm})$

D $P = (2 \times 24 \text{ cm}) + (2 \times 8 \text{ cm})$

GRADE 4 AF 1.4

6. Dan has a collection of 18 model sports cars. What is the prime factorization of 18?

A $2^2 \times 9$ **C** 2×3^2

B $2^2 \times 3^2$ **D** $2^2 \times 6$

KEY NS 1.4 page 12

Education Place
Visit www.eduplace.com/camap/ for **Test-Taking Tips** and **Extra Practice**.

Reading & Writing Math

Vocabulary

Many numbers break down in different ways.

Use the **Word Bank** to match each term with its definition.

1. A _____ is one of two or more numbers that are multiplied to give a product.

2. A _____ is a whole number that has exactly two factors, 1 and itself.

3. A _____ is a whole number that has more than two factors.

4. The _____ tells how many times the base is a factor.

You can show a number as the product of its prime factors by making a **factor tree**.

Step 1:	Write any pair of factors for the number 72.
Step 2:	Write a pair of factors for each number until all the factors are prime numbers.
Step 3:	Write the prime factor of the number. The prime factorization of 72 is $3 \times 3 \times 2 \times 2 \times 2$.

Writing Explain why the number 1 is neither a prime nor a composite number. Use the words in the Word Bank in your explanation.

Reading Check out this book in your library. *On Beyond a Million: An Amazing Math Journey,* by David M. Schwartz.

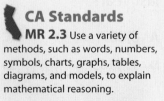

CA Standards

MR 2.3 Use a variety of methods, such as words, numbers, symbols, charts, graphs, tables, diagrams, and models, to explain mathematical reasoning.

Also NS 1.3, KEY NS 1.4

Standards-Based Extra Practice

Prepares for KEY **NS 1.4** page 8

Set A

Use division to find the factors of each number. Then write if the number is *prime* or *composite*.

1. 5   **2.** 20   **3.** 26   **4.** 31

Solve.

5. Paula wants to arrange 18 posters in an array. How many different arrays can she make? Describe the arrays.

KEY **NS 1.4** page 12

Set B

Write the prime factorization of each number. If the number is prime, write *prime*.

1. 12   **2.** 13   **3.** 25   **4.** 36

Solve.

5. Sam says that the prime factorization of 24 is $2 \times 2 \times 6$. Is he right? Explain.

NS 1.3, KEY **NS 1.4** page 14

Set C

Write the prime factorization. Use exponents if possible. If the number is prime, write *prime*.

1. 44   **2.** 36   **3.** 47   **4.** 50

Solve.

5. The California highway system has about 30,000 signs. This can be written as $3 \times 10 \times 10 \times 10 \times 10$. Write the number of signs using exponents.

KEY **NS 1.4** page 16

Set D

Find the greatest common factor (GCF) of the numbers.

1. 6, 18   **2.** 12, 9   **3.** 16, 20   **4.** 4, 17

Solve.

5. Mario is arranging 63 paperback books and 36 hardcover books in equal rows. Each row must be all paperback or all hardcover books. What is the greatest number of books he can put in a row?

Education Place
Visit www.eduplace.com/camap/ for
Test-Taking Tips and **Extra Practice**.

Chapter Review/Test

Vocabulary and Concepts ———————————————— NS 1.3, KEY NS 1.4, MR 2.3

Write the best word to complete each sentence.

1. In the number 3^2, the 3 is the base, and the 2 is the _____.

2. The number 28 has more than two factors, so it is _____.

3. If two numbers have some of the same factors, those factors are called _____ factors.

4. The number 5 is _____, because it has exactly two factors.

Skills ———————————————————————————— NS 1.3, KEY NS 1.4

Find the factors of the number. Write if the number is *prime* **or** *composite***.**

5. 18   6. 29   7. 24   8. 40   9. 35

Write the expression as a product of the factors. Then find the value.

10. 1^6 11. 4^3 12. 9^2 13. 2^5 14. 3^3

Write the prime factorization of each number. Use exponents if possible. Find the greatest common factor (GCF) of the numbers.

15. 16, 12   16. 20, 18   17. 5, 7   18. 15, 21

Problem Solving and Reasoning ——————— Prepares for KEY NS 1.4, MR 1.0, MR 2.3

Solve.

19. Sienna is arranging 12 jars of spices on shelves. She wants an equal number of jars on each shelf. What are all the possible ways she can arrange the spices on the shelves?

20. Chelsea made 32 muffins for the bake sale. She needs to package them in boxes, with an equal number of muffins in each box. How many different ways can she package the muffins?

Writing Math Explain   Why is the number 1 neither prime nor composite? Explain.

Spiral Review and Test Practice

1. Which of the following is the number 372,601,000?

A three hundred seventy-two thousand, six hundred one

B three hundred seventy-two million, sixty-one thousand

C three hundred seventy-two million, six hundred one thousand

D three hundred seventy-two million, six hundred thousand

> **Test Tip**
> Write each number in the answer choices in standard form before choosing the correct answer.

GRADE 4 KEY NS 1.1

2. What is 820,568 rounded to the nearest hundred?

A 820,500 **C** 820,600

B 820,568 **D** 821,000

GRADE 4 KEY NS 1.3

3. $4,659 + 3,375 =$

A 7,034

B 7,934

C 8,024

D 8,034

> **Test Tip**
> Estimate first to rule out some answer choices.

GRADE 4 KEY NS 3.1

4. Which number has only two different factors?

A 25

B 16

C 12

D 7

KEY NS 1.4 page 8

5. What is the prime factorization of 36?

A $2 \times 2 \times 9$

B $2 \times 3 \times 6$

C $2 \times 2 \times 3 \times 3$

D $2 \times 2 \times 2 \times 3$

KEY NS 1.4 page 12

6. What is the prime factorization of 12?

A $2^2 \times 3^2$

B 2×3^2

C $2^2 \times 3$

D 3×4

KEY NS 1.4 page 14

Education Place
Visit www.eduplace.com/camap/ for
Test-Taking Tips and **Extra Practice**.

Chapter 2

Fractions and Mixed Numbers

Sea urchin shells, like those above, are found along the coast of California.

Vocabulary and Concepts   GRADE 4 NS 1.5, MR 2.3

Match each word with a definition.

1. fraction   **a.** the total number of parts

2. numerator   **b.** a number that names part of a whole or set

3. denominator   **c.** the number of parts that are shaded

Skills   GRADE 4 NS 1.7

Write the fraction for the shaded part.

4.   **5.**   **6.**   **7.**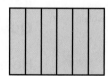

Problem Solving and Reasoning   GRADE 4 NS 1.7

8. One watermelon was cut into fourths. Another watermelon was cut into sixths. Which watermelon was cut into larger pieces?

Vocabulary

Visualize It!

equivalent fractions

fractions that show different numbers with the same value

$$\frac{3}{4} = \frac{6}{8}$$

mixed number

a number made up of a whole number and a fraction

$1\frac{2}{3}$

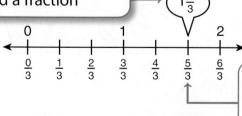

0			1			2
$\frac{0}{3}$	$\frac{1}{3}$	$\frac{2}{3}$	$\frac{3}{3}$	$\frac{4}{3}$	$\frac{5}{3}$	$\frac{6}{3}$

improper fraction

a fraction that has a numerator that is greater than or equal to its denominator

Language Tip

Math words that look alike in English and Spanish often have the same meaning.

English	Spanish
fraction	**fracción**
equivalent	**equivalente**

See **English-Spanish Glossary** pages 628–642.

The improper fraction $\frac{5}{3}$ and the mixed number $1\frac{2}{3}$ are equivalent.

Education Place Visit www.eduplace.com/camap/ for the **eGlossary** and **eGames**.

CA Standards MR 2.3 Use a variety of methods, such as words, numbers, symbols, charts, graphs, tables, diagrams, and models, to explain mathematical reasoning. **Also NS 1.0**

CA Standards
KEY **NS 1.5** Identify and represent on a number line decimals, fractions, mixed numbers, and positive and negative integers.

MR 2.3 Use a variety of methods, such as words, numbers, symbols, charts, graphs, tables, diagrams, and models, to explain mathematical reasoning.

Hands On
Represent Fractions

Objective Represent fractions in a model, on a number line, and as a division problem.

▶ **Explore**

In Chapter 1, you worked with whole numbers. In this lesson, you will work with another kind of number—fractions. You will model fractions in three ways.

Question What are some different ways to model fractions?

Here are two different ways to show $\frac{3}{4}$, $\frac{8}{4}$, and $\frac{9}{4}$.

---

1 Draw a model.

The denominator tells how many equal parts each whole must have. The numerator tells how many parts to shade.

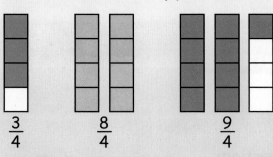

$\frac{3}{4}$　　　$\frac{8}{4}$　　　$\frac{9}{4}$

---

2 Use a number line.

The denominator tells how many equal sections each whole must be divided into.

The numerator tells how many sections to count, starting from 0. Draw a dot where you stop counting.

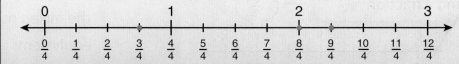

▶ **Extend**

You can use fractions to show division.

Jen made 6 pancakes for herself and 3 friends.
How can she share 6 pancakes equally between 4 people?

6 pancakes divided by 4 → $6 \div 4 = \frac{6}{4}$

1 How many whole pancakes can each person have?

1 whole pancake with 2 left over

2 How can the remaining pancakes be shared?

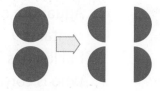

Each person gets another half pancake.

3 How many pancakes does each person get in all?

$6 \div 4 = \frac{6}{4} = 1\frac{1}{2}$

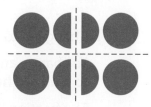

Each person gets $1\frac{1}{2}$ pancakes.

Use the fractions below for problems 1–4.

$\frac{1}{2}$ $\frac{8}{2}$ $\frac{5}{2}$

1. Draw a shaded model for each fraction.

2. Draw a number line and show the position of each fraction.

3. Draw and shade models to show each fraction as a division problem.

4. Write a division sentence for each fraction.

Writing Math

Explain You have 5 sandwiches and you want to equally share them among 3 people. How many sandwiches does each person get? Explain your thinking.

CA Standards

KEY NS 1.5 Identify and represent on a number line decimals, fractions, mixed numbers, and positive and negative integers.

MR 2.6 Make precise calculations and check the validity of the results from the context of the problem.

Also MR 1.1, KEY AF 1.2

Vocabulary

improper fraction

mixed number

Fractions and Mixed Numbers

Objective Represent, identify, and write fractions and mixed numbers on a number line.

▶ Learn by Example

In this lesson, you will focus on fractions that are equal to or greater than 1.

Sherry and Mike watch the zebra sharks feeding at the Aquarium of the Pacific in Long Beach. The feed bucket contains 9 fish. Each weighs $\frac{1}{4}$ pound. Mike says that the bucket has $\frac{9}{4}$ pounds of fish. Sherry says it has $2\frac{1}{4}$ pounds. Who is correct? Show both numbers on a number line.

You can compare the numbers in two ways.

① Change $\frac{9}{4}$ to a mixed number.

To change an **improper fraction** to a **mixed number**, you can divide.

The fraction bar stands for "divided by." So $\frac{9}{4}$ means "9 divided by 4."

$$\begin{array}{r} 2 \\ 4\overline{)9} \\ -8 \\ \hline 1 \end{array}$$
← number of wholes

← number of fourths

So $\frac{9}{4}$ is equal to $2\frac{1}{4}$.

② Change $2\frac{1}{4}$ to an improper fraction.

To change a mixed number to an improper fraction, you can multiply and add.

$$2\frac{1}{4} = \frac{9}{4}$$
← $(4 \times 2) + 1$

← denominator stays the same

③ Compare the fractions on a number line. Since both numbers share the same place on a number line, $\frac{9}{4}$ and $2\frac{1}{4}$ are the same.

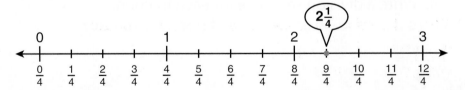

Zebra shark at the Aquarium of the Pacific in Long Beach, CA

Solution: Both Sherry and Mike are correct. $\frac{9}{4} = 2\frac{1}{4}$

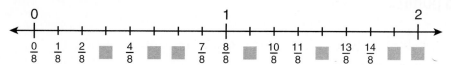
1. Look at the number line below. Write each missing fraction as an improper fraction. Then draw a picture to represent each missing fraction.

Ask Yourself
- How can I use a pattern to find the missing fraction?
- How can I use division to check my answers?

0   1   2

$\frac{0}{8}$ $\frac{1}{8}$ $\frac{2}{8}$ ■ $\frac{4}{8}$ ■   ■ $\frac{7}{8}$ $\frac{8}{8}$ ■ $\frac{10}{8}$ $\frac{11}{8}$ ■ $\frac{13}{8}$ $\frac{14}{8}$ ■   ■

Write the improper fraction as a mixed number or a whole number.

2. $\frac{7}{2}$ 3. $\frac{3}{2}$ 4. $\frac{8}{2}$ 5. $\frac{5}{2}$

Write the mixed number as an improper fraction.

6. $4\frac{1}{2}$ 7. $7\frac{1}{2}$ 8. $3\frac{1}{8}$ 9. $6\frac{5}{7}$

 Math Talk How can you tell whether a fraction can be written as either a mixed number or a whole number?

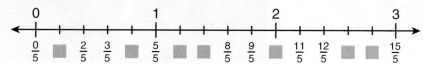
10. Look at the number line below. Write each missing fraction. Then draw a picture to represent each missing fraction.

0   1   2   3

$\frac{0}{5}$ ■ $\frac{2}{5}$ $\frac{3}{5}$ ■ $\frac{5}{5}$ ■   ■ $\frac{8}{5}$ $\frac{9}{5}$ ■ $\frac{11}{5}$ $\frac{12}{5}$ ■   ■ $\frac{15}{5}$

Write the improper fraction as a mixed number or a whole number.

11. $\frac{10}{5}$ 12. $\frac{8}{5}$ 13. $\frac{15}{7}$ 14. $\frac{9}{4}$ 15. $\frac{12}{5}$

Write the mixed number as an improper fraction.

16. $2\frac{3}{4}$ 17. $2\frac{3}{5}$ 18. $5\frac{2}{3}$ 19. $4\frac{2}{7}$ 20. $6\frac{1}{6}$

X **Algebra** Variables **If *m* and *n* are whole numbers not equal to zero, explain how *m* and *n* are related.**

21. $\frac{m}{n}$ is a fraction between 0 and 1.   22. $\frac{m}{n}$ is a fraction between 1 and 2.

Solve.

23. Pete saw 5 Atlantic and 3 horned puffins at the aquarium's diving birds exhibit. Write a fraction to show how many of the puffins were horned puffins.

24. The snake that Edita saw at the zoo is $5\frac{1}{4}$ feet longer than her arm. Write this number as an improper fraction.

History-Social Science Link

Solve.

25. If 11 salmon were split into 4 pieces each, how many salmon slices were there?

26. If each salmon is split into 6 pieces and there were 42 pieces, how many whole salmon were there?

27. There are 18 pieces of salmon ready to be traded. Each is $\frac{1}{4}$ of a whole salmon. Write the amount of salmon as an improper fraction and a mixed number.

28. Twenty-four salmon slices are hung to dry on lines. Each line has an equal number of salmon. In how many ways can the slices be arranged if each line holds between 5 and 12 slices? Explain.

Salmon Fishing in the Northwest

The economy of many Northwest Indian tribes depended on salmon fishing. Cleaned salmon were split into thin slices and hung to dry in the sun. This preserved the salmon for eating and trading.

History-Social Science 5.1.1

 Spiral Review and Test Practice

Find the prime factorization for the number. Use exponents. KEY **NS 1.4** page 14

29. 45

30. 42

31. 36

32. 28

Write the letter of the correct answer. KEY **NS 1.5**

33. Which point on the number line *best* represents $2\frac{3}{5}$?

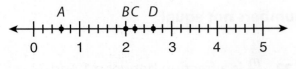

A A   **B** B   **C** C   **D** D

Extra Practice See page 43, Set A.

Key Standards Review

Need Help?
See Key Standards Handbook.

Use any method to find the factors of the number. Then write if each number is *prime* or *composite*. **KEY NS 1.4**

1. 31   **2.** 22   **3.** 13   **4.** 30

5. 16   **6.** 41   **7.** 19   **8.** 35

9. 28   **10.** 47   **11.** 29   **12.** 38

Logical Thinking

Mystery Fraction NS 1.0, NS 2.0

Use the clues to find the mystery fraction.

1. Clues:
- Its numerator and denominator are both prime numbers.
- Its numerator is greater than its denominator.
- Its numerator and denominator differ by 2.
- The sum of its numerator and denominator is 21, 22, 23, or 24.

2. Clues:
- Its denominator is greater than its numerator.
- Its denominator is a product of three prime numbers.
- Its denominator is greater than 10 and less than 15.
- The numerator is three times the greatest prime factor of the denominator.

3. Clues:
- Its numerator is greater than its denominator.
- Its numerator and denominator have a sum of 26.
- Its denominator is a prime number.
- Its denominator is greater than 10.

CA Standards
Prepares for

KEY **NS 2.3** Solve simple problems, including ones arising in concrete situations, involving the addition and subtraction of fractions and mixed numbers (like and unlike denominators of 20 or less), and express answers in the simplest form.

KEY **NS 1.5** Identify and represent on a number line decimals, fractions, mixed numbers, and positive and negative integers.

Also MR 1.0, MR 2.3

Vocabulary

equivalent fractions

simplest form

Materials
Fraction tiles

Equivalent Fractions and Simplest Form

Objective Find equivalent fractions and write fractions in simplest form.

▶ **Learn by Example**

At the San Diego Zoo, four sixths of the 12 lions are sleeping in the sun. How many lions are sleeping in the sun? Find fractions with different denominators that are equivalent to $\frac{4}{6}$.

Different Ways to Find Equivalent Fractions

Way 1   **You can use models or number lines.**

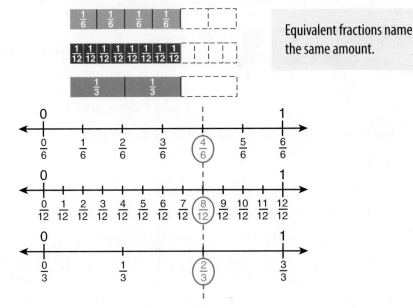

Equivalent fractions name the same amount.

Way 2   **You can multiply.**
Find the number to multiply the denominator by to obtain the new denominator. Multiply the numerator and the denominator by that number.

$$\frac{4}{6} = \frac{8}{12}$$

Way 3   **You can divide.**
Find the number to divide the denominator by to obtain the new denominator. Divide the numerator and the denominator by that number.

$$\frac{4}{6} = \frac{2}{3}$$

Solution: 8 of the 12 lions are sleeping in the sun.
$\frac{4}{6}$, $\frac{8}{12}$, and $\frac{2}{3}$ are **equivalent fractions**.

Another Example

In the previous example, you found $\frac{2}{3}$ by dividing the numerator and the denominator of $\frac{4}{6}$ by the GCF of 4 and 6. $\frac{2}{3}$ is $\frac{4}{6}$ and $\frac{8}{12}$ in **simplest form**. Here is another way to find simplest form.

> **Vocabulary Tip**
> **GCF** stands for **Greatest Common Factor**.

$$\frac{8}{12} = \frac{\overset{1}{\cancel{2}} \times \overset{1}{\cancel{2}} \times 2}{\underset{1}{\cancel{2}} \times \underset{1}{\cancel{2}} \times 3} = \frac{2}{3}$$

Write the prime factorization of the numerator and the denominator. Then cancel common factors and multiply.

▶ Guided Practice

Complete.

> **Ask Yourself**
> Did I multiply or divide the numerator and denominator by the same number?

1. $\frac{12}{18} = \frac{4}{6}$

2. $\frac{21}{12} = \frac{\square}{4}$

3. $\frac{4}{9} = \frac{\square}{54}$

Simplify the fraction.

4. $\frac{4}{36}$

5. $\frac{22}{10}$

6. $\frac{27}{45}$

7. $\frac{42}{24}$

Guided Problem Solving

8. Three fifths of the fish in a tank are clownfish. There are 20 fish in the tank. How many fish are clownfish?

   a. Understand What are you asked to find?

   b. Plan/Solve Write an equation. Use ▇ to stand for the number you need to find. Which equation can you solve to find the answer?

     A $\frac{3}{5} = \frac{\square}{20}$ **B** $\frac{3}{5} = \frac{20}{\square}$

   c. Look Back Read the problem again. Is your answer more or less than 20? Does that make sense?

Tomato Anemonefish (clownfish)

 Math Talk In Exercise 3, how did you decide whether to multiply or divide to find the missing numerator?

Practice and Problem Solving

Complete.

9. $\dfrac{1}{3} = \dfrac{\square}{9}$

10. $\dfrac{15}{35} = \dfrac{\square}{7}$

11. $\dfrac{3}{10} = \dfrac{9}{\square}$

12. $1\dfrac{3}{12} = \dfrac{\square}{4}$

13. $4 = \dfrac{\square}{6}$

Simplify the fraction.

14. $\dfrac{5}{10}$

15. $\dfrac{39}{15}$

16. $\dfrac{15}{18}$

17. $\dfrac{26}{18}$

18. $\dfrac{28}{42}$

19. $\dfrac{22}{30}$

 ## Science Link

Solve.

20. By weight, the fraction of chloride ions in sea salt is $\dfrac{55}{100}$. What is this fraction in simplest form?

21. The fraction of sodium ions in sea salt is about $\dfrac{30}{100}$. Express this fraction in 10ths and 20ths.

22. What fraction of sea salt is neither sodium nor chloride? Express the answer in 20ths.

23. Of all the water found on Earth, $\dfrac{98}{100}$ is salt water found in the oceans. Write this fraction in simplest form.

Salt Water

- Even though sea water is salty, it is not easy to see the salt because salts dissolve in water.

- The most common salt in sea water is sodium chloride (NaCl), or ordinary table salt.

- In water, sodium chloride separates into parts called ions.

Science PS 1.i

 ## Spiral Review and Test Practice

Write the prime factorization of the number. Use exponents if possible. KEY NS 1.4 pages 12 and 14

24. 42

25. 31

26. 49

27. 50

Write the letter of the correct answer. KEY NS 2.3

28. Which shows $\dfrac{24}{36}$ in simplest form?

   A $\dfrac{12}{18}$ **B** $\dfrac{8}{12}$ **C** $\dfrac{6}{9}$ **D** $\dfrac{2}{3}$

36

Extra Practice See page 43, Set B.

Quilting Squares

Sarima is a quilter who enjoys sewing quilts in all kinds of shapes, sizes, and colors. She will be sewing these large ribbon pattern squares together to create a quilt for her sister.

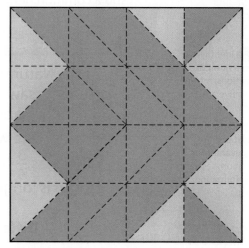

large ribbon pattern square

Use Sarima's quilt square to solve. Write your answers in simplest form.

1. What fraction of the large ribbon pattern square is gold? pink? blue?

2. Sarima finished a quilt using 20 of the large squares. Will the fraction of colors be different for the large quilt? Explain.

3. The world's largest quilt is made of panels that are 6 ft by 3 ft. They are sewn together in groups of 8 panels to form a square. Draw the square. What is its perimeter?

4. **Create and Solve** Draw a quilt pattern. Use it to write a word problem using fractions.

CA Standards
Prepares for KEY **NS 2.3**,
MG 1.4, MR 2.3, MR 2.4

CA Standards
KEY NS 1.5 Identify and represent on a number line decimals, fractions, mixed numbers, and positive and negative integers.

MR 1.1 Analyze problems by identifying relationships, distinguishing relevant from irrelevant information, sequencing and prioritizing information, and observing patterns.

Vocabulary

equivalent fractions

common denominator

Compare Fractions

Objective Compare fractions using a number line and a common denominator.

▶ **Learn by Example**

At the Natural History Museum, students saw the teeth of a Smilodon saber-toothed cat on display. One was $\frac{2}{3}$ foot and the other was $\frac{3}{4}$ foot long. Which length is longer?

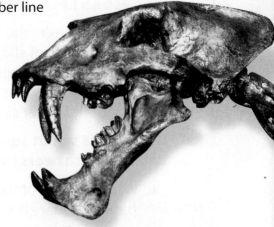

Different Ways to Compare Unlike Fractions

Way 1   Use a number line.

$\frac{2}{3}$ is to the left of $\frac{3}{4}$.

So, $\frac{2}{3} < \frac{3}{4}$

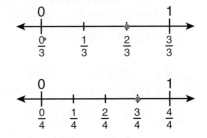

Way 2   Find a **common denominator**.

1 Find a common denominator by finding the product of the denominators of the fractions.

$3 \times 4 = 12$, so 12 is a common denominator for $\frac{2}{3}$ and $\frac{3}{4}$.

2 Use the common denominator to find **equivalent fractions**.

   $\frac{2}{3} = \frac{8}{12}$ $\frac{3}{4} = \frac{9}{12}$

3 To compare the fractions, compare the numerators.
Since $8 < 9$, $\frac{8}{12} < \frac{9}{12}$. So, $\frac{2}{3} < \frac{3}{4}$

Solution: $\frac{3}{4}$ foot is longer than $\frac{2}{3}$ foot.

Compare the fractions. Write <, >, or = for the ⬭.

1. $\frac{5}{7}$ ⬭ $\frac{3}{4}$ 2. $\frac{8}{9}$ ⬭ $\frac{2}{3}$ 3. $\frac{6}{7}$ ⬭ $\frac{13}{15}$

(123) Math Talk How can you compare $\frac{2}{3}$ and $\frac{2}{5}$ without finding a common denominator?

Ask Yourself
• Did I find a common denominator?
• Did I use a number line?

▶ **Practice and Problem Solving**

Compare the fractions. Write <, >, or = for the ⬭.

4. $\frac{3}{8}$ ⬭ $\frac{5}{12}$ 5. $\frac{9}{10}$ ⬭ $\frac{5}{6}$ 6. $\frac{6}{7}$ ⬭ $\frac{12}{14}$ 7. $\frac{5}{8}$ ⬭ $\frac{6}{10}$ 8. $\frac{3}{9}$ ⬭ $\frac{2}{3}$

9. $\frac{6}{8}$ ⬭ $\frac{3}{4}$ 10. $\frac{4}{5}$ ⬭ $\frac{2}{3}$ 11. $\frac{8}{5}$ ⬭ $\frac{3}{5}$ 12. $\frac{4}{10}$ ⬭ $\frac{2}{5}$ 13. $\frac{3}{8}$ ⬭ $\frac{6}{7}$

14. James asked visitors at the aquarium about their favorite animal. One fourth of the people chose a type of fish. Three eighths chose dolphins. Which animal did more people choose?

15. One owl at the San Diego Zoo measured $\frac{1}{4}$ of a foot. Another owl measured 5 inches. Which owl was longer?

Hint
There are 12 inches in a foot.

Bottlenosed Dolphins

✓ **Spiral Review and Test Practice**

List the factors of each number. Then find the greatest common factor (GCF) of the numbers. KEY **NS 2.2** page 16

16. 8, 24   17. 16, 32   18. 25, 40   19. 10, 35

Write the letter of the correct answer. KEY **NS 1.5**

20. Which letter on the number line best identifies a location less than $\frac{2}{3}$?

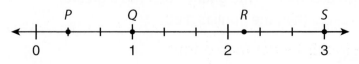

A P **B** Q **C** R **D** S

CA Standards

MR 1.2 Determine when and how to break a problem into simpler parts.

SDAP 1.3 Use fractions and percentages to compare data sets of different sizes.

Also SDAP 1.0, MR 1.1, MR 2.0, MR 2.3, MR 2.4, MR 3.0, MR 3.1, MR 3.2, MR 3.3

Problem Solving Plan
Compare Data Sets

Objective Use fractions to analyze and compare data sets of different sizes.

▶ **Learn by Example**

The table shows the amount of food that two animals at the San Diego Zoo ate in one day.

Which animal's diet contains the greater fraction of leaves?

Daily Diet of Animal		
Animal	**Amount of Food Eaten in One Day (lb)**	**Amount of Leaves in One Day (lb)**
Giraffe	75	25
Gorilla	40	8

UNDERSTAND

A giraffe ate 25 lb of leaves out of a possible 75 lb of food.

lb is the abbreviation for pounds.

A gorilla ate 8 lb of leaves out of a possible 40 lb of food.

PLAN

Find the fraction of the giraffe's food that is leaves.

Find the fraction of the gorilla's food that is leaves.

SOLVE

Giraffe	**Gorilla**	Compare the fractions.
$\frac{25}{75}$ or $\frac{1}{3}$	$\frac{8}{40}$ or $\frac{1}{5}$	$\frac{1}{3} > \frac{1}{5}$

Since $\frac{1}{3}$ is greater than $\frac{1}{5}$, the giraffe's diet has a greater fraction of leaves than the gorilla's diet.

LOOK BACK

Did you answer the question that was asked?

Think

Simplifying the fractions sometimes makes them easier to compare.

Guided Problem Solving

Solve using the Ask Yourself questions.

1. Bernice has 12 stuffed animals and Henri has 8 stuffed animals from the zoo's gift shop. Bernice has 3 pandas and Henri has 4 pandas. Whose collection has the greater fraction of pandas?

 Math Talk Do you need to first write fractions in simplest form before you compare them? Explain.

> **Ask Yourself**
> - Can I simplify the fractions to help me compare them?
> - What denominator should I use to write like fractions?

Independent Problem Solving

Solve. Explain why your answer makes sense. Use the table for Problems 2–3.

2. Which group of animals has the greatest fraction of males?

3. Which group of animals has the greatest fraction of females?

Animal	Male	Female
Elephants	0	3
Hippos	1	2
Lions	3	3
Polar Bears	1	3

4. **Multistep** For 5 years, a researcher at a zoo records that an owl lays 6 eggs each year and a bald eagle lays 3 eggs. If 25 of the owl's eggs hatch and 14 of the bald eagle's eggs hatch, which bird hatched a greater fraction of eggs?

5. Batai has 9 zoo animal postcards, and three of them are reptiles. Leon has 15 postcards and 5 of them are reptiles. Who has the greater fraction of reptile postcards?

6. **Challenge** Two classes go to the zoo. Class A has 32 students. Half the students go on a safari and half go to a snake exhibit. Eighteen of the students in Class B go to the snake exhibit and 12 go on the safari. Which class had the greatest fraction of students at the snake exhibit?

7. **Create and Solve** Change the numbers in Problem 1 so that the following is the answer: Both Henri and Bernice's collections have the same fraction of pandas.

California Kingsnake

Reading & Writing Math

Vocabulary

Different fractions can be equivalent to one another—they represent the same amount or the same point on a number line.

Read the number line.

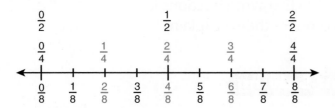

1. What fraction is equivalent to $\frac{2}{8}$?

2. What fractions are equivalent to $\frac{1}{2}$?

3. What fraction is equivalent to $\frac{3}{4}$?

Read the number line below. Identify the fractions at the points marked. Show a fraction in two ways if you can. Tell if the fraction is a mixed number or an improper fraction.

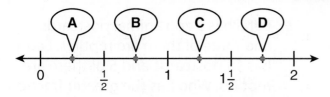

Writing You're the teacher! Write a letter to a student who does not understand the difference between a mixed number and an improper fraction.

Reading Look for this book in your library. *Polar Bear Math: Learning About Fractions from Klondike and Snow,* by Ann Whitehead Nagda and Cindy Bickel

CA Standards
MR 2.3 Use a variety of methods, such as words, numbers, symbols, charts, graphs, tables, diagrams, and models, to explain mathematical reasoning.

Also KEY NS 1.5

Standards-Based Extra Practice

Set A ———————————————————————————— KEY **NS 1.5** page 30

Write each improper fraction as a mixed number or a whole number.

1. $\frac{8}{4}$ **2.** $\frac{16}{3}$ **3.** $\frac{11}{8}$ **4.** $\frac{17}{6}$

5. $\frac{9}{3}$ **6.** $\frac{18}{3}$ **7.** $\frac{12}{11}$ **8.** $\frac{7}{4}$

Write each mixed number as an improper fraction.

9. $3\frac{5}{6}$ **10.** $2\frac{1}{4}$ **11.** $4\frac{1}{3}$ **12.** $1\frac{3}{4}$

13. $2\frac{4}{5}$ **14.** $3\frac{1}{7}$ **15.** $2\frac{5}{6}$ **16.** $5\frac{2}{3}$

Solve.

17. Myra used $2\frac{5}{8}$ yards of material to make a backpack. What is this number as an improper fraction?

Set B ———————————————————————————— Prepares for KEY **NS 2.3** page 34

Complete.

1. $\frac{4}{5} = \frac{\blacksquare}{15}$ **2.** $\frac{1}{6} = \frac{5}{\blacksquare}$ **3.** $5 = \frac{\blacksquare}{5}$ **4.** $\frac{18}{24} = \frac{3}{\blacksquare}$

5. $\frac{9}{21} = \frac{\blacksquare}{7}$ **6.** $\frac{7}{8} = \frac{\blacksquare}{32}$ **7.** $\frac{1}{4} = \frac{8}{\blacksquare}$ **8.** $12 = \frac{\blacksquare}{2}$

Solve.

9. Nadia is delivering glass containers to the recycling center. Five fifteenths of the containers are clear glass. What is this number in simplest form?

Set C ———————————————————————————— Prepares for KEY **NS 1.5** page 38

Compare these fractions. Write <, >, or = for each ⬭.

1. $\frac{1}{3}$ ⬭ $\frac{4}{9}$ **2.** $\frac{2}{8}$ ⬭ $\frac{1}{4}$ **3.** $\frac{5}{6}$ ⬭ $\frac{3}{4}$ **4.** $\frac{9}{10}$ ⬭ $\frac{1}{5}$

Solve.

5. Nathan bought $\frac{5}{8}$ pound of cole slaw and $\frac{2}{3}$ pound of pasta salad at the deli. Did he buy more cole slaw or pasta salad?

Education Place
Visit www.eduplace.com/camap/ for
Test-Taking Tips and **Extra Practice.**

Chapter Review/Test

Vocabulary and Concepts ——————————————— Prepares for KEY NS 2.3, MR 2.3

Write the best word to complete each sentence.

1. A fraction whose numerator is greater than or equal to its denominator is called an _____ fraction.

2. The number $6\frac{1}{3}$ is an example of a _____.

Skills ————————————————————————— Prepares for KEY NS 2.3

Write each improper fraction as a mixed number, and each mixed number as an improper fraction.

3. $\frac{9}{2}$

4. $\frac{15}{4}$

5. $3\frac{2}{5}$

6. $1\frac{5}{9}$

Simplify the fraction.

7. $\frac{12}{18}$

8. $\frac{15}{25}$

9. $\frac{28}{21}$

10. $\frac{16}{44}$

Compare the fractions. Write $<$, $>$, or $=$ for each ⬤.

11. $\frac{3}{4}$ ⬤ $\frac{9}{12}$

12. $\frac{7}{8}$ ⬤ $\frac{5}{12}$

13. $\frac{3}{8}$ ⬤ $\frac{5}{16}$

Problem Solving and Reasoning ——— Prepares for KEY NS 2.3, SDAP 1.3, MR 1.2, MR 2.3

Solve.

14. Antwan and Tran are eating lunch in the cafeteria. Antwan cuts his chicken into 9 pieces and eats 6 of the pieces. Tran cuts his chicken into 6 pieces and eats 4 pieces. Who ate the greater fraction of their chicken?

15. Naomi asked 10 boys and 8 girls whether they prefer dogs or cats. Six of the boys and 4 of the girls preferred dogs. Who had the greater fraction of people that prefer cats, the boys or the girls?

Writing Math How can you use the greatest common factor of the numerator and denominator to simplify a fraction?

Spiral Review and Test Practice

1. Pedro is moving to a city that has a population of about two hundred fifty-three thousand. What is this number in standard form?

A 253

C 253,000

B 200,053

D 253,000,000

GRADE 4 KEY NS 1.1

2. Which of the following is the number 671,085,000?

A six hundred seventy-one million, eighty hundred five thousand

B six hundred seventy-one million, eighty-five thousand

C six hundred seventy-one million, eighty-five

D six hundred seventy million, eighty-five thousand

GRADE 4 KEY NS 1.1

3. What is 40,000,000 + 8,000 + 3 + 200,000,000 + 70,000 + 500 in standard form?

A 420,078,503

B 240,078,503

C 240,070,503

D 483,275

Test Tip
Write the numbers in the question in a vertical list. Line up the digits by place value.

GRADE 4 KEY NS 1.1

4. What is the greatest common factor (GCF) of 12 and 20?

A 2

B 4

C 5

D 6

Test Tip
Read *all* the words in the question. Do you need to find a common factor or the greatest common factor?

KEY NS 1.4 page 16

5. Which point on the number line *best* represents $2\frac{3}{4}$?

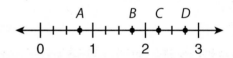

A A

C C

B B

D D

KEY NS 1.5 page 30

6. What is $\frac{36}{48}$ in simplest form?

A $\frac{9}{12}$

B $\frac{3}{8}$

C $\frac{3}{4}$

D $\frac{6}{8}$

KEY NS 2.3 page 34

Education Place
Visit www.eduplace.com/camap/ for
Test-Taking Tips and **Extra Practice**.

Chapter 2 Spiral Review and Test Practice   **45**

Unit 1 Review/Test

Vocabulary and Concepts ———————————————— NS 1.3, KEY NS 1.4, MR 2.3 Chapters 1–2

Fill in the blank to complete each sentence.

1. The fractions $\frac{3}{5}$ and $\frac{6}{10}$ are _____.

2. The expression $24 = 2 \times 2 \times 2 \times 3$ is called the _____ of the number.

3. The mixed number $3\frac{1}{2}$ can also be written as $\frac{7}{2}$, which is an _____.

4. A counting number that has exactly two different _____ is a prime number.

5. When writing exponents, the repeated factor in the product is called the _____.

Skills ——————————————— NS 1.3, KEY NS 1.4, KEY NS 1.5, Prepares for KEY NS 2.3 Chapter 1, Lesson 4

Write each expression using exponents.

6. $4 \times 4 \times 4 \times 4 \times 4 \times 4$

7. $9 \times 9 \times 9$

8. $2 \times 2 \times 2 \times 2 \times 2$

9. 7×7

List the factors of each number. Circle the common factors. Then find the greatest common factor (GCF) of the numbers. Chapter 1, Lesson 5

10. $2, 14$

11. $15, 27$

12. $12, 18$

13. $20, 30$

Complete.

14. $\frac{8}{\square} = \frac{2}{5}$

15. $\frac{\square}{12} = \frac{5}{6}$

16. $\frac{\square}{30} = \frac{9}{10}$

17. $\frac{15}{20} = \frac{\square}{4}$

Compare. Write <, >, or = for each ⬭. Chapter 2, Lesson 4

18. $\frac{3}{5}$ ⬭ $\frac{9}{15}$

19. $\frac{4}{7}$ ⬭ $\frac{2}{3}$

20. $\frac{7}{9}$ ⬭ $\frac{7}{12}$

21. $\frac{2}{11}$ ⬭ $\frac{6}{33}$

Problem Solving and Reasoning ——————— NS 1.3, KEY NS 1.4, KEY NS 1.5, MR 2.3 Chapters 1–2

Solve.

22. Jacinta made sandwiches for the homeless shelter. $\frac{3}{5}$ of the sandwiches she made were ham. $\frac{1}{4}$ of the sandwiches were turkey. Did she make more ham or turkey sandwiches?

23. Rosita has 16 trophies to arrange in her bookcase. She wants each shelf to have an equal number of trophies. In how many ways can the trophies be arranged?

Solve.

24. Pat planted between 20 and 30 seeds. The number of seeds has four prime factors. How many seeds did he plant? Write the prime factorization for the number.

25. Terrance told his friend Marcus that 4^3 is the same as 3^4. Is he correct? Explain why or why not.

Writing Math What is a real-life situation in which knowing how to find the greatest common factor of two numbers would be helpful?

Performance Assessment

Feeding Time at the Aquarium

NS 1.0, MR 1.0, MR 2.0, MR 2.3

Kendra is a volunteer at the aquarium. One of her jobs is to thaw the fish that will be fed to the harbor seals and sea lions. She needs to figure how many pounds of fish to remove from the freezer.

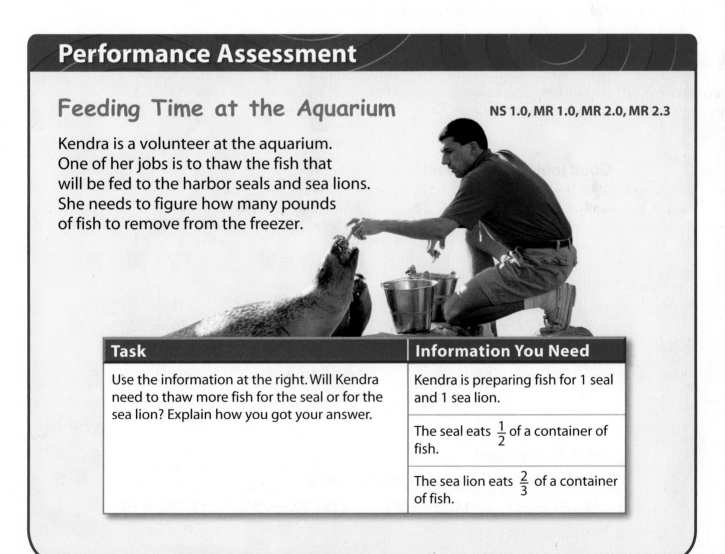

Task	Information You Need
Use the information at the right. Will Kendra need to thaw more fish for the seal or for the sea lion? Explain how you got your answer.	Kendra is preparing fish for 1 seal and 1 sea lion.
	The seal eats $\frac{1}{2}$ of a container of fish.
	The sea lion eats $\frac{2}{3}$ of a container of fish.

Go Fast, Go Far

Unit 1 Mental Math Strategies

Shift a Few

Adding will be quick to do.
Before you start, just shift a few!

To add 48 and 27, I add 2 to the first number and take 2 away from the second number. Then I have 50 + 25. I can add that in my head and get 75.

1. 48 + 27
Shift a few.   ↖ 2 ↓   ↓
50 + 25 = 75

2. 49 + 56
Shift a few.   ↖ 1 ↓   ↓
☐ + ☐ = ☐

3. 29 + 32
Shift a few.   ↖ 1 ↓   ↓
☐ + ☐ = ☐

Good job! Now try these!

4. 18 + 84
Shift a few.   ↖ ☐ ↗ ↓   ↓
☐ + ☐ = ☐

5. 37 + 55
Shift a few.   ↖ ☐ ↗ ↓   ↓
☐ + ☐ = ☐

6. 39 + 78
Shift a few.   ↖ ☐ ↗ ↓   ↓
☐ + ☐ = ☐

7. 27 + 76
Shift a few.   ↖ ☐ ↗ ↓   ↓
☐ + ☐ = ☐

8. 49 + 83
Shift a few.   ↖ ☐ ↗ ↓   ↓
☐ + ☐ = ☐

9. 76 + 95
Shift a few.   ↖ ☐ ↗ ↓   ↓
☐ + ☐ = ☐

Take It Further!
Now try doing all the steps in your head!

10. 39 + 23   **11.** 39 + 84   **12.** 77 + 23   **13.** 28 + 66

Good For You!

48

Unit

2

Equivalence: Fractions and Decimals

BIG IDEAS!

- Each place value to the left of another is ten times greater than the one to the right.

- A decimal is another name for a fraction, and both can be represented on a number line.

Chapter 3
Place Value Through Thousandths

Chapter 4
Relate Fractions and Decimals

Songs and Games

 Math Music Track 2: *The Number Is*
eGames at
www.eduplace.com/camap/

Math Readers

This colorful carpet is from the city of Pushkar in Rajasthan in northern India.

Game

Digit Challenge

Object of the Game Use your number tiles to make the greatest number.

Materials
- Number Tiles (Four sets 0–9)
- Learning Tool 12: Digit Challenge (1 per player)

Set Up
Shuffle all the number tiles and place them in a stack. Give each player a Digit Challenge game board.

Number of Players 2–4

How to Play

1 Each player draws a number tile and places it on his or her game board. Once placed, the tile cannot be moved.

2 Repeat Step 1 until each player has placed 6 tiles. The player who makes the greatest number scores a point.

3 Return all the tiles to the stack and shuffle. Repeat steps 1–2. The first player to score a total of 10 points is the winner.

CA Standards
Prepares for NS 1.1 Estimate, round, and manipulate very large (e.g., millions) and very small (e.g., thousandths) numbers.

Also MR 1.0, MR 2.0

Education Place
Visit www.eduplace.com/camap/ for **Brain Teasers** and **eGames** to play.

Reading When you read a story, you can look at the illustrations to help you visualize or picture what is happening. To visualize math, it can be helpful to show the information and numbers in a word problem in a different way.

Read the problem. Use the place-value charts to help you visualize the numbers.

United States Olympic athlete Brian Martin, from Palo Alto, CA, has won 2 medals in the luge event. Which of his practice times was better, forty seven and sixty-nine thousandths seconds or forty seven and two hundredths seconds?

tenths	ones		tenths	hundredths	thousandths
4	7	.	0	6	9

tenths	ones		tenths	hundredths
4	7	.	0	2

Writing Work with a partner to visualize the numbers in different ways. Here are four possibilities:

- Use place-value models.
- Write mixed numbers.
- Use standard form.
- Use a number line.

Which way do you prefer to use to help you visualize the numbers and solve the problem?

> 47.069 has 6 hundredths.
> 47.02 has 2 hundredths.
> 47.02 is the better time.

Place Value Through Thousandths

Check What You Know

Vocabulary and Concepts GRADE 4 NS 1.0, MR 2.3

Choose the best word to complete each sentence.

1. Use _____ to determine the value of a digit.

2. On the place-value chart, a group of 3 digits set off by a comma is a _____.

3. A _____ is a number with one or more digits to the right of the ones place.

Skills GRADE 4 KEY NS 1.2

Compare. Write >, =, or < for each ⬭.

4. 8.19 ⬭ 8.09

5. 3.5 ⬭ 5.3

6. 9.2 ⬭ 9.20

7. 7.45 ⬭ 7.48

8. 6.07 ⬭ 8.4

9. 11.70 ⬭ 11.07

Problem Solving and Reasoning GRADE 4 KEY NS 1.2

10. A pack of Big Bob's Baseball Cards costs $2.32. A pack of Little Larry's Baseball Cards costs $2.23. Which pack is the more expensive?

Vocabulary

Visualize It!

A **decimal** is a number with one or more **digits** to the right of the decimal point.

Read the word form of the number below as five-hundred eighty-four thousandths.

ones	.	tenths	hundredths	thousandths
0	.	5	8	4

↑ decimal point

Language Tip

Math words that look alike in English and Spanish often have the same meaning.

English	Spanish
value	valor
digit	digito
decimal	decimal

See **English-Spanish Glossary** pages 628–642.

Education Place Visit www.eduplace.com/camap/ for the **eGlossary** and **eGames**.

CA Standards MR 2.3 Use a variety of methods, such as words, numbers, symbols, charts, graphs, tables, diagrams, and models, to explain mathematical reasoning. **Also NS 1.1**

Chapter 3   53

CA Standards

NS 1.1 Estimate, round, and manipulate very large (e.g., millions) and very small (e.g., thousandths) numbers.

Also NS 1.0, MR 1.1, MR 2.3

Vocabulary

decimal

decimal point

thousandths

Materials
- Learning Tool 13 (Thousandths of a Dollar)
- Bill Set and Coin Set
- eManipulatives (optional) www.eduplace.com/camap/

Think

$= \frac{1}{100}$
of a dollar

$\frac{1}{10}$ of a penny $=$

$\frac{1}{1,000}$ of a dollar

Hands On
Represent Whole Numbers and Decimals

Objective Model decimals using money.

▶ **Explore**

A **decimal** is a number with one or more digits to the right of the **decimal point.** The **thousandths** place is 3 digits to the right of the decimal point.

Question How can you model numbers in the thousandths?

Gas is priced to the thousandths place. At the beginning of 2007, in California, the average cost for 5 gallons of gas was $13.245.

Here are some ways to show $13.245.

---

1 Model $13.245 with bills, coins, and the pictures from the Learning Tool.

---

2 Write the number in fraction notation.

$\$13\frac{245}{1,000}$ Since the 5 is in the thousandths place, the denominator should be 1,000.

---

3 Round the number to the nearest cent. If the thousandths place is 5 or greater, increase the hundredths place by 1. If the digit is less than 5, do not change the hundredths place. Drop the thousandths place.

$13.24\underline{5}$
↓
13.25 ←   Since the digit in the thousands place is a 5, round up.

▶ **Extend**

Use bills and coins to help you write the missing number.

	Word Form	Decimal Notation	Fraction Notation
1.	two dollars and thirty cents	$2.30	2\frac{3}{10}$
2.	four dollars and three thousandths of a dollar		4\frac{3}{1,000}$
3.	one dollar and twenty-four cents	$1.24	
4.	eight hundred fifteen dollars and three hundred twenty-one thousandths of a dollar		815\frac{321}{1,000}$
5.	one thousand, seventy-three dollars and five cents	$1,073.05	

> **Hint**
> The word *and* indicates a decimal point.

Round the amount to the nearest cent.

6. twenty-three and four hundred eleven thousandths of a dollar

7. five hundred eighty-six thousandths of a dollar

8. one and two hundred sixty-five thousandths of a dollar

9. twelve and four hundred ninety-six thousandths of a dollar

10. $30.109 **11.** $5.932 **12.** $120.428 **13.** $2.884

14. $3,345.055 **15.** $54.637 **16.** $8.282 **17.** $23.346

18. $15.036 **19.** $1,200.977 **20.** $45.452 **21.** $917.511

22. $53.231 **23.** $7,168.189 **24.** $305.655 **25.** $375.201

Writing Math

What's Wrong? Sarah represented the value of a one-dollar bill plus a penny as $1.001. Explain what she did wrong.

LESSON 2

CA Standards

NS 1.0 Students compute with very large and very small numbers, positive integers, decimals, and fractions and understand the relationship between decimals, fractions, and percents. They understand the relative magnitude of numbers.

NS 1.3 Understand and compute positive integer powers of nonnegative integers; compute examples as repeated multiplication.

Also NS 1.1, MR 1.0, MR 1.1, MR 3.0, MR 3.1

Vocabulary

place value

period

standard form

expanded form

power of 10

word form

Place Value Through Billions

Objective Read and write numbers through billions in standard, expanded, and word forms.

▶ **Learn by Example**

The area of the United States is 2,403,354,240 acres. What are some different ways to write this number?

Look at the chart for **place value**. In a number, each group of 3 digits from right to left is called a **period**. Each period is a group of hundreds, tens, and ones separated by a comma.

Billions			Millions			Thousands			Ones		
hundred billions	ten billions	billions	hundred millions	ten millions	millions	hundred thousands	ten thousands	thousands	hundreds	tens	ones
0	0	2,	4	0	3,	3	5	4,	2	4	0

The value of a digit in a number is determined by its place. For example, in the number 2,403,3<u>5</u>4,240, the 5 has a value of 50,000 or 5 × 10,000.

Different Ways to Read and Write 2,403,354,240

Way 1   Use standard form.

2,403,354,240

Way 2   Use expanded form.

Expanded form shows the sum of the value of the digits.

2,000,000,000 + 400,000,000 + 3,000,000 + 300,000 + 50,000 + 4,000 + 200 + 40

Way 3   Use expanded form with exponents.

Each place is represented by a **power of 10**.

$(2 \times 10^9) + (4 \times 10^8) + (3 \times 10^6) + (3 \times 10^5) + (5 \times 10^4) + (4 \times 10^3) + (2 \times 10^2) + (4 \times 10^1)$

Way 4   Use word form.

two billion, four hundred three million, three hundred fifty-four thousand, two hundred forty

Think

Note the pattern:
$1,000 = 10^3$
$100 = 10^2$
$10 = 10^1$
$1 = 10^0$

Write the number in standard form and in word form.

1. $40,000 + 5,000 + 70 + 9$

2. $100,000,000 + 9,000,000 + 300 + 40 + 2$

3. $80,000,000,000 + 300,000,000 + 4,000,000 + 600,000 + 7,000$

Write each number in expanded form using exponents.

4. 68,341   5. 2,507,950   6. 7,342,005,300

Ask Yourself
What are the periods in the number?

Guided Problem Solving

Use the questions to solve this problem.

7. The population of the United States is about 300,000,000. Use that number to help you choose the best estimate for the population of the world.

   A 650,000,000   **B** 6,500,000   **C** 6,500,000,000

   a. **Understand** What do you need to do?

   b. **Plan/Solve** Compare each number with 300,000,000. Which answer makes more sense? Write the better estimate for the world population.

   c. **Look Back** Did you do what the problem asked?

8. Look at your answer to problem 7. Write the estimated population of the world in word form.

(123) Math Talk Look back at Exercise 6. How did you know what exponent to use for each power of 10?

▶ **Practice and Problem Solving**

Write the number in standard form and in word form.

9. $20,000,000 + 4,000,000 + 70,000 + 9,000 + 100 + 20 + 9$

10. $300,000,000 + 90,000,000 + 2,000,000 + 30,000 + 4,000 + 20 + 5$

11. $14,000,000,000 + 500 + 80 + 9$

Write the number in expanded form using exponents.

12. 78,000,000,001

13. 200,000,700

14. 19,600,030

15. 3,406

16. 602,500,000

17. 9,080,030,070

Solve.

18. The average distance between Earth and the sun is 92,950,000 miles. Write this number in expanded form using exponents.

19. The lengths of all the rivers in the United States add up to about three million, five hundred thousand miles. Write this number in standard form.

History-Social Science Link

Solve.

20. What was California's population in 1850? Use exponents to write it in expanded form.

21. What is the value of the 7 in the population of California in 2000?

22. **Justify** Do you think the population of California today is more or less than one billion? Explain your reasoning.

23. By how much did the population increase between 1850 and 1890?

24. Estimate the population increase between 1950 and 2000. Write your estimate in word form.

Early nineteenth-century explorers like Lewis and Clark helped spark California's amazing population growth. This chart shows how California's population has grown since it became a state in 1850.

California's Population

Year	Population
1850	92,597
1890	1,213,398
1950	10,586,223
2000	33,871,648

History–Social Science 5.8.3

Spiral Review and Test Practice

Write the prime factorization for each number using exponents. KEY **NS 1.4** page 14

25. 4

26. 36

27. 42

28. 50

Write the letter of the correct answer. NS 1.0

29. What is the standard form of nine hundred sixty-four million, ten thousand, six hundred fifty-eight?

    A 964,658   **B** 964,010,658   **C** 964,100,658   **D** 9,640,010,658

Extra Practice See page 71, Set A.

Relative Magnitude

Sometimes the same number can seem very large, very small, or about right.

When does 1,000,000 seem very large?

Few people in the world are able to spend $1,000,000 on a work of art. So it is big news when it happens.

One million dollars is a large amount of money to spend on a single painting.

Millions Spent on Modern Art

Picassos accounted for more than $164 million of the auction total, and were eight of the ten most expensive works. His cubist "Woman Sitting in an Armchair," sold for over $24 million.

When does 1,000,000 seem to be small?

Major Hollywood movies cost tens of millions of dollars to make, even as much as $100,000,000.

One million dollars seems a small amount of money to make a movie.

Low Budget Film Big Hit!

Made with a budget of only $1,000,000, the film has nevertheless done well in screenings abroad because of its presentation and grand scale. The screenwriter said the film has a certain unmatched authenticity.

When does 1,000,000 seem about right?

There are many cities in the world with populations of 1,000,000 or more.

One million seems about right for the population of a major city.

When does 1,000 seem large? small? about right? Explain your thinking.

Urban Populations (rounded)

Münich, Germany	1,315,000
Philadelphia, U.S.	1,463,000
Zigong, China	1,052,000
San Jose, CA	960,000

CA Standards
NS 1.0, NS 1.1, MR 2.3

LESSON 3

CA Standards
NS 1.0 Students compute with very large and very small numbers, positive integers, decimals, and fractions and understand the relationship between decimals, fractions, and percents. They understand the relative magnitude of numbers.
Also AF 1.1, MR 2.3

Place Value Through Thousandths

Objective Read and write decimals through thousandths.

▶ **Learn by Example**

The land area of the United States is 0.062 of the land area on Earth.

Write 0.062 in word form.

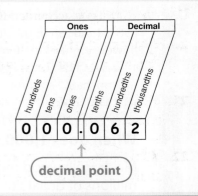

- Write the decimal in the place-value chart.

- The last digit after the decimal point tells how to name the decimal parts.

Solution: The word form of 0.062 is sixty-two thousandths.

Another Example
Write 4.035 in word form.

four and thirty-five thousandths

Use the word *and* to indicate the decimal point.

Ask Yourself

· How can I use the word form to find the last place in the decimal?

· What word do I write for the decimal point?

▶ **Guided Practice**

Write the decimal in standard form.

1. five tenths   **2.** four and sixteen thousandths

Write the decimal in word form.

3. 2.7   **4.** 0.15   **5.** 0.094

 Math Talk How does the value of the last digit help you read a decimal?

Write the decimal in standard form.

6. nine hundredths

7. one hundred thirty-eight thousandths

8. twenty-five thousandths

9. ten and twenty-four hundredths

Write the decimal in word form.

10. 0.019   11. 0.3   12. 0.34   13. 25.4   14. 0.789

15. 4.306   16. 0.082   17. 3.17   18. 11.35   19. 0.007

 Real World Data

Use the table for Problems 20–23.

20. What part of the Earth's land area does North America cover? Write the decimal in word form.

21. Which continent covers one hundred twenty-one thousandths of Earth's land area?

22. Which continent or region covers the smallest amount of Earth's land area?

23. Which continents cover more than two tenths of Earth's land area?

Land Area	
Continent	**Part or Land Area**
Africa	0.205
Antarctica	0.097
Asia	0.214
Europe	0.157
North America	0.148
Oceania	0.058
South America	0.121

 Spiral Review and Test Practice

Write the number in standard form. NS 1.0 page 56

24. 30,000 + 4,000 + 8

25. 2,000,000 + 30,000 + 700 + 90

26. six hundred billion, five hundred sixty-three thousand, eight hundred fifty-five

Write the letter of the correct answer. NS 1.0

27. What is three and fourteen thousandths in standard form?

   A 0.314   **B** 3.014   **C** 3.104   **D** 3.14

CA Standards

NS 1.0 Students compute with very large and very small numbers, positive integers, decimals, and fractions and understand the relationship between decimals, fractions, and percents. They understand the relative magnitude of numbers.

MR 2.0 Students use strategies, skills, and concepts in finding solutions.

Also MR 2.3, KEY NS 1.5

Compare and Order Whole Numbers and Decimals

Objective Compare and order large whole numbers and small decimals.

▶ **Learn by Example**

The table shows some of the populations of the largest cities in the United States in 2005, as estimated by the U.S. Census Bureau. Which city had a greater population, Phoenix or Philadelphia?

Los Angeles	3,844,829
Chicago	2,842,518
Houston	2,016,582
Philadelphia	1,463,281
Phoenix	1,461,575

Example 1

1 Compare 1,461,575 and 1,463,281. Line up the numbers by place value:

    1,461,575
    1,463,281

2 Start from the left. Compare the digits until they are different.

    1,461,575
    1,463,281   3 > 1
    1,463,281 > 1,461,575

Solution: Philadelphia had a greater population than Phoenix.

You can use the same method to order three or more numbers. Order the populations of Chicago, Houston, and Los Angeles from greatest to least.

Los Angeles, CA

Example 2

1 Line up the numbers by place value. Compare the digits, starting at the left.

    2,842,518
    2,016,582
    3,844,829   3 > 2

3,844,829 is the greatest number.

2 Continue comparing.

    2,842,518   8 > 0
    2,016,582

    2,842,518 > 2,016,582

    3,844,829 > 2,842,518 >
    2,016,582

Solution: The populations from greatest to least are 3,844,829; 2,842,518; 2,016,582.

You can use the same steps to compare and order decimals.
Order 4, 4.32, and 4.317 from least to greatest.

Example 3

① Align the decimal points. Write zeros if necessary to make the same number of decimal places.

4.000 ← | **Adding zeros to the end of a decimal does not change its value.**
4.320 ←
4.317

② Starting from the left, compare the digits until they are different.

4.000 ← (0 < 3)
4.320
4.317

4.000 is the least of the 3 numbers.

③ Continue comparing.

4.320
4.317 ← (1 < 2)

4.000 < 4.317 < 4.320

Solution: 4; 4.317; 4.320

▶ **Guided Practice**

Compare. Write >, <, or = for the ⬤.

1. 25,431 ⬤ 25,313

2. 4,569,102 ⬤ 4,569,500

3. 0.6 ⬤ 0.53

4. 4.153 ⬤ 4.182

5. 7 ⬤ 7.109

6. 28.1 ⬤ 28.01

Ask Yourself
- Are the numbers lined up by place value or the decimal point?
- Where are the digits different?

Order the set of numbers from greatest to least.

7. 43,055; 422,007; 42,007

8. 812,661; 82,811,121; 82,935,661

9. 0.0825; 0.56; 0.8

10. 1.3; 1.52; 2.08

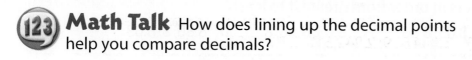 **Math Talk** How does lining up the decimal points help you compare decimals?

Compare. Write >, <, or = for the ●.

11. 164,275,808 ● 4,291,005

12. 90,456,292 ● 89,509,765

13. 17 ● 16.882   **14.** 2.454 ● 2.462   **15.** 3.631 ● 3.7   **16.** 9.9 ● 10.1

Order the set of numbers from least to greatest.

17. 3,906,211; 4,031,232; 4,029,306

18. 265,616,845; 1,264,678,784; 257,724,925

19. 3.55; 3.472; 4.14

20. 0.72; 7.2; 7

 Science Link

Use the Fun Facts to solve Problems 21–24.

21. Argon's (Ar) atomic weight is 39.95. Use symbols to compare its atomic weight with oxygen (O).

22. Compare fluorine's (F) atomic weight with krypton's (Kr) atomic weight. Write > or <.

23. Order the following elements from least to greatest according to their atomic weights: selenium (Se), iodine (I), and bromine (Br).

24. Look at the atomic weight of tellurium (Te). If you add two zeros at the end of the decimal, will the atomic weight change?

 **Fun Facts**

Some Chemical Elements

- Elements are the building blocks of matter.

- Scientists organize the elements in the periodic table. A small section of the periodic table is shown.

- Each box in the table represents an element.

8	9	10
O	**F**	**Ne**
16.00	19.00	20.18
16	17	18
S	**Cl**	**Ar**
32.07	35.45	39.95
34	35	36
Se	**Br**	**Kr**
78.96	79.90	83.80
52	53	54
Te	**I**	**Xe**
127.6	126.9	131.3

atomic number ⟶
atomic symbol ⟶
atomic weight ⟶

Science PS 1.d

✓ Spiral Review and Test Practice

Write the improper fraction as a mixed number or a whole number. **KEY** NS 2.3 page 30

25. $\frac{5}{3}$ **26.** $\frac{10}{5}$ **27.** $\frac{13}{6}$ **28.** $\frac{8}{7}$

Write the letter of the correct answer. NS 1.0

29. Which shows the numbers in order from greatest to least?

A 8.86; 8.03; 8   **B** 8; 8.03; 8.86   **C** 8.03; 8.86; 8   **D** 8.86; 8; 8.03

Extra Practice See page 71, Set C.

Key Standards Review

Need Help?
See Key Standards Handbook.

Write the missing fraction or mixed number that should go in the shaded box. KEY **NS 1.5**

1.

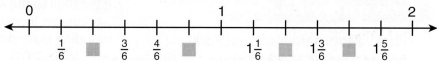

Write the factors that complete each factor tree. Then use exponents to write the prime factorization. KEY **NS 1.4**

2.

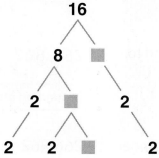

3.

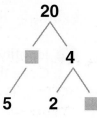

Number Shuffle NS 1.1

Use the digits 1–9 to fill in the spaces provided. Place four digits to the left of the decimal and three digits to the right of the decimal to create the number described. Do not use a digit more than once.

☐ ☐ ☐ ☐ . ☐ ☐ ☐

1. a number with more than seven tenths

2. a number with less than 3 thousandths

3. a number with more than eight thousandths and more than six tenths

CA Standards

NS 1.1 Estimate, round, and manipulate very large (e.g., millions) and very small (e.g., thousandths) numbers.

MR 1.0 Students make decisions about how to approach problems.

Round Whole Numbers and Decimals

Objective Round whole numbers and decimals.

▶ **Learn by Example**

Rocky Mountain National Park has an area of 266,862 acres.

How can you use rounding rules to round 266,862 to the nearest thousand?

Rounding Rules

If the digit to the right is 5 or greater, increase the rounding place digit by 1.

If the digit to the right is less than 5, do not change the rounding place digit.

Example 1

1 Identify the place you want to round to. Circle the digit to the right.

266,⑧62

↑ rounding place

2 Use rounding rules to round the number.

266,862
↓
267,000

Since 8 > 5, change the 6 to 7. Change digits to the right to zeros.

Solution: 266,862 rounded to the nearest thousand is 267,000.

How can you round 0.607 to the nearest hundredth?

Example 2

1 Identify the place you want to round to. Circle the digit to the right.

0.60⑦

↑ rounding place

2 Use rounding rules to round the number.

0.607
↓
0.61

Since 7 > 5, change 0 to 1. Drop all digits to the right.

Solution: 0.607 rounded to the nearest hundredth is 0.61.

▶ Guided Practice

Round to the place indicated by the underlined digit.

1. 783,256

2. 24,592,124

3. 674,129,811

4. 0.572

5. 0.145

6. 3.957

7. 8,236,008

8. 24.451

9. 395,156

10. 1.457

11. 54,311,728 1

12. 7,305,295

Ask Yourself
- Is the digit to the right of the rounding place 5 or greater?
- Do I change the rounding place digit or leave it the same?

(123) Math Talk Why is the digit in the hundreds place used to round a number to the nearest thousand?

▶ Practice and Problem Solving

Round to the place indicated by the underlined digit.

13. 5,261

14. 574,238

15. 3,489,112

16. 659,324,721

17. 8,923,452

18. 168,034,526

19. 6,493,451,723

20. 24,376,563,321

21. 0.457

22. 6.459

23. 3.219

24. 4.09

25. 12.09

26. 0.568

27. 0.143

28. 27.353

29. Right or Wrong? Avery collects baseball cards. He has 4,794 cards in his collection. He said that he has about 4,000 cards in his collection. Is Avery right or wrong? Explain your reasoning.

30. Scott weighs a bunch of green grapes on a digital scale. The grapes weigh 2 pounds, 12 ounces. What is the weight of the grapes rounded to the nearest pound?

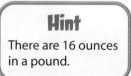

Hint
There are 16 ounces in a pound.

✓ Spiral Review and Test Practice

Write each fraction in simplest form. **KEY** NS 2.3 page 34

31. $\frac{5}{20}$

32. $\frac{8}{10}$

33. $\frac{12}{16}$

34. $\frac{9}{18}$

Write the letter of the correct answer. NS 1.1

35. What is 10.724 rounded to the nearest hundredth?

A 10   **B** 10.8   **C** 10.73   **D** 10.72

 Extra Practice See page 71, Set D.

CA Standards

MR 2.5 Indicate the relative advantages of exact and approximate solutions to problems and give answers to a specified degree of accuracy.

NS 1.1 Estimate, round, and manipulate very large (e.g., millions) and very small (e.g., thousandths) numbers.

Also NS 1.0, MR 1.0, MR 1.1, MR 2.0, MR 2.3, MR 2.4, MR 3.0, MR 3.1, MR 3.2, MR 3.3

Problem Solving Plan
Estimate or Exact?

Objective Determine when to use estimates and when to use exact answers to solve a problem.

▶ **Learn Through Reasoning**

The results for California's 2006 election for governor are shown in the table.

California Election Results for Governor, 2006	
Candidate	**Votes**
Angelides	3,376,732
Camejo	205,995
Jordan	69,934
Noonan	61,901
Olivier	114,329
Schwarzenegger	4,850,157

Example 1

Sometimes you need an exact answer to a problem.

> How many more votes did the winning candidate receive compared to the candidate who got the second highest number of votes?

Find the difference.
$$\begin{array}{r} 4{,}850{,}157 \\ -\ 3{,}376{,}732 \\ \hline 1{,}473{,}425 \end{array}$$

The winning candidate received 1,473,425 more votes.

Vocabulary Tip

A **candidate** is a person running for office.

Example 2

Sometimes a problem asks only for an estimate.

> About how many people voted for California's governor in the 2006 election?

Use your rounding rules to find an estimate.

$$\begin{array}{rcl} 3{,}376{,}732 & \rightarrow & 3{,}000{,}000 \\ 205{,}995 & \rightarrow & 200{,}000 \\ 69{,}934 & \rightarrow & 70{,}000 \\ 61{,}901 & \rightarrow & 70{,}000 \\ 114{,}329 & \rightarrow & 100{,}000 \\ 4{,}850{,}157 & \rightarrow & +\ 5{,}000{,}000 \\ \hline & & 8{,}440{,}000 \end{array}$$

About 8,440,000 people voted for California's governor.

Example 3

Sometimes an estimate is all you need to solve a problem.

> If all votes for non-winning candidates had gone to the second-place candidate, would he have won the election?

Use high and low estimates for the number of votes that the other four non-winning candidates received.

Add 700,000 to the second-place winner's 3,376,732 votes. He could not have won the election.

68

▶ Guided Problem Solving

Solve using the Ask Yourself question.

Ask Yourself
Does the question ask for an exact answer or estimate?

1. The table shows the population of the five largest cites in the United States in the year 2004. About what is the difference between the populations of Houston and Los Angeles? Round each population to the nearest million.

City	New York, NY	Los Angeles, CA	Chicago, IL	Houston, TX
Population	8,143,197	3,844,829	2,842,518	2,016,582

 Math Talk Find the actual difference between the population of Houston and Los Angeles. Round the difference to the nearest million. Compare your answer to the answer in Problem 1. What do you notice? Explain.

▶ Independent Problem Solving

Use the table to solve Problems 2–3.
Explain why you used an estimate or an exact answer.

2. The first U.S. Census was taken in 1790. How many more people were counted in 2000 than in 1790?

3. Between which two periods did the population increase by about 15,000,000 people?

4. Shamali wants to save up 360,000 frequent flyer miles for a first class, round-trip ticket to India. She already has 127,392 miles. How many more miles does she need?

5. **Challenge** One month, Company A's website had 4,731,020 visitors. Its two biggest competitors had 2,763,812 visitors and 3,174,209 visitors. Is the total number of visitors to the competitors' websites greater or less than that of Company A? Tell how you found your answer.

6. **Create and Solve** Use the numbers from the population table to write and solve two problems, one with an estimated answer and one with an exact answer.

U.S. Population Growth	
Year	**Population**
1790	3,929,214
1800	5,308,483
1850	23,191,876
1900	76,212,168
1950	152,271,417
2000	281,421,906

Reading & Writing Math

Vocabulary

Look at the number in the place-value chart. Use this number to complete the word web.

Billions			Millions			Thousands			Ones		
hundreds	tens	ones	hundreds	tens	ones	hundreds	tens	ones	hundreds	tens	ones
		8 ,	8	2	7 ,	6	1	0 ,	7	3	1

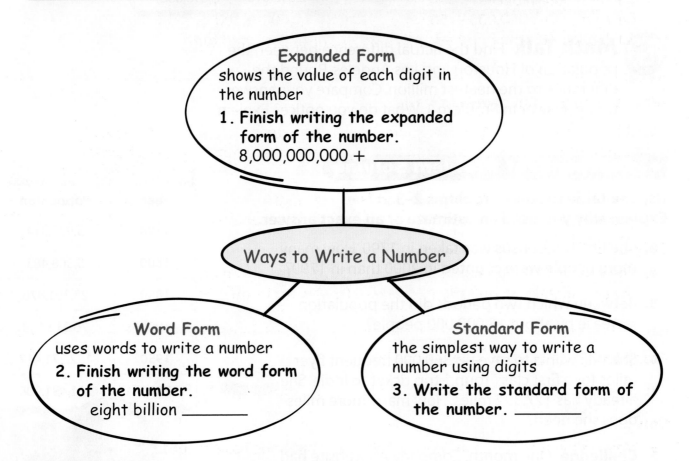

Expanded Form
shows the value of each digit in the number
1. Finish writing the expanded form of the number.
8,000,000,000 + _____

Ways to Write a Number

Word Form
uses words to write a number
2. Finish writing the word form of the number.
eight billion _____

Standard Form
the simplest way to write a number using digits
3. Write the standard form of the number. _____

Writing How can you write the number 8,827,610,731.347 in word form?

Reading Look for this book in your library. *Digging for Bird Dinosaurs: An Expedition to Madagascar,* by Nic Bishop.

CA Standards
MR 2.3 Use a variety of methods, such as words, numbers, symbols, charts, graphs, tables, diagrams, and models, to explain mathematical reasoning.
Also NS 1.0

Standards-Based Extra Practice

Set A ———————————————————————————————————— NS 1.0, NS 1.3 page 56

Write each number in expanded form using exponents.

1. 4,308,500   **2.** 3,983   **3.** 8,380,677,000   **4.** 3,000,500,000

Solve.

5. The population of Los Angeles County in the year 2000 can
be written as 9,000,000 + 500,000 + 10,000 + 9,000 + 300 +
30 + 8. What is the population in standard form and word form?

Set B —— NS 1.0 page 60

Write the decimal in standard form.

1. thirty-two
hundredths

2. twelve and
six tenths

3. sixteen
thousandths

4. six and three
hundred six
thousandths

5. forty-two
hundredths

6. fifty-five and five
tenths

7. eight
thousandths

8. six hundred
and one tenth

Solve.

9. The winner of the swim meet finished 0.08 minutes ahead of
the swimmer in second place. What is 0.08 in word form?

Set C —— NS 1.0 page 62

Compare. Write >, <, or = for each ⬤.

1. 22 ⬤ 22.22   **2.** 0.58 ⬤ 0.61   **3.** 16.509 ⬤ 17.122   **4.** 6.5 5.6

Solve.

5. Mavis is training to run in a 5-kilometer road race. She has a record
of her three best practice times. They are 28.02; 27.23; and 28.31.
Write the practice times in order from least to greatest.

Set D —— NS 1.1 page 66

Round to the place indicated by the underlined digit.

1. 0.1<u>5</u>4   **2.** 13<u>3</u>,698   **3.** 39,28<u>8</u>,313   **4.** <u>0</u>.82

Solve.

5. Brett filled the tank of his car with 17.65 gallons of gas.
What is this number rounded to the nearest tenth?

Education Place
Visit www.eduplace.com/camap/ for
Test-Taking Tips and **Extra Practice**.

Chapter Review/Test

Vocabulary and Concepts ———————————— NS 1.0, MR 2.3

Write the best word to complete each sentence.

1. In the number 3,207,408 the 4 has a value of 400. The value of a digit in a number is called its _____ value.

2. When a number is written in expanded form with exponents, each place is represented by a power of _____.

3. A _____ is a number with one or more digits to the right of the decimal point.

Skills ———————————————————— NS 1.0, NS 1.1

Write the number in standard form and in word form.

4. 70,000,000 + 1,000,000 + 800,000 + 20,000 + 1,000 + 10

5. 9,000,000 + 900,000 + 90,000 + 9,000 + 900 + 90 + 9

6. 10,000,000,000 + 2,000,000,000 + 300,000 + 30,000

Write the decimal in word form.

7. 2.02   8. 0.608   9. 10.19   10. 38.1

Order the set of numbers from least to greatest.

11. 8.307; 9.001; 8.318   12. 7,308,102; 6,103,309; 6,114,558   13. 12.102; 12.012; 12

Problem Solving and Reasoning ———————— NS 1.1, MR 2.0, MR 2.3, MR 2.5

Solve.

14. Elevations in Joshua Tree National Park range from a low of 536 feet to a high of 5,184 feet. What is the difference in elevation from the highest to the lowest point?

15. The population of Orange County was 2,410,556 in 1990, and 2,846,289 in 2000. Find the actual difference in population from 1990 to 2000. Then round the difference to the nearest thousand.

Writing Math **Analyze** How are comparing and ordering whole numbers and decimals similar?

Spiral Review and Test Practice

1. What is 8 + 200,000 + 10 + 30,000 in standard form?

A 821,300

B 320,018

C 230,081

D 230,018

NS 1.0 page 56

2. Which of the following has the greatest value?

A 3,212,048

Test Tip
Look at the suffix in the word *greatest*. Think about what it tells you to look for.

B 3,211,057

C 3,212,057

D 3,211,067

NS 1.0 page 62

3. What is 50,000,000 + 70,000 + 2,000,000 + 3,000 + 6 in standard form?

A 52,037,006

B 52,073,006

C 52,073,060

D 520,073,006

NS 1.1 page 56

4. Which letter on the number line best identifies a location less than $\frac{3}{5}$?

Test Tip
Read the question carefully. Look for key words such as *more than*, *less than*, or *equal to*.

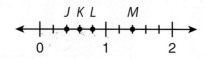

A J

C L

B K

D M

KEY NS 1.5 page 38

5. What is the standard form of three hundred twenty million, fourteen thousand, eight hundred seven?

A 300,014,807

C 320,014,807

B 320,000,807

D 320,140,807

NS 1.1 page 56

6. What is two and fifty-one thousandths in standard form?

A 0.051

C 2.51

B 2.051

D 251

NS 1.1 page 60

Relate Fractions and Decimals

The popsicle was invented by San Francisco native Frank Epperson.

Vocabulary and Concepts   GRADE 4 NS 1.5, MR 2.3

Match each word with a definition.

1. equivalent fractions

2. mixed number

a. Fractions that name the same amount.

b. A number made up of a whole number and a fraction.

Skills   GRADE 4 KEY NS 1.2

Compare. Write >, <, or = for each ⬤.

4. 2.19 ⬤ 2.019

5. $\frac{3}{8}$ ⬤ $\frac{3}{4}$

6. 1.3 ⬤ 1.30

7. 4.602 ⬤ 4.62

8. $\frac{4}{5}$ ⬤ $\frac{8}{10}$

9. $5\frac{1}{2}$ ⬤ $\frac{9}{2}$

Problem Solving and Reasoning   GRADE 4 NS 1.6

10. About $\frac{3}{10}$ of the players in a basketball league are left-handed. Express the fraction of the team that are right-handed as a decimal.

Vocabulary

Visualize It!

Word	Fraction	Decimal	Equals
tenth	$\frac{1}{10}$	0.1	one of 10 equal parts
hundredth	$\frac{1}{100}$	0.01	one of 100 equal parts
thousandth	$\frac{1}{1,000}$	0.001	one of 1,000 equal parts

Language Tip

Math words that look alike in English and Spanish often have the same meaning.

English	Spanish
equivalent	equivalentes
mixed number	número mixto

See **English-Spanish Glossary** pages 628–642.

 Education Place Visit www.eduplace.com/camap/ for the **eGlossary** and **eGames**.

CA Standards MR 2.3 Use a variety of methods, such as words, numbers, symbols, charts, graphs, tables, diagrams, and models, to explain mathematical reasoning. **Also NS 1.0**

Chapter 4   75

CA Standards

KEY NS 1.5 Identify and represent on a number line decimals, fractions, mixed numbers, and positive and negative integers.

MR 2.3 Use a variety of methods, such as words, numbers, symbols, charts, graphs, tables, diagrams, and models, to explain mathematical reasoning.

Also KEY NS 1.2, **MR 3.3**

Materials

• Learning Tool 52 (Decimal-Fraction Number Lines)
• Straightedge
• Colored pencils (blue and red)

Hands On
Fractions and Decimals

Objective Identify decimal equivalents of common fractions.

▶ **Explore**

In Chapter 3, you learned to write fractions with denominators of 10, 100, and 1000 and their decimal equivalents.

Question How can you find decimal equivalents for other fractions?

In a sports car race, the first place car finished the race $\frac{3}{4}$ seconds ahead of the second place car. What is the decimal equivalent of $\frac{3}{4}$?

1 Use the Learning Tool. Find the number line for fourths.

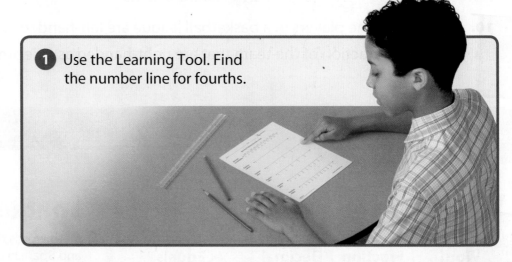

California Speedway Fontana, CA

2 Find the point for $\frac{3}{4}$. Place a straightedge vertically so it crosses all of the number lines and draw a vertical line with your blue colored pencil. Find the decimal that the blue line passes through.

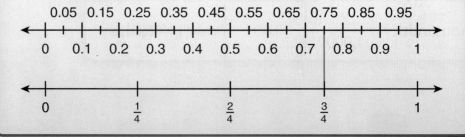

0.05 0.15 0.25 0.35 0.45 0.55 0.65 0.75 0.85 0.95

0   0.1   0.2   0.3   0.4   0.5   0.6   0.7   0.8   0.9   1

0        $\frac{1}{4}$ $\frac{2}{4}$ $\frac{3}{4}$ 1

Solution: 0.75 is equivalent to $\frac{3}{4}$.

You can use the other number lines on the Learning Tool to find decimal equivalents of fractions with other denominators.

Find the decimal equivalent of $\frac{2}{10}$.

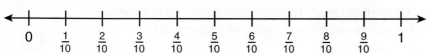

1 Find the number line for tenths.

---

2 Find the point for $\frac{2}{10}$. Place a straightedge vertically so it crosses all of the number lines and draw a vertical line with your red colored pencil.

Find the decimal that the red line passes through.

▶ **Extend**

Use the Learning Tool. Write the fraction as a decimal.

1. $\frac{7}{10}$ **2.** $\frac{4}{5}$ **3.** $\frac{1}{2}$

4. $\frac{6}{8}$ **5.** $\frac{1}{5}$ **6.** $\frac{2}{8}$

7. $\frac{3}{5}$ **8.** $\frac{1}{4}$ **9.** $\frac{8}{10}$

10. $\frac{5}{10}$ **11.** $\frac{2}{5}$ **12.** $\frac{4}{8}$

13. $\frac{1}{5}$ **14.** $\frac{3}{10}$ **15.** $\frac{2}{4}$

16. $\frac{9}{10}$ **17.** $\frac{4}{10}$ **18.** $\frac{6}{10}$

19. Draw another number line at the bottom of Learning Tool 52 that you could use to find the decimal equivalent of $\frac{17}{20}$.

20. Look back at Exercises 1–18. List the fractions that equal 0.5. Explain why more than one fraction can have the same decimal equivalent.

Writing Math

Explain How can you use the number lines to compare 0.6 and $\frac{3}{8}$? Which number is larger?

CA Standards

KEY **NS 1.2** Interpret percents as a part of a hundred; find decimal and percent equivalents for common fractions and explain why they represent the same value; compute a given percent of a whole number.

MR 2.3 Use a variety of methods, such as words, numbers, symbols, charts, graphs, tables, diagrams, and models, to explain mathematical reasoning.

Also KEY NS 1.5, MR 2.0, MR 3.0, MR 3.2

Equivalent Fractions and Decimals

Objective Change decimals to fractions and mixed numbers, and change mixed numbers and fractions to decimals.

▶ **Learn by Example**

The Rose Bowl Stadium was built in 1922 and grew as college football became more popular. The original capacity was $\frac{3}{5}$ of its capacity today. Write $\frac{3}{5}$ as a decimal.

Rose Bowl Stadium in Pasadena, CA

Think

If you are converting a mixed number to a decimal, write the whole number to the left of the decimal point.

Example 1

1 Find an equivalent fraction with a denominator that is a power of 10.

$$\overset{\times 2}{\frac{3}{5}} = \frac{6}{10}\underset{\times 2}{}$$

2 Convert the fraction to a decimal.

$$\frac{6}{10} = 0.6$$

Solution: The original Rose Bowl Stadium had 0.6 of its capacity today.

You can also convert decimals to fractions or mixed numbers.

Write 0.55 as a fraction in simplest form.

Example 2

1 Write the decimal as a fraction with a power of 10 as the denominator.

$$0.55 = \frac{55}{100}$$

2 Write the fraction in simplest form.

$$\frac{55}{100} = \frac{11}{20}$$

Write the fraction or mixed number as a decimal.

1. $\frac{1}{2}$ **2.** $1\frac{3}{10}$ **3.** $2\frac{3}{4}$

Write the decimal as a fraction or mixed number in simplest form.

4. 0.17   **5.** 1.2   **6.** 3.5

Ask Yourself
Did I express each fraction or mixed number in simplest form?

Guided Problem Solving

Use the questions to solve this problem.

7. In 1891, the Monrovia Town Band was the first marching band in the Rose Bowl Parade. Now many marching bands are part of the parade. In one year, $\frac{1}{4}$ of the bands who applied to march were accepted. Write the fraction as a decimal.

   a. Understand What do you need to find?

   b. Plan Find a fraction equivalent to $\frac{1}{4}$ with a power of ten in the denominator. What power of 10 will you use?

   c. Solve Use your plan to write the decimal.

   d. Look Back Look at the solution. How can you use a 10 × 10 grid to check your answer?

University of Southern California Marching Band in the Rose Bowl Parade

8. Suppose $\frac{3}{4}$ of the bands who applied to march were accepted. Write the decimal equivalent of $\frac{3}{4}$. Explain two ways you could use to find the answer.

123 Math Talk When you write a decimal in the form of an equivalent fraction, why is it important to use a denominator that is a power of 10?

Write the decimal as a fraction or mixed number in simplest form.

9. 0.8   **10.** 0.13   **11.** 0.75   **12.** 3.6   **13.** 4.5   **14.** 7.25

Write the fraction or mixed number as a decimal.

15. $\frac{1}{5}$ **16.** $\frac{7}{10}$ **17.** $\frac{3}{25}$ **18.** $2\frac{7}{10}$ **19.** $3\frac{3}{4}$ **20.** $5\frac{3}{100}$

Use the number line for Problems 21–22.

21. Write the decimal represented by point A.

22. Write the fraction represented by point C.

23. Right or Wrong? Each flat represents one whole. Marnie says the shaded parts of the flats show that $2.3 = 2\frac{3}{100}$. Do you agree? Explain your reasoning.

 Science Link

Solve.

24. Because MESSENGER flies by other planets during its long journey, the spacecraft will travel 4.9 billion miles before it begins orbiting Mercury. Write 4.9 as a mixed number.

25. MESSENGER's journey to Mercury will take more than 6.5 years. Write the number as a mixed number in simplest form.

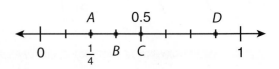

Messages from Mercury

- Mercury is the closest planet to the sun.

- The MESSENGER spacecraft was launched in 2004 and will enter Mercury's orbit in March 2011. It will study the characteristics of Mercury for one Earth year.

- MESSENGER gains momentum for its journey from the gravity of other planets.

Science ES 5.b, ES 5.c

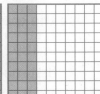

 Spiral Review and Test Practice

Write each improper fraction as a mixed number or a whole number. KEY NS 1.5 page 30

26. $\frac{5}{2}$ **27.** $\frac{15}{4}$ **28.** $\frac{6}{3}$ **29.** $\frac{8}{3}$

Write the letter of the correct answer. KEY NS 1.2

30. What is the decimal equivalent of $2\frac{4}{5}$?

   A 2.45   **B** 2.8   **C** 0.28   **D** 28.0

    Extra Practice See page 89, Set A.

Key Standards Review

Need Help?
See Key Standards Handbook.

Between which two letters does $4\frac{1}{3}$ fall on each number line? **KEY NS 1.5**

1.

2.
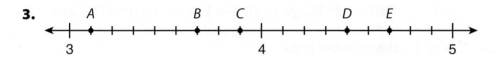

3.

Write each prime factorization. Use exponents if possible.
KEY NS 1.4

4. 15   **5.** 48   **6.** 16

7. 30   **8.** 36   **9.** 22

10. 45   **11.** 27   **12.** 42

13. 28   **14.** 32   **15.** 40

Challenge

Problem Solving

Batting Averages **KEY NS 1.2**

A good batting average is 0.300 or more. In this case, we say that a player is "batting three hundred." That means the batter would probably get about 300 hits out of every 1,000 times at bat. If a player gets a hit once in every 3 times at bat, is that player "batting more or less than 300"?

CA Standards

KEY NS 1.2 Interpret percents as a part of a hundred; find decimal and percent equivalents for common fractions and explain why they represent the same value; compute a given percent of a whole number.

KEY NS 1.5 Identify and represent on a number line decimals, fractions, mixed numbers, and positive and negative integers.

Also MR 2.3

Compare and Order Fractions and Decimals

Objective Compare and order decimals, fractions, and mixed numbers.

▶ **Learn by Example**

You can use what you know about finding equivalent fractions, mixed numbers, and decimals to put different numbers in order.

Order $\frac{4}{5}$, $1\frac{9}{10}$, and 1.25.

Different Ways to Order Fractions and Decimals

Way 1 Use number lines.

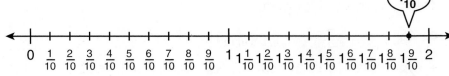

The number farthest to the left has the least value. The number farthest to the right has the greatest value.

$$\frac{4}{5} < 1.25 < 1\frac{9}{10}$$

Way 2 Write fractions and mixed numbers as equivalent decimals.

$$\frac{4}{5} = \frac{8}{10} = 0.8 \qquad 1\frac{9}{10} = 1.9 \qquad 1.25$$

Order the decimals.

$$0.8 < 1.25 < 1.9$$

So, $\frac{4}{5} < 1.25 < 1\frac{9}{10}$.

Solution: $\frac{4}{5} < 1.25 < 1\frac{9}{10}$

Guided Practice

Order the set of numbers from least to greatest.

1. $2\frac{17}{20}$, 2.75, $2\frac{4}{5}$

2. $\frac{7}{20}$, $1\frac{1}{4}$, 0.82

3. $\frac{9}{25}$, 0.09, 0.19

Ask Yourself
Will I write the numbers in the same form or use a number line?

123 Math Talk How do you know what power of 10 to use as a denominator when writing a decimal as an equivalent fraction?

Practice and Problem Solving

Order the set of numbers from least to greatest.

4. $\frac{1}{2}$, 0.55, 2.5

5. $\frac{4}{5}$, $\frac{1}{100}$, $2\frac{3}{4}$

6. $\frac{3}{10}$, 0.25, $\frac{3}{2}$

7. $\frac{9}{15}$, 0.3, $\frac{4}{5}$

Solve.

8. Penny cuts three lengths of ribbons. The ribbons are $1\frac{3}{4}$ ft, $1\frac{7}{12}$ ft, and 1.5 ft. Show all three of these lengths on a number line. Then list the lengths from shortest to longest.

9. **Challenge** Manuel had two pieces of lumber that were six feet long. He cut 0.5 feet from one 6-foot piece and $\frac{1}{4}$ foot from the second piece of lumber. After the cuts, how long is the shorter piece? the longer piece?

 Spiral Review and Test Practice

Write each number in standard form. NS 1.0 pages 56 and 60

10. four billion, twelve million, five hundred sixty-nine

11. forty-five thousandths

Choose the letter of the correct answer. KEY NS 1.5, KEY NS 1.2

12. Which of the following is true?

A $\frac{3}{4} < \frac{1}{4} < 1\frac{3}{8}$ B $1\frac{1}{2} < 1\frac{3}{8} < 1.2$ C $\frac{3}{4} < 1.2 < 1\frac{3}{8}$ D $1\frac{3}{8} > \frac{6}{8} > 1\frac{2}{8}$

CA Standards

KEY NS 1.5 Identify and represent on a number line decimals, fractions, mixed numbers, and positive and negative integers.

MR 3.3 Develop generalizations of the results obtained and apply them in other circumstances.

Also KEY NS 1.2

Vocabulary

unit fraction

Mental Math: Fraction and Decimal Equivalents

Objective To compare and order fractions, mixed numbers, and decimals using mental math.

▶ **Learn by Example**

In this lesson, you will learn how to convert fractions to decimals and decimals to fractions in your head.

The table shows the decimal equivalents for some **unit fractions.** Unit fractions are fractions that have 1 in the numerator. Learning these equivalents will help you solve problems involving non-unit fractions mentally.

Common Fraction-Decimal Equivalents

Fraction	Decimal
$\frac{1}{2}$	0.5
$\frac{1}{4}$	0.25
$\frac{1}{5}$	0.2
$\frac{1}{8}$	0.125
$\frac{1}{10}$	0.1

Think

$\frac{1}{2} = 0.50$ $\frac{1}{5} = 0.20,$

$\frac{2}{5} = 2 \times 0.20 =$
$0.20 + 0.20 = 0.40$

$0.50 > 0.40$

$2.50 > 2.40,$
so $2\frac{1}{2} > 2\frac{2}{5}$

Place $\frac{4}{5}$, $\frac{3}{10}$, $\frac{1}{4}$, and $\frac{3}{8}$ on the number line.

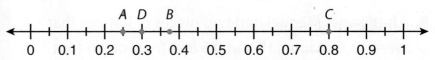

1 Use decimal equivalents to identify the points for the unit fractions.

$\frac{1}{4} = 0.25$ So, Point A represents $\frac{1}{4}$.

2 Use decimal equivalents of unit fractions to find decimal equivalents of non-unit fractions.

$\frac{1}{5} = 0.2$ So $\frac{4}{5} = 0.2 + 0.2 + 0.2 + 0.2 = 0.8$
So, Point C represents $\frac{4}{5}$.

$\frac{1}{10} = 0.1$ So $\frac{3}{10} = 0.1 + 0.1 + 0.1 = 0.3$
So, Point D represents $\frac{3}{10}$.

$\frac{1}{8} = 0.125$ So $\frac{3}{8} = 0.125 + 0.125 + 0.125 = 0.375$
So, Point B represents $\frac{3}{8}$.

Solution: Point A is $\frac{1}{4}$, Point B is $\frac{3}{8}$, Point C is $\frac{4}{5}$, and Point D is $\frac{3}{10}$

▶ Guided Practice

Use the number line and mental math to complete Exercises 1–2.

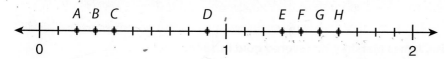

$$\overset{\quad\quad A\quad\quad B\ \ C\quad\quad\quad\quad DE\quad\quad F\quad\quad G}{\longleftarrow\!\underset{0}{\mid}\!+\!+\!\blacklozenge\!+\!+\!\blacklozenge\!+\blacklozenge\!\bullet\!+\!\underset{1}{\mid}\!+\!+\!\bullet\!\bullet\!+\!\blacklozenge\!+\!+\!\blacklozenge\!+\!+\!\underset{2}{\mid}\!\longrightarrow}$$

1. Write the decimal and the fraction in simplest form for point *B*.

2. Which point represents $\frac{5}{4}$? Explain your answer.

 Math Talk How does knowing decimal equivalents for some fractions help you find decimal equivalents of other fractions with the same denominator?

▶ Practice and Problem Solving

Use the number line to complete Exercises 3–4.

$$\overset{\quad\quad A\ B\ \ C\quad\quad\quad\quad D\quad\quad\quad E\ F\ G\ H}{\longleftarrow\!\underset{0}{\mid}\!+\!\blacklozenge\!\blacklozenge\!+\!\blacklozenge\!+\!+\!+\!+\!+\!\blacklozenge\!\underset{1}{\mid}\!+\!+\!+\!\blacklozenge\!\blacklozenge\!\blacklozenge\!+\!\blacklozenge\!+\!+\!\underset{2}{\mid}\!\longrightarrow}$$

3. Write the mixed number for point *H*.

4. Which point represents 1.3?

Solve using mental math.

5. Will says that $0.45 = \frac{4}{5}$. Is he correct? Explain.

6. **Challenge** Dora's mother drove Dora $\frac{7}{8}$ of the way to school. She walked the rest of the way. She lives 1 mile from the school. Sebby walked 0.78 mile to school. Who had the longer walk?

✓ Spiral Review and Test Practice

Compare. Write >, < or = for the ⬭. NS 1.0 page 62

7. 27 ⬭ 26.942

8. 5.426 ⬭ 5.462

9. 4,051,376 ⬭ 4,059,886

Write the letter of the correct answer. KEY NS 1.5

10. Which letter on the number line identifies the location of 3.75?

A P   **C** R

B Q   **D** S

$$\overset{\quad\quad\quad\quad\quad P\quad Q\quad\quad\quad\quad R\ \ S}{\longleftarrow\!\underset{3}{\mid}\!+\!\blacklozenge\!+\!\blacklozenge\!+\!+\!+\!\blacklozenge\!+\!\blacklozenge\!+\!+\!\underset{4}{\mid}\!\longrightarrow}$$

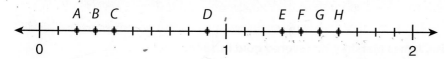

Ask Yourself

Which unit fraction equivalent can help me?

LESSON 5

Field Trip...

Coloma, CA

CA Standards
MR 1.0, MR 1.1,
MR 2.0, MR 2.3,
NS 1.0, NS 1.3,
KEY NS 1.4, KEY NS 1.5

Problem Solving

Objective Use skills and strategies to solve word problems.

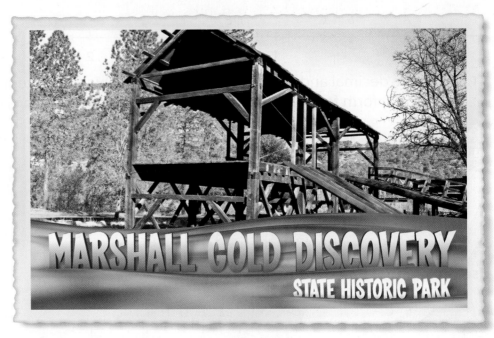

At this site, James Marshall discovered gold in 1848.

The discovery of gold in 1848 started the Gold Rush era and set off a huge movement of people to the California area.

Solve. Tell which strategy or method you used.

1. A gold digger found a nugget that weighed exactly 8 ounces. He wants to make smaller nuggets whose weights are factors of 8. List the possible sizes of nuggets that he could make.

2. Mrs. Chen's class visits the gold discovery site for half an hour. They listen to a tour guide at the Sawmill Replica for 0.2 hour. Then they visit the Morrison Cabin for $\frac{3}{8}$ hour. At which site did they spend the most time?

3. Fool's gold, also known as pyrite, has a pale yellow color that often looks and feels like gold, but it is not. Suppose a miner finds three nuggets of pyrite with the following weights: $\frac{1}{2}$ ounce, 0.1 ounce, and $\frac{3}{4}$ ounce. Show these numbers on a number line and order them from least to greatest.

Problem Solving On Tests

Select a Strategy
- Write an Equation
- Work Backward
- Guess and Check
- Choose the Operation
- Estimate

1. Gary has a collection of 54 rare stamps. What is the prime factorization of 54?

A $2^2 \times 3^2$ **C** 2×3^3

B $2^3 \times 7$ **D** $3^2 \times 5$

KEY **NS 1.4** page 12

2. Jasmine wrote the prime factorization of a number as 3^4. Which of the following is 3^4?

A $3 + 3 + 3 + 3$ **C** $4 + 4 + 4$

B $3 \times 3 \times 3 \times 3$ **D** $4 \times 4 \times 4$

NS 1.3 page 14

3. Julie drew the number line shown below. Which letter on the number line best identifies the location of $1\frac{2}{5}$?

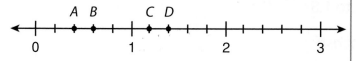

A A   **C** C

B B   **D** D

KEY **NS 1.5** page 30

4. Carla has 24 tubes of toothpaste and 40 toothbrushes. She puts the toothpaste equally into bags. The toothbrushes are put into bags in the same amount as the toothpaste. What is the greatest common factor (GCF) of 24 and 40?

A 2   **C** 6

B 4   **D** 8

KEY **NS 1.4** page 16

5. Reggie added two fractions and got a sum of $\frac{8}{12}$. Which shows $\frac{8}{12}$ written in simplest form?

A $\frac{1}{3}$

B $\frac{2}{3}$

C $\frac{4}{6}$

D $\frac{4}{3}$

> **Test Tip**
> To find the simplest form, divide the numerator and denominator by the Greatest Common Factor.

KEY **NS 2.3** page 34

6. The total area of California is 163,707 square miles. What is this value rounded to the nearest thousand square miles?

A 160,000   **C** 164,000

B 163,000   **D** 164,707

NS 1.1 page 66

7. A package weighs 16.526 pounds. What is this value rounded to the nearest tenth of a pound?

A 16.5

B 16.53

C 17

D 20

> **Test Tip**
> Apply rounding rules for whole numbers to decimals.

NS 1.1 page 66

Education Place
Visit www.eduplace.com/camap/ for
Test-Taking Tips and **Extra Practice**.

Chapter 4 Lesson 5   87

Reading & Writing Math

Vocabulary

Fractions and decimals are two ways of representing parts of a whole. Sometimes a fraction and a decimal represent the same value.

Use the number line for Exercises 1–6.

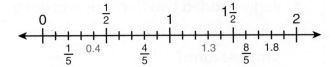

1. What **decimal** is **equivalent** to $\frac{1}{5}$?

2. What **fraction** is equivalent to 0.4?

3. What **improper fraction** is equivalent to 1.3?

4. What **mixed number** is equivalent to 1.3?

5. What **decimal** is equivalent to $\frac{8}{5}$?

6. What **improper fraction** is equivalent to 1.8?

7. Order these numbers from *greatest* to *least*:

$$1\frac{1}{2} \quad 0.5 \quad 1.2 \quad 1 \quad \frac{3}{8}$$

Writing How did you figure out how to order the numbers in question 7? Explain your reasoning.

Reading Check out this book in your library.
Funny and Fabulous Fraction Stories, by Dan Greenberg

CA Standards
MR 2.3 Use a variety of methods, such as words, numbers, symbols, charts, graphs, tables, diagrams, and models, to explain mathematical reasoning.

Also KEY NS 1.5

Standards-Based Extra Practice

Set A ────────────────────────────────────── NS 1.0 page 78

Write each fraction or mixed number as a decimal.

1. $2\frac{1}{5}$ **2.** $\frac{3}{50}$ **3.** $12\frac{9}{10}$ **4.** $4\frac{1}{25}$

5. $7\frac{3}{4}$ **6.** $18\frac{7}{100}$ **7.** $3\frac{1}{2}$ **8.** $\frac{3}{5}$

9. $10\frac{1}{4}$ **10.** $\frac{1}{10}$ **11.** $\frac{13}{100}$ **12.** $16\frac{7}{20}$

Solve.

13. Emma is making a scrapbook for her mother. She finished $\frac{2}{5}$ of the scrapbook. What decimal represents the part of the scrapbook she finished?

Set B ────────────────────────────────────── KEY **NS 1.5** page 82

Order each set of numbers from least to greatest. Use a number line to help you.

1. $1.85; 1.58; 1\frac{3}{5}$ **2.** $7.4; 7\frac{1}{5}; 8\frac{1}{2}$ **3.** $\frac{4}{5}; \frac{3}{4}; 0.79$ **4.** $5.88; 5.78; 5\frac{9}{10}$

5. $1\frac{37}{100}; 1\frac{47}{100}; 1.05$ **6.** $0.75; \frac{7}{10}; 0.8$ **7.** $2.5; 2.55; 2\frac{49}{100}$ **8.** $4\frac{3}{4}; 3\frac{3}{4}; 3.77$

Solve.

9. Miles filled two bags with old toys when he cleaned the attic. The first bag weighs 5.79 pounds and the second bag weighs $5\frac{4}{5}$ pounds. Which bag weighs more?

Set C ────────────────────────────────────── KEY **NS 1.5** page 84

Use the number line to complete Exercises 1–4.

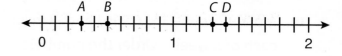

1. Write the mixed number for point *C*.

2. Write the decimal and the fraction in simplest form for point *B*.

3. Write the mixed number for point *D*.

4. Which point represents 0.3?

5. Carrie lives 6.7 miles from the ice skating rink. Jerome lives $6\frac{3}{5}$ miles from the same rink. Who lives closer to the skating rink?

Education Place
Visit www.eduplace.com/camap/ for
Test-Taking Tips and **Extra Practice**.

Chapter Review/Test

Vocabulary and Concepts ———————————————— NS 1.0, MR 2.3

Write the best word to complete each sentence.

1. A fraction with a numerator of 1 is called a _____ fraction.

2. To write a fraction as a decimal, write an equivalent fraction with a denominator that is a power of _____.

Skills ——————————————————————————————— NS 1.0, KEY NS 1.5

Write the fraction or mixed number as a decimal.

3. $\frac{3}{4}$

4. $1\frac{9}{10}$

5. $4\frac{2}{5}$

6. $2\frac{3}{25}$

Write the decimal as a fraction or mixed number in simplest form.

7. 1.5

8. 0.25

9. 8.2

10. 0.05

Compare. Write $<$, $>$, or $=$ for each ⬤.

11. $\frac{1}{2}$ ⬤ 0.2

12. $1\frac{1}{4}$ ⬤ 1.3

13. 0.67 ⬤ $\frac{7}{10}$

Order the set of numbers from least to greatest.

14. 5.3 $5\frac{3}{5}$ 5.4

15. $\frac{1}{10}$ 0.25 $\frac{1}{5}$

16. 3.77 $3\frac{3}{4}$ 3.7

Problem Solving and Reasoning ———————— NS 1.3, KEY NS 1.5, MR 1.0, MR 2.3

Solve.

17. Mount McKinley is the highest point in the U.S. at about 2×10^4 feet. Write the height in standard form.

18. Lamont walked 2.7 miles on Saturday. On Sunday he road his bike $2\frac{2}{3}$ miles. On which day did he travel more miles?

19. A plant grew $\frac{3}{4}$ in., 0.9 in., and $\frac{4}{5}$ in. in each of 3 weeks. Order the numbers from least to greatest.

20. Gina has one dozen eggs. She divides the eggs into more than 1 basket. How many baskets could she use?

Writing Math What are three different ways to order fractions and decimals? When would you use each?

Spiral Review and Test Practice

1. What is 20,000,000 + 10,000 + 300,000,000 + 8,000 + 500 + 6 in standard form?

A 320,180,506

B 320,018,560

C 320,018,506

D 32,018,506

GRADE 4 KEY NS 1.1 page 56

2. What is 306,249 rounded to the nearest hundred?

A 306,300

B 306,250

C 306,200

D 306,000

NS 1.1 page 66

3. 4,932 + 2,086 =

A 7,028

B 7,018

C 6,918

D 6,018

Test Tip
Use the inverse operation to check your answer.

GRADE 4 KEY NS 3.1

4. What is 13.526 rounded to the nearest hundredth?

A 13.5

B 13.52

C 13.53

D 14

NS 1.1 page 66

5. What is the decimal 0.3 written as a fraction?

A $\dfrac{3}{10}$

B $\dfrac{3}{100}$

C $\dfrac{1}{3}$

D $\dfrac{0}{3}$

KEY NS 1.2 page 78

6. What is the mixed number $1\dfrac{3}{5}$ written as a decimal?

A 0.16

B 0.6

C 1.35

D 1.6

Test Tip
Use number sense to rule out some answer choices.

KEY NS 1.2 page 78

Education Place
Visit www.eduplace.com/camap/ for **Test-Taking Tips** and **Extra Practice**.

Unit 2 Review/Test

Vocabulary and Concepts ————————————— NS 1.0, MR 1.1, MR 2.3 Chapter 3

Write *true* or *false*.

1. To compare numbers, write them in a place-value chart and compare the digits from left to right.

2. The number 3,000,000 + 400,000 + 20,000 + 9,000 + 800 + 70 + 5 is written in standard form.

3. When a number is written in word form, the decimal point is indicated by the word *point*.

4. On a place-value chart, each group of 3 digits from right to left is called a period.

5. One tenth of a penny is equivalent to $\frac{1}{100}$ of a dollar.

Skills ————————————————————— NS 1.0 Chapter 3, Lesson 2

Write each number in standard form and in word form.

6. 3,000 + 400 + 8

7. 70,000,000,000 + 300,000,000 + 6,000

8. 4,000,000 + 200,000 + 60,000 + 30

9. 500,000 + 20,000 + 8,000 + 300 + 50 + 2

Write each decimal in word form. Chapter 3, Lesson 3

10. 0.248

11. 8.38

12. 18.9

13. 0.902

Write each fraction or mixed number as a decimal. Chapter 4, Lesson 2

14. $26\frac{2}{5}$

15. $\frac{59}{100}$

16. $18\frac{3}{20}$

17. $\frac{19}{50}$

Compare. Write <, >, or = for each ⬭ **.** Chapter 4, Lesson 3

18. 0.87 ⬭ $\frac{3}{4}$

19. 7.9 ⬭ $7\frac{9}{10}$

20. $1\frac{19}{20}$ ⬭ $1\frac{17}{20}$

21. 0.18 ⬭ $\frac{1}{5}$

Problem Solving and Reasoning ———— NS 1.0, NS 1.1, KEY NS 1.5, MR 2.3 Chapters 3–4

Solve.

22. An Astronomical Unit (AU) is approximately the mean distance between the Earth and the Sun. 1 AU = 149,597,870.691 kilometers. Round this number to the nearest thousand kilometers.

23. Liam wants to find the closest park. The distances between his house and three parks are: 3.25 miles, 3.52 miles, and 3.48 miles. Order the distances from the closest to the farthest.

Solve.

24. Portia wants to put $1\frac{1}{2}$ hours of music on a CD. So far, she has $1\frac{1}{4}$ hours. Portia adds four more songs. She now has 1.5 hours of music on the CD. Does she now have too much time? Explain your answer.

25. Louis counts his money. He has one dollar-bill, two dimes, and eight pennies. He writes this amount as $1.028. Is he correct? Explain your thinking.

Writing Math How is knowing how to change mixed numbers and fractions to decimals useful?

Performance Assessment

Charlene's New Rug

KEY **NS 1.2**, NS 1.0

Charlene's mother is letting her pick out a rug for the bedroom she shares with her sister. Charlene wants to get the longest rug she can to fit in the space and stay within her budget. Charlene makes a list of possibilities to show her mother. The chart shows the rugs she is considering.

	Length in inches	Width in inches	Price
Rug A	97.35	38.5	$44.78
Rug B	$96\frac{3}{4}$	$39\frac{1}{4}$	$44.87
Rug C	98.2	39.75	$45.82
Rug D	$98\frac{1}{2}$	$38\frac{1}{2}$	$45.25
Rug E	$97\frac{7}{10}$	$39\frac{1}{3}$	$42.90
Rug F	$98\frac{3}{20}$	38	$45.49

Task	Information You Need
Use the information above and to the right. Eliminate any rugs that are too large for Charlene's room or that cost too much. Then make two lists, the first with longest to shortest rugs, the second with the least expensive to most expensive rugs.	The rug can be up to 98.2 inches long.
	The width of Charlene's room is 78 inches.
	Charlene can't spend more than $45.50.

Make 99

A simple strategy of mine, is first to make a 99!

First I take 3 away from 602 to get 599. I must also take 3 away from 345, and I get 342.

1.
$$\begin{array}{r} 602 \\ -\ 345 \\ \hline \end{array}$$
Take 3 from 602. →
Take 3 from 345. →
$$\begin{array}{r} 599 \\ -\ 342 \\ \hline 257 \end{array}$$

2.
$$\begin{array}{r} 208 \\ -\ 59 \\ \hline \end{array}$$
Take 9 from 208. →
Take 9 from 59. →
$$-\ \blacksquare$$

3.
$$\begin{array}{r} 102 \\ -\ 54 \\ \hline \end{array}$$
Take ■ from 102. →
Take ■ from 54. →
$$-\ \blacksquare$$

4.
$$\begin{array}{r} 506 \\ -\ 227 \\ \hline \end{array}$$
Take ■ from ■. →
Take ■ from ■. →
$$-\ \blacksquare$$

Good job! Now try these!

5.
$$\begin{array}{r} 803 \\ -\ 346 \\ \hline \end{array}$$
→ ■
$$-\ \blacksquare$$

6.
$$\begin{array}{r} 105 \\ -\ 79 \\ \hline \end{array}$$
→ ■
$$-\ \blacksquare$$

7.
$$\begin{array}{r} 401 \\ -\ 265 \\ \hline \end{array}$$
→ ■
$$-\ \blacksquare$$

8.
$$\begin{array}{r} 704 \\ -\ 126 \\ \hline \end{array}$$
→ ■
$$-\ \blacksquare$$

9.
$$\begin{array}{r} 600 \\ -\ 495 \\ \hline \end{array}$$
→ ■
$$-\ \blacksquare$$

10.
$$\begin{array}{r} 807 \\ -\ 798 \\ \hline \end{array}$$
→ ■
$$-\ \blacksquare$$

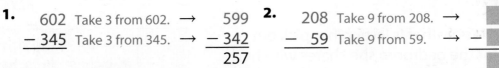

Take It Further!

Now try doing all the steps in your head!

11.
$$\begin{array}{r} 203 \\ -\ 179 \\ \hline \end{array}$$

12.
$$\begin{array}{r} 501 \\ -\ 386 \\ \hline \end{array}$$

13.
$$\begin{array}{r} 307 \\ -\ 298 \\ \hline \end{array}$$

14.
$$\begin{array}{r} 908 \\ -\ 149 \\ \hline \end{array}$$

Unit 3

Algebra

BIG IDEAS!

- You can solve problems by finding the value of variables in an equation.
- You can use the Distributive, Commutative, Associative, Identity, and Equality Properties to solve equations.

Chapter 5
Expressions and Equations

Chapter 6
Properties

Songs and Games

Math Music Track 3:
Properties

eGames at
www.eduplace.com/camap/

Math Readers

This is a closeup of an ox cart wheel from the town of Sarchi in Costa Rica.

Game

Make It Even

Object of the Game Make an expression equal to an even number.

Materials
Number Tiles (Three sets 0–9, two sets +, −)

Number of Players 2

Set Up
Give each player a set of symbol tiles. Shuffle the number tiles and place them face down in a stack.

How to Play

1 Each player draws 3 number tiles from the stack. Players use the number tiles and one or two of their symbol tiles to make an expression.

2 A player's score is the value of the expression. If the value is an even number, the score is doubled.

3 Return all the tiles to the deck and shuffle. Repeat steps 1–2.

4 The player with the highest score after 4 rounds wins.

CA Standards
Prepares for KEY AF 1.2 Use a letter to represent an unknown number; write and evaluate simple algebraic expressions in one variable by substitution.

Also MR 1.0, MR 2.0

Education Place
Visit www.eduplace.com/camap/ for **Brain Teasers** and **eGames** to play.

Reading When you read a story, you interpret the words, sentences, and paragraphs. When you read math, you have to go beyond words. Often you must analyze graphs and tables to get the information you need.

Read the problem. Study the function table.

Vann works part-time for the Transit Authority. He earns $12 an hour. The input column of the function table shows the number of hours (x) that he works. The output column shows how much he earns (y). What is the rule for the function table?

The rule shows how the input (h) is related to the output (e).

Rule: ?	
Input (x)	Output (y)
1	$12
2	$24
3	$36
4	$48

amount earned

number of hours

→ 1 × $12
→ 2 × $12
→ 3 × $12
→ 4 × $12

The rule for this table is multiply by $12. $y = x \cdot \$12$

Writing Keith drives a limo to the airport. He can take 4 passengers at a time. Write a problem that can be answered by using this information and a function table. Ask a classmate to solve the problem.

Expressions and Equations

Check What You Know

Vocabulary and Concepts GRADE 4 AF 1.0, MR 2.3

Choose the best word to complete each sentence.

1. _____, such as addition and subtraction, are opposites and "undo" each other.

2. A combination of numbers, variables, and operation signs is a(n) _____ .

3. A _____ is a rule that gives exactly one output value for each input value.

Skills GRADE 4 AF 1.1

Determine the missing number in each number sentence.

3. $4 + \blacksquare = 7$

4. $\blacksquare + 8 = 13$

5. $9 - \blacksquare = 5$

6. $\blacksquare - 7 = 10$

7. $16 + \blacksquare = 34$

8. $\blacksquare - 35 = 47$

Problem Solving and Reasoning GRADE 4 KEY NS 3.0

9. Tony had \$37. After he was paid for his part-time job, he had \$72. How much was Tony paid?

10. Tina had \$56. After she bought a DVD, she had \$29 left. How much did the DVD cost?

Vocabulary

Visualize It!

$$y + 6 = 14$$

Language Tips

The word *equation* has the same Latin root as "equal." In an equation, the left side is equal to the right side.

Math words that look alike in English and Spanish often have the same meaning.

English	Spanish
equation	**ecuación**
variable	**variable**

See **English-Spanish Glossary** pages 628–642.

variable

A letter that stands for a number in an algebraic expression.

In this equation, *y* is a variable.

equation

A mathematical sentence that shows that two expressions have the same value.

Here $y + 6$ has the same value as 14.

Education Place Visit www.eduplace.com/camap/ for the **eGlossary** and **eGames**.

CA Standards MR 2.3 Use a variety of methods, such as words, numbers, symbols, charts, graphs, tables, diagrams, and models, to explain mathematical reasoning. **Also KEY AF 1.2**

Chapter 5   99

CA Standards

MR 1.1 Analyze problems by identifying relationships, distinguishing relevant from irrelevant information, sequencing and prioritizing information, and observing patterns.

Prepares for KEY AF 1.2
Use a letter to represent an unknown number; write and evaluate simple algebraic expressions in one variable by substitution.

Also NS 1.0, MR 2.3, MR 2.4, MR 3.0, MR 3.2, MR 3.3

Vocabulary

function rule

function table

Materials
Learning Tool 10
(Centimeter Grid)

Hands On
Algebra and Patterns

Objective Extend patterns using models and find function rules.

▶ **Explore**

In this lesson, you will use a rule to describe a pattern.

If the same pattern continues, how many squares would be in Figure 10?

Question How can I find a rule to describe this pattern?

Figure 1   **Figure 2**   **Figure 3**

---

1 Look at how the figure changes each time. Make a **function table** to organize the input and output values.

Figure Number	1	2	3				← input
Number of Squares	3	4	5				← output

---

2 Color and label the next two figures on the Learning Tool.

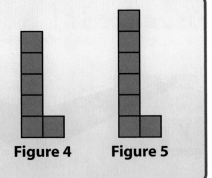

Figure 4   **Figure 5**

---

3 Continue the table.

Figure Number	1	2	3	4	5			← input
Number of Squares	3	4	5	6	7			← output

4 Write a **function rule** to describe the pattern. You can use the function rule to find the output value for any input value.

Rule: The output number is the input number plus 2.

Use the rule to find the number of squares in Figure 10.

Figure Number	1	2	3	4	5	10
Number of Squares	3	4	5	6	7	12

Think

In this pattern, the number of squares is always 2 more than the figure number.

Solution: There will be 12 squares in Figure 10.

▶ **Extend**

Draw a figure that could come next in the pattern. Write a function rule to describe your pattern. Then complete the table.

1.

Figure 1   **Figure 2**   **Figure 3**

Figure	1	2	3	4	10
Number of Dots					

2.

 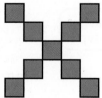 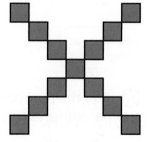

Figure 1   **Figure 2**   **Figure 3**

Figure	1	2	3	4	10
Number of Squares					

Writing Math

Can you use the function table if the input number is a very large number? Look at the table in Exercise 1. What would the output be if the input number is 1,000,000?

LESSON 2

CA Standards

NS 1.3 Understand and compute positive integer powers of nonnegative integers; compute examples as repeated multiplication.

Prepares for KEY AF 1.2
Use a letter to represent an unknown number; write and evaluate simple algebraic expressions in one variable by substitution.

Also MR 1.0, MR 1.2, MR 2.0

Vocabulary

order of operations

expression

Simplify Expressions

Objective Simplify expressions using the order of operations.

 Learn by Example

You know that a numerical **expression** can be a number or numbers with operations. In this lesson, you will learn a set of rules that will help you find the value of an expression. The rules are called the **order of operations**.

Order of Operations
1. Simplify the terms within **p**arentheses.
2. Simplify the terms with **e**xponents.
3. **M**ultiply and **d**ivide from left to right.
4. **A**dd and **s**ubtract from left to right.

Ms. Lang drives a San Francisco cable car. When she begins her route, there are 35 passengers. At the first stop, 5 passengers get off at the front door and 10 passengers get off at the back door. At the next stop, 2 passengers get on. How many passengers are on the cable car after the second stop?

Order of Operations

$$35 \quad - \quad (5 + 10) \quad + \quad 2$$

Number at beginning | Number that get off at first stop | Number that get on at second stop

① Add the numbers inside the parentheses first.
$35 - (5 + 10) + 2$
$= 35 - 15 + 2$

② Since there are no exponents in the expression, move on to the next operation.

③ There is nothing to multiply or divide. Move on to the next operation.

④ Add or subtract from left to right.
$= 35 - 15 + 2$
$= 20 + 2$
$= 22$

Solution: There are 22 passengers on the cable car after the second stop.

Another Example

Find the value of $15 - (10 - 1) + 4^2 \times 3$.

$15 - (10 - 1) + 4^2 \times 3$

$= 15 - 9 + 4^2 \times 3$ ← Find the value of the expression inside parentheses.

$= 15 - 9 + 16 \times 3$ ← Find the value of the term with an exponent. $4^2 = 4 \times 4$

$= 15 - 9 + 48$ ← Multiply and divide from left to right.

$= 6 + 48$ ← Add and subtract from left to right.

$= 54$

▶ Guided Practice

Find the value of each expression.

1. $(14 + 2) - 5$

2. $25 - (5 + 10) - 5$

3. $4 + 3 \times 8$

4. $20 - 2 \times 4$

5. $4^2 - (4 + 3)$

6. $20 - 4^2$

7. $3 \times 8 + 5^2$

8. $65 - 4^3 + 10$

9. $10 - 2^3$

> **Ask Yourself**
> • Which operation should I do first?
> • Have I simplified the expression completely?

(123) Math Talk Do $2 + 5 \times 10$ and $2 + (5 \times 10)$ have the same value? Explain.

▶ Practice and Problem Solving

Find the value of each expression.

10. $(4 + 5) - (4 + 2)$

11. $19 + (4 - 3)$

12. $1 + 6 \times 9$

13. $100 - 2 \times 10$

14. $30 - (1 + 9) + 6^2$

15. $120 - 8^2$

16. $8^2 - 2 \times 5$

17. $20 + 3^3 - 10$

18. $100 + (4 + 4)$

✓ Spiral Review and Test Practice

Write each fraction in simplest form. KEY **NS 2.3** page 34

19. $\frac{12}{24}$

20. $\frac{12}{16}$

21. $\frac{21}{24}$

22. $\frac{15}{18}$

Write the letter of the correct answer. NS 1.3

23. Find the value of $4^3 + 1$.

    A 13   **B** 17   **C** 65   **D** 125

Extra Practice See page 117, Set A.

CA Standards

KEY AF 1.2 Use a letter to represent an unknown number; write and evaluate simple algebraic expressions in one variable substitution.

AF 1.0 Students use variables in simple expressions, compute the value of the expression for specific values of the variable, and plot and interpret the results.

Also NS 1.3, MR 1.1, MR 1.2, MR 2.0, MR 3.0, MR 3.1, MR 3.3

Vocabulary

algebraic expression

evaluate

variable

Write and Evaluate Expressions

Objective Write and evaluate numerical and algebraic expressions.

▶ **Learn by Example**

A **variable** is any letter, such as x or n, that you use to stand for a number. When an expression contains a variable, like $n + 5$, it is called an **algebraic expression**.

One day, Los Angeles International Airport (LAX) had 3 more than twice the number of flights of San Diego International Airport (SAN). Write an algebraic expression for the number of flights at LAX.

Write an Expression

① Decide what variable to use for the missing value.

Suppose there are n flights a day at SAN.

② Decide and write the first operation.

Show twice the number of flights: $2n$

> Remember $2n$ is another way to write $2 \times n$.

③ Decide and write any other operations.

$2n + 3$ shows 3 more than twice the number of flights.

Solution: $2n + 3$ shows the number of flights at LAX.

To **evaluate** an expression, substitute a number for the variable and find the value of the expression.

If SAN had 20 flights that day, how many flights did LAX have?

Think

Remember to use order of operations.

Evaluate an Expression

① Write the expression.

$2n + 3$

↑ variable

② Substitute 20 for n.

$2 \times 20 + 3$

↑ number

③ Find the value.

$2 \times 20 + 3 = 40 + 3$

$2 \times 20 + 3 = 43$

Solution: If SAN has 20 flights in one day, LAX had 43 flights.

Write an algebraic expression for each exercise.
Use the variable *n* to represent the unknown number.

1. a number to the third power plus 6

2. 8 less than twice a number

Translate the algebraic expression into words.

3. $3k + 9$ **4.** $11 - 2z$ **5.** $14 + t^2$ **6.** $b^3 - 4$

Evaluate the expression when $t = 3$.

7. $4t + 11$ **8.** $22 - 3t$ **9.** $t^4 - 1$ **10.** $13 + 10t$

11. $27 + 2t$ **12.** $6t - 5$ **13.** $(t + 1) \div 2$ **14.** $4 + 3t$

Guided Problem Solving

Use the questions to solve this problem.

15. A San Francisco company rents bicycles for $7 per hour and tandem bicycles (two-seaters) for $11 per hour. Suppose a family rents a tandem bicycle for the parents and a single bicycle for each child. Write an algebraic expression for finding the bicycle rental cost per hour.

   a. Understand What is the cost of the parents' bicycle? What is the cost for one child's bicycle?

   b. Plan Use *n* to represent the number of children. What is the cost per hour of the children's bicycles?

   c. Solve Write an expression for the total bicycle rental cost.

   d. Look Back Read the problem again. Does your expression match the situation in the problem?

16. In Problem 15, what will be the cost for a family with two parents and 5 children?

⟨123⟩ Math Talk How can an algebraic expression have different values?

Practice and Problem Solving

Write an algebraic expression for the word phrase. Use the variable *n* to represent the unknown number.

17. subtract 10 from double a number

18. 9 plus a number to the fourth power

19. a number divided by 3

20. 6 is reduced by a number

 Algebra Expressions **Translate the algebraic expression into words.**

21. $6x - 14$ **22.** $35 - g$ **23.** $2m + 7$ **24.** $10p - 9$ **25.** $27 + w^2$

Evaluate the expression when $p = 18$ and $m = 20$.

26. $12 + p$ **27.** $44 - m$ **28.** $p + 20$ **29.** $m - (2 + 7)$

30. $2p - 18$ **31.** $3 + 5p$ **32.** $60 - 2m$ **33.** $m^2 - 10$

 Real World Data

Paul's grandfather designed the gardens shown. Use the diagram for problems 34–35.

34. Suppose there are *x* trees in a garden. Write an algebraic expression for the number of flowers in that garden.

35. Suppose Paul's grandfather creates another garden that fits this pattern. The number of trees is 12. What is the number of flowers?

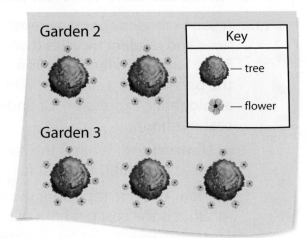

Garden 2

Garden 3

Key	
— tree	
— flower	

Spiral Review and Test Practice

Solve. NS 1.1 page 66

36. The distance from a point on the equator, through Earth's center, to another point on the equator is 12,756 kilometers. What is 12,756 rounded to the nearest thousand?

37. What is 3,459.488 rounded to the nearest ten?

Write the letter of the correct answer. KEY **AF 1.2**

38. If $n = 2$, what is the value of $5 + 6n$?

   A 13   **B** 17   **C** 22   **D** 60

Extra Practice See page 117, Set B.

Key Standards Review

Need Help?
See Key Standards Handbook.

Use the number lines to answer each problem. **KEY** NS 1.5

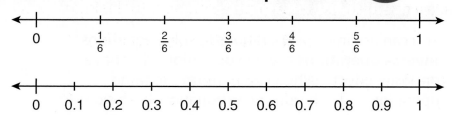

1. The distance between the school and the library is $\frac{2}{6}$ miles. The distance between the school and the grocery store is 0.9 miles. Which trip is longer?

2. A park is surrounded by four fences. Two parallel sides of the park measure $\frac{3}{6}$ miles. The other two fences measure 0.8 miles. What shape is the park?

Write the number for each prime factorization. KEY NS 1.4

3. $2^2 \times 7$

4. 3^3

5. $3^2 \times 5$

6. $2^3 \times 5$

7. $2^2 \times 5$

8. 2^5

Challenge

Critical Thinking

Decades and Centuries KEY AF 1.2

Match each phrase with the expression that represents it. A *decade* is 10 years and a *century* is 100 years.

a. $10 - n$ **b.** $\frac{n}{10}$ **c.** $100 - n$ **d.** $n + 10$ **e.** $10 \times n$ **f.** $100 \times n$

1. the number of decades in n years

2. the number of years in n decades

3. Serena's age a decade from now if she is n years old now

4. Mr. Cecotti's age n years ago if he is a century old now

5. the number of years left in the decade if n years have passed

6. the number of years in n centuries

CA Standards

KEY **AF 1.2** Use a letter to represent an unknown number; write and evaluate simple algebraic expressions in one variable substitution.

MR 1.1 Analyze problems by identifying relationships, distinguishing relevant from irrelevant information, sequencing and prioritizing information, and observing patterns.

Also MR 1.2, MR 2.3

Vocabulary

equation

inverse
 operations

Write and Solve Equations

Objective Write and solve equations with an unknown variable.

▶ **Learn by Example**

You can use inverse operations to solve equations. **Inverse operations** are two operations that have opposite effects. When you perform the same operation on both sides of an equation, both sides remain equal.

Inverse Operations
addition ⟺ subtraction
multiplication ⟺ division

Charlie is riding the Bay Area Rapid Transit (BART) from Fruitvale to Union City. He will arrive in 18 minutes. The whole trip takes 24 minutes. How long has Charlie been on the train? Write and solve an **equation** about Charlie's trip.

① Write the equation. Let n represent how long Charlie has been on the train.

$$n + 18 = 24$$

| minutes riding | minutes left | total minutes |

② Solve for n. Use the inverse operation to undo the operation in the equation.

$$n + 18 = 24$$
$$n + 18 - 18 = 24 - 18$$
$$n + 0 = 6$$
$$n = 6$$

Solution: Charlie has been on the train for 6 minutes.

Other Examples

Solve: $x - 8 = 27$.

$$x - 8 + 8 = 27 + 8$$
$$x + 0 = 35$$
$$x = 35$$

Solve: $4m = 36$.

$$4m \div 4 = 36 \div 4$$
$$1m = 9$$
$$m = 9$$

▶ **Guided Practice**

Solve and check.

1. $x + 6 = 14$
2. $n - 4 = 19$
3. $5 + d = 17$

4. $y - 2 = 16$
5. $3x = 12$
6. $5a = 100$

Ask Yourself

What operation can I use to undo the operation in the equation?

Choose the equation that represents the situation. Then use the equation to solve the problem.

7. Mr. Rincon spent $4.50 on a BART ticket and a magazine. The BART ticket cost $2.00. How much did the magazine cost?

   A. $\$4.50 + n = \$2.00$
   B. $\$2.00 + n = \$4.50$

 Math Talk Addition and subtraction are called inverse operations. Explain why.

Commuters board a BART train.

▶ **Practice and Problem Solving**

Solve and check.

8. $y + 4 = 11$
9. $n - 10 = 20$
10. $7 + x = 19$
11. $r - 13 = 15$

12. $2n = 10$
13. $6a = 36$
14. $7 + n = 16$
15. $y - 5 = 12$

16. $20 + w = 32$
17. $p - 5 = 6$
18. $7x = 21$
19. $8c = 40$

20. $4 + w = 7$
21. $x - 9 = 22$
22. $17 + d = 50$
23. $2y = 16$

Solve.

24. **Multistep** Mr. Singer gave an equal amount of money to each of 3 nephews to spend at the mall. He gave them a total of $24. The oldest nephew spent half the money his uncle gave him. How much did the oldest nephew spend?

Choose the equation that represents the situation. Then use the equation to solve the problem.

25. Margie took a cab home from the airport. The fare was $24. Margie gave the driver $28 and told him to keep the change as a tip. How much was the driver's tip?

 A. $24 + n = $28

 B. $28 + n = $24

26. Ms. Star started the month with a full book of bus tickets. She used 24 tickets during the month. She had 16 tickets left in the book at the end of the month. How many tickets are in a full book?

 A. $n - 24 = 16$

 B. $n + 16 = 24$

27. Tavon rides his bicycle on a trail that is a loop. Last week he rode 6 times around the loop for a total of 18 miles. How many miles is the loop?

 A. $6 + n = 18$ **B.** $6n = 18$

 Science Link

Use the Fun Facts to answer Problems 28–29.

28. The equation $72 - x = 28$ represents the difference between the average heart rates of a human and a horse. What is the average heart rate of a horse?

29. A cow's heart beats about 60 times a minute. Write an equation to represent how many times faster a mouse's heart beats than a cow's. Solve the equation.

Heart Rates

- Your heart is an organ that pumps blood throughout your body. Blood carries nutrients and oxygen your cells need to live.

- An adult human heart beats at an average of about 72 beats per minute. Other animals have different heart rates.

- Heart rates are related to size. A small animal, like a mouse, may have a heart rate of 600 beats a minute. That's ten beats every second!

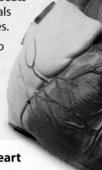

Model of human heart

Science LS 2.a, 2.b

 Spiral Review and Test Practice

Write the decimal as a fraction. Simplify your answer. NS 1.0, KEY **NS 1.5** page 78

30. 0.75   **31.** 0.3   **32.** 0.5   **33.** 0.25

Write the letter of the correct answer. KEY **AF 1.2**

34. Derek has 6 more video games than Jason. Derek has 11 games. Which equation shows how many games Jason has?

 A $n + 6 = 11$ **B** $11 + 6 = n$ **C** $n - 6 = 11$ **D** $6 - n = 11$

Extra Practice See page 117, Set C.

Game

Equation Countdown

Object of the Game Create equations that match given values of a variable.

Materials
- Learning Tool 14 (Variable Cards) (1 set)
- Stopwatch or timer

Number of Players 2

Set Up
One player shuffles the variable cards and places them face down in a pile.

How to Play

1 A player sets the timer for five minutes. Each player takes one variable card. The object of the game is to write equations that are true when the variable in the equation is substituted for the value shown on the card. For example, if the variable card shows $n = 4$ the player may write $4n = 16$, $2n + 4 = 12$, and so on.

2 Players record their equations. Players check each other's equations when time is up.

$n = 4$

3 At the end of the game, players add their points to see who has won. Points are awarded as follows:
- 2 points for each correct equation
- 1 extra point for using more than one operation in an equation
- 2 points for using parentheses in an equation

CA Standards

AF 1.0 Students use variables in simple expressions, compute the value of the expression for specific values of the variable, and plot and interpret the results.

KEY AF 1.2 Use a letter to represent an unknown number; write and evaluate simple algebraic expressions in one variable by substitution.

Also MR 1.0

Education Place
Visit www.eduplace.com/camap/ for **Brain Teasers** and **eGames** to play.

Chapter 5 Lesson 4 **111**

CA Standards

KEY AF 1.5 Solve problems involving linear functions with integer values; write the equation; and graph the resulting ordered pairs of integers on a grid.

AF 1.0 Students use variables in simple expressions, compute the value of the expression for specific values of the variable, and plot and interpret the results.

Also **AF 1.1, KEY SDAP 1.5, MR 1.1, MR 2.3, MR 3.0**

Vocabulary

ordered pair

Variables and Functions

Objective Use equations with two variables to represent functions and find function values.

▶ **Learn by Example**

A function is a rule that pairs one number, the input, with exactly one other number, the output. You can represent a function as an equation or as a set of **ordered pairs**. You write the ordered pair as (input, output).

Look at the pattern. Write the rule. How many squares will there be in Figure 10?

   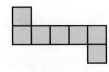

Figure 1   **Figure 2**   **Figure 3**   **Figure 4**

Different Ways to Represent Functions

Way 1 **Use one variable.**

The input is the figure number, F. The output, or number of squares, is $F + 3$.
Rule: Output $= F + 3$.

So if $F = 10$ then the output is $10 + 3$ or 13 squares.

Write the ordered pairs: (1, 4) (2, 5) (3, 6) (4, 7) (10, 13)

Output $= F + 3$	
F	$F + 3$
1	4
2	5
3	6
4	7
10	13

Way 2 **Use two variables.**

Let $x =$ the figure number.
Let $y =$ the number of squares.
Rule: $y = x + 3$.

If x is 10 then $y = 10 + 3$ or 13.

Write the ordered pairs: (1, 4) (2, 5) (3, 6) (4, 7) (10, 13)

$y = x + 3$	
x	y
1	4
2	5
3	6
4	7
10	13

Think

Inputs and outputs are often represented by the variables x and y.

Solution: There will be 13 squares in Figure 10.

Copy and complete the function table.

Ask Yourself
• What pattern does the function table show?
• How do I find the value of the output?

1.

$y = 5 + x$	
x	y
4	
3	
2	

2.

$y = 2x - 3$	
x	y
3	
4	
5	

3.

$p = 5 + 5n$	
n	p
1	
2	
3	

(123) Math Talk Write the numbers in the table from Exercise 3 as ordered pairs.

▶ **Practice and Problem Solving**

Copy and complete the function table.

4. $y = 12 \div x$

x	y
1	
2	
3	

5. $y = 9x$

x	y
0	
	9
2	

6. $y = 3x + \frac{3}{4}$

x	y
0	
3	
10	

7. $y = 20 - 4x$

x	y
0	
2	
4	

Write an equation. Then, find the value of y for the given value of x.

8.

x	10	12	50	70
y	5	6	25	35

if $x = 18$ $y = \blacksquare$

9.

x	0	2	4	6
y	8	18	28	38

if $x = 8$ $y = \blacksquare$

10.

x	2	4	6	8
y	4	16	36	64

if $x = 10$ $y = \blacksquare$

✓ **Spiral Review and Test Practice**

Compare. Write $<$, $>$, or $=$ for the ⬭ **. NS 1.0, KEY NS 1.5** page 82

11. $\frac{1}{2}$ ⬭ 0.4

12. $\frac{1}{4}$ ⬭ 0.3

13. 1.75 ⬭ $1\frac{3}{4}$

14. $\frac{9}{20}$ ⬭ 0.6

Write the letter of the correct answer. KEY AF 1.5

15. Which equation could have been used to create this function table?

x	y
1	6
2	7
3	8

A $y = \frac{x}{6}$ **B** $y = 6x$ **C** $y = x + 5$ **D** $y = x - 5$

CA Standards
KEY **AF 1.2** Use a letter to represent an unknown number; write and evaluate simple algebraic expressions in one variable by substitution.

MR 2.4 Express the solution clearly and logically by using the appropriate mathematical notation and terms and clear language; support solutions with evidence in both verbal and symbolic work.

Also MR 1.1, MR 2.0, MR 2.3, MR 3.0, MR 3.1, MR 3.2, MR 3.3

Problem Solving Strategy
Write an Expression

Objective Write an expression to help solve problems.

▶ **Learn by Example**

In previous lessons, you learned to write and evaluate expressions. In this lesson, you will use those skills to solve problems.

Glenda works at a camera store. She makes $400 a week, plus an extra $4 for each camera she sells. Write an expression to represent how much Glenda is paid each week. Then find how much money Glenda will be paid if she sells 23 cameras in a week.

UNDERSTAND

Glenda is paid $400 in a week, plus $4 for each camera she sells. The number of cameras sold will change from week to week. The problem asks how much money she will make in a week if she sells 23 cameras.

PLAN

You can write an expression by using a variable, c, to represent the number of cameras Glenda sells in a week.

$400 per week	$400
Plus $4 for each camera sold.	$400 + \$4 \times c$

SOLVE

Substitute the number of cameras sold, 23, for the variable, and evaluate the expression. Remember the order of operations.

$400 + 4 \times c$
$400 + 4 \times 23$
$400 + 92$
492

If Glenda sells 23 cameras, she will make $492 in a week.

LOOK BACK

Work backwards using inverse operations to check your answer.

▶ **Guided Problem Solving**

Use the Ask Yourself questions to help you solve this problem.

1. Paulo exercises every morning. He does a number of push-ups. Then he subtracts the number of push-ups he did from 40, and does twice this many crunches. If Paulo does 25 push-ups one morning, how many crunches will he do? Write an expression to solve the problem.

 Math Talk When do you use a variable in an expression instead of a number?

Ask Yourself
- What operations will I use to solve the problem?
- What will my variable represent?
- Should I use parentheses in my expression?

▶ **Independent Problem Solving**

Write an expression to solve each problem.

2. Ron made a batch of cookies. He gave two to his sister, and then half of what was left to his parents. If he started with 12 cookies, how many does he have left?

3. Sasha makes pottery for her family and friends. On Monday she had a certain number of bowls. On Tuesday, she made 8 more and gave away 5. On Wednesday, she gave away 3 in the morning and 4 in the afternoon. On Thursday, she gave away 1 and made 4. If she started with 9 bowls, how many did she have at the end of the day on Thursday?

4. Bradford sells hats for $5 each. At a craft fair, he sold 38 hats. Bradford paid $60 to rent his booth. How much did he earn at the craft fair?

5. Keenan participated in a walk for charity. His sponsor, Mrs. Diaz, agreed to donate $5.00 plus $2.00 for each mile Keenan walked. If Keenan walked 8 miles, how much did Mrs. Diaz donate?

6. **Challenge** Phoebe is three years older than her sister, Kate. Phoebe's mother is four times as old as Kate. Phoebe's father is a year younger than her mother. If Phoebe's father is 35, how old is Phoebe?

7. **Create and Solve** Write a word problem that can be solved using an expression with at least two operations and one variable.

Reading & Writing **Math**

Vocabulary

You use **inverse operations** to solve equations.

The Rand School is having a raffle to raise money for the 5th grade graduation party. To have enough money for the party, they need to sell a total of 750 raffle tickets. They still need to sell 356 tickets. How many tickets have they already sold?

Complete the web to show different ways to solve this problem.

Solving Problems with Equations

Write an addition equation.
$356 + n = 750$
What operation will you use to solve the equation?
Solve:

Write a subtraction equation.
$750 - 356 = n$
What operation will you use to solve the equation?
Solve:

Which equation was easier to solve?

Writing Write a word problem that can be solved with an addition equation or a subtraction equation. Make a web like the one above for your problem. Solve each equation.

Reading Check out this book in your library. *Math Curse,* by Jon Scieszka.

> **CA Standards**
> **MR 2.3** Use a variety of methods, such as words, numbers, symbols, charts, graphs, tables, diagrams, and models, to explain mathematical reasoning.
>
> **Also KEY AF 1.2**

Standards-Based Extra Practice

Set A ——————————————————————————— NS 1.3 page 102

Find the value of each expression.

1. $3^2 - (2 + 3)$ **2.** $17 - 2^2$ **3.** $(2 \times 4) + 4^2$ **4.** $18 - (1 \times 9)$

Solve.

5. Rachel bought 3 T-shirts for $8 each and 1 baseball cap for $7. Write an expression you could simplify to find how much Rachel spent in all.

Set B ——————————————————————————— AF 1.0 page 104

Write an algebraic expression for each exercise. Use the variable x to represent the unknown number.

1. 5 plus a number to the third power   **2.** 18 is added to a number   **3.** six times a number plus 4   **4.** a number divided by 5

Solve.

5. There were 18 students at the park. If n students leave, write an expression that describes the number of students at the park now.

Set C ——————————————————————————— KEY **AF 1.2** page 108

Solve and check.

1. $d - 3 = 6$ **2.** $7 + n = 13$ **3.** $x - 8 = 16$ **4.** $8n = 24$

Solve.

5. Adrian used 6 lemons to make lemonade. She has 18 lemons left. How many lemons did Adrian start with?

Set D ——————————————————————————— AF 1.0 page 112

Write an equation. Then, find the value of y for the given value of x.

1.

x	y
1	4
2	8
3	12

If $x = 7$, $y = $ ▨

2.

x	y
2	8
4	6
6	4

If $x = 5$, $y = $ ▨

3.

x	y
1	24
2	12
3	8

If $x = 6$, $y = $ ▨

4.

x	y
0	$\frac{1}{2}$
2	$4\frac{1}{2}$
4	$8\frac{1}{2}$

If $x = 3$, $y = $ ▨

Solve.

5. Kate does volunteer work at the senior citizens center. In 2 days, she worked 6 hours; in 3 days she worked 9 hours; and in 4 days, she worked 12 hours. Write an equation that relates the number of days Kate worked (x) to the number of hours she worked (y).

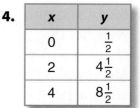

Education Place
Visit www.eduplace.com/camap/ for
Test-Taking Tips and **Extra Practice**.

Chapter Review/Test

Vocabulary and Concepts ────────────── KEY **AF 1.2**, MR 2.3

Write the best word to complete each sentence.

1. A _____ matches each input value with exactly one output value.

2. A _____ is any letter that is used to represent a number.

Skills ────────────── NS 1.3, AF 1.0, KEY **AF 1.2**, KEY **AF 1.5**

Find the value of each expression.

3. $(8 + 1) - (5 + 2)$ 4. $60 - 2 \times 10$ 5. $100 - 4^3$ 6. $40 + (6 - 3)$

Evaluate the expression when $k = 4$ and $q = 10$.

7. $5q - 4$ 8. $7 + 2k$ 9. $6^2 - q$ 10. $9k - (5 - 1)$

Copy and complete the function table.

11.

$y = x + 6$	
x	y
0	
3	
8	

12.

$y = 30 - 2x$	
x	y
5	
8	
11	

13.

$y = 24 \div x$	
x	y
2	
3	
6	

Problem Solving and Reasoning ────── KEY **AF 1.2**, MR 1.1, MR 2.0, MR 2.3, MR 2.4

Write an expression to solve each problem.

14. Meryl's neighbor pays her to watch and walk her dog while she is away. Meryl charges $10, plus $4 for each walk. If Meryl walks the dog 2 times, how much will she have earned?

15. Greg lives 3 times further from school than Ben does. Eve lives 2 miles closer to school than Greg does. If Eve lives 16 miles from school, how many miles away does Ben live?

Writing Math How can you find the equation for a function table when you know the x- and y-values?

Spiral Review and Test Practice

1. Which of the following is 802,319,000?

A eight hundred twenty million, three hundred nineteen thousand

B eight hundred two million, three hundred nineteen thousand

C eight hundred two million, nineteen thousand

D eight hundred two million, three hundred nineteen

NS 1.1 page 56

2. Which of the following has the greatest value?

A 5,069,207

B 5,059,207

C 5,068,907

D 5,078,207

NS 1.0 page 62

3. What is the value of the expression $(9 + 4) + 6$?

A 19

B 18

C 13

D 7

Test Tip
Think about the addition properties when you add.

NS 2.0 page 102

4. Which point on the number line *best* represents 0.6?

KEY **NS 1.5** page 82

5. Simplify $2^3 + 4$.

A 8

B 10

C 12

D 216

Test Tip
Compute first, then look for your answer in the answer choices.

NS 1.3 page 102

6. If $A = 3$, what is the value of $4 \times A + 2$?

A 6

B 8

C 14

D 24

KEY **AF 1.2** page 104

Properties

Check What You Know

Vocabulary and Concepts GRADE 4 AF 1.0, MR 2.3

Match each word with a definition.

1. Identity Property of Multiplication

2. Commutative Property of Multiplication

3. Zero Property of Multiplication

a. states that if a number is multiplied by 0, the product is 0

b. states that the product of 1 and any number is that number

c. states that the order of factors does not change the product

Skills AF 1.0

Find the value of the variable.

3. $8 + p = 69$

4. $13x = 65$

5. $89 - y = 77$

6. $10 - n = 7$

7. $16 + b = 134$

8. $k - 35 = 147$

Problem Solving and Reasoning AF 1.0

9. Dwight is paid $22 for each lawn he mows. This month, Dwight made $198. Write an equation with a variable that shows how many lawns (*l*) Dwight mowed.

10. Natalie had 85 string bracelets. She wants to sell them in groups of 5. Write an equation with a variable to show how many groups (*g*) Natalie can make?

Vocabulary

Visualize It!

Distributive Property

For any values of a, b, and c:
$a(b + c) = (a \times b) + (a \times c)$

10   8

6

$6(10 + 8) = (6 \times 10) + (6 \times 8)$
$108 = 108$

Language Tips

In everyday language, an object's *value* is what the object is worth. In mathematics, a value is the quantity for which a symbol stands. In the equation $4 + x = 6$, the value of the symbol x is 2.

Math words that look alike in English and Spanish often have the same meaning.

English	Spanish
property	propiedad
multiplication	multiplicación

See **English-Spanish Glossary** pages 628–642.

Education Place Visit www.eduplace.com/camap/ for the **eGlossary** and **eGames**.

CA Standards MR 2.3 Use a variety of methods, such as words, numbers, symbols, charts, graphs, tables, diagrams, and models, to explain mathematical reasoning. **Also AF 1.3**

Chapter 6   121

CA Standards

AF 1.3 Know and use the distributive property in equations and expressions with variables.

MR 2.3 Use a variety of methods, such as words, numbers, symbols, charts, graphs, tables, diagrams, and models, to explain mathematical reasoning.

Also MR 1.0, MR 1.2

Vocabulary

Distributive Property

partial product

Materials
• Workmat 4
• Straightedge

Think

How can I use the facts I already know?

Hands On
Model the Distributive Property

Objective Use the Distributive Property to multiply.

▶ **Explore**

In this lesson, you will use basic multiplication facts and models to help you solve more complex multiplication problems.

Question How can you use an array to find a product?

Troy buys a display case for his die-cast car collection. It has 5 shelves. Each shelf holds 16 cars. How many model cars can it hold in all? Draw an array and find the area.

1 Draw a rectangle 5 units wide and 16 units long on your workmat.

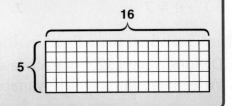

2 You can divide the rectangle into two parts to make it easier to find the area. Divide your rectangle. Shade and label each part.

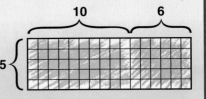

3 Find the area of the rectangle. The **Distributive Property** allows you break a multiplication expression into **partial products**. You can then add the partial products to find the product.

$$Area = L \times W$$
$$= 5 \times 16$$
$$= 5 \times (10 + 6)$$
$$= (5 \times 10) + (5 \times 6) \leftarrow \boxed{\text{partial products}}$$
$$= 50 + 30$$
$$= 80$$

Solution: The case can hold 80 cars.

▶ **Extend**

Show the partial products and find the sum. Then write a multiplication sentence for finding the area.

1.

2.

3.

4.

5.

6.

7.

8.

Draw and divide a rectangle to show the partial products. Use the Distributive Property to find the product.

9. 6 × 18	**10.** 7 × 25	**11.** 8 × 34	**12.** 9 × 42
13. 7 × 36	**14.** 3 × 41	**15.** 3 × 54	**16.** 8 × 23
17. 2 × 29	**18.** 5 × 12	**19.** 4 × 21	**20.** 6 × 33
21. 3 × 32	**22.** 2 × 58	**23.** 7 × 14	**24.** 5 × 21
25. 4 × 36	**26.** 9 × 27	**27.** 2 × 44	**28.** 3 × 17

Writing Math

Reasoning When you use the Distributive Property to find areas of rectangles, why does it make sense to separate the rectangles so you get groups of 10?

LESSON 2

CA Standards

AF 1.3 Know and use the distributive property in equations and expressions with variables.

MR 1.1 Analyze problems by identifying relationships, distinguishing relevant from irrelevant information, sequencing and prioritizing information, and observing patterns.

Also KEY AF 1.2, MR 1.2, MR 2.2, MR 2.3, MR 3.3

Vocabulary

Distributive Property

Use the Distributive Property

Objective Use the Distributive Property in equations with variables.

▶ **Learn by Example**

In the last lesson, you broke a number apart (in tens and ones) and found the product. In this lesson, you will break apart numbers in other ways and use the **Distributive Property** to find the product.

Jillian and Eric are collecting drink bottles. Jillian collects 4 drink bottles and Eric collects 8 drink bottles. In California, one drink bottle can be exchanged for a 5 cent per bottle refund. How many cents will Jillian and Eric collect if they redeem all their bottles?

In this problem:

a = 5 cent refund
b = Jillian's bottles (4)
c = Eric's bottles (8)

Distributive Property
For any values of a, b, and c: $a(b + c) = (a \times b) + (a \times c)$

Way 1 Find the number of bottles first. Then find the total amount of cents they collected.

$a(b + c) = $ ▦

$5 \times (4 + 8) = $ ▦

$5 \times 12 = $ ▦

$5 \times 12 = $ **60 cents**

Way 2 Find the amount of cents Jillian will get and the amount Eric will get. Then find the total amount of cents.

$(a \times b) + (a \times c) = $ ▦

$(5 \times 4) + (5 \times 8) = $ ▦

$20 + 40 = $ ▦

$20 + 40 = $ **60 cents**

Because of the Distributive Property, both expressions have the same value.

Solution: Jillian and Eric can collect 60 cents for their bottles.

▶ Guided Practice

Use the Distributive Property to find the value of the variable.

1. $5 \times 23 = (5 \times 12) + (5 \times m)$ **2.** $9 \times 32 = (9 \times 30) + (9 \times a)$

3. $c \times 11 = (7 \times 9) + (7 \times 2)$ **4.** $4 \times y = (4 \times 25) + (4 \times 21)$

 Math Talk When you use the Distributive Property to rewrite an expression, will the result always be the same? Explain.

Ask Yourself

Do both sides of the equation have the same value?

▶ Practice and Problem Solving

Use the Distributive Property to find the value of the variable.

5. $8 \times 62 = (8 \times 50) + (8 \times d)$ **6.** $4 \times 68 = (4 \times 60) + (4 \times a)$

7. $y \times 79 = (6 \times 70) + (6 \times 9)$ **8.** $3 \times z = (3 \times 33) + (3 \times 9)$

 Real World Data

Use the table for Problems 9–11.

9. Raheem has 7 sedimentary rocks and 5 igneous rocks in her collection. Al has twice as many of each. Write two different expressions to show Al's collection.

10. Ben has 3 times as many rocks as Doug and Lindsay put together. How many rocks does Ben have? Write an equation to solve the problem.

11. Michelle has 5 small rocks and x large rocks. Jen has 2 times as many rocks as Michelle. How many large rocks are in Michelle's collection?

Number of Rocks in Each Collection	
Doug	4
Jen	16
Raheem	12
Lindsay	7

✓ Spiral Review and Test Practice

Simplify. KEY NS 2.3 page 34

12. $\frac{25}{40}$ **13.** $\frac{12}{42}$ **14.** $\frac{8}{20}$ **15.** $\frac{15}{27}$

Write the letter of the correct answer. AF 1.3

16. What value of m makes this equation true? $5 \times 27 = (5 \times 20) + (5 \times m)$

   A 2   **B** 5   **C** 7   **D** 9

CA Standards

KEY **AF 1.2** Use a letter to represent an unknown; write and evaluate simple algebraic expressions in one variable by substitution.

MR 1.1 Analyze problems by identifying relationships, distinguishing relevant from irrelevant information, sequencing and prioritizing information, and observing patterns.

Also MR 1.2, MR 2.2, MR 2.3, MR 3.3

Vocabulary

Commutative Property of Addition

Associative Property of Addition

Identity Property of Addition

Properties of Addition

Objective Use properties to evaluate expressions and solve equations.

▶ **Learn by Example**

You already know how to write and evaluate expressions. In this lesson you will see how properties of addition can help you evaluate those expressions.

Properties of Addition

Commutative Property

The order in which numbers are added does not affect their sum.

$$3 + 8 = 8 + 3$$

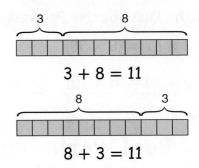

$$3 + 8 = 11$$

$$8 + 3 = 11$$

Associative Property

The way in which numbers are grouped does not affect their sum.

$$(2 + 6) + 4 = 2 + (6 + 4)$$

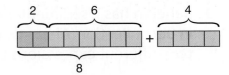

$$(2 + 6) + 4 = 8 + 4 = 12$$

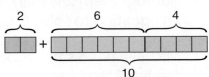

Identity Property

The sum of any number and zero is that number.

$$5 + 0 = 5$$
$$0 + 5 = 5$$

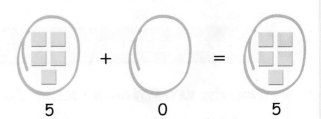

$$5 \qquad 0 \qquad 5$$

The properties of addition also can be shown using variables.

Properties of Addition

Commutative Property	Associative Property	Identity Property
For any addends a and b,	For any addends a, b, and c,	For any addend a,
$a + b = b + a$	$(a + b) + c = a + (b + c)$	$a + 0 = a$

▶ **Guided Practice**

Find the missing number. Identify the property you used.

1. ▨ $+ 7 = 7 + 3$

2. $(3 + 2) + 5 = 3 + ($ ▨ $+ 5)$

3. $0 + 3{,}250 =$ ▨

4. $(18 + 3) + 9 =$ ▨ $+ (18 + 3)$

5. $5 + 48 + 52 =$ ▨

6. $0 + 789 =$ ▨

 Math Talk Why can there not be a Commutative Property for subtraction? Use an example to explain.

▶ **Practice and Problem Solving**

Find the missing number. Identify the property you used.

7. $38 +$ ▨ $= 38$

8. $51 + (37 + 9) = ($ ▨ $+ 37) + 9$

9. $93 + 18 = 18 +$ ▨

Use mental math. Identify the property or properties you used.

10. $3 + 75 + 25$

11. $456 + 0$

12. $37 + 1 + 999$

 Spiral Review and Test Practice

Write the value of the underlined digit. NS 1.0 pages 56 and 60

13. $5{,}3\underline{8}7{,}296$

14. $2.8\underline{7}3$

15. $49{,}\underline{0}05{,}287$

16. $52.79\underline{6}$

Write the letter of the correct answer. AF 1.0, KEY **AF 1.2**

17. Which expression has the same value as $a + b$?

    A $b + a$ **B** $a \times b$ **C** $a + b + c$ **D** $b - a$

Ask Yourself
Did I identify which properties I used?

CA Standards
KEY **AF 1.2** Use a letter to represent an unknown; write and evaluate simple algebraic expressions in one variable by substitution.

Also MR 1.0, MR 1.1, MR 2.3, MR 3.0

Vocabulary

Commutative Property of Multiplication

Associative Property of Multiplication

Zero Property of Multiplication

Identity Property of Multiplication

Vocabulary Tip

Identity means "sameness." To get the same number in addition, you add 0. To get the same number in multiplication, you multiply by 1.

Properties of Multiplication

Objective Use properties to evaluate expressions and solve equations.

▶ **Learn by Example**

In this lesson, you will see how properties of multiplication can help you evaluate expressions.

Properties of Multiplication

Commutative Property

Changing the order of numbers does not change their product.

$3 \times 20 = 20 \times 3$

Associative Property

Changing the grouping of numbers does not change their product.

$3 \times (4 \times 9) = (3 \times 4) \times 9$

Zero Property

The product of any number and 0 is 0.

$15 \times 0 = 0$

Identity Property

The product of any number and 1 is that number.

$45 \times 1 = 45$

The properties of multiplication can also be shown using variables.

Properties of Multiplication

Commutative Property

For any factors a and b,

$a \times b = b \times a$

Associative Property

For any factors a, b, and c,

$a \times (b \times c) = (a \times b) \times c$

Zero Property

For any factor a,

$a \times 0 = 0$

Identity Property

For any factor a,

$a \times 1 = a$

Complete. Identify the property you used.

1. $(3 \times 12) \times 30 = 3 \times (12 \times \boxed{})$

2. $a \times 65 = \boxed{} \times a$

3. $785 \times \boxed{} = 785$

4. $43 \times 0 = \boxed{}$

5. $1 \times \boxed{} = 385$

6. $b \times 0 = \boxed{}$

Ask Yourself

What property can I use?

Guided Problem Solving

Use the questions to solve this problem.

7. Charlie says that there is an Associative Property of Division because $(8 \div 2) \div 1 = 8 \div (2 \div 1)$. Is Charlie correct?

   a. **Understand** If Charlie's example is true, does that mean there is an Associative Property of Division?

   b. **Plan** Check Charlie's example and try some other examples.

   c. **Solve** Do any of your examples show that there is NOT an Associative Property of Division? Is Charlie correct or not?

   d. **Look Back** Why did Charlie's example work?

8. If there is an Identity Property for division, then for any value of a these equations will be true:

   $a \div 1 = a$ $1 \div a = a$

   Do you think there is an Identity Property for division?

(123) **Math Talk** How can you evaluate the expression $a \times b \times c \times 0$ without substituting or multiplying?

Complete. Identify the property you used.

9. $(24 \times 16) \times 0 = $ ▇

10. $4 \times (16 \times 1) = 4 \times$ ▇

11. $3 \times 24 = 24 \times$ ▇

12. $(15 \times 4) \times 2 = $ ▇ $\times (4 \times 2)$

13. ▇ $\times 486 = 486$

14. $z \times$ ▇ $= 0$

Compare. Write >, <, or = for the ⬭.

15. $(6 \times 2) \times 30$ ⬭ $(6 \times 30) \times 20$

16. $a \times 6 \times 5$ ⬭ $6 \times a \times 5$

Science Link

Solve.

17. A low flow showerhead uses $\frac{7}{10}$ of the water used by a regular showerhead. For every 100 gallons that a regular showerhead uses, how many gallons does a low flow showerhead use? How many gallons of water are saved?

18. A cow can drink 35 gallons of water a day. How many gallons of water can a cow drink in 2 weeks?

19. Suppose a person uses 40 gallons of water a day for personal use. Use the Associative Property of Multiplication to show two ways to find the amount of water a person could use in a year (52 weeks in a year).

Fun Facts

Water Conservation

- Since fresh water resources are limited, it is important to conserve water.
- The Water Conservation Garden in El Cajon, CA teaches gardeners how to use water wisely.
- Home owners can use low flow showerheads to reduce water use.

California poppy

Science ES 3.d

✓ Spiral Review and Test Practice

Simplify. Evaluate, given $n = 5$. AF 1.0, KEY **AF 1.2**, AF 1.3 page 102

20. $(3 + n) - (4 + 1)$

21. $(4 \times n) - 6$

22. $n + (2 \times 5)$

Write the letter of the correct answer. KEY **AF 1.2**

23. What value for m makes this equation true?

$(46 \times 3) \times m = 46 \times (3 \times 7)$

A 3 **B** 7 **C** 21 **D** 138

Extra Practice See page 135, Set C.

Key Standards Review

Need Help?
See Key Standards Handbook.

Write the letter that represents the fraction or decimal. KEY **NS 1.5**

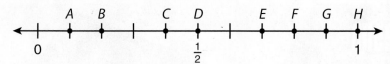

0      $\frac{1}{2}$ 1

1. $\frac{9}{10}$ **2.** 0.2   **3.** $\frac{5}{10}$ **4.** 0.8

5. 0.1   **6.** $\frac{1}{1}$ **7.** 0.4   **8.** $\frac{7}{10}$

Use a variable to write an expression for each word phrase. KEY **AF 1.2**

9. a number multiplied by 12

10. 9 more than a number

11. 5 times a number is decreased by 4

12. (a number divided by 8) plus 7 more

13. (12 times a number) is decreased by 8

14. 13 more than (a number divided by 3)

Problem Solving

Properties

Write *true* or *false*. Give examples to support your answer.
For any counting numbers *a*, *b*, and *c*: KEY **AF 1.2**

1. $(a + b) - c = a + (b - c)$

2. $a + b = b + a$

3. $a \div b = b \div a$

4. $(a \times b) \times 0 = 0$

> **Hint**
> The counting numbers are 1, 2, 3, 4 … and so on.

Explain how the product of the pairs of numbers are related. NS 1.0

5. 25×4; 50×4

6. 12×30; 36×10

7. 8×50; 5×80

8. 43×10; 86×20

9. 333×30; 111×90

10. 360×18; 180×18

LESSON 5

Field Trip...

Fresno, CA

CA Standards
MR 1.0, MR 1.1
Prepares for
KEY NS 2.3, Prepares
for KEY NS 1.5, AF 1.3,
KEY AF 1.2

Problem Solving

Objective Use skills and strategies to solve word problems.

The Fresno Metropolitan Museum, "The Met," has been visited by more than 2 million people since it opened in 1984.

Solve. Tell which strategy or method you used.

Collections	Pieces
Salazar	100
Native American	1300
Ansel Adams	50
Jigsaw Puzzle	1200
Landscape Painting	36
Arts and Crafts	200
Petesch Caricature	150

1. The Met has about 3,000 pieces within all the collections. Rewrite each separate collection as a fraction of all the collections. Simplify each fraction and place them in order from least to greatest.

2. Suppose the Met is holding separate lectures on fossils in three halls. Each hall holds 75 chairs. Maya wants to find the total number of chairs she needs by using the Distributive Property. Look at the equation. What values should she use for m and n? How many chairs does she need?

$$3 \times 75 = (3 \times m) + (3 \times n)$$

3. The Met holds a 5-day winter camp for students. They offer 30 different hands-on science exhibits. Write and solve an equation that helps you find the number of exhibits you must go to everyday if you want to see all 30 exhibits. Let n stand for the number of exhibits.

Problem Solving On Tests

Select a Strategy
- Draw a Picture
- Write an Equation
- Guess and Check
- Choose the Operation
- Estimate

1. As of July 1, 2005, the estimated population of the United States was two hundred ninety-six million, five hundred seven thousand, sixty-one. Which is the standard form of this number?

A 296,570,610

B 296,507,610

C 296,507,601

D 296,507,061

Test Tip
Use the commas and the place value words to help name the standard form of the number.

NS 1.0 page 56

2. Grace bought 1.25 pounds of apples. Which point on the number line *best* represents 1.25?

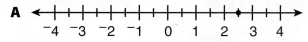

A
B
C
D

KEY NS 1.5 page 62

3. Katherine's scores at the last gymnastics meet were 6.08, 6, and 6.39. Which shows these scores in order from greatest to least?

A 6.08, 6.39, 6

B 6, 6.39, 6.08

C 6.39, 6.08, 6

D 6, 6.08, 6.39

Test Tip
Try saying the word form for each number to help order the numbers from greatest to least.

NS 1.0 page 62

4. The length of a wooden board is 0.4 meters. What is the decimal 0.4 written as a fraction?

A $\frac{4}{100}$ B $\frac{1}{4}$ C $\frac{1}{25}$ D $\frac{2}{5}$

NS 1.0 page 78

5. One of the highest peaks in the Lake Tahoe Basin is Monument Peak at a height of 10,067 feet. What is this value rounded to the nearest hundred feet?

A 10,000   C 10,700

B 10,100   D 11,000

NS 1.1 page 66

6. Jeremy gave this equation to Saul to solve. If $N = 6$, what is the value of $3 \times N - 2$?

A 12   B 16   C 22   D 34

KEY AF 1.2 page 104

7. Which situation could be described by the expression $p + 3\frac{1}{2}$?

A Greg read p pages yesterday, and $3\frac{1}{2}$ pages more today.

B Greg read p pages yesterday, and $3\frac{1}{2}$ pages fewer today.

C Greg read $3\frac{1}{2}$ pages yesterday, and p pages fewer today.

D Greg read $3\frac{1}{2}$ pages yesterday, and p times as many pages today.

KEY AF 1.2 page 102

Education Place
Visit www.eduplace.com/camap/ for **Test-Taking Tips** and **Extra Practice**.

Chapter 6 Lesson 5   **133**

Reading & Writing Math

Vocabulary

Use the **properties of addition** and **multiplication** to solve problems.

Complete the Word Web.

Associative Property of Addition
When you change the way the **addends** are grouped the **sum** stays the same.

$$3 + (2 + 6) = (3 + 2) + 6$$
$$3 + \underline{\quad} = \underline{\quad} + 6$$
$$11 = \underline{\quad}$$

Associative Property of Multiplication
When you change the way the **factors** are grouped the **product** stays the same.

$$3 \times (2 \times 6) = (3 \times 2) \times 6$$
$$3 \times \underline{\quad} = \underline{\quad} \times 6$$
$$36 = \underline{\quad}$$

Properties of Addition and Multiplication

Commutative Property of Addition
When you change the order of the **addends**, the **sum** stays the same.

$$5 + 4 = 4 + \underline{\quad}$$

Commutative Property of Multiplication
When you change the order of the **factors**, the **product** stays the same.

$$5 \times 4 = 4 \times \underline{\quad}$$

Identity Property of Addition
When you add zero to a number, the **sum** is that number.

$$6 + 0 = \underline{\quad}$$

Identity Property of Multiplication
When you multiply a number by one, the **product** is that number.

$$6 \times 1 = \underline{\quad}$$

Writing Explain how you would use the **Distributive Property**. Write a problem that you can solve using the Distributive Property.

Reading Look for this book in your library.
Olympic Math, by Sharon Vogt

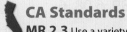 **CA Standards**
MR 2.3 Use a variety of methods, such as words, numbers, symbols, charts, graphs, tables, diagrams, and models, to explain mathematical reasoning.
Also AF 1.3

Standards-Based Extra Practice

Set A ────────────────────────────────────── AF 1.3 page 124

Use the Distributive Property to find the value of the variable.

1. $y \times 18 = (5 \times 10) + (5 \times 8)$ **2.** $2 \times 23 = (2 \times 12) + (2 \times c)$ **3.** $7 \times y = (7 \times 16) + (7 \times 13)$

4. $6 \times 14 = (6 \times 9) + (6 \times a)$ **5.** $2 \times d = (2 \times 8) + (2 \times 9)$ **6.** $4 \times 32 = (4 \times 18) + (4 \times y)$

7. $a \times 12 = (8 \times 5) + (8 \times 7)$ **8.** $9 \times c = (9 \times 5) + (9 \times 3)$ **9.** $4 \times 21 = (4 \times 7) + (4 \times a)$

Solve.

10. Matthew has 4 large and 3 small movie posters. Karl has twice as many movie posters. Write two different expressions to show the number of movie posters Karl has.

Set B ────────────────────────────────────── KEY **AF 1.2** page 126

Find the missing number. Identify the property or properties you used.

1. $387 + 0 = \blacksquare$

2. $21 + 4 + 10 = (21 + 10) + \blacksquare$

3. $22 + (13 + 2) = (22 + \blacksquare) + 2$

4. $35 + \blacksquare = 35$

5. $6 + 12 = 12 + \blacksquare$

6. $15 + (5 + 6) = (\blacksquare + 5) + 6$

Solve.

7. Marilyn bought supplies. She paid $8 for paper, $5 for a notebook, and $2 for a marker. How much did she spend in all? Identify the property or properties you used to solve the problem.

Set C ────────────────────────────────────── KEY **AF 1.2** page 128

Complete. Identify the property you used.

1. $5 \times 2 = \blacksquare \times 5$

2. $16 \times 0 = \blacksquare$

3. $283 \times \blacksquare = 283$

4. $(5 \times 3) \times 10 = 5 \times (3 \times \blacksquare)$ **5.** $(4 \times 6) \times 2 = 4 \times (6 \times \blacksquare)$ **6.** $c \times 21 = \blacksquare \times c$

7. $(4 \times 2) \times 5 = \blacksquare \times (2 \times 5)$ **8.** $(2 \times 13) \times 0 = \blacksquare$ **9.** $(2 \times 6) \times 3 = \blacksquare \times (6 \times 3)$

Solve.

10. Alan pasted 2 photos in each of 4 rows on 6 pages of his scrapbook. How many photos did he paste in his scrapbook? Identify the property you used.

Education Place
Visit www.eduplace.com/camap/ for
Test-Taking Tips and **Extra Practice**.

Chapter Review/Test

Vocabulary and Concepts ———————————————— KEY **AF 1.2**, MR 2.3, AF 1.3

Write the best word to complete each sentence.

1. $2 \times (3 \times 4) = (2 \times 3) \times 4$ is an example of the _____ Property of Multiplication.

2. The _____ Property of Multiplication states that the product of any number and 0 is 0.

3. The _____ Property allows you to break a multiplication problem into partial products.

Skills ———————————————————————————— AF 1.3, KEY **AF 1.2**

Use the Distributive Property to find the value of the variable.

4. $4 \times 27 = (4 \times 20) + (4 \times b)$

5. $2 \times 38 = (2 \times 30) + (2 \times c)$

6. $y \times 60 = (2 \times 50) + (2 \times 10)$

7. $3 \times d = (3 \times 4) + (3 \times 5)$

8. $6 \times 12 = (6 \times y) \times (6 \times 7)$

9. $c \times 19 = (8 \times 9) + (8 \times 10)$

Find the missing number. Identify the property you used.

10. $(5 + 2) + 3 = 5 + (\blacksquare + 3)$

11. $9 \times 2 = \blacksquare \times 9$

12. $\blacksquare + 438 = 438$

Problem Solving and Reasoning ———— KEY **AF 1.2**, AF 1.3, MR 1.0, MR 1.1, MR 1.2, MR 2.3

Solve.

13. Kim makes a mirror frame. She uses 27 shells of 3 different kinds. Write and solve an equation to show how many of each kind of shell Kim needs if she uses an equal number of each kind.

14. Juanita rides her bicycle 3 times a week. Each time she rides, she travels 14 miles. Use the Distributive Property to find the number of miles she rides each week.

15. Max thinks if he can work 3 hours two times a week, he'll earn the same amount as if he works 2 hours three times a week. Is he correct? Explain.

Writing Math State 4 properties of multiplication and give an example of each.

Spiral Review and Test Practice

1. What is 38,275,461 rounded to the nearest ten million?

A 40,000,000

B 38,300,000

C 38,000,000

D 30,000,000

NS 1.1 page 66

2. The population of the city where Andrea lives is 274,536. The population of the city where Andrea's grandmother lives is 318,195. To the nearest thousand, about how many people live in these two cities?

A 592,000   **C** 594,000

B 593,000   **D** 500,000

NS 1.1 page 68

3. $36,000 - 9,472 =$

A 36,528

B 33,472

Test Tip
Estimate first to rule out some answer choices.

C 26,628

D 26,528

GRADE 4 KEY NS 3.1

4. Sam lives 7 more miles from the beach than Kim. Sam lives 13 miles from the beach. Which equation can be solved to find how many miles Kim lives from the beach?

A $n - 7 = 13$

B $13 + 7 = n$

Test Tip
Draw a picture to help you understand the problem.

C $n + 7 = 13$

D $7 - n = 13$

KEY AF 1.2 page 108

5. What value for y makes this equation true?

$$7 \times 34 = (7 \times 30) + (7 \times y)$$

A 3   **C** 30

B 4   **D** 40

AF 1.3 page 124

6. If $x = 4$, what is the value of $52 + x + 33$?

A 85

B 87

C 89

D 125

KEY AF 1.2 page 126

Education Place
Visit www.eduplace.com/camap/ for
Test-Taking Tips and **Extra Practice**.

Unit 3 Review/Test

Vocabulary and Concepts

Write the best word to complete each sentence.

1. According to the _____, changing the order of factors does not change their product.

2. You can use a _____ to find the output value for any given input value.

3. The expression $a(b + c) = (a \times b) + (a \times c)$ represents the _____.

4. A mathematical expression that contains variables is called an _____.

5. The _____ says that the way in which numbers are grouped does not affect their sum.

Skills

Simplify.

6. $12 + (2 \times 3)$ 7. $(5 + 8) - (3 + 6)$ 8. $20 - (2 + 1) + 2^2$ 9. $21 + (8 - 6)$

Solve and check. Chapter 5, Lesson 3

10. $11 + a = 25$ 11. $n + 12 = 21$ 12. $x - 5 = 17$ 13. $4y = 20$

Find the missing number. Identify the property you used. Chapter 6, Lesson 3

14. $0 + 29 = \blacksquare$

15. $(4 + 2) + 8 = 4 + (\blacksquare + 8)$

16. $19 + (1 + 7) = (\blacksquare + 1) + 7$

17. $13 + 3 = 3 + \blacksquare$

18. $y \times 7 = \blacksquare \times y$

19. $20 \times 0 = \blacksquare$

20. $12 \times \blacksquare = 12$

21. $(2 \times 6) \times 4 = 2 \times (6 \times \blacksquare)$

Problem Solving and Reasoning

Write an expression or equation to solve each problem.

22. Eli's grandfather agreed to pay Eli $15 to paint a fence. His grandfather gave him $20 and told him to keep the change. How much extra money did Eli receive?

23. Sonia rides her bicycle 1 mile from home to her friend's house, goes for a bike ride with her friend, than rides home. Write the expression to show the total number of miles she rides.

Write an expression or equation to solve each problem.

24. Zina is doing a puzzle with her cousin. They have placed 200 pieces already. They have 50 pieces left to place. How many pieces total are in the puzzle?

25. Ed's father gave him and his sister the same amount of money to spend at the museum. He gave them a total of $18. Ed spent one third of his money. How much did Ed spend?

Writing Math Explain how the Associative Property of Addition can help you evaluate expressions and solve equations.

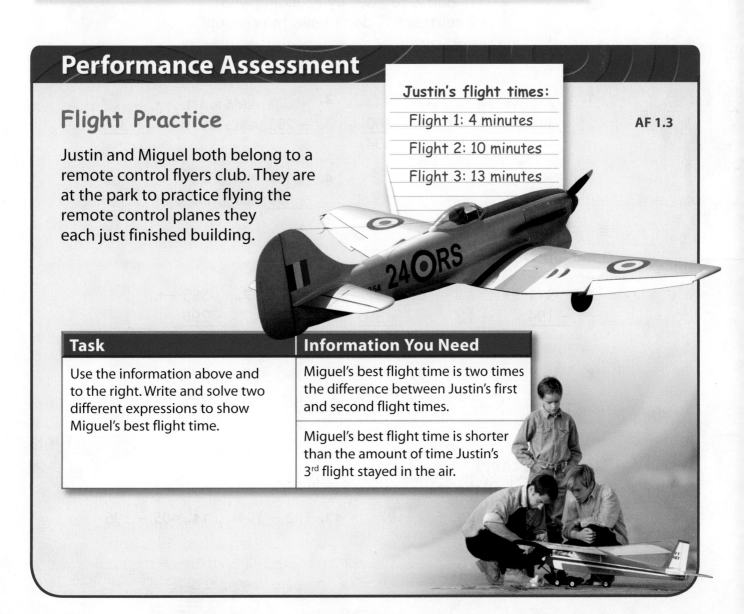

Performance Assessment

Flight Practice

Justin and Miguel both belong to a remote control flyers club. They are at the park to practice flying the remote control planes they each just finished building.

Justin's flight times:

Flight 1: 4 minutes

Flight 2: 10 minutes

Flight 3: 13 minutes

AF 1.3

Task	Information You Need
Use the information above and to the right. Write and solve two different expressions to show Miguel's best flight time.	Miguel's best flight time is two times the difference between Justin's first and second flight times.
	Miguel's best flight time is shorter than the amount of time Justin's 3rd flight stayed in the air.

Greg Tang's Go Fast, Go Far

Unit 3 Mental Math Strategies

Round to Subtract

Here's a really clever act.
Round the number you subtract!

To subtract 398, I round to 400. To do that, I added 2 to 398, so I have to add 2 to 732. By rounding what I subtract, I don't have to regroup!

1.
```
  732  Add 2 to 732. →    734
– 398  Add 2 to 398. → – 400
                        334
```

2.
```
  571  Add 5 to 571. →   ▮
– 295  Add 5 to 295. → – 300
                        ▮
```

3.
```
  906  Add ▮ to 906. →   ▮
– 497  Add ▮ to 497. → – ▮
                        ▮
```

4.
```
  131  Add ▮ to ▮. →   ▮
–  93  Add ▮ to ▮. → – ▮
                      ▮
```

Good job! Now try these!

5.
```
  311 →   ▮
– 194  – ▮
        ▮
```

6.
```
  923 →   ▮
– 595  – ▮
        ▮
```

7.
```
  585 →   ▮
– 298  – ▮
        ▮
```

8.
```
  162 →   ▮
–  93  – ▮
        ▮
```

9.
```
  707 →   ▮
– 499  – ▮
        ▮
```

10.
```
  922 →   ▮
– 896  – ▮
        ▮
```

Good For You!

Take It Further!

Now try doing all the steps in your head!

11. 844 – 698   **12.** 603 – 97   **13.** 782 – 194   **14.** 405 – 396

Add and Subtract Fractions and Mixed Numbers

BIG IDEAS!

- You can add fractions by using equivalency to make a common denominator.

- When adding or subtracting mixed numbers you sometimes regroup as you do for whole numbers.

Chapter 7
Add and Subtract Fractions

Chapter 8
Add with Mixed Numbers

Chapter 9
Subtract with Mixed Numbers

Songs and Games

Math Music Track 4: *Like and Unlike Denominators*

eGames at
www.eduplace.com/camap/

Math Readers

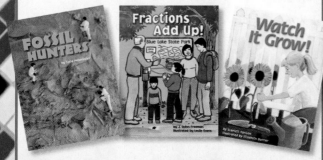

A starburst tile pattern on the California Dome in Balboa Park, San Diego, CA

Game

Action Fractions

Object of the Game Practice comparing fractions.

Materials
Learning Tool 15: Number/Symbol Cards
(2 sets of number cards labeled 1, 2, 3, 4, 6, 8)

Number of Players 2

Set Up
Give each player 2 sets of number cards.
Players shuffle their cards and place them face
down in a stack.

How to Play

1 One player shuffles and deals all cards facedown.
Players stack their cards.

2 Players take 3 cards from the top of their stacks.
Using 2 of the 3 cards, each player makes a
fraction whose numerator is less than or equal to
its denominator. The unused card is returned to
the bottom of the player's stack.

3 Players compare the fractions. The player
with the greater fraction earns 1 point. If the
fractions are equivalent, each player earns 1 point.

4 Repeat Steps 2 and 3. The player with
more points after all the cards
have been used is the winner.

CA Standards
Prepares for KEY **NS 2.3** Solve
simple problems, including ones arising in
concrete situations, involving the addition and
subtraction of fractions and mixed numbers
(like and unlike denominators of 20 or less), and
express answers in the simplest form.

Also MR 1.0

Education Place
Visit www.eduplace.com/camap/ for
Brain Teasers and **eGames** to play.

Reading To get the right answer to a mathematics problem, you need to make sure you understand the question.

Problem 1

Three friends ordered a pizza with 8 slices. Jeanette ate $\frac{2}{8}$ of a pizza. Marissa ate $\frac{4}{8}$ of a pizza. Ariel ate the rest. How many slices of Pizza did Ariel eat?

A. 1 slice

B. 2 slices

C. 4 slices

D. 6 slices

Writing Now it's your turn. Answer Problem 2. Then write about how you solved the problem, step by step.

Problem 2

The Perez family ordered a large pizza for dinner. A large pizza is divided into 8 slices. Marco ate $\frac{3}{8}$ of the pizza. Ramon ate 1 slice more than Marco. Emilio ate the rest. How much of the pizza did Emilio eat?

A. $\frac{1}{8}$ of the pizza

B. $\frac{2}{8}$ of the pizza

C. $\frac{4}{8}$ of the pizza

D. $\frac{5}{8}$ of the pizza

Thinking Through the Problem

Understand the question You want to know how many slices Ariel ate. Will your answer be a fraction or whole number?

Plan Find out what fraction of the pizza Ariel ate. Look at the numerator to tell how many pizza slices Ariel ate.

Solve Follow your plan. Write the answer to the problem.

Look Back Use fraction tiles to check your answer.

The correct answer is **B.**

I always check to see if I answered the question that was asked.

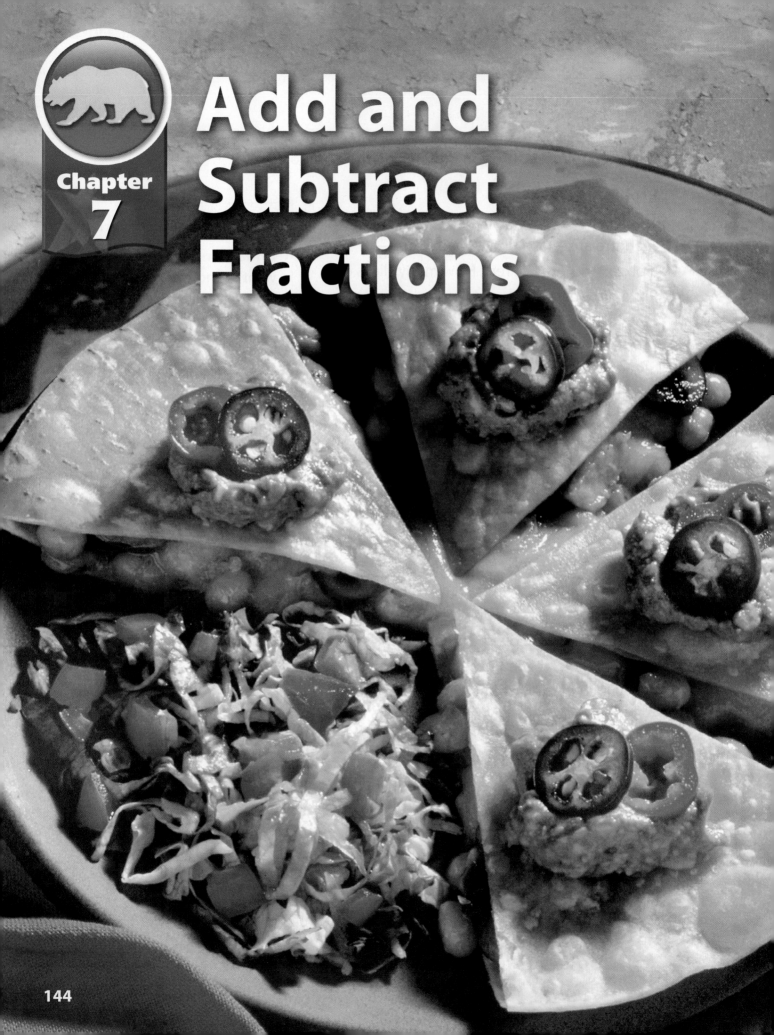

Vocabulary and Concepts GRADE 4 NS 1.5, MR 2.3

Tell what the word means and give an example.

1. unit fraction

2. common denominator

Skills GRADE 4 NS 1.5

Complete.

3. $\dfrac{9}{21} = \dfrac{\square}{7}$

4. $3\dfrac{2}{3} = \dfrac{\square}{6}$

5. $6 = \dfrac{\square}{8}$

6. $3\dfrac{3}{5} = 3\dfrac{6}{\square}$

7. $\dfrac{\square}{12} = 1\dfrac{3}{4}$

8. $\dfrac{5}{15} = \dfrac{1}{\square}$

Write each mixed number as an equivalent improper fraction.

9. $4\dfrac{2}{5}$

9. $6\dfrac{1}{3}$

10. $2\dfrac{3}{8}$

Problem Solving and Reasoning GRADE 4 NS 1.5

10. The class voted on blue, red, or purple as their class color. One-fourth of the class voted for blue and $\dfrac{1}{8}$ of the class voted for purple. What fraction of the class voted for red?

Vocabulary

Visualize It!

A **mixed number** is made up of a whole number and a fraction.

$$\dfrac{4}{4} \quad + \quad \dfrac{3}{4} \quad = \quad \dfrac{7}{4} \text{ or } 1\dfrac{3}{4}$$

$\dfrac{7}{4}$ and $1\dfrac{3}{4}$ are equivalent.

Language Tip

Math words that look alike in English and Spanish often have the same meaning.

English	Spanish
sum	suma
difference	diferencia

See **English-Spanish Glossary** pages 628–642.

Education Place Visit www.eduplace.com/camap/ for the **eGlossary** and **eGames**.

CA Standards
KEY NS 2.3 Solve simple problems, including ones arising in concrete situations, involving the addition and subtraction of fractions and mixed numbers (like and unlike denominators of 20 or less), and express answers in the simplest form.

MR 3.2 Note the method of deriving the solution and demonstrate a conceptual understanding of the derivation by solving similar problems.
Also NS 2.0, MR 2.3, MR 3.0

Materials
Fraction tiles

Hands On
Add and Subtract Fractions with Like Denominators

Objective Explore adding and subtracting fractions with like denominators.

▶ **Explore**

You can use models to add and subtract fractions that have the same denominator.

Question How can you use fraction tiles to add and subtract fractions with like denominators?

Jesse is hiking along a 1-mile trail in the Lake Tahoe area. She hikes $\frac{1}{8}$ mile and stops to take a photograph of the scenery. After another $\frac{3}{8}$ mile, she stops again to take more photographs. How far has she hiked?

Use fraction tiles to add the fractions.

1 Show $\frac{1}{8}$.

2 Add $\frac{3}{8}$.

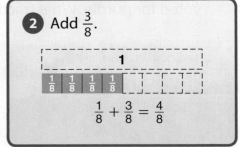

$$\frac{1}{8} + \frac{3}{8} = \frac{4}{8}$$

3 Simplify if possible.

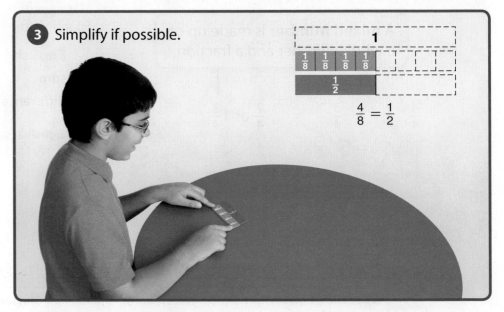

$$\frac{4}{8} = \frac{1}{2}$$

Solution: Jesse has hiked $\frac{1}{2}$ mile.

The next day, Jesse hiked a $\frac{7}{8}$ mile trail. She photographed an osprey at the $\frac{5}{8}$ mile point. How far from the end of the trail did Jesse see the osprey?

1 Model $\frac{7}{8}$.

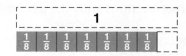

---

2 Subtract $\frac{5}{8}$.

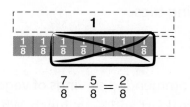

$$\frac{7}{8} - \frac{5}{8} = \frac{2}{8}$$

---

3 Simplify.

▶ **Extend**

Use fraction tiles to find the sum or difference. Simplify if possible.

1. $\frac{3}{10} + \frac{4}{10}$ **2.** $\frac{5}{8} + \frac{2}{8}$ **3.** $\frac{5}{6} - \frac{1}{6}$ **4.** $\frac{1}{3} + \frac{1}{3}$

5. $\frac{4}{5} - \frac{2}{5}$ **6.** $\frac{3}{8} + \frac{3}{8}$ **7.** $\frac{5}{8} - \frac{2}{8}$ **8.** $\frac{7}{10} - \frac{3}{10}$

Use the model for Problems 9–10.

9. Create and Solve Write an addition problem that can be modeled by the fraction tiles shown. Give it to a classmate to solve.

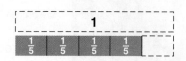

10. Suppose three of the $\frac{1}{5}$ tiles were removed. What subtraction sentence would that model?

Writing Math

Explain How could you know the denominator of the sum of $\frac{5}{12}$ and $\frac{2}{12}$ without using fraction tiles? What will the numerator be?

LESSON 2

CA Standards
KEY NS 2.3 Solve simple problems, including ones arising in concrete situations, involving the addition and subtraction of fractions and mixed numbers (like and unlike denominators of 20 or less), and express answers in the simplest form.

MR 1.1 Analyze problems by identifying relationships, distinguishing relevant from irrelevant information, sequencing and prioritizing information, and observing patterns.

Also NS 2.0, MR 1.2, MR 3.2, MR 3.3

Add and Subtract Fractions with Like Denominators

Objective Add and subtract fractions with like denominators.

▶ **Learn by Example**

In this lesson, you will learn how to add and subtract fractions without using tiles.

Example 1

Manuel eats the recommended servings of vegetables each day. He ate $\frac{1}{10}$ at breakfast and $\frac{7}{10}$ at lunch. What fraction of the recommended servings of vegetables has he eaten?

1 Add.

$$\frac{1}{10} + \frac{7}{10} = \frac{8}{10}$$

> To add fractions with like denominators, add the numerators and keep the same denominator.

2 Simplify if possible.

$$\frac{1}{10} + \frac{7}{10} = \frac{8}{10} = \frac{4}{5}$$

Solution: Manuel has eaten $\frac{4}{5}$ of the recommended servings of vegetables.

Example 2

Elsy's recipe for grilled eggplant uses $\frac{7}{8}$ cup of diced eggplant. Tran's recipe calls for $\frac{3}{8}$ cup. How much more eggplant does Elsy's recipe need than Tran's recipe?

1 Subtract.

$$\frac{7}{8} - \frac{3}{8} = \frac{4}{8}$$

> To subtract fractions with like denominators, subtract the numerators and keep the same denominator.

2 Simplify if possible.

$$\frac{7}{8} - \frac{3}{8} = \frac{4}{8} = \frac{1}{2}$$

Solution: Elsy's recipe needs $\frac{1}{2}$ cup more eggplant.

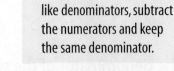

Add or subtract. Write the answer in simplest form.

1. $\frac{3}{4} + \frac{1}{4}$ 2. $\frac{5}{8} - \frac{1}{8}$ 3. $\frac{1}{5} + \frac{3}{5}$ 4. $\frac{5}{12} - \frac{3}{12}$

5. $\frac{3}{10} + \frac{3}{10}$ 6. $\frac{7}{12} - \frac{1}{12}$ 7. $\frac{5}{8} + \frac{1}{8}$ 8. $\frac{5}{6} - \frac{1}{6}$

Guided Problem Solving

Use the questions to solve this problem.

9. Letitia has $\frac{5}{16}$ cup each of sliced strawberries and sliced bananas. Does she have enough fruit to make a recipe that requires $\frac{1}{2}$ cup of sliced fruit?

   a. **Understand** What operation will tell you how much fruit Letitia has? What else do you need to find?

   b. **Plan** Find the sum of $\frac{5}{16} + \frac{5}{16}$. Then compare the sum to $\frac{1}{2}$.

   c. **Solve** Answer the question.

   d. **Look Back** Did you answer the question that was asked?

10. **Suppose** Letitia had $\frac{3}{16}$ cups of strawberries and $\frac{5}{16}$ cup of bananas. Will she have enough for the recipe? Explain your answer.

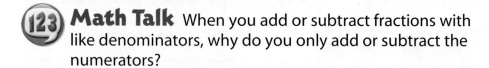 **Math Talk** When you add or subtract fractions with like denominators, why do you only add or subtract the numerators?

▶ **Practice and Problem Solving**

Add or subtract. Write the answer in simplest form.

11. $\frac{1}{6} + \frac{1}{6}$ 12. $\frac{1}{9} + \frac{7}{9}$ 13. $\frac{11}{12} - \frac{5}{12}$ 14. $\frac{1}{16} + \frac{9}{16}$

15. $\frac{9}{10} - \frac{3}{10}$ 16. $\frac{3}{16} + \frac{3}{16}$ 17. $\frac{4}{15} + \frac{1}{15}$ 18. $\frac{1}{9} + \frac{5}{9}$

Solve. Write each answer in simplest form.

19. Maria gets $\frac{5}{8}$ of the daily recommended amount of calcium from milk. She gets $\frac{1}{8}$ of it from cheese. How much of the recommended amount of calcium does Maria get from milk and cheese?

20. Multistep Tara had a bunch of celery with 12 stalks. She spread peanut butter on 4 stalks. She used 3 stalks in a salad. What fraction of the bunch of celery was left?

 ## Science Link

Solve. Write the answer in simplest form.

21. You need $\frac{1}{2}$ tablespoon of yeast to make herb bread. You only have a $\frac{1}{4}$ tablespoon measurer. How many $\frac{1}{4}$ tablespoons of yeast do you need to use?

22. Peter measured $\frac{2}{3}$ cup of plain flour. How much does he need to pour out if he only needs $\frac{1}{3}$ cup for his recipe?

23. Alisa crushed $\frac{1}{4}$ teaspoon of fresh chives. She needs $\frac{3}{4}$ teaspoon. How much more does Alisa need for the recipe?

24. Challenge Nick made a loaf of bread and sliced it into 9 equal pieces. He and his friends ate 6 pieces. His sister Tania made the same amount of bread and cut it into 12 equal pieces. She and her friends ate 7 pieces. Who had more bread left? Explain.

 **Fun Facts**

Yeast

- Yeasts are single-cell organisms that can only be seen with a microscope.
- Unlike plants, yeasts cannot use light energy to make their food. They use sugars as food.
- Combining sugar and yeast in a bread recipe produces carbon dioxide that helps the bread dough rise.

A group of yeast cells

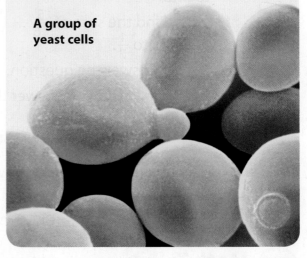

Science LS 2.g

 ## Spiral Review and Test Practice

Evaluate the expression when $n = 2$. AF 1.0, KEY **AF 1.2** page 104

25. $11 + n$ **26.** $8 - n$ **27.** $n + 4$ **28.** $3 + n$

Write the letter of the correct answer. KEY **NS 2.3**

29. Daria mixed $\frac{3}{8}$ cup raisins and $\frac{3}{8}$ cup peanuts for a snack. What fraction of a cup was her snack?

     A $\frac{9}{8}$ cup   **B** $\frac{7}{8}$ cup   **C** $\frac{6}{16}$ cup   **D** $\frac{3}{4}$ cup

Extra Practice See pages 162, Set B.

Key Standards Review

Need Help?
See Key Standards Handbook.

Write three mixed numbers that represent points *A*, *B*, and *C*. KEY **NS 1.5**

1.

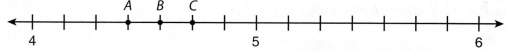

Translate each expression into words. KEY **AF 1.2**

2. $10p$

3. $(n + 3) + 4$

4. $4a \times 2$

5. $9t + 8$

6. $6d - 6$

7. $2 + (7y)$

8. $9 + (8 \div x)$

9. $5s + 7$

10. $1 + (s \div 2)$

Challenge

Logical Thinking

Check It Out KEY **NS 2.3**

Change one digit or the operation sign in each number sentence to make it true.

1. $\dfrac{2}{4} + \dfrac{1}{4} = \dfrac{4}{4}$

2. $\dfrac{7}{8} - \dfrac{2}{8} = \dfrac{4}{8}$

3. $\dfrac{5}{8} - \dfrac{2}{8} = \dfrac{7}{8}$

4. $\dfrac{2}{5} + \dfrac{2}{5} = 1$

5. $\dfrac{4}{7} - \dfrac{2}{7} = \dfrac{6}{7}$

6. $\dfrac{3}{9} + \dfrac{2}{9} = \dfrac{4}{9}$

Use Mental Math to add. Look for fractions with a sum of 1.

7. $\dfrac{7}{8} + \dfrac{1}{8} + \dfrac{5}{8} + \dfrac{3}{8}$

8. $\dfrac{6}{11} + \dfrac{8}{11} + \dfrac{5}{11} + \dfrac{3}{11}$

9. $\dfrac{4}{6} + \dfrac{2}{6}$

10. $\dfrac{3}{9} + \dfrac{4}{9} + \dfrac{6}{9}$

11. $\dfrac{5}{7} + \dfrac{4}{7} + \dfrac{2}{7} + \dfrac{2}{7}$

12. $\dfrac{8}{7} + \dfrac{6}{7}$

13. $\dfrac{7}{13} + \dfrac{12}{13} + \dfrac{4}{13} + \dfrac{1}{13} + \dfrac{5}{13}$

14. $\dfrac{4}{5} + \dfrac{4}{5} + \dfrac{4}{5} + \dfrac{4}{5} + \dfrac{4}{5}$

CA Standards
KEY NS 2.3 Solve simple problems, including ones arising in concrete situations, involving the addition and subtraction of fractions and mixed numbers (like and unlike denominators of 20 or less), and express answers in the simplest form.

MR 3.2 Note the method of deriving the solution and demonstrate a conceptual understanding of the derivation by solving similar problems.
Also NS 2.0, MR 2.3

Materials
Fraction tiles

Hands On
Add and Subtract Fractions with Unlike Denominators

Objective Explore adding and subtracting fractions with unlike denominators.

▶ **Explore**

You have learned how fraction tiles can be used to add and subtract fractions that have like denominators. In this lesson you will use what you've learned to add and subtract fractions that have unlike denominators.

Question How can you use fraction tiles to add and subtract fractions with unlike denominators?

A recipe for trail mix calls for $\frac{1}{8}$ cup of almonds and $\frac{1}{4}$ cup of peanuts. How many cups of nuts does the trail mix contain?

Use fraction tiles to add.

Trail Mix
$\frac{1}{4}$ cup yogurt-covered peanuts
$\frac{1}{8}$ cup almonds
$\frac{3}{4}$ cup granola
Fruit:
$\frac{2}{4}$ cup dried cherries
$\frac{3}{4}$ cup dried apricots

Hint
Always look at the greater denominator and try those tiles first.

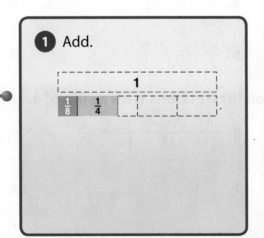

1 Add.

2 Make a row of tiles the same length using like tiles.

Solution: The trail mix contains $\frac{3}{8}$ cup of nuts.

Gina had $\frac{2}{3}$ liter of water in her water bottle when she started her bicycle ride. At the end of her ride she had $\frac{1}{4}$ liter left. How much water did she drink during her bicycle ride?

1 Model the fractions and compare.

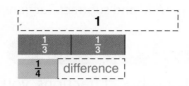

2 Find fraction tiles with like units that fill in the space that shows the difference.

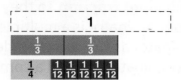

Solution: Gina drank $\frac{5}{12}$ liter of water.

Hint
Sometimes using the greater denominator does not work. Multiplying the denominators can help you find the right tiles to use.

▶ **Extend**

Use fraction tiles to find the sum or difference.

1. $\frac{3}{10} + \frac{3}{5}$ **2.** $\frac{1}{2} - \frac{3}{8}$ **3.** $\frac{2}{3} + \frac{1}{6}$

4. $\frac{7}{12} - \frac{1}{6}$ **5.** $\frac{1}{3} + \frac{1}{4}$ **6.** $\frac{3}{5} - \frac{1}{2}$

7. $\frac{2}{5} + \frac{1}{2}$ **8.** $\frac{3}{4} - \frac{1}{3}$ **9.** $\frac{8}{12} - \frac{2}{3}$

10. $\frac{1}{4} + \frac{1}{3}$ **11.** $\frac{4}{5} - \frac{1}{2}$ **12.** $\frac{1}{2} + \frac{1}{4}$

13. $\frac{5}{6} - \frac{1}{3}$ **14.** $\frac{3}{5} + \frac{1}{10}$ **15.** $\frac{2}{4} - \frac{1}{3}$

16. $\frac{3}{8} + \frac{1}{4}$ **17.** $\frac{3}{8} + \frac{1}{2}$ **18.** $\frac{1}{6} + \frac{2}{3}$

19. $\frac{3}{5} - \frac{2}{10}$ **20.** $\frac{5}{12} - \frac{1}{3}$

Writing Math

Explain why you cannot always use tiles with the greater denominator to show the sum or difference of two fractions with unlike denominators.

CA Standards

KEY NS2.3 Solve simple problems, including ones arising in concrete situations, involving the addition and subtraction of fractions and mixed numbers (like and unlike denominators of 20 or less), and express answers in the simplest form.

Also NS 2.0, MR 1.2

Vocabulary

equivalent fraction

common denominator

Add and Subtract Fractions with Unlike Denominators

Objective Add and subtract fractions with unlike denominators.

▶ **Learn by Example**

To add or subtract fractions, you need to rewrite each fraction as an **equivalent fraction** so they share a **common denominator**. If one denominator is a multiple of the other, use the greater denominator as the common denominator. Otherwise, multiply the denominators to find a common denominator.

When asked to name their favorite fruit, $\frac{1}{5}$ of the students in Ethan's class chose apples and $\frac{1}{4}$ chose bananas. What fraction of the students surveyed chose apples or bananas?

Think

You cannot use the greater denominator as a common denominator because 5 is not a multiple of 4.

---

1 Find a common denominator. Use the product of the denominators.

$$5 \times 4 = 20$$

↑
(common denominator)

$$\frac{1}{5} \overset{\times 4}{\underset{\times 4}{=}} \frac{4}{20} \qquad \frac{1}{4} \overset{\times 5}{\underset{\times 5}{=}} \frac{5}{20}$$

2 Rewrite the problem. Then add.

$$\frac{1}{5} + \frac{1}{4} = \frac{4}{20} + \frac{5}{20}$$
$$= \frac{9}{20}$$

You can also write the problem in vertical form.

$$\begin{array}{r} \frac{1}{5} = \frac{4}{20} \\ + \frac{1}{4} = \frac{5}{20} \\ \hline \frac{9}{20} \end{array}$$

Solution: $\frac{9}{20}$ of the students surveyed chose apples or bananas.

Another Example

Find $\frac{5}{12} - \frac{1}{6}$.

1 Find a common denominator. Since 12 is a multiple of 6, you can use 12 as a common denominator.

$$\frac{1}{6} = \frac{2}{12}$$

2 Rewrite the problem. Then subtract. Write the answer in simplest form.

$$\frac{5}{12} = \frac{5}{12}$$
$$-\frac{1}{6} = \frac{2}{12}$$
$$\frac{3}{12} = \frac{1}{4}$$

▶ Guided Practice

Add or subtract. Write the answer in simplest form.

1. $\frac{1}{8}$
    $+ \frac{1}{4}$

2. $\frac{1}{3}$
    $+ \frac{2}{5}$

3. $\frac{1}{2}$
    $- \frac{1}{4}$

4. $\frac{2}{3}$
    $- \frac{1}{2}$

5. $\frac{1}{2} + \frac{2}{9}$

6. $\frac{1}{3} + \frac{1}{2}$

7. $\frac{1}{2} + \frac{3}{10}$

8. $\frac{1}{6} + \frac{1}{3}$

9. $\frac{1}{2} - \frac{3}{8}$

10. $\frac{4}{5} - \frac{1}{4}$

11. $\frac{1}{2} - \frac{2}{5}$

12. $\frac{3}{4} - \frac{3}{16}$

Ask Yourself
- Did I find a common denominator?
- Is my answer in simplest form?

 Math Talk Why do you need to find equivalent fractions with the same denominator before adding or subtracting fractions?

▶ Practice and Problem Solving

Add or subtract. Write the answer in simplest form.

13. $\frac{1}{3}$
    $+ \frac{1}{4}$

14. $\frac{3}{8}$
    $+ \frac{1}{4}$

15. $\frac{7}{8}$
    $- \frac{1}{2}$

16. $\frac{3}{4}$
    $- \frac{1}{2}$

17. $\frac{11}{12}$
    $- \frac{1}{3}$

18. $\frac{3}{4} - \frac{2}{5}$

19. $\frac{4}{5} - \frac{3}{4}$

20. $\frac{3}{8} - \frac{1}{16}$

21. $\frac{1}{2} + \frac{1}{4}$

22. $\frac{2}{3} + \frac{1}{5}$

23. $\frac{3}{4} - \frac{1}{3}$

24. $\frac{1}{8} + \frac{1}{2}$

25. $\frac{9}{10} - \frac{1}{2}$

26. $\frac{1}{3} + \frac{5}{12}$

27. $\frac{1}{5} + \frac{1}{3}$

Solve.

28. Jana had $\frac{1}{4}$ cup yogurt during breakfast. She had $\frac{1}{2}$ cup yogurt with her lunch. How much yogurt did Jana eat in all?

29. Enrique mixed $\frac{1}{2}$ quart of orange juice, $\frac{1}{4}$ quart of pineapple juice, and $\frac{1}{8}$ quart of grape juice. How much juice did he mix?

 Real World Data

The circle graph shows the fractional part of the land that a farmer uses to grow each type of crop.

30. What fraction of the land is used to grow carrots and tomatoes?

31. Right or Wrong? Zack says that the fraction of land used to grow berries is the same as the fraction of land used to grow lettuce and peas. Is he right or wrong? Explain.

32. Challenge Next year, the farmer plans to grow a second variety of berries on the land he usually uses for lettuce. How much greater will the berry part of the farm be than the part of the farm used to grow peas? Show your work.

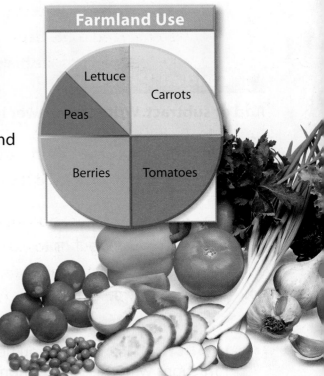

Farmland Use

Lettuce · Carrots · Peas · Berries · Tomatoes

 Spiral Review and Test Practice

Write the fraction or mixed number in decimal form. KEY **NS 1.2**, NS 1.0 page 104

33. $\frac{1}{4}$

34. $1\frac{3}{4}$

35. $\frac{2}{5}$

36. $2\frac{1}{2}$

Write the letter of the correct answer. KEY **NS 2.3**

37. Tomás drank $\frac{1}{3}$ quart of orange juice in the morning. He drank $\frac{1}{4}$ quart of orange juice after school. How much more orange juice did Tomás drink in the morning than after school?

A $\frac{1}{12}$ **B** $\frac{1}{7}$ **C** $\frac{5}{12}$ **D** $\frac{7}{12}$

Extra Practice See pages 163, Set D.

Feeding Time

Some veterinarians work at special wildlife centers, animal parks, and zoos. These types of veterinarians take care of abandoned and injured animals.

Baby tiger cub fed in Ramona, CA.

1. Leanne mixed $\frac{1}{3}$ cup ground vegetables, $\frac{1}{3}$ cup ground mealworms, and $\frac{1}{4}$ cup warm water to feed some baby birds. How many cups of feed does she make?

2. Humboldt penguin chicks are fed ground up food through eyedroppers. If $\frac{3}{16}$ of an eyedropper of ground vitamins was mixed with $\frac{5}{8}$ of an eyedropper of ground fish, would the eyedropper be full?

3. A veterinarian at a zoo might spend $\frac{3}{8}$ of her work day making the rounds to examine animals and $\frac{1}{4}$ of her work day treating animals. What part of the work day is left for other tasks?

CA Standards
KEY **NS 2.3**, MR 2.6

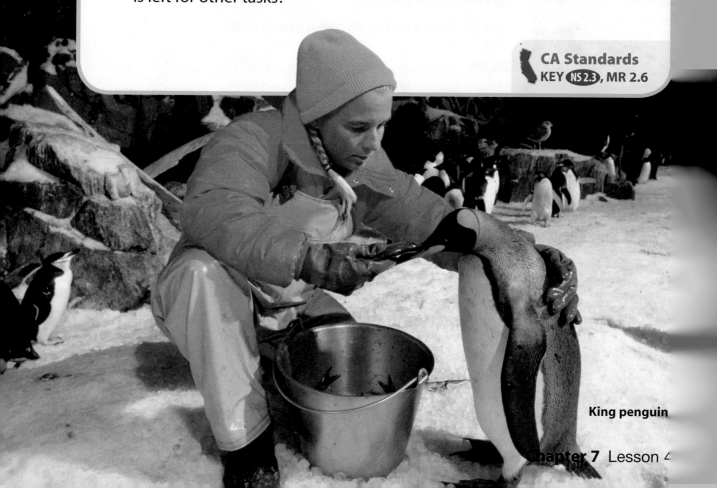

King penguin

CA Standards

MR 2.6 Make precise calculations and check the validity of the results from the context of the problem.

KEY NS 2.3 Solve simple problems, including ones arising in concrete situations, involving the addition and subtraction of fractions and mixed numbers (like and unlike denominators of 20 or less), and express answers in the simplest form.

Also MR 1.1, MR 1.2, MR 2.0, MR 2.3, MR 2.4, MR 3.0, MR 3.1, MR 3.2

Problem Solving Strategy
Work Backward

Objective Work backward to solve problems.

▶ **Learn by Example**

Sometimes you can start with what you know in a problem and work backward.

> Laurie rode her bike on Friday. On Saturday, she rode $\frac{1}{2}$ mile more than on Friday. On Sunday, she rode $\frac{1}{4}$ mile less than on Saturday. On Monday, she rode $\frac{1}{8}$ mile more than on Sunday. Laurie rode $\frac{5}{8}$ mile on Monday. How many miles did Laurie ride on Friday?

UNDERSTAND

Laurie rode $\frac{5}{8}$ mile on Monday.

How many miles did Laurie ride on Friday?

PLAN

Start with what you know.

Work backward and use inverse operations.

SOLVE

Monday	Sunday	Saturday	Friday
$\frac{5}{8}$ mile	$\frac{4}{8}$ mile	$\frac{6}{8}$ mile	$\frac{2}{8}$ mile
This is $\frac{1}{8}$ mile more than on Sunday.	This is $\frac{1}{4}$ mile less than on Saturday.	This is $\frac{1}{2}$ mile more than on Friday.	

Subtract $\frac{1}{8}$.　　Add $\frac{1}{4}$.　　Subtract $\frac{1}{2}$.

Laurie rode $\frac{2}{8}$ or $\frac{1}{4}$ mile on Friday.

LOOK BACK

Is your answer reasonable? Begin with the distance Laurie rode on Friday. Work the problem in the other direction.

Think

Addition and subtraction are inverse operations.

Multiplication and division are inverse operations.

▶ Guided Problem Solving

Solve using the Ask Yourself questions.

1. Sonja and Adam need ice for their fruit smoothie. They have $\frac{1}{4}$ cup more raspberries than ice. They have $\frac{1}{8}$ cup more bananas than raspberries. They have $\frac{1}{2}$ cup of bananas. How many cups of ice do they have?

 Math Talk How can you check your answer?

Ask Yourself
• Did I choose the right information to start with?
• What operation will I use for each step?

▶ Independent Problem Solving

**Use the Work Backward strategy to solve.
Explain why your answer makes sense.**

2. A veterinarian was feeding a retriever. She gave $\frac{1}{3}$ pound more food to the retriever than to a beagle. She gave $\frac{2}{5}$ pound more food to the beagle than to a Chihuahua. She gave the Chihuahua $\frac{1}{5}$ pound of food. How much food did the retriever get?

3. Patty lives $\frac{1}{4}$ mile farther from a stadium than Leo. Rafael lives $\frac{1}{2}$ mile closer to the stadium than Patty. Leo lives $\frac{3}{8}$ mile from the stadium. How far does Rafael live from the stadium?

4. Paul bought blue paint for a mural. He bought $\frac{1}{4}$ gallon more green paint than blue paint. He bought $\frac{3}{8}$ gallon less red paint than green paint. He bought $\frac{3}{16}$ gallon more white paint than red paint. If he bought $\frac{3}{4}$ gallon white paint, how much blue paint did he buy?

5. **Challenge** On Tuesday the Dunns used $\frac{1}{3}$ of a tank of gas more than on Monday. On Wednesday, they used $\frac{1}{5}$ of a tank less than on Monday. On Thursday, they used $\frac{1}{5}$ of a tank less than on Tuesday. They used $\frac{3}{5}$ of a tank on Thursday. How much gas did they use on Wednesday?

6. **Create and Solve** Rewrite Problem 1 so that the answer to how many cups of ice are needed is $\frac{1}{4}$ cup of ice.

Reading & Writing **Math**

Vocabulary

Complete the labels that show how to add and subtract fractions.

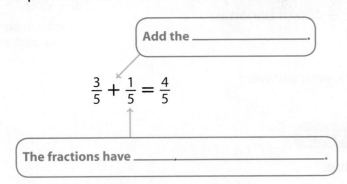

Add the _____.

$$\frac{3}{5} + \frac{1}{5} = \frac{4}{5}$$

The fractions have _____.

$$\frac{7}{8} = \frac{7}{8}$$
$$- \frac{1}{4} = \frac{2}{8}$$
$$\frac{5}{8}$$

$\frac{1}{4}$ and $\frac{2}{8}$ are _____.

Word Bank

common denominators

equivalent fractions

numerators

mixed number

Writing Can you rewrite any two fractions so that they have a common denominator? Tell why or why not.

Reading Check out this book in your library. *Fraction Fun* by David A. Adler

CA Standards

MR 2.3 Use a variety of methods, such as words, numbers, symbols, charts, graphs, tables, diagrams, and models, to explain mathematical reasoning.

Also NS 2.0, KEY NS 2.3

Standards-Based Extra Practice

Use fraction tiles to find the sum or difference. Simplify if possible.

1. $\frac{3}{5} + \frac{1}{5}$ 2. $\frac{3}{4} - \frac{2}{4}$ 3. $\frac{2}{10} + \frac{4}{10}$

   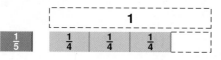   

4. $\frac{1}{10} + \frac{3}{10}$ 5. $\frac{3}{12} + \frac{4}{12}$ 6. $\frac{4}{6} + \frac{1}{6}$

7. $\frac{4}{5} - \frac{1}{5}$ 8. $\frac{3}{8} + \frac{3}{8}$ 9. $\frac{1}{4} + \frac{2}{4}$

10. $\frac{3}{3} - \frac{2}{3}$ 11. $\frac{3}{4} - \frac{1}{4}$ 12. $\frac{7}{8} - \frac{3}{8}$

13. $\frac{5}{6} - \frac{3}{6}$ 14. $\frac{3}{5} - \frac{1}{5}$ 15. $\frac{2}{10} + \frac{6}{10}$

16. $\frac{11}{12} - \frac{9}{12}$ 17. $\frac{1}{10} + \frac{3}{10}$ 18. $\frac{1}{3} + \frac{1}{3}$

19. $\frac{6}{8} - \frac{5}{8}$ 20. $\frac{2}{8} + \frac{5}{8}$ 21. $\frac{3}{5} + \frac{2}{5}$

Solve.

22. Meredith used $\frac{3}{8}$ of an orange to make an orange smoothie. She used $\frac{1}{8}$ of the orange in a salad. What fraction of the orange did Meredith use in all?

23. Jackson walked $\frac{9}{10}$ of a mile through Yosemite National Park. He backtracked $\frac{2}{10}$ of a mile before stopping to take some photographs. How far will Jackson have to walk to return to where he started?

24. Vincent picked vegetables from his garden. He washed and sliced the vegetables to make a salad. He has $\frac{9}{12}$ cups of cauliflower and $\frac{6}{12}$ cups of tomatoes. How much more cauliflower than tomatoes does Vincent have?

Education Place
Visit www.eduplace.com/camap/
for **Extra Practice**.

Standards-Based Extra Practice

Set B ── KEY **NS 2.3** page 148

Add or subtract. Write each answer in simplest form.

1. $\dfrac{13}{16} - \dfrac{4}{16}$

2. $\dfrac{6}{8} + \dfrac{2}{8}$

3. $\dfrac{1}{2} + \dfrac{1}{2}$

4. $\dfrac{3}{4} - \dfrac{1}{4}$

5. $\dfrac{3}{5} - \dfrac{2}{5}$

6. $\dfrac{1}{9} + \dfrac{7}{9}$

7. $\dfrac{2}{6} + \dfrac{1}{6}$

8. $\dfrac{13}{15} - \dfrac{11}{15}$

9. $\dfrac{12}{18} + \dfrac{3}{18}$

10. $\dfrac{19}{20} - \dfrac{9}{20}$

11. $\dfrac{6}{10} + \dfrac{1}{10}$

12. $\dfrac{7}{8} - \dfrac{2}{8}$

13. $\dfrac{7}{7} - \dfrac{2}{7}$

14. $\dfrac{1}{5} + \dfrac{1}{5}$

15. $\dfrac{4}{9} - \dfrac{1}{9}$

16. $\dfrac{10}{11} - \dfrac{9}{11}$

17. $\dfrac{1}{3} + \dfrac{2}{3}$

18. $\dfrac{9}{10} - \dfrac{2}{10}$

19. $\dfrac{5}{15} + \dfrac{9}{15}$

20. $\dfrac{1}{8} + \dfrac{2}{8}$

21. $\dfrac{3}{11} + \dfrac{1}{11}$

Solve.

22. James made a pan of vegetable lasagna. He and his friends ate $\dfrac{2}{12}$ of the lasagna. His sisters ate $\dfrac{1}{12}$ of the lasagna. How much more of the lasagna did James and his friends eat?

23. Shawn ate $\dfrac{3}{16}$ cup of broccoli and $\dfrac{7}{16}$ cup of carrots with his dinner. What fraction of a cup of vegetables did he eat in all?

24. Angela kept track of her calorie intake for one week. She got $\dfrac{1}{4}$ of her calories from fat and $\dfrac{2}{4}$ from carbohydrates. What fraction of her calories were from fat and carbohydrates combined?

25. Ralph used a scale to measure the weight of some ingredients for his bean soup. The beans weigh $\dfrac{1}{3}$ pound and the chopped onions weigh $\dfrac{2}{3}$ pound. How much more do the chopped onions weigh than the beans?

26. Joel likes to eat cottage cheese with blueberries. On Thursday, he ate $\dfrac{6}{12}$ pound of cottage cheese and on Friday, he ate $\dfrac{2}{12}$ pound of cottage cheese. How much cottage cheese did he eat?

Standards-Based Extra Practice

Set C —————————————————————————— KEY **NS 2.3** page 152

Use fraction tiles to find the sum or difference.

1. $\frac{3}{4} - \frac{1}{2}$

2. $\frac{7}{12} + \frac{1}{3}$

3. $\frac{1}{5} + \frac{2}{3}$

4. $\frac{1}{2} + \frac{3}{8}$

5. $\frac{4}{5} - \frac{2}{3}$

6. $\frac{1}{3} + \frac{4}{9}$

7. $\frac{5}{8} - \frac{1}{4}$

8. $\frac{9}{16} - \frac{1}{4}$

9. $\frac{13}{15} - \frac{3}{5}$

10. $\frac{1}{2} - \frac{1}{5}$

11. $\frac{5}{6} - \frac{2}{3}$

12. $\frac{5}{18} + \frac{1}{9}$

Solve.

13. Damian drank $\frac{1}{8}$ liter of a sports drink after playing a basketball game. He drank $\frac{1}{4}$ liter of the sports drink when he got home. What part of a liter of the sports drink did Damian drink in all?

14. Gloria and Carmen are meeting at the library to work on a school project. Gloria walks $\frac{3}{5}$ miles and Carmen walks $\frac{1}{3}$ mile. How much farther does Gloria walk than Carmen?

Set D —————————————————————————— KEY **NS 2.3**, MR 2.3 page 154

Add or subtract. Write each answer in simplest form.

1. $\frac{5}{8} - \frac{1}{2}$

2. $\frac{2}{3} - \frac{1}{6}$

3. $\frac{1}{4} + \frac{5}{8}$

4. $\frac{9}{10} - \frac{1}{5}$

5. $\frac{5}{6} - \frac{2}{3}$

6. $\frac{5}{7} + \frac{2}{14}$

7. $\frac{3}{5} + \frac{3}{10}$

8. $\frac{11}{12} - \frac{3}{4}$

9. $\frac{7}{20} - \frac{1}{10}$

Solve.

10. Harold took a survey of his friends' favorite sports. One half prefer soccer. One eighth prefer football. What fraction of Harold's friends prefer either soccer or football?

11. Mark poured $\frac{3}{4}$ cup of oat bran cereal in a bowl. He ate $\frac{3}{8}$ of a cup. How much cereal is left?

Education Place
Visit www.eduplace.com/camap/
for **Extra Practice**.

Chapter Review/Test

Vocabulary and Concepts ———————————— KEY **NS 2.3**, MR 2.3

Write the best word to complete each sentence.

1. To subtract fractions that have common denominators, subtract their _____.

2. Equivalent fractions have the same _____.

3. One way to find a common denominator is to _____ the denominators of the fractions.

Skills ———————————————————————— KEY **NS 2.3**

Add or subtract. Write the answer in simplest form.

4. $\frac{12}{14} + \frac{2}{14}$ 5. $\frac{2}{10} + \frac{4}{10}$ 6. $\frac{6}{7} - \frac{6}{7}$ 7. $\frac{2}{8} + \frac{5}{8}$

8. $\frac{1}{3} + \frac{2}{3}$ 9. $\frac{1}{2} - \frac{1}{5}$ 10. $\frac{5}{15} + \frac{3}{5}$ 11. $\frac{1}{8} + \frac{1}{4}$

12. $\frac{3}{4} + \frac{1}{5}$ 13. $\frac{5}{16} + \frac{7}{16}$ 14. $\frac{17}{18} - \frac{5}{6}$ 15. $\frac{1}{2} + \frac{1}{3}$

16. $\frac{7}{10} - \frac{1}{5}$ 17. $\frac{8}{12} - \frac{1}{3}$ 18. $\frac{1}{4} + \frac{2}{10} + \frac{2}{5}$

Problem Solving and Reasoning ———————— KEY **NS 2.3**, MR 1.1, MR 2.3, MR 3.1

Solve.

19. Anika makes an avocado salad. She uses $\frac{1}{4}$ cup more lettuce than tomatoes, $\frac{5}{12}$ cup less onions than lettuce, and $\frac{3}{4}$ cup more avocado than onions. If she uses $\frac{11}{12}$ cup of avocado, what fraction of a cup of tomatoes does she use?

20. Matt ran $\frac{1}{5}$ mile less on Monday than on Tuesday. He ran $\frac{1}{2}$ mile less on Wednesday than he did on Monday. He ran $\frac{7}{10}$ mile more on Friday than on Wednesday. If Matt ran $\frac{4}{5}$ mile on Friday, how far did he run on Tuesday?

Writing Math **Explain** How would you subtract two fractions that have unlike denominators?

Spiral Review and Test Practice

1. Which of the following has the greatest value?

A 73,109,400

B 73,198,400

C 73,207,500

D 73,208,400

NS 1.0 page 62

2. What is the value of the expression $9 + 0$?

A 900

B 90

C 9

D 0

NS 1.0 page 126

3. $86,314 - 52,974 =$

A 23,340

B 33,340

C 34,340

D 34,660

NS 1.0 page 68

4. Which equation could have been used to create this function table?

x	y
1	9
2	10
3	11
4	12

Test Tip
Check your answer by substituting the x- and y-values from the table in the equation you chose.

A $y = x - 8$

B $y = x + 8$

C $y = 8x$

D $y = \frac{8}{x}$

KEY **AF 1.5** page 112

5. If $y = 9$, what is the value of $(y \times 2) \times 5$?

A 90

B 80

C 18

D 10

KEY **AF 1.2** page 128

6. It takes Natalie $\frac{5}{12}$ hour to ride her bike to the library and $\frac{1}{12}$ hour to ride her bike from the library to the post office. How much time does it take Natalie to ride her bike to the library and then to the post office?

A $\frac{1}{3}$ hour

B $\frac{1}{4}$ hour

C $\frac{1}{2}$ hour

D $\frac{7}{12}$ hour

Test Tip
Show the fractions on a number line to help understand the problem.

KEY **NS 2.3** page 148

Education Place
Visit www.eduplace.com/camap/ for
Test-Taking Tips and **Extra Practice**.

Add with Mixed Numbers

Vocabulary and Concepts GRADE 4 NS 1.5, MR 2.3

Tell what the word means and give an example.

1. mixed number

2. fraction

Skills KEY NS 1.4, KEY NS 1.5

Find the Greatest Common Factor for each set of numbers.

3. 40 and 80   **4.** 71 and 15   **5.** 76 and 4

6. 36 and 99   **7.** 50 and 27

Write each improper fraction as a mixed number in simplest form.

8. $\dfrac{14}{3}$ **9.** $\dfrac{88}{6}$

Problem Solving and Reasoning GRADE 4 KEY NS 3.0

10. Sula had 83 pens and 27 gift boxes. What is the greatest number of pens she could put in each gift box to be sure that each box has the same number of pens.

Vocabulary

Visualize It!

$$\frac{11}{8} = 1\frac{3}{8}$$

A **mixed number** is made up of a whole number and a fraction.

Language Tip

Math words that look alike in English and Spanish often have the same meaning.

English	Spanish
sum	suma
mixed number	número mixto

See **English-Spanish Glossary** pages 628–642.

 Education Place Visit www.eduplace.com/camap/ for the **eGlossary** and **eGames**.

CA Standards

KEY NS 2.3 Solve simple problems, including ones arising in concrete situations, involving the addition and subtraction of fractions and mixed numbers (like and unlike denominators of 20 or less), and express answers in the simplest form.

MR 2.3 Use a variety of methods, such as words, numbers, symbols, charts, graphs, tables, diagrams, and models, to explain mathematical reasoning.

Also MR 2.4

Vocabulary

mixed number

$$1\frac{3}{4}$$

whole ↗   ↖ fraction
number part   part

Materials
fraction tiles

Hands On
Sums Greater Than 1

Objective Explore adding fractions whose sum is greater than 1.

▶ **Explore**

You already learned how to add fractions with like and unlike denominators. In this lesson, you will learn how to add fractions with sums greater than 1.

Question How can you model adding fractions when the sum is greater than 1?

Mike and his brother are planning to hike the American Discovery Trail in California. Mike is making trail mix for the hike. His recipe calls for $\frac{5}{8}$ cup of peanuts and $\frac{1}{2}$ cup of raisins. How many cups of trail mix does this recipe make?

1 Set up your addition.

Place five $\frac{1}{8}$ tiles and one $\frac{1}{2}$ tile under the one whole tile.

$$\frac{5}{8} + \frac{1}{2}$$

2 Find a common denominator.

You can use $\frac{1}{8}$ tiles to make a row that is the same length as the sum of $\frac{5}{8}$ and $\frac{1}{2}$.

This shows that the common denominator is 8.

$$\frac{5}{8} + \frac{1}{2}$$

$$\frac{5}{8} + \frac{4}{8}$$

3 Find the sum.

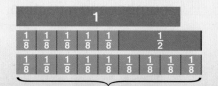

$$\frac{5}{8} + \frac{4}{8} = \frac{9}{8}$$

4 Write the sum as a **mixed number**.

Compare $\frac{9}{8}$ to the one whole tile. You can add another $\frac{1}{8}$ tile to the whole to make the rows equal.

$$\frac{9}{8} = \frac{8}{8} + \frac{1}{8} = 1\frac{1}{8}$$

Solution: Mike made $1\frac{1}{8}$ cups of trail mix.

▶ **Extend**

Write the equation illustrated by the model. Write the sum as a mixed number in simplest form.

1.

2.

Use models to add. Write each sum as a mixed number in simplest form.

3. $\frac{7}{9} + \frac{2}{3}$ **4.** $\frac{3}{4} + \frac{1}{3}$ **5.** $\frac{2}{3} + \frac{5}{6}$

6. $\frac{7}{12} + \frac{3}{4}$

7. $\begin{array}{r} \frac{4}{5} \\ + \frac{2}{3} \\ \hline \end{array}$

8. $\begin{array}{r} \frac{9}{10} \\ + \frac{3}{5} \\ \hline \end{array}$

9. $\begin{array}{r} \frac{7}{12} \\ + \frac{1}{2} \\ \hline \end{array}$

10. $\begin{array}{r} \frac{1}{2} \\ + \frac{7}{10} \\ \hline \end{array}$

11. $\begin{array}{r} \frac{1}{4} \\ + \frac{7}{8} \\ \hline \end{array}$

Writing Math

Explain When you use fraction tiles to find the sum of two fractions, how can you tell whether or not your answer will be a mixed number?

CA Standards

KEY NS 2.3 Solve simple problems, including ones arising in concrete situations, involving the addition and subtraction of fractions and mixed numbers (like and unlike denominators of 20 or less), and express answers in the simplest form.

MR 2.4 Express the solution clearly and logically by using the appropriate mathematical notation and terms and clear language; support solutions with evidence in both verbal and symbolic work.

Also NS 1.0, MR 1.1, MR 2.2, MR 2.3, MR 2.6

Add a Fraction and a Mixed Number

Objective Add a fraction and a mixed number with like and unlike denominators.

▶ **Learn by Example**

Mrs. Chang spent $3\frac{1}{2}$ hours gardening on Saturday. She spends $\frac{2}{3}$ hour working in her garden on Sunday. How many hours did Mrs. Chang spend gardening that weekend?

1 Since the denominators are different, find a common denominator.

2 Rewrite the fractions as equivalent fractions with the common denominator.

$$3\frac{1}{2} = 3\frac{3}{6}$$
$$+ \frac{2}{3} = + \frac{4}{6}$$

$\frac{1}{2} \overset{\times 3}{=} \frac{3}{6}$ $\overset{\times 3}{}$

$\frac{2}{3} \overset{\times 2}{=} \frac{4}{6}$ $\overset{\times 2}{}$

> 3 is not a multiple of both 2 and 3, so use the product of the denominators. $2 \times 3 = 6$

3 Add the fractions. Then add the whole numbers.

$$3\frac{1}{2} = 3\frac{3}{6}$$
$$+ \frac{2}{3} = + \frac{4}{6}$$
$$\overline{\qquad \quad 3\frac{7}{6}}$$

$6\overline{)7}$
$\underline{-6}$
1

$\frac{7}{6} = 1\frac{1}{6}$

4 Simplify the sum if possible. $\quad 3\frac{7}{6} = 3 + 1\frac{1}{6} = 4\frac{1}{6}$

Solution: Mrs. Chang spent $4\frac{1}{6}$ hours gardening that weekend.

Add. Write the sum in simplest form.

1. $4\frac{1}{6} + \frac{1}{6}$ 2. $\frac{1}{4} + 2\frac{1}{4}$ 3. $4\frac{3}{7} + \frac{5}{7}$ 4. $\frac{5}{9} + 4\frac{4}{9}$

5. $\frac{1}{5}$ 6. $6\frac{2}{3}$ 7. $2\frac{1}{2}$ 8. $\frac{9}{12}$
   $+1\frac{1}{4}$ $+\frac{1}{4}$ $+\frac{2}{3}$ $+3\frac{1}{2}$
   ‾‾‾‾‾   ‾‾‾‾‾   ‾‾‾‾‾   ‾‾‾‾‾

> **Ask Yourself**
> • Did I use a common denominator to add the fractions?
> • Did I write each sum in simplest form?

Guided Problem Solving

Use the questions to solve this problem.

9. Sonya is using ribbon to decorate the curtains for her bedroom. She bought $1\frac{1}{3}$ yards of blue ribbon, $\frac{5}{6}$ yard of yellow ribbon, and $\frac{9}{12}$ yard of red ribbon. Sonya uses all of the blue and red ribbon. How many yards of blue and red ribbon does Sonya use?

   a. **Understand** What information is needed to answer this question? What information is not needed?

   b. **Plan** What should you use as the common denominator?

   c. **Solve** Add the lengths of the blue and red ribbons. Write the answer in simplest form.

   d. **Look Back** Does your answer make sense? Explain.

(123) Math Talk How do you know when a mixed number is not in simplest form?

▶ **Practice and Problem Solving**

Add. Write the sum in simplest form.

10. $2\frac{1}{8} + \frac{3}{8}$ 11. $\frac{1}{6} + 3\frac{1}{6}$ 12. $\frac{7}{12} + 5\frac{3}{4}$ 13. $1\frac{4}{5} + \frac{6}{5}$ 14. $2\frac{1}{4} + \frac{1}{2}$

15. $\frac{1}{4}$ 16. $9\frac{3}{7}$ 17. $3\frac{7}{12}$ 18. $\frac{8}{14}$ 19. $5\frac{3}{10}$
    $+3\frac{1}{8}$ $+\frac{1}{2}$ $+\frac{3}{6}$ $+2\frac{5}{7}$ $+\frac{4}{5}$
    ‾‾‾‾‾   ‾‾‾‾‾   ‾‾‾‾‾   ‾‾‾‾‾   ‾‾‾‾‾

Write each mixed number in simplest form.

20. $5\frac{7}{6}$ **21.** $8\frac{3}{9}$ **22.** $4\frac{21}{7}$ **23.** $10\frac{8}{3}$ **24.** $6\frac{9}{7}$

 # History-Social Science Link

Solve. Write answers in simplest form.

25. A park ranger from the Victory Center led Callie's family on a $\frac{1}{2}$ hour Yorktown Battlefield Siege Line Walking Tour and then a $\frac{3}{4}$ hour walking tour of the historical buildings in Yorktown. Afterwards, the family sat down for lunch for $1\frac{1}{3}$ hours. How long did they spend on tours with the park ranger?

26. At the 1780s farm, visitors can help weed the garden and water the plants. Larry helped by carrying $1\frac{1}{2}$ quarts of water. Melissa carried $\frac{5}{8}$ quart. How many quarts of water did they carry in all?

Battle of Yorktown

- Yorktown, Virginia is the site of the October 19, 1781 surrender of British soldiers to American and French forces under General George Washington.

- Yorktown Victory Center and the nearby Museum of the American Revolution have exhibits describing the surrender, the daily life of ordinary soldiers, and a re-created 1780s farm.

History-Social Science 5.6.1

 ## Spiral Review and Test Practice

Copy and complete the function table. Write an equation for the function rule. KEY **AF 1.5** page 112

27. Rule: _____

Week	x	1	2	3	4	5	6	7
Total Money Saved ($)	y	3	6	9				

Write the letter of the correct answer. KEY **NS 2.3**

28. Latoya made a healthy smoothie using $1\frac{1}{4}$ cups of yogurt and $\frac{1}{3}$ cup of raspberries. How many cups of smoothie did Latoya make?

   A $1\frac{1}{12}$ **B** $1\frac{1}{6}$ **C** $1\frac{2}{7}$ **D** $1\frac{7}{12}$

Extra Practice See page 181, Set A.

Key Standards Review

Need Help?
See Key Standards Handbook.

Evaluate each expression when $n = 16$. KEY **AF 1.2**

1. $n + (41 - 33)$

2. $18 + n$

3. $(8 - 8) + n - (32 - 28)$

4. $n + (25 \div 5)$

5. $(47 + n) \times 2$

6. $(n - 14) + (n - 16)$

7. $(n + n) \div 32$

8. $(29 - n) \times (n - n)$

9. $n + (6 + 5) - (13 - 8)$

Add or Subtract. Write each sum or difference in simplest form. KEY **NS 2.3**

10. $\dfrac{1}{4} + \dfrac{1}{8}$

11. $\dfrac{5}{12} - \dfrac{1}{6}$

12. $\dfrac{1}{3} + \dfrac{1}{5}$

13. $\dfrac{3}{5} + \dfrac{3}{15}$

14. $\dfrac{1}{2} - \dfrac{4}{9}$

15. $\dfrac{2}{3} + \dfrac{2}{9}$

16. $\dfrac{3}{4} - \dfrac{1}{8}$

17. $\dfrac{1}{2} + \dfrac{1}{6}$

18. $\dfrac{5}{6} - \dfrac{1}{2}$

Challenge

Number Sense

Magic Squares KEY NS 2.3

Copy and complete this fraction magic square.

In a magic square, each row, column, and diagonal has the same sum.

In the magic square at the right, each row, column, and diagonal should have a sum of $1\dfrac{1}{2}$, and each missing numerator is a different number from 1 to 9.

Can you find another way to complete the fraction magic square?

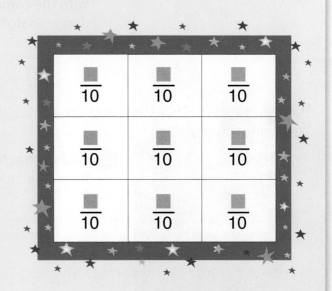

CA Standards

KEY NS 2.3 Solve simple problems, including ones arising in concrete situations, involving the addition and subtraction of fractions and mixed numbers (like and unlike denominators of 20 or less), and express answers in the simplest form.

MR 2.4 Express the solution clearly and logically by using the appropriate mathematical notation and terms and clear language; support solutions with evidence in both verbal and symbolic work.

Also NS 1.0, NS 2.0, KEY AF 1.2, MR 2.2, MR 2.3

Add Mixed Numbers with and without Regrouping

Objective Add two mixed numbers with and without regrouping.

▶ **Learn by Example**

In this lesson, you will use what you learned about adding fractions and mixed numbers to add two mixed numbers.

Evelyn walks each day to stay healthy. Her journal shows the number of miles she walked on Monday and Tuesday. How many miles did she walk in the two days?

Walking Journal	
Monday	$3\frac{1}{2}$ miles
Tuesday	$2\frac{4}{5}$ miles

1 Find a common denominator.

You can use 10 as the common denominator.
$2 \times 5 = 10$

2 Rewrite the fractions as equivalent fractions with the common denominator.

$$3\frac{1}{2} = 3\frac{5}{10}$$
$$+ 2\frac{4}{5} = + 2\frac{8}{10}$$

$$\frac{1}{2} \xrightarrow{\times 5} = \frac{5}{10} \xleftarrow{\times 5}$$

$$\frac{4}{5} \xrightarrow{\times 2} = \frac{8}{10} \xleftarrow{\times 2}$$

3 Add the fractions. Add the whole numbers.

$$3\frac{1}{2} = 3\frac{5}{10}$$
$$+ 2\frac{4}{5} = + 2\frac{8}{10}$$
$$5\frac{13}{10}$$

4 Simplify the sum if possible.

$$5\frac{13}{10} = 5 + 1\frac{3}{10} = 6\frac{3}{10}$$

Solution: Evelyn walked $6\frac{3}{10}$ miles in the two days.

Another Example

Evaluate $4\frac{1}{6} + y$ **if** $y = 5\frac{1}{3}$.

$$4\frac{1}{6} + y = 4\frac{1}{6} + 5\frac{1}{3}$$

$$4\frac{1}{6} = \quad 4\frac{1}{6}$$

$$+ 5\frac{1}{3} = + 5\frac{2}{6}$$

$$\overline{\qquad \qquad} \quad \overline{\qquad \qquad}$$

$$9\frac{3}{6} = 9\frac{1}{2}$$

> Since 6 is a multiple of 3, use 6 as the common denominator.

Solution: When the value of y is $5\frac{1}{3}$, then $4\frac{1}{6} + y = 9\frac{1}{2}$.

▶ **Guided Practice**

Add. Write the sum in simplest form.

1. $5\frac{1}{6} + 3\frac{1}{6}$

2. $3\frac{5}{7} + 6\frac{3}{7}$

3. $3\frac{1}{3} + 1\frac{1}{2}$

4. $2\frac{3}{10} + 6\frac{1}{5}$

5. $4\frac{3}{4} + 2\frac{1}{3}$

6. $2\frac{9}{10} + 3\frac{3}{5}$

7. $\quad 2\frac{2}{3}$
$\quad + 3\frac{2}{3}$
$\quad \overline{\qquad}$

8. $\quad 2\frac{5}{6}$
$\quad + 4\frac{5}{12}$
$\quad \overline{\qquad}$

9. $\quad 1\frac{1}{2}$
$\quad + 4\frac{2}{5}$
$\quad \overline{\qquad}$

Ask Yourself
• Did I use a common denominator to add the fractions?
• Did I write each sum in simplest form?

123 Math Talk Look back at Exercise 2. Without adding the fractions, how do you know that your answer will be more than 9?

▶ **Practice and Problem Solving**

Add. Write the sum in simplest form.

10. $2\frac{2}{5} + 1\frac{1}{5}$

11. $4\frac{1}{4} + 3\frac{3}{4}$

12. $6\frac{3}{4} + 2\frac{1}{8}$

13. $5\frac{4}{5} + 2\frac{2}{3}$

14. $3\frac{2}{5} + 1\frac{1}{3}$

15. $3\frac{8}{20} + 1\frac{4}{10}$

16. $6\frac{9}{12} + 2\frac{1}{6}$

17. $1\frac{7}{15} + 4\frac{3}{5}$

18. $\quad 5\frac{1}{3}$
$\quad + 2\frac{1}{3}$
$\quad \overline{\qquad}$

19. $\quad 5\frac{5}{14}$
$\quad + 4\frac{9}{14}$
$\quad \overline{\qquad}$

20. $\quad 3\frac{7}{9}$
$\quad + 2\frac{1}{3}$
$\quad \overline{\qquad}$

21. $\quad 5\frac{7}{16}$
$\quad + 5\frac{3}{8}$
$\quad \overline{\qquad}$

Algebra Expressions

Evaluate the expression. Write your answer in simplest form.

22. Evaluate $3\frac{7}{12} + y$ if $y = 2\frac{3}{4}$.

23. Evaluate $2\frac{2}{4} + y$ if $y = 3\frac{2}{3}$.

24. Evaluate $1\frac{9}{10} + y$ if $y = 4\frac{4}{5}$.

25. Evaluate $4\frac{1}{2} + y$ if $y = 3\frac{5}{9}$.

26. Evaluate $2\frac{2}{4} + y$ if $y = 4\frac{8}{12}$.

27. Evaluate $3\frac{3}{4} + y$ if $y = 3\frac{3}{5}$.

 ## Science Link

Use the table to solve Problems 28–30. Write answers in simplest form.

28. A microclimate is the weather of a small area within a larger region. Coastal mountains and valleys have created a microclimate in the small town of Bonny Doon. What is the total rainfall in Bonny Doon for November and December?

29. What is the total rainfall in San Francisco for November and December?

30. Challenge Find the total rainfall for the months listed for both places. Write each total as a mixed number and as a decimal.

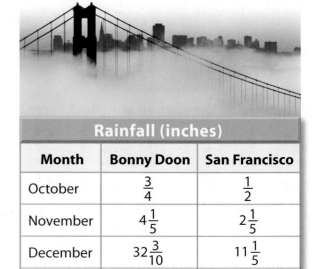

Rainfall (inches)		
Month	**Bonny Doon**	**San Francisco**
October	$\frac{3}{4}$	$\frac{1}{2}$
November	$4\frac{1}{5}$	$2\frac{1}{5}$
December	$32\frac{3}{10}$	$11\frac{1}{5}$
January	13	$3\frac{1}{2}$
February	$5\frac{7}{10}$	$2\frac{4}{5}$

Science ES 4.d

Spiral Review and Test Practice

Solve. KEY NS 2.3 page 168

31. $6 + \frac{3}{4}$ **32.** $\frac{1}{2} + 2$ **33.** $\frac{5}{8} + 3$ **34.** $9 + \frac{7}{8}$

Write the letter of the correct answer. KEY NS 2.3

35. Randy filled his fish tank with $1\frac{2}{3}$ gallons of water. Then he added $1\frac{3}{4}$ gallons of water. How many gallons of water did Randy pour into his fish tank?

A $2\frac{5}{7}$ **B** $2\frac{17}{12}$ **C** $3\frac{5}{12}$ **D** $3\frac{17}{12}$

Extra Practice See page 181, Set B.

Mixed Number Match Up

Use numbers from the box to solve. Some numbers may be used more than once and others may not be used at all.

$$5\frac{4}{5} \qquad \frac{5}{6} \qquad \frac{11}{20} \qquad 2\frac{8}{15}$$

$$\frac{3}{4} \qquad 6\frac{1}{12} \qquad \frac{1}{2} \qquad 6\frac{2}{9}$$

$$4\frac{3}{5} \qquad 2\frac{1}{3} \qquad 1\frac{3}{7} \qquad 2\frac{1}{4}$$

1. $2\frac{3}{4} + x = 3\frac{1}{4}$

2. $3\frac{7}{9} + n = 4\frac{11}{18}$

3. $p + 1\frac{7}{15} = 6\frac{1}{15}$

4. $c + 4\frac{8}{10} = 10\frac{3}{5}$

5. $a + 2\frac{2}{3} = 8\frac{3}{4}$

6. $3\frac{7}{9} + r = 6\frac{1}{9}$

7. $5\frac{5}{14} + t = 6\frac{11}{14}$

8. $4\frac{1}{5} + k = 6\frac{9}{20}$

9. Choose three numbers from the box that make this equation true.

$$w + x + y = 3\frac{1}{2}$$

10. Write Your Own Write an equation that can be solved using one of the numbers from the box.

CA Standards
KEY **AF 1.2**, KEY **NS 2.3**,
MR 1.0

Berkeley, CA

CA Standards
MR 1.1, MR 2.0,
MR 2.3, MR 3.1

NS 1.0, KEY **NS 1.5**,
KEY **NS 2.3**, KEY **AF 1.2**,
KEY **AF 1.5**

Problem Solving

Objective Use skills and strategies to solve word problems.

Hall of Health

Hands-on Health Museum

Exhibits and displays at the Hall of Health teach students about good health.

Solve. Tell which strategy or method you used.

1. On Monday, Aiden ran 2 miles. On Wednesday, he ran $1\frac{1}{2}$ miles. On Friday, he ran $\frac{3}{4}$ miles. How many total miles did he run in 3 days?

2. On Monday, Lucy drinks $7\frac{2}{3}$ ounces of soy milk and eats $\frac{1}{2}$ of a pear. On Tuesday, she drinks 7.5 ounces of soy milk and eats $\frac{3}{4}$ cup of granola. Which day did Lucy drink more milk? Use a number line to help you.

3. Luisa kept track of how many minutes she jumped rope each day.

   a. Write an equation using x to represent the day and y to represent the minutes Luisa jumped rope.

   b. If the pattern continues, use your equation to find how many minutes Luisa would exercise on Day 8.

   c. Is it reasonable to think that this pattern would continue for a whole year? Explain.

Minutes of Jumping Rope	
Day	Minutes
1	6
2	7
3	8
4	9
5	10

Problem Solving On Tests

Select a Strategy
- Write an Equation
- Work Backward
- Guess and Check
- Choose the Operation
- Make an Organized List

1. The table shows the number of students that have perfect attendance. Which statement is true?

Class	Number of students	Number with perfect attendance
Mr. Klein	28	7
Mrs. Walker	20	6

A Mr. Klein's class has the greater fraction of students with perfect attendance.

Test Tip
Set up each class as a fraction in simplest form.

B Mrs. Walker's class has the greater fraction of students with perfect attendance.

C The two classes have an equal fraction of students with perfect attendance.

D The attendance records cannot be compared because there are more students in one class than in the other.

SDAP 1.3 page 40

2. Josh ran a distance of seven and fifteen thousandths miles. What is seven and fifteen thousandths written in standard form?

A 0.715   B 7.015   C 7.105   D 7.15

NS 1.0 page 60

3. The school van can seat 9 passengers. Which expression represents the product of n and 9?

A $9n$ B $9 \div n$ C $n \div 9$ D $n + 9$

KEY AF 1.2 page 102

4. Mark worked 8 hours a day for 6 days. On one of the days, he needed to take off 5 hours. If $h = 8$, what is the value of $6h - 5$?

A 9

B 18

C 43

D 63

Test Tip
Determine which operation to do first. Then replace the variable with the number.

KEY AF 1.2 page 104

5. Frank bought 6 tickets to a music concert, each priced at $85. What value of c makes this equation true?

$$6 \times 85 = (6 \times 80) + (6 \times c)$$

A 5   B 6   C 80   D 85

AF 1.3 page 124

6. Sue made bracelets on 3 different occasions. She made 13 one week and 39 during another week. If $b = 7$, what is the value of $13 + (b + 39)$?

A 46

B 59

C 66

D 598

Test Tip
To help simplify the expression, try using the Associative Property of Addition.

KEY AF 1.2 page 126

Education Place
Visit www.eduplace.com/camap/ for **Test-Taking Tips** and **Extra Practice**.

Reading & Writing Math

Vocabulary

Use the Word Bank to help you explain how to add **mixed numbers**.

$$3\frac{2}{5} + 5\frac{2}{3}$$

Word Bank

fractions

unlike denominators

equivalent fractions

whole numbers

Step 1: Look at the fractions. The two fractions have _____ . In order to add, the fractions must have a common denominator. The common denominator is _____ .

Step 2: Write _____ with the common denominator.

$$3\frac{2}{5} = 3\,\frac{}{}$$

$$+\,5\frac{2}{3} = +\,5\,\frac{}{}$$

Step 3: Add the _____ .
Add the _____ .

Step 4: Simplify the sum, if possible.

$$3\frac{2}{5} = 3$$

$$+\,5\frac{2}{3} = +\,5$$

Writing
How are improper fractions and mixed numbers alike? How are they different?

Reading
Check out this book in your library.
Math Game 1: Rescue Alice from the Evil Math King
by Tori Jung

CA Standards
MR 2.3 Use a variety of methods, such as words, numbers, symbols, charts, graphs, tables, diagrams, and models, to explain mathematical reasoning.

Also NS 2.0, KEY NS 2.3

Standards-Based Extra Practice

Add. Write each sum in simplest form.

1. $\frac{2}{5}$
    $+ 1\frac{1}{5}$

2. $\frac{1}{4}$
    $+ 3\frac{3}{8}$

3. $\frac{5}{6}$
    $+ 5\frac{1}{4}$

4. $\frac{5}{16}$
    $+ 2\frac{3}{16}$

5. $\frac{2}{3}$
    $+ 5\frac{1}{6}$

6. $1\frac{1}{4}$
    $+ \frac{1}{3}$

7. $\frac{7}{8}$
    $+ 3\frac{1}{16}$

8. $\frac{2}{3}$
    $+ 1\frac{1}{6}$

Solve.

9. Allie planted flowers for $1\frac{1}{8}$ hours and mowed the lawn for $\frac{3}{4}$ hours. How many hours did Allie work in the yard?

10. Janelle put $\frac{2}{3}$ cup of cherries and $1\frac{5}{6}$ cups of grapes in a bowl. How many cups of fruit are in the bowl?

Add. Write each sum in simplest form.

1. $1\frac{2}{3} + 3\frac{1}{3}$

2. $4\frac{1}{8} + 4\frac{1}{8}$

3. $9\frac{1}{5} + 1\frac{6}{10}$

4. $1\frac{1}{7} + 2\frac{3}{14}$

Evaluate the expression. Write each answer in simplest form.

5. Evaluate $3\frac{1}{6} + y$, if $y = 7\frac{2}{3}$

6. Evaluate $1\frac{1}{4} + y$, if $y = 4\frac{1}{4}$

7. Evaluate $2\frac{1}{8} + y$, if $y = 19\frac{2}{4}$

8. Evaluate $11\frac{3}{5} + y$, if $y = 5\frac{1}{4}$

Solve.

9. Lauren walked $3\frac{1}{4}$ miles around Golden Gate Park in San Francisco. The next day she walked $4\frac{1}{8}$ miles. How many miles did Lauren walk on both days?

10. Huong uses $3\frac{2}{3}$ cups of peanuts and $3\frac{2}{3}$ cups of walnuts to make a nut mix. How many cups of nuts does she use in all?

Education Place
Visit www.eduplace.com/camap/
for **Extra Practice**.

Chapter 8 Extra Practice **181**

Chapter Review/Test

Vocabulary and Concepts ──────────────── KEY NS 2.3, MR 2.3

Write the best term to complete each sentence.

1. A _____ has a whole number and a part.

2. An _____ can have a numerator greater than its denominator.

Skills ──────────────────────── KEY NS 2.3, KEY AF 1.2

Add. Write the sum in simplest form.

3. $\frac{12}{15} + \frac{2}{3}$

4. $\frac{8}{10} + \frac{4}{10}$

5. $1\frac{2}{3} + \frac{5}{9}$

6. $\frac{3}{8} + 1\frac{3}{4}$

7. $4\frac{1}{2} + 5\frac{3}{8}$

8. $7\frac{8}{9} + 2\frac{5}{18}$

9. $5\frac{1}{4} + 6\frac{2}{3}$

10. $5\frac{1}{6} + 2\frac{3}{18}$

Evaluate the expression. Write the answer in simplest form.

11. Evaluate $x + 22\frac{1}{6}$ if $x = 3\frac{1}{3}$

12. Evaluate $x + 7\frac{3}{4}$ if $x = 4\frac{5}{16}$

Problem Solving and Reasoning ──────── KEY NS 2.3, KEY AF 1.5, MR 1.1, MR 2.3, MR 2.4

Solve.

13. After visiting the Hall of Health, Mario decided to keep an exercise diary. He walked $2\frac{1}{2}$ miles on Wednesday and $3\frac{1}{4}$ miles on Thursday. What was the total distance Mario walked?

14. Shania made a healthy trail mix. She used $2\frac{4}{5}$ cups of raisins, $4\frac{3}{5}$ cups of peanuts, and $1\frac{9}{10}$ cups of almonds. How many cups of trail mix did she make?

15. Henry kept track of how many minutes he rode his bike each day. If d = the day and m = the number of minutes, write an equation showing how to find the number of minutes he biked on any given day. How many minutes will he bike on day 11?

Bike Record			
Day (d)	1	2	3
Minutes (m)	$25\frac{1}{4}$	$26\frac{1}{4}$	$27\frac{1}{4}$

Writing Math Ami says that she can tell that the sum of $2\frac{3}{8}$ and $3\frac{5}{16}$ is less than 6 without adding. How does she know this?

Spiral Review and Test Practice

1. $5,794 + 2,845 =$

A 7,639

B 8,539

C 8,639

D 8,640

NS 1.0 page 68

2. What is the difference between 37,421 and 8,049 when both numbers are rounded to the nearest thousand?

A 30,000

B 29,400

C 29,000

D 28,000

NS 1.1 page 66

3. What value for x makes this number sentence true?

$$(7 - 4) + 5 = 2 + x$$

A 3

B 6

C 8

D 16

Test Tip
You can check your answer by replacing x with the number you chose and solving the equation.

KEY **AF 1.2** page 108

4. What value for y makes this equation true?

$$5 \times 28 = (5 \times 20) + (5 \times y)$$

A 80   C 8

B 20   D 2

AF 1.3 page 124

5. The population of New York City in 2005 was 19,254,630. What is this value rounded to the nearest thousand?

A 19,300,000

B 19,255,000

C 19,254,600

D 19,254,000

NS 1.1 page 66

6. $1\frac{1}{2} + \frac{3}{4} =$

A $1\frac{1}{4}$

B $1\frac{1}{2}$

C 2

D $2\frac{1}{4}$

Test Tip
When you add or subtract fractions and mixed numbers, use vertical form.

KEY **NS 2.3** page 170

Education Place
Visit www.eduplace.com/camap/ for **Test-Taking Tips** and **Extra Practice**.

Chapter 8 Spiral Review and Test Practice **183**

Chapter 9

Subtract with Mixed Numbers

Vocabulary and Concepts KEY NS 1.4, KEY NS 1.5, MR 2.3

Tell what the word means and give an example. pages 16 and 30

1. greatest common factor (GCF)

2. mixed number

Skills KEY NS 1.5, KEY NS 2.3

Complete. pages 30 and 34

3. $\dfrac{14}{8} = \boxed{}\dfrac{3}{4}$

4. $\dfrac{22}{5} = 4\boxed{}$

5. $6 = \dfrac{\boxed{}}{8}$

6. $3\dfrac{8}{\boxed{}} = \dfrac{41}{11}$

7. $\dfrac{\boxed{}}{6} = \dfrac{1}{3}$

Write each sum in simplest form. page 170

8. $1\dfrac{3}{4} + \dfrac{3}{4}$

9. $4\dfrac{2}{7} + 2\dfrac{6}{7}$

Problem Solving and Reasoning KEY NS 2.3

10. Emily ate $1\dfrac{1}{2}$ slices of pizza. Felix ate $2\dfrac{2}{3}$ slices of pizza. How many slices of pizza did Emily and Felix eat in all?

Vocabulary

Visualize It!

You can subtract a mixed number from a whole number.

Rename $\longrightarrow 5 - 1\dfrac{1}{4}$

$$4 + \dfrac{4}{4}\!\!\!\!\boxed{1} - 1\dfrac{1}{4} = 3\dfrac{3}{4}$$

Subtract whole numbers

Subtract fractions

Language Tip

Math words that look alike in English and Spanish often have the same meaning.

English	Spanish
difference	diferencia
denominator	denominador

See **English-Spanish Glossary** pages 628–642.

 Education Place Visit www.eduplace.com/camap/ for the **eGlossary** and **eGames**.

CA Standards MR 2.3 Use a variety of methods, such as words, numbers, symbols, charts, graphs, tables, diagrams, and models, to explain mathematical reasoning. **Also KEY NS 2.3**

Chapter 9   185

CA Standards

KEY NS 2.3 Solve simple problems, including ones arising in concrete situations, involving the addition and subtraction of fractions and mixed numbers (like and unlike denominators of 20 or less) and express answers in simplest form.

NS 2.0 Students perform calculations and solve problems involving addition, subtraction, and simple multiplication and division of fractions and decimals.

Also MR 2.3, MR 3.2

Materials
• Fraction tiles
• Markers

Hands On
Rename to Subtract

Objective Explore how to rename a whole number to subtract mixed numbers.

▶ Explore

In Chapter 8, you learned how to regroup when adding mixed numbers. In this chapter, you will rename whole numbers to subtract fractions.

Question How can you use fraction tiles to help rename a whole number as a fraction?

Max and Sam are building a doghouse. For the door frame, they need 2 feet of board. They have $1\frac{5}{8}$ feet of board. How much more board do they need?

Work with a partner. Use fraction tiles to model $2 - 1\frac{5}{8}$.

> **1** Use two whole fraction tiles to represent the 2 feet.
>
> | 1 | | 1 |

> **Hint**
> Rename one whole using a fraction with the same denominator as the fraction or mixed number you are subtracting.

> **2** Rename one whole tile as $\frac{8}{8}$ using eight $\frac{1}{8}$ tiles.
>
> | 1 | | $\frac{1}{8}$ $\frac{1}{8}$ $\frac{1}{8}$ $\frac{1}{8}$ $\frac{1}{8}$ $\frac{1}{8}$ $\frac{1}{8}$ $\frac{1}{8}$ |

> **3** Subtract $1\frac{5}{8}$ by taking away the whole tile and 5 of the $\frac{1}{8}$ tiles.
>
> $\frac{1}{8}$ $\frac{1}{8}$ $\frac{1}{8}$

> **4** Count the number of $\frac{1}{8}$ tiles remaining.
>
> There are three $\frac{1}{8}$ tiles remaining.

Solution: Max and Sam need $\frac{3}{8}$ foot of board for the door frame.

▶ **Extend**

Choose the model you would use to find the difference. Then find the difference.

1. $2 - 1\frac{1}{3}$

A. [1] [$\frac{1}{3}$ | $\frac{1}{3}$ | $\frac{1}{3}$]

B. [1] [$\frac{1}{5}$ | $\frac{1}{5}$ | $\frac{1}{5}$ | $\frac{1}{5}$ | $\frac{1}{5}$]

2. $2 - 1\frac{9}{10}$

A. [1] [$\frac{1}{8}$ | $\frac{1}{8}$ | $\frac{1}{8}$ | $\frac{1}{8}$ | $\frac{1}{8}$ | $\frac{1}{8}$ | $\frac{1}{8}$ | $\frac{1}{8}$]

B. [1] [$\frac{1}{10}$ | $\frac{1}{10}$ | $\frac{1}{10}$ | $\frac{1}{10}$ | $\frac{1}{10}$ | $\frac{1}{10}$ | $\frac{1}{10}$ | $\frac{1}{10}$ | $\frac{1}{10}$ | $\frac{1}{10}$]

3. $2 - 1\frac{3}{4}$

A. [1] [$\frac{1}{2}$ | $\frac{1}{2}$]

B. [1] [$\frac{1}{4}$ | $\frac{1}{4}$ | $\frac{1}{4}$ | $\frac{1}{4}$]

Use fraction tiles to rename one whole. Subtract the mixed number from the whole number. Sketch your model.

4. $4 - 2\frac{2}{3}$ **5.** $3 - 1\frac{5}{12}$ **6.** $2 - 1\frac{1}{6}$

7. $3 - 2\frac{1}{5}$ **8.** $2 - 1\frac{7}{10}$ **9.** $4 - 1\frac{3}{5}$

10. $2 - 1\frac{2}{4}$ **11.** $3 - 2\frac{7}{10}$ **12.** $2 - \frac{7}{8}$

13. Sketch three different ways to show the number 2 as a mixed number.

14. Suppose you are being asked to model the expression $4 - 2\frac{4}{4}$. You have 4 whole tiles. Do you need to rename to subtract? Explain.

Writing Math

Leslie says that 3 can be renamed as $2\frac{3}{3}$ and Jules says 3 can be renamed as $2\frac{4}{4}$. Explain why both of them are correct.

CA Standards
KEY NS 2.3 Solve simple problems, including ones arising in concrete situations, involving the addition and subtraction of fractions and mixed numbers (like and unlike denominators of 20 or less) and express answers in simplest form.

NS 2.0 Students perform calculations and solve problems involving addition, subtraction, and simple multiplication and division of fractions and decimals.

Also NS 1.0, MR 2.4, MR 2.6

Rename to Subtract

Objective Rename a whole number as a mixed number to subtract.

▶ **Learn by Example**

In Lesson 1, you modeled renaming whole numbers using fraction tiles. In this lesson, you will practice renaming to subtract mixed numbers from whole numbers.

The Guzman family needs 5 bags of cement for their patio. They need $1\frac{2}{3}$ bags for their front porch. How much more do they need for their patio?

Find $5 - 1\frac{2}{3}$.

---

1 Rename 5 as $4 + 1$. Then rename 1, using 3 for the denominator.

$$5 = 4 + 1$$
$$4 + \frac{3}{3} = 4\frac{3}{3}$$

---

2 Subtract the fractions.

$$5 = \quad 4\frac{3}{3}$$
$$- 1\frac{2}{3} = -1\frac{2}{3}$$
$$\overline{\qquad \frac{1}{3}}$$

---

3 Subtract the whole numbers.

$$5 = \quad 4\frac{3}{3}$$
$$- 1\frac{2}{3} = -1\frac{2}{3}$$
$$\overline{\quad 3\frac{1}{3}}$$

---

4 Use addition to check your work.

$$3\frac{1}{3}$$
$$+ 1\frac{2}{3}$$
$$\overline{4\frac{3}{3} = 5}$$

Rocky Creek Bridge, near Monterey, CA, is built of concrete.

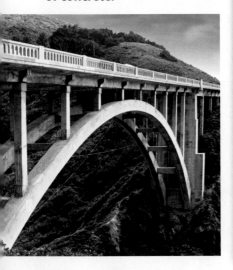

Solution: The Guzman family needs $3\frac{1}{3}$ more bags for their patio.

Subtract. Check your answer.

1. $6 - 4\frac{1}{5}$

2. $10 - 8\frac{4}{9}$

3. $16 - 7\frac{7}{20}$

4. $7 - 4\frac{1}{5}$

5. $21 - 1\frac{5}{12}$

6. $45 - 11\frac{5}{7}$

 Math Talk When you subtract a fraction from a whole number, why do you need to rename the whole number?

▶ **Practice and Problem Solving**

Subtract.

7. $\begin{array}{r} 5 \\ -\ 3\frac{3}{4} \\ \hline \end{array}$

8. $\begin{array}{r} 2 \\ -\ 1\frac{5}{8} \\ \hline \end{array}$

9. $\begin{array}{r} 55 \\ -\ 23\frac{1}{2} \\ \hline \end{array}$

10. $\begin{array}{r} 6 \\ -\ \frac{2}{15} \\ \hline \end{array}$

11. $\begin{array}{r} 7 \\ -\ 4\frac{1}{5} \\ \hline \end{array}$

12. $14 - 13\frac{3}{7}$

13. $24 - 20\frac{1}{12}$

14. $62 - 18\frac{9}{20}$

15. $35 - 16\frac{1}{24}$

Solve.

16. Rikku spent 3 hours helping her friends build scenery for a play. Gordon helped build for $1\frac{1}{4}$ hours. How much more time did Rikku work on the scenery?

17. Johan is building a fence for his dog. Johan's dog can jump up to $4\frac{1}{2}$ feet. If the fence is 8 feet tall, how much higher would the dog need to jump to get over the fence?

 Spiral Review and Test Practice

Write the decimal as a fraction or mixed number. KEY **NS 1.5** page 78

18. 0.5

19. 0.75

20. 1.2

21. 0.9

22. 3.83

Write the fraction as a decimal. KEY **NS 1.5** page 78

23. $\frac{1}{4}$

24. $\frac{32}{100}$

25. $\frac{1}{2}$

26. $\frac{7}{10}$

27. $\frac{3}{5}$

Write the letter of the correct answer. KEY **NS 2.3**

28. Find $4 - 2\frac{1}{6}$.

A $1\frac{5}{6}$ B $2\frac{3}{6}$ C $2\frac{5}{6}$ D 3

LESSON 3

CA Standards
KEY **NS 2.3** Solve simple problems, including ones arising in concrete situations, involving the addition and subtraction of fractions and mixed numbers (like and unlike denominators of 20 or less) and express answers in simplest form.

NS 2.0 Students perform calculations and solve problems involving addition, subtraction, and simple multiplication and division of fractions and decimals.

Also NS 1.0, MR 1.1, MR 1.2, MR 2.2, MR 3.2

Subtract Mixed Numbers with Like Denominators

Objective Subtract mixed numbers with like denominators.

▶ **Learn by Example**

Rolf spent $7\frac{1}{4}$ hours constructing a wooden planter for his grandmother. His sister spent $1\frac{3}{4}$ hours painting it. How many more hours did it take to construct the planter than to paint it?

Find $7\frac{1}{4} - 1\frac{3}{4}$.

---

1 Rename $7\frac{1}{4}$.

Rename one whole to have the same denominator as the fraction.

$$7\frac{1}{4} = 7 + \frac{1}{4}$$
$$= 6 + 1 + \frac{1}{4}$$
$$= 6 + \frac{4}{4} + \frac{1}{4}$$
$$= 6 + \frac{5}{4}$$

---

2 Subtract the fractions.

$$7\frac{1}{4} = \quad 6\frac{5}{4}$$
$$- 1\frac{3}{4} = - 1\frac{3}{4}$$
$$\overline{\qquad \frac{2}{4}}$$

---

3 Subtract the whole numbers.

$$7\frac{1}{4} = \quad 6\frac{5}{4}$$
$$- 3\frac{3}{4} = - 1\frac{3}{4}$$
$$\overline{\qquad 5\frac{2}{4}}$$

---

4 Write the difference in simplest form.

$$5\frac{2}{4} = 5\frac{1}{2}$$

Vocabulary Tip

A fraction is in **simplest form** when the numerator and denominator have 1 as the greatest common factor.

Solution: It took $5\frac{1}{2}$ more hours to construct the planter than to paint it.

Subtract. Write the difference in simplest form.

1. $8\frac{3}{8} - 2\frac{5}{8}$ 2. $10\frac{1}{9} - 9\frac{4}{9}$ 3. $58\frac{9}{20} - 19\frac{9}{20}$

 Math Talk How do you know what denominator to use when you rename?

► **Practice and Problem Solving**

Subtract. Write the difference in simplest form.

4. $2\frac{2}{8}$
$-1\frac{5}{8}$

5. $2\frac{1}{6}$
$-1\frac{5}{6}$

6. $4\frac{1}{8}$
$-2\frac{1}{8}$

7. $5\frac{2}{9}$
$-3\frac{8}{9}$

8. $32\frac{1}{5}$
$-21\frac{4}{5}$

9. $21\frac{2}{7} - 16\frac{4}{7}$ 10. $31\frac{5}{9} - 11\frac{8}{9}$ 11. $76\frac{3}{20} - 25\frac{11}{20}$ 12. $42\frac{3}{10} - 4\frac{9}{10}$

 Real World Data

Use the table to solve problems 13–15. Write the answer in simplest form.

13. In June, how much more rain did San Benito County receive than Ventura County?

14. In May, how much more rain did Ventura County receive than San Benito County?

15. **Multistep** Compare the rainfall of both counties for the first three months of the year. Which county received more rain? How much more did it receive?

Rainfall (inches)		
	San Benito County	**Ventura County**
Jan	$4\frac{42}{100}$	$7\frac{97}{100}$
Feb	$2\frac{86}{100}$	$7\frac{22}{100}$
Mar	$3\frac{55}{100}$	$2\frac{17}{100}$
Apr	$1\frac{86}{100}$	$1\frac{87}{100}$
May	$\frac{50}{100}$	$1\frac{54}{100}$
Jun	$\frac{24}{100}$	$\frac{7}{100}$

 Spiral Review and Test Practice

Find the missing number. Identify the property you used. **KEY AF 1.2** page 126

16. $41 + 6 = 6 + \blacksquare$ 17. $23 + (55 + 7) = (\blacksquare + 55) + 7$ 18. $68 + \blacksquare = 68$

Write the letter of the correct answer. **KEY NS 2.3**

19. Find $5\frac{3}{5} - 1\frac{4}{5}$.

A $5\frac{1}{5}$ B $4\frac{4}{5}$ C $4\frac{1}{5}$ D $3\frac{4}{5}$

CA Standards
KEY NS 2.3 Solve simple problems, including ones arising in concrete situations, involving the addition and subtraction of fractions and mixed numbers (like and unlike denominators of 20 or less) and express answers in simplest form.

NS 2.0 Students perform calculations and solve problems involving addition, subtraction, and simple multiplication and division of fractions and decimals.

Also NS 1.0, MR 1.2, MR 2.4, MR 2.2, MR 2.3

Subtract Mixed Numbers

Objective Subtract mixed numbers with unlike denominators.

▶ **Learn by Example**

The oak tree named "Old Glory" was the largest tree ever transplanted. It was moved to a new park in Los Angeles on January 20, 2004.

In 2004, Old Glory was $16\frac{1}{6}$ feet around. That same year, the oak tree in Annie's yard was $5\frac{1}{2}$ feet around. How much larger was Old Glory's circumference compared to Annie's tree?

$$16\frac{1}{6} - 5\frac{1}{2} = \bigcirc$$

---

1 Find a common denominator.

You can use the larger denominator, 6, as the common denominator.

$$16\frac{1}{6} = \quad 16\frac{\square}{6}$$
$$- 5\frac{1}{2} = - 5\frac{\square}{6}$$

---

2 Write equivalent fractions.

$$16\frac{1}{6} = \quad 16\frac{1}{6}$$
$$- 5\frac{1}{2} = - 5\frac{3}{6}$$

---

3 Rename mixed numbers if necessary.

You cannot subtract $\frac{3}{6}$ from $\frac{1}{6}$. Rename one whole.

$$16\frac{1}{6} = \quad 15\frac{7}{6}$$
$$- 5\frac{1}{2} = - 5\frac{3}{6}$$

---

4 Subtract. Make sure your answer is in simplest form.

$$16\frac{1}{6} = \quad 15\frac{7}{6}$$
$$- 5\frac{1}{2} = - 5\frac{3}{6}$$
$$\overline{\qquad 10\frac{4}{6} = 10\frac{2}{3}}$$

Solution: Old Glory was $10\frac{2}{3}$ feet farther around than Annie's tree.

► Guided Practice

Subtract. Write the difference in simplest form.

Ask Yourself
- Did I rename when necessary?
- Did I simplify the difference?

1. $4\frac{1}{3}$
$-2\frac{1}{5}$

2. $9\frac{9}{10}$
$-4\frac{2}{5}$

3. $4\frac{1}{2}$
$-2\frac{7}{10}$

4. $8\frac{5}{12}$
$-6\frac{5}{6}$

5. $5\frac{5}{6} - 1\frac{1}{3}$

6. $25\frac{7}{8} - 3\frac{1}{2}$

7. $11\frac{1}{4} - 8\frac{1}{2}$

Guided Problem Solving

Use the questions to solve this problem.

8. Marvin and his mom are buying board for a tree house. They need $30\frac{1}{5}$ feet of board. They have $7\frac{3}{4}$ feet already. How much more board do they need?

   a. Understand What operation can you use to solve the problem?

   b. Plan What common denominator can you use?

   c. Solve Rename and subtract.

     Marvin and his mom need ◯ feet of board.

   d. Look Back Is your answer in simplest form?

(123) Math Talk The value of a number does not change when it is renamed correctly. Explain why.

► Practice and Problem Solving

Subtract. Write the difference in simplest form.

9. $9\frac{6}{8}$
$-2\frac{1}{2}$

10. $7\frac{1}{2}$
-3

11. $7\frac{3}{16}$
$-6\frac{1}{8}$

12. $3\frac{4}{5}$
$-1\frac{4}{20}$

13. $4\frac{1}{5}$
$-3\frac{3}{10}$

14. $4\frac{7}{10} - 1\frac{1}{5}$

15. $2\frac{1}{2} - 1\frac{2}{3}$

16. $6\frac{3}{4} - 3\frac{5}{8}$

17. $2\frac{5}{2} - 1\frac{4}{5}$

Algebra Expressions **Evaluate the expression**
when $a = 3\frac{3}{4}$, $b = 5\frac{1}{8}$, and $c = 1\frac{1}{2}$.

18. $a - c$ **19.** $b - a$ **20.** $b - c$ **21.** $(a + c) - b$

Write $>$, $<$ **or** $=$ **for the** ⬭.

22. $3\frac{3}{8} - 1\frac{1}{4}$ ⬭ $4 - 2\frac{2}{3}$ **23.** $8\frac{1}{4} - 3\frac{1}{2}$ ⬭ $6\frac{3}{4} - 2$ **24.** $6\frac{1}{4} - 4\frac{5}{8}$ ⬭ $10 - 7\frac{1}{8}$

 Science Link

Solve.

25. Steel is an alloy, or a mixture of pure metals. Another common alloy is bronze. Bronze is about $\frac{3}{5}$ copper. Rose gold is about $\frac{1}{4}$ copper. How much more copper is in bronze than rose gold?

26. Challenge Brass is about $\frac{2}{3}$ copper and $\frac{1}{3}$ zinc. Is the amount of copper in bronze from question 25 closer to the amount of copper in brass or the amount of zinc in brass? by how much?

The Golden Gate Bridge

- The main cables of the Golden Gate Bridge are made of steel.
- The major element in steel is iron.
- About 1% of the steel in the cables is made up of a combination of carbon, manganese, phosphorus, sulfur, and silicon.

Science **PS 1.c**

Spiral Review and Test Practice

Add. Write the sum in simplest form. KEY **NS 2.3** pages 170, 174

27. $8\frac{1}{4} + \frac{1}{4}$ **28.** $9\frac{5}{8} + 4\frac{1}{2}$ **29.** $2\frac{1}{4} + 8\frac{1}{2}$ **30.** $5\frac{2}{3} + \frac{1}{6}$ **31.** $1\frac{1}{2} + 1\frac{4}{5}$

Write the letter of the correct answer. KEY **NS 2.3**

32. Lim is laying a brick path in his garden. Today, Lim completed $10\frac{1}{3}$ feet. Yesterday, he laid $2\frac{1}{2}$ feet less than he did today. How many feet of brick did Lim lay yesterday?

A $7\frac{5}{6}$ **B** $8\frac{1}{6}$ **C** $8\frac{5}{6}$ **D** 9

Extra Practice See page 199, Set C.

Key Standards Review

Need Help?
See Key Standards Handbook.

Make a factor tree. Then write the prime factorization for each number using exponents. KEY **NS 1.4**

1. 9

2. 8

3. 17

4. 16

5. 14

6. 21

7. 18

8. 23

Add. Write each sum in simplest form. KEY **NS 2.3**

9. $2\frac{1}{6} + 3\frac{1}{6}$

10. $4\frac{3}{4} + 5\frac{3}{4}$

11. $3\frac{5}{8} + 2\frac{3}{8}$

12. $3\frac{3}{4} + 3\frac{7}{8}$

13. $4\frac{1}{2} + 5\frac{3}{4}$

14. $2\frac{1}{5} + 3\frac{2}{5}$

15. $2\frac{1}{2} + 3\frac{1}{8}$

16. $6\frac{3}{4} + 7\frac{5}{6}$

17. $4\frac{2}{3} + 8\frac{5}{9}$

Challenge — Mental Math

Count On, Count Back KEY **NS 2.3**

Add or subtract mixed numbers and fractions mentally by counting on or back to make the next whole.

Add $5\frac{3}{4} + \frac{3}{4}$.   Think: $5\frac{3}{4} + \frac{1}{4} = 6$; $6 + \frac{1}{2} = 6\frac{1}{2}$

Subtract $5\frac{2}{5} - \frac{3}{5}$.   Think: $5\frac{2}{5} - \frac{2}{5} = 5$; $5 - \frac{1}{5} = 4\frac{4}{5}$

Count on or back to find the answer.

1. $2\frac{5}{9} + \frac{5}{9}$

2. $4\frac{9}{16} + \frac{9}{16}$

3. $3\frac{2}{5} - \frac{4}{5}$

4. $5\frac{1}{8} - \frac{5}{8}$

5. $3\frac{4}{9} + \frac{7}{9}$

6. $7\frac{3}{5} - \frac{4}{5}$

7. $2\frac{5}{7} + \frac{5}{7}$

8. $4\frac{1}{6} - \frac{5}{6}$

9. $8\frac{1}{4} + \frac{3}{4}$

CA Standards

KEY NS 2.3 Solve simple problems, including ones arising in concrete situations, involving the addition and subtraction of fractions and mixed numbers (like and unlike denominators of 20 or less), and express answers in the simplest form.

MR 2.3 Use a variety of methods, such as words, numbers, symbols, charts, graphs, tables, diagrams, and models, to explain mathematical reasoning.

Also AF 1.0, KEY AF 1.2, MR 1.1, MR 1.2, MR 2.0, MR 2.4, MR 3.0, MR 3.1, MR 3.2, MR 3.3

Vocabulary

function rule

Problem Solving Strategy
Patterns in Tables

Objective Find and use patterns in tables to solve problems.

▶ **Learn by Example**

Joshua makes walking sticks. The table shows the height of four walking sticks with and without tops. He decided to make his friend a walking stick that is $5\frac{1}{12}$ feet high. What was the height of this walking stick before the top was attached?

Joshua's Walking Sticks	
Height with Top (x)	**Height without Top (y)**
$4\frac{11}{12}$ ft	$4\frac{2}{3}$ ft
5 ft	$4\frac{3}{4}$ ft
$5\frac{1}{2}$ ft	$5\frac{1}{4}$ ft
$5\frac{3}{8}$ ft	$5\frac{1}{8}$ ft

UNDERSTAND

The height of the walking stick with a top is $5\frac{1}{12}$ ft.

The height of the walking stick without a top is unknown.

PLAN

You need to know the height of the top.

Find a pattern in the table and write a **function rule**. Use the function rule to answer the question.

SOLVE

Look for a pattern by finding the difference between the height of walking sticks with and without tops.

Use the pattern to write a function rule using the two variables.

$$x - \frac{1}{4} = y$$

Use the function rule to answer the question.

$$5\frac{1}{12} - \frac{1}{4} = 4\frac{5}{6}$$

The walking stick was $4\frac{5}{6}$ feet before the top was attached.

LOOK BACK

Look back at the problem. Does your answer make sense?

Guided Problem Solving

Use the Ask Yourself questions to help you solve this problem.

1. The chart shows the lengths of some flutes, and the position of the first key, in inches, from the end of the flute. Where would the first key fall on a flute $15\frac{1}{2}$ inches long?

Flute Length (x)	$15\frac{3}{4}$	$15\frac{1}{4}$	$14\frac{3}{8}$	$16\frac{1}{2}$
Key Position (y)	$13\frac{5}{8}$	$13\frac{1}{8}$	$12\frac{1}{4}$	$14\frac{3}{8}$

 Math Talk How does a function rule show a pattern?

Ask Yourself
- Did I use the correct function rule for the pattern?
- What value am I looking for?
- Did I answer the question the problem asked?

Independent Problem Solving

Find a pattern. Write a function rule to solve. Explain why your answer makes sense.

2. Alejandro paints portraits of his friends. He puts each portrait in a frame. The table shows the height of each portrait, and its height when framed. What will be the height of a portrait $4\frac{1}{4}$ feet tall when framed?

Height Without Frame (x)	Height With Frame (y)
$4\frac{2}{3}$ ft	$5\frac{5}{12}$ ft
$5\frac{5}{12}$ ft	$6\frac{1}{6}$ ft
$3\frac{1}{2}$ ft	$4\frac{1}{4}$ ft
$6\frac{1}{3}$ ft	$7\frac{1}{12}$ ft

3. Mira takes the bus to her part-time job. The chart shows the length of her shifts for one week and her total work and travel time for each day. If Mira works a $3\frac{1}{2}$ hour shift, how long will she spend on work and travel?

Shift Time (s)	$2\frac{3}{4}$ hr	$5\frac{1}{2}$ hr	4 hr	$5\frac{3}{4}$ hr
Total Time (t)	$3\frac{5}{12}$ hr	$6\frac{1}{6}$ hr	$4\frac{2}{3}$ hr	$6\frac{5}{12}$ hr

4. **Multistep** Sandy and her friends are building a playhouse for a daycare center. Each vertical beam is sunk into the ground to keep it in place. The chart shows the length of several beams and their height above the ground. Simplify the fractions, and find the height above ground of a beam $9\frac{1}{4}$ feet long.

Length of Beam (l)	Height Above Ground (h)
$11\frac{5}{6}$ ft	$9\frac{4}{8}$ ft
8 ft	$5\frac{6}{9}$ ft
$12\frac{1}{2}$ ft	$10\frac{3}{18}$ ft
$11\frac{1}{12}$ ft	$8\frac{15}{20}$ ft

5. **Challenge** Convert the data in Problem 3 to minutes and solve the new problem. Write your answer in minutes.

6. **Create and Solve** Write a word problem that can be solved using the function rule $y = x - 1\frac{1}{2}$.

Reading & Writing Math

Vocabulary

Complete the labels to show how to subtract mixed numbers.

$$5\frac{1}{2} - 2\frac{3}{4} = \bigcirc$$

Step 1: Find a _____ .	$5\frac{1}{2} =$	$5\frac{\blacksquare}{4}$
	$-\ 2\frac{3}{4} = -$	$2\frac{\blacksquare}{4}$
Step 2: Write _____ .	$5\frac{1}{2} =$	$5\frac{2}{4}$
	$-\ 2\frac{3}{4} = -$	$2\frac{3}{4}$
Step 3: _____ mixed numbers.	$5\frac{1}{2} =$	$4\frac{6}{4}$
	$-\ 2\frac{3}{4} = -$	$2\frac{3}{4}$
Step 4: Subtract. Make sure your answer is in _____ .	$5\frac{1}{2} =$	$4\frac{6}{4}$
	$-\ 2\frac{3}{4} = -$	$2\frac{3}{4}$
		$2\frac{3}{4}$

Word Bank

improper fraction

common denominator

rename

equivalent fractions

mixed number

simplest form

Writing How is subtracting mixed numbers like adding mixed numbers? How is it different?

Reading Look for this book in your library.
The Number Devil: A Mathematical Adventure,
by Hans Magnus Enzensberger

 **CA Standards**

MR 2.3 Use a variety of methods, such as words, numbers, symbols, charts, graphs, tables, diagrams, and models, to explain mathematical reasoning.

Also NS 2.0, KEY NS 2.3

Standards-Based Extra Practice

Set A ——————————————————————— KEY **NS 2.3**, NS 2.0 page 188

Subtract. Check your answers.

1. $12 - 9\frac{1}{3}$ **2.** $7 - 2\frac{1}{4}$ **3.** $5 - \frac{3}{8}$ **4.** $19 - 14\frac{3}{5}$

5. $15 - 1\frac{1}{12}$ **6.** $5 - 3\frac{4}{5}$ **7.** $16 - \frac{3}{12}$ **8.** $11 - 2\frac{5}{6}$

Solve.

9. Jeremiah is building a tree house. The opening for the door is $2\frac{5}{8}$ feet wide. He has a board that is 6 feet wide. How much should Jeremiah cut off the board so it will fit in the opening?

Set B ——————————————————————— KEY **NS 2.3**, NS 2.0 page 190

Subtract. Write the difference in simplest form.

1. $5\frac{1}{3} - 3\frac{2}{3}$ **2.** $12\frac{3}{8} - 6\frac{7}{8}$ **3.** $9\frac{1}{5} - 3\frac{3}{5}$ **4.** $14\frac{5}{7} - 5\frac{6}{7}$

5. $34\frac{1}{4} - 17\frac{3}{4}$ **6.** $16\frac{1}{7} - 3\frac{4}{7}$ **7.** $18\frac{1}{6} - 2\frac{3}{6}$ **8.** $19\frac{1}{5} - 3\frac{3}{5}$

Solve.

9. Jackie made a chest out of wood. It took her $3\frac{1}{4}$ hours to design the chest and $1\frac{3}{4}$ hours to build the chest. How much longer did it take Jackie to design the chest than to build it?

Set C ——————————————————————— KEY **NS 2.3**, NS 2.0 page 192

Subtract. Write the difference in simplest form.

1. $6\frac{5}{6} - 3\frac{2}{3}$ **2.** $8\frac{1}{8} - 5\frac{3}{4}$ **3.** $2\frac{2}{7} - 1\frac{5}{14}$ **4.** $5\frac{3}{16} - 4\frac{3}{4}$

5. $8\frac{3}{5} - 2\frac{1}{10}$ **6.** $7\frac{1}{16} - 3\frac{2}{8}$ **7.** $7\frac{3}{4} - 3\frac{1}{8}$ **8.** $19\frac{1}{12} - 2\frac{2}{3}$

Write $>$, $<$ or $=$ for the ⬤.

9. $6\frac{1}{8} - 2\frac{1}{2}$ ⬤ $9 - 6\frac{1}{8}$ **10.** $8\frac{2}{3} - 1\frac{1}{3}$ ⬤ $19\frac{5}{6} - 12$ **11.** $3\frac{1}{4} - 1\frac{1}{2}$ ⬤ $4 - 1\frac{2}{5}$

Solve.

12. A basketball trophy is $8\frac{3}{16}$ inches tall. A soccer trophy is $7\frac{5}{8}$ inches tall. How much shorter is the soccer trophy than the basketball trophy?

Education Place
Visit www.eduplace.com/camap/
for **Extra Practice**.

Chapter Review/Test

Vocabulary and Concepts ——————————————— NS 1.0, MR 2.3

Write the best term to complete each sentence.

1. To subtract $1\frac{1}{8}$ from 4, rename 4 as a _____ number.

2. If the greatest common factor of the numerator and denominator of a fraction is 1, then the fraction is written in _____.

Skills ——————————————————————————— KEY NS 2.3

Subtract. Write the difference in simplest form.

3. $8 - 1\frac{1}{9}$

4. $18 - 5\frac{5}{6}$

5. $34\frac{1}{5} - 2\frac{4}{5}$

6. $5\frac{3}{16} - 1\frac{7}{16}$

7. $4\frac{1}{4} - 3\frac{1}{3}$

8. $6\frac{3}{5} - 1\frac{1}{2}$

9. $8\frac{3}{7} - 2\frac{3}{14}$

10. $78\frac{1}{6} - 59\frac{5}{12}$

Write >, < or = for the ⬤.

11. $8\frac{5}{12} - 5\frac{1}{12}$ ⬤ $6\frac{1}{6} - 2\frac{1}{3}$

12. $10\frac{3}{9} - 7\frac{2}{3}$ ⬤ $2\frac{5}{8} - 1\frac{1}{2}$

13. $3\frac{1}{2} - \frac{1}{4}$ ⬤ $6 - 2\frac{3}{4}$

Problem Solving and Reasoning ——————— KEY NS 2.3, KEY AF 1.5, MR 1.1, MR 2.3

Write a function rule to solve.

14. Gideon builds wooden boxes for his uncle's workshop. The table shows the length and height of each box. The width of each box remains the same. What would be the height of a box that is $23\frac{1}{4}$ inches long?

Box length (l)	Box height (h)
$5\frac{1}{4}$	$7\frac{11}{12}$
9	$11\frac{2}{3}$
$2\frac{1}{6}$	$4\frac{5}{6}$

15. Sarah helps her father build a deck by cutting boards of different lengths. The table shows the length of each piece of wood before and after it is cut. How long will a board $22\frac{3}{8}$ feet long be once Sarah has cut it?

Original board length (x)	New board length (y)
$15\frac{1}{8}$	$11\frac{7}{8}$
$17\frac{3}{4}$	$14\frac{1}{2}$
20	$16\frac{3}{4}$

Writing Math **Right or Wrong** Jacob says that $4\frac{1}{3} - 2\frac{2}{3} = 2\frac{1}{3}$. Is he correct? Explain.

Spiral Review and Test Practice

1. $54,200 - 31,168 =$

  A 23,168

  B 23,132

  C 23,032

  D 22,032

NS 1.0 page 68

---

2. What is the value of the expression $47 - (12 + 8) + 3$?

  A 70

  B 46

  C 30

  D 24

Test Tip
Remember to follow the order of operations.

NS 1.0 page 104

---

3. If $n = 4$, what is the value of $5n - 3$?

  A 2

  B 6

  C 17

  D 20

KEY AF 1.2 page 104

4. Ruben ran $\frac{2}{3}$ mile in the morning. He ran $\frac{1}{4}$ mile in the afternoon. How much farther did Ruben run in the morning than in the afternoon?

  A $\frac{1}{12}$ mile

  B $\frac{1}{3}$ mile

  C $\frac{5}{12}$ mile

  D $\frac{11}{12}$ mile

Test Tip
Look for word clues that help you decide what operation to use.

KEY NS 2.3 page 154

---

5. Sally poured $1\frac{5}{6}$ quarts of grape juice in a pitcher. She added $1\frac{1}{3}$ quarts of cranberry juice. How many quarts of juice are in the pitcher?

  A $\frac{1}{2}$ **C** $2\frac{2}{3}$

  B $2\frac{1}{6}$ **D** $3\frac{1}{6}$

KEY NS 2.3 page 174

---

6. $5 - 3\frac{1}{8} =$

  A $\frac{7}{8}$ **C** $2\frac{1}{8}$

  B $1\frac{7}{8}$ **D** $2\frac{7}{8}$

KEY NS 2.3 page 188

Education Place
Visit www.eduplace.com/camap/ for
Test-Taking Tips and **Extra Practice**.

Chapter 9 Spiral Review and Test Practice **201**

Unit 4 Review/Test

Vocabulary and Concepts ———————————————— KEY **NS 2.3** Chapters 7–8

Fill in the blank to complete each sentence.

1. A number that has a whole part and a fraction part is called a _____.

2. When you add two fractions, the answer is called the _____.

3. When you subtract two fractions, the answer is called the _____.

4. The top number in a fraction is called the _____.

5. The bottom number in a fraction is called the _____.

Skills ———————————————————————— KEY **NS 2.3** Chapters 7–8

Add. Write each answer in simplest form.

6. $\frac{2}{3} + \frac{1}{3}$ 7. $\frac{1}{5} + \frac{3}{5}$ 8. $\frac{2}{7} + \frac{1}{2}$ 9. $\frac{3}{8} + \frac{3}{4}$

10. $2\frac{3}{8} + 1\frac{5}{8}$ 11. $\frac{4}{7} + 6\frac{6}{7}$ 12. $2\frac{1}{2} + 4\frac{7}{8}$ 13. $\frac{4}{9} + 2\frac{2}{3}$

Subtract. Write each answer in simplest form. Chapters 7–9

14. $\frac{5}{8} - \frac{3}{8}$ 15. $\frac{7}{10} - \frac{5}{10}$ 16. $\frac{5}{8} - \frac{1}{4}$ 17. $\frac{2}{3} - \frac{1}{9}$

18. $6 - 2\frac{1}{3}$ 19. $4\frac{3}{5} - 2\frac{4}{5}$ 20. $6\frac{5}{7} - 3\frac{1}{2}$ 21. $4\frac{1}{6} - 1\frac{5}{9}$

Problem Solving and Reasoning ————————— KEY **NS 2.3**, **MR 1.0** Chapters 7–8

Solve.

22. Tom has to build a dog house in 3 days. He built $\frac{3}{8}$ of it on the first day and $\frac{1}{2}$ of it on the second day. How much does he have left to build?

23. Chad built a deck and a shed. He used $\frac{2}{3}$ of the wood for the deck and $\frac{1}{4}$ of it for the shed. How much of his wood did he use?

Solve.

24. Meghan ran $2\frac{1}{5}$ miles on Monday and $1\frac{2}{5}$ miles on Tuesday. How far did she run on both days?

25. Sheena exercised for $\frac{3}{4}$ of an hour on Saturday. Sunday she only exercised for $\frac{1}{3}$ of an hour. How much longer did she exercise on Saturday?

Writing Math Explain how you can find a common denominator.

Performance Assessment

KEY NS 2.3

Get Healthy, Get Rewards!

Jessica's aerobics teacher has created an exercise program. Every time Jessica exercises, she earns points. When she gets enough points, she can earn rewards.

Excerise	Length of time	reward points
jumping jacks	$\frac{1}{4}$ hour	10
jogging	$\frac{1}{3}$ hour	8
walking	$\frac{3}{4}$ hour	12
lift weights	$\frac{3}{4}$ hour	10
jump rope	$\frac{1}{5}$ hour	8

Reward	Points Needed
gift card	50
water bottle	25
cooler	40
bike	200
running shoes	100

Task	Information You Need
Use the information above and to the right. Figure out how long Jessica will have to do each of her exercises and how many points she will earn for each exercise.	Jessica wants at least enough points to earn a bike and a pair of running shoes.
	She only wants to walk, lift weights, and do jumping jacks.
	She wants to do each exercise for the same amount of time.

Greg Tang's Go Fast, Go Far

Unit 4 Mental Math Strategies

Place Value Multiply

These problems can be fast to do.
Be sure to think of place value.

Remember 10 × 10 = 100. To find 30 × 40,
I multiply 3 tens by 4 tens to get 12 hundreds.
My answer for 30 × 40 is 1,200.

1. 30 × 40 = 3 tens × 4 tens
     = 3 × 4 × tens × tens
     = 12 hundreds
     = 1,200

2. 80 × 60 = 8 tens × 6 tens
     = 8 × 6 × tens × tens
     = ▢ hundreds
     = ▢

3. 50 × 30 = ▢ tens × ▢ tens
     = ▢ × ▢ × tens × tens
     = ▢ hundreds
     = ▢

4. 50 × 40 = ▢ tens × ▢ tens
     = ▢ × ▢ × tens × tens
     = ▢ hundreds
     = ▢

Good job! Now try these!

5. 20 × 70 = ▢ hundreds
     = ▢

6. 30 × 80 = ▢ hundreds
     = ▢

7. 70 × 40 = ▢ hundreds
     = ▢

8. 60 × 60 = ▢ hundreds
     = ▢

Go Faster!

Take It Further!

Now try doing all the steps in your head!

9. 40 × 60   **10.** 90 × 30   **11.** 50 × 80   **12.** 70 × 60

Multiply and Divide Fractions

BIG IDEAS!

- When you multiply two fractions, the product is less than either fraction.

- Since division is another way of writing multiplication, you can rewrite division with fractions as multiplication with fractions.

Chapter 10
Multiply Fractions

Chapter 11
Divide Fractions

Songs and Games

Math Music Track 5:
Divide by a Fraction

eGames at
www.eduplace.com/camap/

Math Readers

Predict the Quotient

Object of the Game Determine which divisors will divide evenly into given dividends.

Materials
- Counters
- Workmat 1 (for recording)
- Learning Tool 17: Predict the Quotient
- Learning Tool 15: Number/Symbol Cards
  (1 set labeled 2–9)

Set Up

Players shuffle the number cards and place them face down in a stack. Each player gets a Predict the Quotient game board and will use Workmat 1.

Number of Players 2

How to Play

1 Players take turns picking a number card from the stack.

2 After players pick a card, they choose one number from their Predict the Quotient game board that they think is divisible by the number shown on the number card.

> A number is divisible by a second number if it can be divided by the second number without a remainder.

3 The player completes the division problem on their Workmat. If there is no remainder, the player places a counter on the game board.

4 The first player to cover all the spaces on his or her game board is the winner.

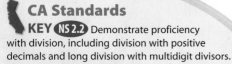

CA Standards
KEY NS 2.2 Demonstrate proficiency with division, including division with positive decimals and long division with multidigit divisors.

Also MR 1.0

Education Place
Visit www.eduplace.com/camap/ for
Brain Teasers and **eGames** to play.

Reading In both reading and math, you should ask yourself, "What's the point?" or "What is this all about?" If you can answer the question, you know the big idea.

Delia takes notes to help her understand the big ideas in math. She has just started to take notes on Unit 5.

Big Idea	Notes/Examples
• When you multiply two fractions, the product is less than the fraction.	When you multiply a counting number by a fraction, you are finding a part of the counting number, so the product is less than the counting number. $2 \times \frac{3}{4} = \frac{6}{4}$, or $1\frac{1}{2}$
• Since division is another way of writing multiplication, you can rewrite division with fractions as multiplication with fractions.	You can use an area model to see that $1\frac{1}{2}$ is $\frac{3}{4}$ of 2.

Writing Make a Big Idea Chart for Unit 5 like the one above. Make your own notes as you work through the unit.

If $\frac{3}{4}$ of 2 is a fractional part of 2, then $\frac{3}{4}$ of a fraction must be a fractional part of a fraction!

Multiply Fractions

Vocabulary and Concepts GRADE 4 NS 1.5, MR 2.3

Tell what the word means and give an example.

1. improper fraction

2. simplest form

Skills KEY NS 2.3

Complete. pages 30, 34, and 170

3. $1\frac{7}{8} + 6\frac{1}{8} = \blacksquare$

4. $\frac{4}{15} = \frac{20}{\blacksquare}$

5. $6 = \frac{\blacksquare}{6}$

6. $3\frac{8}{\blacksquare} = 3\frac{72}{99}$

7. $\frac{\blacksquare}{6} = \frac{63}{54}$

Write each mixed number as an equivalent improper fraction. page 30

8. $4\frac{2}{5}$

9. $6\frac{1}{3}$

Problem Solving and Reasoning KEY NS 2.3 page 170

10. A fruit punch recipe calls for $\frac{5}{8}$ cup orange juice and $1\frac{5}{8}$ cup cranberry juice. What is the total amount of both juices?

Vocabulary

Visualize It!

You can **multiply** to add fractions quickly.

$$\frac{3}{4} + \frac{3}{4} + \frac{3}{4} = 3 \times \frac{3}{4} = \frac{9}{4} \text{ or } 2\frac{1}{4}$$

Language Tip

Math words that look similar in English and Spanish often have the same meaning.

English	Spanish
factor	factor
multiply	multiplicar

See **English-Spanish Glossary** pages 628–642.

 Education Place Visit www.eduplace.com/camap/ for the **eGlossary** and **eGames**.

CA Standards

NS 2.4 Understand the concept of multiplication and division of fractions.

Also MR 1.1, MR 2.2, MR 2.3, MR 2.4, MR 2.6, MR 3.0, MR 3.2

Materials
Markers: blue and red

Hands On
Multiply Whole Numbers and Fractions

Objective Use an area model to multiply a whole number by a fraction.

▶ **Explore**

A juice container holds 2 quarts. It is $\frac{3}{4}$ full.
How many quarts of juice are in the container?
You need to find $\frac{3}{4} \times 2$.

Question How can you use an area model to multiply a fraction by a whole number?

1 Draw two squares.
Shade the two squares blue.

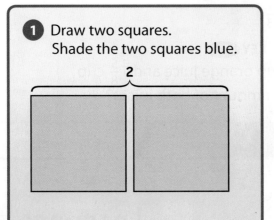

2 Draw lines to separate the squares into fourths. Shade $\frac{3}{4}$ of each square red.

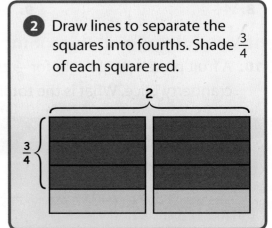

3 To find the product, count the fourths that are shaded purple.

$$\frac{3}{4} \times 2 = \frac{6}{4}$$

number of fourths shaded purple
number of fourths in 1 square

Write your answer in simplest form. $\frac{6}{4} = 1\frac{2}{4} = 1\frac{1}{2}$

4 Check your work.

$1 \times 2 = 2$, so $\frac{3}{4} \times 2 < 2$.

Is your answer less than 2?

Solution: There are $1\frac{1}{2}$ quarts of juice in the container.

▶ **Extend**

Write the answer in simplest form.

1.

$\frac{3}{8} \times 3 = \blacksquare$

2.
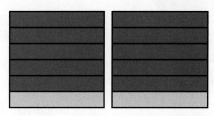

$\frac{5}{6} \times 2 = \blacksquare$

3.
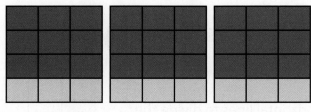

$\frac{3}{4} \times 3 = \blacksquare$

Use models. Write the answer in simplest form.

4. $\frac{1}{3} \times 4 = \blacksquare$

5. $\frac{2}{3} \times 3 = \blacksquare$

6. $\frac{1}{6} \times 2 = \blacksquare$

7. $3 \times \frac{3}{4} = \blacksquare$

8. $5 \times \frac{3}{5} = \blacksquare$

9. $2 \times \frac{3}{5} = \blacksquare$

10. $\frac{1}{2} \times 4 = \blacksquare$

11. $\frac{4}{5} \times 2 = \blacksquare$

12. $5 \times \frac{2}{3} = \blacksquare$

13. $\frac{1}{2} \times 3 = \blacksquare$

14. $\frac{2}{3} \times 9 = \blacksquare$

15. $\frac{1}{5} \times 8 = \blacksquare$

16. $2 \times \frac{4}{5} = \blacksquare$

17. $5 \times \frac{3}{4} = \blacksquare$

18. $0 \times \frac{1}{5} = \blacksquare$

> **Think**
> Because of the Commutative Property of Multiplication, $3 \times \frac{3}{4}$ and $\frac{3}{4} \times 3$ have the same product.

19. **X Algebra** Properties Explain how you found the answer to Exercise 18.

Writing Math

Generalize When you multiply a whole number (not zero) by a fraction less than one, will the product be less than or greater than the whole number? Explain.

CA Standards

NS 2.4 Understand the concept of multiplication and division of fractions.

NS 2.5 Compute and perform simple multiplication and division of fractions and apply those procedures to solving problems.

Also KEY NS 1.4, NS 2.0, MR 1.0, MR 2.0, MR 2.3

Materials
markers: blue and red

Multiply Fractions

Objective Find the product of two fractions.

▶ **Learn by Example**

A class spent $\frac{3}{4}$ hour practicing for a play. They spent $\frac{5}{6}$ of the time singing. What fraction of an hour did they spend singing? To find a fraction of a fraction, you find the product of the two fractions.

To find $\frac{5}{6}$ of $\frac{3}{4}$, multiply $\frac{5}{6} \times \frac{3}{4}$.

Different Ways to Multiply Fractions

Way 1 **Use an area model.**

1 Use horizontal lines to divide the square into sixths.

Use vertical lines to divide the square into fourths.

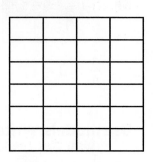

2 Shade the square to show $\frac{5}{6} \times \frac{3}{4}$.

$\frac{3}{4}$ of the square is shaded red.

$\frac{5}{6}$ of the square is shaded blue.

Count the boxes that are purple. $\frac{15}{24}$ or $\frac{5}{8}$ of the whole is shaded.

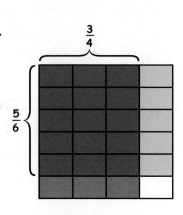

Way 2 **Use multiplication, then simplify.**

1 Multiply the numerators. Multiply the denominators.

$$\frac{5}{6} \times \frac{3}{4} = \frac{5 \times 3}{6 \times 4} = \frac{15}{24}$$

2 Simplify the product if possible.

$$\frac{15}{24} = \mathbf{1}\frac{3 \times 5}{3 \times 8} = \frac{5}{8}$$

$$\frac{15}{24} \overset{\div 3}{\underset{\div 3}{=}} \frac{5}{8}$$

Way 3   Simplify using prime factorization, then multiply.

1 Rewrite using prime factorization.

2 Use common factors to simplify.

3 Multiply.

$$\frac{5}{6} \times \frac{3}{4} = \frac{5 \times 3}{2 \times 3 \times 2 \times 2}$$

$$\frac{5}{6} \times \frac{3}{4} = \frac{5 \times \overset{1}{\cancel{3}}}{2 \times \underset{1}{\cancel{3}} \times 2 \times 2}$$

$$\frac{5 \times 1}{2 \times 1 \times 2 \times 2} = \frac{5}{8}$$

Solution: The class spent $\frac{5}{8}$ hour singing.

▶ Guided Practice

Multiply. Write the answer in simplest form.

1. $\frac{2}{3} \times \frac{3}{5}$ **2.** $\frac{3}{8} \times \frac{4}{5}$ **3.** $\frac{5}{6} \times \frac{3}{10}$

Ask Yourself
• Can I use prime factorization?
• Did I write my answer in simplest form?

Guided Problem Solving

Use the questions to solve this problem.

4. Two fifths of a class is in the drama club. One fourth of the drama club are in a play. What fraction of the class is in a play?

   a. Understand What do you need to find?

   b. Plan What strategy will you choose?

   c. Solve Use your strategy to solve. $\frac{1}{4} \times \frac{2}{5} = \bigcirc$

   d. Look How can you check your answer?

(123) Math Talk When you simplify $\frac{5 \times 3}{2 \times 3 \times 2 \times 2}$, why can you cross out those factors that are common to the numerator and denominator?

▶ Practice and Problem Solving

Multiply. Write the answer in simplest form.

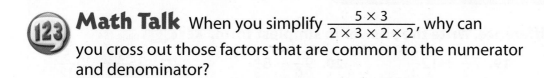

5. $\frac{1}{5} \times \frac{5}{8}$ **6.** $\frac{2}{5} \times \frac{5}{8}$ **7.** $\frac{3}{5} \times \frac{4}{7}$ **8.** $\frac{4}{5} \times \frac{5}{12}$

9. $\frac{1}{8} \cdot 6$ **10.** $\frac{3}{8} \cdot 4$ **11.** $9 \cdot \frac{5}{8}$ **12.** $8 \cdot \frac{1}{6}$

Solve. Write your answer in simplest form.

13. A recipe calls for $\frac{1}{2}$ cup of flour. If you cut the recipe in half, how much flour do you need?

14. Mrs. Alonzo bought $\frac{3}{4}$ yard of fabric. She used $\frac{1}{2}$ of it. How much fabric does she have left?

 Science Link

Solve. Show your work.

15. Half of the water taken from the Colorado River each year is shared by California, Arizona, and Nevada. California gets about $\frac{3}{5}$ of that share. How much of the water taken from the Colorado River is used in California each year?

16. The total length of the Colorado River is about 1,500 miles. About $\frac{1}{3}$ of the Colorado River runs through Arizona. Approximately how many miles of the river run through Arizona?

17. On average, each person in San Diego uses about 88 gallons of water each day. How much water would each person need to conserve in order to save $\frac{1}{8}$ of the water used in San Diego?

Colorado River

- The Colorado River flows through or touches Colorado, Utah, Nevada, Arizona, and California.
- The river supplies water to almost all of the states in the Southwest.

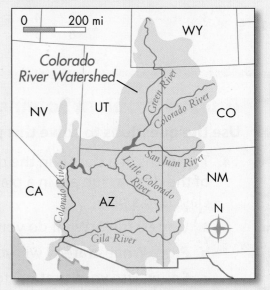

Science ES 3.d, 3.e

 Spiral Review and Test Practice

Find the sum or difference. Write the answer in simplest form. KEY **NS 2.3** page 154

18. $5\frac{3}{4} + 4\frac{1}{2}$

19. $7\frac{1}{2} + 12\frac{2}{3}$

20. $9\frac{1}{6} - 8\frac{2}{3}$

21. $25\frac{3}{4} - 20\frac{5}{12}$

22. $6\frac{3}{4} + 5\frac{7}{12}$

23. $8\frac{2}{3} - 4\frac{1}{9}$

24. $3\frac{3}{6} + 2\frac{2}{3}$

25. $10\frac{2}{5} - 8\frac{3}{10}$

Write the letter of the correct answer. NS 2.4

26. $\frac{1}{3} \cdot \frac{1}{5} =$

A $\frac{1}{15}$ **B** $\frac{2}{15}$ **C** $\frac{2}{8}$ **D** $\frac{1}{8}$

Extra Practice See page 223, Set B.

Key Standards Review

Need Help?
See Key Standards Handbook.

Write each fraction or decimal as a mixed number in simplest form. Then label each point on the number line. **KEY NS 1.5**

1.

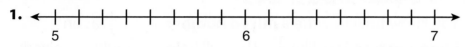

5   6   7

A. $\dfrac{44}{8}$ **B.** 6.75   **C.** $\dfrac{55}{8}$ **D.** 5.25

Subtract. Write each difference in simplest form. **KEY NS 2.3**

2. $2\dfrac{1}{3} - \dfrac{2}{3}$ **3.** $5\dfrac{1}{6} - 2\dfrac{5}{6}$ **4.** $3\dfrac{1}{4} - 1\dfrac{3}{8}$

5. $9\dfrac{5}{6} - 4\dfrac{1}{3}$ **6.** $5\dfrac{3}{8} - 4\dfrac{7}{8}$ **7.** $4\dfrac{1}{8} - 2\dfrac{7}{16}$

8. $8\dfrac{1}{8} - 5\dfrac{7}{8}$ **9.** $3\dfrac{1}{12} - 1\dfrac{5}{6}$ **10.** $4\dfrac{5}{6} - 2\dfrac{1}{6}$

Challenge Problem Solving

Fraction Detective NS 2.5, KEY NS 2.3

Use the fractions at the right to answer Exercises 1–4. Find two fractions to fit each description.

$\dfrac{1}{2}$ $\dfrac{1}{3}$ $\dfrac{1}{4}$ $\dfrac{2}{3}$ $\dfrac{3}{4}$

1. The product is $\dfrac{1}{8}$, and the sum is $\dfrac{3}{4}$.

2. Both the product and the difference are equal to $\dfrac{1}{12}$.

3. The product is $\dfrac{1}{2}$, and the difference is $\dfrac{1}{12}$.

4. The product is $\dfrac{1}{6}$, and the sum is less than 1.

CA Standards

NS 2.5 Compute and perform simple multiplication and division of fractions and apply those procedures to solving problems.

NS 2.4 Understand the concept of multiplication and division of fractions.

Also KEY **NS 1.4**, KEY **AF 1.5**, MR 1.0, MR 2.0, MR 2.3

Vocabulary

mixed number

improper fraction

Multiply with Mixed Numbers

Objective Find products of fractions and mixed numbers.

▶ **Learn by Example**

You know how to write a **mixed number**, like $2\frac{3}{4}$, as an **improper fraction**, like $\frac{11}{4}$. This will help you multiply mixed numbers.

> Max will juggle and do yo-yo tricks at his brother's party. The party will last $1\frac{3}{4}$ hours. Max plans to spend $\frac{2}{3}$ of that time performing. How long will Max perform?

Multiply. $\frac{2}{3} \times 1\frac{3}{4} = n$

---

1 Write the mixed number as an improper fraction.

$1\frac{3}{4} = \frac{7}{4}$

$(4 \times 1) + 3 = 7$

or

$1\frac{3}{4} = \frac{4}{4} + \frac{3}{4} = \frac{7}{4}$

---

2 Use common factors to simplify. Then multiply.

$\frac{2}{3} \times \frac{7}{4} = \frac{\overset{1}{\cancel{2}} \times 7}{3 \times \underset{1}{\cancel{2}} \times 2}$

$= \frac{7}{6}$

---

3 Simplify. Write the fraction as a mixed number if you can.

$\frac{7}{6} = 1\frac{1}{6}$

$\begin{array}{r} 1\frac{1}{6} \\ 6\overline{)7} \\ -6 \\ \hline 1 \end{array}$

or

$\frac{7}{6} = \frac{6}{6} + \frac{1}{6} = 1\frac{1}{6}$

Solution: Max will perform for $1\frac{1}{6}$ hours.

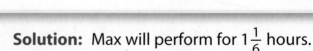

Multiply. Write the answer in simplest form.

1. $\frac{4}{5} \times 1\frac{2}{3}$

2. $2\frac{3}{4} \times 1\frac{1}{2}$

3. $6 \times 2\frac{3}{4}$

⟨x⟩ Algebra Functions **Complete the function table.**
Write the answer in simplest form.

4.

Rule: $y = 1\frac{1}{2}x$			
x	$\frac{3}{4}$	$1\frac{1}{2}$	4	5
y				

5.

Rule: $2\frac{3}{4}x$			
x	$\frac{1}{4}$	$\frac{3}{4}$	$1\frac{1}{2}$	2
y				

(123) Math Talk Is the product of two mixed numbers always greater than 1?

► **Practice and Problem Solving**

Multiply. Write the answer in simplest form.

6. $1\frac{5}{6} \times \frac{1}{3}$

7. $\frac{3}{4} \times 2\frac{1}{3}$

8. $1\frac{7}{9} \times 2$

9. $5 \times 4\frac{1}{5}$

10. $2\frac{1}{3} \times 2\frac{3}{4}$

11. $3\frac{1}{2} \times \frac{4}{5}$

12. $3 \times 4\frac{5}{6}$

13. $2\frac{5}{6} \times 2\frac{1}{4}$

14. $\frac{3}{8} \cdot 1\frac{1}{4}$

15. $3\frac{5}{8} \cdot 2\frac{1}{2}$

16. $1\frac{7}{9} \cdot \frac{1}{12}$

17. $3\frac{1}{8} \cdot 4$

18. $2\frac{1}{5} \cdot \frac{2}{3}$

19. $3 \cdot 2\frac{2}{3}$

20. $4\frac{5}{8} \cdot 2\frac{2}{3}$

Solve.

21. **Measurement** For the yo-yo trick, "Rock the Baby," Max places his fingers halfway down the string. The string is $2\frac{3}{4}$ feet long. How long is each half?

22. Vicki bought a yo-yo with a string that was $\frac{5}{8}$ of her height. Use the photo to the right to help you find the length of the string.

23. A clown worked 40 jobs this year. $\frac{5}{8}$ were from repeat customers. How many of the clown's jobs were from new customers?

24. **Right or Wrong?** A clown earned $12 for each hour he worked. He worked $1\frac{1}{2}$ hours, so he expected to be paid $16. Was he right? Explain.

Vicki's height

$4\frac{4}{5}$ ft

Algebra Functions Copy and complete the function table.
Write the answers in simplest form.

25.

Rule: $y = \frac{1}{4}x$			
x	$2\frac{1}{8}$	$2\frac{1}{4}$	$2\frac{3}{8}$	$2\frac{1}{2}$
y				

26.

Rule: $y = 8x$			
x	$3\frac{3}{4}$	4	$4\frac{1}{4}$	$4\frac{1}{2}$
y				

 Real World Data

Solve. Show your work.

27. The record high temperature in Sacramento is 43°C. How much greater is the hottest temperature on Earth?

28. California is the most populous state in the United States. The population of the entire country is about $8\frac{1}{3}$ times as large as California's. About how many people live in the United States?

29. The oldest living tree on earth is about $\frac{1}{10}$ as tall as the tallest tree on earth. Approximately how tall is the oldest living tree on earth?

Bristlecone pine tree, White Mountains, CA

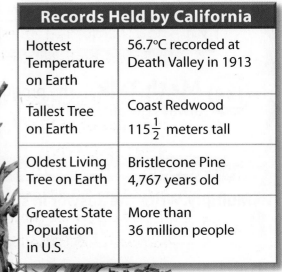

Records Held by California	
Hottest Temperature on Earth	56.7°C recorded at Death Valley in 1913
Tallest Tree on Earth	Coast Redwood $115\frac{1}{2}$ meters tall
Oldest Living Tree on Earth	Bristlecone Pine 4,767 years old
Greatest State Population in U.S.	More than 36 million people

Spiral Review and Test Practice

Subtract. Write the answer in simplest form. KEY **NS 2.3** page 192

30. $12 - \frac{5}{6}$

31. $7\frac{1}{2} - 3\frac{3}{4}$

32. $12\frac{2}{3} - 9\frac{5}{6}$

33. $11\frac{1}{4} - 9$

Write the letter of the correct answer. NS 2.5

34. $10 \times 1\frac{1}{3} =$

    A $2\frac{1}{3}$ **B** $8\frac{2}{3}$ **C** 10 **D** $13\frac{1}{3}$

Extra Practice See page 223, Set C.

Zoom!

A test driver tests all different kinds of new cars. He might test a family car one week and an exotic sports car the next week.

1. When Bill test drives a family car, he does $\frac{1}{5}$ city driving, $\frac{1}{5}$ suburban driving, and $\frac{3}{5}$ highway driving. If he drives for $12\frac{1}{3}$ miles, how many miles are highway driving?

2. One of the sports cars Bill tests sells for $4\frac{3}{4}$ times the value of a $10,000 family car. What is the value of the sports car?

3. Speed tests may take place on closed airport runways. If $\frac{1}{2}$ of a $2\frac{1}{4}$-mile runway at Los Angeles International Airport (LAX) is used for a test drive, how many miles long is the test drive?

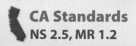

CA Standards
NS 2.5, MR 1.2

Problem Solving

Objective Use skills and strategies to solve word problems.

Carlsbad, CA

CA Standards
MR 1.0, MR 1.2,
MR 2.0, MR 2.3,
NS 2.4, NS 1.0,
Prepares for
KEY **NS1.4**, NS 2.0,
KEY **NS2.3**, SDAP 1.0

Students get 'hands-on' experience during tours at Carlsbad's Museum of Making Music.

At Carlsbad's Museum of Making Music, visitors learn how popular music was shaped. Special exhibits and performances are regularly held at the museum. In the Music Ventures Fieldtrip Program, students can try out the instruments themselves.

Solve. Tell which strategy or method you used.

1. Three-sixths of the orchestra plays woodwind instruments. If $\frac{1}{4}$ of them are flute players, what fraction of the orchestra are flute players? Write the fraction in simplest form.

2. Brad's orchestra has 60 musicians and Clara's orchestra has 80 musicians. If both orchestras each have 20 violinists, whose orchestra has the greater fraction of violinists?

3. A concert hall seats 1,126 people. Each ticket costs $100. If the concert hall plays twenty sold-out shows, how much money did the concert hall collect from ticket sales?

4. Suppose 36 instruments are on display in equal rows. How many different arrangements of instruments can be made if each row contains at least 2 instruments?

Problem Solving On Tests

Select a Strategy
- Draw a Picture
- Write an Equation
- Work Backward
- Guess and Check
- Choose the Operation

1. Jan works 4 hours more than Julie. If x equals Jan's hours and y equals Julie's hours, which equation could have been used to create this function table?

   A $y = x + 6$

   B $y = x - 6$

   C $y = x - 4$

   D $y = x + 4$

   KEY **AF 1.5** page 112

2. Jay wrote this equation for Bart to solve. What value for w makes this equation true?

   $$(27 \times 5) \times w = 27 \times (5 \times 20)$$

   A 4   **B** 5   **C** 20   **D** 100

   KEY **AF 1.2** page 128

3. Eric mixed $\frac{5}{8}$ pint of orange juice with $\frac{1}{8}$ pint of water. What fraction of a pint was his drink?

   A $\frac{3}{8}$ pint **B** $\frac{1}{2}$ pint **C** $\frac{3}{4}$ pint **D** $\frac{7}{8}$ pint

   KEY **NS 2.3** page 148

4. Juanita jogged $\frac{2}{3}$ mile on Tuesday. On Wednesday, she jogged $\frac{1}{2}$ mile. How much farther did she jog on Tuesday than on Wednesday?

   A $\frac{1}{6}$ mile

   B $\frac{1}{5}$ mile

   C $\frac{1}{3}$ mile

   D $\frac{3}{5}$ mile

   Test Tip
   Remember to make equivalent fractions with like denominators before adding or subtracting.

   KEY **NS 2.3** page 154

5. Mrs. Parker needs $2\frac{1}{4}$ yards of blue material to make a curtain, and $\frac{2}{3}$ yard of white material to make the trim. What is the total amount of material Mrs. Parker needs to buy?

   A $2\frac{3}{7}$ yards   **C** $2\frac{7}{12}$ yards

   B $2\frac{3}{12}$ yards   **D** $2\frac{11}{12}$ yards

   KEY **NS 2.3** page 174

6. Coach Connor brought $3\frac{1}{2}$ gallons of water to the soccer game. His assistant bought $2\frac{3}{4}$ gallons of water. What was the total amount of water the coaches brought to the game?

   A $5\frac{5}{8}$ gallons   **C** 6 gallons

   B $5\frac{2}{3}$ gallons   **D** $6\frac{1}{4}$ gallons

   KEY **NS 2.3** page 174

7. Carlos has $4\frac{1}{5}$ pounds of potatoes. If he uses $2\frac{3}{5}$ pounds of the potatoes to make potato salad, how many pounds of potatoes will he have left?

   A $1\frac{2}{5}$ pounds   **C** $2\frac{2}{5}$ pounds

   B $1\frac{3}{5}$ pounds   **D** $2\frac{3}{5}$ pounds

   KEY **NS 2.3** page 190

Education Place
Visit www.eduplace.com/camap/ for
Test-Taking Tips and **Extra Practice**.

Reading & Writing Math

Vocabulary

When you multiply mixed numbers, rewrite them as **improper fractions**. Use common factors to **simplify**, then multiply. Write your product in **simplest form**.

Complete the table to find the product.

$1\frac{1}{2} \times 1\frac{1}{6}$	
Step 1: Rewrite mixed numbers as improper fractions.	$1\frac{1}{2} = \dfrac{\blacksquare}{\blacksquare}$ $1\frac{1}{6} = \dfrac{\blacksquare}{\blacksquare}$
Step 2: Use common factors to simplify. Then multiply.	
Step 3: Simplify. Write the fraction as a mixed number if you can.	

Writing Write a problem that could be solved by multiplying mixed numbers. Challenge a classmate to solve your problem.

Reading Look for this book in your library. *Further Adventures of Penrose the Mathematical Cat* by Theoni Pappas

CA Standards

MR 2.3 Use a variety of methods, such as words, numbers, symbols, charts, graphs, tables, diagrams, and models, to explain mathematical reasoning.

Also NS 2.4, NS 2.5

 Standards-Based Extra Practice

Set A —— NS 2.4 page 210

Write each answer in simplest form.

1. $3 \times \frac{1}{2} = \blacksquare$

2. $\frac{1}{4} \times 4 = \blacksquare$

Use models. Write the answer in simplest form.

3. $2 \times \frac{3}{5}$

4. $4 \times \frac{1}{3}$

5. $\frac{4}{5} \times 5$

6. $\frac{3}{4} \times 5$

7. $\frac{1}{3} \times 6$

8. $7 \times \frac{2}{3}$

9. $8 \times \frac{3}{5}$

10. $\frac{5}{7} \times 10$

Set B —— NS 2.5 page 212

Multiply. Write your answer in simplest form.

1. $\frac{5}{6} \times \frac{2}{3}$

2. $\frac{3}{4} \times \frac{7}{8}$

3. $\frac{3}{10} \times \frac{4}{5}$

4. $\frac{1}{2} \times \frac{4}{9}$

5. $\frac{3}{8} \times \frac{1}{3}$

6. $\frac{1}{9} \times \frac{5}{8}$

7. $\frac{2}{7} \times \frac{4}{8}$

8. $\frac{2}{5} \times \frac{3}{8}$

Solve.

9. Justin played his guitar for $\frac{3}{4}$ hour. He played his favorite song for $\frac{1}{3}$ of that time. How much time did Justin spend playing his favorite song?

Set C ———————————————————————————————————— NS 2.5, NS 2.4 page 216

Multiply. Write the answer in simplest form.

1. $\frac{1}{3} \times 4\frac{2}{3}$

2. $4\frac{1}{5} \times 6\frac{2}{3}$

3. $4 \times 1\frac{1}{2}$

4. $4\frac{1}{6} \times 2$

5. $5\frac{5}{6} \times 4\frac{4}{5}$

6. $7\frac{2}{7} \times 4\frac{5}{9}$

7. $8 \times 5\frac{3}{4}$

8. $12 \times 2\frac{1}{6}$

Solve.

9. Mr. Santana travels $12\frac{1}{2}$ miles to his job. He rides a bus for $\frac{5}{6}$ of the distance. How many miles does Mr. Santana ride the bus?

Education Place
Visit www.eduplace.com/camap/
for **Extra Practice**.

Chapter 10 Extra Practice **223**

Chapter Review/Test

Vocabulary and Concepts ————————————— NS 2.4, MR 2.3

Write the best word to complete each sentence.

1. To find $\frac{3}{4}$ of $\frac{2}{5}$, _____ the fractions.

2. To multiply two mixed numbers, rewrite the mixed numbers as _____ fractions.

Skills ————————————————————————— NS 2.4, NS 2.5

Multiply. Write the answer in simplest form.

3. $6 \times \frac{1}{4}$

4. $2 \times \frac{2}{3}$

5. $5 \times \frac{1}{10}$

6. $\frac{3}{4} \times 28$

7. $\frac{2}{5} \times 12$

8. $\frac{1}{3} \times \frac{2}{5}$

9. $\frac{2}{3} \times \frac{3}{8}$

10. $\frac{4}{7} \times \frac{1}{2}$

11. $\frac{2}{9} \times \frac{3}{4}$

12. $\frac{5}{6} \times \frac{3}{8}$

13. $2\frac{1}{3} \times \frac{4}{5}$

14. $\frac{1}{7} \times 2\frac{1}{3}$

Problem Solving and Reasoning ————— NS 2.4, NS 2.5, MR 1.0, MR 2.0, MR 2.3

Solve.

15. There are 36 swimmers on the swim team. Five-ninths of the swimmers are girls. How many of the swimmers are girls?

16. A bottle of energy drink contains $\frac{9}{10}$ liter. Coach Donavan buys 15 bottles. How many liters of energy drink did he buy?

17. A museum has 240 paintings. Of these, $\frac{1}{4}$ were painted by women. One-half of these paintings are of flowers. How many paintings of flowers are there?

18. Last year, $\frac{1}{5}$ of the rooms at the museum were closed for repairs. If the museum has 35 rooms, how many of the rooms were open last year?

19. Mr. Lennox has three boards, each of which measures $4\frac{1}{2}$ feet long. He needs $2\frac{1}{3}$ of the boards for the top of a railing he is building. How long is the railing?

20. The museum tour lasts $\frac{2}{5}$ of an hour. The tour guide gives 10 tours every day. How many hours does she spend giving tours each week?

Writing Math Adrianna multiplied $2\frac{1}{2} \times \frac{1}{5}$ and got $2\frac{1}{10}$. Explain what Adrianna did wrong, and describe how you would find the correct answer.

Spiral Review and Test Practice

$\frac{3}{10} = \frac{1}{5}$

1. $3,207 - 1,508 =$

  A 1,699

  B 1,709

  C 1,799

  D 2,301

NS 1.0 page 126

2. $37 + 21 = \square + 37$

  A 16

  B 21

  C 37

  D 58

KEY AF 1.2 page 126

3. Which of the following is another way to write $(4 \times 5) \times 2$?

  A $(4 + 5) + 2$

  B $4 \times (2 \times 5)$

  C $(4 \times 5) + 2$

  D $(3 \times 4) \times 3$

NS 1.0 page 128

4. Edna did two chores in the garden. She planted flowers for $\frac{3}{10}$ hour and weeded for $\frac{1}{10}$ hour. How much time did Edna spend working in the garden?

  A $\frac{1}{5}$ hour   **C** $\frac{1}{2}$ hour

  B $\frac{2}{5}$ hour   **D** $\frac{4}{5}$ hour

KEY NS 2.3 page 148

5. $4\frac{3}{8} - 2\frac{5}{8} =$

$1\frac{6}{8} =$

  A $\frac{3}{4}$

  B 1

  C $1\frac{3}{4}$

  D $2\frac{1}{4}$

> **Test Tip**
> You can check your answer by using the inverse operation.

KEY NS 2.3 page 190

6. $\frac{1}{5} \cdot \frac{1}{4} =$

  A 1

  B $\frac{2}{9}$

  C $\frac{1}{9}$

  D $\frac{1}{20}$

> **Test Tip**
> The symbol • means to multiply.

NS 2.5 page 212

Education Place
Visit www.eduplace.com/camap/ for
Test-Taking Tips and **Extra Practice.**

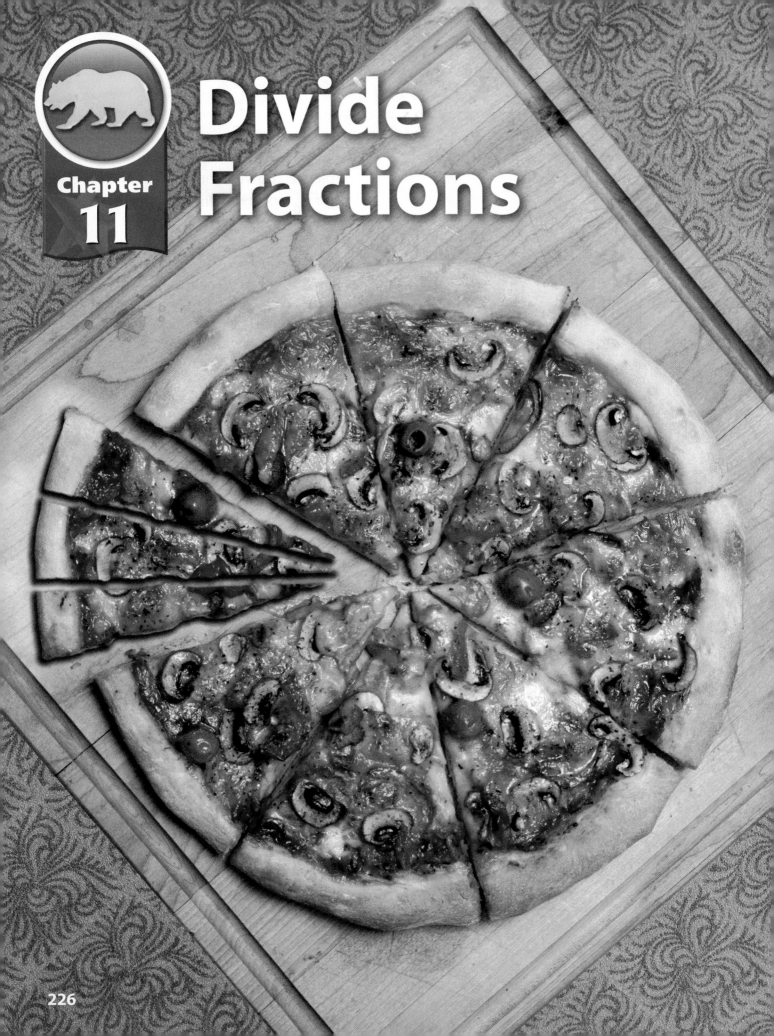

Chapter 11

Divide Fractions

Vocabulary and Concepts GRADE 4 NS 1.5, MR 2.3

Write the best word to complete each sentence.

1. To find a fraction of a fraction, you find the _____ of the two fractions.

2. A fraction is in _____ when the greatest common factor of its numerator and denominator is 1.

Skills NS 2.4 pages 210, 212, and 216

Multiply. Write each number in simplest form.

3. $3 \times \frac{2}{3}$

4. $\frac{1}{6} \times \frac{3}{4}$

5. $3\frac{1}{5} \times \frac{5}{8}$

6. $\frac{1}{2} \times \frac{1}{2}$

7. $2 \times 2\frac{2}{7}$

8. $5 \times \frac{3}{4}$

9. $4\frac{1}{2} \times 2\frac{1}{3}$

Problem Solving and Reasoning NS 2.4

10. A piece of ribbon is $\frac{1}{2}$ yard long. Mary uses $\frac{3}{4}$ of the piece of ribbon to trim her dress. How long was the piece of ribbon Mary used?

Vocabulary

Visualize It!

Divide a Whole Number by a Unit Fraction

Using a model.

$3 \div \frac{1}{5}$

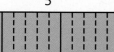

15 parts in all

$3 \div \frac{1}{5} = 15$

Using the **reciprocal**.

$3 \div \frac{1}{5}$

$3 \times \frac{5}{1}$

Find the reciprocal of $\frac{1}{5}$, then multiply.

Language Tip

Math words that look similar in English and Spanish often have the same meaning.

English	Spanish
equivalent	equivalente
fraction	fracción

See **English-Spanish Glossary** pages 628–642.

Education Place Visit www.eduplace.com/camap/ for the **eGlossary** and **eGames**.

CA Standards MR 2.3 Use a variety of methods, such as words, numbers, symbols, charts, graphs, tables, diagrams, and models, to explain mathematical reasoning. **Also NS 2.4**

Chapter 11   227

CA Standards

NS 2.4 Understand the concept of multiplication and division of fractions.

NS 2.5 Compute and perform simple multiplication and division of fractions and apply these procedures to solving problems.

Also MR 2.0, MR 2.3, MR 2.6, NS 1.0, NS 2.0

Vocabulary

unit fraction

Materials
Fraction Tiles

Think
How many half-cup scoops make four cups?

Hands On
Divide by a Unit Fraction

Objective Use models to divide with unit fractions.

▶ **Explore**

Krista is making bread. The recipe calls for 4 cups of flour. Krista has a measuring scoop that is $\frac{1}{2}$ cup. How many scoops of flour should Krista use?

Question How can you use fraction strips to divide a whole number by a **unit fraction**?

1 Use the fraction strips. Use 1 strip to model each cup of flour.

| 1 |
| 1 |
| 1 |
| 1 |

2 Model Krista's scoop with a fraction strip.

| $\frac{1}{2}$ | $\frac{1}{2}$ |

3 Cover the four 1 strips with $\frac{1}{2}$ strips. Count how many $\frac{1}{2}$ strips there are.

$\frac{1}{2}$	$\frac{1}{2}$
$\frac{1}{2}$	$\frac{1}{2}$
$\frac{1}{2}$	$\frac{1}{2}$
$\frac{1}{2}$	$\frac{1}{2}$

4 Record.

$$4 \div \frac{1}{2} = 8$$

Check
Check by multiplying.
$$8 \times \frac{1}{2} = 4$$

Solution: Krista needs to scoop 8 times to have 4 cups of flour.

What if Krista had to use a $\frac{1}{3}$ cup scoop to measure the 4 cups of flour? How many $\frac{1}{3}$ cup scoops of flour does Krista need?

1 Use fraction strips to model 4 cups of flour.

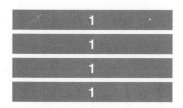

2 Which fraction strips can you use to model the $\frac{1}{3}$ cup scoops?

How many thirds can you take out of 4 whole strips?

3 Model 4 cups divided by $\frac{1}{3}$ cup with fraction strips.

4 Write the equation:

$4 \div \frac{1}{3} = \bigcirc$

Check by multiplying.

▶ **Extend**

Match each question with one of the models. Write A, B, or C. Then write a division equation and solve.

1. What is 3 divided by $\frac{1}{4}$?   **2.** What is 3 divided by $\frac{1}{2}$?   **3.** What is 3 divided by $\frac{1}{6}$?

A

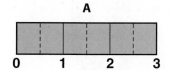

B

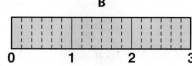

C

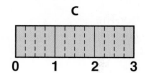

Model with fraction strips. Solve.

4. $1 \div \frac{1}{2} = \blacksquare$ **5.** $1 \div \frac{1}{3} = \blacksquare$ **6.** $1 \div \frac{1}{4} = \blacksquare$ **7.** $2 \div \frac{1}{5} = \blacksquare$

8. $3 \div \frac{1}{6} = \blacksquare$ **9.** $3 \div \frac{1}{2} = \blacksquare$ **10.** $5 \div \frac{1}{8} = \blacksquare$ **11.** $5 \div \frac{1}{3} = \blacksquare$

12. $4 \div \frac{1}{3} = \blacksquare$ **13.** $4 \div \frac{1}{4} = \blacksquare$ **14.** $6 \div \frac{1}{7} = \blacksquare$ **15.** $2 \div \frac{1}{9} = \blacksquare$

16. $4 \div \frac{1}{6} = \blacksquare$ **17.** $8 \div \frac{1}{3} = \blacksquare$ **18.** $8 \div \frac{1}{4} = \blacksquare$ **19.** $3 \div \frac{1}{4} = \blacksquare$

Writing Math

Explain How would you explain to another student how to divide a whole number by a unit fraction?

CA Standards

NS 2.5 Compute and perform simple multiplication and division of fractions and apply these procedures to solving problems.

NS 2.4 Understand the concept of multiplication and division of fractions.

Also KEY **AF 1.5**, **MR 1.0**, **MR 2.0, MR 2.3, MR 2.6, NS 2.0**

Vocabulary

reciprocal

> **Think**
>
> 3 is the divisor. The reciprocal of 3 is $\frac{1}{3}$.

Divide Fractions by a Counting Number

Objective Use reciprocals to divide fractions by a counting number.

▶ **Learn by Example**

The **reciprocal** of $\frac{2}{3}$ is $\frac{3}{2}$. The reciprocal of 4 is $\frac{1}{4}$.

The product of a fraction and its reciprocal is always 1.

$$\frac{2}{3} \times \frac{3}{2} = \frac{\overset{1}{2} \times \overset{1}{3}}{\underset{1}{3} \times \underset{1}{2}} = 1 \qquad \frac{4}{1} \times \frac{1}{4} = \frac{\overset{1}{4} \times 1}{1 \times \underset{1}{4}} = 1$$

Three friends want to share $\frac{1}{2}$ of a pizza equally. How much pizza does each person get?

Different Ways to Divide a Fraction by a Counting Number

Way 1 **Use a model.**

  ❶ Show $\frac{1}{2}$ of a pizza.   ❷ Make 3 equal portions.

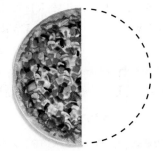 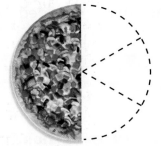

- - - - - - - - - -

Way 2 **Multiply by the reciprocal of the divisor.**

$$\frac{1}{2} \div 3 \;=\; \frac{1}{2} \div \frac{3}{1} \;=\; \frac{1}{2} \times \frac{1}{3} = \frac{1}{6}$$

Solution: Each person gets $\frac{1}{6}$ of a pizza.

> **Check**
>
> **Multiply to check.**
>
> $\frac{1}{6} \times 3$
>
> $\frac{1}{6} \times \frac{3}{1} = \frac{1 \times 3}{6 \times 1} = \frac{3}{6} = \frac{1}{2}$

Ask Yourself
• Did I multiply by the reciprocal?
• Did I write my answer in simplest form?

▶ Guided Practice

Divide. Show your work. Multiply to check.

1. $6 \div 8$

2. $\dfrac{1}{2} \div 7$

3. $\dfrac{4}{3} \div 12$

4. $\dfrac{3}{4} \div 10$

5. $\dfrac{6}{8} \div 3$

6. $\dfrac{6}{11} \div 2$

7. $\dfrac{14}{15} \div 7$

8. $\dfrac{15}{16} \div 5$

𝗫 Algebra Functions **Copy and complete each function table.**

9.

Rule: $y = x \div 3$			
x	$\dfrac{3}{4}$	$\dfrac{9}{10}$	$\dfrac{6}{7}$	$\dfrac{12}{15}$
y				

10.

Rule: $y = x \div 2$			
x	$\dfrac{7}{8}$	$\dfrac{3}{4}$	$\dfrac{9}{10}$	$\dfrac{5}{6}$
y				

Guided Problem Solving

Use the questions to solve this problem.

11. Josie is making tomato sauce. Her recipe calls for $\dfrac{3}{4}$ cup of tomato paste. The recipe makes enough for 6 pizzas. How much tomato paste is on each pizza?

  a. Understand How much tomato paste is in the recipe? How many pizzas can you make?

  b. Plan What do you need to find?

  c. Solve What strategy will you choose? Write the answer.

  d. Check Back How can you check that your answer is reasonable?

123 Math Talk When you divide a fraction by a whole number, is the result smaller or larger than the fraction? Explain.

▶ Practice and Problem Solving

Divide. Show your work. Simplify your answer.

12. $\dfrac{3}{2} \div 7$

13. $\dfrac{7}{3} \div 21$

14. $\dfrac{8}{3} \div 2$

15. $\dfrac{4}{3} \div 3$

16. $\dfrac{4}{3} \div 4$

Algebra Functions **Copy and complete the function tables.**

17.

Rule: $y = x \div 7$				
x	$\frac{14}{15}$	$\frac{7}{9}$	$\frac{21}{4}$	$\frac{35}{35}$
y	☐	☐	☐	☐

18.

Rule: $y = x \div 5$				
x	$\frac{5}{4}$	$\frac{2}{3}$	$\frac{3}{4}$	$\frac{12}{12}$
y	☐	☐	☐	☐

 ## Science Link

Solve.

19. Sheldon thoroughly mixes 5 cups of flour, $\frac{3}{4}$ cup of sugar, and $\frac{1}{5}$ tablespoon of salt. He then divides the mixture into three equal parts. How much of each ingredient is in each part?

20. A recipe that makes 8 servings calls for 2 cups of flour. How much flour should be used to make only 5 servings?

21. Nancy put $\frac{5}{8}$ cup of sugar into her cornbread batter. She then sees that the recipe calls for only $\frac{5}{16}$ cup of sugar. What could Nancy do to fix her cornbread batter?

Food Chemistry

- The physical properties of sugar, salt, and flour are similar—color, texture, and hardness.
- The chemical properties of sugar, salt, and flour are different.
- You can taste the differences when chemical receptors in your mouth and nose react with particles from food.

Science PS 1.f

Spiral Review and Test Practice

**Write an algebraic expression for each word phrase.
Use *n* to represent the unknown number.** **KEY** **AF 1.2** pages 126, 128

22. 8 less than a number **23.** 5 more than a number **24.** 25 times a number

Write the letter of the correct answer. **NS 2.4, NS 2.5**

25. A salad serves 8 people. Emma put $\frac{2}{3}$ cup of dressing on the salad. How much salad dressing is there in each serving?

A $\frac{1}{12}$ cup **B** $5\frac{1}{3}$ cups **C** $\frac{10}{3}$ cups **D** 12 cups

Extra Practice See page 243, Set A.

Key Standards Review

Need Help?
See Key Standards Handbook.

Write the letter of the point on the number line that represents the fraction or decimal in Exercises 1–5. KEY **NS 1.5**

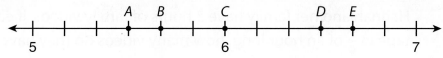

1. $\frac{17}{3}$ 2. 6.5   3. $\frac{36}{6}$ 4. $\frac{40}{6}$ 5. 5.5

Find the prime factorization of each number. KEY **NS 1.4**

6. 15   7. 45   8. 18

9. 27   10. 30   11. 42

12. 38   13. 16   14. 34

15. 26   16. 50   17. 44

 **Number Sense**

Who's Operating? KEY **NS 2.3**, NS 2.5

Combine three fractions with two operations to equal a given number. Use the following symbols: +, −, ×, and ÷.

1. $\frac{3}{4}$ ⬭ $\frac{1}{4}$ ⬭ $\frac{1}{3}$ = 1   2. $\frac{3}{4}$ ⬭ $\frac{1}{2}$ ⬭ $\frac{1}{8}$ = 3   3. $\frac{5}{8}$ ⬭ $\frac{1}{2}$ ⬭ $\frac{1}{4}$ = $\frac{1}{16}$

4. $\frac{9}{10}$ ⬭ $\frac{1}{2}$ ⬭ $\frac{1}{4}$ = $\frac{13}{20}$ 5. $\frac{3}{4}$ ⬭ $\frac{1}{5}$ ⬭ $\frac{2}{5}$ = $\frac{19}{20}$ 6. $\frac{2}{4}$ ⬭ $\frac{1}{4}$ ⬭ $\frac{4}{4}$ = 1

7. $\frac{5}{6}$ ⬭ $\frac{1}{6}$ ⬭ $\frac{1}{10}$ = $\frac{1}{2}$ 8. $\frac{4}{5}$ ⬭ $\frac{1}{5}$ ⬭ 1 = 0   9. $\frac{2}{9}$ ⬭ $\frac{5}{9}$ ⬭ $\frac{8}{9}$ = $1\frac{13}{45}$

CA Standards

NS 2.5 Compute and perform simple multiplication and division of fractions and apply those procedures to solving problems.

NS 2.4 Understand the concept of multiplication and division of fractions.

Also NS 2.0, MR 1.0, MR 1.1, MR 2.0, MR 2.3

Vocabulary

reciprocal

Divide by a Fraction

Objective Use reciprocals to divide by a fraction.

▶ **Learn by Example**

Hannah and her family have 3 hours of family videos. If each tape is $\frac{3}{4}$ of an hour long, how many videos do they have?

$$3 \div \frac{3}{4} = x$$

Different Ways to Divide by a Fraction

Way 1 **Draw a diagram.**

1 Draw a number strip to represent the hours. Since you divide by fourths, divide each hour into fourths.

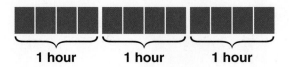

1 hour   1 hour   1 hour

$$3 \div \frac{1}{4} = 3 \times 4 = 12$$

Think

How many fourths are in 3?

2 Divide the number strip into groups of 3 fourths. Then count the number of groups.

12 fourths ÷ 3 fourths = 4

$$12 \div 3 = 4$$

Think

The product of a fraction and its reciprocal is always 1.

$$\frac{3}{4} \times \frac{4}{3} = \frac{\overset{1}{\cancel{3}} \times \overset{1}{\cancel{4}}}{\underset{1}{\cancel{4}} \times \underset{1}{\cancel{3}}} = 1$$

Way 2 **Multiply by the reciprocal.**

1 Write a multiplication problem using the reciprocal of the divisor.

$$3 \div \frac{3}{4} = 3 \times \frac{4}{3}$$

2 Look for common factors. Multiply.

$$3 \times \frac{4}{3} = \frac{\overset{1}{\cancel{3}} \times 4}{\underset{1}{\cancel{3}}} = 4$$

Solution: The family has 4 videos.

Divide. Write the answer in simplest form.

1. $\frac{1}{2} \div \frac{7}{12}$ 2. $1\frac{5}{6} \div \frac{2}{3}$ 3. $3 \div \frac{1}{2}$

4. $\frac{5}{12} \div \frac{1}{4}$ 5. $4 \div \frac{3}{6}$ 6. $\frac{4}{9} \div \frac{2}{3}$

 Math Talk Why does multiplying by 2 give the same answer as dividing by $\frac{1}{2}$?

► **Practice and Problem Solving**

Divide. Write the answer in simplest form.

7. $\frac{1}{2} \div \frac{3}{4}$ 8. $5 \div \frac{2}{3}$ 9. $\frac{5}{6} \div \frac{5}{12}$ 10. $\frac{1}{3} \div \frac{1}{4}$ 11. $2 \div \frac{3}{8}$

12. $\frac{7}{12} \div \frac{3}{4}$ 13. $\frac{3}{4} \div \frac{1}{3}$ 14. $\frac{2}{3} \div \frac{1}{6}$ 15. $\frac{7}{12} \div \frac{1}{12}$ 16. $\frac{7}{8} \div \frac{1}{2}$

Solve.

17. Three-eighths of the people in a survey said they watched television last night. If 600 people watched television, how many people took part in the survey?

18. **Estimate** Find a number that, when divided by $\frac{3}{4}$, gives a quotient between $\frac{1}{2}$ and $\frac{2}{3}$.

Add. Write the answer in simplest form. KEY **NS 2.3** page 174

19. $7\frac{1}{28} + 2\frac{3}{8} = \blacksquare$ 20. $3\frac{5}{6} + 4\frac{1}{3} = \blacksquare$ 21. $5\frac{3}{4} + 9\frac{2}{3} = \blacksquare$

Write the letter of the correct answer. NS 2.5

22. $\frac{1}{2} \div \frac{1}{8} = $

   A $\frac{2}{12}$ **B** $\frac{1}{12}$ **C** $\frac{1}{2}$ **D** 4

LESSON 4

CA Standards

NS 2.5 Compute and perform simple multiplication and division of fractions and apply those procedures to solving problems.

NS 2.4 Understand the concept of multiplication and division of fractions. Also KEY **NS 1.4**, AF 1.0, MR 1.0, MR 1.1, MR 2.0, MR 2.3

Vocabulary

mixed number

improper fraction

reciprocal

Divide with Mixed Numbers

Objective Use improper fractions and reciprocals to divide with mixed numbers.

▶ **Learn by Example**

You can use what you know about dividing by fractions to divide by mixed numbers. When you divide with mixed numbers, first rewrite them as improper fractions and follow the same steps.

A snowmobile tank holds $8\frac{1}{2}$ gallons of gas. Marty used $1\frac{1}{4}$ gallons today. What fraction of the gas in the tank did he use?

Write the fraction as division.

$$\frac{1\frac{1}{4}}{8\frac{1}{2}} = 1\frac{1}{4} \div 8\frac{1}{2}$$

Divide by a Mixed Number

1 Write the mixed numbers as improper fractions.

$$1\frac{1}{4} \div 8\frac{1}{2} = \frac{5}{4} \div \frac{17}{2}$$

2 Write a multiplication problem using the reciprocal of the divisor.

$$\frac{5}{4} \div \frac{17}{2} = \frac{5}{4} \times \frac{2}{17}$$

3 Look for common factors.

$$\frac{5}{4} \times \frac{2}{17} = \frac{5 \times 2}{4 \times 17}$$

$$= \frac{5 \times \overset{1}{2}}{2 \times \underset{1}{2} \times 17}$$

4 Multiply. Write the answer in simplest form.

$$\frac{5 \times \overset{1}{2}}{2 \times \underset{1}{2} \times 17} = \frac{5}{34}$$

Solution: Marty used $\frac{5}{34}$ of the gas in the tank.

236

Another Example

Divide by a whole number.

1 Write the mixed numbers as improper fractions.

$$6\frac{3}{4} \div 3 = \frac{27}{4} \div \frac{3}{1}$$

2 Write a multiplication problem using the reciprocal of the divisor.

$$\frac{27}{4} \div \frac{3}{1} = \frac{27}{4} \times \frac{1}{3}$$

3 Look for common factors.

$$\frac{27 \times 1}{4 \times 3} = \frac{9 \times \overset{1}{\cancel{3}} \times 1}{4 \times \underset{1}{\cancel{3}}}$$

4 Multiply. Write answer in simplest form.

$$9 \times \frac{1}{4} = \frac{9}{4} = 2\frac{1}{4}$$

▶ **Guided Practice**

Divide. Write the answer in simplest form.

1. $\frac{2}{3} \div 4\frac{2}{5}$

2. $11 \div 1\frac{1}{2}$

3. $8\frac{2}{3} \div 12\frac{1}{2}$

4. $\frac{1}{4} \div 1\frac{1}{4}$

5. $\frac{5}{8} \div 5$

6. $1\frac{5}{9} \div \frac{7}{8}$

7. $\frac{4}{7} \div 2$

8. $7\frac{1}{3} \div 2\frac{3}{4}$

9. $\frac{9}{10} \div 1\frac{4}{5}$

Ask Yourself
• Did I write improper fractions?
• Did I multiply by the reciprocal?
• Is my solution in simplest form?

(123) Math Talk How are the reciprocals of unit fractions and counting numbers related?

▶ **Practice and Problem Solving**

Divide. Write the answer in simplest form.

10. $\frac{3}{4} \div 1\frac{2}{3}$

11. $10 \div 3\frac{1}{5}$

12. $\frac{7}{4} \div 7\frac{3}{4}$

13. $1\frac{1}{5} \div 3\frac{7}{8}$

14. $7\frac{1}{2} \div 2\frac{5}{8}$

15. $\frac{2}{3} \div 1\frac{1}{3}$

16. $\frac{3}{5} \div 6$

17. $\frac{3}{4} \div 2\frac{1}{2}$

18. $\frac{1}{6} \div 2\frac{1}{3}$

19. $\frac{2}{3} \div 2\frac{2}{3}$

20. $\frac{4}{5} \div 1\frac{1}{2}$

21. $\frac{5}{6} \div 3\frac{1}{3}$

22. $\frac{2}{5} \div 4\frac{2}{5}$

23. $\frac{1}{8} \div 1\frac{1}{2}$

24. $\frac{5}{6} \div 1\frac{5}{6}$

25. $\frac{7}{8} \div 2\frac{1}{2}$

26. $\frac{7}{10} \div 1\frac{3}{7}$

27. $6 \div 3\frac{1}{3}$

28. $1\frac{1}{4} \div 2\frac{1}{2}$

29. $\frac{3}{4} \div 2\frac{3}{8}$

Solve the problems below.

30. Measurement Draw a line segment that is $3\frac{1}{8}$ inches long. If you divide the line segment into five equal lengths, how long will each piece be? Show it on your line.

31. Glennis drew a line segment that was $9\frac{3}{5}$ inches long. Then she divided it into line segments that were each $1\frac{1}{5}$ inches long. How many line segments did she make?

 Algebra Expressions **Rewrite each expression as a whole number or a fraction in simplest form.**

32. $n \div 2$ **33.** $3n \div 3m$ **34.** $\frac{1}{a} \div \frac{1}{a}$ **35.** $6x \div 3x$

 Real World Data

Use the schedule for Problems 36–39.

36. What fraction of Beth's Monday class schedule does ballet represent?

37. Last Monday, Beth was late for her Jazz class. She missed $\frac{1}{3}$ of the class. How much time is that?

38. One of Beth's teachers divides each hour of class into thirds. She uses those six sessions to work with different groups. Which class is this?

39. Beth's Tuesday schedule is like Monday's, except ballet class is half as long, and jazz class is twice as long. Explain why her total time is the same.

Beth's Monday Schedule	
Class	**Number of Hours**
Modern Dance	2
Ballet	$2\frac{1}{2}$
Jazz	$1\frac{1}{4}$
Character	$1\frac{1}{2}$
Strength Training	$\frac{3}{4}$

Spiral Review and Test Practice

Multiply. Write the answer in simplest form. NS 2.4, NS 2.5 pages 210, 212, 216

40. $4\frac{1}{2} \times \frac{2}{3}$ **41.** $\frac{3}{4} \times \frac{1}{3}$ **42.** $12 \times \frac{5}{6}$ **43.** $2\frac{1}{4} \times \frac{1}{9}$

Write the letter of the correct answer. NS 2.5

44. $\frac{3}{8} \div \frac{1}{3} =$

   A $\frac{4}{11}$ **B** $\frac{9}{8}$ **C** $\frac{8}{9}$ **D** $\frac{17}{24}$

Extra Practice See page 243, Set C.

Division Scramble

Object of the Game Practice dividing fractions by making the greatest possible quotient.

Materials
- Learning Tool 16 (Division Scramble Game Board) (2 per player)
- Learning Tool 15 (Number/Symbol Cards) (1 set labeled 1 to 10)

Number of Players 2

Set Up
Shuffle the Number Cards and place them face down in a stack. Each player gets a Division Scramble Game Board.

How to Play

1 In turn each player takes one card from the stack and places that card face up on his or her game board. Once placed, a card cannot be moved.

2 The game continues until each player has four cards placed on his or her game board.

3 Each player then divides the fractions displayed on the game board. The player whose example has the greater quotient wins.

4 Shuffle the number cards and play again. This time the player whose example has the lesser quotient wins.

CA Standards

NS 2.4 Understand the concept of multiplication and division of fractions.

NS 2.5 Compute and perform simple multiplication and division of fractions and apply these procedures to solving problems.

Also MR 1.0, MR 2.0

Education Place
Visit www.eduplace.com/camap/ for **Brain Teasers** and **eGames** to play.

Chapter 11 Lesson 4 **239**

CA Standards

MR 2.6 Make precise calculations and check the validity of the results from the context of the problem.

NS 2.5 Compute and perform simple multiplication and division of fractions and apply these procedures to solving problems.

Also NS 2.4, KEY NS 2.3,
MR 1.1, MR 2.0, MR 2.1,
MR 2.3, MR 2.4, MR 3.0,
MR 3.1, MR 3.2, MR 3.3

Problem Solving Plan
Reasonable Answers

Objective Determine if the answers to problems are reasonable.

▶ **Learn Through Reasoning**

After you solve a problem, look back at the problem and decide whether the answer is reasonable.

Example 1

Sometimes answers are unreasonable because the problem is misinterpreted.

> Mr. Costa makes sandwiches for the class picnic. He buys $6\frac{1}{2}$ pounds of turkey and uses $\frac{1}{4}$ pound in each sandwich. How many sandwiches can he make?

Tanya says Mr. Costa can make 2 sandwiches.

Her answer is unreasonable. Each sandwich has $\frac{1}{4}$ pound of turkey, so the number of sandwiches that Mr. Costa can make using $6\frac{1}{2}$ pounds of turkey should be much greater than 2.

Example 2

Sometimes an answer does not make sense.

> Alison made $5\frac{3}{4}$ cups of popcorn. She gave $1\frac{1}{4}$ cups of popcorn to each of her friends. How many friends received popcorn?

Alison says that $4\frac{3}{5}$ friends received popcorn.

Alison's answer is unreasonable because there cannot be a part of a friend.

Example 3

Sometimes the calculations are incorrect.

> Luis made 3 different yogurt parfaits in $\frac{1}{4}$ hour. He spent the same amount of time making each parfait. How long did it take Luis to make 1 parfait?

Luis says that he spent $\frac{3}{4}$ hour making each parfait.

His answer is unreasonable. He spent $\frac{1}{4}$ hour making all 3 parfaits, so the time he spent making each parfait should be less than $\frac{1}{4}$ hour, not more.

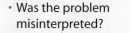

▶ Guided Problem Solving

Solve using the Ask Yourself questions. Tell whether the statement in blue is reasonable or unreasonable. Explain your answer.

Ask Yourself
- Was the problem misinterpreted?
- Does your answer make sense?
- Are the calculations correct?

1. Denny bought $\frac{2}{3}$ pound of mushrooms. He divided the mushrooms equally among 4 pizzas. **That means he put $\frac{1}{3}$ pound of mushrooms on each pizza.**

(123) Math Talk How can you quickly check if an answer is unreasonable because of incorrect calculations?

▶ Independent Problem Solving

Tell whether each statement in blue is reasonable or unreasonable. Explain your answer.

2. Myra put $4\frac{1}{2}$ pounds of vegetables in a salad. She used different types of vegetables. Each type of vegetable weighed $1\frac{1}{8}$ pounds. **That means there are 4 different types of vegetables in Myra's salad.**

3. **Multistep** Sanita was preparing fruit on a skewer. She left $\frac{1}{8}$ of the skewer open at each end and covered the rest with fruit. Twelve inches of the skewer was covered with fruit. **So, the skewer was 16 inches long.**

4. There are 25 students in cooking class. Twelve of the students are girls. **So, $\frac{1}{3}$ of the students are boys.**

5. **Challenge** Tao has $5\frac{1}{2}$ hours for cooking lessons. Each lesson is $\frac{2}{3}$ of an hour long with $\frac{1}{4}$ hour between lessons. **In $5\frac{1}{2}$ hours, she can give at least 6 lessons.**

6. **Create and Solve** Write and solve a word problem that uses division of fractions or mixed numbers. Explain why your answer is reasonable.

Reading & Writing

Vocabulary

To divide fractions, you can write the **reciprocal** of the divisor.

Write the reciprocal of each fraction or mixed number.

1. $\frac{3}{5}$ **2.** $2\frac{1}{4}$ **3.** $7\frac{2}{3}$

Complete the table to find the quotient.

$3\frac{3}{5} \div 1\frac{2}{5}$	
Step 1: Rewrite mixed numbers as improper fractions.	$3\frac{3}{5} = \frac{\blacksquare}{\blacksquare}$ $1\frac{2}{5} = \frac{\blacksquare}{\blacksquare}$
Step 2: Write a multiplication problem using the reciprocal of the divisor.	
Step 3: Look for common factors.	
Step 4: Multiply. Write the answer in simplest form.	

Writing Explain how adding and subtracting fractions is different from multiplying and dividing fractions.

Reading Check out this book in your library. *Cool Math* by Christy Maganzini

CA Standards

MR 2.3 Use a variety of methods, such as words, numbers, symbols, charts, graphs, tables, diagrams, and models, to explain mathematical reasoning.

Also NS 2.4, NS 2.5

Standards-Based Extra Practice

Set A ——————————————————————— NS 2.5, NS 2.4 page 230

Divide. Show your work. Multiply to check.

1. $\frac{1}{6} \div 2$

2. $\frac{1}{4} \div 6$

3. $\frac{2}{3} \div 2$

4. $\frac{1}{7} \div 7$

5. $\frac{5}{12} \div 4$

6. $\frac{9}{7} \div 4$

7. $\frac{1}{5} \div 8$

8. $\frac{2}{5} \div 4$

Solve.

9. Torrez made $\frac{4}{5}$ gallon of orange juice. He is serving an equal amount to each of 8 friends. How many gallons of orange juice will each friend get?

Set B ——————————————————————— NS 2.5, NS 2.4 page 234

Divide. Write answers in simplest form.

1. $\frac{3}{8} \div \frac{2}{3}$

2. $\frac{1}{4} \div \frac{3}{5}$

3. $\frac{1}{3} \div \frac{2}{5}$

4. $\frac{4}{7} \div \frac{7}{10}$

5. $\frac{5}{8} \div \frac{1}{4}$

6. $\frac{2}{7} \div \frac{2}{3}$

7. $\frac{1}{5} \div \frac{1}{8}$

8. $\frac{3}{4} \div \frac{1}{4}$

Solve.

9. Nancy has $\frac{3}{4}$ yard of ribbon. She is cutting it into pieces that are each $\frac{3}{8}$ yard long. How many pieces of ribbon will she have?

Set C ——————————————————————— NS 2.5, NS 2.4 page 236

Divide. Write answers in simplest form.

1. $\frac{2}{5} \div 5\frac{2}{3}$

2. $\frac{3}{4} \div 1\frac{3}{5}$

3. $\frac{1}{5} \div 2\frac{3}{5}$

4. $\frac{4}{8} \div 1\frac{3}{10}$

5. $\frac{3}{7} \div 2\frac{1}{4}$

6. $\frac{2}{3} \div 5\frac{1}{3}$

7. $\frac{2}{5} \div 1\frac{1}{8}$

8. $1\frac{1}{2} \div 4\frac{2}{3}$

Solve.

9. Harry ran $\frac{7}{8}$ miles in $8\frac{3}{4}$ minutes. If he ran the same distance each minute, how many miles did he run in 1 minute?

Education Place
Visit www.eduplace.com/camap/
for **Extra Practice**.

Chapter Review/Test

Vocabulary and Concepts ——————————————— NS 2.4, NS 2.5

Write the best word to complete each sentence.

1. The _____ of a number is the number inverted.

2. An _____ has a numerator that is greater than or equal to its denominator.

3. A _____ is written as a whole number and a fraction.

Skills ——————————————————————————— NS 2.4, NS 2.5

Divide. Write answers in simplest form.

4. $4 \div \frac{1}{5}$

5. $2 \div 6$

6. $\frac{1}{9} \div \frac{1}{3}$

7. $\frac{1}{4} \div 2$

8. $\frac{5}{3} \div 4$

9. $\frac{2}{5} \div 12$

10. $\frac{4}{7} \div 5$

11. $8 \div 2\frac{1}{2}$

12. $\frac{3}{5} \div \frac{2}{5}$

13. $\frac{1}{7} \div \frac{3}{4}$

14. $\frac{4}{3} \div 3$

15. $1\frac{1}{9} \div 2\frac{2}{3}$

16. $\frac{5}{7} \div \frac{1}{4}$

17. $\frac{2}{3} \div 1\frac{2}{3}$

18. $\frac{3}{4} \div 2\frac{1}{3}$

19. $2\frac{1}{8} \div \frac{1}{4}$

20. $3\frac{3}{5} \div 1\frac{5}{7}$

21. $6\frac{2}{3} \div \frac{5}{6}$

22. $5\frac{1}{4} \div 3\frac{7}{8}$

Problem Solving and Reasoning ——————— NS 2.4, NS 2.5, MR 2.3, MR 3.1

Solve.

22. Hank uses $4\frac{1}{2}$ cups of flour to make 12 bagels. How much flour is in each bagel?

23. Chris took an 8-mile hike. He walked $3\frac{1}{5}$ miles each hour. How many hours did it take him to complete his hike?

24. Carol has 2 cups of raisins to divide equally among 3 friends. She calculates that each friend will receive $1\frac{1}{2}$ cups of raisins. Is her answer reasonable? Explain.

Writing Math Kristin is planning a dinner for 8 people. She has 6 cups of rice. She wants to serve each person $\frac{3}{4}$ cup of rice. Will she have enough rice? Explain how you found your answer.

Spiral Review and Test Practice

1. $(24 + 13) + 41 = \square + 41$

  A 4

  B 37

  C 41

  D 78

                    NS 1.0 page 126

2. Which statement is true?

  A $(16 - 4) \times 3 = 16 - (4 \times 3)$

  B $(16 - 4) \times 3 < 16 - (4 \times 3)$

  C $(16 - 4) \times 3 = 16 - 4 \times 3$

  D $(16 - 4) \times 3 > 16 - (4 \times 3)$

                    NS 1.0 page 128

3. If $n = 4$, what is the value of $12 - n$?

  A 3

  B 8

  C 12

  D 16

            KEY AF 1.2 page 108

4. Carlos made a batch of mixed nuts. He used $1\frac{5}{6}$ fewer cups of almonds than cashews. He used $3\frac{1}{2}$ cups of cashews. How many cups of almonds are in the mixed nuts?

  A $2\frac{2}{3}$ cups

  B $2\frac{1}{3}$ cups

  C $1\frac{2}{3}$ cups

  D $\frac{2}{3}$ cups

> **Test Tip**
> Look for clue words that help you decide what operation to use.

                    KEY NS 2.3 page 192

5. $2\frac{3}{4} \cdot 1\frac{1}{2} =$

  A $1\frac{1}{8}$ **C** $4\frac{1}{8}$

  B $2\frac{1}{3}$ **D** $4\frac{1}{4}$

          NS 2.4, NS 2.5 page 216

6. Lisa used $\frac{3}{4}$ cup of flour to make 6 muffins. How much flour is in each muffin?

  A 8 cups

  B $4\frac{1}{2}$ cups

  C $\frac{11}{12}$ cup

  D $\frac{1}{8}$ cup

> **Test Tip**
> Decide if your answer is reasonable for the situation described in the problem.

                    NS 2.5 page 230

Unit 5 Review/Test

Vocabulary and Concepts ———————————— NS 2.4, MR 2.3 Chapters 10 and 11

Write the best term to complete each sentence.

1. The _____ of a number is the number inverted.

2. A fraction that has a greater numerator than denominator is called an _____.

3. The top number in a fraction is called the _____.

4. When you multiply two fractions, the answer is called the _____.

5. A fraction that has a whole number next to it is called a _____.

Skills ————————————————————— NS 2.4, NS 2.5

Multiply. Write your answer in simplest form. Chapter 10, Lessons 1–3

6. $5 \times \frac{2}{7}$

7. $12 \times \frac{1}{5}$

8. $\frac{1}{7} \times 23$

9. $\frac{3}{8} \times 24$

10. $\frac{5}{9} \times \frac{2}{3}$

11. $\frac{7}{11} \times \frac{6}{8}$

12. $3\frac{1}{2} \times \frac{3}{7}$

13. $8\frac{2}{5} \times 1\frac{3}{7}$

Divide. Write your answer in simplest form. Chapter 11, Lessons 1–4

14. $30 \div \frac{1}{5}$

15. $9 \div \frac{1}{3}$

16. $\frac{2}{7} \div \frac{2}{5}$

17. $\frac{3}{8} \div \frac{3}{4}$

18. $\frac{6}{7} \div \frac{3}{4}$

19. $\frac{2}{6} \div 1\frac{2}{3}$

20. $\frac{1}{3} \div 2\frac{5}{9}$

21. $\frac{7}{9} \div 2\frac{1}{10}$

Problem Solving and Reasoning ———————— NS 2.4, NS 2.5, MR 1.1, MR 2.6

Solve. Chapters 10–11

22. Bella eats $\frac{1}{5}$ of an apple every day. If she eats the same fraction of an apple, every day for a whole year, how many apples will she eat?

23. Lily has $\frac{1}{2}$ of her sandwich left. She wants to give an equal piece to each of 5 friends. What fraction of the whole sandwich will each friend get?

Solve.

24. In the choir, $\frac{1}{2}$ of the members are boys and $\frac{1}{2}$ are girls. If $\frac{1}{4}$ of the boys are 5th graders, what fraction of the whole choir is 5th grade boys?

25. Seth has a $10 bill. He needs quarters to do laundry. How many quarters can he get for his $10 bill?

Writing Math How are division and multiplication of fractions the same? What makes them different?

Performance Assessment

Mrs. Thompson's Tea Party

KEY **NS 2.3**, NS 2.5, MR 1.1, MR 2.6

Mrs. Thompson is hosting a tea party. She's expecting 12 guests. Help her figure out what she needs to buy at the store, before she bakes.

Walnut Delights

$\frac{1}{3}$ cup flour

$\frac{3}{4}$ cup honey

$\frac{1}{8}$ cup butter

$\frac{1}{4}$ cup vanilla

$\frac{2}{3}$ cup chopped walnuts

Fruit and Nut Snack

$2\frac{1}{4}$ cup bananas

3 cups sliced apples

$\frac{2}{3}$ cup honey

$1\frac{1}{2}$ cups peanut butter

$1\frac{1}{2}$ cups chopped walnuts

Puffed-Rice Treats

$6\frac{1}{2}$ cups puffed rice

$3\frac{1}{4}$ cups marshmallows

$\frac{2}{3}$ cup chopped walnuts

$\frac{1}{4}$ cup butter

Task	Information You Need
Use the information above and to the right. When Mrs. Thompson goes to the store, how much butter, walnuts, and honey does she need to buy?	Each guest gets one of each dessert.
	The Walnut Delights recipe makes 6 servings.
	The Fruit and Nut Snack recipe makes 4 servings.
	The Puffed-Rice Treats recipe makes 12 treats.
	Mrs. Thompson doesn't want any food left over!

Go Fast, Go Far
Unit 5 Mental Math Strategies

Multiply by 50

When 50's what you multiply, half 100's worth a try!

Instead of 50 × 44, I start with 100 × 44 which is 4,400. Then I take half of 4,400 to get 2,200.

1. 50 × 44 → 4,400 → 2,200
 100 × 44 Take half.

2. 50 × 86 → 8,600 → ☐
 100 × 44 Take half.

3. 50 × 120 → ☐ → ☐
 100 × 120 Take half.

2. 50 × 440 → ☐ → ☐
 100 × 440 Take half.

Good job! Now try these!

5. 50 × 64 → ☐ → ☐

6. 50 × 250 → ☐ → ☐

7. 50 × 88 → ☐ → ☐

8. 50 × 170 → ☐ → ☐

9. 50 × 26 → ☐ → ☐

10. 50 × 462 → ☐ → ☐

Take It Further!
Now try doing all the steps in your head!

11. 50 × 94

12. 50 × 28

13. 50 × 130

14. 50 × 420

6

Operations with Decimals

BIG IDEAS!

- A decimal is the same as a fraction with a denominator of a power of 10.

- You can add and subtract decimals like whole numbers and then place the decimal point.

- You can multiply and divide decimals like whole numbers and then place the decimal point.

Chapter 12
Add and Subtract through Thousandths

Chapter 13
Multiply Decimals

Chapter 14
Divide Decimals

Chapter 15
Divide by Two-Digit Divisors

Songs and Games

Math Music Track 6: *My New Book*

eGames at
www.eduplace.com/camap/

Math Readers

A Hundredth of a Second

Seeking the Lowest Price

Doubling Every Day

Niagara Falls Numbers

Game

It All Adds Up

Object of the Game Practice adding money to make whole dollars.

Materials
- Counters
- Stopwatch or timer
- Learning Tool 18: Decimal Cards (1 set)
- Learning Tool 19: It All Adds Up Game Board

Set Up
Give each student a game board. Players shuffle the Decimal Cards and place them face down in a stack.

Number of Players 2

How to Play

1 Player 1 takes the top card from the stack. He or she has 1 minute to match the amount shown on the Decimal Card with an amount on their game board to make $1.00.

2 If the sum is $1.00, the player places a counter on the matching space on their game board. If the player makes an incorrect match or takes longer than one minute, he or she loses the turn and places the Decimal Card at the bottom of the stack.

3 Play continues until a player places four counters in a row horizontally, vertically, or diagonally on their game board. That player wins the game.

CA Standards
KEY NS 2.1 Add, subtract, multiply, and divide with decimals; add with negative integers; subtract positive integers from negative integers; and verify the reasonableness of the results.

Also MR 1.0, MR 2.0

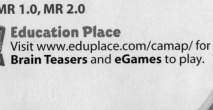
Education Place
Visit www.eduplace.com/camap/ for **Brain Teasers** and **eGames** to play.

Reading You can use a graphic organizer to help you organize information and understand a reading selection. You can also use a graphic organizer to help you organize information and solve a word problem.

Lucy used a diagram to help her solve the following word problem.

Problem 1

A season's pass to Lunar Park costs $42.95. Serena has saved $15.96. How much more money does she need?

A part-part-whole diagram helps me see how the numbers are related.

Cost of season's pass:	
$42.95	
Money saved:	**Money needed:**
$15.96	?

You know the cost of the pass and the amount of money that Serena has saved. You can subtract to find the amount she still needs.

Writing Read Problem 2. Then use a graphic organizer to help you organize the information and solve the problem.

Problem 2

At the park, Serena bought a snack for $3.99. Then she bought a souvenir for $5.95. How much did Serena spend?

Add and Subtract Through Thousandths

Enjoying a ride at the Los Angeles County Fair in Pomona, CA

Check What You Know

Vocabulary and Concepts NS 1.0, MR 2.3

Choose the best term to complete each sentence. pages 54 and 60

1. A _____ is used to separate dollars and cents in money.

2. The _____ of the 3 in 18.739 is 3 hundredths.

Skills GRADE 4 NS 2.0

Add or subtract.

3. $ 35.98
    + 56.73

4. $ 68.19
    − 37.84

5. $ 582.31
    + 74.64

6. $ 568.18
    − 22.58

7. $ 948.74
    − 654.18

8. $ 472.68
    + 339.87

Problem Solving and Reasoning GRADE 4 KEY NS 3.0

9. In 2006, there were 5,416 species of mammals in the world. Of those, 1,093 were listed as being endangered. How many species of mammals were not listed as being endangered?

Vocabulary

Visualize It!

Use models to add decimals.

```
  2.45
+ 1.34
  3.79
```

Language Tips

The word *decimeter* contains the Latin root *deci*, meaning "ten." What other words do you know that contain the root *deci*?

Math words that look similar in English and Spanish often have the same meaning.

English	Spanish
decimeter	decímetro
centimeter	centímetro
millimeter	milímetro

See **English-Spanish Glossary** pages 628–642.

Education Place Visit www.eduplace.com/camap/ for the **eGlossary** and **eGames**.

CA Standards MR 2.3 Use a variety of methods, such as words, numbers, symbols, charts, graphs, tables, diagrams, and models, to explain mathematical reasoning. **Also NS 2.0**

Chapter 12   253

CA Standards
KEY NS 2.1 Add, subtract, multiply and divide with decimals; add with negative integers; subtract positive integers from negative integers; and verify the reasonableness of the results.

MR 2.3 Use a variety of methods, such as words, numbers, symbols, charts, graphs, tables, diagrams, and models, to explain mathematical reasoning.

Also NS 1.0, NS 1.1, MR 1.1

Materials
• Learning Tool 13
  (Thousandths of a Dollar)
• Bill and Coin Set

Hands On
Add and Subtract Decimals

Objective Use models to add and subtract decimals.

▶ **Explore**

Question How can you use models to add and subtract decimals?

Todd is a computer programmer working on a Rushing River simulation ride. Todd needs to program the first rapid to last 1.381 minutes and the next rapid to last 2.233 minutes. How many minutes of the simulation were rapids?

$1.381 + 2.233 = n$

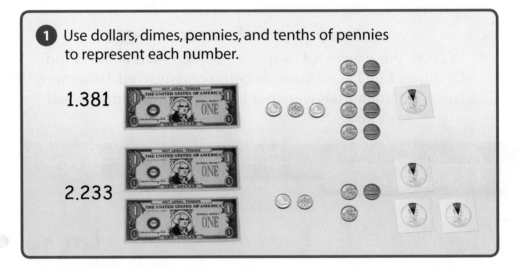

1 Use dollars, dimes, pennies, and tenths of pennies to represent each number.

1.381

2.233

Think

One tenth of a penny is one thousandth of a dollar.

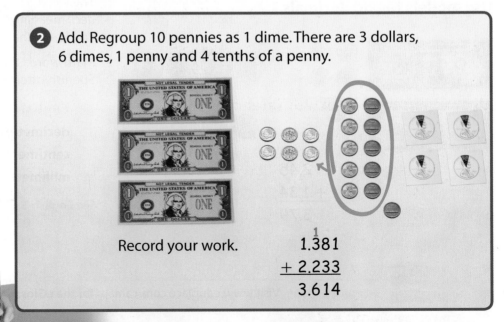

2 Add. Regroup 10 pennies as 1 dime. There are 3 dollars, 6 dimes, 1 penny and 4 tenths of a penny.

Record your work.

$$\begin{array}{r} \overset{1}{1.381} \\ +\ 2.233 \\ \hline 3.614 \end{array}$$

Solution: There are 3.614 minutes of rapids.

Now try 4.582 − 3.215 = n

1 Show 4.582 with models.

2 Subtract 3.215. Regroup 1 penny as 10 tenths of a penny.

 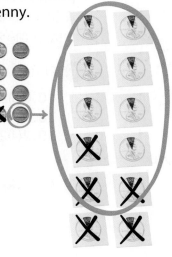

Record your work.

$$\begin{array}{r} \overset{7\,1}{4.5\cancel{8}\cancel{2}} \\ -\ 3.215 \\ \hline 1.367 \end{array}$$

▶ **Extend**

Use models to find each sum.

1. $5.20 + $3.18   **2.** 0.675 + 0.411   **3.** $4.56 + $3.20

4. 3.289   **5.** $48.35   **6.**   4.632
  + 1.331   + 29.46   + 5.02

Use models to find each difference.

7. 17.645 − 3.20   **8.** $6.39 − $5.07   **9.** 28.362 − 8.75

10. $12.00   **11.**   78.066   **12.** $8.96
  −   9.75   −   2.37   −   5.87

Writing Math

Connect How is subtracting decimals similar to subtracting whole numbers?

CA Standards

KEY **NS 2.1** Add, subtract, multiply, and divide with decimals; add with negative integers; subtract positive integers from negative integers; and verify the reasonableness of the results.

MR 2.5 Indicate the relative advantages of exact and approximate solutions to problems and give answers to a specified degree of accuracy.

Also NS 1.0, NS 1.1, MR 1.2

Estimate Sums and Differences

Objective Estimate decimal sums and differences.

▶ **Learn by Example**

A racecar driver had three practice laps. About how much time did it take to complete all three practice laps?

First Practice Lap	40.058 seconds
Second Practice Lap	38.978 seconds
Third Practice Lap	39.242 seconds

1 Round each number to the nearest tenth of a second.

40.0⑤8   5 = 5 so round up   40.058 → 40.1
38.9⑦8   7 > 5 so round up   38.978 → 39.0
39.2④2   4 < 5 so round down   39.242 → 39.2

2 Add the rounded numbers to estimate the sum.

$$\begin{array}{r} 40.1 \\ 39.0 \\ +\ 39.2 \\ \hline 118.3 \end{array}$$

Solution: The practice laps took about 118.3 seconds.

Another Example

Estimate the difference.   0.139 − 0.038

1 Round each number to the nearest tenth.

0.1③9   3 < 5 so round down   0.139 → 0.1
0.0③8   3 < 5 so round down   0.038 → 0.0

2 Subtract the rounded numbers to estimate the difference.

$$\begin{array}{r} 0.1 \\ -\ 0.0 \\ \hline 0.1 \end{array}$$

▶ **Guided Practice**

Estimate by rounding each number to the nearest tenth.

1. $0.638 + 0.199$

2. $21.375 - 10.243$

3. $14.333 + 32.671$

4. $59.848 - 17.004$

Ask Yourself

• Did I follow the rounding rules?

• Did I estimate to the given place?

Estimate by rounding each number to the nearest whole number.

5. 4.302 − 2.499   **6.** 5.067 + 0.872   **7.** 9.382 − 5.019   **8.** 11.901 + 2.052

 Math Talk How is rounding a decimal like rounding a whole number?

▶ **Practice and Problem Solving**

Estimate by rounding each number to the nearest tenth.

9. 23.249 + 1.452   **10.** 2.382 − 2.377   **11.** 31.761 + 9.056

12. 4.733 − 2.471   **13.** 2.098 + 7.704   **14.** 40.651 − 10.622

Estimate by rounding each number to the nearest whole number.

15. 3.01 + 3.49   **16.** 12.65 − 2.81   **17.** 403.02 + 286.97

18. 75.11 − 25.306   **19.** 12.67 + 1.21   **20.** 0.053 + 0.034

 Real World Data

Use the table to solve.

21. Which ride takes longer, Space Mountain or the Colossus? About how much longer?

22. Write the names of the roller coasters in order from the shortest to longest rides.

23. Multistep Marlinda arrived at Space Mountain at 8:05 A.M. She waited in line for 9 minutes before her first ride. She liked the ride so much, she rode it again. She waited in line for 13 minutes. At what time did her second ride finish?

Roller Coaster	Length (in min.)
Big Thunder Mountain Railroad	3.25
Space Mountain	2.47
Colossus	1.45
Déjà Vu	1.32
Giant Dipper	1.75

 Spiral Review and Test Practice

Subtract. Write each answer in simplest form. **KEY** NS 2.3 pages 188, 190, 192

24. $5 - 1\frac{1}{4}$ **25.** $7\frac{3}{8} - 3\frac{5}{8}$ **26.** $5 - 4\frac{4}{5}$ **27.** $47\frac{9}{18} - 38\frac{9}{18}$

Write the letter of the correct answer. **KEY** NS 2.1

28. 8.239 + 1.447 =

  A 96.86   **B** 86.86   **C** 9.686   **D** 8.686

CA Standards

KEY NS 2.1 Add, subtract, multiply and divide with decimals; add with negative integers; subtract positive integers from negative integers; and verify the reasonableness of the results.

MR 2.1 Use estimation to verify the reasonableness of calculated results.

Also NS 1.0, NS 1.1, MR 2.3, MR 2.5

Add and Subtract Decimals

Objective Add and subtract decimals.

▶ **Learn by Example**

Joe walked 0.4 mile to the roller coaster, 0.5 mile to Crazy Critter, and finally 0.75 mile to Tipsy Turvy. How many miles did Joe walk?

Think

- Line up the digits in the addends. Use the decimal points as a guide.
- Add zeros as necessary.
- Regroup as necessary.

Add decimals.

1 Line up the decimals. Add the hundredths.

$$
\begin{array}{r}
0.40 \\
0.50 \\
+\ 0.75 \\
\hline
5
\end{array}
$$

2 Add the tenths.

$$
\begin{array}{r}
\overset{1}{0}.40 \\
0.50 \\
+\ 0.75 \\
\hline
65
\end{array}
$$

3 Add the ones.

$$
\begin{array}{r}
\overset{1}{0}.40 \\
0.50 \\
+\ 0.75 \\
\hline
1.65
\end{array}
$$

Check
Estimate to check.

0.4	rounds to	0
0.5	rounds to	1
0.75	rounds to	1

$0 + 1 + 1 = 2$

1.65 is close to 2.

Solution: Joe walked 1.65 miles.

Another Example

Subtract $54 - 48.75$

Subtract the hundredths, tenths, and ones. Write the decimal point in the answer.

$$
\begin{array}{r}
\overset{13}{\cancel{4}} \overset{9}{\cancel{3}} \overset{10}{\cancel{9}} \cancel{10} \\
\cancel{5}\cancel{4}.\cancel{0}\cancel{0} \\
-\ 48.75 \\
\hline
5.25
\end{array}
$$
↳ decimal point

Check
Estimate to check.

| 48.75 | rounds to | 49 |

$54 - 49 = 5$

5.25 is close to 5.

Solution: $54 - 48.75 = 5.25$

Add. Estimate to check your answer.

1.	2.	3.	4.
5.3	90.9	3.787	28.87
+ 6.4	+ 29.1	+ 0.43	+ 54.81

Subtract. Estimate to check your answer.

5.	6.	7.	8.
4.02	65.4	98.2	0.887
− 1.24	− 13.5	− 8.83	− 0.03

Ask Yourself
- Have I lined up the digits correctly?
- Have I included zeros when I need them to subtract?
- Have I regrouped correctly?

Guided Problem Solving

Use the questions to solve this problem.

9. At the Super Park Complex a tram travels in two directions. Is the route from the Tram Post to Super Safari shorter if you travel through the Enchanted Forest or if you travel through Crocodile Canyon?

a. **Understand** What two distances do you have to compare?

b. **Plan** Try estimating the distances. Round each distance from the map to the nearest whole number.

c. **Solve** Can you answer the question using your estimates? If not, find the exact answer.

d. **Look Back** Did you answer the question?

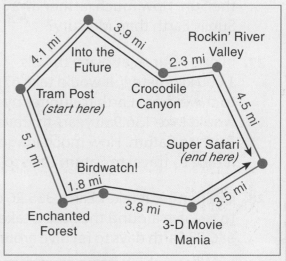

10. Is the difference between both routes in Problem 9 more or less than $\frac{1}{2}$ of a mile? Show your work.

123 **Math Talk** Does rounding each addend to the nearest whole number always give you an estimate that is the same as the actual sum rounded to the nearest whole number?

▶ **Practice and Problem Solving**

Add. Estimate to check your answer.

11.	12.	13.	14.	15.
8.49	9.527	5.619	$51.70	4.56
+ 4.59	+ 3.75	+ 0.75	+ 83.62	+ 3.7

Subtract. Estimate to check your answer.

16.	5.6 − 4.9	17.	3.45 − 0.79	18.	57.681 − 24.925	19.	$28.09 − 17.99	20.	83.66 − 35.3
21.	$35.07 − 16.55	22.	63.341 − 46.258	23.	$46.35 − 28.78	24.	56.368 − 28.462	25.	62.56 − 37.821

 ## Science Link

Solve. Use estimation to check.

26. Mercury is 57.9 million kilometers from the Sun. Earth is 149.6 million kilometers from the Sun. How much farther away from the Sun is Earth than Mercury?

27. In one hour, a jet plane travels 1,000 kilometers. It would take 67.123 years to travel from Earth to Jupiter by jet. It would take 136.986 years to travel from Earth to Saturn. How much longer would it take to travel to Saturn than to Jupiter?

28. **Challenge** It takes Earth 365.26 days to revolve around the Sun. It takes Mars 686.98 Earth days to revolve around the Sun.

   a. What is the difference, in days, between the time it takes Earth to revolve around the Sun and the time it takes Mars to revolve around the Sun?

   b. Does Mars take twice as long as Earth to revolve around the Sun?

The Solar System

- The Sun and the bodies that revolve around it make up the solar system.
- The solar system is a small part of a much larger system called the Milky Way galaxy.
- Earth is one of the many planets that revolve around the Sun or another star.
- The Sun is the largest part of the solar system and its gravity holds the other parts in their positions.

Science Link ES 5.b

 ## Spiral Review and Test Practice

Subtract. KEY NS 2.3 page 188

29. $5 - \dfrac{1}{2}$ 30. $8 - \dfrac{3}{5}$ 31. $4 - \dfrac{1}{8}$ 32. $6 - \dfrac{2}{3}$

Write the letter of the correct answer. KEY NS 2.1

33. Rianna jogged for 4.35 miles on Monday and 3.56 miles on Tuesday. How many miles did she jog in all?

   A 7.01   **B** 7.71   **C** 7.81   **D** 7.91

Extra Practice See page 265, Set B.

Key Standards Review

Need Help?
See Key Standards Handbook.

Name the letter on the number line that represents each expression. KEY **NS 1.5**, KEY **NS 2.3**, NS 2.4

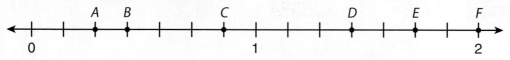

1. $1\frac{2}{7} - \frac{3}{7}$

2. $1\frac{3}{7} + \frac{4}{7}$

3. $\frac{2}{7} + \frac{2}{14}$

4. $\frac{4}{7} \div 2$

5. $\frac{8}{7} + \frac{4}{7}$

6. $1\frac{1}{7} + \frac{2}{7}$

Evaluate each expression when $n = 18$. KEY **AF 1.2**

7. $n + (54 - 27)$

8. $18 + n$

9. $(9 - 9) + n - (37 - 19)$

10. $n + (36 \div 6)$

11. $(65 + n) \times 3$

12. $(n - 9) \times (n - 16)$

13. $(n + n) \div 4$

14. $(27 - n) \times (n - n)$

15. $n + (16 + 5) - (34 - 5)$

 Explore

Zero Sum-Thing KEY **NS 2.1**

If you subtract $2 - 2$, you know the answer is zero. If you add 4 and then subtract 1 and then subtract 3, the answer is also zero. These are zero sums. Adding and subtracting the same amount is the same as adding 0. Do you think this also works with decimals?

1. Write your birthday or another date as a decimal. For example, July 19 becomes 7.19.

- Add 2.06.
- Subtract 1.32.
- Subtract 0.08.
- Add 3.5.
- Subtract 2.16.
- Subtract 2.

2. What do you notice? Why did this work?

3. Use decimals to make up your own zero sum challenge.

$$\begin{array}{r} 7.19 \\ +\ 2.06 \\ \hline 9.25 \\ -\ 1.32 \\ \hline 7.93 \\ -\ 0.08 \\ \hline 7.85 \\ +\ 3.5 \\ \hline 11.35 \\ -\ 2.16 \\ \hline 9.19 \\ -\ 2.00 \\ \hline 7.19 \end{array}$$

Santa Cruz, CA

CA Standards
MR 1.0, MR 1.2,
MR 2.0,

KEY **AF 1.2**,

NS 2.0, KEY **NS 2.1**,

KEY **NS 2.2**,

NS 2.4

Problem Solving

Objective Use skills and strategies to solve word problems.

The Santa Cruz Beach Boardwalk is California's oldest amusement park and has been home to the Looff carousel since 1911.

Solve. Tell which strategy or method you used.

1. The Santa Cruz Beach Boardwalk has more than 34 rides. Rides cost between 3 to 6 tickets and tickets are 65 cents each. Use the table to answer the questions below.

   a. Hanh has a $20 bill. She bought enough tickets to ride the Giant Dipper three times. How much money does she have left?

   b. How many times can Hanh ride the Space Race using the money she has left?

2. The distance between the Looff carousel and the Giant Dipper is x feet. Which expression could you use to find how far you've walked from one ride to the other if you are halfway between them?

   a. $x + \frac{1}{2}$ **b.** $x \div 2$ **c.** $x + 2$ **d.** $x - \frac{1}{2}$

3. The Santa Cruz Beach Boardwalk is a half-mile long. Write an equation to find how many feet long the Boardwalk is. Hint: 1 mile = 5,280 feet.

Boardwalk Rides	
Ride	**Tickets**
Red Baron	3
Giant Dipper	6
Looff Carousel	4
Space Race	5
Cyclone	4

The Giant Dipper, a classic wooden roller coaster, opened in 1924.

Problem Solving On Tests

Select a Strategy
- Draw a Picture
- Write an Equation
- Work Backward
- Guess and Check
- Choose the Operation

1. Hannah needs $2\frac{7}{8}$ cups of flour to make a cake. Her sister needs $1\frac{3}{4}$ cups of flour to make brownies. What is the total amount of flour the girls need for their baking projects?

A $3\frac{5}{6}$ cups   **C** $4\frac{1}{2}$ cups

B $4\frac{1}{4}$ cups   **D** $4\frac{5}{8}$ cups

KEY **NS 2.3** page 174

2. Mr. Turner bought $15\frac{1}{3}$ feet of fencing to finish fencing his yard. He only used $10\frac{1}{2}$ feet of the fencing he bought. How much fencing did he have left?

A $4\frac{1}{2}$ feet   **C** $5\frac{1}{6}$ feet

B $4\frac{5}{6}$ feet   **D** $5\frac{5}{6}$ feet

KEY **NS 2.3** page 192

3. Of the students in Ella's class, $\frac{1}{2}$ are girls. Of the girls in her class, $\frac{1}{3}$ sing in the Girls' Glee Club. What fraction of the girls sings in the Girls' Glee Club?

A $\frac{1}{6}$ **C** $\frac{2}{5}$

B $\frac{1}{5}$ **D** $\frac{5}{6}$

Test Tip
Remember to multiply the numerators and denominators and simplify, if necessary.

NS 2.5 page 212

4. A case of soymilk contains 8 boxes of soymilk. Mack's Deli has $9\frac{3}{4}$ cases of soymilk left after the weekend. How many boxes of soymilk do they have?

A $17\frac{3}{4}$ **B** 23   **C** $72\frac{3}{4}$ **D** 78

KEY **NS 2.3** page 216

5. A recipe for pudding calls for $\frac{2}{3}$ cup of sugar. The recipe makes 6 servings. How much sugar is in each serving?

A $\frac{1}{12}$ cup   **C** $\frac{1}{6}$ cup

B $\frac{1}{9}$ cup   **D** $\frac{1}{4}$ cup

NS 2.4 and NS 2.5 page 230

6. A bag contains $\frac{11}{12}$ pound of peanuts. Raul wants to divide the peanuts into individual servings. How many servings of peanuts can Raul make, if each serving size is $\frac{1}{3}$ pound?

A $\frac{4}{11}$

B $2\frac{7}{12}$

C $2\frac{3}{4}$

D $3\frac{1}{6}$

Test Tip
Remember to invert the divisor to find the reciprocal before dividing fractions.

NS 2.5 page 234

7. Sara has $1\frac{1}{2}$ yards of ribbon. She divided the ribbon into $\frac{5}{6}$ pieces. If $r = \frac{5}{6}$, what is the value of $1\frac{1}{2} \div r$?

A $\frac{5}{9}$ **B** $1\frac{1}{4}$ **C** $1\frac{3}{5}$ **D** $1\frac{4}{5}$

NS 2.5 and KEY **AF 1.2** page 236

Education Place
Visit www.eduplace.com/camap/ for **Test-Taking Tips** and **Extra Practice**.

Chapter 12 Lesson 4   **263**

Reading & Writing **Math**

Vocabulary

Pedro is doing his math homework. Look at Pedro's math homework and his answers.

A. $48.2 - 3.74$

$$
\begin{array}{r}
\overset{7\ 12}{4\cancel{8}.\cancel{2}} \\
-3.74 \\
\hline
1.08
\end{array}
$$

B. $2.981 + 23.71$

$$
\begin{array}{r}
2.981 \\
+23.71 \\
\hline
26.69
\end{array}
$$

C. $9 - 2.87$

$$
\begin{array}{r}
\overset{8\ 10\ 10}{\cancel{9}.\cancel{0}\cancel{0}} \\
-2.87 \\
\hline
6.23
\end{array}
$$

Answer these questions about Pedro's math homework.

1. What mistake did Pedro make in Problem A? What would you tell Pedro to do to fix this mistake?

2. What mistake did Pedro make in Problem B? What would you tell Pedro to do to fix this mistake?

3. What mistake did Pedro make in Problem C? What would you tell Pedro to do to fix this mistake?

4. Copy the problems. Find the correct answers.

Writing Write a note to Pedro. Tell him what you did to fix his mistakes. Give him some advice on how he can avoid mistakes like this in the future.

Reading Check out this book in your library.
The $1.00 Word Riddle Book by Marilyn Burns

CA Standards

MR 2.3 Use a variety of methods, such as words, numbers, symbols, charts, graphs, tables, diagrams, and models, to explain mathematical reasoning.

Also KEY NS 2.1

Standards-Based Extra Practice

Set A ────────────────────────────────── KEY **NS 2.1** page 256

Estimate by rounding each number to the nearest tenth.

1. 4.625 + 8.194   **2.** 9.715 − 5.891   **3.** 0.944 + 4.449

4. 9.156 − 7.644   **5.** 37.556 − 34.292   **6.** 12.114 + 0.059

Estimate by rounding each number to the nearest whole number.

7. 4.155 + 6.511   **8.** 11.31 − 8.604   **9.** 8.486 − 5.51

Solve.

10. A miniature house has two levels. The height of the first level is 4.64 centimeters. The height of the second level is 3.914 centimeters. Round to the nearest tenth to estimate the height of the miniature house.

11. Nick had $8.79 in his pocket. He bought a book for $5.41. Round to the nearest dollar to estimate how much money Nick has left.

Set B ────────────────────────────────── KEY **NS 2.1** page 258

Add or subtract. Estimate to check your answer.

1.   9.001
       + 4.61

2.   14.2
       − 11.191

3.   4.267
       + 6.84

4.   0.811
       − 0.64

5.   5.464
       + 2.48

6.   6.812
       − 4.09

7.   8.6
       + 4.816

8.   11.916
       − 0.11

Solve.

9. Ben drove from San Diego to Los Angeles in 3.75 hours. It took him 2.8 hours to drive back. How many hours did Ben drive in all?

10. David ran the first part of a race in 12.264 seconds and the second part in 11.516 seconds. How much longer did it take David to run the first part of the race than the second part?

Education Place
Visit www.eduplace.com/camap/
for more **Extra Practice**.

Chapter 12 Extra Practice   **265**

Chapter Review/Test

Vocabulary and Concepts ———————————— NS 1.0, NS 1.1, KEY **NS 2.1**, MR 2.3

Write the best word to complete each sentence.

1. When rounding a decimal to the nearest whole number, round down if the number in the _____ place is less than 5.

2. You can round decimals to _____ sums and differences.

3. The second place to the right of the decimal is the _____ place.

4. When adding and subtracting decimals, _____ the decimal points.

Skills ————————————————————————— NS 1.1, KEY **NS 2.1**

Estimate the sum or difference by rounding each number to the nearest tenth. Check that your answer is reasonable.

5. $8.196 + 12.422$ 6. $9.819 - 4.655$ 7. $0.944 - 0.094$ 8. $18.050 + 12.951$

Add or subtract. Estimate to check your answer.

9. $2.914 + 4.605$ 10. $8.1 - 3.9$ 11. $12.01 + 18.909$ 12. $\$4.55 - \$3.87$

13. $5.007 + 4.8$ 14. $\$9.61 + \$12.40$ 15. $13.876 - 8.98$ 16. $62.152 - 5.052$

Problem Solving and Reasoning ———— NS 1.1, KEY **NS 2.1**, MR 2.1, MR 2.3, MR 2.5

Solve.

17. Danny's first ride down the water slide lasted 4.791 seconds. His second ride lasted 5.433 seconds. To the nearest second, what was the total time for both rides?

18. The topsy-turvy ride lasts 38.53 seconds. Riders are in a sideways position for 26.43 seconds. The rest of the time they are upside down. How many seconds are the riders upside down?

19. Patricia drove 1.6 hours to pick up her cousin. She then drove 2.35 hours to the amusement park. How many hours did Patricia drive?

20. Anissa bought a funnel cake for $3.95, a drink for $4.60, and a pretzel for $2.85. How much did she spend?

Writing Math When rounding decimals to the tenths place, how do you know whether to round up or down?

Spiral Review and Test Practice

1. $2{,}605 + 6{,}478 =$

  A 8,073

  B 8,083

  C 9,083

  D 9,183

NS 1.0 page 126

2. $65 + 14 = 14 + \square$

  A 14

  B 51

  C 65

  D 79

KEY AF 1.2 page 126

3. If $4 \times 8 = 32$, then what is $32 \div 4$?

  A 2

  B 8

  C 28

  D 128

> **Test Tip**
> Look for number relationships when you see the words *if* and *then* in a question.

KEY NS 2.2 page 128

4. Fidel brought $2\frac{3}{4}$ pounds of potato salad and $1\frac{2}{3}$ pounds of macaroni salad to the class picnic. How much salad did Fidel bring to the picnic?

  A $\frac{1}{12}$ pound

  B $\frac{5}{12}$ pound

  C $2\frac{5}{12}$ pounds

  D $4\frac{5}{12}$ pounds

KEY NS 2.3 page 174

5. $\frac{5}{6} \div \frac{2}{3} =$

  A $\frac{5}{9}$

  B $\frac{4}{5}$

  C $1\frac{1}{4}$

  D $7\frac{1}{2}$

> **Test Tip**
> Remember to rewrite a fraction division problem as a multiplication problem.

NS 2.4, NS 2.5 page 234

6. What is the sum of $4.506 + 2.71$ when both addends are rounded to the nearest tenth?

  A 8   **C** 7.3

  B 7.4   **D** 7.2

NS 1.1, KEY NS 2.1 page 256

Education Place
Visit www.eduplace.com/camap/ for **Test-Taking Tips** and **Extra Practice**.

Chapter 12 Spiral Review and Test Practice   **267**

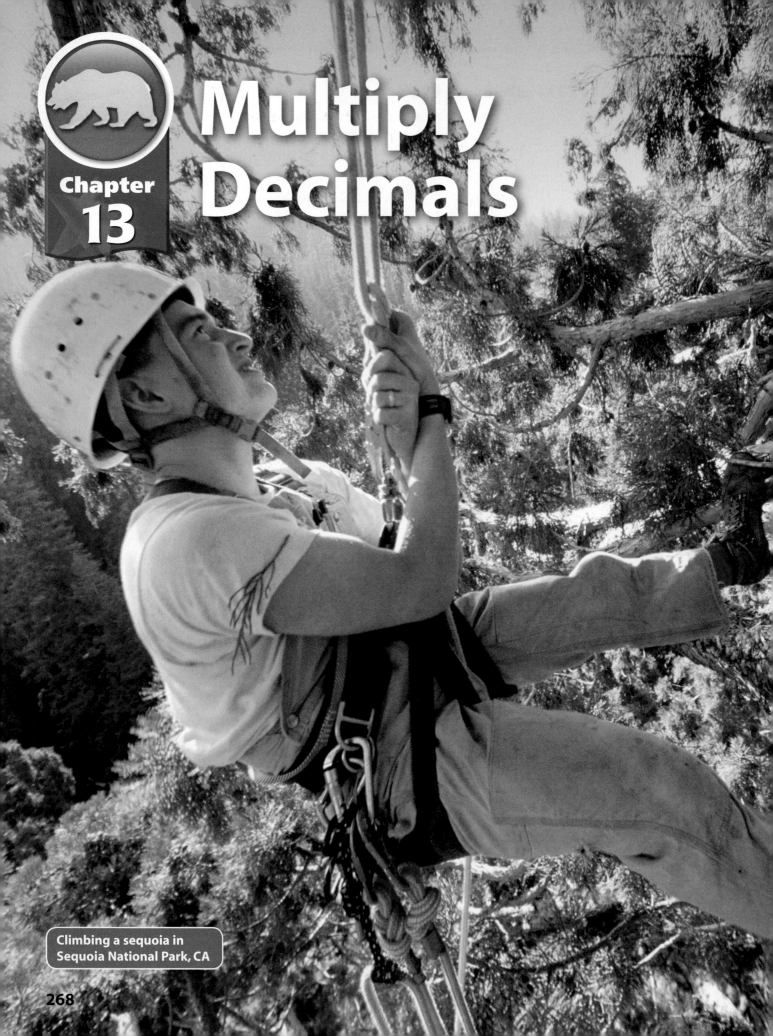

Multiply Decimals

Chapter 13

Climbing a sequoia in Sequoia National Park, CA

Check What You Know

Vocabulary and Concepts NS 1.0, MR 2.3

Choose the best word to complete each sentence. pages 60 and 258

1. To add decimals, align the decimal point in the ____ with the decimal points in the addends.

2. In the number 5.107, the digit 7 is in the ____ place.

Skills NS 1.1

Round to the place indicated by the underlined digit. page 66

3. 14.<u>0</u>8

4. 6.2<u>5</u>2

5. <u>0</u>.584

6. 3.<u>2</u>19

Add. Estimate to check your answer. page 258

7.
$$\begin{array}{r} 3.435 \\ +\ 18.9 \\ \hline \end{array}$$

8.
$$\begin{array}{r} 322.01 \\ +\ 253.187 \\ \hline \end{array}$$

9.
$$\begin{array}{r} 22.22 \\ +\ 333.888 \\ \hline \end{array}$$

Problem Solving and Reasoning KEY NS 2.1

10. In a ski race, Pilar was 0.32 second behind Billy. Wendy was 0.565 second behind Billy. How many seconds behind Pilar was Wendy?

Vocabulary

Visualize It!

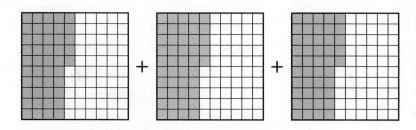

To add decimals quickly you can **multiply**.

$$0.45 + 0.45 + 0.45 = 3 \times 0.45 = 1.35$$

Language Tip

Math words that look alike in English and Spanish often have the same meaning.

English	Spanish
decimal	decimal
decimal point	punto decimal

See **English-Spanish Glossary** pages 628–642.

Education Place Visit www.eduplace.com/camap/ for the **eGlossary** and **eGames**.

CA Standards MR 2.3 Use a variety of methods, such as words, numbers, symbols, charts, graphs, tables, diagrams, and models, to explain mathematical reasoning. **Also KEY NS 2.1**

Chapter 13   269

CA Standards

KEY NS 2.1 Add, subtract, multiply, and divide with decimals; add with negative integers; subtract positive integers from negative integers; and verify the reasonableness of the results.

MR 2.3 Use a variety of methods, such as words, numbers, symbols, charts, graphs, tables, diagrams, and models, to explain mathematical reasoning.

Also NS 2.0, MR 1.2

Materials

- Learning Tool 20 (Hundredths Models)
- Crayons or colored pencils (yellow and blue)

Think

If I shade 89 squares on each hundredths model, I will still shade the same number of squares.

Hands On
Multiply Decimals

Objective Use models to explore multiplication of decimals.

▶ **Explore**

You already know how to multiply with fractions. In this chapter, you will learn how to multiply with decimals.

Question How can you use a model to show multiplying with decimals?

Sonya is a jeweler. She made a pair of gold earrings. Each earring has 0.89 gram of gold. How much gold is in both earrings?

1 Use two hundredths models. Each complete model represents 1 gram of gold. Shade 0.89 two times. Use blue and yellow for each group of 89 hundredths.

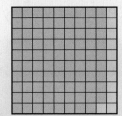 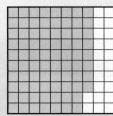

0.89 blue   0.89 yellow

$2 \times 0.89 = 0.89 + 0.89$

2 Count the shaded hundredths. There are 178 shaded hundredths. This is one whole and 78 hundredths.

$2 \times 0.89 = 1.78.$

Solution: There are 1.78 grams of gold in both earrings.

You can use models to multiply a decimal by a decimal.
The model is like the model you use to multiply fractions.

Find 0.2 × 1.5

1 Use two hundredths models.
Shade 1.5 in blue.

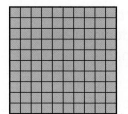

2 Shade 0.2 of each hundredths model
in yellow. Count the green squares.

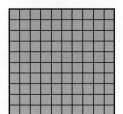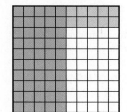

There are 30 hundredths shaded green.

0.2 × 1.5 = 0.30

▶ **Extend**

Use models to multiply. Write the product as a decimal.

1. 4 × 0.24   **2.** 0.3 × 1.2   **3.** 0.12 × 5

4. 0.5 × 0.62   **5.** 3 × 0.42   **6.** 2 × 0.65

7. 0.25 × 4   **8.** 0.6 × 1.2   **9.** 0.1 × 3.2

10. 3 × 0.15   **11.** 4 × 0.2   **12.** 0.3 × 1.5

13. Challenge Sonya also makes silver bracelets. There are
1.5 grams of silver in one bracelet. How much silver is in
12 bracelets?

> **Hint**
> Break the problem
> down into parts. Use
> models to find the
> silver in 2 bracelets.
> Then use a fact you
> know.

Write the multiplication equation that the model shows.

14.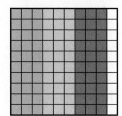

15.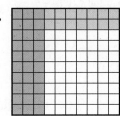

Writing Math

When you multiply a whole number and a decimal less than 1, will
the product always be less than the whole number? Explain.

LESSON 2

CA Standards
KEY NS 2.1 Add, subtract, multiply, and divide with decimals; add with negative integers; subtract positive integers from negative integers; and verify the reasonableness of the results.

Also NS 1.0, NS 2.0, AF 1.0, MR 1.2, MR 2.2, MR 2.6

Multiply Whole Numbers and Decimals

Objective Find the product of a whole number and a decimal.

▶ **Learn by Example**

In Lesson 1, you used models to multiply with decimals. In this lesson, you will learn how to place the decimal point in the product of a whole number and a decimal.

> Carla sells jewelry made by local artists. A customer is interested in a bracelet that is 7 inches long. The customer asks Carla for the length of the bracelet in centimeters. There are 2.54 centimeters in 1 inch. What is the length of the bracelet in centimeters?

Example 1

Find 7×2.54

1 Multiply. Ignore the decimal point.

$$
\begin{array}{r}
254 \\
\times\ 7 \\
\hline
1778
\end{array}
$$

> Multiply like you would when multiplying whole numbers.

2 Place the decimal point in the product.

The number of decimal places in the product must be equal to the total number of decimal places in the factors.

$$
\begin{array}{rl}
2.54 & \leftarrow \quad \text{2 decimal places} \\
\times\ 7 & \leftarrow \quad + \text{0 decimal places} \\
\hline
17.78 & \leftarrow \quad \text{2 decimal places}
\end{array}
$$

Solution: The bracelet is 17.78 centimeters long.

Example 2

Find 12×0.65

$$
\begin{array}{rl}
12 & \leftarrow \quad \text{0 decimal places} \\
\times\ 0.65 & \leftarrow \quad + \text{2 decimal places} \\
\hline
60 & \\
+\ 720 & \\
\hline
7.80 & \leftarrow \quad \text{2 decimal places}
\end{array}
$$

> Check the number of decimal places in the product before you drop any ending zeros.
> $7.80 = 7.8$

Solution: $12 \times 0.65 = 7.80$

Other Examples

Multiply 0.008 by 10, 100, and 1,000.

$0.008 \times 10 = 0.08$ ⟵ The decimal moves one place to the right.

$0.008 \times 100 = 0.8$ ⟵ The decimal moves two places to the right.

$0.008 \times 1,000 = 8$ ⟵ The decimal moves three places to the right.

▶ Guided Practice

Find the product.

1. 4×1.3
2. 2.6×5
3. 0.59×8
4. 3×1.82
5. 3.25×16
6. 0.51×7
7. 6×2.25
8. 3.3×5
9. 18×0.52
10. 2.34×10
11. 100×4.2
12. $1.105 \times 1,000$

Ask Yourself

- Did my product have the correct number of decimal places before I dropped any ending zeros?
- Did I drop any ending zeros in my product?

(123) Math Talk How many places does the decimal point move when you multiply a decimal number by 10? by 100? by 1,000? What pattern do you see?

▶ Practice and Problem Solving

Find the product.

13. 6×2.4
14. 3.8×2
15. 0.13×5
16. 50.2×6
17. 12×0.56
18. 16×9.5
19. 35×0.86
20. 3×31.44
21. 7×4.28
22. 8.2×5
23. 23×0.72
24. 0.16×15
25. 100×0.098
26. $1,000 \times 2.07$
27. 84.077×100
28. 0.442×10

𝓍 Algebra Expressions

Find one value of n that makes the statement true.

29. $8 \times n$ is between 24 and 30
30. $n \times 76$ is between 160 and 200
31. $12 \times n$ is between 60 and 70
32. $n \times 30$ is between 90 and 120

Solve.

33. Carla sold 8 charm bracelets. The price of each bracelet was $8.95. How much money did Carla collect for the 8 charm bracelets?

34. Ryan is making beaded bracelets. Each bead is 0.35 inches long. He uses 16 beads for each bracelet. How many inches long are 3 bracelets?

35. Multistep Lisa earns $9.00 per hour. She worked 2.5 hours on Friday and 6.5 hours on Saturday. After taxes, she gets to keep 0.9 of her earnings. How much does Lisa get to keep?

36. Joe earns $9.00 per hour working in a shoe store. One week, he worked 12.5 hours. Another week, he worked 15 hours. How much did Joe earn for both weeks?

 Science Link

Solve.

37. Hematite is a molecule that is part of rust. About 0.7 of hematite is iron. How much iron is in 15 grams of hematite?

38. Hydrogen is a part of ordinary water. About 0.11 of water is hydrogen. If Gurmeet drinks 460 grams of water, how many grams of hydrogen does he drink?

39. Challenge About 0.89 of water is oxygen. About 0.73 of carbon dioxide is oxygen. Which contains more oxygen, 120 grams of water or 165 grams of carbon dioxide? By how much?

Atoms and Molecules

- Every person, animal, and object is made up of atoms. Atoms can be bonded together to form a molecule.

- Molecules are everywhere! When two oxygen atoms join a carbon atom, it is called carbon dioxide. One oxygen atom joined to two hydrogen atoms is called water.

- Atoms of different elements have different masses. The mass of a molecule is related to the mass of the atoms that make up the molecule.

Science PS1.b, PS1.g

 Spiral Review and Test Practice

Write the name of the property that matches the equation. KEY **AF 1.2** page 126

40. $a + 7 = 7 + a$

41. $(3 + w) + 9 = 3 + (w + 9)$

42. $b + 0 = b$

43. $11 + m = m + 11$

Write the letter of the correct answer. KEY **NS 2.1**

44. Edward can run 340 yards in 1 minute. How many yards can he run in 4.5 minutes?

   A 153   **B** 1,510   **C** 1,350   **D** 1,530

Extra Practice See page 289, Set A.

Key Standards Review

Need Help?
See Key Standards Handbook.

Solve. Write each answer in simplest form. KEY NS 2.3

1. At the carnival, Margeaux spent $\frac{2}{5}$ of her tickets on games and $\frac{3}{10}$ on rides. What fraction of her tickets did she spend?

2. Sojung bought a pencil sharpener for 35 cents and an eraser for a quarter. What fraction of a dollar did she spend on them?

Add or subtract. Estimate to check that your answer is reasonable. KEY NS 2.1

3. $2.4 + 3.6$

4. $62.35 + 7.9$

5. $5.75 - 0.69$

6. $67.4 - 23.07$

7. $6.57 + 32.35$

8. $\$8.32 + \$27.91$

9. $35.62 - 9.86$

10. $\$19.95 - \$11.99$

Challenge Number Sense

Decimal Multiplication KEY NS 2.1

Choose two numbers to solve each problem.

1. Find the greatest product.

2. Find the least product.

3. Find two numbers with a product of 3.52.

4. Find two numbers with a product of 2.2.

5. Find two numbers with a product of 1.3.

6. **Analyze** What are the greatest and least numbers? How did these numbers help you find the answers to some of the problems?

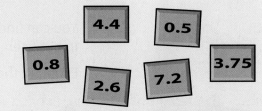

CA Standards
NS 1.1 Students estimate, round, and manipulate very large (e.g., millions) and small (e.g., thousandths) numbers.

KEY NS 2.1 Add, subtract, multiply, and divide with decimals; add with negative integers; subtract positive integers from negative integers; and verify the reasonableness of the results.

Also NS 2.0, MR 2.1

Materials
Workmat 3

Estimate Products

Objective Estimate products of decimals.

▶ **Learn by Example**

A conductor wants to copy a rehearsal schedule for each of the 77 musicians in the orchestra. It costs $0.11 for each copy. About how much will it cost to make all the copies?

Since the problem asks *about* how much it will cost, you can estimate. Use fractions and a number line to help.

Estimate the product of 77 × $0.11

Example 1

① Round the factors.

$$77 \longrightarrow 80$$
$$\$0.11 \longrightarrow \$0.10 \text{ or } \frac{1}{10} \text{ dollar}$$

Multiply.

$$80 \times \frac{1}{10} = \frac{80}{10} = 8$$

Solution: It will cost about $8 to make the copies.

Sometimes you can use estimation to check if your answer is reasonable. Four hundred twenty people went to the symphony one evening. That night, 0.75 of the audience was adults. Rinaldo says that there were about 310 adults in the audience. Is that reasonable?

Example 2

You can find a high and low estimate. The actual product will be in between.

Estimate the product of 0.75 × 420.

① Find a low estimate.

$$0.7 \times 400 = 280$$

② Find a high estimate.

$$0.8 \times 450 = 360$$

Solution: The product of 0.75 × 420 is between 280 and 360. It is reasonable.

Conductor Michael Tilson Thomas leads the San Francisco Symphony Orchestra.

Estimate the product. Write an equation to show the rounded numbers you used.

Ask Yourself
To what whole number or decimal can I round a decimal?

1. 4.91 × 17
2. 213 × 0.22
3. 765 × 1.9
4. 6,082 × 0.52

5. 92 × 4.14
6. 31 × 0.53
7. 7.899 × 609
8. 3.6 × 467

 Math Talk Find the actual product of 563 × 2.6. Tell how you can use a high and low estimate to check if your answer is reasonable.

▶ **Practice and Problem Solving**

Estimate the product. Write an equation to show the rounded numbers you used.

9. 8.32 × 51
10. 9 × 0.121
11. 14.8 × 49
12. 315 × 0.511

13. 7.6 × 37
14. 0.55 × 75
15. 3.1 × 62
16. 28 × 11.88

Use the table to solve problems 17–18. Show your work.

17. Last week, the orchestra rehearsed 4 times. About how many miles did Mr. Belmont travel to and from rehearsal last week?

18. In one month, the orchestra rehearsed 13 times. Ms. Lin attended all of the rehearsals. Ms. Parson missed 3. Which of these musicians traveled more miles for rehearsal that month? About how many more miles did she travel?

Distance to Rehearsal from Musician's House	
Musician	**Distance (mi)**
Mr. Belmont	20.25
Mr. Carlin	4.9
Ms. Lin	19.7
Ms. Parson	29.85

 Spiral Review and Test Practice

Add. Write the answer in simplest form. KEY NS 2.3 page 174

19. $4\frac{3}{5} + 5\frac{1}{10}$
20. $3\frac{5}{8} + 2\frac{1}{3}$
21. $5\frac{3}{4} + 7\frac{7}{10}$

Write the letter of the correct answer. KEY NS 2.1

22. Which is the best estimate for the product 146 × 0.98?

   A 14.6   B 146   C 1460   D 980

CA Standards
KEY **NS 2.1** Add, subtract, multiply and divide with decimals; add with negative integers; subtract positive integers form negative integers; and verify the reasonableness of the results.

Also AF 1.3, NS 1.0, NS 2.0, MR 2.1, MR 2.2, MR 2.3

Multiply Decimals

Objective Find the product of two decimals.

▶ **Learn by Example**

The parking lot at a shopping mall covers 0.8 acre. A section that is 0.4 of the parking lot is reserved for compact cars. How large is the area reserved for compact cars?

Example 1

1 Multiply. Ignore the decimal points.

$$\begin{array}{r} 8 \\ \times\ 4 \\ \hline 32 \end{array}$$

2 Place the decimal point in the product.

$$\begin{array}{r} 0.8 \leftarrow \quad \text{1 decimal place} \\ \times\ 0.4 \leftarrow \quad +\ \text{1 decimal place} \\ \hline 0.32 \leftarrow \quad \text{2 decimal places} \end{array}$$

Solution: The area reserved for compact cars is 0.32 acre.

Hint
The symbol ≈ means "about equal to."

Sometimes the factors have different numbers of decimal places. You can still multiply first and then add the decimal places.

Find 0.81 × 0.7

Check
Estimate to check.

Low Estimate	High Estimate
0.8 ≈ 0	0.8 ≈ 1
× 0.4 ≈ × 0	× 0.4 ≈ × 1
0	1

0.32 is between 0 and 1. It is reasonable.

Example 2

$$\begin{array}{r} 0.81 \leftarrow \quad \text{2 decimal places} \\ \times\ 0.7 \leftarrow \quad +\ \text{1 decimal place} \\ \hline 0.567 \leftarrow \quad \text{3 decimal places} \end{array}$$

$$\frac{81}{100} \times \frac{7}{10} = \frac{567}{1000}$$

$$\frac{567}{1000} = 0.567$$

Solution: 0.81 × 0.7 = 0.567

Another Example

$$\begin{array}{r} 1.52 \leftarrow \quad \text{2 decimal places} \\ \times\ 4.3 \leftarrow \quad +\ \text{1 decimal place} \\ \hline 456 \\ +\ 6080 \\ \hline 6.536 \leftarrow \quad \text{3 decimal places} \end{array}$$

Check
Estimate to check.

Low Estimate	High Estimate
1.52 ≈ 1.00	1.52 ≈ 2.00
× 4.3 ≈ × 4.00	× 4.3 ≈ × 5.00
4.00	10.00

6.536 is between 4.00 and 10.00.

Multiply. Estimate to make sure your answer is reasonable.

1. 0.7×0.3 2. 0.7×0.56 3. 0.6×0.09 4. 1.29×3.7

5. 0.6×0.8 6. 0.89×0.2 7. 8.4×0.55 8. 3.29×1.7

Ask Yourself
Does my product have the correct number of decimal places?

Compare. Write <, >, or = for the ⬤.

9. 0.4×0.2 ⬤ 0.5×0.3 10. 1.2×3.5 ⬤ 2.9×0.5 11. 7.23×0.2 ⬤ 3.56×0.7

 Math Talk Why would 21 be an unreasonable answer to 0.3×0.7?

► **Practice and Problem Solving**

Multiply. Estimate to make sure your answer is reasonable.

12. 0.4×0.4 13. 0.8×0.3 14. 0.3×0.5 15. 0.6×0.9

16. 1.7×0.6 17. 2.2×2.3 18. 0.51×0.4 19. 3.45×1.7

Algebra Equations
Tell whether the value of a is 0.3, 0.03, 3.0, or 3.3.

20. $a \times 5 = 0.15$ 21. $a \times 0.1 = 0.33$ 22. $14 \times a = 4.2$

23. $a^2 = 0.09$ 24. $3 \times 0.01 = a$ 25. $a \times 2 = 6.6$

26. $0.6 \times a = 0.18$ 27. $a \times 0.11 = 0.33$ 28. $a^2 = 9$

Compare. Write <, >, or = for the ⬤.

29. 0.3×0.6 ⬤ 0.9×2.0 30. 0.8×0.5 ⬤ 0.9×0.4 31. 7×0.3 ⬤ 3×0.7

32. 0.1×0.2 ⬤ 0.2×0.02 33. 0.5×8 ⬤ 5×0.8 34. 9×0.01 ⬤ 0.6×1

35. Shane walks 1.2 miles to school. Michael's home is 0.6 of the way between Shane's home and school. How far has Shane walked when he reaches Michael's home on the way to school?

36. **Multistep** Emma's home is 0.4 of the way between Shane's home and Michael's home. How far is Emma's from school?

37. At a bookstore, a book costs $11.95. If you bought the same book at a school book sale, you would pay 0.4 of that amount. How much does the book cost at the book sale?

History-Social Science Link

Use the chart to solve.

38. If a settler purchased 1.5 pounds of baking soda, what was the cost?

39. If a child needed half the supplies that an adult needed, how many pounds of dried fruit would a child have needed? What would the cost have been?

40. Find the total cost of food needed for one adult on the Oregon Trail.

41. A settler buys the necessary amount of cornmeal and bacon for his journey. How much does he pay? Use the Distributive Property to write and solve an equation for the cost.

42. Create and Solve Write and solve a word problem that uses the information from the table.

Packing for the Oregon Trail

In the mid 1800s settlers traveled west on the Oregon Trail. They carried their food and belongings in covered wagons or on the backs of mules. The chart shows the cost of food needed for the trip.

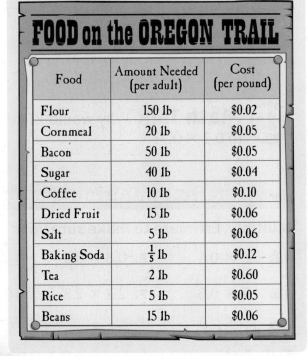

FOOD on the OREGON TRAIL

Food	Amount Needed (per adult)	Cost (per pound)
Flour	150 lb	$0.02
Cornmeal	20 lb	$0.05
Bacon	50 lb	$0.05
Sugar	40 lb	$0.04
Coffee	10 lb	$0.10
Dried Fruit	15 lb	$0.06
Salt	5 lb	$0.06
Baking Soda	$\frac{1}{5}$ lb	$0.12
Tea	2 lb	$0.60
Rice	5 lb	$0.05
Beans	15 lb	$0.06

History-Social Science 5.8.4

Oregon Trail reenactment

Spiral Review and Test Practice

Complete the multiplication sentence. NS 2.4, NS 2.5 page 212

43. $\frac{1}{5} \times$ ___ $= \frac{4}{5}$ **44.** $\frac{4}{5} \times$ ___ $= 40$ **45.** ___ $\times \frac{1}{6} = 2$

46. ___ $\times 22 = 4\frac{1}{8}$ **47.** $28 \times$ ___ $= 3\frac{8}{9}$ **48.** $15 \times$ ___ $= 1\frac{2}{3}$

Write the letter of the correct answer. KEY NS 2.1

49. $24.08 \times 0.7 =$

    A 14.806   **B** 16.856   **C** 24.78   **D** 168.56

Extra Practice See page 289, Set C.

Ride the Rapids

Alexa is a whitewater rafting guide. She explains the classification of the rapids to her beginner passengers. Class I is flat water. As the classes increase to Class V, the height of the waves and drops increase and the number of obstacles, such as rocks in the river, also increases.

1. Today the Class II waves on California's South Fork American River trip are averaging 1.9 feet. If the Class V waves are 4 times as high, what will be their height?

2. The seating space on one of the rafts is 3.5m long and 2.5m wide. What is the area of this rectangular seating space?

3. The first rapids are encountered 0.012 of the way along a 20.5-mile trip. About how many miles from the start of the trip is that?

A family whitewater rafting on the American River near Sacramento, CA

CA Standards
NS 2.5, MG 1.4, MR 2.4

White water rafting on the Kern River, CA

CA Standards

KEY **NS 2.1** Add, subtract, multiply and divide with decimals; add with negative integers; subtract positive integers from negative integers; and verify the reasonableness of the results.

MR 2.1 Use estimation to verify the reasonableness of calculated results.

Also NS 1.0, NS 2.0, MR 1.2, MR 3.0, MR 3.1, MR 3.2, MR 3.3

Zeros in the Product

Objective Decide when to write zeros in the products of decimal factors.

▶ **Learn by Example**

Sometimes you need to write zeros in a product before you can place the decimal point.

A store sells pencils for $0.80 each. The store is located in a place where the sales tax is 0.05 of the total price. How much is the sales tax on one of the pencils?

1 Multiply. Ignore the decimal points.

$$\begin{array}{r} 8 \\ \times\ 5 \\ \hline 40 \end{array}$$

2 Place the decimal point in the product.

$$\begin{array}{rl} 0.8 & \leftarrow \quad \text{1 decimal place} \\ \times\ 0.05 & \leftarrow \quad +\ \text{2 decimal places} \\ \hline 40 & \leftarrow \quad \text{3 decimal places} \end{array}$$

3 Write the number of zeros in front of the product that are needed to place the decimal point correctly.

$$\begin{array}{rl} 0.8 & \\ \times\ 0.05 & \\ \hline 0.040 & \leftarrow \text{3 decimal places} \end{array}$$

Solution: The sales tax is $0.04 for an $0.80 pencil.

Check

Before you multiply, estimate to know where to put the decimal point in your answer.

0.80 ⟶ 1

0.05 × 1 = 0.05

The tax will be a little less than $0.05, so $0.04 is reasonable.

Think

You can compare the exact answer to the estimate. $0.04 is a little less than $0.05. So the answer is reasonable.

Another Example

Find 0.15 × 0.04

$$\begin{array}{rl} 0.15 & \leftarrow \quad \text{2 decimal places} \\ \times\ 0.04 & \leftarrow \quad +\ \text{2 decimal places} \\ \hline 0.0060 & \leftarrow \quad \text{4 decimal places} \end{array}$$

$$\frac{15}{100} \times \frac{4}{100} = \frac{60}{10,000}$$

$$\frac{60}{10,000} = 0.0060$$

Multiply. Check to see if your answer is reasonable.

Ask Yourself
Do I have the correct number of decimal places in the product?

1. 0.2
   × 0.4

2. 0.03
   × 2

3. 0.42
   × 0.20

4. 0.233
   × 2

5. 0.1
   × 0.7

6. 0.04
   × 0.2

7. 0.34
   × 0.1

8. 0.7
   × 0.04

9. 0.05 × 1.3

10. 0.4 × 0.03

11. 0.002 × 4

12. 1.2 × 0.03

13. 0.06 × 1.3

14. 0.03 × 0.02

15. 0.09 × 0.5

16. 7.1 × 0.003

Hint
When you calculate sales tax, always round up to the next penny.

Guided Problem Solving

Use the questions to solve this problem.

17. The price of a notebook is $2.19. The sales tax will be 0.04 of the purchase price. How much will the notebook cost, including the sales tax?

   a. **Understand** How much is the notebook before sales tax?

   b. **Plan** What operation will you use to find the amount of sales tax? What will you do to find the total cost?

   c. **Solve** Carry out your plan and solve the problem.

   d. **Look Back** Does your answer make sense? Check your work with estimation.

$2.19

18. Look back at Problem 17. Suppose the price of the notebook is $2.00. What would be the total cost including tax? Explain how you can solve the problem using mental math.

123 Math Talk Why can 0.040 be written as 0.04?

Multiply. Check to see if the answer is reasonable.

19.   4
    × 0.2

20.   0.4
    × 0.2

21.   0.04
    × 0.2

22.   0.04
    × 2

23.   3.04
    × 0.2

24.   8
    × 0.4

25.   0.8
    × 0.4

26.   0.08
    × 0.4

27.   0.8
    × 0.04

28.   4.8
    × 0.04

 Real World Data

Use the table to solve Problems 29–32.

29. A belt costs $12.40. How much will the sales tax be if it is sold in Nevada?

30. A pair of pants costs $21.95. Including sales tax, what will the pants cost in Kansas? In Missouri?

31. **Challenge** A department store chain has stores in each state in the table. At all the stores a certain hat sells for $32.80 and a certain wallet sells for $15.18. You have $50.00. Do you have enough to buy the items in California? In Colorado? Explain.

32. **Create and Solve** Write your own problem using the information in this table. Exchange problems with a classmate and solve.

State	Sales Tax Rate
Colorado	0.029
Kansas	0.053
Nevada	0.065
California	0.0625
Missouri	0.0425

 Spiral Review and Test Practice

Round the numbers to the nearest tenth to estimate the sum or difference. KEY **NS 2.1** page 256

33. 0.93 + 0.39

34. 4.35 + 4.53

35. 16.09 − 0.11

36. 7.47 − 3.58

Write the letter of the correct answer. KEY **NS 2.1**

37. 2.4 × 0.03

   A 0.072   **B** 0.077   **C** 0.72   **D** 0.720

Extra Practice See page 289, Set D.

Practice Multiplying Decimals

Multiply.

1.   4.3
   × 5
	2. 3.7
	   × 8
		3. 8.1
		   × 2
			4. 5.5
			   × 7

5.   12
   × 0.4
	6. 1.5
	   × 8
		7. 0.13
		   × 4
			8. 1.8
			   × 6

9.   1.22
   × 4
	10. 13.01
	   × 8
		11. 23.1
		   × 7
			12. 25
			   × 4.5

13. 120×0.003 **14.** 31×1.8 **15.** 1.6×23 **16.** 20×0.45

17. 4×10.6 **18.** 0.02×78 **19.** 32×0.005 **20.** 2.713×3

21. 18×9.4 **22.** 1.35×6 **23.** 22×0.52 **24.** 30.5×4

25. 12×12.1 **26.** 3×0.267 **27.** 2.015×5 **28.** 42×1.11

29. 5×2.2 **30.** 3×0.12 **31.** 2.75×7 **32.** 12.5×4

33. 8×4.2 **34.** 14.1×2 **35.** 7.6×3 **36.** 9×3.9

37. 5.2×7 **38.** 3.172×5 **39.** 14×0.28 **40.** 17×9.5

Estimate each product.

41.   9.438
   × 22
	42. 5.872
	   × 48
		43. 483
		   × 1.7
			44. 735
			   × 0.56

45. 582×5.3 **46.** 239×7.7 **47.** 42×3.14 **48.** 57×0.31

Solve.

49. Caleb has $45. A jacket originally priced at $65 is now on sale for 0.25 off the original price. Does Caleb have enough money to buy the jacket? Explain your answer.

50. Last week, Felicia worked 4.5 hours on both Monday and Wednesday. She worked 6.5 hours on both Tuesday and Thursday. If she earns $7.50 an hour, how much did Felicia earn last week?

CA Standards

NS 1.0 Students compute with very large and very small numbers, positive integers, decimals, and fractions and understand the relationship between decimals, fractions, and percents. They understand the relative magnitudes of numbers.

MR 2.5 Indicate the relative advantages of exact and approximate solutions to problems and give answers to a specified degree of accuracy.

Also NS 1.1, NS 2.0, MR 1.0, MR 2.0, MR 2.3, MR 2.4, MR 3.0, MR 3.1, MR 3.2, MR 3.3

Problem Solving Plan
Estimate or Exact?

Objective Use estimates and exact answers to solve problems.

▶ Learn Through Reasoning

Sometimes the same problem can be solved in different ways to fit different situations.

> A high school builds a new football stadium. The stadium cost $7,549,705 to build, and the school agrees to pay this bill in 5 equal yearly payments. About how much will the school pay in one year?

Find an Exact Answer

The contractor who built the stadium sends the school a bill for each payment. She wants to make sure every dollar and cent is accounted for.

Find an exact answer.

$7,549,705 \div 5 = \$1,509,941$

Use an Estimate

A local newspaper reporter is writing a story about the stadium. He wants to let people know about how much the stadium will cost per year.

Find an estimate. Round to the nearest hundred thousand.

$7,549,705 is about $7,500,000.

Divide by the number of payments.

$7,500,000 \div 5 = \$1,500,000$

Solve Using an Estimate

The school can spend up to $1,600,000 dollars per year on the stadium. Is the stadium too expensive?

Find a high estimate. Round up to the nearest million.

$7,549,705 is about $8,000,000.

$8,000,000 \div 5 = \$1,600,000$

Because you rounded up, you know each payment will be less than your estimate.

The school will pay less than $1,600,000 per year, so the stadium is not too expensive.

Guided Problem Solving

1. Ana has $20.00 to buy flowers for actors to wear in the school play. The flowers cost $0.70 each, and she wants to buy 34.

   a. Does Ana have enough money? How do you know?

   b. If Ana has enough money, how much change will she receive? If she doesn't have enough, how much more does she need?

   c. A different type of flower costs $0.40 each. About how much less money would Ana spend if she bought this type of flower?

(123) Math Talk Think of times you might need a rough estimate, a close estimate, or an exact answer.

▶ **Independent Problem Solving**

Use the table at right to solve problems 2–4.

2. Which is greater, the difference in weight between TJ and Linus, or the difference between Linus and Abbey? By how much?

3. Does Abbey weigh more or less than the other three pets together? Tell how you can estimate to find the answer.

4. Robert bought Mo from a pet store that had 38 turtles about Mo's size. About how much more did the 38 turtles weigh than TJ?

5. **Challenge** Milos is taking a taxi service from Sacramento to San Jose. The driver will charge him $1.75 per mile, plus a $15.00 flat fee. Milos wants a high estimate of the cost of the trip to make sure he brings enough money. If the trip is 124 miles, what is a good estimate for Milos? How much will the trip actually cost?

6. **Create and Solve** Write a problem in which one person wants an estimate and another wants an exact answer.

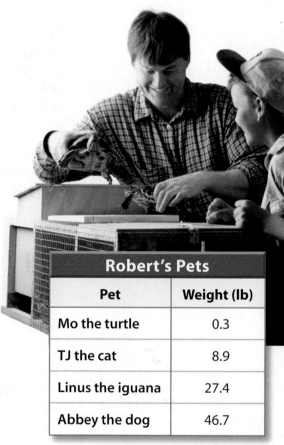

Robert's Pets	
Pet	**Weight (lb)**
Mo the turtle	0.3
TJ the cat	8.9
Linus the iguana	27.4
Abbey the dog	46.7

Reading & Writing Math

Vocabulary

In this chapter, you learned how to multiply decimals and how to multiply whole numbers and decimals.

Soula and Cole were studying for a Math quiz. They drew the models below to help them practice multiplying decimals.

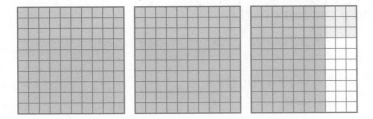

1. What problem does the model show?

2. How can Soula and Cole find the answer to this math problem? What should they do?

3. Solve the problem.

Writing The next practice problem is 4.7×0.62. Write a note to Soula and Cole. Tell them how to model and solve this new problem.

Reading Check out this book in your library. *If You Made a Million* by David M. Schwartz

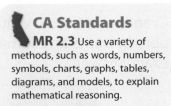

CA Standards
MR 2.3 Use a variety of methods, such as words, numbers, symbols, charts, graphs, tables, diagrams, and models, to explain mathematical reasoning.
Also KEY NS 2.1

Standards-Based Extra Practice

Set A ————————————————————————— KEY **NS 2.1** page 272

Find each product.

1. 10 × 5.14
2. 7 × 2.65
3. 1.744 × 6
4. 5.80 × 4

5. 8 × 2.716
6. 6 × 5.92
7. 3.14 × 2
8. 9.09 × 9

Solve.

9. Michelle needs 3.6 cups of flour to make one loaf of bread. How many cups of flour does she need to make 5 loaves of bread?

Set B ————————————————————————— NS 1.1, KEY **NS 2.1** page 276

Estimate each product. Write an equation to show the rounded numbers you used.

1. 5.244 × 9
2. 807 × 4.9
3. 5.96 × 11
4. 82 × 2.158

Solve.

5. Audra sells candles for $3.96 each. She sold 319 candles for a fundraiser. Estimate how much money Audra made for the fundraiser.

Set C ————————————————————————— KEY **NS 2.1** page 278

Multiply. Estimate to make sure your answer is reasonable.

1. 4.2 × 3.7
2. 2.6 × 1.51
3. 3.14 × 2.6
4. 19.6 × 5.07

Solve.

5. A new highway is 24.8 miles long. Six tenths of the highway passes through a desert. How many miles of the highway pass through the desert?

Set D ————————————————————————— KEY **NS 2.1** page 282

Multiply. Check to see if your answer is reasonable.

1. 0.02 × 1.65
2. 0.06 × 0.5
3. 0.03 × 1.2
4. 2.4 × 0.03

Solve.

5. Pat earned $25.20 babysitting. She saved 0.05 of her earnings. How much did Pat save?

Education Place
Visit www.eduplace.com/camap/
for more **Extra Practice**.

Chapter Review/Test

Vocabulary and Concepts ———————————— NS 1.1, KEY NS 2.1, MR 2.3

Write the best word to complete each sentence.

1. When you multiply two decimals, the answer is the _____.

2. In the expression 3.2 × 5, the numbers 3.2 and 5 are _____.

3. When you multiply a decimal by 10, move the decimal point 1 place to the _____.

4. To find a low estimate for the product of two decimals, round both factors _____.

5. When multiplying two factors that each have 1 decimal place, place the decimal point in the product _____ places to the left.

Skills ——————————————————————— NS 1.1

Estimate. Write an equation to show the rounded numbers.

6. 6.849 × 11	**7.** 10.124 × 14	**8.** 103 × 2.89	**9.** $8.14 × 19

Multiply.

10. 4.9 × 8	**11.** 4 × 6.1	**12.** 10.2 × 1.6	**13.** 3.1 × 9.6
14. 0.5 × 0.08	**15.** 5.09 × 1,000	**16.** 0.64 × 5.7	**17.** 8 × 1.01
18. 3.9 × 1.64	**19.** 8.1 × 4.05	**20.** 0.1 × 0.2	**21.** 0.3 × 0.03

Problem Solving and Reasoning ——————— NS 1.1, KEY NS 2.1, MR 2.1, MR 2.3

Solve.

22. Shaun mows 13 yards each day. He uses 0.61 gallons of gas for each yard. How much gas does he use in one day?

23. Cashews are sold for $4.20 per pound. Sharon buys 2.3 pounds of cashews. What is the total cost?

24. Lucy drives 30.12 miles each way to the beach. In July she drove to the beach three times. How many miles did Lucy drive to and from the beach?

25. The price of a hair clip is $0.75. The sales tax is 0.04 of the purchase price. How much is the sales tax on the hair clip?

Writing Math Use estimation to check Problem 24. Is your answer reasonable? Explain.

Spiral Review and Test Practice

1. $8 \times (4 + 2) = \square \times 6$

   A 6

   B 8

   C 32

   D 48

> **Test Tip**
> Check your answer by evaluating the expressions on both sides of the equation.

KEY **AF 1.2** page 128

2. Which equation could have been used to create this function table?

   A $y = x - 18$

   B $y = x + 7$

   C $y = 7x$

   D $y = x \div 7$

x	y
21	3
35	5
56	8

KEY **AF 1.5** page 112

3. A grocery store chain prints 3,256 circulars every week. How many circulars do they print in 4 weeks?

   A 12,024

   B 12,824

   C 13,004

   D 13,024

NS 1.0 page 128

4. $1\frac{3}{4} \div 2\frac{1}{3} =$

   A $4\frac{1}{12}$

   C $1\frac{1}{3}$

   B $2\frac{1}{4}$

   D $\frac{3}{4}$

NS 2.4, NS 2.5 page 236

5. Selma had ribbon that was 3.42 meters long. She used 1.8 meters to wrap a gift. How long was the piece of ribbon that was left?

   A 1.6 meters

   B 1.62 meters

   C 3.24 meters

   D 5.22 meters

> **Test Tip**
> Solving a problem first using simpler numbers can help you solve the actual problem.

KEY **NS 2.1** page 258

6. Sam can walk 4 miles per hour. At this rate, how many miles can Sam walk in 2.25 hours?

   A 1.75

   B 8

   C 9

   D 900

KEY **NS 2.1** page 272

Education Place
Visit www.eduplace.com/camap/ for **Test-Taking Tips** and **Extra Practice**.

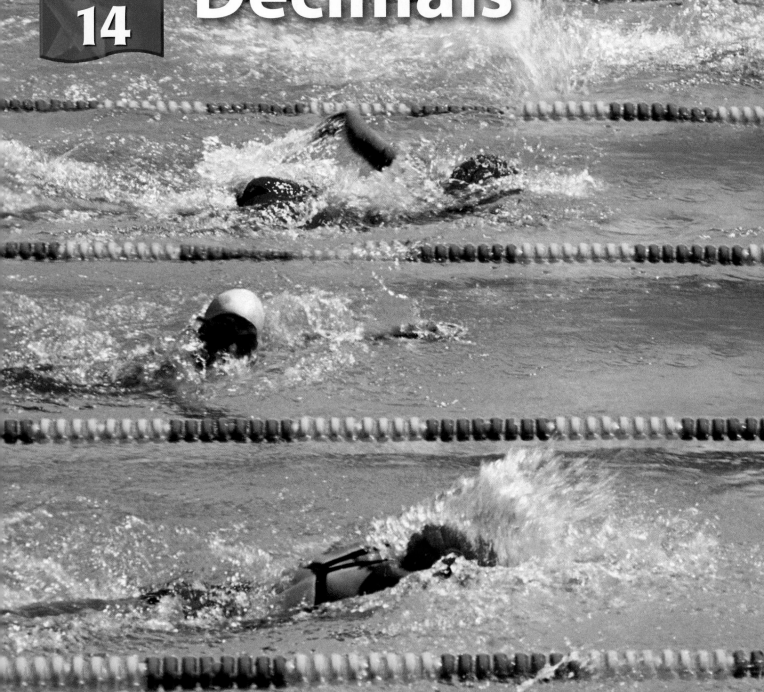

Divide
Decimals

Vocabulary and Concepts NS 1.0, MR 2.3

Choose the best word to complete each sentence. pages 60 and 108

1. In the number 297.321, the digit 3 is in the _____ place.

2. In the equation 72 ÷ 12 = 6, the number 6 is the _____.

Skills NS 1.1

Round to the place indicated by the underlined digit. page 66

3. 5.<u>2</u>1

4. <u>9</u>.562

5. 0.7<u>1</u>6

6. 34.<u>6</u>71

Divide. Write answers in simplest form. pages 230, 234

7. $5 \div \frac{1}{10}$

8. $\frac{9}{10} \div \frac{3}{10}$

9. $\frac{49}{100} \div 7$

Problem Solving and Reasoning NS 2.4

10. Rhonda pours $6\frac{3}{10}$ liters of milk into 3 bottles. Each bottle contains the same amount of milk. How much milk is in each bottle?

Vocabulary

Visualize It!

$2.4 \div 0.4 = 0.6$

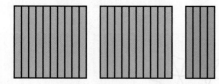

Regroup the tenths as 4 equal groups

0.6 in each group

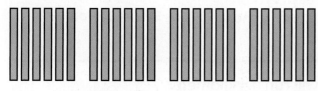

Language Tip

Math words that look alike in English and Spanish often have the same meaning.

English	Spanish
digit	dígito
value	valor

See **English-Spanish Glossary** pages 628–642.

 Education Place Visit www.eduplace.com/camap/ for the **eGlossary** and **eGames**.

CA Standards MR 2.3 Use a variety of methods, such as words, numbers, symbols, charts, graphs, tables, diagrams, and models, to explain mathematical reasoning. **Also KEY NS 2.2**

Chapter 14   293

CA Standards

KEY NS 2.1 Add, subtract, multiply, and divide with decimals; add with negative integers; subtract positive integers from negative integers; and verify the reasonableness of the results.

KEY NS 2.2 Demonstrate proficiency with division, including division with positive decimals and long division with multidigit divisors.

Also NS 1.0, NS 2.0, MR 2.3

Materials
- Learning Tool 21 (Tenths)
- Scissors
- Crayons (red, blue, and yellow)

Hands On
Division with Decimals

Objective Use models to divide with decimals.

▶ **Explore**

You can model dividing decimals by separating into equal groups.

Question How can you use models to divide with decimals?

Four students will run a relay race of 1.6 kilometers. How far will each student run?

Use the Learning Tool. Color one whole model red, one blue, and one yellow.

Divide Decimal by Whole Number

$1.6 \div 4 = n$

1 Show 1.6 using the models.

2 Cut the models apart to show tenths. You should have 16 tenths.

3 Divide the tenths into 4 equal groups.

4 Count the tenths in each group. Write a division equation to show your answer.

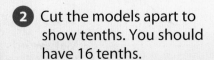

$$1.6 \div 4 = 0.4 \text{ or } \frac{4}{10}$$

Solution: Each student will run 0.4 kilometer.

Divide Whole Number by Whole Number
$3 \div 2 = n$

1 Show 3 wholes using the models.

2 Cut one of the models apart and make 2 equal groups from the 3 wholes.

3 Write a division equation to show your answer.

Divide Whole Number by Decimal
$2 \div 0.4 = n$

1 Show 2 wholes using the models.

2 Cut both models apart and make as many equal groups as possible with 4 tenths in each group.

3 Write a division equation to show your answer.

Divide Decimal by Decimal
$1.8 \div 0.6 = n$

1 Show 1.8 using the models.

2 Cut apart the models and make as many equal groups as possible with 6 tenths in each group.

3 Write a division equation to show your answer.

▶ **Extend**

Use tenths models to divide.
Check your answers by multiplying.

1. $2.4 \div 3$ **2.** $1 \div 2$

3. $3 \div 0.5$ **4.** $1.2 \div 0.2$

5. $2.8 \div 4$ **6.** $3 \div 0.6$

Writing Math

How might you decide whether to use the divisor as the number of equal groups or the number in each group?

Vocabulary

reciprocal

$\frac{8}{1}$ and $\frac{1}{8}$ are reciprocals.

$\frac{2}{5}$ and $\frac{5}{2}$ are reciprocals.

Divide Decimals by Whole Numbers

Objective Divide a decimal by a whole number.

▶ **Learn by Example**

Eli rides his bike 8 times around a track. If Eli rides a total of 9.6 kilometers on the track, how long is the track?

Since Eli rides the same distance 8 times, you need to divide.

Different Ways to Divide 9.6 by 8

Way 1   **Use decimals.**

1 Divide as you do with whole numbers. Ignore the decimal point.

$$\begin{array}{r} 1\,2 \\ 8\overline{)9.6} \\ -8\downarrow \\ \hline 1\,6 \\ -1\,6 \\ \hline 0 \end{array}$$

2 Put a decimal point in the quotient directly above the decimal point in the dividend.

$$\begin{array}{r} 1.2 \\ 8\overline{)9.6} \\ -8\downarrow \\ \hline 1\,6 \\ -1\,6 \\ \hline 0 \end{array}$$

- - - - - - - - - -

Way 2   **Use fractions.**

1 Write the decimal as a fraction. $9.6 = 9\frac{6}{10} = \frac{96}{10}$

2 Rewrite the division as a multiplication. Use the reciprocal of the divisor. Multiply.

$$\frac{96}{10} \times \frac{1}{8} = \frac{96 \times 1}{10 \times 8} = \frac{96}{80}$$

3 Simplify if possible. Write the quotient as a decimal.

$$\frac{96}{80} = \frac{12}{10} = 1\frac{2}{10} = 1.2$$

Solution: The track is 1.2 kilometers.

Another Example
Quotient Less Than One

$$\begin{array}{r} \$0.92 \\ 7\overline{)\$6.44} \\ -63\downarrow \\ \hline 14 \\ -14 \\ \hline 0 \end{array}$$

Check
Estimate to check.

$6.44 \longrightarrow 7$

$7 \div 7 = 1$

$0.92 \longrightarrow 1$

Divide. Check your answer.

1. $15.60 ÷ 3
2. 8.45 ÷ 5
3. $4.80 ÷ 6

4. 82.8 ÷ 3
5. 0.84 ÷ 4
6. $1.76 ÷ 8

(123) Math Talk Why is it important to line up the quotient and the dividend correctly when you divide with decimals?

 Practice and Problem Solving

Divide. Check your answer.

7. 8.1 ÷ 9
8. $76.60 ÷ 2
9. 65.5 ÷ 5
10. $0.90 ÷ 3

11. $6.40 ÷ 8
12. 31.8 ÷ 6
13. 26.8 ÷ 4
14. 0.82 ÷ 2

 Real World Data

Use the chart for Problem 15.

The chart shows the distance in kilometers and the time in minutes for three bicyclists.

15. What was Mike's speed?

16. **Challenge** Yesterday, Javier bicycled 1.75 miles in 7 minutes. Today he bicycled 2.4 miles in 8 minutes. How much faster did Javier bicycle today than yesterday?

Rider	Distance (km)	Speed (km per min)	Time (min)
Tony	2.16	0.27	8
Luis	1.74	0.29	6
Mike	2.7	■	9

✓ **Spiral Review and Test Practice**

Simplify. Prepares for KEY **AF 1.2** page 102

17. (9 + 30) − 5
18. 6 + (8 × 4)
19. (31 − 2) − (15 − 5)
20. 12 − (6 − 4)

Write the letter of the correct answer. KEY **NS 2.1**, KEY **NS 2.2**

21. 57.2 ÷ 4 =

    A 1.43   **B** 1.53   **C** 14.3   **D** 15.3

Extra Practice See page 309, Set A.

CA Standards

KEY NS 2.1 Add, subtract, multiply, and divide with decimals; add with negative integers; subtract positive integers from negative integers; and verify the reasonableness of the results.

KEY NS 2.2 Demonstrate proficiency with division, including division with positive decimals and long division with multidigit divisors.

Also MR 1.2, MR 2.3

Divide Whole Numbers with Decimal Quotients

Objective Divide a whole number by a whole number and write the quotient as a decimal.

▶ **Learn by Example**

Lara will volunteer at the Special Olympics for 3 hours. She will work at 4 different events. She will spend the same amount of time at each event. What part of an hour will she spend at each event?

Since Lara will spend the same amount of time at each event, you need to divide.

$3 \div 4 = n$

1 Write a decimal point in the dividend and a zero in the tenths place of the dividend.

$$4)\overline{3} \longrightarrow 4)\overline{3.0}$$

> Since the dividend is less than the divisor, the answer will not be a whole number.

2 Divide.

$$\begin{array}{r} 0.7 \\ 4)\overline{3.0} \\ -28 \\ \hline 2 \end{array}$$

3 To write the answer without a remainder, you can add zeros in the dividend and continue dividing.

$$\begin{array}{r} 0.75 \\ 4)\overline{3.00} \\ -28\downarrow \\ \hline 20 \\ -20 \\ \hline 0 \end{array}$$

Solution: Lara will spend 0.75 hour at each event.

Other Examples

A. Fraction as Decimal

Write $\frac{3}{8}$ as a decimal.

$$\frac{3}{8} \rightarrow \begin{array}{r} 0.375 \\ 8)\overline{3.000} \\ -24\downarrow \\ \hline 60 \\ -56\downarrow \\ \hline 40 \\ -40 \\ \hline 0 \end{array}$$

> Divide the numerator by the denominator.

$\frac{3}{8} = 0.375$

B. Remainder as Decimal

Find $14 \div 5$.

$$\begin{array}{r} 2.8 \\ 5)\overline{14.0} \\ -10\downarrow \\ \hline 40 \\ -40 \\ \hline 0 \end{array}$$

Winning a race at the Special Olympics

Write each quotient as a decimal. Multiply to check.

1. $4 \div 5$ **2.** $7 \div 4$ **3.** $9 \div 6$ **4.** $21 \div 8$

Write each fraction as a decimal.

5. $\dfrac{1}{5}$ **6.** $\dfrac{7}{8}$ **7.** $\dfrac{5}{4}$ **8.** $\dfrac{8}{5}$

Ask Yourself
- Did I place the first digit of the quotient correctly?
- Did I write zeros in the dividend until there was no remainder?

123 Math Talk Explain why 3, 3.0, and 3.00 represent the same number.

▶ **Practice and Problem Solving**

Write each quotient as a decimal. Multiply to check.

9. $6\overline{)3}$ **10.** $5\overline{)19}$ **11.** $8\overline{)14}$ **12.** $27 \div 4$ **13.** $41 \div 5$

Write each fraction as a decimal.

14. $\dfrac{2}{5}$ **15.** $\dfrac{1}{8}$ **16.** $\dfrac{11}{5}$ **17.** $\dfrac{13}{8}$ **18.** $\dfrac{45}{6}$

19. Analyze The distance around a track is $\dfrac{1}{4}$ mile.
  a. Use division to find the decimal equivalent of $\dfrac{1}{4}$.
  b. Write a fraction equivalent to $\dfrac{1}{4}$ with a denominator that is a power of 10. Write the fraction as a decimal.
  c. Did you get the same answer for parts a and b?

20. Challenge Alexis ran 3 times around a track each day for 5 days. The distance around the track is $\dfrac{3}{8}$ mile. How far did Alexis run in all? Write your answer as a decimal.

Wheel chair race at the Special Olympics

✓ **Spiral Review and Test Practice**

Add or subtract. Write your answer in simplest form. NS 2.0, KEY **NS 2.3** page 154

21. $\dfrac{1}{3} + \dfrac{1}{9}$ **22.** $\dfrac{5}{16} + \dfrac{1}{8}$ **23.** $\dfrac{3}{8} - \dfrac{1}{4}$ **24.** $\dfrac{9}{10} - \dfrac{3}{5}$

Write the letter of the correct answer. KEY **NS 2.1**

25. $16 \div 5 =$

  A 3   **B** 32   **C** 3.2   **D** 3.3

CA Standards

KEY NS 2.1 Add, subtract, multiply, and divide with decimals; add with negative integers; subtract positive integers from negative integers; and verify the reasonableness of the results.

KEY NS 2.2 Demonstrate proficiency with division, including division with positive decimals and long division with multidigit divisors.

Also KEY AF 1.2, NS 1.0, NS 1.3, NS 2.4, NS 2.5, MR 1.0, MR 1.2, MR 3.0, MR 3.1

Think

10, 10^2, 10^3, ... or 10, 100, 1,000, ... are powers of 10.

Divide a Whole Number by a Decimal

Objective Divide a whole number by a decimal.

▶ **Learn by Example**

Janice skates 3 miles in 0.6 hour. What is Janice's speed?

Different Ways to Find 3 ÷ 0.6

Way 1   Use decimals.

① Write a decimal point and a zero in the dividend.

$$0.6\overline{)3} \longrightarrow 0.6\overline{)3.0}$$

② Multiply the divisor and dividend by the same power of 10.

$$\frac{3.0}{0.6} = \frac{30}{6}$$
(×10)

③ Move the decimal point one place to the right in the dividend and divisor. Place a decimal point in the quotient directly above the new decimal point in the dividend. Then divide.

Moving the decimal point 1 place to the right is the same as multiplying by 10.

$$0.6\overline{)3.0} \longrightarrow 6\overline{)30.} \quad 3 \div 0.6 = 5$$

- -

Way 2   Use fractions.

① Write both numbers as fractions. Rewrite the division as a multiplication. Use the reciprocal of the divisor.

$$\frac{3}{1} \div \frac{6}{10} \longrightarrow \frac{3}{1} \times \frac{10}{6}$$

② Multiply.

$$\frac{3}{1} \times \frac{10}{6} = \frac{3 \times 10}{1 \times 6} = \frac{30}{6}$$

③ Simplify if possible.

$$\frac{30}{6} = \frac{5}{1} \text{ or } 5$$

Solution: Janice's speed is 5 miles per hour.

Other Examples

A. Divide by Hundredths

12 ÷ 0.05

Multiply the divisor and dividend by 100.

Show it by moving both decimal points two places to the right. Place a decimal point in the quotient directly above the new decimal point in the dividend. Then divide.

$$
\begin{array}{r}
240. \\
0.05\overline{)12.00} \\
-10 \\
\hline
20 \\
-20 \\
\hline
0
\end{array}
$$

B. Quotient is a Decimal

5 ÷ 0.4

If needed, write one or more zeros in the dividend after the decimal point.

Place a decimal point in the quotient directly above the new decimal point in the dividend. Then divide.

$$
\begin{array}{r}
12.5 \\
0.4\overline{)5.00} \\
-4 \\
\hline
10 \\
-8 \\
\hline
20 \\
-20 \\
\hline
0
\end{array}
$$

▶ Guided Practice

Divide. Multiply to check.

1. $0.8\overline{)4}$

2. $0.02\overline{)3}$

3. $0.8\overline{)10}$

4. 6 ÷ 0.03

5. 7 ÷ 0.2

6. 5 ÷ 0.8

Ask Yourself

Did I multiply the divisor and dividend by the same power of 10 to get a whole number in the divisor?

Guided Problem Solving

Use the questions to solve this problem.

7. Ian skates 4 miles in 24 minutes. What is Ian's speed in miles per hour?

a. **Understand** You are given the distance in miles and the time in minutes. You need to find the speed in *miles* per *hour*. You need to first find the time in *hours*. How many minutes are in an hour?

b. **Plan** Break the problem into parts. First, write 24 minutes as a fraction of an hour. Then simplify the fraction and write it as a decimal. The decimal is Ian's skating time in hours.

c. **Solve** Use the distance in miles and the time in hours to find the speed in miles per hour.

d. **Look Back** Solve the problem in another way. Show your work. Begin by finding the number of minutes it takes Ian to skate 1 mile.

 Math Talk Why do you move the decimal point the same number of places in the dividend and the divisor?

Divide. Multiply to check.

8. $0.5\overline{)25}$
9. $0.01\overline{)6}$
10. $0.4\overline{)3}$
11. $0.7\overline{)28}$
12. $0.6\overline{)15}$

13. $11 \div 0.05$
14. $24 \div 0.8$
15. $24 \div 0.08$
16. $13 \div 0.4$
17. $13 \div 0.04$

18. Multistep Beth is in a cross-country ski race. She travels 5 kilometers in 48 minutes. What is Beth's speed in kilometers per hour?

19. Challenge Carl skates 3 kilometers in 15 minutes. Alex skates 5 kilometers in 30 minutes. Who has a faster speed? How much faster, in kilometers per hour?

 Science Link

Solve.

20. A 20-gram sample of bronze contains 8 grams of tin. What fraction of the sample's mass is tin? Write the fraction as a decimal.

21. A 20-gram sample of brass has 6 grams of zinc. What fraction of the sample's mass is zinc? Write the fraction as a decimal.

22. A brass sample with a mass of 6 grams is divided into 0.5-gram samples. How many 0.5-gram samples are there?

23. Eight hundredths of the mass of a stainless steel sample is nickel. If the stainless steel sample has a mass of 25 grams, what is the mass of the nickel?

Alloys

- Mixtures of two or more metals are called alloys.
- Bronze is an alloy of copper and tin.
- Sterling silver is an alloy of silver and copper.
- Many musical instruments are made of alloys. For example, copper and zinc make up brass.

Science PS 1.c

✓ **Spiral Review and Test Practice**

Divide. Simplify your answer. NS 2.4, NS 2.5 page 230

24. $\frac{1}{3} \div 3$
25. $\frac{4}{6} \div 2$
26. $\frac{1}{5} \div 4$
27. $\frac{3}{8} \div 5$

Write the letter of the correct answer. KEY NS 2.2

28. $72 \div 0.09 =$

A 800   B 8   C 0.8   D 0.008

Extra Practice See page 309, Set C.

Key Standards Review

Need Help?
See Key Standards Handbook.

Solve. Write each sum in simplest form. KEY **NS 2.3**

1. Suppose $\frac{7}{10}$ of your class read a book before bed and $\frac{2}{5}$ watch television. How much more of the class reads a book than watches television?

2. Seth jogs $2\frac{1}{2}$ miles every Saturday. If he has already jogged $1\frac{2}{3}$ miles, how many more miles does he have to go?

Multiply. KEY **NS 2.1**

3. 2×0.8

4. 7×0.4

5. 8×2.03

6. 6×4.51

Estimate the product by rounding each factor to the nearest whole number. KEY **NS 2.1**

7. 0.83×6

8. 5.22×4

9. 3×7.95

10. 7×6.14

Multiply. Estimate to check. KEY **NS 2.1**

11. 0.7×0.2

12. 3.2×1.5

13. 0.3×0.04

14. 0.09×0.8

Challenge — Mental Math

Mental Division KEY **NS 2.1**, KEY **NS 2.2**

Three apples were cut in half. This is the same as saying that the three apples were divided by 0.5. Study how dividing by 0.5 can be done mentally.

$$3 \div 0.5 \text{ is the same as } 3 \times 2 = 6$$

Divide mentally.

1. $16 \div 0.5$

2. $75 \div 0.5$

3. $1.4 \div 0.5$

4. $1.9 \div 0.5$

5. $23 \div 0.5$

6. $45 \div 0.5$

7. $3.5 \div 0.5$

8. $2.7 \div 0.5$

CA Standards

KEY NS 2.1 Add, subtract, multiply, and divide with decimals; add with negative integers; subtract positive integers from negative integers; and verify the reasonableness of the results.

KEY NS 2.2 Demonstrate proficiency with division, including division with positive decimals and long division with multidigit divisors.

Also NS 1.0, NS 1.3, NS 2.4, NS 2.5, MR 2.1

Think

When dividing by a decimal, multiply the divisor by a power of 10 to change it to a whole number. 10, 10^2, 10^3, ... or 10, 100, 1,000 ... are powers of 10.

Divide a Decimal by a Decimal

Objective Divide a decimal by a decimal.

▶ **Learn by Example**

A long distance swimmer swam 2.6 miles at a speed of 0.8 mile per hour. How long did it take?

To find distance, you multiply the speed by the time. So, you can find the time by dividing the distance by the speed.

$$\boxed{\text{distance in miles}} \longrightarrow 2.6 \div 0.8 \longleftarrow \boxed{\text{speed in miles per hour}}$$

Different Ways to Find 2.6 ÷ 0.8

Way 1 **Use decimals.**

1 Multiply the divisor and dividend by the same power of 10. Write a decimal point in the quotient.

$$0.8\overline{)2.6}$$
$$\begin{array}{r} 3. \\ -24 \\ \hline 2 \end{array}$$

$$\frac{2.6}{0.8} \xrightarrow{\times 10} = \frac{26}{6} \xleftarrow{\times 10}$$

2 If needed, write zeros after the decimal point in the dividend to continue dividing.

$$\begin{array}{r} 3.25 \\ 0.8\overline{)2.6.00} \\ -24 \\ \hline 20 \\ -16 \\ \hline 40 \\ -40 \\ \hline 0 \end{array}$$

Check
Estimate to check.

$2.6 \longrightarrow 3$

$0.8 \longrightarrow 1$

$3 \div 1 = 3$

A quotient of 3.25 is reasonable.

Way 2 **Use fractions.**

1 Write the decimals as a mixed number and a fraction.

$$2\frac{6}{10} \div \frac{8}{10}$$

2 Write the mixed number as an improper fraction. Rewrite the division as a multiplication.

$$\frac{26}{10} \div \frac{8}{10} \longrightarrow \frac{26}{10} \times \frac{10}{8}$$

3 Rewrite using factors. Divide by common factors. Multiply.

$$\frac{26 \times 10}{10 \times 8} = \frac{\overset{1}{\cancel{2}} \times 13 \times \overset{1}{\cancel{2}} \times \overset{1}{\cancel{5}}}{\underset{1}{\cancel{2}} \times \underset{1}{\cancel{5}} \times \underset{1}{\cancel{2}} \times 4} = \frac{13}{4}$$

4 Simplify the answer if necessary.

$$\frac{13}{4} = 3\frac{1}{4} = 3.25$$

Solution: It took 3.25 hours.

Divide. Estimate to check that your answer is reasonable.

1. $0.9\overline{)1.8}$ **2.** $0.3\overline{)1.74}$ **3.** $0.2\overline{)0.706}$

4. $0.352 \div 0.08$ **5.** $1.44 \div 0.5$ **6.** $12.6 \div 0.09$

123 Math Talk How do you know which power of 10 to use when simplifying decimal division?

Ask Yourself
- Do I need to write any zeros after the dividend?
- Did I place the decimal point correctly?

▶ **Practice and Problem Solving**

Divide. Estimate to check that your answer is reasonable.

7. $0.8\overline{)2.4}$ **8.** $0.8\overline{)0.24}$ **9.** $0.5\overline{)38.5}$ **10.** $0.5\overline{)3.85}$ **11.** $0.05\overline{)0.385}$

12. $0.3\overline{)6.66}$ **13.** $0.2\overline{)14.7}$ **14.** $0.4\overline{)12.5}$ **15.** $0.4\overline{)100.4}$ **16.** $0.1\overline{)4.56}$

17. $1.12 \div 0.8$ **18.** $11.2 \div 0.08$ **19.** $4.2 \div 0.7$ **20.** $0.525 \div 0.7$ **21.** $0.001 \div 0.01$

Solve.

22. Catherine was swimming at the local pool. She swam 1.3 miles at a rate of 0.5 mile per hour. How long did it take for her to swim 1.3 miles?

23. Challenge Shane trains for the swimming part of a triathalon by swimming 50-meter laps. How many laps does Shane need to swim to cover 1.5 km?

✓ **Spiral Review and Test Practice**

Find the product. NS 2.0, KEY **NS 2.1** page 272

24. 26×5.3 **25.** 4.3×5 **26.** 100×3.684 **27.** $6.325 \times 1,000$

Write the letter of the correct answer. KEY **NS 2.1**, KEY **NS 2.2**

28. $0.85 \div 0.5 =$

A 0.017 **B** 0.17 **C** 0.35 **D** 1.7

CA Standards

MR 2.2 Apply strategies and results from simpler problems to more complex problems.

KEY NS 2.2 Demonstrate proficiency with division, including division with positive decimals and long division with multidigit divisors.

Also KEY NS 2.1, MR 1.1, MR 2.0, MR 2.3, MR 2.4, MR 3.0, MR 3.1, MR 3.2, MR 3.3

Problem Solving Strategy
Use a Simpler Problem

Objective Use a simpler problem to solve a complex problem.

▶ **Learn by Example**

Mr. Clark is in the Blossom Trail 10K run in Sanger, California. He trains for the run on a 0.5-mile track. How many laps will he have to run to cover the distance of the 10K?

UNDERSTAND

- The distance of the race is 10 kilometers.
- 10 kilometers is about 6.2 miles.
- One lap around the track is 0.5 mile.

> 10 kilometers is about 6.2 miles

PLAN

You can use simpler numbers to help you decide how to solve the problem.

SOLVE

1 Choose simpler numbers to decide how to solve the problem.

What if the race is 10 miles and one lap around the track is 2 miles long?

Divide.

$10 \div 2 = 5$

2 Reread the problem. Solve using the original numbers.

Divide.

$$
\begin{array}{r}
12.4 \\
0.5\overline{)6.2\,0} \\
-5 \\
\hline
1\,2 \\
-1\,0 \\
\hline
2\,0 \\
-2\,0 \\
\hline
0
\end{array}
$$

So, Mr. Clark will run 12.4 laps around the track.

LOOK BACK

Is your answer reasonable? Check your answer using inverse operations.

Think

It's often easier to add, subtract, multiply, or divide with numbers like 10 or 2.

▶ Guided Problem Solving

Solve using the Ask Yourself questions.

1. Shauntal is training for a running race. She runs on a half-mile track and would have to run 52.4 laps in order to cover the distance of her race. How many miles is Shauntal's upcoming race? Show your work.

123 Math Talk Look back at Problem 1. Why is the answer less than 52.4?

Ask Yourself
• Can I use simpler numbers to decide how to solve the problem?
• What operations should I use?

▶ Independent Problem Solving

Solve. You can use a simpler problem. Explain why your answer makes sense.

2. Darlene needs Canadian money when she goes skiing in Canada. If a U.S. dollar is worth 1.174 of a Canadian dollar, how much Canadian money will she get for 50 U.S. dollars?

3. A new sports stadium can seat 16,854 spectators. That is $1\frac{1}{2}$ times more spectators than the old stadium could seat. How many spectators could be seated in the old stadium?

Hint
You may want to write $1\frac{1}{2}$ as a decimal.

4. A runner finished a 22-mile race in $2\frac{3}{4}$ hours. What was the runner's average speed in the race?

5. Toni hiked 7,545 feet up Mt. Shasta in one day. In the same day, Dave hiked $\frac{3}{4}$ the distance that Toni hiked. How far did Dave hike?

6. **Challenge** The Bay to Breakers race is 7.46 miles in length. After a runner has completed $\frac{1}{4}$ of the race, she slows down for her first water break. She takes a second water break after completing $\frac{3}{4}$ of the race. Did she run more or less than 4 miles between breaks?

Bay to Breakers race

7. **Create and Solve** Write and solve a word problem that can be solved using operations with fractions or decimals. You may find it helpful to write a simpler problem first.

Vocabulary

In this chapter, you learned how to divide decimals by decimals, and how to divide decimals by whole numbers.

Choose a word from the word bank to label each part of the equation.

> **Word Bank**
> **dividend**
> **quotient**
> **divisor**

$$12.5 \div 0.4 = 31.25$$

1. _____   2. _____   3. _____

4. Nina is framing a painting for her school's art show. The painting is square and is a total of 61.6 inches around. How long is each side of the painting?

   A. Sketch a model of the problem.

   B. Solve the problem. Divide and place the decimal point in the quotient.

   C. The frame is 64 inches around. Nina puts a decorative mark every 0.8 inch around the frame. How many marks will be on the frame?

Writing How was the division in part B similar to the division in part C? How was it different?

Reading Look for this book in your library. *Delightful Decimals and Perfect Percents,* by Lynette Long.

> **CA Standards**
> **MR 2.3** Use a variety of methods, such as words, numbers, symbols, charts, graphs, tables, diagrams, and models, to explain mathematical reasoning.
>
> **Also KEY NS 2.1, KEY NS 2.2**

Standards-Based Extra Practice

Set A ———————————— KEY **NS 2.1**, KEY **NS 2.2** page 296
Divide. Check your answer.

1. 1.64 ÷ 2   **2.** 9.33 ÷ 3   **3.** 19.5 ÷ 5   **4.** 8.64 ÷ 4

Solve.

5. Delmont has $9.45. He wants to give an equal amount to each of his 3 children. How much money will each child get?

Set B ———————————— KEY **NS 2.1**, KEY **NS 2.2** page 298
Write each quotient as a decimal. Multiply to check.

1. 9 ÷ 2   **2.** 13 ÷ 4   **3.** 4 ÷ 5   **4.** 12 ÷ 8   **5.** 3 ÷ 6

6. 5 ÷ 4   **7.** 7 ÷ 4   **8.** 2 ÷ 5   **9.** 2 ÷ 8   **10.** 19 ÷ 8

Solve.

11. Beth picked 6 pounds of apples. She gave them to 8 friends who shared them equally. How many pounds of apples did each friend get?

Set C ———————————— KEY **NS 2.1**, KEY **NS 2.2** page 300
Divide. Multiply to check.

1. 6 ÷ 0.2   **2.** 15 ÷ 0.04   **3.** 4 ÷ 0.05   **4.** 6 ÷ 0.8

5. 2 ÷ 0.04   **6.** 12 ÷ 0.3   **7.** 9 ÷ 0.02   **8.** 25 ÷ 0.5

Solve.

9. Brenda used 24 feet of material to make pot holders. If she used 0.8 foot for each pot holder, how many pot holders did she make?

Set D ———————————— KEY **NS 2.1**, KEY **NS 2.2** page 304
Divide. Estimate to check that your answer is reasonable.

1. 2.8 ÷ 0.8   **2.** 9.95 ÷ 0.05   **3.** 3.08 ÷ 0.2   **4.** 0.756 ÷ 0.3

Solve.

5. A walking trail around a park is 0.8 miles long. Jim walks a total of 4.8 miles on the trail. How many times does he walk around the park?

Education Place
Visit www.eduplace.com/camap/
for more **Extra Practice**.

Chapter 14 Extra Practice   **309**

Chapter Review/Test

Vocabulary and Concepts ———————————————— KEY NS 2.1, KEY NS 2.2, MR 2.3

Write the best word to complete each sentence.

1. In the equation $26 \div 1.3 = 20$, the number 26 is the _____.

2. In the equation $4.8 \div 0.2 = 24$, the number 0.2 is the _____.

3. In the equation $9 \div 5 = 1.8$, the number 1.8 is the _____.

Skills ————————————————————————————— KEY NS 2.1, KEY NS 2.2

Divide. Multiply to check.

4. $2.8 \div 7$ 5. $0.425 \div 0.5$ 6. $12.8 \div 4$ 7. $14.4 \div 0.2$

8. $6.25 \div 0.05$ 9. $9.6 \div 0.8$ 10. $9 \div 0.6$ 11. $24 \div 0.5$

Write each quotient as a decimal. Multiply to check.

12. $13 \div 5$ 13. $21 \div 4$ 14. $3 \div 12$ 15. $7 \div 8$

Write each fraction as a decimal.

16. $\frac{9}{100}$ 17. $\frac{5}{8}$ 18. $\frac{3}{10}$ 19. $\frac{7}{5}$

Problem Solving and Reasoning ———————— KEY NS 2.1, KEY NS 2.2, MR 2.1, MR 2.3

Solve. Multiply or estimate to check your answer.

20. Lin ran around a track 6 times. If she ran a total of 7.8 miles, what is the distance around the track?

21. Matt swam 0.25 miles at a rate of 0.5 miles per hour. How long did it take?

22. Tammy lives $\frac{3}{8}$ mile from her school. Write this distance as a decimal.

23. Katie drives 10 miles in 0.2 hour. What is Katie's speed in miles per hour?

24. Addison cooked 5.6 pound of spaghetti for a dinner party. The serving for each person is 0.4 pound. How many people can be served?

25. Kirk bought 4.2 pounds of peanuts. He divided the peanuts into 7 bags of equal weight. What is the weight of each bag of peanuts?

Writing Math Describe how you could solve Problem 23 using fractions instead of decimals.

Spiral Review and Test Practice

1. $11 + (32 + 46) = 11 + \square$

A 11

B 67

C 78

D 89

KEY **AF 1.2** page 126

2. What value for x makes this equation true?

$x - 24 = 45$

A 21

B 24

C 45

D 69

KEY **AF 1.2** page 108

3. $31 \times 40 =$

A 124

B 1,160

C 1,200

D 1,240

NS 1.0 page 128

4. What is the sum of $52.47 + 34.261$ when both addends are rounded to the nearest tenth?

A 86   **C** 86.7

B 86.6   **D** 86.8

NS 1.1, KEY **NS 2.1** page 256

5. Which of the following is the best estimate for the product 88×0.12?

A 8

B 9

C 18

D 900

> **Test Tip**
> The word *best* tells you that other answers may be correct but you need to choose the *best* answer.

NS 1.1, KEY **NS 2.1** page 276

6. Elena bought 6 pounds of seafood. She saved $5.70 by using her store discount card. How much did she save per pound of seafood?

A $0.90

B $0.95

C $90

D $95

> **Test Tip**
> The word *per* means *for each*.

KEY **NS 2.1** page 296

Education Place
Visit www.eduplace.com/camap/ for
Test-Taking Tips and **Extra Practice**.

Chapter 14 Spiral Review and Test Practice   **311**

Divide by Two-Digit Divisors

The Silicon Valley in California is known for innovations in computer technology.

Check What You Know

Vocabulary and Concepts KEY NS2.2, MR 2.3

Tell what the word means and give an example.

1. quotient

2. remainder

Skills KEY NS2.2

Divide and check.

3. $3\overline{)639}$

4. $4\overline{)1,204}$

5. $6\overline{)438}$

6. $5\overline{)1,560}$

7. $9\overline{)3,645}$

8. $8\overline{)4,584}$

Problem Solving and Reasoning KEY NS2.2

9. Natalia has 7 days to read a 112-page book for English class. She plans to read the same number of pages each day. How many pages will Natalia need to read each day?

10. David is putting his model cars in boxes. He has 70 cars and 6 boxes. If David puts the same number of cars into each box, how many cars will be left over?

Vocabulary

Visualize It!

When you divide, you can **estimate** to get an approximation of the **quotient**.

$4\overline{)276}$

↓

$4\overline{)280}$ ← Adjust the **dividend** to a number that is **compatible** with the **divisor,** 4. Use mental math to divide 280 by 4.

↓

$4\overline{)280}$ 70 ← The **quotient** will be about 70.

Language Tip

Math words that look alike in English and Spanish often have the same meaning.

English	Spanish
dividend	dividendo
divisor	divisor
quotient	cociente
compatible numbers	números compatibles
estimation	estimación

See **English-Spanish Glossary** pages 628–642.

Education Place Visit www.eduplace.com/camap/ for the **eGlossary** and **eGames**.

CA Standards MR 2.3 Use a variety of methods, such as words, numbers, symbols, charts, graphs, tables, diagrams, and models, to explain mathematical reasoning. **Also KEY** NS2.2

Chapter 15 313

CA Standards

KEY NS 2.2 Demonstrate proficiency with division, including division with positive decimals and long division with multidigit divisors.

MR 2.2 Apply strategies and results from simpler problems to more complex problems.

Also NS 1.0, MR 1.1, MR 1.0, MR 1.2, MR 2.3, MR 2.0, MR 3.2, MR 3.3, MR 3.0

Materials
• Workmat 1
• Learning Tool 22 ($20 bills) (2 copies per team)

Hands On
Divide with Multiples of 10, 100, and 1,000

Objective Use basic facts and patterns of zeros to divide mentally.

▶ Explore

Question How can you use basic facts and patterns to divide mentally?

Divide your class into 10 teams. Model a pattern that will help you find 60,000 ÷ 20.

1 Use $20 bills to make piles of $100. Stop once you have made $600. How many bills did you use?

2 Make a table like the one shown. Record the quotient for 600 ÷ 20.

Total Money	Division Equation
$60	60 ÷ 20 = 3
$600	600 ÷ 20 = ◯
$6,000	6,000 ÷ 20 = ◯
$60,000	60,000 ÷ 20 = ◯

3 Combine the money from all 10 teams to make $6,000. Count the number of $20 bills. How many bills does your class have? Record the quotient for 6,000 ÷ 20 in the table.

4 Suppose 10 classes combine all their money so that there is $60,000. Find a pattern of zeros in the table.

Use your pattern to find the quotient for 60,000 ÷ 20. Record the quotient in the table.

Solution: 60,000 ÷ 20 = 3,000

▶ **Extend**

Use basic facts and patterns to find the quotients.

1. $49 \div 7$
490 ÷ 70
4,900 ÷ 70
49,000 ÷ 70

2. $64 \div 8$
640 ÷ 80
6,400 ÷ 80
64,000 ÷ 80

3. $20 \div 5$
200 ÷ 50
2,000 ÷ 50
20,000 ÷ 50

4. **Analyze** What do you notice about the pattern of zeros in Exercises 1 and 2? Why doesn't Exercise 3 follow the same pattern?

Use mental math to find the quotient.

5. $25 \div 5$

6. $250 \div 50$

7. $2,500 \div 50$

8. $25,000 \div 50$

9. $54 \div 9$

10. $540 \div 90$

11. $5,400 \div 90$

12. $54,000 \div 90$

13. $4,800 \div 60$

14. $48,000 \div 60$

15. $90\overline{)3,600}$

16. $90\overline{)36,000}$

17. $40\overline{)2,000}$

18. $40\overline{)20,000}$

19. $30\overline{)210}$

20. $30\overline{)2,100}$

21. $40\overline{)32,000}$

22. $90\overline{)63,000}$

23. $80\overline{)4,000}$

24. $30\overline{)15,000,000}$

25. Suppose another zero was added to the dividend in Exercise 24. How would you change the quotient to match?

26. Find $24 \div 6$, $240 \div 60$, $2,400 \div 600$, and $24,000 \div 6,000$. What can you do to divide mentally when both the dividend and the divisor end in the same number of zeros?

Writing Math

Right or Wrong Luisa says that 40,000 divided by 50 is 8,000. Is Luisa right or wrong? Explain your thinking.

CA Standards

KEY NS 2.2 Demonstrate proficiency with division, including division with positive decimals and long division with multidigit divisors.

MR 2.2 Apply strategies and results from simpler problems to more complex problems.

Also NS 1.0, NS 1.1, MR 2.1, MR 2.0, MR 2.3, MR 3.0, MR 3.2

Vocabulary

compatible numbers

Estimate Quotients

Objective Estimate by using basic facts and multiples of 10 to find compatible numbers.

▶ **Learn by Example**

One way to estimate is to find **compatible numbers**, numbers you can calculate easily in your head.

On June 4, 1876, a train called the *Transcontinental Express* arrived in San Francisco from New York City. The trip covered about 3,500 miles and took about 84 hours to complete. About how many miles did the train travel per hour?

Estimate $84\overline{)3,500}$

Think

What basic fact is close to 35 ÷ 8?

Example 1

1 Find compatible numbers that are close to the numbers in the problem.

$84\overline{)3,500}$
$\downarrow \qquad \downarrow$
$80\overline{)3,200}$

> 80 and 3,200 are compatible numbers since 32 ÷ 8 = 4.

2 Use the compatible numbers to estimate the quotient.

$\dfrac{40}{80\overline{)3,200}}$

So, $84\overline{)3,500}$ is **about** 40.

Solution: The train traveled about 40 miles per hour.

Example 2

Estimate 30,845 ÷ 52

$52\overline{)30,845}$
$\downarrow \qquad \downarrow 600$
$50\overline{)30,000}$

> 50 and 30,000 are compatible numbers since 30 ÷ 5 = 6.

So, 30,845 ÷ 52 is **about** 600.

▶ Guided Practice

Use compatible numbers to estimate the quotient.

1. 257 ÷ 48

250 ÷ ■ = ■

2. 3,489 ÷ 67

3,500 ÷ ■ = ■

3. 48,891 ÷ 63

■ ÷ 60 = ■

Ask Yourself
- What basic fact can I use?
- What is the quotient of the compatible numbers?

4. 805 ÷ 42

5. 5,158 ÷ 19

6. 29,622 ÷ 11

7. 44)‾7‾4‾8‾

8. 28)‾9‾4‾5‾

9. 49)‾1‾8‾9‾

10. 81)‾2‾,‾3‾9‾5‾

11. 39)‾3‾,‾7‾8‾6‾

12. 67)‾4‾,‾8‾8‾4‾

13. 44)‾7‾6‾,‾8‾8‾0‾

14. 81)‾2‾3‾,‾9‾5‾0‾

15. 48)‾9‾9‾,‾9‾5‾4‾

Guided Problem Solving

Use the questions to solve this problem.

16. Albert says that 4,464 ÷ 24 is 186. Carmen says that the quotient is 18. Whose quotient is reasonable? Estimate to check.

   a. Understand What are you being asked to do?

   b. Plan What do you need to do to solve the problem?

   c. Solve Estimate the quotient.

   4,464 ÷ 24

   ◯ ÷ ◯ = ◯

   Explain whose quotient is reasonable.

   d. Look Back Reread the problem. Did you answer the question completely?

17. Analyze To estimate 54,106 ÷ 86, Marshal used the compatible numbers 56,000 and 80. Eva used the compatible numbers 54,000 and 90. Whose estimate will be closer to the actual quotient? Explain your thinking.

 Math Talk How can an estimate help you know whether a quotient is reasonable? Use an example to explain your answer.

Use compatible numbers to estimate the quotient.

18. $637 \div 78$
$640 \div \blacksquare = \blacksquare$

19. $4,485 \div 89$
$4,500 \div \blacksquare = \blacksquare$

20. $83,456 \div 19$
$\blacksquare \div 20 = \blacksquare$

21. $79\overline{)481}$

22. $48\overline{)946}$

23. $68\overline{)558}$

24. $81\overline{)7,243}$

25. $58\overline{)5,495}$

26. $89\overline{)6,240}$

27. $27\overline{)62,390}$

28. $46\overline{)23,904}$

29. $32\overline{)93,841}$

30. Challenge Describe how you could use compatible numbers to estimate $29,456,351 \div 62$.

 Real World Data

Use the table for problems 31–33.

31. About how many miles did John Glenn travel each minute in orbit?

32. What was the difference between the closest and farthest points from Earth during his orbits?

33. Create and Solve Use the data in the table to write and solve your own problem.

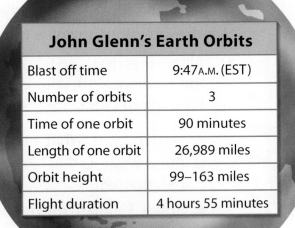

John Glenn's Earth Orbits	
Blast off time	9:47 A.M. (EST)
Number of orbits	3
Time of one orbit	90 minutes
Length of one orbit	26,989 miles
Orbit height	99–163 miles
Flight duration	4 hours 55 minutes

 Spiral Review and Test Practice

Use the Distributive Property to find the value of the variable. AF 1.3 page 124

34. $7 \times 45 = (7 \times 40) + (7 \times a)$

35. $5 \times 79 = (5 \times 70) + (5 \times d)$

36. $n \times 36 = (4 \times 30) + (4 \times 6)$

37. $6 \times m = (6 \times 20) + (6 \times 5)$

Write the letter of the correct answer. KEY **NS 2.2**, MR 2.1

38. Which is the best estimate for $73,360 \div 94$?

A 80 **B** 800 **C** 8,000 **D** 80,000

Extra Practice See page 331, Set A.

Key Standards Review

Need Help?
See Key Standards Handbook.

Evaluate each expression. KEY **AF 1.2**

1. $(s - 6) \div 2$, if $s = 8$

2. $(t + 7) \times 5$, if $t = 4$

3. $3n + 2$, if $n = 8$

4. $2c - 9$, if $c = 15$

5. $(18 - f) \div 3$, if $f = 12$

6. $18 - (f \div 3)$, if $f = 12$

7. $(24 \div t) \times 2$, if $t = 8$

8. $7p \times (3p + 4)$, if $p = 2$

9. $32 - (x \div 2)$, if $x = 24$

Divide and check. KEY **NS 2.1**, KEY **NS 2.2**

10. $8\overline{)70}$

11. $5\overline{)10.2}$

12. $0.2\overline{)26}$

13. $5.4 \div 6$

14. $9.3 \div 3$

15. $12.35 \div 5$

16. $0.3\overline{)78}$

17. $0.5\overline{)6.5}$

18. $0.3\overline{)15}$

 Challenge — Estimate

Compare Quotients KEY **NS 2.2**

You can compare quotients without dividing.

You know $24 \div 4 = 6$.

Is $24 \div 8$ less than or greater than 6?   Is $36 \div 4$ less than or greater than 6?

$\boxed{\text{same dividend, greater divisor}} \rightarrow \boxed{\text{lesser quotient}}$ $\boxed{\text{greater dividend, same divisor}} \rightarrow \boxed{\text{greater quotient}}$

Is the quotient greater than or less than $24 \div 4$?

1. $24 \div 3$

2. $24 \div 12$

3. $16 \div 4$

4. $32 \div 4$

5. $28 \div 4$

6. $24 \div 6$

7. $28 \div 4$

8. $40 \div 4$

Divide by Two-Digit Divisors

Objective Divide with dividends up to three digits and two-digit divisors.

▶ **Learn by Example**

From 1842 to 1868, more than half a million people moved west. The Oregon Trail was a popular route for wagon trains to take. A train left Independence, Missouri and arrived in Fort Laramie, Wyoming 45 days later. How many miles did the train travel each day?

Find 675 ÷ 45

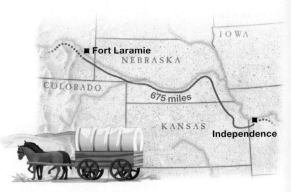

CA Standards

KEY NS 2.2 Demonstrate proficiency with division, including division with positive decimals and long division with multidigit divisors.

KEY NS 2.1 Add, subtract, multiply, and divide with decimals; add with negative integers; subtract positive integers from negative integers; and verify the reasonableness of the results.

Also NS 1.0, MR 1.2, MR 2.1

Hint

Use compatible numbers to help you place each digit in the quotient.

---

1 Estimate to predict the first digit in the quotient.

$$45\overline{)675} \longrightarrow 50\overline{)500}^{\,10}$$

$$\begin{array}{r} 1 \\ 45\overline{)675} \\ -45 \\ \hline 22 \end{array}$$

2 Bring down the ones. Divide and record if there is a remainder.

$$45\overline{)225} \longrightarrow 50\overline{)250}^{\,5}$$

$$\begin{array}{r} 15 \\ 45\overline{)675} \\ -45 \\ \hline 225 \\ -225 \\ \hline 0 \end{array}$$

Check
15 × 45 = 675

Solution: The wagon train traveled 15 miles each day.

Other Examples

A. Divide a whole number by a decimal.

Find 70 ÷ 3.5

$$\begin{array}{r} 20 \\ 3.5\overline{)70.0} \\ -70 \\ \hline 00 \\ -00 \\ \hline 0 \end{array}$$

Check
20 × 3.5 = 70

B. Divide a decimal by a decimal.

Find 6.75 ÷ 4.5

$$\begin{array}{r} 1.5 \\ 4.5\overline{)6.75} \\ -45 \\ \hline 225 \\ -225 \\ \hline 0 \end{array}$$

Check
1.5 × 4.5 = 6.75

Divide. Check your answer.

1. $43\overline{)86}$ 2. $21\overline{)63}$ 3. $3.1\overline{)93}$

4. $945 \div 45$ 5. $88.2 \div 4.2$ 6. $8.8 \div 4.4$

 Math Talk When do you add zeros to the dividend?

Ask Yourself
• What basic fact can I use to estimate the first digit of the quotient?
• Is my quotient reasonable?

▶ **Practice and Problem Solving**

Divide. Check your answer.

7. $27\overline{)81}$ 8. $4.2\overline{)1.26}$ 9. $3.3\overline{)9.9}$ 10. $2.1\overline{)8.4}$

11. $12\overline{)1.68}$ 12. $2.4\overline{)192}$ 13. $1.5\overline{)4.5}$ 14. $11\overline{)132}$

15. $300 \div 75$ 16. $82 \div 4.1$ 17. $6.3 \div 42$ 18. $2.1 \div 1.5$

19. $17.6 \div 1.1$ 20. $780 \div 26$ 21. $7.35 \div 3.5$ 22. $6.2 \div 3.1$

Solve.

23. A family spent $260 for oxen to pull their wagon along the Oregon Trail. If each ox costs $65, how many oxen did they buy?

24. A family saved the same amount each month for two years to get $792 they needed for oxen and supplies for their trip west. How much did they save each month?

25. **Multistep** A wagon train had 94.5 pounds of flour for cooking. Five families shared the flour equally. How many ounces did each family get?

✔ **Spiral Review and Test Practice**

Solve. Write the answer in simplest form. NS 2.5 pages 212, 216

26. $\frac{1}{7} \times \frac{1}{9}$ 27. $\frac{3}{4} \times \frac{5}{6}$ 28. $2\frac{2}{3} \times \frac{1}{8}$ 29. $3\frac{5}{6} \times 1\frac{1}{5}$

Write the letter of the correct answer. KEY NS 2.2

30. Joshua had a rope that was 33.6 meters long. He cut it into pieces that were each 4.2 meters long. How many pieces were there?

   A 0.08   **B** 0.8   **C** 8   **D** 80

 Extra Practice See page 331, Set B.

Estimated Quotient Is Too Large or Too Small

Objective Adjust the estimate of the quotient when the estimate is too large or too small.

CA Standards
KEY NS 2.2 Demonstrate proficiency with division, including division with positive decimals and long division with multidigit divisors.

KEY NS 2.1 Add, subtract, multiply, and divide with decimals; add with negative integers; subtract positive integers from negative integers; and verify the reasonableness of the results.

Also AF 1.0, KEY AF 1.5, MR 2.0, MR 1.2, MR 2.1

▶ **Learn by Example**

A Model T automobile could go 19 miles on one gallon of gas. How much gas would it use to go 741 miles?

Example 1

Find $19\overline{)741}$

1 Place the first digit. Try 4.

$$\begin{array}{r} 4 \\ 19\overline{)741} \\ -76 \end{array}$$

76 > 74
4 is too large.

2 Adjust. Try 3.

$$\begin{array}{r} 3 \\ 19\overline{)741} \\ -57 \\ \hline 17 \end{array}$$

17 < 19
3 is correct.

3 Try 9.

$$\begin{array}{r} 39 \\ 19\overline{)741} \\ -57\downarrow \\ \hline 171 \\ -171 \\ \hline 0 \end{array}$$

0 < 19

Solution: A Model T would use 39 gallons of gas to go 741 miles.

Think

Estimate first.
$19\overline{)741}$
↓
$800 \div 20 = 40$

Example 2

Find $16\overline{)848}$

Estimate first. $16\overline{)848}$ ⟶ $800 \div 20 = 40$

1 Place the first digit. Try 4.

$$\begin{array}{r} 4 \\ 16\overline{)848} \\ -64 \\ \hline 20 \end{array}$$

20 > 16
4 is too small.

2 Adjust. Try 5.

$$\begin{array}{r} 5 \\ 16\overline{)848} \\ -80 \\ \hline 4 \end{array}$$

4 < 16
5 is correct.

3 Try 3.

$$\begin{array}{r} 53 \\ 16\overline{)848} \\ -80\downarrow \\ \hline 48 \\ -48 \\ \hline 0 \end{array}$$

0 < 16

Solution: $848 \div 16 = 53$

Example 3

Find 8.48 ÷ 1.6

$$1.6\overline{)8.4.8}$$

```
        5.3
1.6 ) 8.4.8
     -8 0
       4 8
      -4 8
         0
```

To work with a whole number divisor, first multiply the divisor and dividend by 10. Then follow the same steps as with whole numbers.

Think

Use estimation to check where to place the decimal point. $8 \div 2 = 4$. So the quotient should be close to 4.

▶ Guided Practice

Divide.

1. $35\overline{)420}$

2. $24\overline{)150}$

3. $2.7\overline{)40.5}$

4. $124 \div 16$

5. $6.48 \div 2.4$

6. $24 \div 1.6$

123 Math Talk How do you know if your estimated quotient is too small?

Ask Yourself

• What basic fact can I use to estimate the first digit of the quotient?

• Was my estimate too large or too small?

▶ Practice and Problem Solving

Divide.

7. $45\overline{)270}$

8. $7.5\overline{)60}$

9. $2.3\overline{)8.05}$

10. $9.9\overline{)1.98}$

11. $64\overline{)384}$

12. $16\overline{)408}$

13. $10\overline{)624}$

14. $6.7\overline{)33.5}$

15. $161 \div 46$

16. $37.2 \div 9.3$

17. $203 \div 29$

18. $6.88 \div 4.3$

Solve.

19. A Model T automobile could travel 45 miles per hour. At this rate, how long would it take a Model T automobile to travel 315 miles?

20. **Multistep** By 1927, an assembly line completed one automobile every 25 seconds. How many automobiles could the assembly line complete in 15 minutes?

An automobile assembly line

Copy and complete the function table.

21.

$y = x \div 30$	
x	y
120	
15	
	9
4.5	

22.

$y = x \div 24$	
x	y
	1
	2
14.4	
2.88	

23.

$y = x \div 2.5$	
x	y
5	
	3
12.5	
120	

 Science Link

24. Each planet in our solar system orbits the Sun at a different speed. With a speed of 48 kilometers per second, Mercury is the fastest planet. How long will it take Mercury to travel 720 kilometers?

25. Neptune can travel 600 kilometers in 120 seconds, or 2 minutes. How many seconds would it take for Mars to travel the same distance?

26. Of the planets, which can travel at least 100 kilometers in 5 seconds?

27. Which will take longer, Earth traveling 950 kilometers or Saturn traveling 520 kilometers?

Fun Facts

Average Orbital Speeds of Planets

Planet	Speed (in kilometers per second)
Mercury	48
Venus	35
Earth	19
Mars	24
Jupiter	13
Saturn	10
Uranus	7
Neptune	5

Science ES 5.a, ES 5.b

 Spiral Review and Test Practice

Add or subtract. KEY NS 2.1 page 258

28. $0.013 + 0.538$ **29.** $4.52 + 2.8$ **30.** $18.7 - 14.69$

Write the letter of the correct answer. KEY NS 2.2

31. $462 \div 3.5 =$

A 0.132   B 1.32   C 13.2   D 132

Extra Practice See page 331, Set C.

Quotient Quest

Object of the Game Practice estimating quotients.

Materials
- Learning Tool 15 (Number/Symbol Cards)
  (4 sets of number cards labeled 1–9)

Number of Players 2

Set Up
Shuffle the number cards and place them face down in a stack. On a piece of paper, each player makes a division frame like the one shown below in Step 1.

How to Play

1 Each player takes 5 cards from the stack. Players arrange their cards in a division frame like the one shown here. The object of the game is to use estimation to help you place the cards so the quotient will be as small as possible.

$$2\,4\,)\,9\,3\,5$$

2 Players divide to find their quotient and compare with each other. The player with the smaller quotient gets 1 point. If both quotients are the same, the smaller remainder gets the point. If the remainders are the same, both players get 1 point.

3 Players take turns dealing the cards, repeating steps 1 and 2. The first player to get a total of 10 points wins.

CA Standards
KEY NS 2.2 Demonstrate proficiency with division, including division with positive decimals and long division with multidigit divisors.

Also MR 1.0, MR 2.0

Education Place
Visit www.eduplace.com/camap/ for **Brain Teasers** and **eGames** to play.

Chapter 15 Lesson 4 **325**

CA Standards
KEY **NS 2.2** Demonstrate proficiency with division, including division with positive decimals and long division with multidigit divisors.

KEY **NS 2.1** Add, subtract, multiply, and divide with decimals; add with negative integers; subtract positive integers from negative integers; and verify the reasonableness of the results.

Also MR 1.0, MR 2.1

Four- and Five-Digit Dividends

Objective Divide four- and five-digit dividends by two-digit divisors.

▶ **Learn by Example**

In the 1850s, stagecoaches delivered letters and packages out West.

Suppose a stagecoach traveled from Missouri to California and back in 42 days. If it traveled 5,376 miles, how many miles did the stagecoach travel each day?

1 Estimate the first digit of the quotient. Then divide the hundreds.

Try 1 hundred.

Think:
$$\frac{100}{40)\overline{4,000}}$$

$$\begin{array}{r} 1 \\ 42\overline{)5,376} \\ -42 \\ \hline 11 \end{array}$$

2 Bring down the tens. Divide the tens.

Try 3 tens.

Think:
$$\frac{30}{40)\overline{1,200}}$$

$$\begin{array}{r} 13 \\ 42\overline{)5,376} \\ -42 \\ \hline 117 \\ -126 \end{array}$$

> **Estimate is too large. Try 2 tens.**

$$\begin{array}{r} 12 \\ 42\overline{)5,376} \\ -42 \\ \hline 117 \\ -84 \\ \hline 33 \end{array}$$

3 Bring down the ones. Divide the ones.

Try 8 ones.

Think:
$$\frac{8}{40)\overline{320}}$$

$$\begin{array}{r} 128 \\ 42\overline{)5,376} \\ -42 \\ \hline 117 \\ -84 \\ \hline 336 \\ -336 \\ \hline 0 \end{array}$$

Check
$128 \times 42 = 5,376$

Solution: The stagecoach traveled 128 miles each day.

Other Examples

A. Find 72,096 ÷ 24

```
         3,004
    24)72,096
      -72
        00
       -0
        09
       -0
        96
       -96
         0
```

B. Find 1,530 ÷ 12

```
        127.5
   12)1,530.0
     -12
       33
      -24
       90
      -84
        6 0
       -6 0
         0
```

C. Find 51.216 ÷ 2.4

```
        2 1.34
   2.4)51.2.16
      -48
        3 2
       -2 4
         81
        -7 2
         96
        -96
          0
```

▶ Guided Practice

Divide. Check your answer.

1. 14)5,628   2. 4.2)4.872   3. 12)24,108   4. 9.2)5,060

 Math Talk Look at your answer to Exercise 2. Does your answer seem reasonable?

Ask Yourself
- Where should I place the first digit?
- Is the estimated digit in the quotient too large or too small?

▶ Practice and Problem Solving

Divide. Check your answer.

5. 17)5,185   6. 7.3)7.373   7. 4.8)2,400   8. 25)6,805

9. **Challenge** Stagecoach drivers usually took about 22 days to cover 2,812 miles. Pony Express riders usually took about 12 days to cover 1,866 miles. Who covered more miles in a day? Explain how you decided.

✓ Spiral Review and Test Practice

Divide. KEY NS 2.1, KEY NS 2.2 pages 296, 298, 300, and 304

10. 8)3.2   11. 5)48   12. 0.9)63   13. 0.3)7.8

Write the letter of the correct answer. KEY NS 2.2

14. 36,520 ÷ 44 =

   A 83   **B** 830   **C** 8210   **D** 8300

CA Standards

KEY NS 2.2 Demonstrate proficiency with division, including division with positive decimals and long division with multidigit divisors.

MR 2.6 Make precise calculations and check the validity of the results from the context of the problem.

Also MR 1.1, MR 1.2, MR 2.0, MR 2.3, MR 2.4, MR 3.0, MR 3.1, MR 3.2, MR 3.3

Problem Solving Plan
Use the Remainder

Objective Determine how to use the remainder in division word problems.

▶ **Learn by Example**

When you solve a problem, sometimes you need to decide how to use the remainder.

Example 1

Sometimes you use the remainder to decide on the answer.

Karen is downloading her favorite songs on CDs. There is room for 80 minutes of music on one CD. How many CDs will Karen use to download 228 minutes of her favorite songs?

$$
\begin{array}{r}
2 \text{ R68} \\
80\overline{)228} \\
-160 \\
\hline
68
\end{array}
$$

Karen will fill 2 CDs and use 1 more CD for the 68 remaining minutes. She will use 3 CDs in all.

Example 2

Sometimes you write the quotient as a decimal.

Mrs. Chang paid $1,071 to buy 12 new printers for the library. What was the price of each printer?

The price of each printer was $89.25.

$$
\begin{array}{r}
89.25 \\
12\overline{)1,071.00} \\
-96 \\
\hline
111 \\
-108 \\
\hline
30 \\
-24 \\
\hline
60 \\
-60 \\
\hline
0
\end{array}
$$

Example 3

Sometimes you write the remainder as a fraction.

Jeremy charges $40 per hour to design websites. He earned $330 in one week. How many hours did he work?

Jeremy worked for $8\frac{1}{4}$ hours.

$$
\begin{array}{r}
8 \ \frac{10}{40} = 8\frac{1}{4} \\
40\overline{)330} \\
-320 \\
\hline
10
\end{array}
$$

▶ Guided Problem Solving

Use the Ask Yourself questions to help you solve this problem.

1. Alfredo pays $54 per month for cell phone service. He used his cell phone for 12 hours in February. What was the cost of using his cell phone per hour?

 Math Talk How does looking at the question in each situation help you decide what to do with the remainder?

▶ Independent Problem Solving

Solve. Explain how you used the remainder.

2. Mr. Gasper built new workstations for the computer lab. He used 175 feet of lumber to make 14 workstations. How much lumber did each workstation require?

3. Members of the Computer Club are setting up tables for their annual banquet. Each table can seat 16 people. If 104 people attend, how many tables will they need?

4. **Multistep** Every month, the Sanchez family pays $45 for basic cable TV service and $24 for each of two movie channels. What is the total cost per day for these services in a 30-day month?

5. A group of 83 students will take a computer class. Each class has 14 students. What is the least number of classes needed?

6. A website had 905 visitors during the month of December. What was the average number of visitors each day?

7. During a science experiment, the temperature of a mixture increased by 26° in 4 hours. What was the average increase in temperature each hour?

8. **Challenge** The answer to the following problem is 3 boxes but the question is missing. What is the question?

   Ms. Snyder ordered 74 ink cartridges. Twenty-eight can fit into a box.

9. **Create and Solve** Write a word problem that has an answer where you write the remainder as a fraction.

Reading & Writing Math

Vocabulary

Shane rushed through his math homework and made some mistakes. Look at his work. Find his errors. Use the words **quotient, divisor, dividend,** and **remainder** to describe what he did wrong. Then copy and correct the problems.

divisor

quotient   remainder

1.
$$
\begin{array}{r}
16 \text{ R16} \\
21\overline{)163} \\
-21 \\
\hline
142 \\
-126 \\
\hline
16
\end{array}
$$

dividend

2.
$$
\begin{array}{r}
30 \text{ R35} \\
38\overline{)149} \\
-114 \\
\hline
35
\end{array}
$$

3.
$$
\begin{array}{r}
1 \text{ R22} \\
16\overline{)182} \\
-16 \\
\hline
22
\end{array}
$$

4.
$$
\begin{array}{r}
13 \text{ R35} \\
45\overline{)621} \\
-45 \\
\hline
170 \\
-135 \\
\hline
35
\end{array}
$$

Writing

When Eve works on her division homework, she always turns her lined paper sideways so the lines go up and down the page instead of across the page.

How does turning her page help Eve when she does her division problems? Do you think this is a good idea? Tell why or why not.

Reading

Look for this book in your library. *Math Mysteries* by Jack Silbert

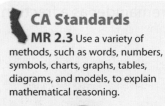

CA Standards

MR 2.3 Use a variety of methods, such as words, numbers, symbols, charts, graphs, tables, diagrams, and models, to explain mathematical reasoning.

Also KEY NS 2.2

Standards-Based Extra Practice

Set A ────────────────────────────── KEY **NS 2.2** page 316

Use compatible numbers to estimate each quotient.

1. 39)‾278‾
2. 61)‾3,591‾
3. 19)‾117‾
4. 52)‾291‾

5. 83)‾1,540‾
6. 12)‾391‾
7. 35)‾7,010‾
8. 64)‾42,156‾

9. Rose Bowl Stadium has a seating capacity of 95,542. If there are 28 sections of seats, estimate how many people can sit in each section.

Set B ────────────────────────────── KEY **NS 2.2** page 320

Divide. Check your answer.

1. 36)‾324‾
2. 19)‾475‾
3. 31)‾527‾
4. 2.2)‾3.08‾

5. 9.0 ÷ 1.8
6. 128 ÷ 16
7. 51.2 ÷ 3.2
8. 98 ÷ 14

9. Dave is putting his collection of 792 baseball cards in a scrapbook. If he puts 18 cards on each page, how many pages will he fill?

Set C ────────────────────────────── KEY **NS 2.2** page 322

Divide.

1. 1.6)‾7.2‾
2. 28)‾420‾
3. 13)‾338‾
4. 5.1)‾25.5‾

5. 627 ÷ 11
6. 32.4 ÷ 1.8
7. 4.41 ÷ 2.1
8. 123 ÷ 41

9. The area of Pete's basement floor is 320 square feet. He used 2.5 gallons of paint to paint the floor. How much did 1 gallon of paint cover?

Set D ────────────────────────────── KEY **NS 2.2** page 326

Divide. Check your answer.

1. 64)‾3,712‾
2. 54)‾1,458‾
3. 49)‾1,862‾
4. 12)‾1,536‾

5. 38,190 ÷ 19
6. 19,241 ÷ 71
7. 31,896 ÷ 9
8. 299.7 ÷ 2.7

9. The traffic light at the corner of Elm Street and Ford Avenue changes 2,880 times in 24 hours. How many times does the traffic light change in 1 hour?

Education Place
Visit www.eduplace.com/camap/
for more **Extra Practice**.

Chapter Review/Test

Vocabulary and Concepts ———————————— KEY NS 2.1, KEY NS 2.2, MR 2.2

Write the best term to complete each sentence.

1. You can estimate a quotient with _____, which are numbers you can use to calculate easily in your head.

2. When dividing with decimals, decide where to place the decimal point in your quotient and then divide as if the numbers were _____.

Skills ———————————————————————— NS 1.1, KEY NS 2.1, KEY NS 2.2

Use mental math to find each quotient.

3. $63 \div 9$ **4.** $630 \div 90$ **5.** $630 \div 9$ **6.** $6,300 \div 90$ **7.** $6,300 \div 9$

Use compatible numbers to estimate each quotient.

8. $997 \div 19$ **9.** $423 \div 58$ **10.** $71,813 \div 910$

11. $627 \div 11$ **12.** $806 \div 93$ **13.** $16,484 \div 82$

Divide. Check your answer.

14. $19.5 \div 6.5$ **15.** $8.8 \div 1.6$ **16.** $3588 \div 23$ **17.** $528 \div 11$

18. $43,152 \div 48$ **19.** $34.2 \div 1.8$ **20.** $16,124 \div 40$ **21.** $432 \div 0.32$

Problem Solving and Reasoning ——————— KEY NS 2.1, KEY NS 2.2, MR 2.1, MR 2.3

Solve.

22. The Morse family drove 775 miles in 19 hours on their vacation. Estimate how many miles they drove each hour.

23. A theater made $6,048 selling tickets to a play. If each ticket cost $18, how many tickets were sold?

24. Roger divides 72 by 10 and writes the quotient as 7R2. How could you use the remainder to write the quotient as a decimal?

25. Nora has a ribbon that is 36.4 centimeters long. She cuts it into pieces that are 2.8 centimeters long. How many pieces are there?

Writing Math How could you use estimation to check the reasonableness of your answer to Problem 25?

Spiral Review and Test Practice

1. What is 75,382,014 rounded to the nearest million?

A 75,000,000

B 75,400,000

C 76,000,000

D 80,000,000

> **Test Tip**
> Read the question again when you finish to be sure that you chose the correct answer.

NS 1.1 page 66

2. What number goes in the box to make this number sentence true?

$(8 - 3) + 4 = 7 + \square$

A 15   **C** 5

B 9   **D** 2

KEY AF 1.2 page 108

3. A bicycle race covers a distance of 364 miles. If 32 cyclists are in the race, how many miles do they ride altogether?

A 396 miles

B 1,820 miles

C 10,448 miles

D 11,648 miles

NS 1.0 page 286

4. 46.08
      $\times$ 0.4

A 16.402

B 18.432

C 184.32

D 18,432

KEY NS 2.1 page 278

5. $22 \div 8 =$

A 2

B 2.75

C 2.76

D 275

> **Test Tip**
> Use the inverse operation to check your answer.

KEY NS 2.1 page 298

6. Which of the following is the best estimate of $47,230 \div 83$?

A 6

B 60

C 600

D 60,000

KEY NS 2.2 page 316

Education Place
Visit www.eduplace.com/camap/ for
Test-Taking Tips and **Extra Practice**.

Chapter 15 Spiral Review and Test Practice **333**

Unit 6 Review/Test

Vocabulary and Concepts ———————————————————— KEY **NS 2.1**, MR 2.3

Fill in the blank to complete each sentence. Chapters 12–15

1. When you multiply two decimals the answer is called the _____.

2. In the number 5.064, the 0 is in the _____ place.

3. In the number 19.387 the 1 is in the _____ place.

4. In the equation 2.3 × 8 = 18.4, 2.3 and 8 are _____.

5. In the number 14.263 the 6 is in the _____ place.

Skills ———————————————————————————————— KEY **NS 2.1**, NS 1.1

Add or subtract. Estimate to check your answer. Chapter 12, Lessons 1–3

6.	2.085	7.	10.681	8.	14.929	9.	15.261
	+ 1.504		− 3.569		+ 23.245		− 13.785

10.	1.05	11.	254.12	12.	43.257	13.	4.06
	+ 0.267		+ 105.002		− 21.998		− 2.851

Multiply or divide. Chapters 13–15

14.	11	15. 27 ÷ 6	16.	27.18	17. 1.44 ÷ 6
	× 4.6			× 19.99	

16.	2.901	17. 5.25 ÷ 0.5	18. 9.75 ÷ 3	19.	2.007
	× 0.805				× 0.901

Use compatible numbers to estimate each quotient.

20. 92)‾4,526   21. 31)‾268   22. 68)‾143   23. 512)‾24,689

Problem Solving and Reasoning

NS 1.1, KEY NS 2.1, MR 1.1 Chapters 12–15

Solve.

24. There are 33.9 million people living in the state of California. If the people were divided into three groups how many million people would there be in each group?

25. Darrell makes $8.65 every hour mowing grass. He mows 4 days a week for 3 hours per day. About how much does he make in a week?

Writing Math What happens to a number if you accidentally place a digit one place to the left of where it belongs?

Performance Assessment

KEY NS 2.1

The President's Challenge

The President's Challenge is a physical fitness test that awards students for their level of fitness. Students must reach a certain level in 5 different events to qualify for awards. The table shows the levels 11-year old boys and girls must achieve for the 50th percentile and the 85th percentile awards.

	11-year old fitness levels									
	85th precentile					**50th percentile**				
	Curl-ups (1 min.)	Shuttle Run	Sit & Reach	1 mi. Run	Pull-Ups (1 min.)	Curl-ups (1 min.)	Shuttle Run	Sit & Reach	1 mi. Run	Pull-Ups (1 min.)
Boys	47	10	31	7:32	6	37	11.1 sec	25	9:20	2
Girls	42	10.5	34	9:02	3	32	11.5	29	11:17	1

Task	Information You Need
Use the information above and to the right to figure out which precentile Ken and Jen achieve in three events. Both are 11 years old. Explain how you got your answers. **Hint:** In running events, a faster time is better.	In every 0.25 minute, Ken did 12 curl-ups.
	Ken reached 26 cm and Jen reached 1.5 times farther than him in the Sit & Reach.
	Jen ran the shuttle run in 10.3 seconds, which was 0.8 seconds faster than Ken.
	Jen did 12 fewer curl ups per minute than Ken.

Greg Tang's Go Fast, Go Far

Unit 6 Mental Math Strategies

Multiply by 11

Eleven can be fast and fun, simply just insert the sum!

I have a fast way to do 11 × 54. I split 54 by putting the 5 in the hundreds place and the 4 in the ones place. Then I insert their sum in the middle, the tens place, and get 594. If the sum is greater than 9, I just regroup!

1. 11 × 54 = 100s 10s 1s `5` `9` `4` = ▢

2. 11 × 78 = 100s 10s 1s `7` `15` `8` = ▢

3. 11 × 17 = 100s 10s 1s `1` ▢ `7` = ▢

4. 11 × 43 = 100s 10s 1s `4` ▢ `3` = ▢

Way to go! Now try these!

5. 11 × 26 = ▢▢▢ = ▢

6. 11 × 59 = ▢▢▢ = ▢

7. 11 × 31 = ▢▢▢ = ▢

8. 11 × 25 = ▢▢▢ = ▢

9. 11 × 46 = ▢▢▢ = ▢

10. 11 × 63 = ▢▢▢ = ▢

Take It Further!

Now try doing all the steps in your head!

11. 11 × 28

12. 11 × 36

13. 11 × 86

14. 11 × 54

Good For You!

Unit
7

Data and Graphs

BIG IDEAS!

- *Mean*, *median*, and *mode* are three ways to interpret the same set of data.

- Each type of graph is suited to display a different type of data.

- Ordered pairs locate and describe specific points on a coordinate grid.

Chapter 16
Graphs and Statistics

Chapter 17
Graphs on a Coordinate Grid

Songs and Games

Math Music Track 7:
Find an Ordered Pair

eGames at
www.eduplace.com/camap/

Math Readers

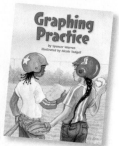

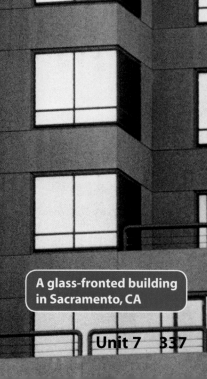

A glass-fronted building in Sacramento, CA

Game

In the Middle

Object of the Game To write a 4-digit number that is the median of a set of numbers.

Materials
- Workmat 1
- 4 Number cubes (labeled 1–6)

Number of Players 3 or 5

How to Play

1 Players take turns tossing all four number cubes at once.

2 Without showing their work to each other, players use the digits on the number cubes to write a 4-digit number on their Workmat. The object of the game is to write a number that will be the median, or middle number.

3 Players place their Workmats side by side to compare numbers. Then they arrange them in order from least to greatest.

4 The player with the middle number wins the round and gets 1 point. If another player has the same number, he or she also gets 1 point. The game ends after 7 rounds. The winner is the player with the most points.

CA Standards
SDAP 1.1 Know the concepts of mean, median, and mode; compute and compare simple examples to show that they may differ.

Also MR 1.0

 Education Place
Visit www.eduplace.com/camap/ for **Brain Teasers** and **eGames** to play.

338

Reading When you read a story, you start at the top of the page, and you read to the bottom. When you read graphs or tables, you often have to look in more than one place and in more than one direction. You need to read closely to find specific information.

Hector tracked the daily high temperature in Lake Tahoe for one week during the month of February. The results are shown in the line graph below. Use the checklist to preview the line graph. What was the high temperature on Friday?

Find:
✓ the title
✓ the heading on the horizontal axis
✓ the heading on the vertical axis
✓ the labels
✓ the number scale
✓ the line of the graph

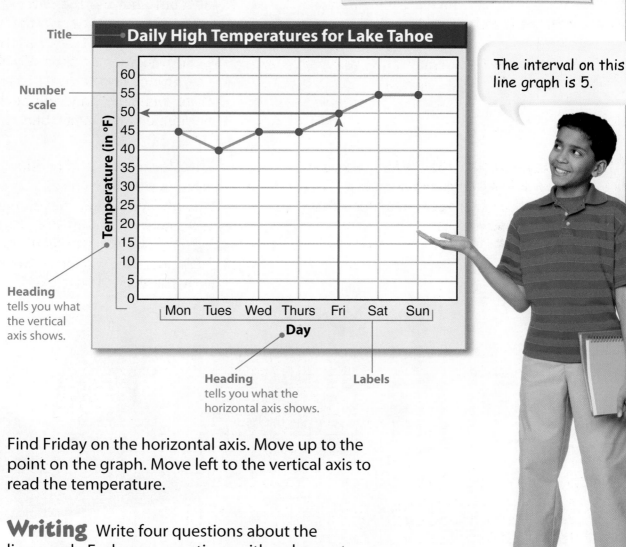

Title

Number scale

Heading
tells you what the vertical axis shows.

Daily High Temperatures for Lake Tahoe

Temperature (in °F)

Mon Tues Wed Thurs Fri Sat Sun

Day

Heading
tells you what the horizontal axis shows.

Labels

The interval on this line graph is 5.

Find Friday on the horizontal axis. Move up to the point on the graph. Move left to the vertical axis to read the temperature.

Writing Write four questions about the line graph. Exchange questions with a classmate and answer them.

Graphs and Statistics

A snowboarder competes at Big Bear Resort in California.

Check What You Know

Vocabulary and Concepts GRADE 4 SDAP 1.0, MR 2.3
Match each term with a definition.

1. bar graph

2. pictograph

a. a graph that uses pictures or symbols to show data

b. one method of collecting data

c. a graph that uses bars to show data

Skills GRADE 4 SDAP 1.0
The graph shows the number of visitors to an amusement park. Use the graph to answer Questions 3–4.

3. When does the daily average equal 120 visitors?

4. On average, how many more daily visitors were there in August than in June?

Problem Solving and Reasoning GRADE 4 SDAP 1.0
5. Jerome surveyed the students in his class to find out the most popular flavor of ice cream. The results are shown in the table. How many more students like Rocky Road than Mint Chip?

Average Daily Visitors	
May	🎡 🎡 🎡
June	🎡 🎡 🎡 🎡
July	🎡 🎡 🎡 🎡 🎡 🎡
August	🎡 🎡 🎡 🎡 🎡
September	🎡 🎡 🎡

Each 🎡 = 40 people

Popular Ice Cream Flavors	
Ice Cream Flavor	**Number of Votes**
Rocky Road	17
Chocolate	8
Mint Chip	12

Vocabulary

Visualize It!

mean 11
The average of a set of data. It is the sum of all of the numbers divided by the number of addends.

5, 6, 7, 7, 9, 10, 11, 13, 14, 15, 19

mode 7
the number that occurs most often

median 10
the middle number

Language Tip
Math words that look alike in English and Spanish often have the same meaning.

English	Spanish
median	**mediana**

See **English-Spanish Glossary** pages 628–642.

Education Place Visit www.eduplace.com/camap/ for the **eGlossary** and **eGames**.

CA Standards MR 2.3 Use a variety of methods, such as words, numbers, symbols, charts, graphs, tables, diagrams, and models, to explain mathematical reasoning. **Also SDAP 1.1**

Chapter 16 341

CA Standards
SDAP 1.1 Know the concept of mean, median, and mode; compute and compare simple examples to show that they may differ.
Also MR 2.3

Vocabulary

mean

average

Materials
2-color counters

Hands On
Model Finding the Mean

Objective Use models to find the mean.

▶ **Explore**

Finding a **mean** is one way to find a number that is typical of the numbers in a group. The mean of a group is sometimes called the **average**. An average tells you what you would most likely find in a group of data.

Question How can you use counters to find the mean of a set of numbers?

A group of fifth-grade students answered a survey about the number of hours they practiced soccer in one week. What is the mean number of hours these students practiced soccer?

Hours Spent at Soccer Practice

1, 2, 2, 4, 5, 4, 2, 4, 3

Think

Each column of counters represents one member of the soccer team. How many columns will you have?

Work in groups.

1. Make columns of counters that model the number of hours each student practiced soccer.

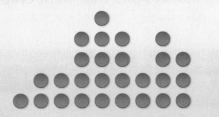

2. Rearrange the columns of counters so that each column has the same number of counters.

342

3 Count the number of counters in each column.

What is the mean, or average, number of hours these students practiced soccer in one week?

▶ **Extend**

Find the mean of each set of numbers. Use counters.

1. 4, 6, 7, 8, 6, 5

2. 8, 6, 7, 6, 7, 8

3. 3, 5, 4, 5, 3, 4

4. 6, 7, 9, 5, 9, 6

Solve.

5. Charlie spent the following number of hours playing basketball each day last week: 2, 3, 2, 1, 3, 4, and 6. What is the mean number of hours that Charlie spent per day playing basketball?

6. Carlotta recorded the number of baskets she scored during each game. What is the mean number of baskets Carlotta made per game?

Game 1				
Game 2	︙卌
Game 3				
Game 4	卌	
Game 5					
Game 6				

7. Challenge Carlotta wants to increase her mean to 5 baskets scored per game. How many baskets in all does Carlotta need to score in Games 7 and 8 to change her mean to 5? Explain how you know.

Writing Math

Predict Look at the numbers 2, 5, 14, 6, and 3. Will the mean of the numbers be closer to 2 or to 14? Explain.

CA Standards

SDAP 1.1 Know the concept of mean, median, and mode; compute and compare simple examples to show that they may differ.

SDAP 1.2 Organize and display single-variable data in appropriate graphs and representations (e.g., histogram, circle graphs) and explain which types of graphs are appropriate for various data sets.

Also KEY NS 2.2 **, MR 2.3, SDAP 1.0**

Vocabulary

mean

median

mode

Mean, Median, and Mode

Objective Find the mean, median, and mode for a set of data.

▶ **Learn by Example**

Kenny went bowling with a group of friends. Their scores in the first game are shown. What are the mean, median, and mode of their scores?

84, 72, 83,
84, 92, 85,
80, 83, 84

Find the Mean

The **mean** is the average of a set of data. It is the sum of all the numbers divided by the number of addends.

1 Add the scores.

$$84 + 72 + 83 + 84 + 92 + 85 + 80 + 83 + 84 = 747$$

2 Divide the sum by the number of addends.

The mean bowling score is 83.

$$
\begin{array}{r}
83 \\
9\overline{)747} \\
-72 \\
\hline
27 \\
-27 \\
\hline
0
\end{array}
$$

Find the Median

The **median** is the middle number when the data are arranged in order.

1 Write the data in order from least to greatest.

72 80 83 83 [84] 84 84
85 92

2 The median is 84.

Find the Mode

The **mode** is the number that occurs most often. There can be more than one mode or no mode.

1 Underline the numbers that occur more than once.

72 80 <u>83</u> <u>83</u> <u>84</u> <u>84</u> <u>84</u>
85 92

2 Find the number that occurs most often. The mode of this set of data is 84.

Other Examples

A. Even Number of Data

For an even number of data, the median is the average of the middle two numbers.

Find the median of 6, 10, 11, 13, 13, and 13.

$$\frac{11 + 13}{2} = 12$$ The median is 12.

B. More Than One Mode

Find the mode of 1, 1, 2, 2, 2, 3, 3, 4, 4, 4, and 7.

1 1 <u>2</u> <u>2</u> <u>2</u> 3 3 <u>4</u> <u>4</u> <u>4</u> 7

The numbers 2 and 4 both occur three times, so both numbers are modes.

► **Guided Practice**

Use the data in the table to complete Exercises 1–3.

Miniature Golf Scores
69, 72, 74, 73, 73, 72, 75, 73, 70, 72, 89, 72, 91

1. What is the mean of the miniature golf scores?

2. What is the median of the scores?

3. What is the mode of the scores?

 Math Talk In what way is finding the median or mode of a set of data different from finding its mean? Explain.

Ask Yourself
- Did I remember the difference between mean, median, and mode?
- Did I arrange the numbers in order?

► **Practice and Problem Solving**

Use the data in the table to complete Exercises 4–6.

4. What is the mean of the number of miles hiked?

5. What is the median of the miles hiked?

6. What is the mode of the miles hiked?

Number of Miles Hiked
12, 7, 13, 14, 14, 12, 12

✓ **Spiral Review and Test Practice**

Subtract. Then simplify your answer. KEY **NS 2.3**, NS 2.0, NS 1.0 page 192

7. $4\frac{2}{3} - 2\frac{1}{3}$ **8.** $5\frac{7}{8} - 3\frac{1}{2}$ **9.** $3\frac{1}{2} - 2\frac{3}{4}$ **10.** $6\frac{5}{6} - 3\frac{1}{3}$

Write the letter of the correct answer. SDAP 1.1

11. Angela's bowling scores were 121, 93, 87, 90, 110, 89, and 110. What is the mean of Angela's scores?

A 93   **B** 100   **C** 110   **D** 700

Extra Practice See page 359, Set A.

CA Standards
KEY **SDAP 1.4** Identify ordered pairs from a graph and interpret the meaning of the data in terms of the situation depicted by the graph.
Also NS 1.0, AF 1.1, KEY AF 1.4, SDAP 1.0, MR 2.3

Vocabulary

line graph

ordered pair

double line graph

Materials
• Workmat 4
• Dry erase markers (blue and red)
• Learning Tool 10 (Centimeter Grid)

Line Graphs

Objective Make and interpret line graphs.

▶ **Learn by Example**

Hannah wore her inline skates at work so she could quickly move around the warehouse. Hannah kept track of the distance she skated. Each half-hour she wrote the total number of miles she had skated.

Distance Skated

Time	8:00	8:30	9:00	9:30	10:00	10:30	11:00	11:30	12:00
Miles Skated	0	2	4	6	9	9	11	13	14

Make a Line Graph

Make a **line graph** to show the data Hannah collected. A line graph shows a set of data over time.

1 Draw the axes. Label the horizontal axis **Time** and the vertical axis **Total Miles Skated**. Choose an appropriate scale and mark equal intervals.

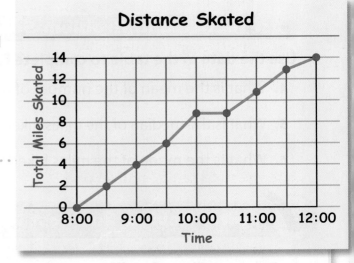

2 Plot the ordered pairs in red. Join the points to make the line graph.

The point on the grid that shows that Hannah skated 0 miles by 8:00 is represented by the **ordered pair** (8:00, 0).

3 Give the graph a title.

Make a Double Line Graph

Maneesh works at the same warehouse with Hannah. He also kept track of the distance he skated around the warehouse.

Distance Skated									
Time	8:00	8:30	9:00	9:30	10:00	10:30	11:00	11:30	12:00
Miles Skated	0	1	2	4	6	6	10	12	13

You can make a **double line graph** to compare two sets of data over time.

Use your graph from Example 1.

1 Plot the ordered pairs for Maneesh in blue. Join the points to make the line graph.

2 Make a key to show what each line represents.

3 Give the graph a new title.

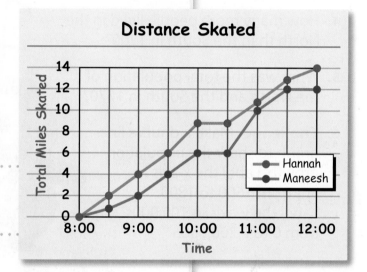

▶ **Guided Practice**

Use the data table for Exercise 1.

Number of Safety Helmets Sold						
	May	**June**	**July**	**Aug.**	**Sept.**	**Oct.**
Brand X	60	45	35	25	20	15

1. Use the safety helmet data to make a line graph.

Ask Yourself
- What scale should I use?
- How should I label the axes?
- Did I include a title?

123 Math Talk Why are line graphs useful for showing data over time?

Practice and Problem Solving

Use the data table for Problems 2–3.

Number of Safety Helmets Sold						
	May	June	July	Aug.	Sept.	Oct.
Brand Y	35	30	30	25	25	22

2. Use your line graph from Exercise 1 and the safety-helmet data to make a double line graph.

3. **Analyze** What conclusions can you draw from the graph?

History-Social Science Link

Use the table to answer Questions 4–6.

4. How many more people lived in the North than the South in 1700?

5. What was the total population of the North and the South in 1770?

6. **Challenge** Make a double line graph to show the population growth. Label the x-axis in 50s from 1600 to 1800. Label the y-axis in 100,000s from 0 to 2,200,000.

Colonial Population Growth		
	North	South
1640	26,634	26,037
1670	111,935	107,400
1700	250,888	223,071
1740	905,563	755,539
1770	2,148,076	1,688,254

History-Social Science 5.4.1

Spiral Review and Test Practice

Write each quotient in simplest form. NS 2.4, NS 2.5, NS 1.0 pages 230, 234, and 236.

7. $\frac{7}{12} \div \frac{9}{10}$ 8. $5\frac{1}{2} \div 6$ 9. $2 \div \frac{2}{3}$ 10. $\frac{4}{5} \div 2\frac{3}{5}$

Write the letter of the correct answer.

KEY **SDAP 1.4**, SDAP 1.0

11. Jamal's grandparents drove him to summer camp. He recorded how many total miles he had traveled at each hour. He arrived at camp at 2:00. At what time was he halfway through his trip?

 A 11:00 **B** 12:00 **C** 1:00 **D** 2:00

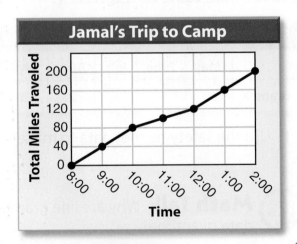

Jamal's Trip to Camp

348

Extra Practice See page 359, Set B.

Choose a Graph Scale

The scale you choose for a graph can affect the appearance of the data.

Here are two graphs that show the same data. What differences do you notice?

1. Which graph makes it look as though sales are increasing more? Why?

2. The zigzag line at the base of the vertical axis on the first graph shows that some numbers have been left out. How would the graph change if these numbers were included?

3. What do you notice when you compare the intervals used on the vertical axes of the two graphs? How do you think the appearance of the graph would change if intervals of 3,000 were used?

4. Make another graph that displays the same data. Adjust the vertical axis on your graph so sales appear to be increasing only a little bit each month.

5. Why is it important to look at how the axes are numbered when you are interpreting a graph?

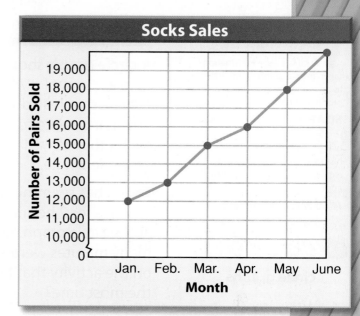

Socks Sales

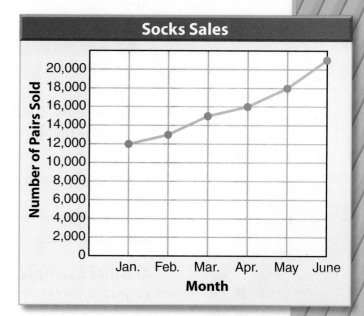

Socks Sales

CA Standards
AF 1.1, SDAP 1.0,
SDAP 1.2, MR 2.3

CA Standards

AF 1.1 Use information taken from a graph or equation to answer questions about a problem situation.

SDAP 1.2 Organize and display single-variable data in appropriate graphs and representations (e.g., histogram, circle graphs) and explain which types of graphs are appropriate for various data sets.

Also MR 2.3, MR 2.0

Vocabulary

circle graphs

Circle Graphs

Objective Use and interpret circle graphs.

▶ **Learn by Example**

A **circle graph** shows data as parts of a whole. A circle graph also shows how parts relate to each other as well as to the whole.

Teresa has swimming practice for 2 hours. Look at the circle graph. How many minutes were spent on the activity that takes the most time?

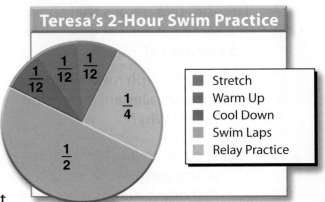

Teresa's 2-Hour Swim Practice

- ■ Stretch
- ■ Warm Up
- ■ Cool Down
- ■ Swim Laps
- ■ Relay Practice

Hint

2 hours = 120 minutes

1. Find the largest section of the circle graph. Lap swim is the largest section.

2. Swimming laps took $\frac{1}{2}$ of the swim practice. The total amount of time that Teresa spent at swim practice was 2 hours, or 120 minutes.

3. Multiply 120 minutes by $\frac{1}{2}$. $120 \times \frac{1}{2} = 60$

Solution: Teresa spent 60 minutes swimming laps.

Another Example

Many newspapers show data in circle graphs. A tilted circle graph can be misleading. Which graph looks like it shows more foreign visitors?

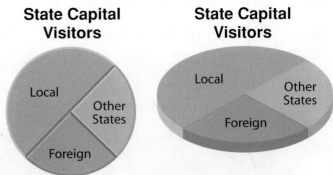

State Capital Visitors

State Capital Visitors

Use the circle graph to answer
Questions 1–2.

Nut Mix

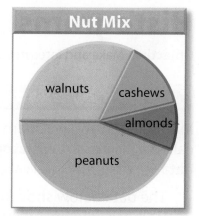

1. If you only like almonds,
   is this a nut mix that
   you would want to buy?
   Explain.

2. Is this mix of nuts more or less
   than $\frac{1}{2}$ peanuts? How can you tell?

 Math Talk Explain why this is a good type of graph to
use to show the data about the nut mix.

Ask Yourself
- What does the
  largest section of the
  circle tell you?
- Does the circle graph
  tell exact amounts of
  each type of nut?

▶ **Practice and Problem Solving**

Use the circle graph to answer Questions 3–5.

The fifth-grade class held a vote to decide what they wanted
to do for their class trip. The circle graph shows the results.

3. What fraction of the class wanted to go bowling?

4. What fraction of the class chose either bowling or
   the amusement park?

5. **Challenge** Arrange all the activities in order from least
   to greatest number of votes.

 Spiral Review and Test Practice

**Estimate each product. Write a multiplication sentence
to show the rounded numbers you used.** NS 2.0, KEY **NS 2.1** page 276

6. 0.97×18 7. 5.301×4.917 8. 22×9.8

Write the letter of the correct answer. SDAP 1.2

9. A circle graph section shows that 10 hours were spent at
   the park. What would a section that is half of the size of
   the park section be labeled?

   A $\frac{1}{2}$ hour   **B** 2 hours   **C** 5 hours   **D** 20 hours

CA Standards

SDAP 1.2 Organize and display single-variable data in appropriate graphs and representations (e.g., histogram, circle graphs) and explain which types of graphs are appropriate for various data sets.

AF 1.1 Use information taken from a graph or equation to answer questions about a problem situation.

Also SDAP 1.1, MR 1.2, MR 2.3, MR 3.0, MR 3.3

Vocabulary

histogram

frequency table

Materials
Learning Tool 10 (Centimeter Grid)

Histograms

Objective Make and interpret a histogram.

▶ **Learn by Example**

In this lesson you will learn about a special type of bar graph called a histogram. A **histogram** is a bar graph that compares data within equal intervals, or groupings.

The data below show the ages of players on a professional ice hockey team. Are more of the players in the 19–24 age group, the 25–30 age group, or the 31–36 age group?

21	24	31	23	25	32	35	23	34
31	30	30	20	19	24	32	32	36
30	19	21	22	24	24	36	32	

Make a histogram. Start by using a **frequency table** to organize the data. A frequency table shows data using tally marks.

Example 1 Make a Frequency Table

① Use tally marks to record the frequencies. Make one tally mark for each player.

② Count the tally marks and write the frequencies.

Intervals	Tally Marks	Frequency
19–24	卌 卌 ǀǀ	12
25–30	ǀǀǀǀ	4
31–36	卌 卌	10

Example 2 Make a Histogram

① Draw and label the vertical axis. Choose an equally spaced scale.

② Label the horizontal axis and list the three age groups.

③ Draw a bar for each age group. Do not leave spaces between the bars.

④ Give the graph a title.

Hockey Players

(Histogram: Number of Players vs Age — 19–24: 12, 25–30: 4, 31–36: 10)

Solution: Most of the players are in the 19–24 age group.

Use the data and histogram on page 352 for Problems 1–2.

1. Which of the three age groups had the fewest players?

2. List the age groups by size from least to greatest.

Ask Yourself
Do I need to know the exact number the bar shows?

Guided Problem Solving

Use the questions to solve this problem.

3. Sherrie made a list of the ages of the players from a professional women's ice hockey team. Which age group has the most players? Make a histogram to answer the question.

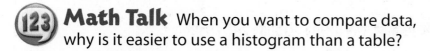

31	34	30	29	28	31	24	19
32	34	20	27	28	29	32	33
36	35	31	22	26	29	31

a. **Understand** What is the youngest age? What is the oldest age? How many years do you need to show on the *x*-axis?

b. **Plan** Make a frequency table of the data. Use 3 equal intervals. How many years are in each interval?

c. **Solve** Use your frequency table to make your histogram.

d. **Look Back** Count the number of players using your histogram. Does it match the number of players in the original list?

4. Make another frequency table and histogram for the data in Problem 3. Use a different number of equal intervals.

(123) Math Talk When you want to compare data, why is it easier to use a histogram than a table?

▶ **Practice and Problem Solving**

The histogram shows the heights of players for the Los Angeles Lakers. Use the histogram for Problems 5–7.

5. In which height group were the most players?

6. How many Lakers players were in the 73–76 inch tall group?

7. **Challenge** How many players were less than 6.75 feet tall?

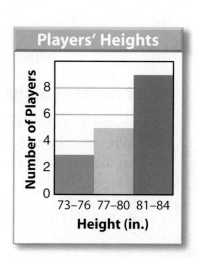

Players' Heights

Number of Players

73–76 77–80 81–84
Height (in.)

Science Link

Use the Fun Facts to answer Questions 8–13.

8. What intervals could you use to arrange the crater data into four equal intervals?

9. Use four intervals to make a histogram.

10. **Predict** Based on the observed data, about what diameter might the next identified crater be? Explain.

11. What is the median diameter of the craters?

12. What is the mean diameter of the craters in the table to the nearest whole number?

13. **What's Wrong?** Deena says the mode of the crater data is 8 km. Explain what is wrong with Deena's answer.

Arizona's Meteor Crater is a little more than 1 km wide.

Science **ES 5.b**

Fun Facts

- Meteorites are bits of matter from our solar system that have landed on Earth, causing craters.
- Scientists have identified 27 craters in the United States.
- Three of the identified craters are 60 km or more in diameter. Two of the craters are less than 0.2 km in diameter.
- The table shows the diameters of the remaining 22 craters.

Diameter (in kilometers) of U.S. Craters										
16	12	1	9	7	7	6	8	4	4	8
13	13	6	3	9	6	8	13	10	12	7

Spiral Review and Test Practice

Divide. Check by multiplying. KEY **NS 2.2** page 314

14. $570 \div 10$

15. $7,200 \div 100$

16. $85,000 \div 1,000$

17. $6,750 \div 100$

Write the letter of the correct answer. SDAP 1.2

18. Students in Mrs. Garcia's class traveled the following number of miles to school: 9, 9, 1, 3, 5, 4, 7, 10, 13, 6, 1, 4. Which is the best choice for intervals for a histogram?

   A 1–5, 6–9, 10–13

   B 1–5, 6–10, 11–16

   C 1–3, 4–6, 7–9, 10–12

   D 1–4, 5–8, 9–12, 13–16

Extra Practice See page 359, Set D.

Key Standards Review

Need Help?
See Key Standards Handbook.

Divide. Then check your work. KEY **NS 2.1**, KEY **NS 2.2**

1. $6\overline{)2.4}$

2. $7\overline{)9.66}$

3. $3.2\overline{)78.4}$

4. $6.4 \div 32$

5. $125.5 \div 5$

6. $30.69 \div 9.9$

7. $8\overline{)3.2}$

8. $4\overline{)0.46}$

9. $7.4\overline{)7.844}$

10. $0.48 \div 12$

11. $32.4 \div 0.8$

12. $19.61 \div 3.7$

13. $3\overline{)21.6}$

14. $0.5\overline{)2.05}$

15. $1.48\overline{)2.96}$

16. $0.32 \div 4$

17. $24.48 \div 1.2$

18. $4.104 \div 3.8$

Challenge

Number Sense

Raise It Up SDAP 1.1

You have a mean of 78 for five quizzes. Each quiz has a possible score of 100.

- Can you raise your mean to 80 after six quizzes?
- Can you raise your mean to 82 after six quizzes?
- If there will be 10 quizzes in all, can you raise your mean to 90?

Explain each of your answers.

Mystery Numbers SDAP 1.1

One number is written on each card. The numbers are ordered from least to greatest. The mean of the numbers is 5, the median is 6, and the mode is 2. What numbers are on the cards?

Problem Solving Plan
Choose an Appropriate Graph

Objective Choose an appropriate graph to display data.

CA Standards

MR 2.3 Use a variety of methods, such as words, numbers, symbols, charts, graphs, tables, diagrams, and models, to explain mathematical reasoning.

SDAP 1.2 Organize and display single-variable data in appropriate graphs and representations (e.g., histogram, circle graphs) and explain which types of graphs are appropriate for various data sets.

Also MR 1.1, MR 1.2, MR 2.0, MR 2.4, MR 3.0, MR 3.1, MR 3.2, MR 3.3

Vocabulary

line graph

circle graph

histogram

▶ **Learn Through Reasoning**

When you display data in a graph, you need to choose the most appropriate graph for the data.

Example 1

The data show change over time, so a **line graph** is appropriate.

Skateboard Sales			
Month	May	June	July
Number of Sales	20	15	30

Skateboard Sales

Example 2

The data show parts of a whole, so a **circle graph** is appropriate.

Sport Survey			
Sport	Soccer	Baseball	Basketball
Number of Votes	2	4	10

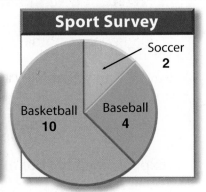

Sport Survey

Soccer **2**

Basketball **10**

Baseball **4**

Example 3

The data are compared in equal intervals, so a **histogram** is appropriate.

Runners' Times			
Minutes	0–4	5–9	10–14
Number of Runners	2	6	4

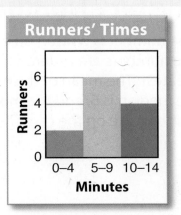

Runners' Times

▶ Guided Problem Solving

Solve using the Ask Yourself questions. Use a graph to display the data set. Explain your choice.

Ask Yourself
- Do the data show change over time? parts of a whole?
- Can the data be compared in equal intervals?

1. Manuel's workout includes stretching for $\frac{1}{2}$ hour, jogging for $\frac{1}{4}$ hour, and lifting weights for $\frac{1}{4}$ hour.

 Math Talk Give an example of data that can be displayed in a double line graph.

▶ Independent Problem Solving

For Problems 2–3, use a graph to display the data set. Explain your choice.

2.

Temperatures on Field Day			
Time	9:00 A.M.	11:00 A.M.	1:00 P.M.
Temp. (°F)	78	84	89

3.

Distance of Hiking Trails				
Miles	0–2	3–5	6–8	9–11
Number of Trails	14	8	5	3

4. **Predict** Look at the data table in Problem 2. Predict if the temperature at 8:00 A.M. would have been higher or lower than the 9:00 A.M. reading. Explain your thinking.

5. **Challenge** An ice skater practiced her program for $\frac{1}{2}$ hour during the first week of training. For the next three weeks, she practiced twice as long as the week before. Choose an appropriate graph to display the data. Explain your choice.

6. **Create and Solve** Use these data for practice times. Make a frequency table. Then show the data in a histogram. Decide what intervals you will use.

Practice Time								
4	5	6	8	8	9	10	10	10
11	12	12	12	12	14	15	15	16
18	18	18	18	22	24	25	26	30

Reading & Writing **Math**

Vocabulary

In this chapter you made and read graphs and **frequency tables.** You also learned how to find **mean, median,** and **mode.** Each provides slightly different information about the same data set.

Mr. Jackson surveyed his fifth-grade students. He asked, "How much do you spend for lunch each day?" The tally chart shows his data.

Lunch	
Amount	**Number of Students**
$1.00	卌 卌		
$1.25	||
$1.50	卌 ||
$1.75	卌 |||
$2.00	|||
$2.25		
$2.50	||

Use the information in the tally chart to answer the questions.

1. What is the mode of this data?

2. What is the median of this data?

Writing Jessica arrived late to class. She told Mr. Jackson she spent $2.25 each day for lunch. Does this change the median or mode? Tell why or why not.

Reading Check out this book in your library. *Tiger Math: Learning to Graph from a Baby Tiger* by Ann Whitehead Nagda

CA Standards
MR 2.3 Use a variety of methods, such as words, numbers, symbols, charts, graphs, tables, diagrams, and models, to explain mathematical reasoning.
Also SDAP 1.1

Standards-Based Extra Practice

Set A ────────────────────────────────────── SDAP 1.1 page 344
Find the mean, median, and mode of each set of data.

1. 6, 4, 4, 3, 8

2. 12, 9, 8, 8, 8

3. Janie's last 5 test scores in English were 83, 97, 83, 88, and 99. What are the mean, median and mode of her test scores?

Set B ────────────────────────────────────── SDAP 1.2 page 346
Use the table to answer Questions 1–4.

1. How many people ran in the marathon in 2002?

2. How many more men than women ran the marathon in 2003?

3. Which year had the most runners? How many?

4. Use the information in the table to make a double line graph.

Marathon Runners		
Year	Men	Women
2001	6,844	3,447
2002	5,411	3,573
2003	6,568	3,436
2004	6,897	5,154

Set C ────────────────────────────────────── AF 1.1 page 350
Use the circle graph to answer Questions 1–3.
Don has 40 minutes before he arrives at school. The circle graph shows what fraction of that time he spends on different activities.

1. How many minutes does Don use to travel to school?

2. Which activity takes him 10 minutes to complete?

3. How many minutes does he spend getting dressed?

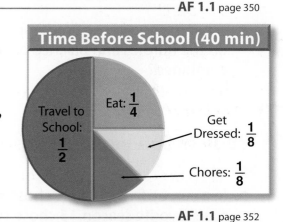

Time Before School (40 min)

Travel to School: $\frac{1}{2}$

Eat: $\frac{1}{4}$

Get Dressed: $\frac{1}{8}$

Chores: $\frac{1}{8}$

Set D ────────────────────────────────────── AF 1.1 page 352
Use the data and the histogram for Problems 1–3.

1. How many bowlers scored less than 151?

2. How many bowlers scored more than 200?

3. Which range of scores did the greatest number of bowlers have?

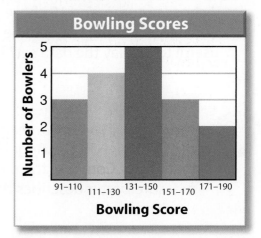

Bowling Scores

Number of Bowlers vs. Bowling Score (91–110, 111–130, 131–150, 151–170, 171–190)

Education Place
Visit www.eduplace.com/camap/ for more **Extra Practice**.

Chapter Review/Test

Vocabulary and Concepts ———————————————— SDAP 1.1, MR 2.3

Write the best word to complete the sentence.

1. The _____ of a data set is the sum of all the addends divided by the number of addends.

Skills ———————————————————————— SDAP 1.1, SDAP 1.2, AF 1.1

Find the mean, median and mode of each set of numbers.

2. 1, 4, 5, 4, 6

3. 0, 6, 6

4. 11, 2, 5, 4, 6, 7, 7

5. 2, 4, 2, 2, 5

Use the circle graph to answer Questions 6–8.

6. How much time is spent on the scooter ride?

7. How much time is spent on the net climb?

8. What fraction of the time is spent on the hurdles and balance beam combined?

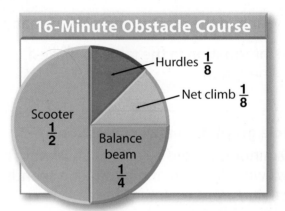

16-Minute Obstacle Course

Hurdles $\frac{1}{8}$

Net climb $\frac{1}{8}$

Scooter $\frac{1}{2}$

Balance beam $\frac{1}{4}$

Problem Solving and Reasoning ———————————— SDAP 1.1, SDAP 1.2, MR 2.3

Solve.

9. In a survey, five students chose spring as their favorite season, 15 chose summer, 7 chose autumn, and 10 chose winter. Which type of graph would be most useful to display the data set? Explain.

10. Victor wants to compare data on game scores for a baseball team using intervals of 0–5, 6–11, and 12–17 runs. Which type of graph would be most useful to display the data set? Explain.

Writing Math Angela scored 92, 91, 87, 41, and 89 on her math tests. Compare the mean and median of her scores. Which measure better describes the set of scores? Explain.

Spiral Review and Test Practice

1. $6{,}431 - 2{,}518 =$

   A 4,913

   B 4,127

   C 3,923

   D 3,913

NS 1.0 page 126

2. Which equation shows the relationship of all the values in the table below?

   A $y = x - 6$

   B $y = x + 15$

   C $y = 6x$

   D $y = x \div 6$

x	y
3	18
5	30
7	42
10	60
12	72

KEY **AF 1.5** page 112

3. Gabriel has a collection of 432 stamps. He put the same number of stamps in each of 4 folders. How many stamps are in each folder?

   A 18

   B 108

   C 172

   D 1,728

> **Test Tip**
> Visualizing a problem can help you decide how to solve the problem.

KEY **NS 2.2** page 240

4. $56 \div 0.08 =$

   A 7

   B 70

   C 700

   D 7,000

KEY **NS 2.1** page 300

5. Karen made 4.8 cups of orange juice. She is serving the juice in glasses that each hold 1.6 cups. How many glasses does she need?

   A 0.3

   B 2

   C 3

   D 7.68

> **Test Tip**
> Reading a problem more than once can help you understand the problem.

KEY **NS 2.1**, KEY **NS 2.2** page 304

6. Elisa recorded the points she scored in 5 computer games.

   107, 74, 121, 85, 138

   What is the median of these numbers?

   A 64   **C** 105

   B 74   **D** 107

SDAP 1.1 page 344

Education Place
Visit www.eduplace.com/camap/ for
Test-Taking Tips and **Extra Practice**.

Chapter 16 Spiral Review and Test Practice   **361**

Graphs on a Coordinate Grid

Vocabulary and Concepts GRADE 4 KEY MG2.0, MR 2.3

Match each word with a definition.

1. coordinates
2. *x*-axis
3. function

a. a rule that pairs each input with one and only one output
b. the horizontal number line on a coordinate grid
c. the numbers in an ordered pair

Skills GRADE 4 KEY AF 1.5

**Study the pattern and complete the function table.
Predict the number of squares in the fourth figure.**

	Figure	Number of squares
4.	1	
5.	2	
6.	3	
7.	4	

Figure 1 Figure 2 Figure 3

Problem Solving and Reasoning GRADE 4 KEY MG 2.0

8. A map shows the location of the school and the library on a coordinate grid. The school is located at the point (2, 3). The library is located at a point 4 units to the right and 5 units up from the school. What ordered pair can be used to locate the library?

Vocabulary

Visualize It!

y-axis
the vertical number line

Point A is named by the **ordered pair** (2, 3). This point is across 2 on the *x*-axis and up 3 on the *y*-axis.

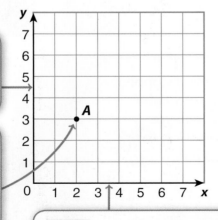

x-axis
the horizontal number line

Language Tip

Words that look alike in English and Spanish often have the same meaning.

English	Spanish
coordinate	coordenada

*See **English-Spanish Glossary** pages 628–642.

Education Place Visit www.eduplace.com/camap/ for the **eGlossary** and **eGames**.

CA Standards MR 2.3 Use a variety of methods, such as words, numbers, symbols, charts, graphs, tables, diagrams, and models, to explain mathematical reasoning. **Also KEY SDAP 1.4**

Chapter 17   363

CA Standards

KEY SDAP 1.4 Identify ordered pairs of data from a graph and interpret the meaning of the data in terms of the situation depicted by the graph.

KEY SDAP 1.5 Know how to write ordered pairs correctly; for example, (x, y).

Also AF 1.1, MR 2.3, MR 2.4

Vocabulary

coordinate grid

***x*-axis**

***y*-axis**

ordered pair

origin

Materials
- Workmat 7
- Learning Tool 10 (Centimeter Grid)

Hands On
Plot Points on a Coordinate Grid

Objective Plot points on a coordinate grid.

▶ **Explore**

A **coordinate grid** is formed by two perpendicular number lines that intersect at the 0 of each line. The horizontal number line is the ***x*-axis**. The vertical line is the ***y*-axis**.

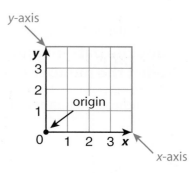

The point where the number lines meet is called the **origin**. You can describe any point on the grid by an **ordered pair** of numbers (x, y). Start at the origin. Move x units to the right and then y units up and then make a dot.

Question How can you plot points on a coordinate grid?

Use Workmat 7 to plot a point at $(3, 6)$.

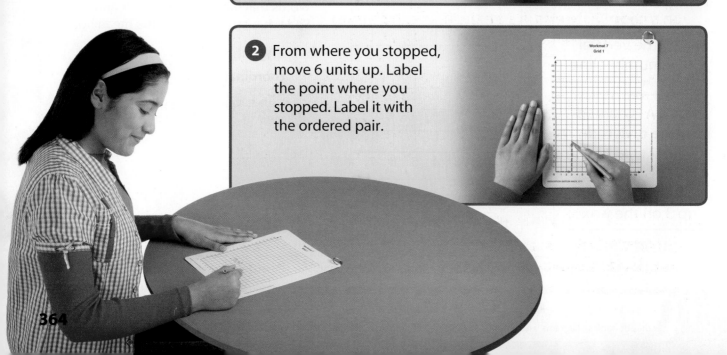

① Start at the origin and move 3 units to the right along the *x*-axis.

② From where you stopped, move 6 units up. Label the point where you stopped. Label it with the ordered pair.

364

▶ **Extend**

**Use Workmat 7 to plot the point and label it with its letter.
Connect the points to make a closed figure. Write the
name of the figure.**

1. *A* (7, 2) *B* (7, 6) *C* (2, 6) *D* (2, 2)

2. *E* (8, 8) *F* (3, 5) *G* (3, 1)

3. *H* (1, 1) *J* (1, 6) *K* (6, 6) *L* (6, 1)

4. *M* (1, 4) *N* (2, 8) *P* (5, 10) *Q* (7, 7) *R* (5, 2)

Write the ordered pair for the point.

5. *A*

6. *B*

7. *C*

8. *D*

9. *E*

10. *F*

11. *G*

12. *H*

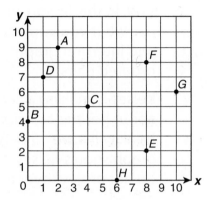

Use Workmat 7 for Exercises 13–16.

13. Mark any 4 points on a coordinate grid so that each point is
the same distance from the *y*-axis. Label the points and write
the coordinates. What do you notice about the coordinates?

14. Mark any 4 points on a coordinate grid so that each point is
the same distance from the *x*-axis. Label the points and write
the coordinates. What do you notice about the coordinates?

15. Josh plotted the points *M* (2, 1), *A* (4, 3), *T* (2, 5), and *H* (0, 3)
on a coordinate grid. Name the figure this makes when he
connects the points.

16. **Create and Solve** Plot 3 points and connect the points
to make a triangle. On a separate piece of paper, write the
coordinates for each vertex. Exchange papers and ask your
partner to plot the vertices of your triangle on his or her
workmat. Use your own workmat to check your partner's work.

Writing Math

Is the location of the point (2, 3) the same as the point (3, 2)?
Use a coordinate grid to help explain your answer.

CA Standards

KEY SDAP 1.4 Identify ordered pairs of data from a graph and interpret the meaning of the data in terms of the situation depicted by the graph.

AF 1.1 Use information taken from a graph or equation to answer questions about a problem situation.

Also KEY SDAP 1.5, MR 1.1, MR 2.3, MR 2.4

Materials

Learning Tool 10 (Centimeter Grid)

Interpret Graphs of Ordered Pairs

Objective Read and interpret graphs of ordered pairs.

▶ **Learn by Example**

You know how to plot ordered pairs as points on a coordinate grid. In this lesson, you will use what you know to read and interpret graphs of ordered pairs.

Kelsey is making a scrapbook about her trip to Arizona. The book will have 15 pages. The graph shows Kelsey's progress on her project over a 10-day period.

How many pages of the scrapbook did Kelsey complete by the third day?

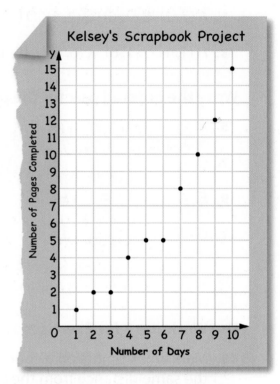

Kelsey's Scrapbook Project

Determine what you know and what you need to find out.

Each ordered pair is named by (x, y). You know the value of x is 3 because the x-axis is labeled "Number of Days" and the problem asks about the third day. This means you need to find the value of y when x is 3.

(3, ?)

1 From the origin, move 3 units right along the x-axis, "Number of Days."

2 Move up to the point marked on the graph.

3 Read the value on the y-axis, "Number of Pages Completed."

When x is 3, y is 2. The ordered pair is (3, 2).

Solution: Kelsey completed 2 pages in 3 days.

▶ Guided Practice

Use the graph of Kelsey's scrapbook project for Problems 1–2.

1. How many pages did Kelsey complete by the second day?

2. How many days did it take Kelsey to complete 5 pages?

Ask Yourself
- Did I move along the horizontal axis to find the value of *x*?
- Did I move along the vertical axis to find the value of *y*?

Guided Problem Solving

Use the questions to solve this problem.

3. Use the graph on page 366. How many pages did Kelsey do on Day 9?

   a. **Understand** What do you need to find?

   b. **Plan** How can you use the information from the graph to help you solve the problem? What operation will you use?

   c. **Solve** Use the information from the graph to solve the problem.

   d. **Look Back** Does your answer make sense?

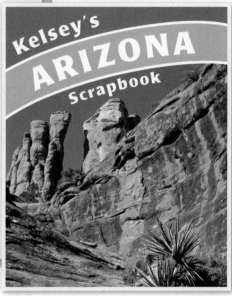

 Math Talk Look at Kelsey's progress. What does it mean when the value of *y* stays the same over two days?

▶ Practice and Problem Solving

Use the graph of Kelsey's scrapbook project for Problems 4–9.

4. How many pages had Kelsey completed by Day 7?

5. What two days did Kelsey not complete any new pages of her scrapbook? How do you know?

6. How many days did it take Kelsey to complete a little more than half of the scrapbook?

7. On which day did Kelsey complete the last page?

8. How many pages did Kelsey complete on Day 1? Day 2? Day 7? Tell how you know.

9. Did Kelsey work faster at the beginning of the project or at the end? How can you use the graph to find the answer?

Science Link

Sometimes coordinate grids are shown without either horizontal or vertical lines. Look carefully at the labels. Sometimes a line can stand for more than one unit.

Use the graph for Problems 10–14.

10. What do you think the dashed horizontal line means?

11. What was the wet bulb temperature at Hour 2?

12. At what hour was the lowest temperature reached?

13. At what hour should the farmers begin spraying water on the plants? At what hour could the water be turned off?

14. For how many hours should farmers spray their plants during this cold spell? Explain.

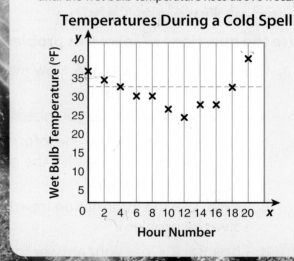

Temperatures During a Cold Spell

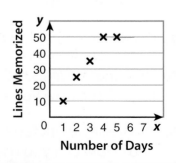

Science ES 3.b

Spiral Review and Test Practice

Copy and complete the function table. KEY **AF 1.2**, KEY **AF 1.5** page 112

15.

$y = x^2$	
x	y
2	4
4	■
6	36
■	64

16.

$y = 20 - 2x$	
x	y
0	■
1	18
2	16
5	■

17.

$y = 3x + 10$	
x	y
1	13
3	19
4	■
7	■

Write the letter of the correct answer. AF 1.1, KEY **SDAP 1.4**

18. Kyle has 50 lines in the school play. How many days does it take for Kyle to memorize half of his lines?

A 1   **B** 2   **C** 3   **D** 4

368

Extra Practice See page 379, Set A.

Key Standards Review

Need Help?
See Key Standards Handbook.

Divide. KEY NS 2.2

1. 42)630

2. 32)832

3. 64)960

4. 910 ÷ 13

5. 969 ÷ 19

6. 768 ÷ 32

7. 90)540

8. 33)1,122

9. 17)561

10. 744 ÷ 24

11. 4,824 ÷ 24

12. 7,089 ÷ 51

13. 34)850

14. 45)62,640

15. 95)7,600

16. 648 ÷ 18

17. 4,608 ÷ 48

18. 12,500 ÷ 25

Challenge Explore

Heart Rate SDAP 1.0, KEY SDAP 1.4

A heart rate is how often a heart beats per minute. The graph shows heart-rate data for an adult man at rest and immediately after exercise. Use the graph to decide if the statement is *true* or *false*. Explain.

1. The man's heart rate rapidly decreases for the first 5 minutes after exercise.

2. The man's heart rate after exercise will probably gradually slow down to 0 beats per minute.

3. The man's heart rate after exercise will probably level off to about 55 beats per minute if he continues to rest.

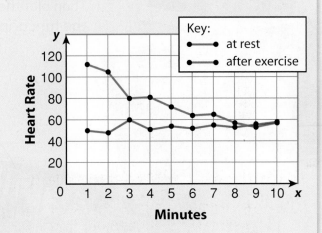

KEY **AF 1.5** Solve problems involving linear functions with integer values; write the equation; and graph the resulting ordered pairs of integers on a grid.

KEY **SDAP 1.5** Know how to write ordered pairs correctly, for example (x, y).

Also AF 1.0, KEY **AF 1.2**, KEY **AF 1.4**, MR 2.3, MR 3.0

Materials

Learning Tool 10 (Centimeter Grid)

Graphs of Functions

Objective Graph functions.

▶ **Learn by Example**

Kirsten ordered historic postcards for $2 each. There was also a shipping charge of $3. Make a graph to show the total cost as a function of the number of postcards Kirsten orders.

1 Make a function table with x and y columns for the function $y = 2x + 3$. Use the numbers 1 through 3 for x.

total cost → $y = 2x + 3$ ← shipping cost

↑ number of postcards ordered

$y = 2x + 3$	
x	**y**
1	
2	
3	

2 Substitute the value of x into the function $y = 2x + 3$ to find the value of y. Then write the ordered pairs.

$y = 2x + 3$		
x	**y**	
1	5	(1, 5)
2	7	(2, 7)
3	9	(3, 9)

3 Use the Learning Tool to make a coordinate grid. Then plot the points from the function table.

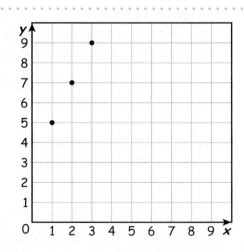

Solve.

1. Mario collects California train postcards. The cards cost $3 each. The equation $y = 20 - 3x$ shows how much change Mario will receive (y) if he buys different numbers of cards (x) with a $20 bill.

   a. Copy and complete the function table.

   b. Write the ordered pairs.

   c. Use the Learning Tool to make a coordinate grid. Then plot the points.

   d. How much change does Mario receive if he buys 6 postcards?

   e. Can he buy 7 postcards? Explain your reasoning.

$y = 20 - 3x$	
x	**y**
5	5
4	8
3	11
2	14

 Math Talk Explain how you can use the graph you made to find Mario's change if he buys 4 postcards.

> **Ask Yourself**
> Did I substitute each value for x in the equation to find the value of y?

▶ **Practice and Problem Solving**

Solve.

2. Jasmine likes old postcards with pictures of California cities. An antique store sells them for $3 each. Jasmine has a coupon for $1 off her total purchase. The equation $y = 3x - 1$ shows how much Jasmine spends (y) if she buys different numbers of antique postcards (x).

   a. Copy and complete the function table.

   b. Write the ordered pairs.

   c. Use the Learning Tool to make a coordinate grid. Then plot the points.

   d. Suppose the coupon was $2 off the total purchase. The rule is $y = 3x - 2$. Create a function table and plot the points.

$y = 3x - 1$	
x	**y**
1	2
2	5
3	8
4	11

847—Hollywood Boulevard at Night, Hollywood, California

History-Social Science Link

3. Suppose you are driving on the Coronado Trail. The equation $y = 123 - x$ shows how many miles to the end of the trail (y) for the number of miles you have driven (x).

a. Copy and complete the function table.

b. Write the ordered pairs.

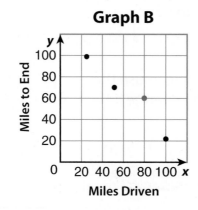

$y = 123 - x$	
x	**y**
100	▨
53	▨
25	▨

The Coronado Trail

- In 1540, Spanish explorer Francisco de Coronado began searching for cities of gold in the area north of Mexico.

- He was the first European to see the Grand Canyon and explore lands that are now Arizona, New Mexico, and Kansas.

- A 123-mile stretch of Coronado's route through Arizona is named the Coronado Trail. Between Morenci and Alpine, AZ, the trail curves about 460 times.

c. Which graph represents the function?

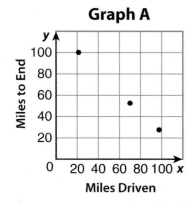

History-Social Science 5.2.3

d. Find one more ordered pair you could plot on the graph.

e. Explain why the green point on Graph B cannot be a point on the graph of this function.

 Spiral Review and Test Practice

Find the mean, median, and mode of the set of data. SDAP 1.1 page 344

4. 13, 2, 3, 6, 9, 8, 4, 8, 10, 10, 6, 5

5. 66, 55, 15, 49, 60, 59, 59, 11, 91, 75

6. 25, 26, 1, 4, 4, 6, 11, 4, 2, 8, 1, 4

Write the letter of the correct answer. KEY **AF 1.5**

7. Which equation could have been used to create this graph?

A $y = x + 1$ **C** $y = 3x + 1$

B $y = x + 2$ **D** $y = 2x + 1$

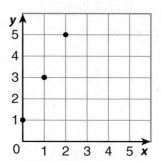

Extra Practice See page 379, Set B.

Math Works! Bike Mechanic

Pedal Power

Mike is a bike mechanic who makes gear repairs to bicycles. Before he makes the repairs, he needs some information to fix the bike. The table shows the number of pedal revolutions and the distance traveled for a bike in tenth gear.

1. Copy and complete the table.

Bike Pedal Revolutions

Pedal Revolutions (x)	1	2	3	4	5	6
Distance in meters (y)	2	4	6			

2. How does the value of *y* compare to the value of *x*?

3. Use the relationship you described in Exercise 2 to write an equation.

4. Graph the ordered pairs from Exercise 1. Connect the points.

5. What is the value of *y* when *x* is 16? 10? 25?

6. Calculate the distance traveled for $\frac{3}{2}$ revolutions, for $\frac{5}{2}$ revolutions, and for $\frac{7}{2}$ revolutions.

CA Standards
KEY **AF 1.2**, KEY **AF 1.5**,
MR 1.1, MR 2.3, MR 3.3

CA Standards

AF 1.0 Students use variables in simple expressions, compute the value of the expression for specific values of the variable, and plot and interpret the results.

KEY AF 1.5 Solve problems involving linear functions with integer values; write the equation; and graph the resulting ordered pairs on a grid.

Also AF 1.1, KEY **AF 1.2**, KEY **AF 1.4**, KEY **SDAP 1.4**, MR 1.1, MR 2.3, MR 3.0, MR 3.2, MR 3.3

Materials

Learning Tool 10 (Centimeter Grid)

Graphs from Patterns

Objective Graph a function that represents a pattern.

▶ **Learn by Example**

Sun Yi made this pattern. The first four figures in her pattern are shown below. How can she graph the function to find the number of square tiles in Figure 10 of this pattern?

Figure 1

Figure 2

Figure 3

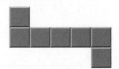

Figure 4

1 Make a function table.

Figure Number	Number of Squares
x	y
1	4
2	5
3	6
4	7

2 Graph the ordered pairs.

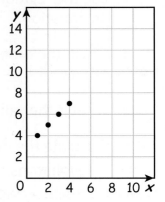

3 Choose the equation for the function.

In this pattern, the number of squares is always three more than the figure number.

A. $y = 3x$

B. $y = x - 3$

C. $y = x + 3$

4 Continue this pattern on the graph to find the ordered pair for Figure 10.

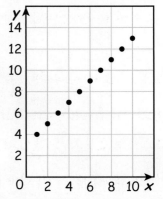

Solution: There are 13 square tiles in Figure 10.

Check

Substitute 10 for x in the equation.

Hint

Use the ordered pairs from your function table to test each equation.

1. How many buttons will be in Figure 10 of this pattern?

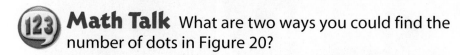

Figure 1   **Figure 2**   **Figure 3**   **Figure 4**

a. Make a function table.

b. Graph the ordered pairs.

c. Choose the equation for the function.

   A $y = x + 2$ **B** $y = 2x$

d. Continue the pattern on the graph until $x = 10$.

Ask Yourself
- Does the graph match the function table?
- Did you use the equation to check your answer?

123 Math Talk What are two ways you could find the number of dots in Figure 20?

 Practice and Problem Solving

2. How many toothpicks will be in Figure 10 of this pattern?

Figure 1   **Figure 2**   **Figure 3**   **Figure 4**

a. Make a function table.

b. Graph the ordered pairs.

c. Choose the equation for the function.

   A $y = 3x + 1$ **B** $y = x + 3$

d. Continue the graph until $x = 10$.

Hint
Substitute values for x and y for each equation.

Spiral Review and Test Practice

Find the mean, median, and mode of the set. SDAP 1.1 page 344

3. 1, 1, 2, 2, 5, 5, 8, 8, 8, 23, 36

4. 7, 7, 8, 12, 14, 20, 29, 31

Write the letter of the correct answer. KEY **AF 1.2**, KEY **AF 1.5**

5. Which equation shows the relationship of all values in the function table?

x	2	3	4	5
y	3	5	7	9

   A $y = x + 1$ **B** $y = 2x - 1$ **C** $y = 2x + 1$ **D** $y = 3x - 3$

LESSON 5

Field Trip...

Chino, CA

CA Standards
MR 1.2, MR 2.0,
MR 2.1, MR 2.3
NS 1.0, SDAP 1.1,
KEY **SDAP 1.5**, Prepares
for KEY **AF 1.5**

Problem Solving

Objective Use skills and strategies to solve word problems.

Many aircraft at The Air Museum Planes of Fame are the only ones of their type that exist today.

Solve. Tell which strategy or method you used.

Airshow Attendance		
Day	**Adults**	**Children**
1	85	27
2	110	23

1. The museum holds an annual 2-day airshow each May. It costs $18.00 for an adult ticket and $5.00 for a child ticket. Use the table to find the mean ticket sale earnings over both days.

2. The museum has a large collection of rare planes. Among these planes is the P-51 Mustang, which cost $50,985 to build in 1945, and the Vought Corsair, which cost $1,500,000. How much more did it cost to build the Vought Corsair than the P-51? Use estimation to check your calculation.

3. The Sopwith Camel was a popular World War II plane. This plane climbs 1,085 feet per minute. Make a function table to show how many feet high the plane was flying after 9 minutes. Then write the ordered pairs.

Problem Solving On Tests

Select a Strategy
- Draw a Picture
- Write an Equation
- Work Backward
- Choose the Operation
- Estimate

1. Jorge has $4\frac{1}{2}$ cups of raisins. He wants to divide the raisins into individual servings. How many servings of raisins can Jorge make, if each serving size is $\frac{3}{4}$ cup?

A $3\frac{3}{8}$ **B** $4\frac{2}{3}$ **C** 6   **D** $7\frac{1}{5}$

NS 2.5 page 236

2. Shana had a cable 7.45 meters long. She cut the cable into two sections. One section was 3.8 meters long. What was the length of the other section?

A 3.55 meters

B 3.65 meters

C 4.45 meters

D 4.65 meters

Test Tip
Remember to line up the decimal points before adding or subtracting.

KEY NS 2.1 page 258

3. Phil makes $8 per hour working at the drugstore. If he works 6.5 hours on Saturday, how much will he earn?

A $46.00   **C** $52.00

B $48.50   **D** $53.00

KEY NS 2.1 page 272

4. Juan owns 25.04 acres of property. Of the entire acreage, 0.6 of it is a pond. How much of the property is the pond?

A 11.084   **C** 15.084

B 15.024   **D** 15.204

KEY NS 2.1 page 278

5. Marissa ran 18.4 miles in 4 hours. If she ran at a constant rate, how many miles did she run each hour?

A 4.24 miles   **C** 4.8 miles

B 4.6 miles   **D** 73.6 miles

KEY NS 2.1 page 296

6. A chemist has 20.52 ounces of a solution. If she pours the solution into beakers, each of which holds 3.8 ounces, how many beakers will she fill?

A 5.4

B 54

C 16.72

D 77.976

Test Tip
Estimate to check your answer.

KEY NS 2.2 page 304

7. Mike walked a total of 43.4 miles. Each day he walked 6.2 miles. How many days did he walk?

A 0.07

B 0.7

C 7

D 70

KEY NS 2.1 page 304

Education Place
Visit www.eduplace.com/camap/ for
Test-Taking Tips and **Extra Practice**.

Chapter 17 Lesson 5   **377**

Vocabulary

In this chapter you learned to find specific locations, or points, on a coordinate grid. You also learned terms to describe parts of a coordinate grid.

Write the mathematical term that is identified by each letter. Choose from the terms in the Word Bank.

A. _____

B. _____

C. _____

D. _____

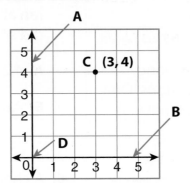

Word Bank

origin

x-axis

ordered pair

y-axis

line graph

coordinate grid

On Workmat 7, plot two points and record their locations.

You can find locations on a map using ordered pairs. Draw a map of your classroom on a coordinate grid. Describe the location of three places using ordered pairs.

Writing Write a description of how to find (5, 2) on a coordinate grid.

Reading Check out this book in your library. *Math Potatoes: Mind-Stretching Brain Food,* by Greg Tang.

CA Standards

MR 2.3 Use a variety of methods, such as words, numbers, symbols, charts, graphs, tables, diagrams, and models, to explain mathematical reasoning.

Also KEY SDAP 1.4, **KEY** SDAP 1.5

Standards-Based Extra Practice

Set A ———————————————————————————— KEY **SDAP 1.4**, AF 1.1 page 366

Use the graph to answer Questions 1–4.

1. How many books did Anna read the second week of vacation?

2. During which week did Anna read 5 books?

3. How many books did Anna read the first week of vacation?

4. During which week did Anna read the most books?

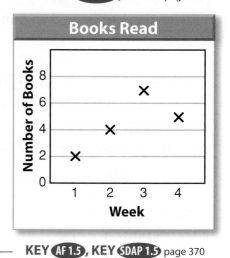

Set B ———————————————————————————— KEY **AF 1.5**, KEY **SDAP 1.5** page 370

Solve.

A catalog sells miniature cars for $6 each. Vince pays $3 for shipping costs no matter how many cars he orders. The equation $y = 6x + 3$ shows how much he pays (y) for different numbers of miniature cars (x).

1. Copy and complete the function table.

2. Write the ordered pairs.

3. Plot the points on grid paper.

$y = 6x + 3$	
x	y
2	■
5	■
8	■
10	■

Set C ———————————————————————————————————— KEY **AF 1.5** page 374

Sandra made this pattern with counters. Use the pattern to solve Problems 1–4.

1. Make a function table for the pattern.

2. Graph the ordered pairs on grid paper.

3. Choose the equation for the function.

Equation A	Equation B
$y = 2x + 2$	$y = x + 4$

4. If Sandra continues the pattern, how many counters will be in Figure 8?

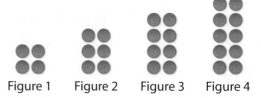

Figure 1   Figure 2   Figure 3   Figure 4

Education Place
Visit www.eduplace.com/camap/
for more **Extra Practice**.

Chapter 17 Extra Practice   **379**

Chapter Review/Test

Vocabulary and Concepts —————————————— KEY **SDAP 1.4**, KEY **SDAP 1.5**, MR 2.3

Write the best word to complete each sentence.

1. The _____ is the horizontal axis on the coordinate grid.

2. The _____ is the vertical axis on the coordinate grid.

Skills ———————————————————————— KEY **SDAP 1.4**, KEY **SDAP 1.5**, KEY **AF 1.5**

Use the graph to answer Questions 3–5.

3. How many pages were completed in 4 days?

4. How many days did it take to complete 14 pages?

5. How many days did it take to complete half the report?

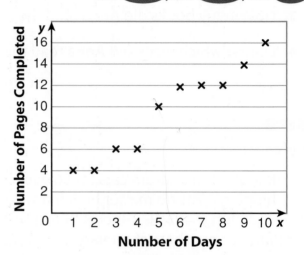

Copy and complete each function table.

6.

y = 4x	
x	y
1	
2	
3	

7.

y = x + 6	
x	y
3	
4	
5	

8.

y = 2x + 1	
x	y
5	
4	
3	

Problem Solving and Reasoning —————————————— KEY **AF 1.5**, MR 2.3

Use the pattern to solve Problems 9–10.

9. If the pattern continues, how many dots will be in the next figure?

10. The equation for the function that describes the pattern is $y = 4x - 3$, where x is the figure number and y is the number of dots. How many dots will be in Figure 10?

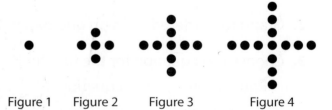

Figure 1   Figure 2   Figure 3   Figure 4

Writing Math How do you know where to plot a point on a coordinate grid if you have an ordered pair?

Spiral Review and Test Practice

1. Rachel met her goal of 100 hours of volunteer work. After what week was she halfway to her goal?

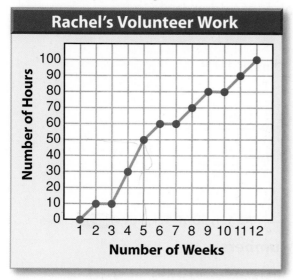

Rachel's Volunteer Work

A Week 3   **C** Week 5

B Week 4   **D** Week 6

KEY **SDAP 1.4** page 366

2. Patty divided 47 stickers among 3 sticker books. If each book has the same number of stickers, how many stickers are left over?

A 0

B 1

Test Tip
Make sure the answer you chose matches the question in the problem.

C 2

D 15

KEY **NS 2.2** page 328

3. The line graph shows the average temperature in Andy's hometown from March through August.

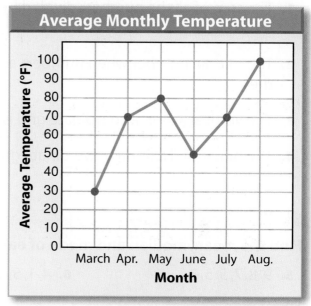

Average Monthly Temperature

Between which two months did the temperature increase twice as much as it did between June and July?

A March and April

B April and May

C May and June

D July and August

Test Tip
You need to take more than one step to solve some problems.

KEY **SDAP 1.4** page 346

Education Place
Visit www.eduplace.com/camap/ for
Test-Taking Tips and **Extra Practice**.

Chapter 17 Spiral Review and Test Practice   **381**

Unit 7 Review/Test

Vocabulary and Concepts ———————————— SDAP 1.1, MR 2.3 Chapters 16–17

Fill in the blank to complete each sentence.

1. The sum of all the numbers divided by the number of addends is the _____.

2. The middle number when numbers are arranged in order is the _____.

3. The vertical axis in a coordinate grid is called the _____.

4. The horizontal axis on a coordinate grid is called the _____.

Skills ———————————— AF 1.1, SDAP 1.1, KEY SDAP 1.4 Chapter 16, Lesson 2

Find the mean, median and mode of each set of numbers.

5. 9, 8, 7, 5, 5, 2

6. 4, 1, 5, 5, 10

7. 0, 0, 11, 9, 10

Plot each point on a coordinate grid. Label each point with its letter. Connect the points to make a closed figure. Write the name of each figure. Chapter 17, Lesson 1

8. A (1, 9) B (1, 2) C (5, 9) D (5, 2)

9. E (6, 2) F (6, 5) G (1, 2)

10. W (1, 1) X (3, 1) Y (2, 3) Z (4, 3)

11. Z (1, 2) Y (5, 2) V (5, 5) U (1, 5)

Use the circle graph to answer Questions 12–13. Chapter 16, Lesson 4

Mrs. Chu held a vote to decide what type of after-school activity the school should run. The circle graph shows the results.

12. Did more than $\frac{1}{2}$ of the students vote for any of the activities? Explain how you know.

13. Which activity did most of the students want?

After-School Activities

Sports

Drawing

Photography

Problem Solving and Reasoning ——— SDAP 1.1, SDAP 1.2, MR 2.3 Chapters 16–17

Solve.

14. Elle, Kim, and Brook each baked 1 dozen muffins for the bake sale. Sheila baked 16 and Mary baked 18. What is the average number of muffins the girls baked?

15. Mr. Briggs wants to plot the temperature outside his classroom every hour for 4 hours. What would be the best type of graph for Mr. Briggs to use? Explain your choice.

 **BIG IDEA!**

Writing Math Explain how ordered pairs, graphs, and functions are all related.

Performance Assessment

On The Right Path

KEY **AF 1.4**, KEY **SDAP 1.5**

Traveling the streets of a city is often like being on a coordinate grid. Planning your trip just takes a little work with ordered pairs.

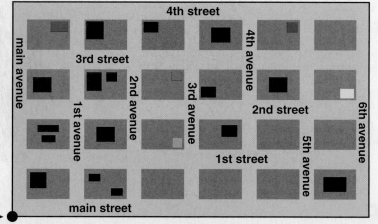

| library |
| bakery |
| snack shop |
| grocery store |
| grandpa's house |

Task	Information You Need
Use the information above and to the right. Find the coordinates for each of your trips. Explain what the numbers in your ordered pairs mean. Then find the average number of blocks traveled per trip.	Drop off books at the library.
	Pick up milk at the grocery store.
	Visit grandpa.
	Visit my uncle who is a baker.

Go Fast, Go Far

Unit 7 Mental Math Strategies

Multiply by 12

A group of 12 is fast to do, start with 10 and then add 2!

I have a fast way to multiply 12 × 5. To find 12 groups of 5, I add 10 groups of 5 to 2 groups of 5 and get 50 + 10 = 60. The secret to big numbers is breaking them into easier, smaller numbers!

1. $12 \times 5 = \boxed{50} + \boxed{10} = \boxed{60}$
          10 × 5 2 × 5

2. $12 \times 7 = \boxed{} + \boxed{14} = \boxed{}$
          10 × 7 2 × 7

3. $12 \times 8 = \boxed{} + \boxed{} = \boxed{}$
          10 × 8 2 × 8

4. $12 \times 9 = \boxed{} + \boxed{} = \boxed{}$
          10 × 9 2 × 9

Very nice work! Keep it up!

5. $12 \times 12 = \boxed{} + \boxed{} = \boxed{}$

6. $12 \times 6 = \boxed{} + \boxed{} = \boxed{}$

7. $12 \times 14 = \boxed{} + \boxed{} = \boxed{}$

8. $12 \times 15 = \boxed{} + \boxed{} = \boxed{}$

9. $12 \times 24 = \boxed{} + \boxed{} = \boxed{}$

10. $12 \times 30 = \boxed{} + \boxed{} = \boxed{}$

Good For You!

Take It Further!
Now try doing all the steps in your head!

11. 12×21

12. 12×34

13. 12×25

14. 12×48

8

Geometry

⭐ BIG IDEAS!

- Angles are measured and compared by the number of degrees of their openings.

- The sum of the angles in any triangle is 180 degrees and the sum of the angles of any quadrilateral is 360 degrees.

- Perpendicular lines intersect at right angles and parallel lines never intersect.

Chapter 18
Angles and Lines

Chapter 19
Triangles and Quadrilaterals

Chapter 20
Geometric Figures

Songs and Games

Math Music Track 8: *Three Angles*
eGames at
www.eduplace.com/camap/

Math Readers

A Roller Coaster of Angles
by Carter W. Ryan

Beautiful Geometry
by Marilyn Eden

If I Designed the Zoo

Game

Three-in-a-Row

Object of the Game Identify and draw geometric figures.

Materials
- Counters
- Learning Tool 23: 3-by-3 Grid
- Learning Tool 24: Geometry Cards (1 set)

Set Up
Give each player a 3-by-3 grid. Players shuffle the Geometry Cards and place them face down in a stack.

Number of Players 2–3

How to Play

1 Each player sketches the following geometric figures in any space on their grid:

- acute angle
- right angle
- obtuse angle

- acute triangle
- right triangle
- obtuse triangle

- parallel lines
- perpendicular lines
- ray

2 Students take turns turning over the top card from the stack.

3 Students place a counter over the drawing on their grid that matches the Geometry Card.

4 The first player to get three in a row horizontally, vertically, or diagonally is the winner.

CA Standards
MG 2.0 Students identify, describe, and classify the properties of, and the relationships between, plane and solid geometric figures.

Also MR 1.0, MR 1.1

Education Place
Visit www.eduplace.com/camap/ for
Brain Teasers and **eGames** to play.

Reading In reading, thinking about what you already know helps you to understand a new topic. You already know a lot about geometry. You can use what you know to move ahead.

Before beginning a chapter on geometry, Lauren lists three things she already knows.

> I remember classifying triangles by the measure of their angles.

Topic: Angles and lines

What do I already know?
1. You can draw a line through any two points.
2. A line goes on without end in both directions.
3. A ray is part of a line. It has one endpoint and goes on without end in one direction.

Writing Think about all the words in your math vocabulary that relate to lines and angles, for example, *line segment, parallel lines,* and *intersecting lines.* Work with a partner to write five more things you know about the topic.

Angles and Lines

Detail of a building at an amusement park in Santa Cruz, CA

Vocabulary and Concepts GRADE 4 MG 3.5, MR 2.3

Choose the best word to complete each sentence.

1. The corner of a doorway is an example of a _____ angle.

2. The hands of a clock at 2:00 form an _____ angle.

3. The hands of a clock at 7:00 form an _____ .

Skills GRADE 4 MG 3.1

Write the name of each figure.

4.

5.

6.

7. Draw two line segments that intersect.

8. Draw two lines that are parallel.

9. Draw an angle that measures about 100°.

Problem Solving and Reasoning GRADE 4 MG 3.5

10. What is one time of day when the hands on a clock form a right angle?

Vocabulary

Visualize It!

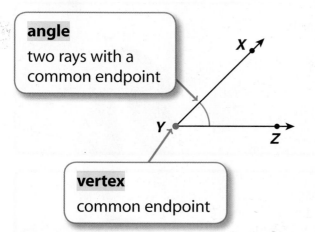

angle

two rays with a common endpoint

vertex

common endpoint

Language Tip

Words that look alike in English and Spanish often have the same meaning.

English	Spanish
line	línea
angle	ángulo

See **English-Spanish Glossary** pages 628–642.

 Education Place Visit www.eduplace.com/camap/ for the **eGlossary** and **eGames**.

CA Standards MR 2.3 Use a variety of methods, such as words, numbers, symbols, charts, graphs, tables, diagrams, and models, to explain mathematical reasoning. **Also KEY MG 2.1**

Chapter 18   389

CA Standards

KEY MG 2.1 Measure, identify, and draw angles, perpendicular and parallel lines, rectangles and triangles by using appropriate tools (e.g., straightedge, ruler, compass, protractor, drawing software).

MR 2.2 Apply strategies and results from simpler problems to more complex problems.

Also MG 2.0, MR 1.0, MR 1.1, MR 2.3, MR 2.4

Vocabulary

ray

angle

vertex

protractor

degrees

Materials
Protractor

Hands On
Measure and Draw Angles

Objective Name, measure, and draw angles.

▶ **Explore**

A **ray** is a part of a line that begins at an endpoint and goes on forever in one direction. Two rays that share an endpoint form an **angle**. The shared endpoint is the **vertex**. A small arc is used to mark the angle and the symbol ∠ is used to identify an angle.

Question How can you use a protractor to measure and draw angles?

What is the measure of ∠*FDE*?

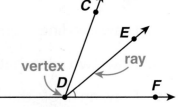

vertex   ray

Ray *DE* and ray *DF* form ∠*EDF*, or ∠*FDE*, or ∠*D*.

1 A **protractor** is a tool used to measure angles in **degrees**. Place the center mark of the protractor on the vertex, *D*.

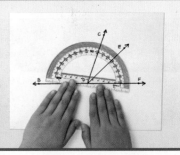

Hint

Protractors often have two scales. It is important to use the same scale in Steps 2 and 3.

2 Line up the 0° mark of the protractor with ray *DF*.

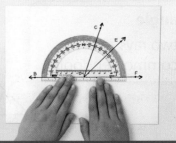

3 Find where ray *DE* passes through the same scale. Read the measure of the angle.

The measure of ∠*FDE* is 44°.

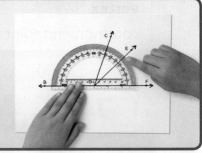

You can also use a protractor to draw an angle with a given number of degrees.

Draw ∠XYZ that measures 75°.

 Draw ray YX and label it as shown.

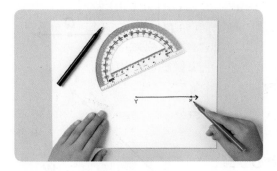

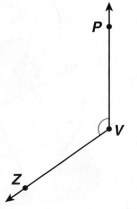 Place the center mark of the protractor on the endpoint, y.

Line up the 0° mark with ray YX.

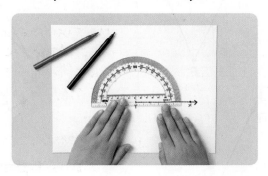

3 Mark a point at 75°. Label the point Z.

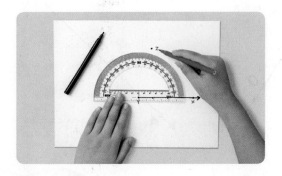

4 Draw a ray from the vertex Y through the point Z.

You can check your work by measuring ∠XYZ. Your angle should be 75°.

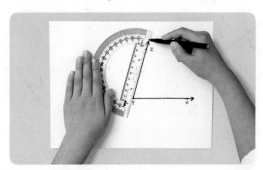

 **Extend**

Estimate the measure of the angle. Then, use a protractor to measure the angle. Write the measure.

1.

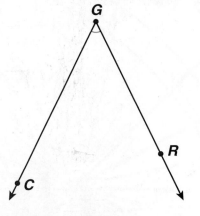

G

R

C

2.

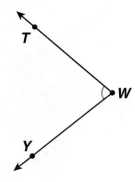

P

V

Z

3.

T

W

Y

Estimate the measure of the angle. Then, use a protractor to measure the angle. Write the measure.

4.

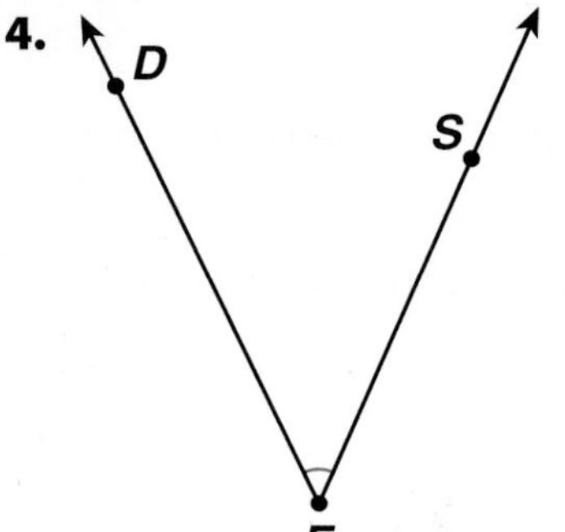

5.

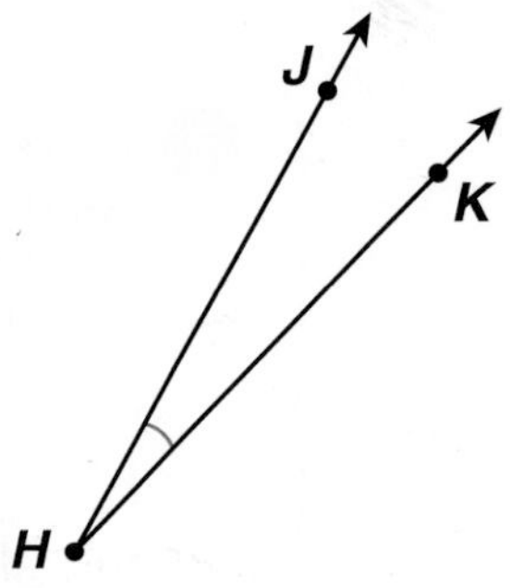

6.

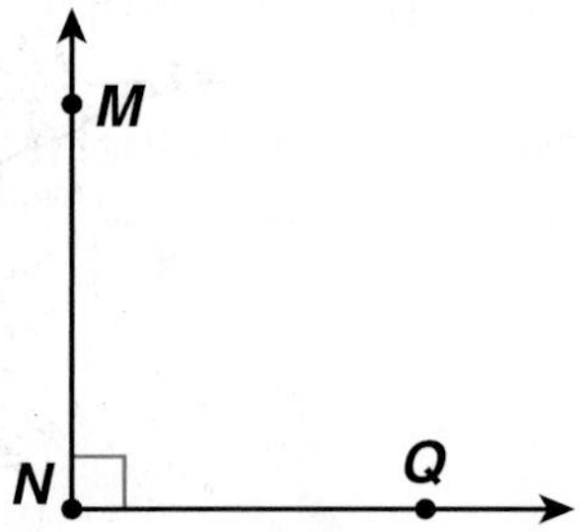

7.

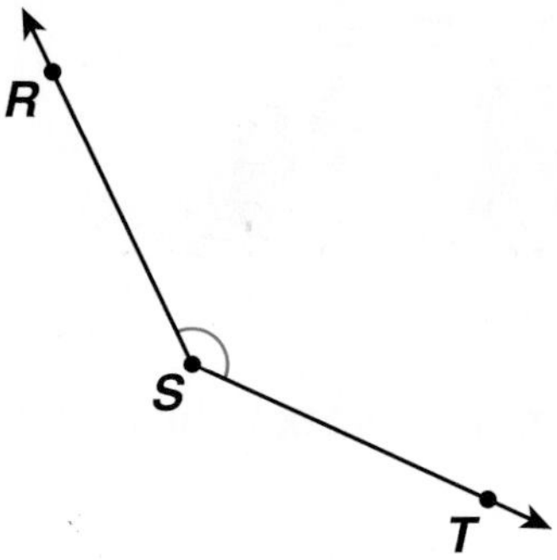

8.

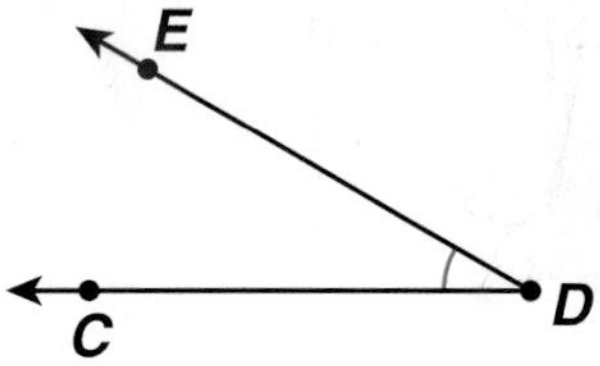

9.

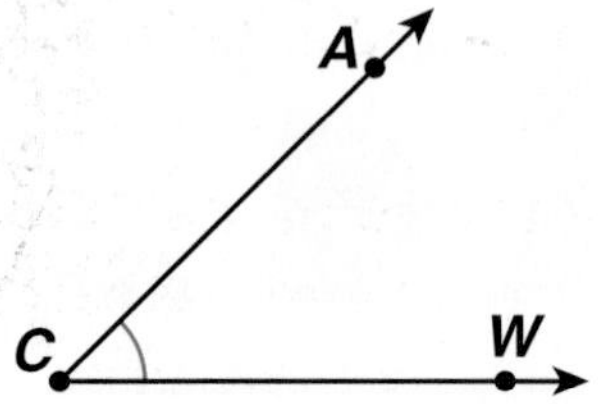

10.

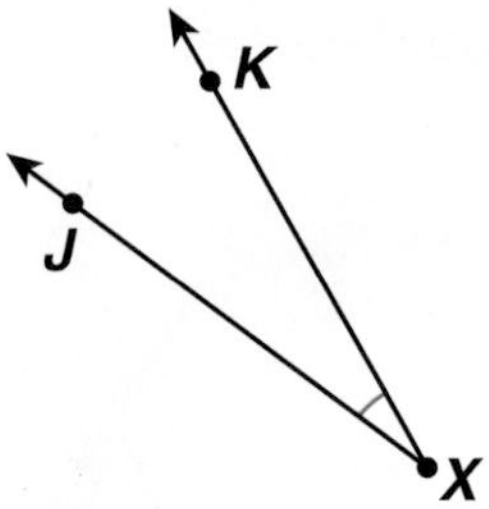

11.

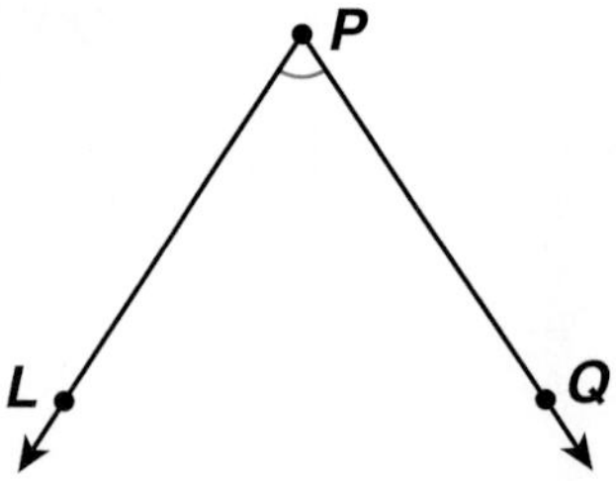

12

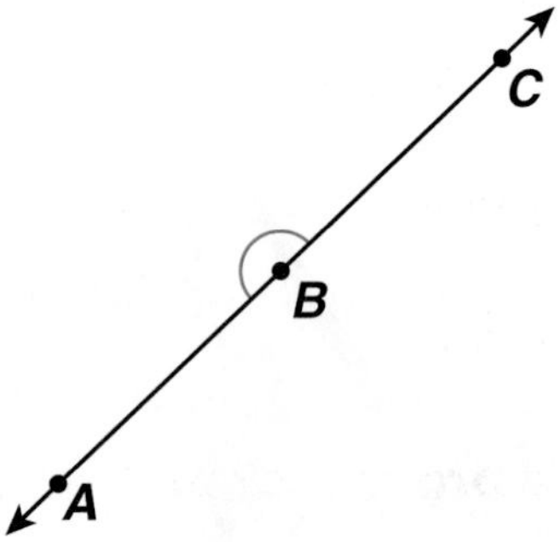

13.

14.

15.

Find the angle. Measure the angle with your protractor and write the measure.

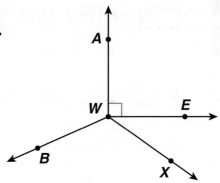

16. ∠AWE

17. ∠EWX

18. ∠BWX

19. ∠AWB

20. Analyze What is the sum of all four angle measures? If any ray in the figure is moved closer to the ray nearest it, will the sum of the angle measures change? Explain.

Write another name for the angle. Then measure the angle with your protractor and write the measure.

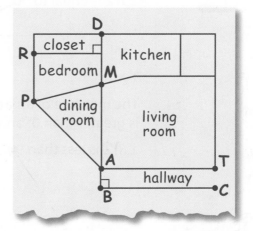

21. ∠ABC

22. ∠DMA

23. ∠PAT

24. ∠RPA

25. ∠RPM

Use a protractor to draw an angle having that measure.

26. 165°	**27.** 90°	**28.** 20°
29. 180°	**30.** 85°	**31.** 30°
32. 55°	**33.** 110°	**34.** 75°
35. 45°	**36.** 120°	**37.** 160°

38. Describe how you could use a protractor to draw an angle greater than 180°.

Writing Math

Analyze How can the outer scale of a protractor be used to measure an angle that opens to the right?

CA Standards
KEY **MG 2.1** Measure,
identify, and draw angles,
perpendicular and parallel lines,
rectangles and triangles by
using appropriate tools
(e.g., straightedge, ruler, compass,
protractor, drawing software).
**Also MG 2.0, MR 1.0,
MR 1.1, MR 2.3, MR 2.4**

Vocabulary

acute

obtuse

right

straight

Materials
Protractor

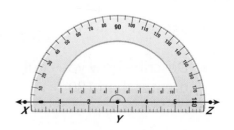

Classify Angles

Objective Classify angles as acute, right, obtuse, or straight.

▶ **Learn by Example**

In this lesson, you will identify angles as acute, right, obtuse, or straight.

Classify Angles

The measure of a **right angle** is equal to 90°.

∠JYZ is equal to 90°.

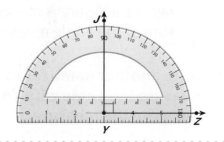

The measure of an **acute angle** is greater than 0° and less than 90°.

∠RYZ is less than 90°.

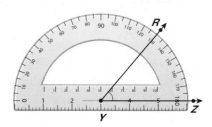

The measure of an **obtuse angle** is greater than 90° and less than 180°.

∠CYZ is between 90° and 180°.

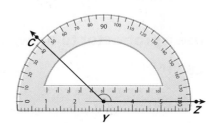

The measure of a **straight angle** is equal to 180°.

∠XYZ is equal to 180°.

**Hetch Hetchy Power Transmission
Tower in California**

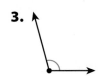
▶ **Guided Practice**

Classify the angle as acute, obtuse, straight, or right.

1.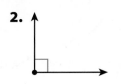

2.

3.

4.

5.

6.

Guided Problem Solving

7. Draw three acute angles so that the sum of the measures is equal to the measure of a straight angle.

   a. **Understand** What kind of angles do you need to draw? Can one of your angles be 90°?

   b. **Plan** What must the sum of the three angle measures be? Decide what angle measures you want to use.

   c. **Solve** Draw the three angles.

   d. **Look Back** Measure each angle. Is each angle acute? Is the sum of the angle measures 180°?

The sum of the angles at the center of the circle is 360°.

(123) **Math Talk** Is the sum of the measures of two acute angles always less than 90°?

▶ **Practice and Problem Solving**

Classify the angle as acute, obtuse, straight, or right.

8.

9.

10.

11.

Classify the angle as acute, obtuse, straight, or right.

12.

13.

14.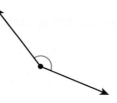

15.

 ## Science Link

Use the circle graph for Problems 16–19.

16. Which section of the circle graph has an angle that measures approximately 170°? Explain.

17. Classify the angle formed by the Silicon section of the graph.

18. What type of angle is formed by the Iron section of the graph?

19. What do you think is the sum of the six angles in the graph? Explain.

Fun Facts

Elements in Earth's Crust by Mass

- Scientists have discovered more than 100 elements.
- Only a few elements make up most of the things on Earth.
- Oxygen is one of the most abundant elements in the universe.

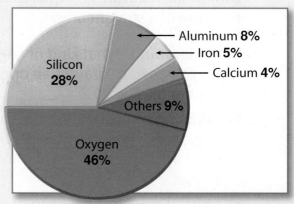

Aluminum **8%**
Iron **5%**
Calcium **4%**
Silicon **28%**
Others **9%**
Oxygen **46%**

Science **PS 1.h**

Spiral Review and Test Practice

Divide. Check your answer. NS 2.0, KEY **NS 2.1**, KEY **NS 2.2** page 296

20. $6\overline{)3.6}$

21. $7\overline{)4.9}$

22. $2\overline{)12.0}$

23. $5\overline{)45.0}$

Write the letter of the correct answer. KEY **MG 2.1**

24. Which describes the angle shown?

   A acute   **B** right   **C** obtuse   **D** straight

Extra Practice See page 405, Set A.

Multiply or divide by using patterns. KEY **NS 2.1**

1. 6.2×10^1

2. $6.5 \div 10^3$

3. $0.8 \div 10^1$

4. 8.34×10^2

5. 11.546×10^2

6. $76 \div 10^3$

7. 27.456×10^3

8. 27.621×10^3

9. $3{,}246 \times 10^2$

10. $7.25 \div 10^1$

11. 19.6×10^3

12. 7.2×10^2

13. $8.67 \div 10^2$

14. $36.44 \div 10^2$

15. $0.045 \div 10^2$

Solve. Write each difference in simplest form. KEY **NS 2.3**

16. Benito's bird feeder holds $4\frac{1}{2}$ cups of bird seed. If the birds eat $2\frac{3}{4}$ cups of seed, how many cups of seed are left in the feeder?

17. Keiko has read $8\frac{2}{5}$ of her books this month for the school book club. Jan has only read $3\frac{3}{4}$ of her books. How much more does Jan have to read to catch up with Keiko?

18. Hector is $5\frac{1}{2}$ feet tall. His younger brother is $4\frac{1}{4}$ feet tall. How much taller is Hector than his younger brother?

 **Visual Thinking**

Angle Measures KEY **MG 2.1**

Tell which group of angles can be arranged from least to greatest. Explain.

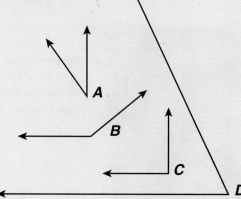

Group 1

Group 2

CA Standards
KEY MG 2.1 Measure, identify, and draw angles, perpendicular and parallel lines, rectangles and triangles by using appropriate tools (e.g., straightedge, ruler, compass, protractor, drawing software).

MR 2.3 Use a variety of methods, such as words, numbers, symbols, charts, graphs, tables, diagrams, and models, to explain mathematical reasoning.
Also MR 1.1, MR 2.4

Vocabulary

line

line segment

parallel lines

intersecting lines

perpendicular lines

Lines and Line Segments

Objective Draw and identify lines, line segments, parallel lines, intersecting lines and perpendicular lines.

▶ **Learn by Example**

A **line** is a straight, continuous, and unending path made up of a collection of points in a plane. A **line segment** is part of a line and has two endpoints.

Pairs of lines and line segments can be classified as intersecting, perpendicular, or parallel.

① **Parallel lines** and line segments lie in the same plane but never intersect.

$\overline{AT} \parallel \overline{BC}$

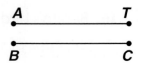

Line segment *AT* is *parallel to* line segment *BC*.

② **Intersecting lines** and line segments have one point in common.

$\overline{PM}$ and $\overline{DA}$ intersect.

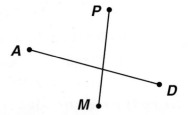

③ **Perpendicular lines** and line segments intersect at right angles.

$\overline{RL} \perp \overline{DA}$

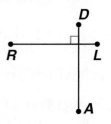

Line segment *RL* is *perpendicular to* line segment *DA*.

Perpendicular and parallel lines in Balboa Park, San Diego.

Another Example

Draw line *PQ* and line *NM* intersecting at point *X*.

- Draw line *PQ* and label it.
- Draw line *NM* intersecting line *PQ*. Label line *NM*.
- Label the point of intersection *X*.

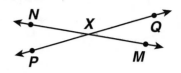

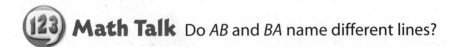

Draw the pair of lines.

1. Line *AB* and line *CD* intersecting at point *E*

2. Line *KM* parallel to line *BT*

Draw the pair of line segments.

3. Line segment *KS* parallel to line segment *HQ*

4. Line segment *FG* perpendicular to line segment *RP*

(123) Math Talk Do *AB* and *BA* name different lines?

▶ **Practice and Problem Solving**

Draw the pair of lines.

5. Line *CD* parallel to line *BA*

6. Line *ST* and line *UV* intersecting at point *Z*

7. Line *AB* perpendicular to line *QN*

Draw the pair of line segments.

8. Line segment *QT* and line segment *CG* intersecting at point *B*

9. Line segment *AS* perpendicular to line segment *FG*

10. Line segment *KX* parallel to line segment *BH*

Oakland Bay Bridge, San Francisco, CA

Identify the relationship between the lines.

11.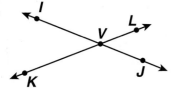

12.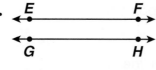

13.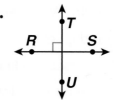

 Real World Data

The map shows the area surrounding City Hall Plaza in Oakland, California. Use the map for Problems 14–16.

14. Name a street that is parallel to International Drive.

15. Name a street that is perpendicular to International Drive.

16. Gianna is waiting for Nina at the southeast corner of 16th Street and San Pablo Ave. What type of angle is formed by the two streets at this point?

 Spiral Review and Test Practice

Divide. Check your answer. KEY NS 2.1 page 300

17. $0.7\overline{)21}$

18. $0.4\overline{)36}$

19. $0.9\overline{)720}$

20. $0.4\overline{)864}$

Write the letter of the correct answer. KEY MG 2.1

21. Which of the following best describes the lines in the figure?

A parallel

B perpendicular

C intersecting

D acute

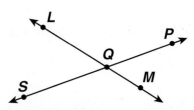

Extra Practice See page 405, Set B.

Triple Concentration

Object of the Game Recognize and name basic geometric shapes and angles.

Materials	**Number of Players** 2
• Learning Tool 25 (Triple Concentration Cards) (1 set)	

How to Play

1 Shuffle the cards. Place them facedown in a 3 by 6 array.

2
- The first player turns up three cards.
- If all the cards match (picture, word name, and symbol), the player collects those cards.
- If the cards do not match, the player turns the cards face down.
- The next player takes a turn.

3 Continue the game until all matches have been made. The player with the most cards wins.

picture	line AB	$\overleftrightarrow{A\,B}$
line segment AB	$\overline{A\,B}$
line segment BC	$\overline{B\,C}$
line BC	$\overleftrightarrow{B\,C}$
parallel lines	$\overleftrightarrow{C\,D} \parallel \overleftrightarrow{F\,G}$
perpendicular lines	$\overleftrightarrow{C\,D} \perp \overleftrightarrow{F\,G}$

LESSON 4

Field Trip...

Petaluma, CA

CA Standards
MR 1.0, MR 1.2,
MR 2.0, MR 2.1,
MR 2.6, NS 1.0, NS 1.1,
KEY **NS 2.1**, KEY **NS 2.2**,
KEY **MG 2.1**

Problem Solving

Objective Use skills and strategies to solve word problems.

Petaluma Adobe was one of the largest ranches in the Mexican Province of California.

Solve. Tell which strategy or method you used.

1. The Petaluma Adobe ranch covers 103.125 square miles. There are 640 acres in one square mile. How many acres is the Petaluma Adobe ranch? Use estimation to check your calculation.

2. In early April, sheep shearing is a local event. It takes 22 minutes to shear the woolen fleece. Geraldo has a herd of 23 sheep that need shearing. How long will it take to shear them all? Give your answer in hours and minutes. Is your answer reasonable?

3. During Fandango (a Mexican celebration), crafters sell and trade at the ranch. One crafter sells rugs for $223 each. The materials used to make the rug cost $53.50. Choose the expression that represents the amount of money the crafter makes selling n rugs. Evaluate the expression for $n = 3$.

   A $(\$223 - \$53.50) \times n$ **B** $\$223 - (\$53.50 \times n)$

4. Draw a rectangle that is 7.5 inches × 5.5 inches. Design a rug of your own that uses at least one 60°, 25°, and 10° angle.

Problem Solving On Tests

Select a Strategy
- Write an Equation
- Work Backward
- Guess and Check
- Choose the Operation
- Estimate

1. Mrs. Clark has two packages to mail. One weighs 6.714 pounds, and the other weighs 2.358 pounds. To the nearest hundredth of a pound, which represents the total weight of the two packages?

   A 8.06 pounds   **C** 9.06 pounds

   B 8.07 pounds   **D** 9.07 pounds

   NS 1.1, KEY **NS 2.1** page 256

2. What is the product of 2.3 and 0.04?

   A 0.072   **C** 0.72

   B 0.092   **D** 0.92

   KEY **NS 2.1** page 282

3. Sarah has $9 in nickels. To find the number of nickels she has, she divides 9 by 0.05. How many nickels does Sarah have?

   A 18   **C** 120

   B 55   **D** 180

   KEY **NS 2.2** page 300

4. Mr. Morrison saves money by buying paper by the case instead of by the package. He saved $6.36 by buying a case of 12 packages of paper. How much did he save per package?

   A $0.53

   B $0.55

   C $0.64

   D $1.89

   Test Tip
   Remember to place the decimal point in the quotient.

   KEY **NS 2.2** page 298

5. A new football stadium has 40,280 seats. If there are 53 sections of seats, and each section contains the same number of seats, how many seats are in each section?

   A 75   **C** 739

   B 695   **D** 760

   Test Tip
   Use the inverse operation to check your work.

   KEY **NS 2.2** page 326

6. Kathleen created 30 pages of art for a children's book. She kept this record of her progress.

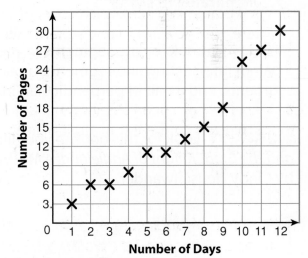

Art for Children's Book

How many days did it take Kathleen to complete half of the pages?

   A 6   **B** 8   **C** 11   **D** 15

   KEY **SDAP 1.4** page 366

Reading & Writing Math

Vocabulary

Measure each angle with a protractor. Give its measure and tell whether it is **acute, obtuse, right,** or **straight.**

1.

2.

3.

4.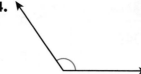

Draw each pair of **lines.**

5. $\overleftrightarrow{AB}$ **intersecting** with $\overleftrightarrow{CD}$

6. $\overleftrightarrow{EF}$ **perpendicular** to $\overleftrightarrow{GH}$

7. $\overleftrightarrow{JK}$ **parallel** to $\overleftrightarrow{LM}$

Writing Look for line segments in your classroom. Find a pair of intersecting line segments, a pair of parallel line segments, and a pair of perpendicular line segments.

Reading Look for this book in your library. *Sir Cumference and the Great Knight of Angleland: A Math Adventure,* by Cindy Neuschwander.

CA Standards

MR 2.3 Use a variety of methods, such as words, numbers, symbols, charts, graphs, tables, diagrams, and models, to explain mathematical reasoning.

Also KEY MG 2.1

Standards-Based Extra Practice

Set A ———————————————————————— KEY **MG 2.1** page 394

Classify each angle as acute, obtuse, straight, or right.

1.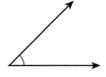

2.

3.

4.

Use a protractor to measure each angle. Write the measure. Classify each angle as acute, obtuse, straight, or right.

5.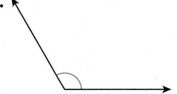

6.

7.

8.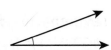

Set B ———————————————————————— KEY **MG 2.1** page 398

Draw each pair of lines.

1. Line *AB* perpendicular to line *LM*

2. Line *GH* and line *DF* intersecting at point *Z*

Draw each pair of line segments.

3. Line segment *FL* parallel to line segment *ST*

4. Line segment *VW* perpendicular to line segment *YZ*

Education Place
Visit www.eduplace.com/camap/
for more **Extra Practice**.

Chapter 18 Extra Practice **405**

Chapter Review/Test

Vocabulary and Concepts ——————————— MG 2.0, KEY MG 2.1, MR 2.3

Write the best word to complete each sentence.

1. A _____ is a tool used to measure angles in degrees.

2. A _____ is part of a line and has two endpoints.

3. _____ lines have one point in common.

Skills ———————————————————————— KEY MG 2.1, KEY MG 2.2

Use a protractor to measure each angle. Write the measure.
Classify each angle as acute, obtuse, straight, or right.

4.
5.
6.

Draw each pair of lines.

7. Line *DW* perpendicular to line *PQ*

8. Line *AB* and line *TW* intersecting at point *J*

9. Line *GJ* parallel to line *KM*

10. Use a protractor to draw an angle measuring 25°.

11. What is the sum of the measures of all four angles?

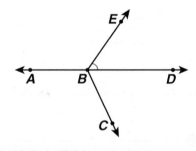

Problem Solving and Reasoning ———— KEY MG 2.1, KEY MG 2.2, MG 2.0, MR 2.2, MR 2.3

Solve. Explain your thinking.

12. Is the sum of the measure of an acute angle and the measure of a right angle always greater than 90°?

13. Is the sum of the measure of an acute angle and the measure of an obtuse angle always greater than 180°?

14. Rob used a protractor to draw an angle with measure 135°. What is the difference in degrees between what he drew and the measure of a straight angle?

15. Maple Street runs parallel to Lincoln Street. Is it possible to have a traffic light at the intersection of the two streets?

Writing Math How are lines and line segments alike? How do they differ? Explain.

Spiral Review and Test Practice

1. Which is closest to the measure of the angle shown below?

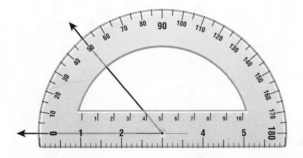

A 40°   **C** 130°

B 50°   **D** 140°

KEY **MG 2.1** page 390

2. What value for x makes this equation true?

$x - 17 = 36$

A 17   **C** 36

B 19   **D** 53

KEY **AF 1.2** page 108

3. Kelly brought 6 bottles of water to soccer practice. Each bottle has a capacity of 500 mL. There are 1,000 milliliters in 1 liter. How many liters of water can the 6 bottles hold?

A $\frac{1}{2}$ L   **C** 6 L

B 3 L   **D** 3,000 L

NS 2.0, MR 1.1 page 240

4. If a section of a circle graph represents 6 hours of participation in sports, how much time would a section half the size of the sports section represent?

A $\frac{1}{2}$ hour

B 3 hours

C 6 hours

D 12 hours

> **Test Tip**
> Drawing a picture can help you understand some problems.

SDAP **1.2** page 350

5. Line p is represented by the equation $y = 3$.

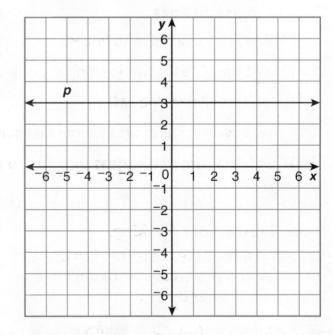

Which ordered pair is located on line p?

A (3, 1)   **C** (1, 3)

B (3, 0)   **D** (0, 0)

KEY **AF 1.4**, KEY **SDAP 1.5** page 364

Education Place
Visit www.eduplace.com/camap/ for
Test-Taking Tips and **Extra Practice.**

19

Triangles and Quadrilaterals

Check What You Know

Vocabulary and Concepts GRADE 4 MG 3.0, MR 2.3

Match the word to its definition. Then draw an example.

1. angle

2. line

3. ray

a. two rays with a common endpoint

b. part of a line that begins at an endpoint and goes on forever in one direction

c. a length that goes on forever in two directions

Skills

Circle the congruent pairs. GRADE 4 MG 3.3

4.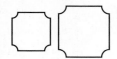

5.

6.

7.

Problem Solving and Reasoning GRADE 4 MG 3.8

8. I am a plane shape. I have two pairs of parallel sides. The two sides in one pair have the same length. The two sides in another pair also have the same length, but the length of the sides in this pair is not as long as the length of the first pair of sides. What am I? Draw me.

Vocabulary

Visualize It!

A **quadrilateral** has 4 sides and 4 angles.	□ ◇ ▱
A **triangle** has 3 sides and 3 angles.	△ ◺

Language Tips

The words *quadrilateral* and *triangle* contain the word roots *quad-*, which means "four," and *tri-*, which means "three". Knowing this helps you remember how many sides and angles quadrilaterals and triangles have.

Math words that look similar in English and Spanish often have the same meaning.

English	Spanish
quadrilateral	cuadrilátero
triangle	triángulo

See **English-Spanish Glossary** pages 628–642.

 Education Place Visit www.eduplace.com/camap/ for the **eGlossary** and **eGames**.

CA Standards MR 2.3 Use a variety of methods, such as words, numbers, symbols, charts, graphs, tables, diagrams, and models, to explain mathematical reasoning. **Also MG 2.0**

Chapter 19   409

CA Standards

KEY MG 2.2 Know that the sum of the angles of any triangle is 180° and the sum of the angles of any quadrilateral is 360° and use this information to solve problems.

KEY MG 2.1 Measure, identify, and draw angles, perpendicular and parallel lines, rectangles and triangles by using appropriate tools (e.g., straightedge, ruler, compass, protractor, drawing software).

Also MG 2.0, MR 2.2, MR 2.3, MR 3.0, MR 3.2, MR 3.3

Vocabulary

straight angle

quadrilateral

Materials
- Straightedge
- Scissors
- Tracing paper

Hands On
Sums of Angle Measures

Objective Find the sum of the measures of the angles in triangles and quadrilaterals.

▶ **Explore**

In this lesson you will learn about the sum of the measures of angles in triangles and in quadrilaterals.

Question What is the sum of the measures of the angles in a triangle?

1 Use a straightedge to draw a triangle.

Cut out the triangle. Label the angles *a*, *b*, and *c*.

2 Tear off the three angles of the triangle.

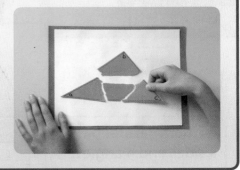

3 Use a straightedge to draw a straight angle.

Arrange the angles of the triangle so that they meet at a point and lie on the straight angle. What does this tell you about the sum of the measures of the angles of the triangle?

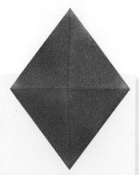

A **quadrilateral** has four sides and four angles.

Question What is the sum of the measures of the angles in a quadrilateral?

1 Use a straightedge to draw a quadrilateral. Label the angles *a*, *b*, *c*, and *d*.

2 Trace your quadrilateral to make a copy of it. Cut out the copy.

3 On your copy, draw a line segment connecting one vertex to the opposite vertex. Cut the quadrilateral along the line you drew.

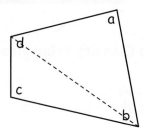

4 What shape are the pieces you cut?

- What is the sum of the measures of the angles in each of those pieces?

- Place the pieces together to fit onto your original quadrilateral.

- What is the sum of the measures of the angles of the quadrilateral?

▶ **Extend**

Trace each figure. Use scissors and a straight angle to find the sum of the measures of the angles for each figure.

1.

2.

3.

4.

5.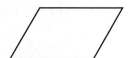

6.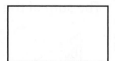

7. **Challenge** A circle is 360°. Show how the four angles from Exercise 4 can be placed so that they meet at a point to form a circle.

Writing Math

Right or Wrong? Amy made a kite. She says the sum of the measures of the angles of the kite is 720°. Is she correct?

CA Standards

KEY **MG 2.2** Know that the sum of angles of any triangle is 180° and the sum of the angles of any quadrilateral is 360° and use this information to solve problems.

MG 2.0 Students identify, describe, and classify the properties of, and the relationships between, plane and solid geometric figures.

Also KEY **MG 2.1**, **MR 2.0, MR 2.3, MR 2.4, MR 2.6, MR 3.0**

Vocabulary

equilateral triangle

isosceles triangle

scalene triangle

right triangle

acute triangle

obtuse triangle

Materials
• Protractor
• Ruler

Triangles

Objective Classify triangles and find missing angle measures.

▶ **Learn by Example**

A triangle is made up of 3 line segments called sides. Each pair of sides has a common endpoint, or vertex, and forms an angle.

Different Ways to Classify Triangles

There are several different types of triangles.
You can classify triangles by the lengths of their sides.

equilateral triangle
All sides are the same length.

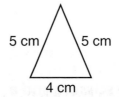

isosceles triangle
At least two sides are the same length.

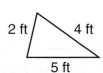

scalene triangle
No sides are the same length.

You can classify triangles by their angle measures.
The sum of the angle measures in any triangle is 180°.

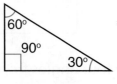

right triangle
one right angle

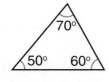

acute triangle
all acute angles

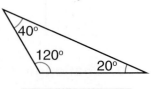

obtuse triangle
one obtuse angle

Another Example
Missing Angle Measure

$x = 180° - (100° + 44°)$

$x = 180° - 144°$, so $x = 36°$

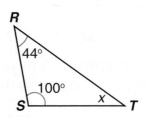

Classify each triangle in two ways.

1.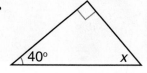

2.

▶

Ask Yourself

• Are the angles acute? obtuse? right?

• How many sides are equal in length?

Find the missing angle measure.

3.
40°   x

4.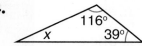
116°
x   39°

(123) Math Talk Is an equilateral triangle also an isosceles triangle? Explain. Can a triangle have two right angles? Explain.

▶ **Practice and Problem Solving**

Classify each triangle in two ways.

5.
2 m
2 m   2 m

6.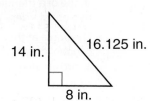
14 in.   16.125 in.
8 in.

7.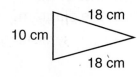
18 cm
10 cm
18 cm

8.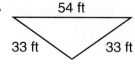
54 ft
33 ft   33 ft

9.

10.

Find the missing angle measures.

11.
80°
40°   x

12.
x   125° 30°

13.
45°
x

14.
60°
60°   x

15.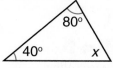
x
30°

16.
36°
72°   x

17.
70°   x
40°

18.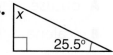
x
25.5°

Use a protractor and a ruler to help you solve Problems 19–21.

19. Try to draw each of the following. If a figure cannot be drawn, explain why.
  a. scalene acute triangle
  b. an equilateral right triangle
  c. a scalene right triangle

20. Analyze Can an isosceles triangle be obtuse? Use a diagram to explain.

21. Challenge In a right triangle, suppose one of the acute angles is twice the size of the other. What is the measure of the smallest angle?

Isosceles triangle in a spider's web

 Science Link

Solve each problem.

22. Classify, in two ways, the triangle that a water molecule makes.

23. What are the measurements of the two unlabeled angles in the diagram?

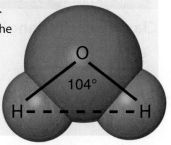

Spiral Review and Test Practice

Solve. KEY **NS 2.2** page 326

24. $7525 \div 25 =$

25. $75.25 \div 2.5 =$

26. $9450 \div 45 =$

27. $94.5 \div 0.45 =$

28. $1875 \div 15 =$

29. $18.75 \div 1.5 =$

Write the letter of the correct answer. MG 2.0

30. What is one name that applies to this triangle?

  A obtuse
  B scalene
  C equilateral
  D right

1.5 inches 1.5 inches
1.5 inches

Test Tip
Ask yourself: What do I know about the lengths of the sides and the measures of the angles?

Extra Practice See page 425, Set A.

Key Standards Review

Need Help?
See Key Standards Handbook.

Solve. Use any method. KEY **AF 1.2**

1. $5x = 25$

2. $64 = 8k$

3. $v \div 6 = 6$

4. $2b = 14$

5. $72 = 9p$

6. $42b = 84$

7. $10g = 110$

8. $c \div 8 = 48$

9. $4x = 48$

10. $4r = 24$

11. $w \div 3 = 9$

12. $7z = 49$

Divide. KEY **NS 2.1**, KEY **NS 2.2**

13. $0.44\overline{)4.62}$

14. $3.4\overline{)8.84}$

15. $0.05\overline{)4.0}$

16. $6.5 \div 25$

17. $1.222 \div 0.52$

18. $21.28 \div 0.7$

19. $0.03\overline{)0.24}$

20. $1.6\overline{)8.8}$

21. $0.03\overline{)1.215}$

22. $61.32 \div 1.4$

23. $46.2 \div 4.4$

24. $2.28 \div 9.5$

Challenge — Problem Solving

What's the Angle? KEY MG 2.2

Find the measure of each angle without using a protractor.

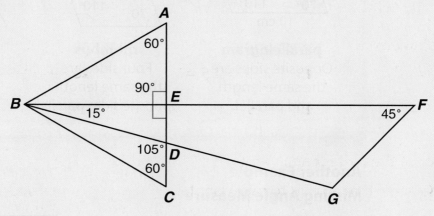

1. $\angle ABE$

2. $\angle CBD$

3. $\angle BGF$

4. $\angle EDB$

CA Standards

KEY MG 2.2 Know that the sum of the angles of any triangle is 180° and the sum of the angles of any quadrilateral is 360° and use this information to solve problems.

MG 2.0 Students identify, describe, and classify the properties of, and the relationships between, plane and solid geometric figures.

Also KEY MG 2.1, MR 2.0, MR 2.3, MR 2.4, MR 2.6, MR 3.0

Vocabulary

quadrilateral

rectangle

square

parallelogram

rhombus

trapezoid

Quadrilaterals

Objective Classify quadrilaterals and find missing angle measures.

▶ **Learn by Example**

A quadrilateral is a four-sided figure. The sum of the angle measures in any quadrilateral is 360°. You can use sides and angles to classify quadrilaterals.

How many different quadrilaterals can you see in Angel Stadium in Anaheim?

Classifying Quadrilaterals

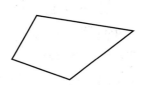

quadrilateral
four sides;
four angles

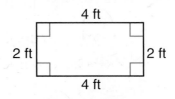

rectangle
Opposite sides are
the same length;
four right angles.

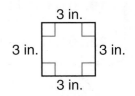

square
Four sides are
the same length;
four right angles.

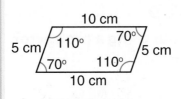

parallelogram
Opposite sides are
the same length
and parallel.

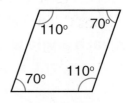

rhombus
Four sides are
the same length;
opposite sides parallel.

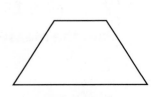

trapezoid
one pair of
parallel sides

Another Example

Missing Angle Measure

Subtract the sum of the known angle measures from 360°.

$x = 360° - (75° + 41° + 132°)$

$x = 360° - 248°$ so, $x = 112°$

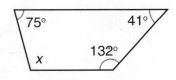

Classify each figure in as many ways as possible. Then find the missing angle measures.

1.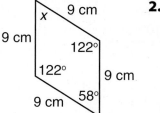

2.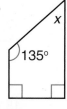

3.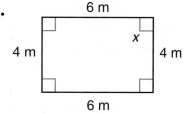

Guided Problem Solving

Use the questions to solve this problem.

4. Alan cut a four-sided figure from a sheet of paper. He used a protractor to find three of the angle measurements. Classify Alan's figure and write an equation to find the missing angle measure.

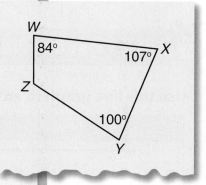

a. Understand What do you need to do to solve this problem?

b. Plan What figure is this? What is the sum of the measures of the angles in this type of figure?

c. Solve Let z equal the measure of $\angle Z$. Write and solve an equation to find the measure of $\angle Z$.

d. Look Back Does the sum of the four angles equal 360°?

(123) **Math Talk** Why can some quadrilaterals be classified in more than one way?

▶ **Practice and Problem Solving**

Classify each figure in as many ways possible. Then find the missing angle measure.

5.

6.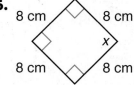

7.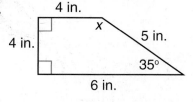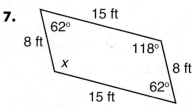

Use this figure to answer Exercises 8–9.

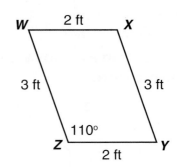

8. What is the measure of ∠X?

9. What is the measure of ∠W?

10. **Challenge** Is every square a rhombus? Is every rhombus a square? Explain.

Solve.

11. Julia is planting this flower bed surrounded by a short fence. The fence has two parallel sides. Classify the figure and write an equation to find the measurement of the missing angle.

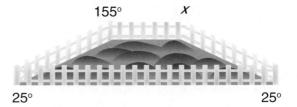

Spiral Review and Test Practice

Use this line graph to answer the questions. AF 1.1 page 346

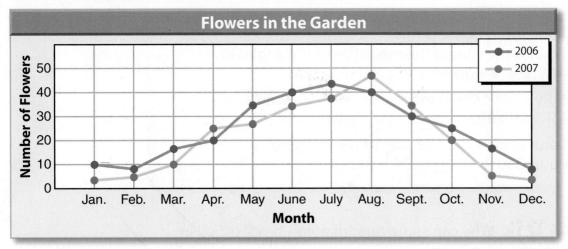

12. In which month and year did the garden have the most flowers?

13. Between which two months was there the greatest increase in the number of flowers?

Write the letter for the correct answer. KEY MG 2.2

14. The two missing angles have the same measure. What is the measure of each angle?

   A 120°   **B** 60°   **C** 90°   **D** 180°

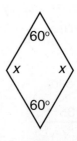

Extra Practice See page 425, Set B.

Find Angle Measures of Polygons

Triangle

Sum of angles = 180°

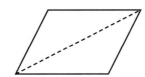

Quadrilateral

Sum of angles = 360°

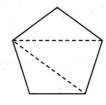

Pentagon

Sum of angles = 540°

1. Copy and complete the table.

Number of Sides	3	4	5	6	7	8	9	10
Number of Triangles	1	2	3					
Sum of Angle Measures	180°	360°	540°					

2. How can you find the sum of the angle measures of any polygon?

3. If *n* = the number of sides of a polygon, write an expression for the sum of the angles of the polygon.

The exposed ends of columns of polished granite, Devils Postpile National Monument, CA

CA Standards
KEY **AF 1.2**, KEY **MG 2.2**, MR 2.3

CA Standards
KEY MG 2.1 Measure, identify, and draw angles, perpendicular and parallel lines, rectangles, and triangles by using appropriate tools (e.g., straightedge, ruler, compass, protractor, drawing software).

MG 2.0 Students identify, describe, and classify the properties of, and the relationships between, plane and solid geometric figures.

Also KEY MG 2.2, MR 2.3, MR 2.4, MR 2.6

Vocabulary

congruent

Materials
• Ruler
• Protractor
• Tracing paper

Congruence

Objective Identify congruent figures.

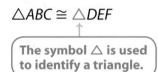 **Learn by Example**

Figures that are the same shape and the same size are called **congruent** figures. The symbol ≅ is used to indicate congruence.

If two figures are congruent, then the corresponding parts of the figures have equal measures.

Different Ways to Check for Congruence

Way 1 **Use a tracing.**

Trace triangle *ABC* and place the tracing on top of triangle *DEF*. You can see that the triangles are congruent.

△*ABC* ≅ △*DEF*

> The symbol △ is used to identify a triangle.

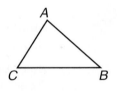

Way 2 **Use a ruler and a protractor.**

Use a ruler to measure the sides of the figures and a protractor to measure the angles. If the corresponding sides and angles are the same measure, the figures are congruent.

quadrilateral *PQRS* ≅ quadrilateral *WXYZ*

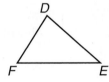

Guided Practice

Use a tracing or a ruler and protractor to see if the two figures are congruent. Write *yes* or *no*.

1.

2.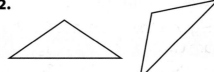

Ask Yourself
- Are the figures the same size and shape?
- Do corresponding sides and angles have the same measure?

 Math Talk Draw three squares. Make two of the squares congruent. Describe the differences of your squares.

Practice and Problem Solving

Use a tracing or a ruler and protractor to see if the two figures are congruent. Write *yes* or *no*.

3.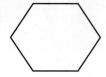

4.

5.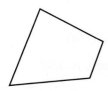

6.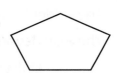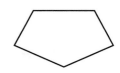

7. **Challenge** There are two figures. Both figures have 4 congruent angles. Both figures have two pairs of parallel sides, but only one of the figures has 4 congruent sides. What are the two figures?

Spiral Review and Test Practice

Divide. NS 1.0, NS 2.0, KEY NS 2.2 page 304

8. $27.3 \div 0.5$

9. $109.6 \div 0.25$

10. $6.07 \div 0.5$

11. $83.6 \div 2.2$

Write the letter for the correct answer. MG 2.0

12. Which two figures are congruent?

A  B   C  D

CA Standards

MR 2.3 Use a variety of methods, such as words, numbers, symbols, charts, graphs, tables, diagrams, and models, to explain mathematical reasoning.

KEY MG 2.2 Know that the sum of the angles of any triangle is 180° and the sum of the angles of any quadrilateral is 360° and use this information to solve problems.

Also MG 2.0, MR 1.1, MR 2.0, MR 2.4, MR 3.0, MR 3.1, MR 3.2

Problem Solving Plan
Missing Angle Problems

Objective Find the missing angle measure in a triangle or a quadrilateral to solve problems.

▶ **Learn by Example**

Marc is trimming some trees in his yard. When he goes inside for lunch, he leaves a ladder leaning against the tool shed.

The ladder, the side of the tool shed, and the ground form a right triangle. The ladder and tool shed form a 30° angle. What are the measures of the other two angles of the triangle?

30°

UNDERSTAND

The ladder forms a 30° angle with the tool shed.

The triangle formed is a right triangle, so one angle is 90°.

The sum of the measures of the angles in any triangle is 180°.

PLAN

Add the measure of the two angles you know.

Subtract the sum from 180° to find the measure of the third angle.

SOLVE

$$\begin{array}{r} 30° \\ + 90° \\ \hline 120° \end{array} \qquad \begin{array}{r} 180° \\ - 120° \\ \hline 60° \end{array}$$

The measures of the other two angles of the triangle are 60° and 90°.

LOOK BACK

Did you answer the question that was asked?

Add the measures of the three angles. Do they total 180°?

Guided Problem Solving

Solve using the Ask Yourself questions. Explain why your answer makes sense.

1. Elias is making a map of the school's playground. The playground is in the shape of a quadrilateral. He figures out that one corner is a 45° angle and another corner is a 110° angle. If another corner is a right angle, what is the measure of the last corner?

(123) **Math Talk** How can making a sketch of a figure help you solve a problem about missing angle measures?

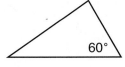 **Independent Problem Solving**

Solve. Explain why your answer makes sense.

2. The stones on a garden walkway are isosceles triangles. Look at the given angle measure. What are the measures of each angle on one of the stones? How do you know?

3. Clara's flowerbed is shaped like a parallelogram. One corner of the flowerbed is a 100° angle. What are the measures of the other three angles in the flowerbed?

4. The triangles below are congruent. Find the measure of angle *x*.

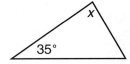

5. **Create and Solve** Write a word problem that can be solved using this diagram.

6. **Challenge** A square and a right triangle are joined to make a trapezoid. The two angles of the right triangle have the same measure. What are the measures of the four angles in the trapezoid? Use a protractor to draw the trapezoid and check your work.

7. A path is shaped like a quadrilateral. Sidney measures three of the angles as 45°, 60°, and 75°. Without measuring the fourth angle, how can she tell that she did something wrong?

Reading & Writing

Vocabulary

Label each triangle. Tell if it is a **right triangle**, an **isosceles triangle**, a **scalene triangle**, an **equilateral triangle**, an **acute triangle**, or an **obtuse triangle.** Triangles may have more than one label.

1.
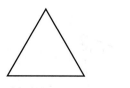

2.

3.
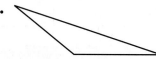

4.
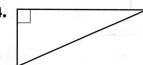

Name each figure and find the missing angle measures.

5.
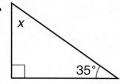
x, $35°$

6.
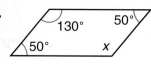
$130°$ $50°$ $50°$ x

7.
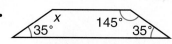
x $145°$ $35°$ $35°$

8.
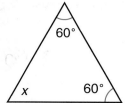
$60°$ $60°$ x

Writing How can you be sure two figures are **congruent**?

Reading Look for this book in your library. *What's Your Angle, Pythagoras? A Math Adventure,* by Julie Ellis.

CA Standards

MR 2.3 Use a variety of methods, such as words, numbers, symbols, charts, graphs, tables, diagrams, and models, to explain mathematical reasoning.

Also MG 2.0, KEY MG 2.2

Standards-Based Extra Practice

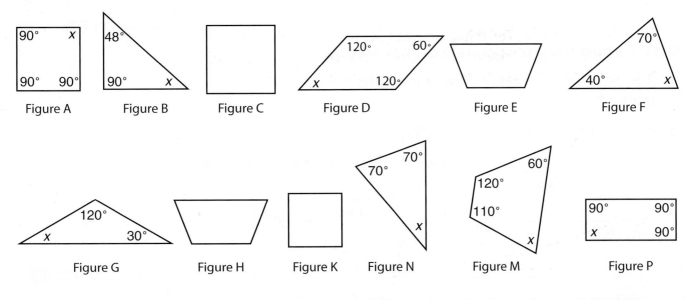

Figure A   Figure B   Figure C   Figure D   Figure E   Figure F

Figure G   Figure H   Figure K   Figure N   Figure M   Figure P

Set A ————————————————————— MG 2.0, KEY MG 2.2 page 412

Find each missing angle measure. Then classify each triangle in two ways.

1. Figure N   **2.** Figure G   **3.** Figure B   **4.** Figure F

Set B ————————————————————— MG 2.0, KEY MG 2.2 page 416

Classify each figure in as many ways as possible. Then find the missing angle measure.

1. Figure M   **2.** Figure P   **3.** Figure D   **4.** Figure A

Set C ————————————————————— MG 2.0, KEY MG 2.1 page 420

Use a ruler to measure the sides and a protractor to measure the angles. Determine if the figures are congruent. Write *yes* or *no*.

1. Figure *A* and Figure *K*   **2.** Figure *M* and Figure *H*   **3.** Figure *F* and Figure *N*

4. Figure *H* and Figure *E*   **5.** Figure *B* and Figure *G*   **6.** Figure *C* and Figure *K*

Education Place
Visit www.eduplace.com/camap/
for more **Extra Practice**.   **Chapter 19** Extra Practice   **425**

Chapter Review/Test

Vocabulary and Concepts

Write the best word to complete each sentence.

1. A triangle with 3 sides of different lengths is a _____ triangle.

2. A triangle with a right angle is called a _____ triangle.

3. A _____ has four sides of equal length and may have four right angles.

4. An _____ triangle has at least two sides that are the same length.

Skills

Find the sum of the measures of the angles for each figure.

5.

6.

7.

Classify each triangle in two ways. Then find the measure of the missing angle.

8. x, 90°, 39°

9. 68°, x, 44°

10. 130°, 24°, x

Classify each figure in as many ways as possible.

11.

12.

13.

Problem Solving and Reasoning

Solve.

14. A triangular flag contains a right angle and an angle that measures 41°. What is the measure of the third angle in the flag?

15. Lanny built a fence around his triangular garden. If two of the angles formed by the fence measure 50°, what is the measure of the third angle?

Writing Math How can you decide if two figures are congruent?

Spiral Review and Test Practice

1.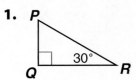

Triangle *PQR* is a right triangle. What is the measure of angle *P*?

A 240°

B 120°

C 105°

D 60°

> **Test Tip**
> Use what you know about the sum of angle measures of a triangle to help you solve the problem.

KEY **MG 2.2** page 412

2. Each of 34 students finished a 26-mile marathon. How many miles did they walk altogether?

A 60

B 272

C 874

D 884

NS 1.0 page 240

3. Which of the following is a prime number?

A 4

B 13

C 16

D 21

KEY **NS 1.4** page 6

4. The ages of students who competed in a spelling bee are 13, 8, 12, 10, 9, 16, 13, 11, 15, 9, and 12. Which of the following is the best choice for intervals in a histogram that shows the data?

A 8–9, 10–11, 12–13, 14–15

B 8–10, 11–13, 14–16, 17–19

C 8–10, 11–13, 14–16

D 8–10, 11–12, 13–16

> **Test Tip**
> Read all answer choices before choosing the correct answer.

SDAP 1.2 page 352

5. Which equation shows the relationship of all the values in the table below?

x	y
2	8
3	11
4	14
5	17
6	20

A $y = 4x$

B $y = 3x + 2$

C $y = 3x - 2$

D $y = 2x + 4$

> **Test Tip**
> Check your answer by substituting *x*-values into your answer choice and solving for *y*.

KEY **AF 1.5** page 112

Education Place
Visit www.eduplace.com/camap/ for **Test-Taking Tips** and **Extra Practice**.

Chapter 19 Spiral Review and Test Practice **427**

Chapter 20

Geometric Figures

Check What You Know

Word Bank

ray
right triangle
quadrilateral
polygon

Vocabulary and Concepts GRADE 4 MG 3.7, MG 3.8, MR 2.3

Match the word to its definition. Then draw an example.

1. A square, a rhombus and a parallelogram are all examples of a _____.

2. A _____ is a part of a line that begins at an endpoint and goes on forever in one direction.

3. A triangle with one 90° angle is called a _____.

Skills KEY MG 2.1

Are the lines perpendicular? page 398

4.

5.

How many pairs of parallel lines does each figure have? page 398

6.   7.   8.   9.

Problem Solving and Reasoning KEY MG 2.2 page 410

10. I am a plane shape. I have no parallel or perpendicular lines. I have 3 angles, whose measures add up to 180°. I also have 3 congruent sides. What am I?

Vocabulary

Visualize It!

parallel	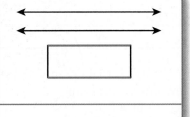
two or more lines that never meet. Some quadrilaterals have parallel lines.	
perpendicular	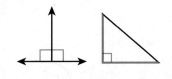
lines that come together to form a right angle. Some polygons have perpendicular lines.	

Language Tip

Math words that look similar in English and Spanish often have the same meaning.

English	Spanish
parallel	paralela
perpendicular	perpendicular

See **English-Spanish Glossary** pages 628–642.

Education Place Visit www.eduplace.com/camap/ for the **eGlossary** and **eGames**.

CA Standards
KEY **MG 2.1** Measure, identify, and draw angles, perpendicular and parallel lines, rectangles, and triangles by using appropriate tools (e.g., straightedge, ruler, compass, protractor, drawing software).

MG 2.0 Students identify, describe, and classify the properties of, and the relationships between, plane geometric figures.

Also MR 1.1, MR 2.3, MR 2.4

Vocabulary

perpendicular

parallel

Materials
- Compass
- Straightedge
- Tracing paper

Hands On
Construct Parallel and Perpendicular Lines

Objective Construct lines that are parallel or perpendicular to a given line.

▶ **Explore**

Perpendicular lines intersect at right angles. **Parallel** lines never intersect. They are always the same distance from each other.

Lines can be named by identifying two of their points or by using lowercase letters like *c* and *d*.

Question How can you use a compass and straightedge to construct parallel or perpendicular lines?

Follow the steps to construct perpendicular lines.

1 Draw line *c* and point *W*. Put the point of the compass on *W*. Draw an arc that intersects the line *c* twice. Label the intersecting points *X* and *Y*.

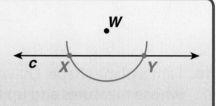

2 Place the point of the compass at *X* and draw an arc. Do the same for *Y*. Label the point where the two arcs intersect *V*.

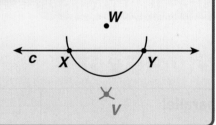

3 Draw a line through points *W* and *V*. Label the new line *d*. Line *d* is perpendicular to line *c*.

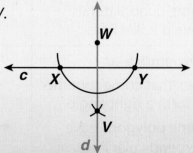

You can write **d ⊥ c** to indicate that the lines are perpendicular.

Follow the steps to construct parallel lines.

1 Draw line *f* and point *Q*. Follow the steps on page 430 to construct line *g* through point *Q* perpendicular to *f*.

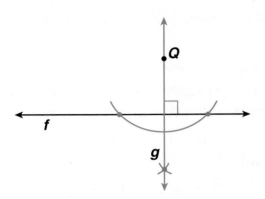

2 Follow the steps again to construct line *e* through point *Q* perpendicular to *g*.

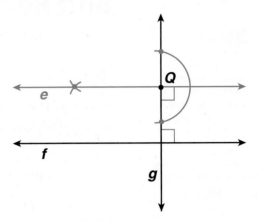

Since *g* is perpendicular to both *e* and *f*, *e* is parallel to *f*. Write *e* ∥ *f*.

▶ **Extend**

Use a compass and straightedge for Exercises 1–5.

1. Draw line *r*. Label a point *Z* that is not on *r*. Construct line *h* so that *h* is perpendicular to *r* and passes through *Z*.

2. Draw a line and label it *m*. Construct line *n* so that *n* is perpendicular to *m*.

3. Trace line segment *AB*. Construct one line segment that is perpendicular, and one line segment that is parallel to $\overline{AB}$.

4. Draw line *x*. Label a point *A* that is not on *x*. Construct line *y* so that *y* is perpendicular to *x* and passes through *A*.

5. Draw a line and label it *e*. Construct line *f* so that *f* is parallel to *e*.

Writing Math

What do you know about two lines that are perpendicular to the same line?

CA Standards
KEY MG 2.1 Measure, identify, and draw angles, perpendicular and parallel lines, rectangles and triangles by using appropriate tools (e.g., straightedge, ruler, compass, protractor, drawing software).

MR 2.0 Students identify, describe, and classify the properties of, and the relationship between, plane geometric figures.

Also MG 2.3, MR 2.4

Materials
• Compass
• Straightedge

Hands On
Construct Triangles and Rectangles

Objective Construct triangles and rectangles.

▶ **Learn With Manipulatives**

You can see both rectangles and triangles on the faces of the Transamerica Pyramid in San Francisco.

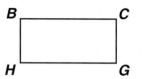

You can construct triangles and rectangles with a compass and a straightedge.

Construct a rectangle, *MNPQ*, congruent to rectangle *BCGH*.

---

① Draw a line. Mark a point on the line. Label the point *Q*.

Q

② Measure $\overline{HG}$ in the rectangle above. Move the slider on your compass to that measure and draw an arc from *Q*. Label the point of intersection *P*.

Q   *P*

③ Construct a line perpendicular to $\overline{QP}$ at *Q*. Construct a second line perpendicular to $\overline{QP}$ at *P*.

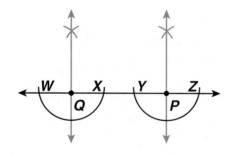

④ Measure $\overline{GC}$ in the rectangle above. Use this measure to draw an arc from *P* and label point *N*. Draw another arc from *Q* and label point *M*. Use a straightedge to draw $\overline{MN}$.

MNPQ ≅ *BCGH*

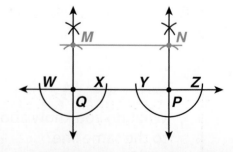

Construct a triangle, *RST*, congruent to equilateral triangle *KLJ*.

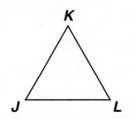

1 Draw a line. Mark a point on the line. Label the point *R*.

2 Measure $\overline{JL}$. Move the slider to that measure and draw an arc from *R*. Label the point of intersection *T*.

3 Without changing the compass measure, draw an arc from point *R* and an arc from point *T*. Label the point where the two arcs intersect *S*.

4 Use a straightedge to draw $\overline{RS}$ and $\overline{TS}$. Write $\triangle RST \cong \triangle JKL$.

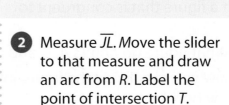

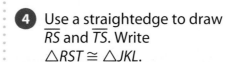

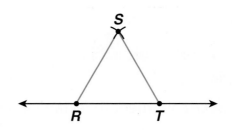

▶ **Guided Practice**

Complete the construction.

1. Construct triangle *PNR* congruent to equilateral triangle *BXY*.

2. Construct rectangle *AEIU* congruent to rectangle *CJNR*.

3. Construct square *CDVW* congruent to square *LMTS*.

Ask Yourself

- Is my figure the same shape?
- Is my figure the same size?

Guided Problem Solving

Use the questions to solve this problem.

4. Claire drew the figure to the right. The distance between A and C is the same as the lengths of $\overline{AB}$ and $\overline{BC}$. Construct a figure that is congruent to Claire's figure.

   a. **Understand** What figure do points A, B, and C form?

   b. **Plan** Sketch how you can divide the figure into two figures you know how to construct.

   c. **Solve** Construct a figure that is congruent to figure ABCDE.

   d. **Look Back** Is your figure the same size and shape as Claire's?

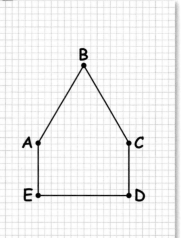

(123) **Math Talk** What does it mean to say two figures are congruent?

Practice and Problem Solving

Complete the construction.

5. Construct rectangle BCEF congruent to rectangle GHTU.

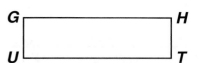

6. Construct triangle RSO congruent to equilateral triangle PQV.

7. Construct a rectangle where at least one of the sides is congruent to $\overline{WX}$.

Spiral Review and Test Practice

Divide. Check your answer. KEY (NS 2.2) pages 320, 322, 326

8. $59\overline{)35{,}424}$ 9. $17\overline{)629}$ 10. $43\overline{)86}$ 11. $17\overline{)5{,}185}$

Write the letter of the correct answer. KEY (MG 2.1)

12. Which of the following best describes the figure?

   A parallel lines   **C** acute angles

   B perpendicular lines   **D** obtuse angles

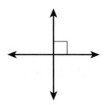

Extra Practice See page 441, Set A.

Key Standards Review

Need Help?
See Key Standards Handbook.

Use a protractor to find the measure of each angle. KEY **MG 2.1**

1.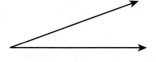

2.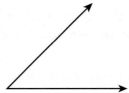

3.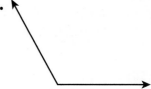

Use a protractor to draw an angle for each measure. KEY **MG 2.1**

4. 130°

5. 30°

6. 90°

Challenge Problem Solving

Constructions Using a Circle KEY **MG 2.1**

Use a compass to draw a circle with center *C* and radius *CQ*.

Do not change the compass opening. Place the compass point at *Q*. Draw a mark on the circle.

Place the compass point on the mark. Draw again. Repeat around the circle.

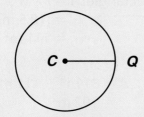

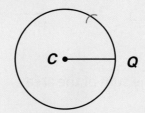

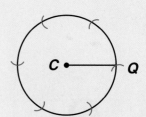

Use the construction above to make the figure.

1. a regular hexagon

2. an equilateral triangle

3. a trapezoid

CA Standards

MG 1.0 Students understand and compute the volumes and areas of simple objects.

KEY NS 2.1 Add, subtract, multiply, and divide with decimals; add with negative integers; subtract positive integers from negative integers; and verify the reasonableness of the results.

Also NS 1.3, AF 1.0, MR 1.0, MR 1.2, MG 1.4

Perimeter and Area of Complex Figures

Objective Find the perimeter and area of complex figures.

▶ **Learn by Example**

Shane's Inspiration in Los Angeles was the first playground in California built so children with and without physical disabilities could play together.

This figure shows the measurements for a new playing court at a playground. What is the area and perimeter of the playing court?

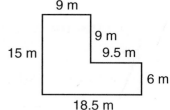

① Divide the complex figure into simple figures. Draw a line that divides the figure into a square and a rectangle.

② Use formulas to find the area of each figure.

$$\text{square: } A = s^2$$
$$= (9\text{ m})^2$$
$$= 81\text{ m}^2$$

$$\text{rectangle: } A = l \times w$$
$$= (18.5\text{ m})(6\text{ m})$$
$$= 111\text{ m}^2$$

③ Find the sum of the areas.

$$A = 81\text{ m}^2 + 111\text{ m}^2$$
$$= 192\text{ m}^2$$

④ Use a formula to find the perimeter of the figure.

$$P = 15\text{ m} + 18.5\text{ m} + 6\text{ m}$$
$$+ 9.5\text{ m} + 9\text{ m} + 9\text{ m}$$
$$= 67\text{ m}$$

Solution: The area of the playing court is 192 m². The perimeter is 67 m.

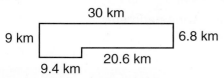 **Guided Practice**

Find the perimeter and area. All corners are right angles.

1.

30 km
9 km
6.8 km
9.4 km
20.6 km

2.
8 in. 1 in.
6 in.
5 in.
10 in.

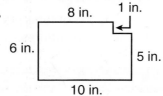 **Ask Yourself**
• Is there a measure missing?
• How can the figure be divided?

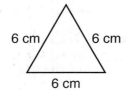 **Math Talk** The figures in Exercises 1 and 2 have 6 sides. How would you find the perimeter of a figure with 7 sides?

Practice and Problem Solving

Find the perimeter and area of the figure. All corners are right angles.

3.
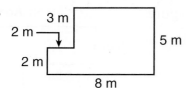
3 m
2 m
2 m
5 m
8 m

4.
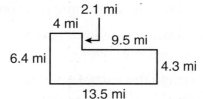
2.1 mi
4 mi
9.5 mi
6.4 mi
4.3 mi
13.5 mi

5.
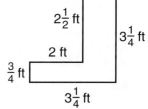
$2\frac{1}{2}$ ft
$3\frac{1}{4}$ ft
2 ft
$\frac{3}{4}$ ft
$3\frac{1}{4}$ ft

 Real World Data

Use the map of a playground for Problems 6–7.

6. Find the area and perimeter of the sandbox.

7. Each hopscotch square is 1 ft². How can you find the area of the hopscotch court? What is the area?

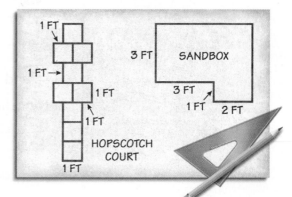

1 FT
1 FT
3 FT SANDBOX
1 FT
3 FT
1 FT 2 FT
1 FT
HOPSCOTCH COURT
1 FT

Spiral Review and Test Practice

Classify the triangle in two ways. MG 2.0, KEY MG 2.1 page 412

8.
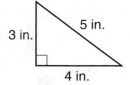
5 in.
3 in.
4 in.

9.
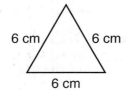
6 cm 6 cm
6 cm

10.

9 ft 9 ft
8 ft

Write the letter of the correct answer. MG 1.0

11. Find the area of this figure.

A 13 cm² **B** 5 cm² **C** 10 cm² **D** 15 cm²

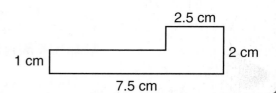
2.5 cm
2 cm
1 cm
7.5 cm

CA Standards

MR 1.2 Determine when and how to break a problem into simpler parts.

MG 1.0 Students understand and compute the volumes and areas of simple objects.

Also NS 1.3, KEY NS 2.1**,
KEY** NS 2.3**, NS 2.5,
KEY** AF 1.2**, MG 1.4,
MR 1.1, MR 2.0, MR 2.4,
MR 3.0, MR 3.1, MR 3.2,
MR 3.3**

Vocabulary

area

Problem Solving Plan
Multistep Problems

Objective Break problems into parts involving perimeter and area of complex figures.

▶ **Learn by Example**

A community group needs to purchase enough grass seed to seed a picnic area. How much money will they need to buy the seed?

Grass Seed Mixture	
Area Covered	**Price List**
1 lb covers 75 m²	1 lb cost $12
4 lb covers 300 m²	4 lb cost $38

UNDERSTAND

You know the picnic area is a complex figure.

You know how many square feet each bag of grass seed will cover.

You know the cost of grass seed.

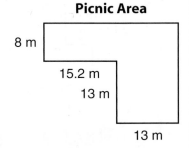

Picnic Area

PLAN

First, find the **area** of the complex figure.

Second, find the cost of the grass seed needed for the picnic area.

SOLVE

① Divide the complex figure.

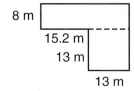

② Find the area of each figure.

Rectangle $A = l \times w$	Square $A = s^2$
$A = 28.2 \times 8$	$A = (13)^2$

Find the sum of the areas.

$225.6 + 169 = 394.6$ m²

③ Find the cost of the grass seed.

Two 1-lb bags and one 4-lb bag will cover 450 m². The cost is $12 + $12 + $38 = $62.

LOOK BACK

Look back at the problem. Did you answer the question?

Guided Problem Solving

Solve using the Ask Yourself questions.

1. Look back at the figure on page 438. The picnic area will be surrounded by a fence. A local business donated 60 meters of fence. How many more meters of fence is needed?

(123) Math Talk Is there a different way to divide the picnic area into simple figures?

<blockquote>
Ask Yourself
- How can the complex figure be divided?
- Do I need to find the perimeter or area?
- What steps should I follow?
</blockquote>

▶ **Independent Problem Solving**

Solve. Explain why your answer makes sense.

2. Kendra is painting the sign at the entrance to the playground.

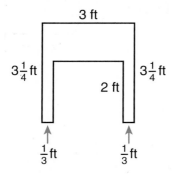

a. She has enough paint to cover 5 ft². Is that enough to cover the front of the sign?

b. Tara is putting a lighting strip around the sign. How many feet of lighting strip will she use?

c. **Challenge** How could you use subtraction to find the area of the sign?

3. A turf company is laying grass. The area of the front lawn is 52.6 m².

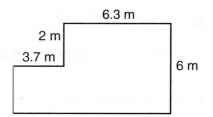

a. What is the length of the blue side? Hint: Divide the complex figure into 2 shapes.

b. Bill wants to enclose the yard with a fence using boards that are 2 meters long. How many boards should he buy?

4. **Create and Solve** Draw a complex figure that can be divided into simple shapes. Write a word problem that can be solved by finding the area of your complex figure.

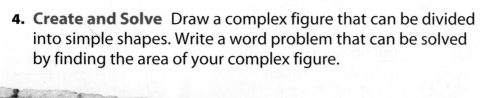

Reading & Writing

Vocabulary

You know how to use formulas to find the perimeter and area of complex figures. The **perimeter** is the distance around a figure. The **area** is the number of square units needed to cover the figure.

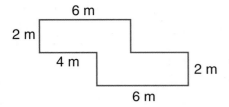

6 m

2 m

4 m

2 m

6 m

1. Find the perimeter of the figure.

2. Find the area of the figure.

You also know how to draw **congruent** figures.

Complete the construction.

3. Construct a triangle *DEF* congruent to right triangle *ABC*.

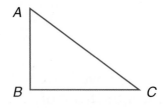

4. Construct a rectangle *HIJK* congruent to rectangle *PQRS*.

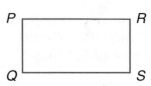

Writing What tools do you need in order to construct perpendicular lines? Parallel lines?

Reading Look for this book in your library. *Grandfather Tang's Story: A Tale Told with Tangrams* by Ann Tompert

CA Standards
MR 2.3 Use a variety of methods, such as words, numbers, symbols, charts, graphs, tables, diagrams, and models, to explain mathematical reasoning.
Also MG 1.0, MG 2.0, KEY MG 2.1

Standards-Based Extra Practice

Complete each construction.

1. Construct triangle *CDE* congruent to equilateral triangle *BXY*.

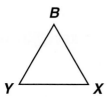

2. Construct rectangle *ABCD* congruent to rectangle *RSUT*.

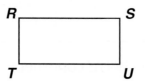

3. Label a point *e*. Construct a square congruent to square *STZV* such that point *e* is one of the corners of the congruent square.

4. Construct triangle *TYQ* congruent to equilateral triangle *MNP*.

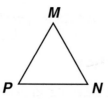

Find the perimeter and area. All corners are right angles.

1.

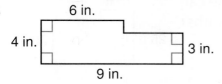

2.

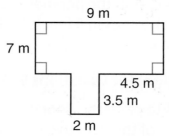

3.

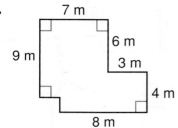

4.

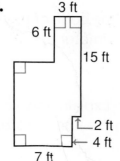

Education Place
Visit www.eduplace.com/camap/
for more **Extra Practice**.

Chapter Review/Test

Vocabulary and Concepts ———————————— MG 2.0, KEY **MG 2.1**, MR 2.3

Write the best word to complete each sentence.

1. Two _____ lines never intersect.

2. A pair of perpendicular lines intersect at a _____ angle.

Skills ———————————————————— MG 1.4, MG 2.0, KEY **MG 2.1**, MG 1.0

3. Construct rectangle *WXYZ* congruent to rectangle *ABCD*.

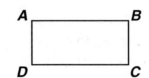

Find the perimeter and area of each figure.

4.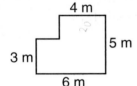
4 m, 20, 5 m, 3 m, 6 m

5.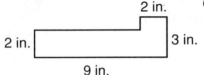
2 in., 2 in., 3 in., 9 in.

6.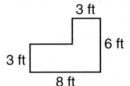
3 ft, 6 ft, 3 ft, 8 ft

Problem Solving and Reasoning ——— MG 1.0, MG 1.4, MG 2.0, KEY **MG 2.1**, MR 2.3

Solve.

7. Jim sketched a patio design. He has enough cement to cover 50 square feet of his patio. Does he need to buy more cement? Explain.

8. Michelle needs to find the perimeter of her garden. If she can buy fencing that comes in 5 feet lengths, how many lengths will she need to buy?

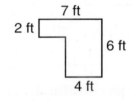
7 ft, 2 ft, 6 ft, 4 ft

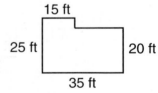
15 ft, 25 ft, 20 ft, 35 ft

Use the figure at right for Questions 9–10.

9. Mr. Ortiz wants to paint the floor of his son's room. What is the area of the floor in square feet?

10. Mr. Ortiz wants to tape the edge of the floor before painting. What is the perimeter of the room?

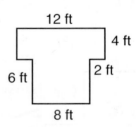
12 ft, 4 ft, 6 ft, 2 ft, 8 ft

Writing Math Explain how you could use subtraction to find the area of the figure shown.

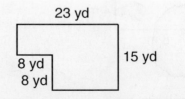
23 yd, 8 yd, 8 yd, 15 yd

Spiral Review and Test Practice

1. Marco drives 1,328 miles every month commuting to his job. How many miles does he drive in 6 months?

A 6,968

C 7,948

B 7,868

D 7,968

NS 1.0, MR 1.1 page 240

2. There are 327 cars parked in a parking garage. An equal number of cars are parked on each of 3 floors. How many cars are parked on each floor of the garage?

A 19

C 109

B 108

D 981

KEY NS 2.2 page 328

3. What is the area of this complex figure?

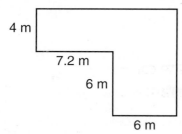

A 36 m²

B 57.6 m²

C 64.8 m²

D 88.8 m²

> **Test Tip**
> Use what you know about finding the area of *parallelograms* to find the area of a complex figure.

KEY MG 1.1 page 436

4. Sarah read 60 books. How many weeks did it take her to read half that many books?

A 5

B 6

C 7

D 8

KEY SDAP 1.4 page 366

5.

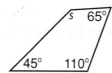

What is the measure of angle *s* in the figure above?

A 360°

B 220°

C 170°

D 140°

KEY MG 2.2 page 416

Education Place
Visit www.eduplace.com/camap/ for
Test-Taking Tips and **Extra Practice**.

Unit 8 Review/Test

Vocabulary and Concepts ———————— MG 2.0, KEY MG 2.1, MR 2.3 Chapters 18 and 20

Choose the best word to complete each sentence.

1. You can construct triangles and rectangles using a straightedge and a _____.

2. An _____ is formed by two rays with a common endpoint.

3. _____ lines intersect at right angles.

4. A _____ is a tool used to measure angles.

5. Figures that are the same size and shape are called _____.

Skills ———————————————— MG 1.4, MG 2.0, KEY MG 2.1, KEY MG 2.2 Chapter 19, Lessons 2–3

Find the measure of the missing angle. Classify the angle as acute, obtuse, straight, or right.

6.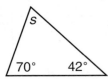
70° 42°

7.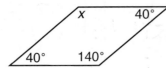
40° 140° x 40°

8.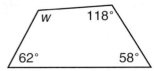
62° 58° w 118°

Use a protractor to draw the angles. Chapter 18, Lesson 1

9. angle *ABC* that measures 125°

10. angle *XYZ* that measures 46°

Use a protractor and a ruler to draw the following triangles. Chapter 18, Lesson 2

11. a right scalene triangle

12. an obtuse isosceles triangle

Find the perimeter and area of each figure. Chapter 20, Lesson 3

13. Figure *C*

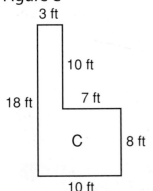

3 ft
10 ft
18 ft
7 ft
C
8 ft
10 ft

14. Figure *D*

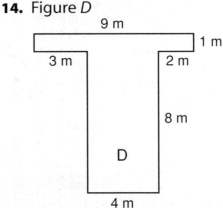

9 m
1 m
3 m
2 m
8 m
D
4 m

Problem Solving and Reasoning — KEY MG 1.1, MG 2.0 Chapters 18–20

Solve.

15. Barry has a garden shaped like a rhombus. One side of the garden is 10 feet long. How long are the other sides?

16. Jolene's garden has 4 congruent sides. She divided it into 2 right triangles. Are the 2 triangles congruent? Explain.

17. Sam's garden is in the shape of a right triangle. Two sides are congruent. What is the measure of the non-right angles?

18. Gloria planted a rectangular garden. Its perimeter is 16 meters. What is the largest area the garden can have?

19. Payton's square garden has an area of 25 ft². What is its perimeter?

20. Raul's garden has only 1 pair of parallel sides. What shape is his garden?

BIG IDEA!

Writing Math How does the measure of an angle help you classify shapes?

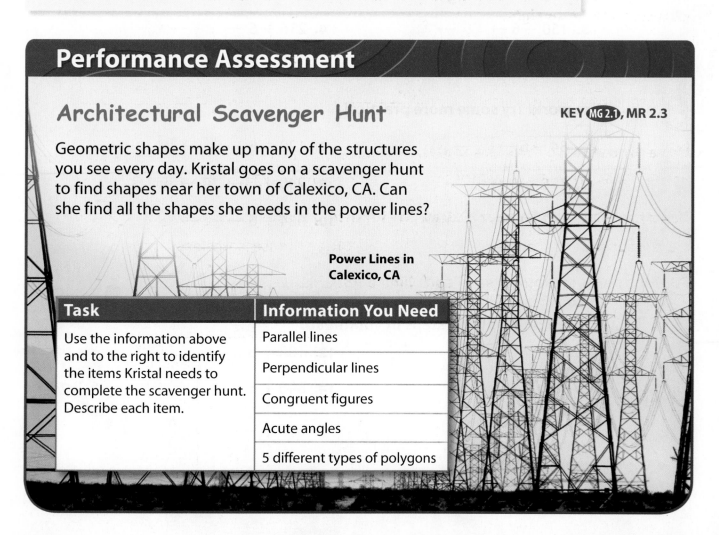

Performance Assessment

Architectural Scavenger Hunt — KEY MG 2.1, MR 2.3

Geometric shapes make up many of the structures you see every day. Kristal goes on a scavenger hunt to find shapes near her town of Calexico, CA. Can she find all the shapes she needs in the power lines?

Power Lines in Calexico, CA

Task	Information You Need
Use the information above and to the right to identify the items Kristal needs to complete the scavenger hunt. Describe each item.	Parallel lines
	Perpendicular lines
	Congruent figures
	Acute angles
	5 different types of polygons

 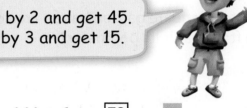

Go Fast, Go Far

Unit 8 Mental Math Strategies

Divide by 6

The answer can be quick to see, divide by 2 and then by 3!

First, I divide 90 by 2 and get 45. Then I divide 45 by 3 and get 15.

1. $90 \div 6 \rightarrow$ 45 $\rightarrow$ 15
Divide 90 by 2.   Divide by 3.

2. $144 \div 6 \rightarrow$ 72 $\rightarrow$ ▢
Divide 144 by 2.   Divide by 3.

3. $150 \div 6 \rightarrow$ ▢ $\rightarrow$ ▢
Divide 150 by 2.   Divide by 3.

4. $216 \div 6 \rightarrow$ ▢ $\rightarrow$ ▢
Divide 216 by 2.   Divide by 3.

Nice work! Try some more practice!

5. $84 \div 6 \rightarrow$ ▢ $\rightarrow$ ▢

6. $120 \div 6 \rightarrow$ ▢ $\rightarrow$ ▢

7. $186 \div 6 \rightarrow$ ▢ $\rightarrow$ ▢

8. $240 \div 6 \rightarrow$ ▢ $\rightarrow$ ▢

9. $162 \div 6 \rightarrow$ ▢ $\rightarrow$ ▢

10. $684 \div 6 \rightarrow$ ▢ $\rightarrow$ ▢

Take It Further!
Now try doing all the steps in your head!

11. $78 \div 6$

12. $108 \div 6$

13. $426 \div 6$

14. $846 \div 6$

Go Faster!

Greg Tang's at top

Greg Tang's

9

Geometry and Measurement

BIG IDEAS!

- The formulas for the area of parallelograms, rectangles, and triangles are related to one another.

- Surface area and volume are two ways to describe solid objects.

Chapter 21
Area

Chapter 22
Solids

Songs and Games

Math Music Track 9: *What Formula?*
eGames at **www.eduplace.com/ camap/**

Math Readers

Catching the Wind
by S. Adio Shevlot

More Than a Guess
by Clayton James
Illustrated by Cheryl Mendenhall

Game

Find the Area

Object of the Game Practice finding the area of different sized rectangles.

Materials
- Learning Tool 26: Rulers
- Learning Tool 27: Rectangle Cards (2 sets)

Set Up
Each player gets a centimeter ruler. Players shuffle the Rectangle Cards and place them face down in a stack.

Number of Players 2

How to Play

1 Players take turns drawing a card from the stack until each player has four cards.

2 Players measure the length and width of each rectangle with a centimeter ruler.

3 Players find the area for each rectangle and add the areas together.

4 The player with the largest sum scores a point.

5 Return all the cards to the stack and shuffle. Repeat steps 1–4. The first player to score a total of 3 points is the winner.

CA Standards

MG 1.0 Students understand and compute the volumes and areas of simple objects.

KEY MG 2.1 Measure, identify, and draw angles, perpendicular and parallel lines, rectangles, and triangles by using appropriate tools (e.g., straightedge, ruler, compass, protractor, drawing software).

Also MR 1.0, MR 2.3

Education Place
Visit www.eduplace.com/camap/ for **Brain Teasers** and **eGames** to play.

Reading You can use a K-W-L chart to help you understand a reading selection. To solve word problems in this unit, you can use a K-W-P-L chart. The chart helps you focus on important information. Here is an example:

Celia wants to carpet a sun porch. The drawing shows the measurements of the room. How many square feet of carpeting does she need?

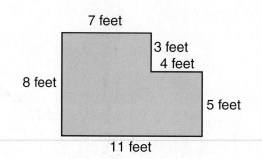

What Do I Know?	What Do I Want to Know?	What Is My Plan to Find Out?	What Did I Learn?
• the measurements of the room	• the area of the room	• Separate the figure into two rectangles. • Find the area of each rectangle. ($A = l \times w$) • Add areas.	

> $7 \times 8 = 56$
> $4 \times 5 = 20$
> The sun porch area is 76 ft².

Writing Celia chooses carpeting that costs $10 per square foot. Can she carpet the room for less than $1,000? Complete the K-W-P-L Chart to help you solve the problem.

What Do I Know?	What Do I Want to Know?	What Is My Plan to Find Out?	What Did I Learn?

Area

Chapter 21

Rice fields near Sacramento, CA

Check What You Know

Vocabulary and Concepts   KEY MG 2.1, MR 2.3

Match the word to its definition, then draw an example.

pages 398 and 430

Word Bank

- **polygon**
- **perpendicular**
- **parallel**
- **triangle**

1. _____ lines intersect to form two right angles.

2. Rectangles and squares are two shapes that have perpendicular and _____ lines.

3. A _____ is a closed figure with three or more angles and sides.

4. A figure with three sides and three angles is called a _____ .

Skills   GRADE 4 MG 3.0, MG 3.1

5. Which figure is not a polygon?

   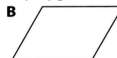   

A   B   C   D

6. I have perpendicular and parallel lines. Which figure am I?

   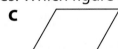

A   B   C   D

Problem Solving and Reasoning   GRADE 4 MG 1.0, MG 1.1

7. The floor of Susanna's tree house is 10 feet long and 10 feet wide. Susanna is covering the floor with square tiles each of which measures 2 feet long and 2 feet wide. How many tiles does Susanna need to completely cover the floor?

Vocabulary

Visualize It !

Area of a Parallelogram

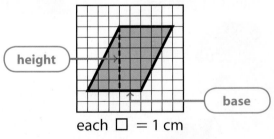

height

base

each □ = 1 cm

Area = base × height
= 5 × 6
= 30 cm²

Language Tip

Math words that look similar in English and Spanish often have the same meaning.

English	Spanish
area	área
polygon	polígono
square unit	unidad cuadrada

See **English-Spanish Glossary** pages 628–642.

Education Place Visit www.eduplace.com/camap/ for the **eGlossary** and **eGames**.

CA Standards **MR 2.3** Use a variety of methods, such as words, numbers, symbols, charts, graphs, tables, diagrams, and models, to explain mathematical reasoning. **Also KEY MG 1.1**

Chapter 21   451

CA Standards

KEY MG 1.1 Derive and use the formula for the area of a triangle and of a parallelogram by comparing it with the formula for the area of a rectangle (i.e., two of the same triangles make a parallelogram with twice the area; a parallelogram is compared with a rectangle of the same area by pasting and cutting a right triangle on the parallelogram).

MG 1.0 Students understand and compute the volumes and areas of simple objects.

Also MG 1.4, MR 2.3, MR 2.4, MR 3.3

Vocabulary

parallelogram

base (of a parallelogram)

height (of a parallelogram)

Materials

• Learning Tool 10 (Centimeter Grid)
• Straightedge
• Scissors
• Colored markers
• Tape

Hands On
Area of Parallelograms

Objective Derive the formula for the area of a parallelogram using the formula for the area of a rectangle.

▶ **Explore**

Question How can you use the area of a rectangle to find the area of a **parallelogram**?

Lee plans to paint a design in the shape of a parallelogram on the dance floor. She needs to know the area to determine how much paint to buy. How many square feet of the floor will be covered by the design?

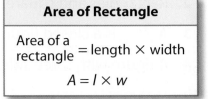

Area of Rectangle
Area of a rectangle = length × width
$A = l \times w$

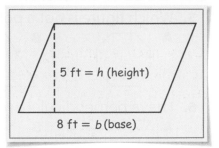

5 ft = h (height)

8 ft = b (base)

In a parallelogram, the **base** can be any side. The **height** is the length of a perpendicular segment extending from a vertex to the base.

1 Copy the parallelogram on grid paper. Use one centimeter to represent each foot. Be sure to draw the height h.

2 Shade the triangle shape on the end of the figure. Emphasize the height h with a colored marker. Cut out the parallelogram.

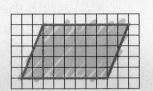

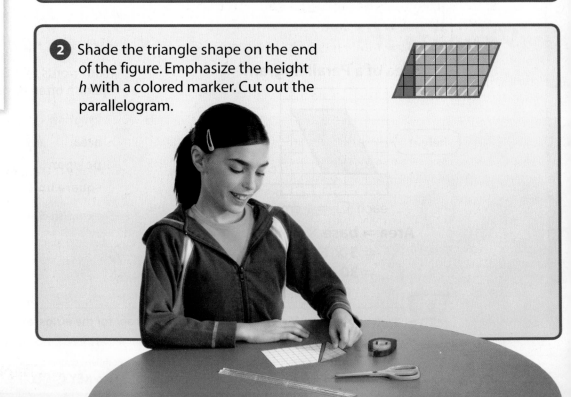

3 Cut out the triangle that you shaded. Move the cut-out triangle to the other side of the parallelogram and tape it in place. What figure have you formed?

What can you say about the area of the rectangle and the area of the parallelogram?

Solution: The painted design will cover 8 × 5 or 40 square feet. Square feet, sq ft, and ft² are three ways of writing the same thing.

▶ **Extend**

Copy each parallelogram on grid paper. Cut and tape to make the parallelogram into a rectangle. Find the area of the rectangle and the parallelogram.

1.

2.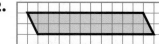

3.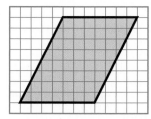

4.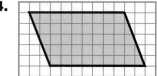

5. Generalize What formula can you use to find the area of a parallelogram? Explain how this formula relates to the formula for finding the area of a rectangle.

A detail of a Frank Lloyd Wright window

Writing Math

Connect Can you multiply the lengths of two adjacent sides to find the area of a rectangle? Can you multiply the lengths of two adjacent sides to find the area of a parallelogram? Explain your answers.

Vocabulary Tip

Adjacent sides of a figure share an endpoint.

CA Standards

KEY MG 1.1 Derive and use the formula for the area of a triangle and of a parallelogram by comparing it with the formula for the area of a rectangle (i.e., two of the same triangles make a parallelogram with twice the area; a parallelogram is compared with a rectangle of the same area by cutting and pasting a right triangle on the parallelogram).

MG 1.0 Students understand and compute the volumes and areas of simple objects.

Also KEY NS 2.1, MG 1.4, MR 1.2, MR 2.3, MR 2.6

Area of Parallelograms

Objective Use a formula to find the area of parallelograms.

▶ Learn by Example

In Lesson 1, you found a formula that could be used to find the area of parallelograms. In this lesson you will use that formula.

Kimberly has designed a set for a play. The set will be in the shape of a parallelogram. The base will be 30 feet and its height will be 15 feet. The technical director needs to know the area of the set so she can mix enough paint. What is the area of the set?

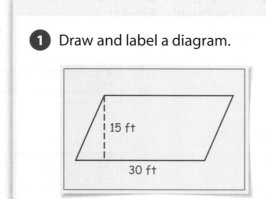

1 Draw and label a diagram.

15 ft

30 ft

2 Use the formula $A = b \times h$ to find the area.

$A = b \times h$
$A = 30 \times 15$
$A = 450$

Think

Area is expressed in square units. Since the base and height are in feet, the area is in square feet (ft²).

Solution: The area of the set is 450 square feet.

Another Example

In this example, the measured height is shown outside the parallelogram.

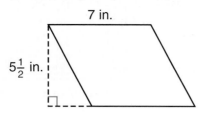

7 in.

$5\frac{1}{2}$ in.

$A = b \times h$
$\quad = 7 \times 5\frac{1}{2}$
$\quad = 38\frac{1}{2}$

The area is $38\frac{1}{2}$ square inches or $38\frac{1}{2}$ in.²

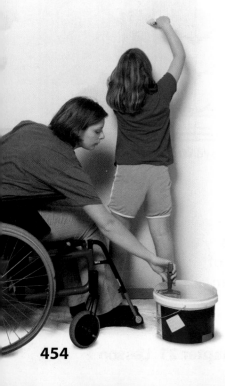

► **Guided Practice**

Find the area of each figure.

1.

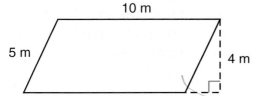

2.

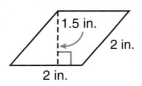

Guided Problem Solving

3. The figure to the right shows the lawn a gardener wants to seed. Five-pound bags of seed cover 2,000 ft² and cost $22.95. How many bags of lawn seed must she buy?

  a. Understand What do you need to find?

  b. Plan Break the problem into parts.
- First, find the _?_ of the parallelogram.
- Then, find the number of _?_ needed.

  c. Solve Follow your plan to solve.

  d. Look Back Did you answer the question?

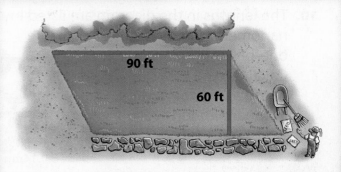

(123) Math Talk Angela says that since a rectangle is a type of parallelogram, you can use the formula $A = b \times h$ to find the area of any rectangle. Is this true? Explain.

► **Practice and Problem Solving**

Find the area of each figure.

4.

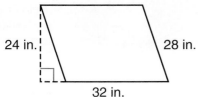

5.

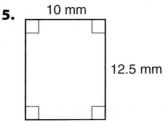

6.

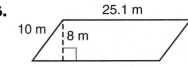

Solve. Draw pictures to help find the solutions.

7. Liam made a parallelogram-shaped tabletop. The long side of the table top is 42 inches. A perpendicular line from one long side to the other is $24\frac{1}{2}$ inches. What is the area of the table top?

8. Pierre designed a parallelogram-shaped parking lot. The height of the parallelogram is 75 meters. The area is 17,700 square meters. What is the length of the parking lot?

 ## Science Link

Use the diagram to solve Problems 9–10.

9. The diagram labels one angle of the parallelogram. What are the measurements of the other three angles?

10. The lengths in the diagram are listed in nanometers. A nanometer is one-billionth of a meter. Calculate the area of the parallelogram in square nanometers.

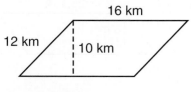

Fun Facts

- What do soot, graphite, and diamond have in common? All are forms of the same element, carbon.
- The differences among these substances come from their different arrangements of carbon atoms.
- Graphite is the "lead" in a lead pencil.
- In graphite, groups of carbon atoms are arranged in the shapes of parallelograms. The diagram shows one such group with carbon atoms labeled A, B, C, and D.

Science PS 1.d

 Spiral Review and Test Practice

Use information from the graph to answer Questions 11–13. AF 1.1 page 350

11. Was more money earned from Fruit and Nuts or from Nursery and Flowers?

12. Which three categories earned about $\frac{3}{4}$ of the money?

13. What two categories earned about half the money?

Write the letter of the correct answer.

14. What is area of this figure? **KEY MG 1.1**

California Agriculture Money Earned

Vegetables

Livestock and Poultry

Fruits and Nuts

Nursery and Flowers

Field Crops

Farm Related

16 km

12 km 10 km

A 56 km **B** 120 km² **C** 160 km² **D** 192 km²

Extra Practice See page 467, Set A.

Find the missing measure in each figure below. KEY MG 2.2

1.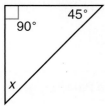

2.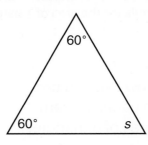

3.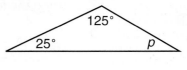

4.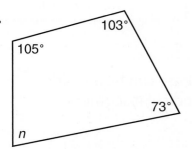

5.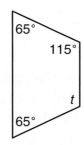

6.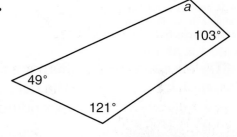

Challenge — Critical Thinking

What's the Area? MG 1.0, KEY MG 1.1

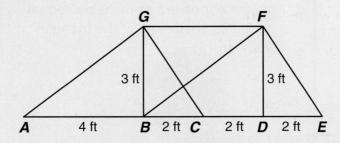

1. What is the area of the polygons shown in the figure?

   a. rectangle *BDFG*   **b.** parallelogram *ABFG*   **c.** parallelogram *CEFG*

2. How are these three polygon areas related? Why?

CA Standards

KEY **MG 1.1** Derive and use the formula for the area of a triangle and of a parallelogram by comparing each with the formula for the area of a rectangle (i.e., two of the same triangles make a parallelogram with twice the area; a parallelogram is compared with a rectangle of the same area by pasting and cutting a right triangle on the parallelogram).

MG 1.0 Students understand and compute the volumes and areas of simple objects.

Also MG 1.4, AF 1.0, KEY AF 1.2, MR 2.3, MR 2.4, MR 3.3

Vocabulary

base (of a triangle)

height (of a triangle)

Materials
• Learning Tool 10
  (Centimeter Grid)
• Straightedge
• Scissors
• Colored markers

Hands On
Area of Triangles

Objective Derive the formula for the area of a triangle using the formula for the area of a parallelogram.

▶ **Explore**

Question How can you use the area of a parallelogram to find the area of a triangle?

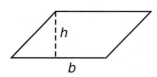

Area of a Parallelogram
Area of a parallelogram $=$ base $\times$ height
$A = b \times h$

Remember, in a parallelogram, the base can be any side. The height is the length of a perpendicular segment extending from a vertex to the base.

1 Draw a parallelogram on grid paper. Make sure that the lengths of the base and the height are whole numbers. Use a colored marker to highlight the height. Find the area.

$b = 8$ cm $h = 3$ cm
$A = 8 \times 3 = 24$ cm²

2 Draw a line from a vertex to the vertex opposite it to make two equal triangles. Shade one of the triangles.

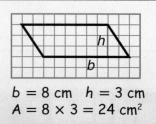

3 Cut out the shaded triangle, and place it on top of the triangle that was not cut out.

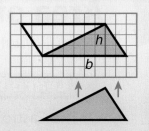

> The **base** of a triangle can be any side. The **height** is perpendicular to the base.

- What do you notice about the area of the parallelogram and the area of the triangle?

- What do you notice about the base and height of the triangle and of the parallelogram?

4 Repeat with another parallelogram having a different base and height. Are your results the same?

▶ **Extend**

Make two copies of each triangle on the same piece of grid paper. Cut out one copy. Place it beside the uncut copy to make a parallelogram. Find the area of the parallelogram. Find the area of the triangle.

1.

2.

3.

4.

5. Analyze Look back at the triangles in Exercises 3 and 4 and the parallelograms they made. What do you notice? What does that tell you about the relationship of the area of a right triangle and the area of a rectangle?

6. Challenge Look to the right at the aerial map of some streets in San Francisco. Many streets form rectangles or parallelograms, but you can see a triangle bordered by S. Van Ness Avenue, Mission St, and Plum St. If the base of the triangle is 120 meters and the height is 180 meters, find the area of the triangle shaped block. Use a diagram to help.

Writing Math

Connect How do you use the formula for the area of a parallelogram to find the area of a triangle? Explain.

CA Standards
KEY **MG 1.1** Derive and use the formula for the area of a triangle and of a parallelogram by comparing each with the formula for the area of a rectangle (i.e., two of the same triangles make a parallelogram with twice the area; a parallelogram is compared with a rectangle of the same area by cutting and pasting a right triangle on the parallelogram).

MG 1.0 Students understand and compute the volumes and areas of simple objects.

Also NS 1.0, KEY **NS 2.1**, MG 1.4, KEY **AF 1.2**, MR 1.0, MR 2.3

Area of a Triangle

Objective Use the formula to find the area of triangles.

▶ **Learn by Example**

The Castro District is a neighborhood in San Francisco. You can see that Duboce Avenue, Market Street, and Castro Street form a triangle. The approximate lengths of these streets are shown on the table. What is the area of this neighborhood?

Street	Length
Duboce Ave.	800 m
Market St.	1,050 m
Castro St.	650 m

The Castro District, San Francisco, CA

Think

Remember to express your answer in square units. 1 square meter can also be written as 1 m² and 1 sq m.

① Find the information you need.

- The base of the triangle, b, is 800 meters.
- The height of the triangle, h, is 650 meters.
- You do not need the other side of the triangle.

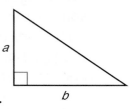

② Use the formula for area of a triangle.

$A = 0.5 \times 800 \times 650$

$= 400 \times 650$

$= 260,000$

Area of a Triangle

$A = \frac{1}{2}b \times h$ or

$A = 0.5b \times h$

Solution: The area of the Castro District is about 260,000 m².

Other Examples

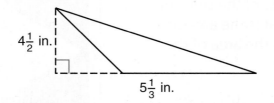

12.5 cm

18.4 cm

$4\frac{1}{2}$ in.

$5\frac{1}{3}$ in.

In this example, the height is shown measured outside the triangle.

The area is 115 cm².   The area is 12 in.²

▶ Guided Practice

Find the area of the figure.

1.

4 in.

5 in.

2.

$2\frac{1}{2}$ yd $7\frac{1}{8}$ yd

$6\frac{1}{4}$ yd

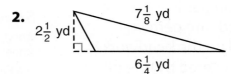

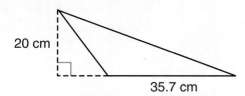

Ask Yourself
- What formula do I use?
- Which segments represent the base and the height?

(123) Math Talk Kyle wants to find the area of the triangle shown. How can he use the Commutative Property of Multiplication and mental math to find the area?

20 cm

35.7 cm

▶ Practice and Problem Solving

Find the area of the figure.

3.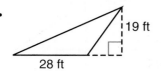

19 ft

28 ft

4.

$2\frac{3}{4}$ yd

$4\frac{1}{3}$ yd

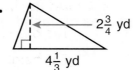

For Problems 5–6, draw and label a diagram to help you solve.

5. A sculptor is making a giant aluminum triangle. The triangle will balance on one point, and its 32-foot base will be parallel to the ground. If the sculpture is 14 feet tall, how many square feet of aluminum is needed for the triangle?

6. The sculptor has a smaller triangular sculpture that he wants to set next to the larger triangle. The smaller triangle measures 4 m tall and has an area of 12 m². What is the length of the base of the triangle?

7. **Challenge** The corners of the yellow pane of glass meet at the midpoints of the sides of the rectangular window. What is the area of each purple triangle? What is the area of the yellow pane?

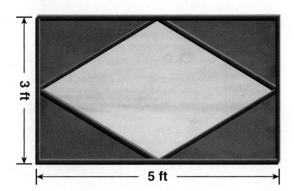

History-Social Science Link

Solve.

8. A modern design using triangles is shown to the right. Suppose the beads are perfectly round and measure 1 cm. Use the beadwork to solve. What is the area covered by one of the purple and pink triangles?

9. Suppose a triangle design was 10 cm wide and 7 cm high. What will be the area covered by beads?

10. A bead strip includes a triangle that has 450 in.² covered by round $\frac{1}{2}$-inch red beads. Sixty beads make up the width of the triangle. What is the height of the triangle?

Southwestern Pueblo Indians
- Woody plants, seashells, and bright-colored stones were used to make beaded designs.
- The bead designs were used on clothing, jewelry, bags, and religious objects.
- The designs often included geometric shapes, such as triangles.

A modern bead design

History-Social Science 5.1.2

Spiral Review and Test Practice

Find the perimeter and area of each figure. MG 1.4

11.
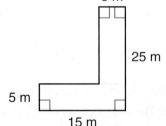
5 m
25 m
5 m
15 m

12.
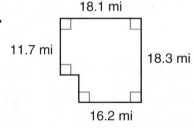
18.1 mi
11.7 mi
18.3 mi
16.2 mi

13.
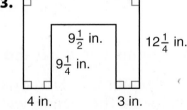
$9\frac{1}{2}$ in.
$9\frac{1}{4}$ in.
$12\frac{1}{4}$ in.
4 in.
3 in.

Write the letter of the correct answer. KEY MG 1.1

14. What is the area of the triangle?

A 18 km²   B 6 km²   C 36 km²   D 120 km²

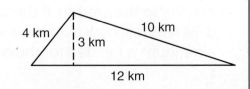
4 km   3 km   10 km   12 km

Extra Practice See page 467, Set B.

Homes in the Area

The Muñoz family is buying a home from a realtor. A realtor is someone who sells homes. When a realtor lists a home for sale, the dimensions of each room are measured.

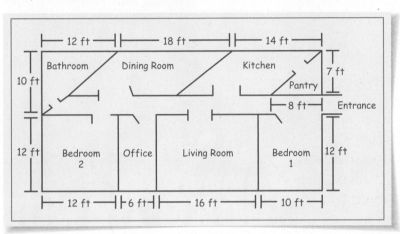

Use the floor plan to solve the problems.

1. What is the area of each room?

   a. Living room   **b.** Dining room   **c.** Kitchen
   d. Bedroom 1   **e.** Bedroom 2   **f.** Bathroom
   g. Pantry   **h.** Office

2. When a realtor advertises the home, what number can she use to describe the total number of square feet of all the rooms combined?

3. **Multistep** Before the owners sell the home, a realtor might suggest that they put new carpeting in the living room and dining room. About how many square yards of carpeting will they need? Hint: There are 9 square feet in 1 square yard.

CA Standards
MG 1.0, MG 1.4,
MR 1.2, MR 2.4

LESSON 5

Field Trip...

Fresno, CA

CA Standards
MR 1.0, MR 1.2,
MR 2.0, MR 2.1,
MR 2.3, MR 2.4,
MR 2.6, NS 1.0,
KEY NS 2.1, NS 2.4,
NS 2.5, KEY NS 2.2,
MG 1.0, KEY MG 1.1

Problem Solving

Objective Use skills and strategies to solve word problems.

The Cobb Ranch in Fresno, California, is home to a 6-acre cornfield maze.

Solve. Tell which strategy or method you used.

1. In one year, California planted 540,000 acres of corn. In the same year, Iowa planted 12,700,000 acres. How many more acres did Iowa need to plant in order to have planted exactly 24 times the amount California planted?

2. Each year, about $28\frac{1}{2}$ billion bushels of corn are produced worldwide. The United States produces about $\frac{4}{10}$ of those bushels. About how many bushels of corn does the United States produce each year?

3. Ethanol fuel is an alternative to gasoline. If one bushel of corn can produce 2.8 gallons of ethanol, how many bushels would you need to produce enough ethanol for a vehicle with a 28-gallon fuel tank?

4. A farmer plants a triangular cornfield maze with a base of $70\frac{1}{2}$ feet and a height of $32\frac{1}{2}$ feet. One bag of corn seeds covers 1 square foot. How many bags of seed are needed? Use estimation to check your answer.

Problem Solving On Tests

Select a Strategy
- Draw a Picture
- Work Backward
- Guess and Check
- Choose the Operation
- Estimate

1. Pete's model sailboat had a sail. One side of the sail looked like the angle shown below. Which of the following *best* describes the angle?

A obtuse

B acute

C right

D straight

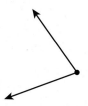

KEY **MG 2.1** page 394

2. Gina has a school banner that looks like a right triangle. She labeled the school banner as *XYZ*. The measure of angle *X* is 25°. What is the measure of angle *Z*?

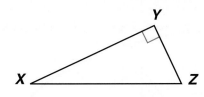

A 25° **B** 65° **C** 75° **D** 90°

KEY **MG 2.2** page 412

3. Gail plans to buy carpet for her bedroom shown below. What is the area of her bedroom?

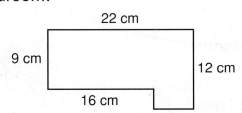

22 cm

9 cm

12 cm

16 cm

A 68 cm²

B 210 cm²

C 216 cm²

D 264 cm²

Test Tip
Divide the figure into simple figures. Then find and combine the area of each simple figure.

MG 1.0 page 436

4. Marla made a graph with the points (2, 3), (1, 1) and (0, −1). Which equation could have been used to create this graph?

A $y = 3x - 2$ **C** $y = x + 2$

B $y = x + \frac{1}{2}$ **D** $y = 2x - 1$

KEY **AF 1.5** page 370

5. Kendra and her family are driving to the beach for a weeklong vacation. The graph shows their progress as they drive across the state.

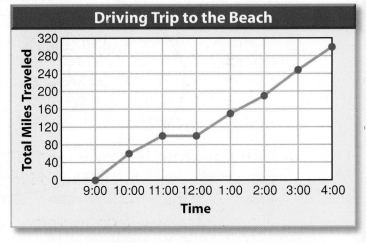

Driving Trip to the Beach

Total Miles Traveled

Time

Kendra and her family arrive at the beach at 4:00. At what time were they halfway to the beach?

A 11:00   **C** 1:00

B 12:00   **D** 2:00

Test Tip
Use clue words in the problem and the graph to interpret the data.

KEY **SDAP 1.4** page 346

Education Place
Visit www.eduplace.com/camap/ for **Test-Taking Tips** and **Extra Practice**.

Chapter 21 Lesson 5   **465**

Reading & Writing Math

Vocabulary

When you are finding the **area** of a parallelogram or a triangle, it's easiest to use a formula.

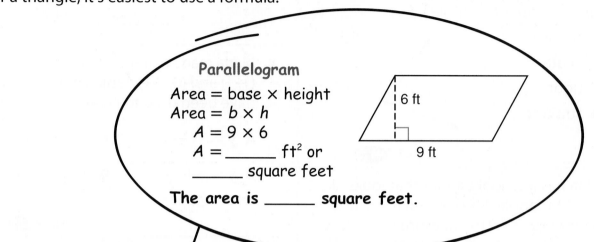

Parallelogram

Area = base × height
Area = $b \times h$
$A = 9 \times 6$
$A = $ _____ ft² or _____ square feet

The area is _____ square feet.

6 ft

9 ft

Formulas for Area

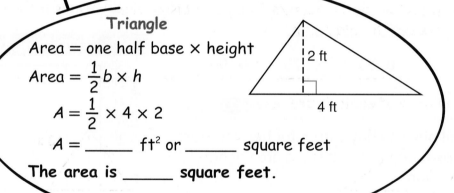

Triangle

Area = one half base × height

Area = $\frac{1}{2} b \times h$

$A = \frac{1}{2} \times 4 \times 2$

$A = $ _____ ft² or _____ square feet

The area is _____ square feet.

2 ft

4 ft

Writing Suppose you wanted to cover the floor of your room with carpet squares. Explain what measurements you would need and why.

Reading Check out this book in your library. *Flatland: A Romance of Many Dimensions* by Edwin A. Abbott

CA Standards
MR 2.3 Use a variety of methods, such as words, numbers, symbols, charts, graphs, tables, diagrams, and models, to explain mathematical reasoning.

Also KEY MG 1.1

Standards-Based Extra Practice

Find the area of each figure.

1.
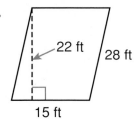

2.
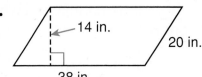

3.
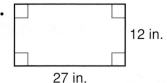

4.
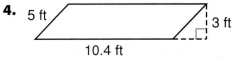

Draw and label a diagram. Then solve the problem.

5. Donald is making a sign in the shape of a parallelogram. The length of the sign is 5.2 feet. The height is 2.8 feet. What is the area of Donald's sign?

Find the area of each figure.

1.
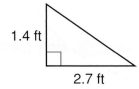

2.
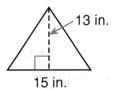

3.
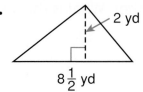

4.
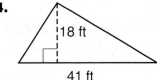

Draw and label a diagram. Then solve the problem.

5. An architect is designing a triangular ice skating rink. The base of the skating rink is 112 feet and the height is 88 feet. What is the area of the ice skating rink?

Education Place
Visit www.eduplace.com/camap/
for more **Extra Practice.**

Chapter Review/Test

Vocabulary and Concepts ———————————————— MG 2.0, MR 2.3

Choose the best word to complete the sentence.

1. A _____ is a quadrilateral whose opposite sides are parallel and congruent.

2. Any side of a parallelogram can be its _____ .

3. The length of a perpendicular segment from a vertex of a triangle to the line that contains the base is the _____ .

Skills ———————————————————————— MG 1.0, KEY **MG 1.1**

Find the area of the figure.

4.
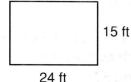
15 ft
24 ft

5.
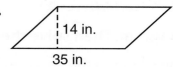
14 in.
35 in.

6.
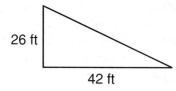
26 ft
42 ft

7.
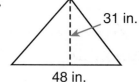
31 in.
48 in.

Problem Solving and Reasoning ——————— MG 1.0, KEY **MG 1.1**, MR 1.1, MR 2.3

Draw and label a diagram to help you.

8. Your room is a rectangle with a length of 42 feet and a width of 22 feet. How much carpeting would you need to buy to cover the floor?

9. There is a world map that measures 48 inches by 60 inches. What is the area?

10. The art room in a school is 52 feet by 62 feet. The cafeteria is 100 feet by 84 feet. How many more square feet is the cafeteria than the art room?

Writing Math How can you use the area of a rectangle to help find the area of a parallelogram?

1. What value for x makes this equation true?

$$x + 31 = 57$$

A 88

B 57

C 31

D 26

KEY **AF 1.2** page 108

2. Which two figures are congruent?

A

B

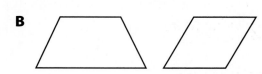

C

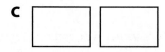

D

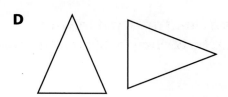

MG 2.0 page 420

3. The line graph shows the amount of money students earned washing cars.

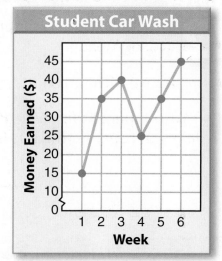

Between which two weeks did earnings increase half as much as they did between Weeks 4 and 5?

A Weeks 1 and 2

B Weeks 2 and 3

C Weeks 3 and 4

D Weeks 5 and 6

Test Tip
Read the graph for understanding before solving the problem.

KEY **SDAP 1.4** page 346

4. In the figure below, *JKML* is a parallelogram.

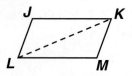

If the area of triangle *JKL* is 24 square meters, what is the area of *JKML*?

A 12 m^2 **C** 36 m^2

B 24 m^2 **D** 48 m^2

KEY **MG 1.1** page 454

Education Place
Visit www.eduplace.com/camap/ for **Test-Taking Tips** and **Extra Practice**.

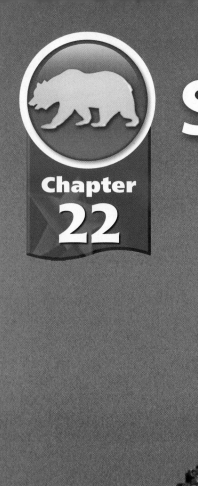

Solids

These are the pyramids at Giza in Egypt.

Vocabulary and Concepts MG 1.0, MR 2.3

Choose the best word to complete each sentence. page 436

1. You use the formula $A = l \times w$ to find the area of a ____ .

2. A solid figure that has six square faces of equal size is a ____ .

3. The distance around a plane figure is ____ .

4. The total area of the surfaces of a solid figure is ____ .

Skills GRADE 4 MG 3.6

Determine the number of cubes needed to build each figure.

5.

6.

Multiply. page 128

7. $2 \times 7 \times 3$

8. $9 \times 4 \times 5$

9. $18 \times 1 \times 8$

Problem Solving and Reasoning GRADE 4 KEY NS 3.2

10. A school has 26 classrooms. Each classroom has 5 rows of desks with 6 desks in each row. How many desks are in the classrooms?

Vocabulary

Visualize It!

rectangular prism

a solid figure with six faces that are rectangles

net

a flat pattern that can be folded to make a solid figure

Language Tips

In everyday language, *volume* describes the loudness of a sound. In mathematics, *volume* describes the size of a three-dimensional object.

Math words that look alike in English and Spanish often have the same meaning.

English	Spanish
cube	cubo
area	área
prism	prisma

See **English-Spanish Glossary** pages 628–642.

 Education Place Visit www.eduplace.com/camap/ for the **eGlossary** and **eGames**.

CA Standards MR 2.3 Use a variety of methods, such as words, numbers, symbols, charts, graphs, tables, diagrams, and models, to explain mathematical reasoning. **Also MG 2.0**

Chapter 22 471

CA Standards

KEY **MG 1.2** Construct a cube and rectangular box from two-dimensional patterns and use these patterns to compute the surface area for these objects.

Also MG 2.0, MG 2.3, MR 2.3

Vocabulary

net

rectangular prism

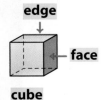

cube

Materials

• Learning Tool 9 (Inch Grid Paper) (2 copies per student)
• Scissors
• Tape

Hands On
Make Solids Using Nets

Objective Identify the nets of solid figures.

▶ **Explore**

Cardboard boxes and other containers are made from nets. A **net** is a flat pattern that can be folded into a solid figure.

Question How can you use a net to make a solid figure?

Mario and Molly are selling toys on the Internet. Each toy has its own box. The boxes come in different shapes and sizes, but are stored unfolded.

---

1 Tape two Learning Tools together. Copy the net shown at the right. Then cut it out.

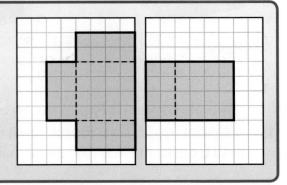

---

2 Fold the net on the dotted lines. Tape the edges together. The net should make a **rectangular prism**, a solid figure with six faces that are rectangles.

Look at these nets.

A.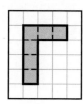

B.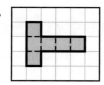

C.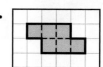

1 Predict whether each pattern is or is not a net for a cube.

2 Copy each pattern onto the Learning Tool. Cut it out, fold it, and tape the edges to check your prediction.

Was your prediction correct?

▶ **Extend**

Predict whether the net forms a rectangular prism, a cube, or neither. Then copy the pattern onto grid paper, cut it out, fold it, and tape it together to check your prediction.

1.

2.

3.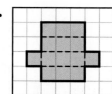

4.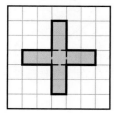

5.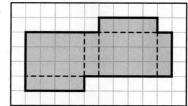

6.

7.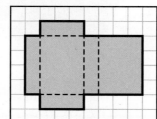

8.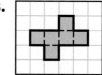

Writing Math

What's Wrong? Dierdre drew this net to make a cube. Will it work? If not, what could Dierdre do to change the net so that it will work?

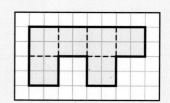

CA Standards

MG 2.3 Visualize and draw two-dimensional views of three-dimensional objects made from rectangular solids.

MG 2.0 Students identify, describe, and classify the properties of, and the relationships between, plane and solid geometric figures.

Also MR 2.3, MR 1.2

Materials
- Learning Tool 10 (Centimeter Grid)
- Unit cube set

Hands On
Draw Views of Solid Figures

Objective Make two-dimensional drawings of solid figures.

▶ **Explore**

Question How can you draw different two-dimensional views of solid figures?

You can use grid paper to show different views of a solid figure.

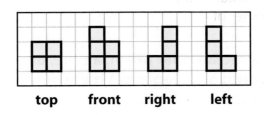

top   front   right   left

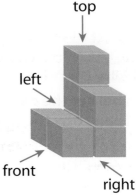

1 Use cubes to build the figure.

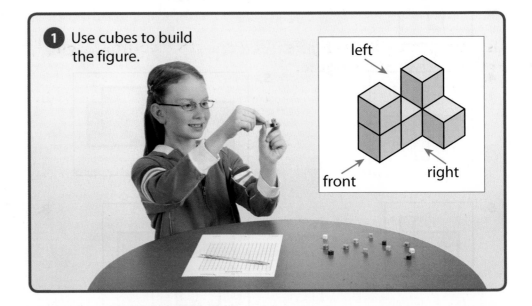

2 Draw these views on grid paper:
- the top view
- the front view
- the view from the right side
- The view from the left side

474

You can use two-dimensional views to build a three-dimensional figure.

    top   front   right   left

1 Look at the top view. What can you say about the bottom of the figure? Use cubes to build the bottom layer of the figure.

2 Use the side and front views to visualize the middle layer and then the top layer of the figure. Build each layer.

3 Compare the figure you built to other students' figures. Is there more than one figure that has these views? Explain.

▶ **Extend**

Use cubes to build the figure. Then draw the top, front, right, and left views of the figure.

1.

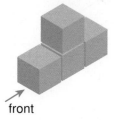

front

2.

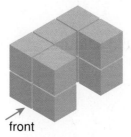

front

3.

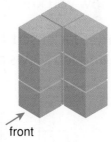

front

4.

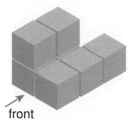

front

5.

front

6.

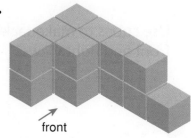

front

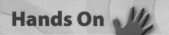
Use the cubes to build a three-dimensional figure with these views. Compare your figures with other students' figures.

7.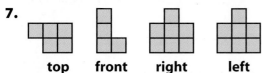

   top   front   right   left

8.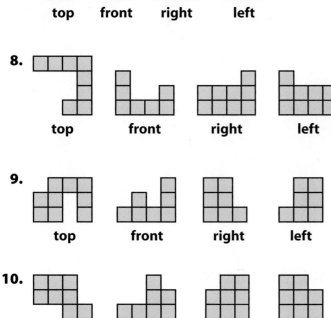

   top   front   right   left

9.

   top   front   right   left

10.

   top   front   right   left

11. **Analyze** A figure has a top view and a side view that are identical. What type of solid figure might this be? Explain how you know.

12. **Challenge** Jack used 14 cubes to build a figure. The top and left views are shown.

    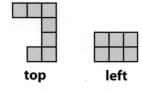

    top   left

    Use cubes to make Jack's figure. Then draw the front and right views.

Writing Math

Analyze Why does the top view tell you how the bottom layer of cubes must be arranged?

Extra Practice See page 489, Set B.

Key Standards Review

Need Help?
See Key Standards Handbook.

Write an expression to represent the area of each figure. KEY **AF 1.2**

1.

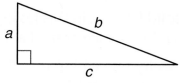

2.

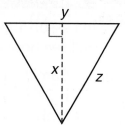

3.

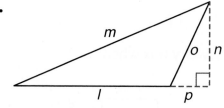

In the figure below, *DEFG* is a parallelogram. Use the figure to answer Problems 4 and 5. KEY **MG 1.1**

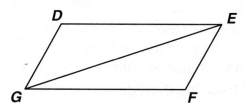

4. If the area of the triangle *EFG* is 31 square inches, what is the area of *DEFG*?

5. If the area of *DEFG* is 56 square inches, what is the area of triangle *DEG*?

Challenge

Visual Thinking

Letter Cube MG 2.3

**Imagine this net is folded to make a cube.
Name the face that is opposite each given face.**

1. face A   **2.** face B   **3.** face C

LESSON 3

CA Standards

MG 1.0 Students understand and compute the volumes and areas of simple objects.

KEY MG 1.2 Construct a cube and rectangular box from two-dimensional patterns and use these patterns to compute the surface area for these objects.

Also NS 1.3, MR 1.1, MR 2.1, MR 2.3, MR 2.4, MR 2.6

Vocabulary

surface area

Materials
Learning Tool 10
(Centimeter Grid)

Surface Area

Objective Use nets to find the surface area of solid figures.

▶ **Learn by Example**

In Lesson 1, you used nets to make solid figures. In this lesson you will see how you can use a net to find the surface area of a figure.

Camilla needs to cover a small jewelry box with paper. The box is 8 centimeters long, 4 centimeters wide, and 2 centimeters high. What is the surface area of the jewelry box?

The net shows the faces of the jewelry box when it is cut apart and laid flat.

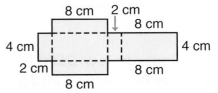

The sum of the areas of the faces is called the **surface area** of the solid figure.

You can use a table like this one to help you find the surface area.

cm² is another way to write *square centimeters*

Face	Length	Width	Area
top	8 cm	4 cm	32 cm²
bottom	8 cm	4 cm	32 cm²
front	4 cm	2 cm	8 cm²
back	4 cm	2 cm	8 cm²
left	3 cm	2 cm	16 cm²
right	3 cm	2 cm	16 cm²
sum			**112 cm²**

Solution: The surface area of the rectangular prism is 112 cm².

Another Example
Surface Area of a Cube

Surface area = 6×5^2
            = 6×25
            = 150 in.²

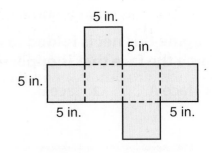

Predict what solid figure each net will make. Then find the surface area of the figure. Each square is 1 cm².

1.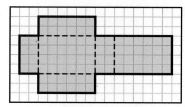

2.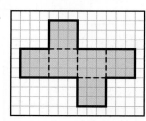

Use the net to determine the surface area of the solid figure.

3.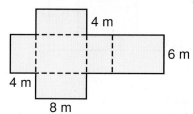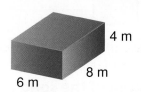

Net A

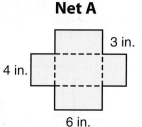

Net B

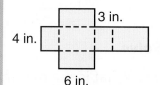

Guided Problem Solving

Use the questions to solve this problem.

4. Julio is wrapping a box that is 6 inches long, 3 inches high, and 4 inches wide. What is the minimum amount of paper needed to wrap the box?

   a. **Understand** What do you need to find out?

   b. **Plan** Choose the net that you can use to help you solve the problem.

   c. **Solve** Use your net to find the area of each face. Record the areas in a table.

   You will need at least ⃝ in.² of wrapping paper.

   d. **Look Back** Did you include every face?

5. Look back at Problem 4. Do you think Julio needs more than the minimum amount of wrapping paper? Explain.

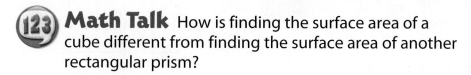 **Math Talk** How is finding the surface area of a cube different from finding the surface area of another rectangular prism?

Predict what solid figure each net will make. Then find the surface area of the figure. Each square is 1 cm².

6.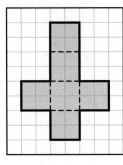

7.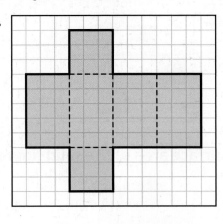

8.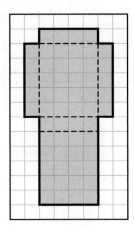

Use the net to determine the surface area of the solid figure.

9.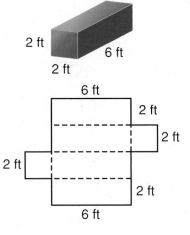

2 ft

6 ft

2 ft

6 ft

2 ft

2 ft

2 ft

2 ft

2 ft

6 ft

10.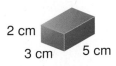

2 cm

3 cm   5 cm

5 cm

5 cm   3 cm

2 cm   2 cm

5 cm

3 cm

Solve.

11. What is the minimum amount of wrapping paper needed to cover a box that is 6 inches long, 4 inches high, and 5 inches wide?

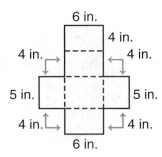

4 in.

6 in.   5 in.

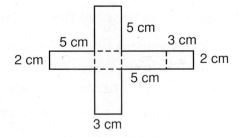

6 in.

4 in.

4 in.   4 in.

5 in.   5 in.

4 in.   4 in.

6 in.

12. Challenge Suppose a cushion is 10.2 cm long, 8.4 cm wide, and 5.2 cm high. What is the minimum amount of cloth needed to cover that cushion?

5.2 cm

10.2 cm   8.4 cm

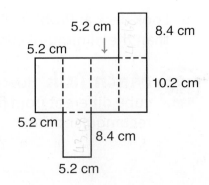

5.2 cm   8.4 cm

5.2 cm

5.2 cm   10.2 cm

5.2 cm

8.4 cm

5.2 cm

480

Real World Data

Use the table to solve Problems 13–16.

Types of Boxes	Length	Width	Height
Cube Box	7 in.	7 in.	7 in.
Long Box	22 in.	6 in.	6 in.
Tall Box	8 in.	8 in.	30 in.
Flat Box	12 in.	9 in.	3 in.
Printers Box	11.25 in.	8.75 in.	6 in.

13. Use grid paper and draw a net for the cube box to help you find the surface area of that box.

14. Use grid paper and draw a net for the tall box to help you find the surface area of that box.

15. Stanley has 575 cm² of wrapping paper to cover a long box. Does he have enough paper to cover the box? Explain your answer.

16. Predict Use estimation to predict if you need more wrapping paper to cover a flat box or a printers box. Calculate to check your prediction.

 Spiral Review and Test Practice

Classify each figure in as many ways as possible. Then find the missing angle measures. KEY **MG 2.2**, KEY **AF 1.2** page 416

17.

8 in.
8
x

18.

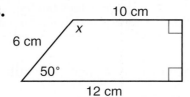
10 cm
x
6 cm
50°
12 cm

19.

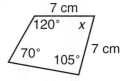
7 cm
120° x
70° 105°
7 cm

Write the letter of the correct answer. KEY **MG 1.2**

20. What is the surface area of the box formed by the pattern below?

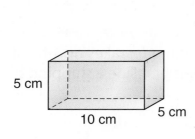
5 cm
10 cm
5 cm

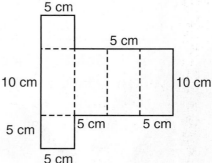
5 cm
5 cm
10 cm
10 cm
5 cm
5 cm
5 cm
5 cm

A 200 cm²   **B** 225 cm²   **C** 250 cm²   **D** 255 cm²

CA Standards
KEY **MG 1.3** Understand the concept of volume and use the appropriate units in common measuring systems (i.e., cubic centimeter [cm³], cubic meter [m3], cubic inch [in.³], cubic yard [yd³]) to compute the volume of rectangular solids.

Also NS 1.0, NS 1.3, MG 1.0, MG 1.4, MR 2.0, MR 2.3, MR 2.4

Vocabulary

cubic unit

1 unit   1 unit
1 unit

volume

Volume

Objective Find the volume of rectangular prisms and cubes.

▶ **Learn by Example**

The volume of a solid figure is the amount of space the figure takes up. Volume is measured in **cubic units**. A cube measuring 1 unit on each edge has a volume of 1 cubic unit.

Joon works in the gift shop at the Discovery Science Center. One of the most popular items is a model of the Solar Cube that measures 1 foot on each side. The cubes come stacked in a shipping box that is 6 feet long, 3 feet wide, and 3 feet high. How many models fit in each box?

The **volume** of a rectangular prism or a cube is the product of the length, the width, and the height.

Volume of a Rectangular Prism

1 Find the volume of the shipping box.

$V = l \times w \times h$

$= 6 \times 3 \times 3$

$= 54$

$= 54 \text{ ft}^3$ ← Cubic feet can be abbreviated ft³ or cu ft

....

2 Find the volume of each solar cube model.

$V = l \times w \times h$

$= 1 \times 1 \times 1$

$= 1$

$= 1 \text{ ft}^3$

Solution: Since each model takes up 1 ft³ of space, 54 Solar Cube models fit inside a shipping box.

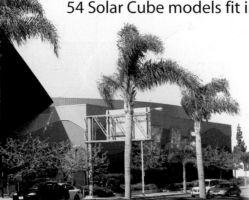

The Solar Cube at the Discovery Science Center, Santa Ana, CA

Another Example
Volume of a Cube

A cube measures 3 feet on each edge.
What is the volume of the cube?

$V = s^3$
$= (3 \text{ ft})^3$
$= (3 \text{ ft}) \times (3 \text{ ft}) \times (3 \text{ ft})$
$= 27 \text{ ft}^3$

3 ft
3 ft   3 ft

Notice that in a cube, the measures of the length, width, and height are all equal. If s represents the side of any face of the cube, then $V = s \times s \times s$ or s^3.

The volume of the box is 27 ft^3.

▶ Guided Practice

Find the volume of each solid figure.

1.

12 m
12 m   12 m

2.
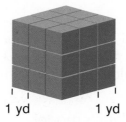
1 yd   1 yd

Ask Yourself
- What formula can I use to find volume?
- Which measures do I use in the formula?
- What units are used to measure volume?

(123) Math Talk How is a unit of volume different from a unit of area?

▶ Practice and Problem Solving

Find the volume of each solid figure.

3.

4.
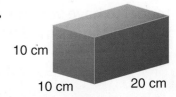
5 cm
2 cm   12 cm

5.
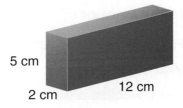
10 cm
10 cm   20 cm

6.

6 in.
6 in.   6 in.

7.
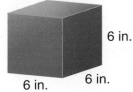
5 cm
4 cm   8 cm

8.
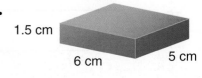
1.5 cm
6 cm   5 cm

9. A cube measures 2 feet on each edge. A rectangular prism is 1 foot long, 3 feet wide, and 2 feet high.

   a. Which box will hold more?

   b. Which box has the greater surface area?

Solve.

10. A restaurant buys the freezer shown at the right.

    a. What is the volume of the freezer in cubic inches?

    b. There are 1,728 cubic inches in one cubic foot. What is a reasonable estimate for the volume of the freezer in cubic feet? Explain how you made your estimate.

30 in.

24 in.

72 in.

11. A box is 2 centimeters wide and 8 centimeters long. It has a volume of 80 cubic centimeters. Find the height of the box.

12. Three boxes have the same volume of 32 cubic in. but different lengths, heights, and widths. What possible dimensions could the boxes have?

 Science Link

Solve.

13. Maria builds a model of a rectangular-shaped reservoir. It is 5 feet long and 4 feet wide. She fills it with water 0.5 foot deep.

    a. Calculate the volume of water in Maria's model.

    b. She drains some of the water. The volume of the remaining water is 2 cubic feet. How deep is the water?

14. Arnold's model reservoir is 2 feet long and 2 feet wide. What must the depth of the water be in his model to have volume equal to the amount of water in Maria's model?

Fun Facts

- A reservoir is a human-made lake, and is used to store fresh water.
- In California, many reservoirs have been built in the Sierra Nevadas.
- These reservoirs store water that will travel to the state's farms and cities.

Hetchy Hetchy Reservoir

Science ES 3.d

 Spiral Review and Test Practice

Find the area of each figure. KEY **MG 1.1** page 454

15.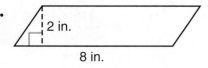

2 in.

8 in.

16.

28 cm

46 cm

Write the letter of the correct answer. KEY **MG 1.3**

17. This rectangular prism has a length of 9 ft, a height of 7 ft, and a width of 4 ft. What is the volume?

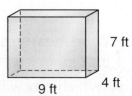

7 ft

9 ft

4 ft

    A 126 cu ft   B 127 cu ft   C 252 cu ft   D 254 cu ft

Extra Practice See page 489, Set D.

Volume of Any Prism

The height of any prism is given by the perpendicular distance between the bases. So the volume of any prism is the same as the volume of a right prism with the same base area and height.

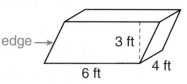

$$V = 6 \times 4 \times 3 = 72 \text{ ft}^3$$

Find the volume of each prism.

1.

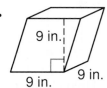

2.

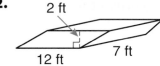

3.

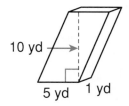

4. **Reasoning** A package of paper that contains 500 sheets is called a ream of paper. What happens to the volume of the paper if it is tilted to one side as shown below?

CA Standards
KEY **MG 1.3**, MR 2.4, MR 3.0

CA Standards

MR 2.4 Express the solution clearly and logically by using the appropriate mathematical notation and terms and clear language; support solutions with evidence in both verbal and symbolic work.

MG 1.4 Differentiate between, and use appropriate units of measures for, two- and three-dimensional objects (i.e., find the perimeter, area, volume).

**Also NS 1.3, KEY MG 1.2,
MG 2.3, KEY AF 1.2,
MR 1.1, MR 2.0, MR 2.3,
MR 3.0, MR 3.1, MR 3.2**

Problem Solving Plan
Perimeter, Area, or Volume?

Objective Solve problems by first determining whether surface area, perimeter, or volume is needed.

▶ **Learn Through Reasoning**

Daniel built a storage bin from the plan shown. Now he needs to use what he knows about perimeter, surface area, and volume to finish the project.

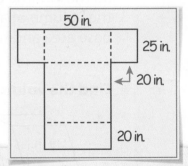

Surface Area

Daniel wants to paint the outside of the box. He will paint every surface except the bottom. How many square feet will he paint?

Add the area of the faces. Do not include the bottom face that Daniel will not paint.

> Top face: $50 \times 25 = 1{,}250$ in.^{2}
> Front and back faces: $2 \times (50 \times 20) = 2{,}000$ in.^{2}
> Side faces: $2 \times (20 \times 25) = 1{,}000$ in.^{2}

> Area is expressed in square units.

Daniel will need to paint 4,250 in.^{2}

Volume

How many cubic inches of space are inside the storage box?

> $V = l \cdot w \cdot h$
> $V = 50 \cdot 25 \cdot 20 = 25{,}000$ in.^{3}

> Volume is expressed in cubic units.

The storage box contains 25,000 in.^{3} of space.

Perimeter

Daniel wants to put a rubber strip around the lid. How many inches of rubber strip does he need?

The inside of the lid has the same width and length as the top and bottom of the storage box.

> $P = 2(l + w)$
> $P = 2(50 + 25)$
> $P = 2(75) = 150$ in.

Daniel needs 150 inches of rubber strip.

▶ Guided Problem Solving

Use the Ask Yourself questions to help you solve this problem.

1. Anna is an artist who is using clear plastic to build benches that will be completely filled with colored sand. Her art will be used in an art gallery.

   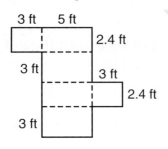

   a. How many square feet of plastic will she need to buy for each bench?

   b. Find the volume of the sand needed to fill the bench.

 Math Talk How do you decide whether you need to find the surface area or volume of a rectangular box?

▶ Independent Problem Solving

Solve. Tell whether you found perimeter, area, or volume.

2. Olivia wants to cover the top, front, back, and sides of a storage locker with fabric. The locker is 12 in. wide, 36 in. high and 36 in. deep.

   a. How much fabric does she need?

   b. How much space is inside the locker?

   c. **Analyze** Olivia wants to place a cube-shaped box inside her locker. The base of the box has a perimeter of 64 inches. Will the box fit in the locker?

3. **Multistep** Elena and her father are planning to put new wallpaper and carpet in her bedroom. The room is 10 feet long, 12 feet wide, and 8 feet high.

   a. How much carpet do they need?

   b. How much wallpaper will they need?

4. Magda wrote this expression to find the surface area in square feet of a cardboard box. $2 \times 7^2 + 4 \times (7 \times 3)$

   a. What is the surface area of the box?

   b. What is the volume of the box?

5. **Challenge** The surface area of a rectangular box is 82 ft². If the length is 7 feet and the width is 3 feet, what is the height?

6. **Create and Solve** Write and solve a problem that is about surface area or volume.

Vocabulary

You can use a **formula** to figure out the **volume** of a rectangular prism. You can create a net to figure out the **surface area** of a solid.

Tony is building a toy box for his nephew. The box is 4 ft long, 2 ft wide and 3 ft high.

1. Draw a **net** for the box.

2. What is the surface area of the box?

3. What is the volume of the box? Write the formula and the answer.

4. Tony wants to cover the bottom of the box with felt. How much felt does he need? Write the formula and the answer.

5. Tony wants to put a decorative trim around the bottom of the box. What length of trim does he need? Write the formula and the answer.

6. Tony's sister told him that she wanted the box to have a volume of 15 ft. Tony said he could not do that. Explain why he could not make a box with a volume of 15 ft.

Writing If you know the area of a square, how can you use it to find the surface area and the volume of a cube with the same length and width of the square?

Reading Check out this book in your library. *A Cloak for the Dreamer* by Aileen Friedman

CA Standards
MR 2.3 Use a variety of methods, such as words, numbers, symbols, charts, graphs, tables, diagrams, and models, to explain mathematical reasoning.

Also MG 1.0, KEY MG 1.2, KEY MG 1.3, MG 1.4

Standards-Based Extra Practice

Set A
KEY **MG 1.2** page 472

Predict whether the net forms a rectangular prism, a cube, or neither. Then copy the pattern onto grid paper, cut it out, fold it, and tape it together to check your prediction.

1.
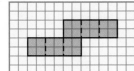

2.
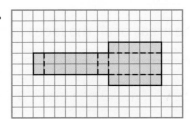

Set B
MG 2.3, MG 2.0 page 474

Draw a top view, a front view, a right side view, and a left side view of the figure on grid paper.

1.

2.

3.

Set C
KEY **MG 1.2** page 478

Predict what solid figure each net will make. Then find the surface area of the figure. Each square is 1 cm².

1.

2.
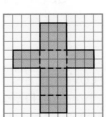

3.
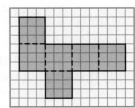

Set D
KEY **MG 1.3** page 482

Find the volume of each solid figure.

1.
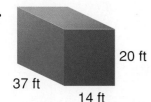
20 ft
37 ft
14 ft

2.
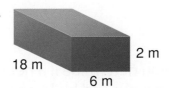
2 m
18 m
6 m

3.
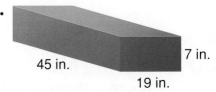
7 in.
45 in.
19 in.

Education Place
Visit www.eduplace.com/camap/ for more **Extra Practice**.

Chapter Review/Test

Vocabulary and Concepts ———————————————— KEY MG 1.2, MR 2.3

Write the best word to complete the sentence.

1. A flat pattern that can be folded to make a solid figure is
   a _____ .

2. The sum of the areas of all the faces of a solid figure is
   the _____ .

Skills ———————————————————— KEY MG 1.2, MG 1.0, KEY MG 1.3

3. Which drawing shows the left side
   view of this figure?

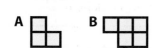

front

A ⌐⌐   B ⌐⌐⌐

4. Find the volume of the solid figure.

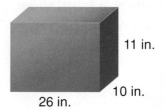

11 in.

10 in.

26 in.

Problem Solving and Reasoning ———————————— KEY MG 1.2, MR 2.3

Solve.

5. Mr. Daniels is using self-adhesive paper to cover all 6 sides of
   a cube. The cube measures 7 inches on each edge. Draw a net
   for the cube. Then find the surface area Mr. Daniels needs
   to cover.

Writing Math How can you determine if a net will work for
a figure without actually cutting it out and building it?

Spiral Review and Test Practice

1. What is the surface area of the box formed by the pattern below?

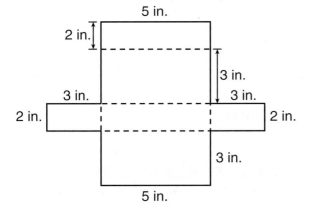

A 50 in.^{2}

B 52 in.^{2}

C 60 in.^{2}

D 62 in.^{2}

> **Test Tip**
> Make an organized list to solve this problem.

KEY **MG 1.2** page 478

2. Which of the following is another way to write the product of 7×25?

A $7 \times 2 \times 5$

B $7 \times 4 \times 6$

C $7 \times 5 \times 5$

D $7 \times 20 \times 5$

KEY **NS 1.4** page 12

3. A section of a circle graph represents 9 votes for a field trip to the art museum. How many votes does a section three times the size of the art museum section represent?

A 3 votes

B 9 votes

C 12 votes

D 27 votes

SDAP **1.2** page 350

4. What is the perimeter of this complex figure?

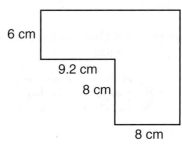

A 31.2 cm

B 55.2 cm

C 62.4 cm

D 167.2 cm^2

> **Test Tip**
> Do the calculations twice to make sure you choose the correct answer.

MG 1.4, KEY **NS 2.1** page 436

Unit 9 Review/Test

Vocabulary and Concepts —————————— KEY **MG 1.2**, MG 2.3, MR 2.3 Chapters 21–22

Choose the best term to complete each sentence.

1. _____ is the measure of the amount of space a solid figure occupies.

2. A _____ is a solid figure with six rectangular faces.

3. _____ is the sum of the areas of all the faces, or surfaces, of a solid figure.

Skills ————————————— KEY **MG 1.1**, KEY **MG 1.2**, KEY **MG 1.3** Chapter 21, Lessons 2–4

Find the area of the figure.

4.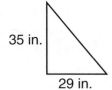
35 in.
29 in.

5.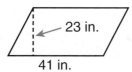
23 in.
41 in.

6.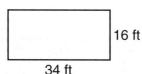
16 ft
34 ft

7.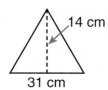
14 cm
31 cm

Use the net to find the surface area of the solid figure. Chapter 22, Lesson 3

8.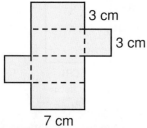
3 cm
3 cm
7 cm

9.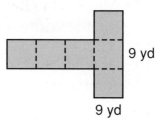
9 yd
9 yd

Find the volume of the solid figure. Chapter 22, Lesson 4

10.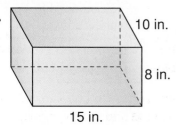
10 in.
8 in.
15 in.

11.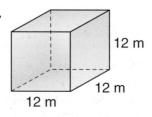
12 m
12 m
12 m

Problem Solving and Reasoning —————— KEY **MG 1.2**, MG 1.4, MR 2.3 Chapters 21–22

Solve. Draw pictures to help find the solutions.

12. Lizzie has a 4 in. × 5 in. photo. She wants to make the length and width 4 times larger. How many times larger will the area of the new picture be?

13. Saba wants to sew a cover for a pillow in the shape of a rectangular prism. If the pillow is 24 inches long, 4 inches wide, and 5 inches high, what is the surface area?

Solve.

14. Mark wants to build a wood frame for a 2 ft by 3 ft oil painting using wood molding. How many inches of molding will he need?

15. What is the area of a triangular rug with a height of 8 feet, and a length of 10 feet?

Writing Math What is the difference between finding the surface area and finding the volume of a rectangular prism?

Performance Assessment

Main Attraction   MG 1.4, MR 1.1

You won a contest to design a family amusement park on about an acre of town land. You decide what to include, and you determine the measurements for each section.

The drawing to the right shows the beginning of Sara's park.

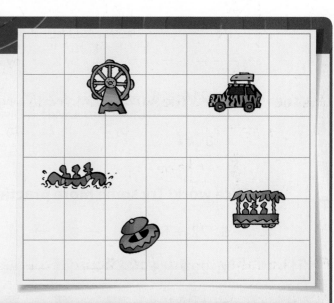

Task	Information You Need
Use the information to the right to create a design for your amusement park. Sketch your plan on grid paper. Find the area and perimeter of the park. Decide how much of the area you will use for each section of the park. Explain your thinking.	The land you have available measures 40 yd x 80 yd.
	Think about including rides, a refreshment area, an entertainment area with a stage and seating, and a souvenir shop.
	Include at least four different types of polygon shapes for your park sections. Be creative!
	Label the dimensions for each section of the park. Include area and perimeter of each section.

Greg Tang's Go Fast, Go Far

Unit 9 Mental Math Strategies

Divide by 8

It's easy to divide by 8. Half three times will work just great!

I have a fast way to do 48 ÷ 8. I take half of 48 which is 24, then half of 24 which is 12, and finally half of 12 which is 6. Dividing by 2 three times is the same as dividing by 8 all at once!

1. 48 ÷ 8 → ⟦24⟧ → ⟦12⟧ → ⟦6⟧
  Divide 48 Divide Divide
  by 2. by 2. by 2.

2. 104 ÷ 8 → ⟦52⟧ → ⟦26⟧ → ▢
  Divide 104 Divide Divide
  by 2. by 2. by 2.

3. 216 ÷ 8 → ▢ → ▢ → ▢
  Divide 216 Divide Divide
  by 2. by 2. by 2.

4. 328 ÷ 8 → ▢ → ▢ → ▢
  Divide 328 Divide Divide
  by 2. by 2. by 2.

Nice work! Try some more practice!

5. 72 ÷ 8 → ▢ → ▢ → ▢

6. 96 ÷ 8 → ▢ → ▢ → ▢

7. 224 ÷ 8 → ▢ → ▢ → ▢

8. 304 ÷ 8 → ▢ → ▢ → ▢

9. 112 ÷ 8 → ▢ → ▢ → ▢

10. 176 ÷ 8 → ▢ → ▢ → ▢

Good For You!

Take It Further!
Now try doing all the steps in your head!

11. 64 ÷ 8

12. 128 ÷ 8

13. 352 ÷ 8

14. 840 ÷ 8

Unit

Percent

BIG IDEAS!

- Percent is another way to write a fraction or a decimal.

- You can use percent to compare data sets or find a part of a number.

Chapter 23
Understand Percent

Chapter 24
Use Percent

Songs and Games

Math Music Track 10: *Are They Equivalent?*

eGames at
www.eduplace.com/camap/

Math Readers

Game

Fraction and Decimal Concentration

Object of the Game Match models of fraction and decimal equivalents.

Materials
- Learning Tool 28: Fraction-Decimal Concentration

Set Up
Players shuffle the game cards and lay them face down in a 5 by 6 array.

Number of Players 2

How to Play

1 Shuffle the game cards and lay them face down in a 5 by 6 array.

2 Players take turns turning over three cards.

3 If all three cards show the same value, the player keeps the cards. If the values do not match, the cards are turned face down.

4 Play continues until all the cards have been matched. The player with the greatest number of matches wins.

CA Standards
KEY NS 1.2 Interpret percents as a part of a hundred; find decimal and percent equivalents for common fractions and explain why they represent the same value; compute a given percent of a whole number.

Also MR 1.1

 Education Place
Visit www.eduplace.com/camap/ for **Brain Teasers** and **eGames** to play.

Reading You use strategies to help you in reading. You also use strategies to help you solve word problems.

In this unit you will solve problems involving fractions, decimals, and percents. You can use strategies to help you solve problems in this unit.

Read this problem:

Andrew rode his bike $2\frac{3}{10}$ miles to get to Ernie's Game Store.

His friend Xavier rode 2.25 miles. Who rode farther?

Before he solves the problem, Juan writes down problem-solving strategies that he knows.

Hmmm. I need to compare $2\frac{3}{10}$ with 2.25.

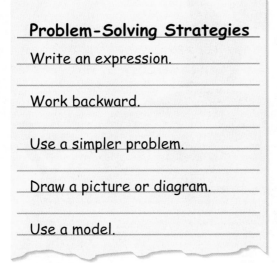

Problem-Solving Strategies

Write an expression.

Work backward.

Use a simpler problem.

Draw a picture or diagram.

Use a model.

Writing Copy the strategies Juan wrote down and add other strategies you know. Then use one of the strategies to solve the problem.

Chapter 23

Understand Percent

Ten-pin bowling: What percent of the pins fell if your score is 8?

Vocabulary and Concepts NS 1.0, MR 2.3

Match each word with a definition. pages 28 and 54

1. fraction
2. decimal
3. mixed number

a. a number with one or more digits to the right of the decimal point

b. a number made up of a whole number and a fraction

c. a number that names a part of a whole, a part of a collection, or a part of a region

Skills NS 1.0

Compare. Write >, <, or = for each 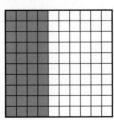 **.** page 82

4. $\frac{3}{5}$ ⬭ 0.5

5. $\frac{1}{4}$ ⬭ 0.75

6. $\frac{3}{10}$ ⬭ 0.03

7. $\frac{4}{25}$ ⬭ 0.25

8. $\frac{7}{50}$ ⬭ 0.14

9. $\frac{2}{5}$ ⬭ 0.2

Problem Solving and Reasoning page 210 NS 1.0

10. One tenth of the players in a basketball league are left-handed. There are 200 players in the league. How many players in the league are left-handed?

Vocabulary

Visualize It!

percent

means "per hundred"

A percent compares a number to 100.

40 of the square units are blue

$$40\% = \frac{40}{100}$$

Language Tip

Math words that look alike in English and Spanish often have the same meaning.

English	Spanish
fraction	fracción
percent	por ciento

See **English-Spanish Glossary** pages 628–642.

Education Place Visit www.eduplace.com/camap/ for the **eGlossary** and **eGames**.

CA Standards MR 2.3 Use a variety of methods, such as words, numbers, symbols, charts, graphs, tables, diagrams, and models, to explain mathematical reasoning. **Also KEY NS 1.2**

Chapter 23   499

CA Standards
KEY NS 1.2 Interpret percents as part of a hundred; find decimal and percent equivalents for common fractions and explain why they represent the same value; compute a given percent of a whole number.

MR 2.3 Use a variety of methods, such as words, numbers, symbols, charts, graphs, tables, diagrams, and models, to explain mathematical reasoning.

Also NS 1.0, MR 2.4

Vocabulary

percent

Materials
- Learning Tool 29 (10 × 10 grid)
- Colored pencils or markers (blue, yellow, green)

Hint
The symbol for percent is %.

Hands On
Model Percent

Objective Explore modeling percents as parts per hundred.

▶ **Explore**

A **percent** compares a number to 100. The word *percent* means "per hundred." So *ten percent* means "ten per hundred," or "ten out of 100." Percents can also be shown in fraction or decimal form.

Question How can you model percents?

Danielle has a collection of 100 game board counters. There are 40 blue counters, 25 yellow counters, and 15 green counters. Model the collection of game board counters on a 10 × 10 grid. Then write each color as a percent, decimal, and fraction of the collection.

① Shade 40 square units blue, 25 square units yellow, and 15 square units green on the 10 × 10 grid.

There are 100 square units total.

② Write each color as a percent of the grid.

blue: 40%   yellow: 25%   green: 15%

③ Write each percent as a decimal.

blue: 0.40   yellow: 0.25   green: 0.15

④ Write each color as a fraction of the grid. Reduce the fractions to simplest form.

blue: $\frac{40}{100} = \frac{2}{5}$

yellow: $\frac{25}{100} = \frac{1}{4}$

green: $\frac{15}{100} = \frac{3}{20}$

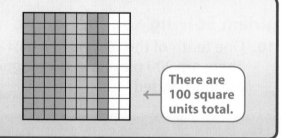

▶ **Extend**

Write the percent of the grid that is shaded. Then write a decimal and a fraction in simplest form for the shaded part.

1.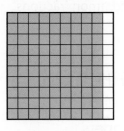

2.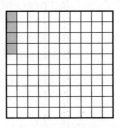

3.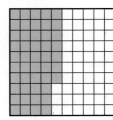

4.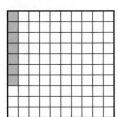

5.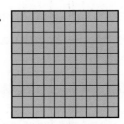

6.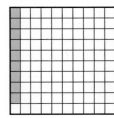

7.

8.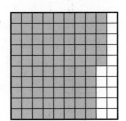

9.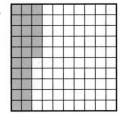

Copy and complete the table. Write the fractions in simplest form.

10.

Decimal Form	Fraction Form	Percent
		50%
0.70		
		38%
0.01		

11.

Decimal Form	Fraction Form	Percent
		6%
0.52		
		22%
0.60		

Math Journal

Writing Math

Use models to show how 9% and 90% are different. Which model shows the decimal 0.9? Which model shows the decimal 0.09?

CA Standards
KEY **NS 1.2** Interpret percents as part of a hundred; find decimal and percent equivalents for common fractions and explain why they represent the same value; compute a given percent of a whole number.

MR 2.3 Use a variety of methods, such as words, numbers, symbols, charts, graphs, tables, diagrams, and models to explain mathematical reasoning.

Also NS 1.0, MR 2.0, MR 2.4, KEY AF 1.2

Materials
Learning Tool 10
(centimeter grid)

Relate Percents to Fractions and Decimals

Objective Find decimal and percent equivalents for common fractions.

▶ Learn by Example

In Lesson 1, you wrote percents as fractions. In this lesson, you will write fractions as percents.

Ernie's Game Store took a survey of 50 shoppers. Thirty shoppers said that their family owns or rents video games. How can you write $\frac{30}{50}$ as a percent?

Different Ways to Write Fractions as Percents

Way 1 Use equivalent fractions.

1 Write the fraction with a denominator of 100.

$$\frac{30}{50} \overset{\times 2}{\underset{\times 2}{=}} \frac{60}{100}$$

2 Write as a percent.

$$\frac{60}{100} = 60\%$$

Way 2 Use division.

1 Divide the numerator by the denominator to find the decimal.

$$\frac{30}{50} \longrightarrow 50\overline{)30.0}^{\,0.6}$$

Add a zero in the dividend.

2 Write the decimal as a percent.

$$0.6 = 0.60 = 60\%$$

Solution: $\frac{30}{50}$ can be written as 60%.

Another Example

Sometimes you must use division to find the equivalent percent.

Write $\frac{3}{8}$ as a percent.

$$\frac{3}{8} \longrightarrow \begin{array}{r} 0.375 \\ 8\overline{)3.000} \\ -\,2\,4 \\ \hline 0\,60 \\ -\,56 \\ \hline 40 \\ -\,40 \\ \hline 0 \end{array}$$

100 is not a multiple of 8. So use division to find the percent.

$\frac{3}{8} = 37.5\,\%$

$$\frac{375}{1{,}000} \overset{\div 10}{\underset{\div 10}{=}} \frac{37.5}{100}$$

► Guided Practice

Find the equivalent percent.

1. $\frac{10}{25}$ 2. $\frac{28}{50}$ 3. $\frac{7}{10}$ 4. $\frac{6}{20}$

5. $\frac{35}{100}$ 6. $\frac{14}{50}$ 7. $\frac{4}{20}$ 8. $\frac{1}{8}$

 Math Talk Which way would you use to write $\frac{1}{8}$ as a percent? Explain your choice.

Ask Yourself

- Can I write an equivalent fraction with a denominator of 100?
- When I divide, do I need to add zeros in the dividend?

► Practice and Problem Solving

Find the equivalent percent.

9. $\frac{6}{25}$ 10. $\frac{8}{10}$ 11. $\frac{30}{50}$ 12. $\frac{7}{8}$ 13. $\frac{2}{20}$

14. $\frac{75}{100}$ 15. $\frac{5}{10}$ 16. $\frac{25}{25}$ 17. $\frac{1}{2}$ 18. $\frac{4}{5}$

19. $\frac{3}{4}$ 20. $\frac{12}{50}$ 21. $\frac{5}{8}$ 22. $\frac{17}{20}$ 23. $\frac{13}{100}$

✗ Algebra Equations
Solve each equation for n.

24. $\frac{25}{100} = \frac{1}{n}$ 25. $\frac{9}{25} = \frac{n}{100}$ 26. $n\% = \frac{7}{20}$ 27. $\frac{23}{50} = n\%$

28. $\frac{20}{100} = \frac{1}{n}$ 29. $\frac{7}{50} = \frac{n}{100}$ 30. $n\% = \frac{13}{25}$ 31. $\frac{12}{40} = n\%$

Solve.

32. Gabi and her brother played checkers after school. Gabi won 3 games. Her brother won 1 game. Write a percent for the number of games each sibling won.

33. Thomas has completed 35 of the 50 squares on a crossword puzzle. What fraction of the squares has he completed? What percent of the puzzle has he completed?

34. Look at the model.

Write the fraction as a percent of the whole.

35. Caitlin took 5 shots on goal during a hockey game. Only one of her shots went into the net. What percent of her shots resulted in goals?

 Real World Data

In a survey, 50 fifth-grade students were asked to name their favorite sport. Use the table to solve problems 36–39.

Favorite Sport	Number of Students
Baseball	25
Soccer	15
Basketball	5
Volleyball	5

36. What percent of students chose baseball as their favorite sport?

37. What decimal can be used to represent the number of students that chose soccer as their favorite sport?

38. What fraction with a denominator of 100 can be used to represent the number of students that chose basketball as their favorite sport?

39. There are 20 students on the fifth-grade soccer team. Nine of them are girls. What percent of the students who are playing soccer are boys? Explain.

 Spiral Review and Test Practice

Write using exponents. Then write the value of the expression. NS 1.3 page 14

40. 4×4

41. $3 \times 3 \times 3$

42. $2 \times 2 \times 2 \times 2$

Write the letter of the correct answer. KEY NS 1.2

43. What is $\frac{5}{8}$ written as a percent?

   A 16%   **B** 58%   **C** 62.5%   **D** 65.2%

Extra Practice See page 515, Set A.

Use what you know about perpendicular, parallel, and congruent line segments to answer each question. KEY **MG 2.1**

1. What kinds of angles are created where two perpendicular lines intersect?

2. What do you know about two lines that are perpendicular to the same line?

3. An equilateral triangle is made up of how many congruent sides?

Use a compass and straightedge to construct each figure. KEY **MG 2.1**

4. Construct triangle *ABC* congruent to triangle *DEF*.

5. Construct rectangle *STUV* congruent to rectangle *MNOP*.

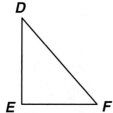

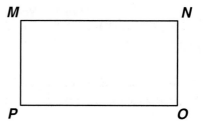

 **Number Sense**

Percent Logic KEY **NS 1.2**

The students at a school took a survey of their favorite day of the school week. Use the graph to answer each question.

1. What percent does the entire circle graph represent?

2. What percent of the students chose Tuesday as their favorite school day?

3. What days did exactly half of the students choose as their favorite school day?

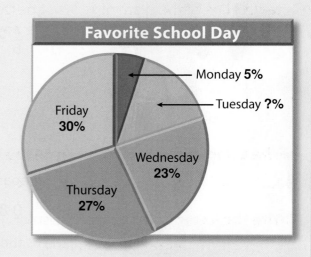

Favorite School Day

Monday 5%
Tuesday ?%
Friday 30%
Wednesday 23%
Thursday 27%

Compare and Order Fractions, Decimals, and Percents

Objective Compare and order fractions, decimals, and percents.

▶ **Learn by Example**

In this lesson, you will learn how to compare and order fractions, decimals, and percents.

On the first of the month, Freddie's Toy Shop had equal numbers of red, blue, and green remote control cars. By the end of the month, $\frac{4}{5}$ of the red, 27% of the blue, and 0.7 of the green cars had been sold. Which color was the most popular for remote control cars that month?

Different Ways to Order

Way 1 **You can use a number line.**

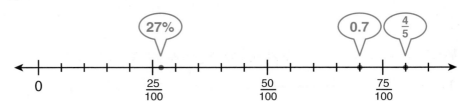

$\frac{4}{5}$ is farthest to the right. $\frac{4}{5} > 0.7 > 27\%$

....

Way 2 **You can rewrite each in decimal form.**

$$\frac{4}{5} = \frac{4}{5} \xrightarrow{\times 20} = \frac{80}{100} = 0.80$$

$$27\% = \frac{27}{100} = 0.27$$

$$0.7 = 0.70$$

Compare 0.80, 0.27, and 0.70.

$$0.80 > 0.70 > 0.27$$

$\frac{4}{5}$ is the greatest number. $\frac{4}{5} > 0.7 > 27\%$

Solution: Red was the most popular remote control car color.

Find the greatest amount.

1. 0.4 $\frac{1}{2}$ 30%

2. $\frac{1}{5}$ 30%   0.25

Find the least amount.

3. $\frac{2}{5}$ 45%   0.19

4. $\frac{9}{20}$ 66%   0.7

 Math Talk How could you write $\frac{9}{20}$ in decimal form by first writing it as a fraction with a denominator of 100?

▶ **Practice and Problem Solving**

Find the greatest amount.

5. $\frac{3}{5}$ 59%   0.62

6. $\frac{3}{8}$ 9%   0.8

7. $\frac{11}{25}$ 0.4   43%

Find the least amount.

8. $\frac{4}{5}$ 0.2   60%

9. $\frac{3}{5}$ 0.4   80%

10. $\frac{4}{5}$ 0.9   85%

Write the numbers in order from greatest to least.

11. $\frac{1}{5}$ 0.1   25%

12. $\frac{3}{20}$ 4%   0.06

13. $\frac{7}{10}$ 0.6   30%

Solve.

14. Write a fraction in simplest form that will make this number sentence true: 42% < ▨ < 0.45

✔ **Spiral Review and Test Practice**

Find the area of the triangle.   MG 1.0, KEY **MG 1.1**, MG 1.4 page 460

15.
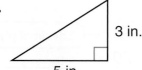
3 in.
5 in.

16.
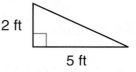
2 ft
5 ft

17.
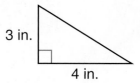
3 in.
4 in.

Write the letter of the correct answer.   KEY **NS 1.2**

18. Which set of numbers is ordered from greatest to least?

A $\frac{11}{20}$ 0.6   0.62

B $\frac{6}{25}$ 0.2   17%

C $\frac{1}{10}$ 0.08   20%

D $\frac{1}{2}$ 0.51   49%

Extra Practice See page 515, Set B.

Chapter 23 **Lesson 3**   **507**

Ask Yourself

- Did I write the numbers in the same form?
- Did I check the order to see if it's reasonable?

CA Standards

KEY NS 1.2 Interpret percents as part of a hundred; find decimal and percent equivalents for common fractions and explain why they represent the same value; compute a given percent of a whole number.

MR 3.2 Note the method of deriving the solution and demonstrate a conceptual understanding of the derivation by solving similar problems.

Also KEY NS 1.5, KEY NS 2.1, NS 2.4, SDAP 1.3

Percent of a Number

Objective Find a percent of a number.

▶ **Learn by Example**

Percent is another way of showing a part of a whole. You can use what you know about multiplying fractions and decimals to find a percent of a number.

The Huntington Beach Kite Party is held every February in Huntington Beach, CA. There are 20 kites entered in one category. If 60% of them are red, how many kites are red in that category?

Different Ways to Find a Percent of a Number

Way 1 **You can write the percent as a fraction and multiply.**

1 Write the percent as a fraction.

$$60\% = \frac{60}{100}$$
$$= \frac{3}{5}$$

2 Multiply.

$$\frac{3}{5} \times 20 = \frac{3 \times 20}{5 \times 1}$$
$$= \frac{60}{5}$$
$$= 12$$

12 is 60% of 20.

Way 2 **You can write the percent in decimal form and multiply.**

1 Write the percent in decimal form.

$$60\% = 60 \text{ hundredths}$$
$$= 0.60$$
$$= 0.6$$

2 Multiply.

$$0.60 \leftarrow \text{2 decimal places}$$
$$\underline{\times\ 20}$$
$$12.00 \leftarrow \text{2 decimal places}$$

$$20 \times 0.6 = 12$$
12 is 60% of 20

Solution: There are 12 red kites.

▶ Guided Practice

Evaluate by writing the percent as a fraction.

1. 35% of 60

2. 80% of 45

3. 5% of 40

4. 12% of 25

Evaluate by writing the percent as a decimal.

5. 40% of 55

6. 75% of 10

7. 16% of 50

8. 15% of 90

Ask Yourself
- Did I write the percent as a fraction?
- Did I write the percent as a decimal?

Guided Problem Solving

Use the questions to solve this problem.

9. There are 25 students in Mrs. Chen's class. On Monday, 32 percent of the class brought their lunch to school. How many students brought their lunch?

   a. **Understand** What are you asked to find out? Do you think your answer will be greater or less than 25? Explain.

   b. **Plan** Decide whether to write 32% as a fraction or decimal.

   c. **Solve** Use your plan to solve the problem. How many students brought their lunch?

   d. **Look Back** Is your answer greater or less than 25? Solve your problem in a different way. Did you get the same answer?

123 Math Talk What is 28% of 66? Explain how you found your answer.

▶ Practice and Problem Solving

Evaluate by writing the percent as a fraction.

10. 65% of 80

11. 70% of 20

12. 25% of 40

13. 15% of 120

14. 50% of 50

15. 10% of 80

16. 25% of 48

17. 20% of 45

Evaluate by writing the percent as a decimal.

18. 90% of 15   **19.** 30% of 35   **20.** 16% of 25   **21.** 28% of 25

 ## Science Link

Solve.

22. A grown great white has about 3,000 teeth in several rows. If about 10% of these are in the front row, about how many teeth are in the front row? Show your work.

23. Suppose a great white shark has 250 teeth in its front row. If it loses 2% of those teeth in one week, how many teeth did it lose that week?

24. Challenge A great white loses teeth and grows new teeth. If a shark lost 240 of its 3,000 teeth in one year, what percent of teeth did it lose?

Great White Sharks

- As with many other animals, the teeth are the first step in a great white shark's digestive system.

- Great white sharks have rows of sharp teeth for shredding their prey.

- Sometimes the sharks swallow things they can't digest. Scientists once even found a cuckoo clock in a great white's stomach.

Science LS 2.c

Spiral Review and Test Practice

Find the volume of the solid figure. MG 1.0, KEY MG 1.3, MG 1.4 page 482

25.
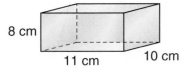
8 cm, 11 cm, 10 cm

26.
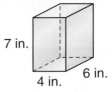
7 in., 4 in., 6 in.

27.
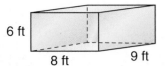
6 ft, 8 ft, 9 ft

28.
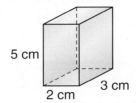
5 cm, 2 cm, 3 cm

Write the letter of the correct answer. KEY NS 1.2

29. What is 25% of 80?

     A 2   **B** 20   **C** 25   **D** 80

     Extra Practice See page 515, Set C.

Plan an Exhibit

Paintings are hung in a museum or gallery in a way that pleases the eye and showcases the artwork best. Curators are in charge of exhibits and must make maximum use of the space available.

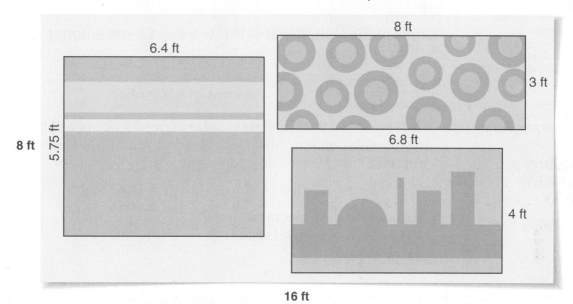

Use the measurements of the art exhibit above to solve.

1. What is the area of the wall space shown?

2. What is the total area of the space covered by all the art pieces?

3. What percent of the total wall is this?

4. What percent of the total wall is not covered by the art?

CA Standards
KEY NS 1.2, KEY NS 2.1,
MG 1.0, MG 1.4, MR 2.4

CA Standards

KEY **NS 1.2** Interpret percents as a part of a hundred; find decimal and percent equivalents for common fractions and explain why they represent the same value; compute a given percent of a whole number.

MR 2.6 Make precise calculations and check the validity of the results from the context of the problem.

Also KEY **NS 2.1**, **AF 1.1**, **KEY** **AF 1.2**, **MR 1.1**, **MR 2.3**, **MR 2.4**

Problem Solving Plan
Percent Problems

Objective Solve problems with percents.

▶ **Learn Through Reasoning**

People in the United States throw away a large amount of trash every day.

Percent of a Number

Each person in the U.S. throws away about 4.5 pounds of trash each day. Twelve percent of the trash is food scraps. About how many pounds of food scraps do people throw away every day?

What number is 12% of 4.5?

Each person throws away about 0.54 pounds of food scraps a day.

$$n = 0.12 \times 4.5$$
$$n = 0.54$$

$$\begin{array}{r} 0.12 \\ \times\ 4.5 \\ \hline 60 \\ 480 \\ \hline 0.540 \end{array}$$

Unknown Percent

About 1.53 pounds of the 4.5 pounds of trash thrown away daily is paper. What percent of trash is paper?

What percent of 4.5 is 1.53?

0.34 = 34%, so 34% of a person's daily trash is paper.

$$4.5 \times n = 1.53$$

To find n, divide 1.53 by 4.5.

$$\begin{array}{r} 0.34 \\ 4.5\overline{)1.530} \\ -1\,35 \\ \hline 180 \\ -180 \\ \hline 0 \end{array}$$

Unknown Total

Every year, each person in the U.S. throws away about 75 pounds of trash that is glass. That is 5% of the total yearly trash. About how many pounds of trash does a person throw away in one year?

5% of what number equals 75?

Each person throws away about 1,500 pounds of trash each year.

$$0.05 \times n = 75$$

To find n, divide 75 by 0.05.

$$\begin{array}{r} 1500 \\ 0.05\overline{)75.00} \\ -5 \\ \hline 25 \\ -25 \\ \hline 0 \end{array}$$

▶ **Guided Problem Solving**

Use the Ask Yourself questions to help you solve this problem.

1. There are 18 students in Jay's class who know how to play chess. That number is 50% of the students in the class. How many students are in Jay's class?

 Math Talk Delma thinks the answer to Problem 1 is 9 students. Explain why her answer is not reasonable.

Ask Yourself
- Will my answer be a percent or a number?
- What number sentence describes the problem?

▶ **Independent Problem Solving**

Solve. Explain why your answer makes sense.

2. Some students like to play word games. In one game, the challenge was to make words with 3 or more letters using the letters given.

   a. Out of the 20 words made, 45% were 3-letter words. How many were 3-letter words?

   b. Three of the 20 words had 5 letters. What percent were 5-letter words?

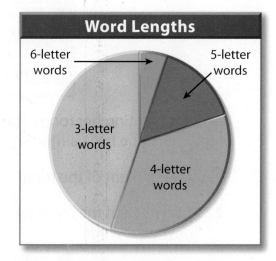

Word Lengths

6-letter words

5-letter words

3-letter words

4-letter words

3. Game Board Gala sells a wide variety of board games. Sixty-five percent of the 20 games sold last week were chess games. How many chess games were sold?

4. In one of Pete's computer games, he scored 245 points or 14% of the total points needed to get to the next level. What is the total number of points needed to get to the next level?

5. **Challenge** Andrea played a word game like the one in Problem 2 using the letters E E T L S F. In her game, there were 30 possible words. Fifty percent of them were 4-letter words. There was one 6-letter word. The number of 3-letter words was 2 more than the number of 5-letter words. What was the percent of 3-letter words and 5-letter words if there were only 3-, 4-, 5-, and 6-letter words?

6. **Create and Solve** Write a percent problem about a game you play.

Reading & Writing **Math**

Vocabulary

A **percent** compares a number to 100. Percents can also be written in fraction or decimal form.

10 ×10 Grid

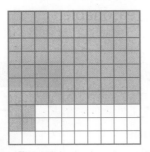

Harriet is painting her room. The model above shows how much of the room she has painted so far.

1. What percent of the room has been painted?

2. How much of the room has not yet been painted? Show your work.

3. Draw a new model that shows how much of the room has not been painted.

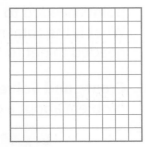

Writing Harriet wants to show the percent of the room she has painted as a fraction. Write a paragraph that tells her how.

Reading Look for this book in your library.
Piece = Part = Portion, by Scott Gifford.

CA Standards

MR 2.3 Use a variety of methods, such as words, numbers, symbols, charts, graphs, tables, diagrams, and models, to explain mathematical reasoning.

Also KEY NS 1.2

Standards-Based Extra Practice

Set A ———————————————————————————————— KEY **NS 1.2** page 502

Find the equivalent percent.

1. $\frac{15}{25}$ 2. $\frac{25}{50}$ 3. $\frac{14}{20}$ 4. $\frac{45}{50}$

5. $\frac{5}{8}$ 6. $\frac{8}{20}$ 7. $\frac{17}{25}$ 8. $\frac{1}{5}$

9. The principal of a school conducted a survey about students' favorite lunch. The results show that $\frac{21}{25}$ of the students prefer pizza. What is $\frac{21}{25}$ as a percent?

Set B ———————————————————————————————— KEY **NS 1.2** page 506

Find the greatest amount.

1. $\frac{3}{5}$ 25% 0.21   2. $\frac{19}{25}$ 50% 0.85   3. $\frac{8}{25}$ 0.42 75%   4. $\frac{20}{50}$ 48% 0.73

Find the least amount.

5. $\frac{2}{5}$ 34% 0.78   6. $\frac{40}{100}$ 0.42 45%   7. $\frac{5}{100}$ 0.65 90%   8. $\frac{5}{5}$ 90% 0.34

9. Lemonade and sparkling water were sold at the school fair. Two fifths of the sales were lemonade and 60% were sparkling water. Which drink was more popular?

Set C ———————————————————————————————— KEY **NS 1.2** page 508

Evaluate by writing the percent as a fraction.

1. 12% of 50   2. 80% of 25   3. 30% of 95   4. 25% of 50

5. 20% of 85   6. 60% of 20   7. 72% of 80   8. 40% of 50

Evaluate by writing the percent as a decimal.

9. 20% of 50   10. 40% of 85   11. 75% of 90   12. 60% of 100

13. 35% of 95   14. 62% of 48   15. 86% of 50   16. 24% of 50

17. There are 28 students in Terry's class. Twenty-five percent of the students brought their lunch to school on Monday. How many students brought their lunch?

Education Place
Visit www.eduplace.com/camap/
for more **Extra Practice**.

Chapter 23 Extra Practice   **515**

Chapter Review/Test

Vocabulary and Concepts ——————————————— KEY NS 1.2, MR 2.3

Choose the best word to complete the sentence.

1. The word _____ means "per hundred."

2. A number with a decimal point in it is a _____ .

Skills ————————————————————————— KEY NS 1.2, NS 1.0

Write the percent of the grid that is shaded. Then write a decimal and a fraction in simplest form for the shaded part.

3.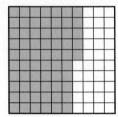

4.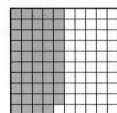

Find the equivalent percent.

5. $\dfrac{15}{50}$ 6. $\dfrac{17}{100}$ 7. $\dfrac{5}{80}$ 8. $\dfrac{8}{20}$

Find the greatest amount.

9. $\dfrac{2}{5}$ 20% 0.15 10. $\dfrac{4}{10}$ 0.51 15% 11. 0.39 $\dfrac{7}{25}$ 35% 12. $\dfrac{10}{100}$ 12% 0.20

Evaluate by writing the percent as a fraction.

13. 20% of 40 14. 10% of 55 15. 30% of 80 16. 5% of 45

Problem Solving and Reasoning ——————— KEY NS 1.2, MR 1.1, MR 2.3

Solve.

17. Forty percent of the 30 bikes that were sold last week were red. How many red bikes were sold?

18. Seventy-two of the 96 fifth-graders in Beekman School like art. What percent of the fifth-graders like art?

19. Members of a sports club were surveyed. Two fifths of the members preferred soccer, and 30% preferred baseball. Which sport was more popular?

20. Your favorite game is on sale for 30% off. The original price is $50. How much will you save by buying it on sale?

Writing Math What is 45% of 80? Explain which method you used.

Spiral Review and Test Practice

1. An electronics store sold 447 picture phones for $68 each. How much was paid for the picture phones in all?

A $515

B $6,258

C $28,376

D $30,396

NS 1.0, MR 1.1 page 240

2. Which fraction represents the largest part of a whole?

A $\frac{1}{10}$

B $\frac{1}{6}$

C $\frac{1}{3}$

D $\frac{1}{8}$

KEY **NS 1.2** page 38

3. What is $\frac{7}{8}$ written as a percent?

A 12.5%

B 78 %

C 87 %

D 87.5%

KEY **NS 1.2** page 502

4. What is the area of the triangle?

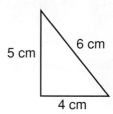

A 15 cm^2

B 10 cm^2

C 20 cm^2

D 40 cm^2

> **Test Tip**
> Decide what information you need and do not need to solve the problem.

KEY **MG 1.1** page 460

5. This rectangular prism has a length of 13 feet, a width of 6 feet, and a height of 2 feet. What is the volume?

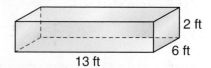

A 21 cu ft

B 26 cu ft

C 78 cu ft

D 156 cu ft

KEY **MG 1.3**, MG 1.4 page 482

Education Place
Visit www.eduplace.com/camap/ for
Test-Taking Tips and **Extra Practice.**

Use Percent

Chapter
24

Check What You Know

Word Bank

circle graph

denominator

tenths

percent

Vocabulary and Concepts KEY NS 1.2, MR 2.3

Choose the best term to complete each sentence. pages 500, 502

1. A ____ compares a number to 100.

2. You read 0.9 as nine ____ .

3. A ____ shows parts of a whole.

Skills KEY NS 1.2

Find the percent by finding an equivalent fraction or dividing the numerator by the denominator. page 502

4. $\dfrac{3}{6}$

5. $\dfrac{7}{10}$

6. $\dfrac{20}{50}$

7. $\dfrac{8}{8}$

8. $\dfrac{4}{40}$

9. $\dfrac{25}{100}$

Problem Solving and Reasoning KEY NS 1.2

10. Twenty-five percent of the students in a survey chose fishing as their favorite summer activity. If 60 students were in the survey, how many chose fishing?

Vocabulary

Visualize It!

thirty-five percent

Model	Percent	Fraction
	35%	$\dfrac{35}{100}$

Language Tip

Math words that look alike in English and Spanish often have the same meaning.

English	Spanish
compare	comparar
graph	gráfica

See **English-Spanish Glossary** pages 628–642.

Education Place Visit www.eduplace.com/camap/ for the **eGlossary** and **eGames**.

CA Standards MR 2.3 Use a variety of methods, such as words, numbers, symbols, charts, graphs, tables, diagrams, and models, to explain mathematical reasoning. **Also KEY NS 1.2, SDAP 1.3**

Chapter 24 519

CA Standards
KEY NS 1.2 Interpret percents as a part of a hundred; find decimal and percent equivalents for common fractions and explain why they represent the same value; compute the given percent of a number.

SDAP 1.2 Organize and display single-variable data in appropriate graphs and representations (e.g. histograms, circle graphs) and explain which types of graphs are appropriate for various data sets.

Also NS 1.0, KEY NS 2.1, KEY MG 2.1, SDAP 1.0, MR 1.0, MR 2.0, MR 2.1, MR 2.3, MR 2.4, MR 3.0, MR 3.3

Vocabulary

circle graph

Materials
• Compass
• Protractor

Think

You can use fractions instead of decimals.

$0.5 = \frac{1}{2}, 0.10 = \frac{1}{10},$

$0.4 = \frac{2}{5}$

Hands On
Make a Circle Graph

Objective Use the concept of percent to make a circle graph.

▶ **Explore**

You will use your understanding of percents to make a **circle graph** that represents data as part of a whole.

Question How can you show the data in the table in a circle graph?

Payments for Purchases	
Method of Payment	**Percent of Customers**
Cash	50%
Check	10%
Credit/Debit Card	40%

1 Find the number of degrees for each section of the circle graph. Multiply each percent by 360° because there are 360° in a circle.

Cash	Check	Credit/Debit
360	360	360
× 0.5	× 0.1	× 0.4
180.0	36.0	144.0

50% of 360° = 180°   10% of 360° = 36°   40% of 360° = 144°

2 Use a compass to draw a circle. Mark the center of the circle with a point. Divide the circle into two equal parts and label one half **Cash**.

3 Use a protractor to draw a 36° angle in the blank half of the circle. Label the section **Check**.

The remaining section measures 144°. You can use your protractor to check the measure. Label the section **Credit/Debit Card**.

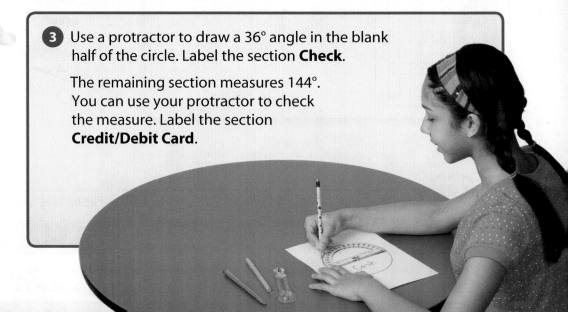

▶ **Extend**

The table shows the results of a survey of 560 shoppers. Use the table for Problems 1–4.

Buying Sneakers	
Type of Store	**Percent of People**
Sporting Goods	25%
Department or Discount	50%
Sneaker	12.5%
Other	12.5%

1. Make a circle graph to display the data.

2. How many shoppers bought sneakers from a sporting goods store?

3. How many shoppers bought sneakers from a department or discount store?

4. How many shoppers bought sneakers from a sneaker store? $\left(12.5\% = 0.125 \text{ or } \frac{1}{8}\right)$

The circle graph shows Mrs. Marco's $3,000 monthly budget. Use the graph to solve Problems 5–9.

5. How much money does Mrs. Marco spend on her rent each month?

6. How much money does Mrs. Marco spend on her car each month?

7. How much money does Mrs. Marco put into savings each month?

8. Mrs. Marco wants to increase her savings to $600 a month. How can Mrs. Marco change her spending to increase her savings? Explain.

9. Mr. Johnson's total monthly budget is $2,000. He budgets 20% for food. Does Mr. Johnson budget more money for food than Mrs. Marco?

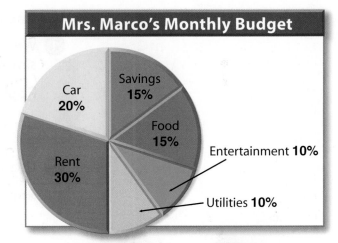

Mrs. Marco's Monthly Budget

Savings 15%
Car 20%
Food 15%
Entertainment **10%**
Rent 30%
Utilities **10%**

> **Vocabulary Tip**
> Utilities include water and electricity.

Writing Math

Explain What should be the sum of all the percents in a circle graph? Explain your answer.

CA Standards

SDAP 1.3 Use fractions and percentages to compare data sets of different sizes.

KEY NS 1.2 Interpret percents as part of a hundred; find decimal and percent equivalents for common fractions and explain why they represent the same value; compute a given percent of a whole number.

Also SDAP 1.0, MR 1.0, MR 1.2, MR 2.0, MR 3.0, MR 3.2, MR 3.3

Compare Data Sets

Objective Use percents and fractions to analyze and compare data sets of different sizes.

▶ Learn by Example

In previous lessons, you learned how fractions, decimals, and percents are related. In this lesson, you will use these ideas to compare sets of data.

Raphael has a collection of 60 stamps. Forty-five are from Mexico. Janine has a collection of 50 stamps. Forty are from Mexico. Who has the greater percent of stamps from Mexico?

Different Ways to Compare Data Sets

Way 1   Use fractions.

1 Write the parts as fractions. Then write each fraction in simplest form.

Raphael: 45 out of 60   **Janine:** 40 out of 50

$$\frac{45}{60} = \frac{3}{4}$$ $$\frac{40}{50} = \frac{4}{5}$$

2 Use a common denominator to compare the fractions.

Raphael: $\frac{3}{4} = \frac{15}{20}$ **Janine:** $\frac{4}{5} = \frac{16}{20}$

$\frac{16}{20} > \frac{15}{20}$ Therefore, $\frac{4}{5} > \frac{3}{4}$

Way 2   Use percents.

1 Write the parts as fractions. Then write each fraction in simplest form.

Raphael: 45 out of 60   **Janine:** 40 out of 50

$$\frac{45}{60} = \frac{3}{4}$$ $$\frac{40}{50} = \frac{4}{5}$$

2 Write each fraction as a percent, and compare.

Raphael: **Janine:**

$$\overset{\times 25}{\frac{3}{4}} = \frac{75}{100} = 75\%$$ $$\overset{\times 20}{\frac{4}{5}} = \frac{80}{100} = 80\%$$

$$80\% > 75\%$$

Solution: Janine has the greater percent of stamps from Mexico.

Compare. Use >, <, or = for the ●.

1. 10 out of 25 ● 6 out of 8

2. 18 out of 36 ● 24 out of 40

3. 1 out of 5 ● 3 out of 30

4. 9 out of 12 ● 24 out of 32

Ask Yourself

• Did I write the fractions in simplest form?

• Did I write the fractions as percents?

Guided Problem Solving

Use the questions to solve this problem.

5. Jim has 40 postcards from National Parks. Twenty are from California. Kimberly has 32 postcards from National Parks. Eight are from California. Whose postcard collection has the greater percent from California?

a. Understand What do you know? What are you asked to find out?

b. Plan Find the percent of California postcards in Jim's collection. Find the percent of California postcards in Kimberly's collection. Compare the percents.

c. Solve Who has the greater percent of California National Park postcards?

d. Look Back How can you use what you know about comparing fractions to check your answer?

6. Right or Wrong? Look back at Problem 5. Suppose Ty has 4 California National Park postcards in his collection of 10 postcards. Kimberly says that since she has 8 postcards from California, she has the greater percent of California postcards. Is Kimberly correct? Explain.

123 Math Talk Is it always necessary to use a common denominator to compare fractions?

Compare. Use >, <, or = for the ⬭.

7. 32 out of 40 ⬭ 21 out of 35

8. 48 out of 60 ⬭ 12 out of 15

9. 10 out of 50 ⬭ 15 out of 60

10. 11 out of 44 ⬭ 2 out of 8

Science Link

Use the Fun Facts to solve Problems 11–13.

11. In a molecule of sugar, which element accounts for 50% of the atoms?

12. What percent of the atoms in a molecule of sugar are either hydrogen or oxygen?

13. Hydrogen peroxide is a substance that is often used to clean a cut. In a molecule of hydrogen peroxide, 50% of the atoms are oxygen. A hydrogen peroxide molecule is made up of 4 atoms. How many more oxygen atoms are there in 5 molecules of sugar than in 5 molecules of hydrogen peroxide?

Fun Facts

Sugar

• A common sugar called glucose is a substance made of the elements carbon, hydrogen, and oxygen. One molecule of glucose contains 6 atoms of carbon, 12 atoms of hydrogen, and 6 atoms of oxygen.

• Glucose is made in plant cells through photosynthesis.

Sugar crystals under a microscope

Science PS 1.b

✓ Spiral Review and Test Practice

Display the data in an appropriate graph. AF 1.1, SDAP 1.2 page 352

14. Two students scored between 61–70 on a math quiz, 6 students scored between 71–80, 12 students scored between 81–90, and 6 students scored between 91–100.

Write the letter of the correct answer. SDAP 1.3

15. Who has the greatest percent of blue marbles?

  A Cora   **C** Rama

  B Chen   **D** Aiden

Name	Total Marbles	Blue Marbles
Cora	20	5
Chen	15	3
Rama	18	6
Aiden	25	5

Extra Practice See page 531, Set A.

Key Standards Review

Need Help?
See Key Standards Handbook.

Write an expression to represent each figure with its given area. Solve for the missing dimension. **KEY AF 1.2**

1. $A = 216$ sq in.

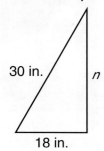

1.

30 in.

n

18 in.

2. $A = 84$ sq ft

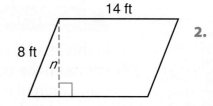

14 ft

8 ft

n

2.

Solve each problem. KEY MG 1.1

3. Oren used 2 congruent triangle-shaped pieces of paper to make a flag in the shape of a parallelogram. One piece has a base of 14 inches and a height of 12 inches. What is the total area of his flag?

4. The banner that hangs over the classroom entrance is a triangle. The banner has a height that is 3 times its base. The area of the banner is 54 square meters. What is its height?

Challenge   Problem Solving

Population Percents   KEY NS 1.2, NS 1.1, SDAP 1.3

Use the graphs at the right to solve.

1. How many more people live in urban areas in California than in Texas?

2. How many people live in rural areas of both states combined?

3. If California's population were 18,000,000, but the percent of people living in urban and rural areas stays the same, which state would have more people living in urban areas? Explain.

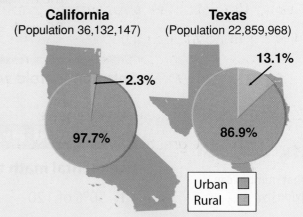

California
(Population 36,132,147)

Texas
(Population 22,859,968)

2.3%

13.1%

97.7%

86.9%

Urban
Rural

CA Standards

KEY NS 1.2 Interpret percents as a part of a hundred; find decimal and percent equivalents for common fractions and explain why they represent the same value; compute the given percent of a number.

NS 1.0 Students compute with very large and very small numbers, positive integers, decimals, and fractions and understand the relationship between decimals, fractions, and percents. They understand the relative magnitudes of numbers.

Also NS 2.4, NS 2.5, KEY SDAP 1.4, KEY SDAP 1.5, MR 1.0, MR 1.2, MR 2.3

Mental Math: Percent of a Number

Objective Find the percent of a number using mental math.

▶ **Learn by Example**

In this lesson, you will learn how to compute the percent of a number using mental math.

A skateboard regularly sells for $80. The skateboard is on sale for 25% off the regular price. How much money will Harold save by buying the skateboard on sale?

Different Ways to Find a Percent of a Number

Way 1   Multiply by $\frac{1}{4}$.

Finding 25% of a number is the same as finding $\frac{1}{4}$ of the number.

$$25\% \times 80 = \frac{1}{4} \times 80$$
$$= \frac{1}{4} \times \frac{80}{1}$$
$$\frac{1 \times 80}{4 \times 1} = \frac{80}{4}$$
$$= 20$$

Way 2   Use mental math. Divide by 4.

Finding 25% of a number is the same as dividing the number by 4.

$$80 \div 4 = 20$$

Solution: Harold will save $20.

▶ **Guided Practice**

Use mental math to find the number.

1. 50% of 120   **2.** 25% of 200   **3.** 10% of 70

 Math Talk Why is finding 25% of a number the same as dividing the number by 4?

Ask Yourself

What number can I divide by?

Use mental math to find the number.

4. 25% of 40   **5.** 50% of 180   **6.** 10% of 48

Hint

Finding 10% of a number is the same as moving the decimal point one place to the left.

7. Multistep A sweatshirt that regularly sells for $35 is on sale for 10% off the regular price. What is the sale price of the sweatshirt?

 Real World Data

Use the graph for Problems 8–10.

8. The Carsons drove from San Jose to Crescent City. At what time did the Carson family complete half of their trip?

9. Write the ordered pair that names the point at which the Carsons had completed 80% of their trip.

10. The Carsons' trip lasted 10 hours. The family stopped at restaurants for their meals. If their meals took up 20% of their time on the trip, how many hours did they spend at restaurants?

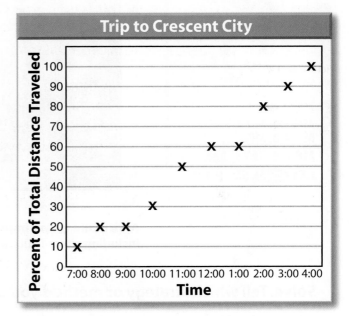

Trip to Crescent City

Spiral Review and Test Practice

Copy and complete the function table. KEY **AF 1.2**, KEY **SDAP 1.4** page 112

11.

$y = x + 2$	
x	**y**
1	
	5
7	
13	

12.

$y = 2x$	
x	**y**
7	
5	
	6
$\frac{1}{4}$	

13.

$y = 2x - 2$	
x	**y**
5	
	12
	20
25	

Write the letter of the correct answer. KEY **NS 1.2**

14. What is 10% of 380?

   A 39   **B** 38   **C** 76   **D** 19

LESSON 4

Field Trip...

Victorville, CA

CA Standards
MR 1.0, MR 1.2,
MR 2.0, MR 2.3,
MR 2.4, KEY NS 1.2,
KEY MG 2.1, SDAP 1.2

Problem Solving

Objective Use skills and strategies to solve word problems.

Agriculture is very important to California's economy. More than 350 crops, including citrus fruits, are planted and harvested in the state.

Solve. Tell which strategy or method you used.

Manuel's Citrus Stand	
Type of Fruit	**Percent of Fruit**
Grapefruit	40%
Lime	10%
Lemon	20%
Orange	30%

1. The table shows what one farmer brings to sell at the farmer's market. Use the table and a protractor to represent the data in a circle graph.

2. Use your graph from Problem 1. Suppose Manuel brings 50 pieces of fruit to sell at his citrus stand. How many more grapefruits does he sell than limes?

3. The High Desert Farmers' Market has 40 spaces available each week for vendors to sell their goods. During one week, thirty of the spaces were occupied. What percent of the spaces were occupied?

4. **Multistep** Three out of every four people that visit the High Desert Farmers' Market buy at least one product. What percentage of people do not buy a product? Explain how you got your answer.

Problem Solving On Tests

Select a Strategy
- Draw a Picture
- Write an Equation
- Guess and Check
- Choose the Operation
- Make a Table

1. Megan has been saving nickels to purchase a stuffed animal. A nickel is worth $0.05. The stuffed animal costs $4.85. How many nickels does Megan need to save?

A 9.7   **B** 97   **C** 100   **D** 970

KEY **NS 2.2** page 304

2. One section of a circle graph represents a bicyclist who rode 12 miles in one day. If another section of the circle graph is $\frac{1}{3}$ the size of that section, how many miles will the section represent?

A $\frac{1}{3}$ mile

B $\frac{1}{4}$ mile

C 4 miles

D 36 miles

AF 1.1 page 350

3. Wanda made a function table that shows the relationship between the number of hours worked and money earned. Which equation shows the relationship of all values in the function table below?

A $y = x + 1$

B $y = 2x - 1$

C $y = 2x + 1$

D $y = x + 2$

Rule: ?	
x	**y**
1	3
2	5
3	7
4	9

KEY **AF 1.5** page 374

4. Tom drew the parallelogram *ABCD* shown below. Then he added a diagonal line to make 2 triangles.

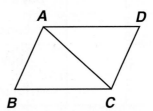

Test Tip
Use what you know about the area of a triangle to find the area of a parallelogram.

What is the area of the parallelogram if the area of the triangle *ABC* is 18 square centimeters?

A 9 cm²   **C** 54 cm²

B 36 cm²   **D** 72 cm²

KEY **MG 1.1** page 454

5. Erin wants to fill a box in the shape of a rectangular prism with sand. The box has a length of 12 centimeters, a height of 9 centimeters, and a width of 7 centimeters. What is the volume of the box?

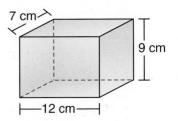

A 192 cm³   **C** 510 cm³

B 255 cm³   **D** 756 cm³

KEY **MG 1.3** page 482

Education Place
Visit www.eduplace.com/camap/ for
Test-Taking Tips and **Extra Practice**.

Reading & Writing Math

Vocabulary

In this chapter, you learned how to use **percent** to solve problems and analyze data.

One month, Akon earned $120. The chart below shows how he will use his money this month.

Fraction of Akon's Earnings	How Akon Uses His Money
$\frac{1}{4}$	buy a video game
$\frac{2}{5}$	bank deposit
$\frac{1}{10}$	buy snacks
$\frac{1}{4}$	save for motor scooter

1. What percent of his allowance will Akon deposit into the bank?

2. How much money will Akon spend on video games?

3. Draw a circle graph that shows the percent of Akon's money he will spend on snacks.

Writing How much money would Akon spend on video games if his allowance was $200 each month? Explain how you arrived at this answer.

Reading Look for this book in your library. *Holes* by Louis Sachar

CA Standards

MR 2.3 Use a variety of methods, such as words, numbers, symbols, charts, graphs, tables, diagrams, and models, to explain mathematical reasoning.

Also KEY NS 1.2, SDAP 1.2

Standards-Based Extra Practice

Set A ———————————————————— KEY **NS 1.2**, SDAP 1.3 page 522

Compare. Use >, <, or = for each ⬤.

1. 1 out of 4 ⬤ 2 out of 20

2. 3 out of 6 ⬤ 50 out of 100

3. 4 out of 12 ⬤ 9 out of 36

4. 20 out of 80 ⬤ 30 out of 90

5. 20 out of 25 ⬤ 3 out of 4

6. 12 out of 40 ⬤ 5 out of 25

7. 4 out of 16 ⬤ 30 out of 60

8. 60 out of 80 ⬤ 8 out of 40

9. Twenty out of 25 dentists in a survey recommend Brand A toothpaste. Twenty-seven out of 36 patients in a survey recommend Brand A toothpaste. Is Brand A toothpaste more popular with dentists or with patients?

Set B ———————————————————— KEY **NS 1.2**, NS 1.0 page 526

Use mental math to find each number.

1. 50% of 140

2. 25% of 80

3. 10% of 90

4. 50% of 350

5. 25% of 40

6. 10% of 60

7. 15% of 60

8. 25% of 100

9. 20% of 60

10. 10% of 100

11. 50% of 20

12. 10% of 70

Use the table to answer the following questions.

13. How many containers of strawberry yogurt were sold?

14. How many containers of vanilla yogurt were sold?

15. How many more containers of blueberry yogurt than banana yogurt were sold?

Yogurt Sales (400 containers sold)	
Flavor	**Percent of Sales**
Vanilla	40%
Strawberry	25%
Blueberry	25%
Banana	10%

Education Place
Visit www.eduplace.com/camap/
for more **Extra Practice**.

Chapter Review/Test

Vocabulary and Concepts ———————— KEY NS 1.2, SDAP 1.2, MR 2.3
Choose the best word to complete the sentence.

1. A _____ graph shows data as part of a whole.

2. A _____ names a part of a whole or a group.

3. The word _____ means "per hundred".

Skills ———————————————— KEY NS 1.2, NS 1.0, SDAP 1.3
Write each set as a fraction in simplest form and as a percent.

4. 45 out of 90   5. 25 out of 100   6. 40 out of 50

Compare. Write >, <, or = for each ⬭.

7. 48 out of 60 ⬭ 12 out of 15   8. 15 out of 20 ⬭ 81 out of 90

9. 34 out of 40 ⬭ 21 out of 35   10. 35 out of 70 ⬭ 9 out of 15

Use mental math to find each number.

11. 50% of 140   12. 25% of 400   13. 40% of 30

14. 20% of 70   15. 25% of 80   16. 75% of 300

Problem Solving and Reasoning ———————— KEY NS 1.2, SDAP 1.2, MR1.1, MR 2.3

The circle graph shows what 420 shoppers planned to buy in a mall. Use the circle graph to solve Problems 17–18.

17. How many shoppers planned to buy electronics?

18. How many shoppers planned to buy jewelry?

19. Three out of every 5 people that visit a store buy at least one item. What percent of people do NOT buy an item? Explain how you got your answer.

20. Thirty percent of Mandy's 50 cat figurines are orange, and 40% of Kate's 40 figurines are orange. Which girl has more orange figurines?

Shopping Plans

Jewelry 5%

Electronics 20%

Shoes 50%

Sporting Goods 25%

Writing Math Explain how you would use mental math to find 20% of 90.

Spiral Review and Test Practice

1. Jerome has a collection of 150 postcards. If 30 of them are from Japan, what percent of the postcards are from Japan?

A 2%

B 5%

C 20%

D 80%

KEY **NS 1.2** page 522

2. Which fraction is equivalent to $\frac{8}{12}$?

A $\frac{1}{6}$

B $\frac{1}{2}$

C $\frac{2}{3}$

D $\frac{12}{8}$

KEY **NS 2.3** page 34

3. Tina used 2.61 meters of yellow ribbon and 1.4 meters of blue ribbon to wrap a package. Approximately how many meters of ribbon did Tina use?

A 2 meters

B 3 meters

C 4 meters

D 5 meters

> **Test Tip**
> The word *approximately* means *about*.

KEY **NS 2.1** page 256

4. What is the surface area of the box formed by the pattern below?

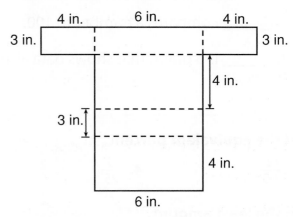

A 108 in.^{2}

B 90 in.^{2}

C 88 in.^{2}

D 84 in.^{2}

KEY **MG 1.2** page 478

5. Which set of numbers is ordered from greatest to least?

A $\frac{4}{5}$, 0.9, 100%

B $\frac{7}{10}$, 90%, 0.07

C $\frac{3}{25}$, 0.09, 3%

D 73%, $\frac{3}{4}$, 0.74

KEY **NS 1.2** page 506

Education Place
Visit www.eduplace.com/camap/ for **Test-Taking Tips** and **Extra Practice**.

Unit 10 Review/Test

Vocabulary and Concepts ———————————— KEY **NS 1.2**, MR **2.3** Chapters 23–24

Choose the best term to complete each sentence.

1. A _____ compares a number to 100.

2. A _____ is a graph that shows data as part of a whole.

Skills ———————————— NS **1.0**, KEY **NS 1.2**, SDAP **1.3**, MR **3.2** Chapter 23, Lessons 2–3

Find the equivalent percent.

3. $\frac{72}{100}$
4. $\frac{5}{25}$
5. $\frac{3}{8}$
6. $\frac{13}{50}$

Find the least amount.

7. $\frac{3}{60}$ $\frac{1}{10}$ 3%
8. $\frac{4}{5}$ 82% 0.75
9. 90% 0.88 $\frac{43}{50}$

Find the greatest amount.

10. $\frac{14}{25}$ 50% 0.65
11. $\frac{3}{10}$ 33% 0.32
12. $\frac{2}{3}$ 60% 0.66

Evaluate by writing the percent as a fraction. Chapter 23, Lesson 4

13. 15% of 80
14. 20% of 65
15. 30% of 75

Compare. Use >, <, or = for each 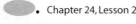 **.** Chapter 24, Lesson 2

16. 20 out of 50 ⬤ 10 out of 100
17. 45 out of 90 ⬤ 5 out of 15

Use mental math to find each number. Chapter 24, Lesson 3

18. 25% of 80
19. 50% of 66
20. 10% of 200
21. 50% of 100

Problem Solving and Reasoning ———————————— KEY **NS 1.2**, MR **2.3** Chapters 23–24

Solve.

22. A trampoline is on sale. The original price is $150, and it is 30% off. How much will be subtracted from the original price?

23. 12 out of every 25 video games sold are action games. What percent of video games sold are action games?

Solve.

24. In a survey that asked students if they prefer red, green, or blue for school colors, 45% of the students said red; $\frac{1}{4}$ said blue, and $\frac{3}{10}$ said green. Which was the favorite color?

25. Twenty-five percent of the 80 T-shirts that were sold last week were blue. The rest were black. How many black T-shirts were sold?

Writing Math How can you use mental math and 10% to help you find a discount at the store if the sale is 40% off?

Performance Assessment

The Lost Data

KEY **NS 1.2**, SDAP 1.2, MR 1.1, MR 1.2, MR 2.3

Heather took a survey of 212 fifth-graders' favorite activities. She was about to display the results in a circle graph, but her dog chewed up the data. Help her figure out which activity and what percent belongs in each section of the graph.

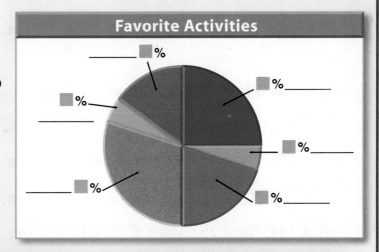

Favorite Activities

Task	Information You Need
Use the information above and to the right to help you solve the problem. Figure out the percent and the color for each choice. The choices were: playing video games, scrapbooking, playing with remote control cars, skateboarding, making models, and biking. Copy and complete the graph.	53 students chose video games.
	$\frac{1}{20}$ of those asked liked scrapbooking.
	Most students answered skateboarding.
	1 out of every 5 students said biking.
	5% like playing with remote control cars.
	The decimal for those who preferred making models was 0.15.

Go Fast, Go Far

Unit 10 Mental Math Strategies

Multiply by 15

Here's a helpful tip for you, 10 plus 5 is fast to do!

I have a fast way to do 15 × 22. I start with 10 × 22, which is 220. To find 5 × 22, I cut 220 in half and get 110. So 15 × 22 is 220 + 110, which is 330.

1. 15 × 22 = $\boxed{220}$ + $\boxed{110}$ = 330
          10 × 22 5 × 22

2. 15 × 46 = $\boxed{460}$ + $\boxed{230}$ = ☐
          10 × 46 5 × 46

3. 15 × 62 = $\boxed{620}$ + ☐ = ☐
          10 × 62 5 × 62

4. 15 × 50 = ☐ + ☐ = ☐
          10 × 50 5 × 50

Good job! Now try these!

5. 15 × 36 = ☐ + ☐ = ☐

6. 15 × 18 = ☐ + ☐ = ☐

7. 15 × 54 = ☐ + ☐ = ☐

8. 15 × 66 = ☐ + ☐ = ☐

9. 15 × 28 = ☐ + ☐ = ☐

10. 15 × 34 = ☐ + ☐ = ☐

11. 15 × 42 = ☐ + ☐ = ☐

12. 15 × 52 = ☐ + ☐ = ☐

Doing Great!

Take It Further!

Now try doing all the steps in your head!

13. 15 × 26

14. 15 × 58

15. 15 × 30

16. 15 × 44

Integers

★ BIG IDEAS!

- You can identify, compare, and order negative numbers on a number line.

- You can model addition and subtraction with negative numbers on a number line.

- There is a set of rules to follow when adding and subtracting integers.

Chapter 25
Understand and Add Integers

Chapter 26
Add and Subtract Integers

Songs and Games

 Math Music Track 11: *Opposite*
eGames at
www.eduplace.com/camap/

Math Readers

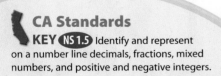

Get to Zero!

Object of the Game Use a number line to prepare for subtraction and addition of integers.

Materials
- Workmat 3
- Counter or penny (1 per player)
- Learning Tool 15: Number/Symbol Cards (1 set labeled 1–10)

Set Up
Each player labels the first number line on Workmat 3 from ⁻10 to 10. Players shuffle the number cards and place them in a stack face down.

Number of Players 2

How to Play

1. To start the game, players take turns taking the top card from the stack. Players then decide whether to assign a positive or negative value to the card. Players place a counter on the number line to match the value they've chosen. This is their starting point. For example, if Player 1 picks 5, he or she can decide to place the counter on either 5 or ⁻5 on the number line.

2. Each player repeats the process picking a number card and moving his or her counter to the right (positive number) or to the left (negative number) on the number line.

3. The first player to land on zero is the winner.

CA Standards
KEY **NS 1.5** Identify and represent on a number line decimals, fractions, mixed numbers, and positive and negative integers.

Also MR 1.0

 Education Place
Visit www.eduplace.com/camap/ for **Brain Teasers** and **eGames** to play.

Reading When you read a story, you can look at the illustrations to help you visualize or picture what is happening. To visualize math, it can be helpful to show the information and numbers in a word problem in a different way.

Read the problem.
Use the thermometer to help you visualize the numbers.

Problem 1
Yesterday's temperature was 6 degrees Celsius. The temperature dropped 8 degrees overnight. What is today's temperature?

I can use the thermometer like a number line.

Writing Read Problem 2. Show the information in a different way to solve the problem.

Problem 2
The temperature is ⁻4°C at noon. It rises 5 degrees over the next three hours. By 7:00 P.M., the temperature falls 6 degrees. What is the temperature at 7:00 P.M.?

°Celsius

Chapter 25

Understand and Add Integers

During the summer, the temperature in Death Valley, CA, can reach more than 100°F.

Check What You Know

Vocabulary and Concepts GRADE 4 KEY NS 1.8, MR 2.3

Choose the best word to complete each sentence.

1. A number less than 0 is a _____ number.

2. A number greater than 0 is a _____ number.

3. A unit used to describe temperature is a _____ .

Skills GRADE 4 KEY NS 1.9

Use the number line for Exercises 4–9. Write a decimal for each point.

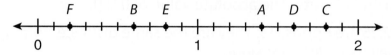

4. A

5. B

6. C

7. D

8. E

9. F

Problem Solving and Reasoning GRADE 4 NS 2.1

10. Rachel used 2.78 yards of string to bundle newspaper for the recycle center. She used 2.69 yards of string to bundle magazines. Did Rachel use more string to bundle newspapers or magazines?

Vocabulary

Visualize It!

°Fahrenheit

positive numbers found above 0° on a thermometer

negative numbers found below 0° on a thermometer

57° is a positive number.

−5° is a negative number.

Language Tips

In everyday language, *positive* and *negative* mean yes and no. In mathematics, *positive* and *negative* mean greater than and less than zero.

Math words that look alike in English and Spanish often have the same meaning.

English	Spanish
positive	positivo
negative	negativo

See **English-Spanish Glossary** pages 628–642.

Education Place Visit www.eduplace.com/camap/ for the **eGlossary** and **eGames**.

CA Standards **MR 2.3** Use a variety of methods, such as words, numbers, symbols, charts, graphs, tables, diagrams, and models, to explain mathematical reasoning. **Also prepares for KEY NS 1.5**

Chapter 25   541

CA Standards
KEY **NS 1.5** Identify and represent on a number line decimals, fractions, mixed numbers, and positive and negative integers.
Also MR 2.0, MR 2.3

Vocabulary

opposite

positive number

negative number

Materials
Workmat 3

Think
Positive numbers can be written with or without a sign.

$$5 = {}^+5$$

Hands On
Integers

Objective Identify numbers and their opposites on a number line.

▶ **Explore**

Every number has an opposite and an absolute value. You can find the **opposite** of a number by changing its sign from + to − or − to +. You can find the absolute value of a number by finding how far from zero it is on a number line.

Zero is its own opposite. The absolute value of 0 is 0.

2.25 and ⁻2.25 are opposites. They are the same distance from zero but they have different signs.

Question How can you use a number line to find absolute value?

Find the absolute value of 2.25 and ⁻2.25.

1 Use Number Line 1 on Workmat 3. Make a number line like the one below.

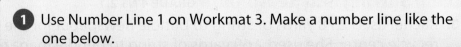

2 Show 2.25 and ⁻2.25 on the number line. 2.25 is to the right of zero, so it is a **positive number**. ⁻2.25 is to the left of zero, so it is a **negative number**.

Read ⁻2.25 as *"negative 2.25."*

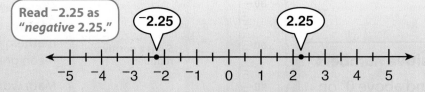

3 Compare the distances between each number and zero.

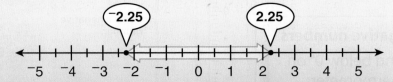

The distance from 0 to 2.25 is the same as the distance from 0 to ⁻2.25.

Solution: The absolute value of both 2.25 and ⁻2.25 is 2.25.

Erase the points you put on your number line. Now use the number line to find the absolute value of 3.5 and its opposite.

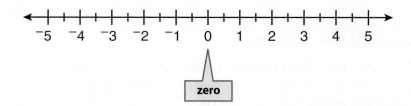

zero

1 Find 3.5 on the number line. Label it F.

2 Find the opposite of 3.5. Label it G.

3 Write the absolute value of ⁻3.5 and 3.5.

▶ **Extend**

Write the opposite of the number. Use the number line to help you.

1. ⁻5	**2.** 1.5	**3.** ⁻9.5	**4.** 0
5. ⁻2	**6.** $-\frac{1}{2}$	**7.** $2\frac{3}{4}$	**8.** $-\frac{7}{8}$
9. 3	**10.** ⁻4.1	**11.** 2.3	**12.** ⁻0.5

Write the absolute value for each number.

13. $-12\frac{3}{4}$	**14.** 225	**15.** ⁻29.3	**16.** 0
17. ⁻300.05	**18.** 16	**19.** ⁻1.05	**20.** 44
21. ⁻21	**22.** ⁻13	**23.** 31.7	**24.** ⁻0.7

Think

• Do I need to change the sign?

• Is the absolute value 0?

Challenge **Find the distance between the numbers on a number line.**

25. 3 and ⁻3 **26.** ⁻4 and 4 **27.** 2.5 and ⁻2.5

28. $-1\frac{1}{2}$ and $1\frac{1}{2}$ **29.** $\frac{3}{7}$ and $-\frac{3}{7}$ **30.** *n* and opposite of *n*

31. Generalize Is there any number that does not have an opposite? Explain.

Writing Math

Analyze Is the absolute value of a number the same as the opposite of that number? Explain.

CA Standards

KEY **NS 1.5** Identify and represent on a number line decimals, fractions, mixed numbers, and positive and negative integers.

Also NS 1.0, MR 2.3, MR 3.2

Vocabulary

integer

negative integer

positive integer

Compare and Order Integers

Objective Compare and order integers.

▶ **Learn by Example**

Whole numbers and their opposites are called **integers**. Whole numbers to the right of zero on a number line are **positive integers**. Whole numbers to the left of zero are **negative integers**. Zero is neither positive nor negative and is also an integer.

You can use a number line to order integers, just as you order other numbers.

> At 0° C, water begins to freeze, and ice crystals shaped like thin plates begin to form. At ⁻4° C, the crystals look like needles. At 1° C, the ice crystals begin to melt. How can you use a number line to order these temperatures from lowest to highest, in other words from least to greatest?

Order Integers

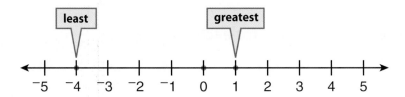

① Locate each integer on the number line.

② The integer farthest to the left has the least value. The integer farthest to the right has the greatest value.

$$^-4 < 0 < 1$$

The temperatures in order from lowest to highest are:

⁻4° C, 0° C, and 1° C.

**Draw a number line from ⁻4 to 4 and label each integer.
Write > or < for the 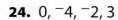.**

1. 1 ⬭ 2   2. ⁻3 ⬭ ⁻1   3. 1 ⬭ ⁻1

 Math Talk If you are comparing two negative integers,
how can you tell which one is greater?

> **Ask Yourself**
>
> Which integer is farther left on the number line?

► **Practice and Problem Solving**

**Draw a number line from ⁻5 to 5 and label each integer.
Write > or < for the ⬭.**

4. ⁻2 ⬭ ⁻1   5. ⁻5 ⬭ ⁻2   6. 5 ⬭ ⁻3   7. 1 ⬭ 0

8. ⁻5 ⬭ 3   9. ⁻5 ⬭ 5   10. ⁻1 ⬭ 1   11. 0 ⬭ 2

**Use your number line from exercises 4–11.
Write an integer to make the statement true.**

12. ▨ < ⁻1   13. ▨ > 0   14. ⁻2 > ▨   15. ⁻5 < ▨

Write the integer that is represented by the labeled point.

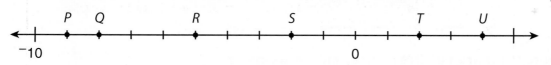

16. point P   17. point S   18. point T   19. point U

**Use the number line below to tell whether the inequality is
true or false.**

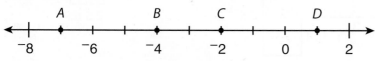

20. D > C   21. A > B   22. C > A   23. B > D

Write the integers in order from least to greatest.

24. 0, ⁻4, ⁻2, 3   25. 2, ⁻2, 4, ⁻5   26. ⁻7, ⁻10, ⁻6, ⁻4

27. ⁻9, 0, ⁻10, ⁻5   28. 3, ⁻7, 0, 4   29. ⁻1, 1, ⁻5, 3

> **Hint**
>
> You can draw a number line if you need help.

Solve.

30. In January, in Barrow, Alaska, normal temperatures range from $^-22°C$ to $^-28°C$. Which is the higher temperature?

31. Right or Wrong? Javier drew this number line. Is it correct? If not, explain why it is incorrect.

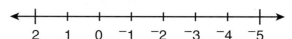

 Science Link

Use the fun facts to solve Problems 32–33.

32. Which kind of ice crystal can form at $^-8°C$, hollow columns or sector plates?

33. Name three temperatures lower than $^-22°$ C at which hollow column crystals form.

34. Ice crystals called dendrites form between $^-12°$ C and $^-16°$ C. Write the integers that are in this temperature range.

35. Create and Solve Use the fun facts to create and solve your own problem.

Fun Facts

- Ice crystals called sector plates look like flowers. Sector plates begin to form at $^-10°$ C.

- Hollow column ice crystals first form between $^-6°$ C and $^-10°$ C. They also form at temperatures lower than $^-22°C$.

Science ES 3.b

Spiral Review and Test Practice

Find the perimeter and area of the figure. MG 1.4 page 436

36.

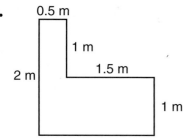

0.5 m
1 m
2 m
1.5 m
1 m

37.

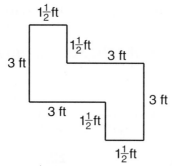

$1\frac{1}{2}$ ft
$1\frac{1}{2}$ ft
3 ft
3 ft
3 ft
3 ft
$1\frac{1}{2}$ ft
$1\frac{1}{2}$ ft

38.

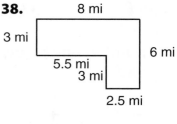

8 mi
3 mi
6 mi
5.5 mi
3 mi
2.5 mi

Write the letter of the correct answer. KEY NS 1.5

39. Which letter on the number line *best* identifies the location of $^-3$?

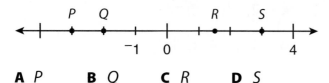

P   Q   R   S
$^-1$ 0   4

A P   **B** Q   **C** R   **D** S

Extra Practice See page 557, Set A.

Key Standards Review

Need Help?
See Key Standards Handbook.

Find the surface area of each figure. KEY MG 1.2

1.

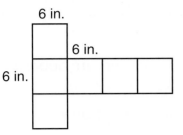

6 in.

6 in.

6 in.

2.

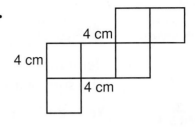

4 cm

4 cm

4 cm

3.

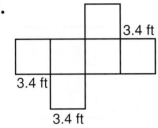

3.4 ft

3.4 ft

3.4 ft

4.

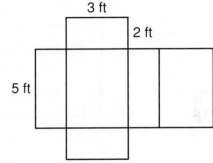

3 ft

2 ft

5 ft

Challenge **Problem Solving**

True or False? KEY NS 2.1

Write *true* or *false*. If false, rewrite the statement so that it is true.

1. The arctic fox lives where the temperature is coldest.

2. The coral snake lives where the temperatures average about 70° colder than where the arctic fox lives.

3. The arctic fox lives where the temperatures average about 10° colder than where the rattlesnake lives.

4. It is not likely that the rattlesnake and the penguin live in the same area.

Average Temperatures Where Animals Live	
Arctic fox	⁻30°C
Coral snake	20°C
Penguin	⁻20°C
Rattlesnake	40°C

CA Standards
KEY **NS 2.1** Add, subtract, multiply, and divide with decimals; add with negative integers; subtract positive integers from negative integers; and verify reasonableness of results.
Also MR 2.0, MR 2.3, MR 3.0, MR 3.2, MR 3.3

Materials
2-color counters

Hands On
Add Integers

Objective Use counters to model addition of integers.

▶ **Explore**

Remember that positive and negative integers are opposites. The sum of an integer and its opposite is 0.

You can use two-color counters to model addition with positive and negative integers.

$$^-3 + 5 = n$$

---

1 Use red counters to represent negative integers.

Let 3 red counters represent $^-3$.

---

2 Use yellow counters to represent positive integers.

Let 5 yellow counters represent 5.

---

3 Match each red counter to a yellow counter.

There are 3 pairs.

The counters that remain represent the sum $^-3 + 5$.

There are 2 yellow counters remaining.

$$^-3 + 5 = 2$$

A red (negative) counter and a yellow (positive) counter represent opposites. The sum of opposites is 0.

▶ **Extend**

Write the addition expression shown by the counters and then find the sum.

1. ○○ ●●●●●●●

2. ●●●● ○○○○○

3. ●●● ○○

4. ○ ●●●●

5. ○○○ ●●

6. ●●●● ○○

7. ●● ○○ ●●

8. ○ ●●● ○○○○

Solve. Use counters to help you.

9. $7 + 3$

10. $^-7 + 4$

11. $^-6 + ^-2$

12. $3 + ^-8$

13. $10 + ^-10$

14. $^-12 + 3$

15. $12 + ^-9$

16. $^-9 + ^-5$

17. $^-7 + ^-3$

18. $^-3 + 8$

19. $6 + 2$

20. $7 + ^-4$

21. $^-1 + 1$

22. $^-3 + 5$

23. $^-3 + ^-5$

24. $3 + ^-5$

Use what you have learned to answer these questions.

25. **Generalize** When you combine two sets of yellow counters, what color represents the answer? What does that tell you about the sum of two positive integers?

26. When you combine two sets of red counters, what color represents the answer? What does that tell you about the sum of two negative integers?

27. When you combine a set of yellow counters and a set of red counters, how can you tell what color counters will represent the answer?

Write About It

Why does a combination of the same number of red and yellow counters represent zero?

LESSON 4

CA Standards

KEY (NS 2.1) Add, subtract, multiply, and divide with decimals; add with negative integers; subtract positive integers from negative integers; and verify reasonableness of results.

KEY (NS 1.5) Identify and represent on a number line decimals, fractions, mixed numbers, and positive and negative integers.

Also MR 2.3, MR 3.2

Materials
Workmat 3

Hint
Write zero near the middle of the number line. Then number the other integers.

Add Integers on a Number Line

Objective Use a number line to add integers.

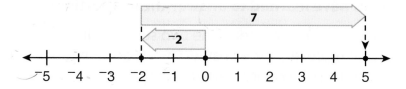 **Learn by Example**

In Lesson 3, you used counters to add positive and negative integers. You can also add with positive and negative integers on a number line.

> Suppose you are playing a game. You can lose points (−) and gain points (+). On your first turn you lose 2 points. On your second turn you win 7 points. What is your score?

Add. $^-2 + 7$

---

1 Draw a number line from $^-5$ to 5 on Workmat 3.

2 Start at 0. To model your first turn (the first addend), move left two units.

3 To model your second turn, start at $^-2$ and move right 7 units to show 7.

4 The number of the point where you stop on the number line is the answer.

$$^-2 + 7 = 5$$

Solution: Your score is 5 points.

Another Example

Sometimes the sum is negative.

$^-5 + 2 = n$

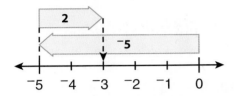

$^-5 + 2 = ^-3$

$^-3 + ^-1 = n$

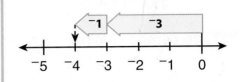

$^-3 + ^-1 = ^-4$

▶ Guided Practice

Use a number line to add.

1. $2 + 4$

2. $^-3 + ^-2$

3. $4 + ^-8$

4. $3 + 7$

5. $^-6 + 6$

6. $^-5 + 0$

Ask Yourself

• Where do I begin on the number line?

• Do I move left or right?

Guided Problem Solving

Use the questions to solve this problem.

7. During a game, Tina's team lost 5 points, won 4 points, won 3 points, and lost 3 points. What is her team's score so far?

a. **Understand** What is the question?

b. **Plan** How can you model the problem to help find the answer?

c. **Solve** Where will you start? Where does each turn take you?

d. **Look Back** How can you check your solution?

(123) **Math Talk** Will the sum of two negative integers always be negative? Explain.

▶ Practice and Problem Solving

Use a number line to add.

8. $11 + ^-5$

9. $^-8 + ^-5$

10. $8 + 7$

11. $^-15 + 15$

12. $12 + ^-18$

13. $^-9 + ^-3$

14. $10 + ^-15$

15. $^-14 + 7$

16. $^-10 + 17$

17. $^-3 + 16$

18. $^-8 + 15$

19. $^-13 + 6$

20. $^-12 + ^-3$

21. $^-15 + 3$

22. $9 + 5$

23. $14 + ^-8$

Evaluate each expression when $x = ^-17$.

24. $6 + x$

25. $^-17 + x$

26. $^-23 + x$

27. $17 + x$

Find each sum. Then compare. Write $>$, $<$, or $=$.

28. $^-5 + 5$ ⬭ $^-4 + 2$

29. $^-6 + 5$ ⬭ $3 + ^-4$

30. $9 + ^-3$ ⬭ $^-2 + 4$

 Real World Data

Use the table to solve Problems 31–36.

31. What is Jack's score after Round 3?

32. **Compare** Who had the greater score after Round 4?

33. What is the total score for Jack and Lily for round 2?

34. What is the total score for Jack and Lily for the first 2 rounds?

35. **Analyze** What does Lily need in order to have a greater score than Jack after Round 5?

36. **Challenge** In the tournament, Tran first gained 19 points. Then he lost 2 times that many points. Then he gained 31 points. How many points did Tran have in all? Explain.

Game Tally		
Round	Jack	Lily
1	Gain 5	Lose 8
2	Lose 4	Gain 3
3	Gain 3	Gain 4
4	Lose 1	Lose 2
5	Lose 1	▢

 Spiral Review and Test Practice

Solve. KEY **NS 1.2** page 526

37. 10% of 225

38. 50% of 24

39. 75% of 800

Write the letter of the correct answer. KEY **NS 2.1**, KEY **AF 1.2**

40. If $n = 43$, what is the value of $^-8 + n$?

   A 51   **B** 35   **C** $^-35$ **D** $^-51$

Extra Practice See page 557, Set B.

Record Weather Data

Ida is a meteorologist in Antarctica. She is a part of a team of researchers who are collecting data on changes in the earth's temperature.

Ida is stationed in Ellsworth, Antarctica. The table below shows the average temperature each month in Ellsworth.

Solve. Draw a number line to help you.

Month	Average Temperature
January	17°F
February	3°F
March	⁻9°F
April	⁻17°F
May	⁻18°F
June	⁻25°F
July	⁻28°F
August	⁻28°F
September	⁻23°F
October	⁻8°F
November	5°F
December	17°F

1. What are the two warmest months in Ellsworth, Antarctica?

2. What are the two coldest months?

3. If the average temperature in June increased by 8°F, what other month would have the same average temperature?

4. Which month's average temperature is 20°F lower than February's average temperature?

5. Ida records the temperature many times each day. On February 12, the temperature at 6:00 A.M. was ⁻5°F. By 12:00 P.M. the temperature had risen 7°F and by 6:00 P.M., it had fallen 3°F. What was the temperature at 6:00 P.M.?

CA Standards
KEY **NS 2.1**, KEY **NS 1.5**, MR 2.6

LESSON 5

Field Trip...

Santa Ana, CA

CA Standards
MR 1.0, MR 2.0,
MR 2.3, MR 2.4

KEY **NS 1.2**, KEY **NS 1.5**,
KEY **NS 2.1**

Problem Solving

Objective Use skills and strategies to solve word problems.

The Discovery Science Center is a hands-on museum where visitors can experience science, technology, and math.

Solve. Tell which strategy or method you used.

1. The Dynamic Earth exhibit at the Science Center teaches about rainfall. The table shows the average yearly rainfall of several places in California.

   a. Which city gets about 10 times as much rainfall as Death Valley?

   b. Show the numbers in the table on a number line.

Average Yearly Rainfall	
Location	**Rainfall**
San Francisco	20.06 in.
Los Angeles	12.15 in.
San Diego	10.28 in.
Death Valley	2.25 in.

2. The record high temperature of 134°F was for Death Valley in California on July 10, 1913. The record low of ⁻45°F was on January 20, 1937 in Boca. Li says the difference between the record low and the record high temperatures is 89°F. Is he correct? Use an equation to explain.

3. Twenty-five students voted for their favorite activity at the Discovery Center. Fifteen students chose the Geyser. What percent of students chose the Geyser?

The Geyser

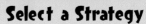
Problem Solving On Tests

Select a Strategy
- Draw a Picture
- Write an Equation
- Work Backward
- Guess and Check
- Choose the Operation

1. Paula used a coordinate grid to show the point (0,5). Which letter represents the point (0,5)?

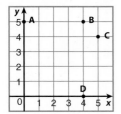

Test Tip
Remember to first find the x-coordinate, then the y-coordinate.

A A

B B

C C

D D

KEY **AF 1.4** page 366

2. Raul used a protractor to measure the angles in this quadrilateral.

What is the measure of angle *m* in the figure?

A 15°

B 90°

C 95°

D 115°

KEY **MG 2.2** page 416

3. Brian received a new comedy DVD movie for his birthday. He asked his friends what part of their movie collection is comedy. Each friend gave Brian the information in a different form. Which set of numbers is ordered from least to greatest?

A $\frac{6}{20}$, 6%, 0.6, 33%

B $\frac{6}{20}$, 0.6, 6%, 33%

C 6%, $\frac{6}{20}$, 33%, 0.6

D 6%, $\frac{6}{20}$, 0.6, 33%

Test Tip
Try changing each number to the same form before comparing and ordering.

KEY **NS 1.2** page 506

4. Tony waits tables at a pizza restaurant. At this restaurant, the tips are divided equally among the wait staff. Which value represents the mean of the data below?

$17.50 $23.55 $18.60 $23.55 $21.80

A $6.05   **C** $21.80

B $21.00   **D** $23.55

SDAP 1.1 page 344

5. There are 25 yogurts in the refrigerator. If 10 yogurts are vanilla flavored, what percent of the yogurt is vanilla?

A 15%   **B** 25%   **C** 40%   **D** 60%

KEY **NS 1.2** page 522

Education Place
Visit www.eduplace.com/camap/ for
Test-Taking Tips and **Extra Practice**.

Chapter 25 Lesson 5   **555**

Vocabulary

You can use a number line to find the **absolute value** of a number, **compare** and **order** integers, and add integers.

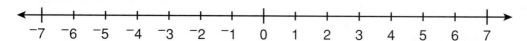

Use the number line to solve the problems.

Find the absolute value of each number.

1. -3 **2.** 6 **3.** 0 **4.** -6

Compare the integers. Write $<$, $>$, or $=$ in the ⬤.

5. -4 ⬤ 4 **6.** 5 ⬤ -6 **7.** 3 ⬤ 0 **8.** 0 ⬤ -3

Find the sum.

9. $-3 + -2$ **10.** $0 + -2$ **11.** $4 + -5$ **12.** $-3 + 3$

13. Max owed his brother 3 dollars. Max got 5 dollars for cleaning the basement. How much money did Max have after he paid his brother back?

Writing Explain how you can use counters to add integers. Explain how you can use a number line.

Reading Check out this book in your library. *Pythagoras Eagle & the Music of Spheres* by Anne Carse Nolting

> **CA Standards**
> **MR 2.3** Use a variety of methods, such as words, numbers, symbols, charts, graphs, tables, diagrams, and models, to explain mathematical reasoning.
>
> **Also KEY NS 1.5, KEY NS 2.1**

Standards-Based Extra Practice

Set A ———————————————————————————————— KEY **NS 1.5** page 544

Draw a number line from ⁻5 to 5 and label each integer. Write >, <, or = for each ⬭.

1. 5 ⬭ 3   **2.** ⁻2 ⬭ 5   **3.** ⁻4 ⬭ ⁻2   **4.** 3 ⬭ ⁻4

5. ⁻5 ⬭ ⁻2   **6.** ⁻3 ⬭ ⁻4   **7.** 0 ⬭ 2   **8.** 2 ⬭ ⁻3

Write the integers in order from least to greatest. Draw a number line if you wish.

9. 0, 5, ⁻3, ⁻1   **10.** 9, 5, ⁻6, ⁻2   **11.** 0, 4, ⁻1, ⁻2   **12.** ⁻8, 6, 0, ⁻4

Solve.

13. The temperature in the morning was ⁻6°F. It was ⁻4°F at night. Was the temperature colder in the morning or at night?

Set B ———————————————————————————— KEY **NS 2.1**, KEY **NS 1.5** page 550

Use a number line to add.

1. ⁻6 + ⁻2   **2.** 9 + 4   **3.** ⁻7 + 4   **4.** 6 + ⁻8

5. ⁻2 + 9   **6.** ⁻5 + ⁻3   **7.** 10 + ⁻4   **8.** ⁻12 + 6

9. 8 + ⁻16   **10.** ⁻2 + 14   **11.** 7 + ⁻21   **12.** ⁻9 + 13

13. ⁻6 + 10   **14.** 5 + 4   **15.** ⁻3 + ⁻12   **16.** 4 + ⁻11

Find each sum. Then compare. Write >, <, or = for each ⬭.

17. ⁻2 + 3 ⬭ 7 + ⁻5   **18.** ⁻9 + 5 ⬭ 3 + ⁻8   **19.** 4 + ⁻6 ⬭ ⁻2 + 5

20. 12 + ⁻7 ⬭ ⁻9 + 7   **21.** ⁻4 + ⁻8 ⬭ 11 + ⁻3   **22.** 3 + ⁻9 ⬭ 6 + ⁻5

Solve.

23. Lisa borrowed 9 books from the library. If she returns 7 of them, how many more books will she still need to return?

Education Place
Visit www.eduplace.com/camap/
for more **Extra Practice**.

Chapter 25 Extra Practice   **557**

Chapter Review/Test

Vocabulary and Concepts

KEY **NS 1.5**, MR 2.3

Write the best word to complete each sentence.

1. Whole numbers and their opposites are _____.

2. Any integer greater than zero is a _____ integer.

3. Numbers that are _____ have the same absolute value, but they have different signs.

Skills

KEY **NS 1.5**, KEY **NS 2.1**

Use the number line for Exercises 4–12.

$$\leftarrow \!\!\! \overset{{}^{-}9 \quad {}^{-}8 \quad {}^{-}7 \quad {}^{-}6 \quad {}^{-}5 \quad {}^{-}4 \quad {}^{-}3 \quad {}^{-}2 \quad {}^{-}1 \quad 0 \quad 1 \quad 2 \quad 3 \quad 4 \quad 5 \quad 6 \quad 7 \quad 8 \quad 9}{\rule{12cm}{0.4pt}} \!\!\! \rightarrow$$

Solve.

4. $^{-}9 + 4$ 5. $6 + 8$ 6. $^{-}7 + {}^{-}1$ 7. $9 + {}^{-}4$

Compare. Write >, < or = for each ⬭.

8. 8 ⬭ $^{-}6$ 9. $^{-}4$ ⬭ $^{-}7$ 10. 2 ⬭ 6 11. $^{-}9$ ⬭ 3 12. $^{-}3$ ⬭ 3

Problem Solving and Reasoning

KEY **NS 1.5**, KEY **NS 2.1**, MR 1.0, MR 2.3

Draw number lines to solve the problems.

13. During a game, Derek lost 14 points on his first turn. On his second turn, he gained 35 points. He lost 17 points on his third turn. What was Derek's score after three turns?

14. The temperature was 67°F at 6:15 A.M. The temperature rose 12 degrees by noon and fell 4 degrees by 5:00 P.M. What was the temperature at 5:00 P.M.?

15. A scientist recorded a set of numbers. Order the numbers from least to greatest.

    3.56 $^{-}4.72$ 0 $-\dfrac{1}{2}$

16. A record high temperature of 122°F was recorded in New Mexico. The record low is $^{-}50$°F. Julie says the difference between the record temperatures is 172°F. Is she correct? Explain.

Writing Math When you add a positive number and a negative number, how can you tell if your answer will be positive or negative?

Spiral Review and Test Practice

1. What number goes in the box to make this number sentence true?

$(16 + {}^-7) + 4 = 3 +$

A 27

B 13

C 10

D 9

KEY **NS 2.1** page 550

2. Which of the following is another way to write the product of 18×6?

A $2 \times 2 \times 3 \times 3 \times 3$

B $2 \times 2 \times 6 \times 6$

C $2 \times 3 \times 2 \times 3 \times 2$

D $9 \times 3 \times 6$

Test Tip
Work backward to check your answer.

KEY **NS 1.4** page 14

3. Which fraction is equivalent to $\frac{3}{5}$?

A $\frac{12}{20}$

B $\frac{6}{15}$

C $\frac{3}{10}$

D $\frac{9}{10}$

KEY **NS 2.3** page 34

4. What is 20% of 350?

A 7

B 20

C 60

D 70

Test Tip
There are different ways to find a percent of a number. Use one way to solve the problem and another way to check your answer.

KEY **NS 1.2** page 508

5. What is 25% of 400?

A 400

B 300

C 100

D 80

Test Tip
Use mental math to help you find the answer.

KEY **NS 1.2** page 526

6.

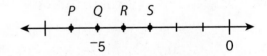

Which letter on the number line best identifies the location of $^-4$?

A S

B R

C Q

D P

KEY **NS 1.5** page 544

Education Place
Visit www.eduplace.com/camap/ for
Test-Taking Tips and **Extra Practice**.

Chapter 25 Spiral Review and Test Practice **559**

Chapter 26

Add and Subtract Integers

Sea and sky at Big Sur, CA

Check What You Know

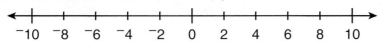

Vocabulary and Concepts KEY NS 1.5, MR 2.3

Choose the best word to complete each sentence. pages 542, 544

1. Whole numbers and their opposites are called _____ .

2. A _____ number is a number less than zero.

3. Every number on a number line has an _____ .

Skills KEY NS 2.1

Use the number line to add. page 550

$$\longleftarrow \;\;{}^{-}10\;\;\;{}^{-}8\;\;\;{}^{-}6\;\;\;{}^{-}4\;\;\;{}^{-}2\;\;\;\;0\;\;\;\;2\;\;\;\;4\;\;\;\;6\;\;\;\;8\;\;\;\;10\;\;\longrightarrow$$

4. $4 + {}^{-}5$

5. ${}^{-}3 + 7$

6. ${}^{-}2 + {}^{-}5$

7. $3 + 6$

8. ${}^{-}1 + {}^{-}8$

9. $9 + {}^{-}12$

Problem Solving and Reasoning KEY NS 1.5

10. The temperature is ${}^{-}2°F$ at Ms. Moreno's house and ${}^{-}4°F$ at school. Is the temperature greater at Ms. Moreno's house or at school?

Vocabulary

Visualize It!

You can use a number line to subtract **positive** and **negative** integers.

$${}^{-}5 - {}^{-}2 = n$$

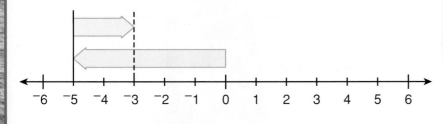

$${}^{-}5 - {}^{-}2 = 3$$

Language Tip

Math words that look alike in English and Spanish often have the same meaning.

English	Spanish
positive	**positivo**
negative	**negativo**

See **English-Spanish Glossary** pages 628–642.

Education Place Visit www.eduplace.com/camap/ for the **eGlossary** and **eGames**.

CA Standards MR 2.3 Use a variety of methods, such as words, numbers, symbols, charts, graphs, tables, diagrams, and models, to explain mathematical reasoning. **Also KEY NS 2.1**

Chapter 26   561

LESSON 1

CA Standards
KEY **NS 2.1** Add, subtract, and multiply with decimals; add with negative integers; subtract positive integers from negative integers; and verify reasonableness of results.

Prepares for GRADE 6 KEY NS 2.3

Also MR 1.0, MR 2.0, MR 2.3

Materials
• Workmat 1
• 2-color counters

Hands On
Subtract Integers

Objective Use counters to model subtraction of integers.

 **Explore**

In Chapter 25, you used counters to model addition with integers. You represented negative integers with red counters and positive integers with yellow. You can do the same to model subtraction.

Question What can you do when there are not enough counters to subtract?

$$^-5 - 2 = n$$

---

1 Use red counters to represent $^-5$.

Place down 5 red counters.

You need to subtract 2, but there are no yellow counters to take away.

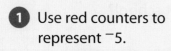

2 Add pairs of red and yellow counters. Each pair represents 0. Remember, adding zero does not change the number.

Add 2 zero pairs so that you can remove 2 yellow counters to subtract 2.

> The sum of $^-1$ and 1 is zero.

3 Take away 2 yellow counters to subtract 2.

The counters that remain represent the answer.

There are only red counters left.

The difference is negative.

Solution: $^-5 - 2 = ^-7$

562

▶ **Extend**

Write a subtraction expression. Then find the difference.

1. ●●●●●●
   Take away 4 reds.

2. ●●●●●
   Take away 3 yellows.

3. ●●●●
   Take away 5 reds.

4. ●●●●
   Take away 6 yellows.

5. ●●●
   Take away 2 yellows.

6. ●●●●●●
   Take away 3 reds.

7. ●●●●●
   Take away 5 reds.

8. ●●●
   Take away 3 yellows.

9. ●
   Take away 3 yellows.

10. ●●
    Take away 5 reds.

Use two-color counters to find the difference.

11. $3 - {}^-6$

12. $2 - {}^-8$

13. ${}^-2 - {}^-6$

14. ${}^-8 - {}^-3$

15. ${}^-8 - {}^-8$

16. $8 - 4$

17. $8 - 8$

18. ${}^-8 - 8$

19. ${}^-4 - {}^-4$

20. ${}^-3 - {}^-7$

21. $5 - {}^-4$

22. $2 - 7$

23. ${}^-9 - {}^-5$

24. $6 - {}^-2$

25. ${}^-4 - 3$

26. $7 - 5$

27. ${}^-1 - 1$

28. ${}^-2 - {}^-8$

29. How can you use the rocks below to model $3 - 6$? What is the difference?

Writing Math

Find ${}^-3 - {}^-4$ and ${}^-3 + 4$. Why is the solution the same?

CA Standards

KEY NS 1.5 Identify and represent on a number line decimals, fractions, mixed numbers, and positive and negative integers.

KEY NS 2.1 Add, subtract, and multiply with decimals; add with negative integers; subtract positive integers from negative integers; and verify reasonableness of results.

Also MR 2.3

Materials
• Workmat 3
• Paper
• Markers

Subtract Integers on a Number Line

Objective Use a number line to subtract integers.

▶ **Learn With Manipulatives**

In Lesson 1, you learned how to use counters to subtract integers. You can also use a number line.

> Suppose that you owe your friend $7. Then your friend says you do not have to pay back $5 of the money you owe. How much, n, do you still owe?

The equation $^-7 - {^-5} = n$ represents this situation. You can use a number line to solve for n.

$$^-7 - {^-5} = n$$

① Make a number line from $^-10$ to 10. Start at 0. To model the first number, move left 7 units to $^-7$.

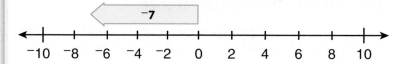

② To model the part you do not have to pay, subtract $^-5$. Move 5 units to the right.

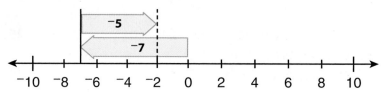

Hint

Write zero near the middle of the number line. Then number the other points.

③ The answer is where you stop on the number line.

$$^-7 - {^-5} = {^-2}$$

$^-7 - {^-5}$ is the same as $^-7 + 5$ because subtracting an integer is the same as adding its opposite.

Solution: You still owe $2.

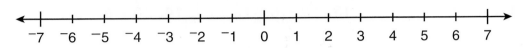

▶ Guided Practice

Use the number line to subtract.

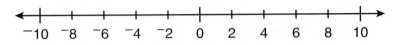

$$^-7 \quad ^-6 \quad ^-5 \quad ^-4 \quad ^-3 \quad ^-2 \quad ^-1 \quad 0 \quad 1 \quad 2 \quad 3 \quad 4 \quad 5 \quad 6 \quad 7$$

1. $^-2 - ^-5$

2. $3 - ^-5$

3. $^-7 - ^-5$

4. $6 - 6$

5. $^-7 - ^-2$

6. $^-1 - 0$

Ask Yourself
• Do I move left or right from 0 for the first integer?
• Which way do I move to subtract the second integer?

Use the number line to complete the pair of number sentences.

$$^-10 \quad ^-8 \quad ^-6 \quad ^-4 \quad ^-2 \quad 0 \quad 2 \quad 4 \quad 6 \quad 8 \quad 10$$

7. $2 - ^-4 = \blacksquare$
$2 + 4 = \blacksquare$

8. $^-8 - ^-6 = \blacksquare$
$^-8 + 6 = \blacksquare$

9. $^-6 - 4 = \blacksquare$
$^-6 + ^-4 = \blacksquare$

Guided Problem Solving

Use the questions to solve this problem.

10. Last month Monica borrowed $6 from Roberto. Today, she loaned Roberto $10 to buy something at the CD store. Who owes whom money, and how much?

　a. Understand You know how much each person borrowed. You want to know who owes money and how much.

　b. Plan Draw a number line. Start with 0 and use arrows to show the money Monica borrowed and then loaned.

　c. Solve Write an equation to find how much money is owed. Who owes that amount?

　d. Look Back How can you check your solution?

 Math Talk Why do you end up at the same point on a number line whether you subtract an integer or add its opposite?

► Practice and Problem Solving

Use the number line to subtract.

11. $^-6 - ^-7 = $ ▨

12. $4 - 6 = $ ▨

13. $^-9 - 6 = $ ▨

14. $10 - 6 = $ ▨

Subtract.

15. $3 - ^-8 = $ ▨

16. $^-8 - ^-1 = $ ▨

17. $2 - ^-5 = $ ▨

18. $3 - 4 = $ ▨

Use the number line to complete each pair of number sentences.

19. $^-9 - ^-9 = $ ▨
$^-9 + 9 = $ ▨

20. $7 - ^-2 = $ ▨
$7 + 2 = $ ▨

21. $10 - ^-3 = $ ▨
$10 + 3 = $ ▨

22. $^-12 - ^-5 = $ ▨
$^-12 + 5 = $ ▨

23. Without the natural greenhouse effect, Earth's average temperature would be 33°C colder than it is. If Earth's average temperature is 15°C, what would the temperature be without the natural greenhouse effect?

 Science Link

Solve. You may use a number line to help.

24. Sean checked his barometer for three days in a row. On Tuesday, it measured 7 mb less than Monday. On Wednesday, it measured 5 mb more than Tuesday. What was the change from Monday to Wednesday?

25. Challenge Sean's barometer measured atmospheric pressure of 1012 mb. Over the next three days, he measured changes of $^-4$, $^-7$, and 4 mb. What was the pressure after 3 days?

 **Fun Facts**

- Earth's atmosphere puts pressure on everything on the planet's surface.
- A barometer measures atmospheric pressure. Changes in pressure can help predict the weather.
- Pressure is often measured in millibars (mb).
- If you see pressure drop more than a millibar in an hour, a storm may be on its way.

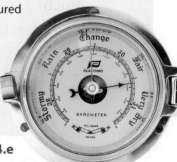

Science ES 4.d, ES 4.e

✓ Spiral Review and Test Practice

Write the decimal as a percent and as a fraction. NS 1.0, KEY **NS 1.2** page 502

26. 0.17

27. 0.05

28. 0.6

29. 0.85

30. 0.3

Write the letter of the correct answer. KEY **NS 2.1**

31. $7 - ^-5$

A 2

B $^-2$

C 75

D 12

Extra Practice See page 575, Set A.

Key Standards Review

Need Help?
See Key Standards Handbook.

Find the volume of each solid figure. KEY **MG 1.3**

1.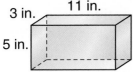
3 in.   11 in.
5 in.

2.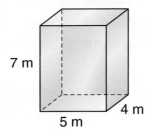
7 m
5 m   4 m

3.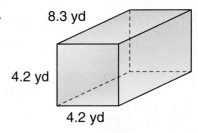
8.3 yd
4.2 yd
4.2 yd

Solve. KEY **NS 1.2**

4. 10% of 330 = n

5. 75% of 44 = n

6. 25% of 28 = n

7. 100% of 17 = n

8. 25% of 124 = n

9. 30% of 60 = n

10. 60% of 30 = n

11. 40% of 10 = n

Order each set from the greatest to the least parts of a unit. KEY **NS 1.2**

12. $\frac{3}{4}$ 0.3   80%

13. $\frac{3}{10}$ 0.2   35%

14. $\frac{11}{20}$ 0.1   25%

Challenge   Problem Solving

Sea Level Integers   KEY **NS 1.5**, KEY **NS 2.1**

The graph shows the elevations (meters above or below sea level) of four cities. Use the graph to solve Problems 1–4.

1. What is Death Valley's elevation?

2. How far above sea level is Shreveport, Louisiana?

3. What is the difference in elevation between Death Valley and Shreveport?

4. Name the city that is closest to sea level.

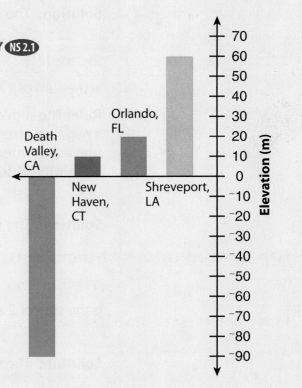

CA Standards
KEY **NS 2.1** Add, subtract, and multiply with decimals; add with negative integers; subtract positive integers from negative integers; and verify reasonableness of results.
Also NS 2.0, AF 1.0, KEY AF 1.2 , KEY AF 1.5 , MR 1.0, MR 2.0

Vocabulary

absolute value

Add and Subtract Integers

Objective Learn rules for adding and subtracting integers.

▶ **Learn by Example**

You already learned that subtracting a negative integer gives the same solution as adding its opposite.

To help predict whether the sum of two integers will be positive or negative, you can use these rules.

Example 1

Is the sum of 2 and 7 positive or negative?

Rule: The sum of two positive integers is positive.

$$2 + 7 = 9$$

Solution: The sum of 2 and 7 is positive.

Example 2

Is the sum of $^-2$ and $^-7$ positive or negative?

Rule: The sum of two negative numbers is negative.

$$^-2 + ^-7 = ^-9$$

Solution: The sum of $^-2$ and $^-7$ is negative.

Example 3

Is the sum of $^-2$ and 7 positive or negative?

Rule: The sum of a positive integer and a negative integer will have the same sign as the integer with the greater **absolute value**.

$$^-2 + 7 = 5$$

Solution: The sum of $^-2$ and 7 is positive.

The absolute value is the distance of a number from 0.

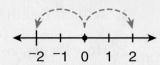

$^-2$ and 2 have the same absolute value, 2

Example 4

Is the sum of 2 and $^-7$ positive or negative?

$$2 + ^-7 = ^-5$$

Solution: The sum of 2 and $^-7$ is negative.

Guided Practice

Decide if the sum or difference is positive or negative. Explain how you decided. Then solve.

1. $1 + 4$

2. $^-4 + 2$

3. $^-9 - 5$

4. $^-2 + ^-6$

5. $7 - ^-3$

6. $4 + ^-8$

Ask Yourself

• Are both signs the same?

• What is the sign of the integer with greatest absolute value?

Guided Problem Solving

Use the questions to solve this problem.

7. You had $20 and bought a pair of flip flops. Now you have $4.50. Write an equation to find out how much the pair of flip flops cost. Solve.

   a. **Understand** Which number represents the whole? Which represents the part?

   b. **Plan** How can you use a variable and integers in an equation to represent the situation?

   c. **Solve** Use n for the unknown. What equation can you write? What does n equal?

   d. **Look Back** How can you check your solution?

 Math Talk Can the rules for deciding the sign of the sum of two integers also be used for deciding the sign of the sum of three or more integers? Explain.

Practice and Problem Solving

Decide if the sum or difference is positive or negative. Explain how you decided. Then solve.

8. $9 + ^-2$

9. $5 + 1$

10. $2 + 4$

11. $^-10 + ^-6$

12. $^-1 - 0$

13. $^-9 - ^-9$

14. $^-6 + ^-10$

15. $^-1 - 3$

16. $8 - ^-6$

17. $^-7 + ^-9$

18. $2 + ^-5$

19. $^-7 - ^-2$

X Algebra Functions **Use the equation to complete the function table.**

20.

y = x + 3	
x	y
⁻9	
⁻3	
3	
6	

21.

y = x − 5	
x	y
7	
2	
⁻3	
⁻8	

22.

y = x + 1	
x	y
⁻8	
⁻6	
⁻4	
⁻2	

 Real World Data

Use the table to solve problems 23–25.

23. In which month do you find the greatest difference between the average high temperature and the average low temperature? What is the absolute value of the difference?

24. On January 10, 1949, at daybreak, the temperature was ⁻7°C. At noon, the temperature was ⁻6°C. At which time was the temperature higher? Explain.

25. The lowest temperature ever recorded in Fresno during September was 2.8°C. How is this temperature similar to the record low for October?

Temperatures (°C) for Fresno, CA				
	January	April	July	October
Average High	12.4	23.7	36.7	26.5
Record High	25.5	37.8	44.4	38.9
Average Low	3.1	8.8	18.5	10.5
Record Low	⁻7.8	0	10	⁻2.8

Chuckchansi stadium, Fresno, CA

Spiral Review and Test Practice

Compare. Write >, <, or = for the ●. **KEY** NS 1.5 page 544

26. ⁻5 ● 1   27. 2 ● 1   28. ⁻12 ● 6   29. 5 ● 5

Write the letter of the correct answer. KEY NS 2.1

30. ⁻7 − 19 = n

   A n = ⁻26   **B** n = 26   **C** n = ⁻12   **D** n = 12

Practice Game

Zero in on Zero

Object of the Game Practice adding and subtracting integers by getting as close to zero as possible.

Materials
Number Cube (labeled 0 – 5)

Number of Players 2

How to Play

1 Each player starts with 5 points.

2 The first player rolls the number cube.

3 He or she chooses to add or subtract the digit on the number cube from his or her total points.

4 Players take turns until each player has had five turns. The player whose total points after five turns is closest to zero wins.

CA Standards
KEY NS 2.1 Add, subtract, multiply, and divide with decimals; add with negative integers; subtract positive integers from negative integers; and verify the reasonableness of the results.

Also MR 1.0, MR 2.0

Education Place
Visit www.eduplace.com/camap/ for **Brain Teasers** and **eGames** to play.

Chapter 26 Lesson 3   **571**

CA Standards
KEY NS 1.5 Identify and represent on a number line decimals, fractions, mixed numbers, and positive and negative integers.

MR 2.3 Use a variety of methods, such as words, numbers, symbols, charts, graphs, tables, diagrams, and models, to explain mathematical reasoning.

Also KEY NS 2.1, MR 1.1, MR 2.0, MR 3.1

Problem Solving Strategy
Use a Number Line

Objective Use a number line to help solve problems involving integers.

▶ **Learn by Example**

You can use a number line to solve problems involving integers.

> When Alma stepped outside, the wind was blowing, which made the actual temperature of 5°F feel 6° colder. Ten minutes later, the wind increased, which made Alma feel 3° colder than when she first stepped out. How cold does it feel to Alma?

UNDERSTAND

The problem asks you to find how cold Alma feels now.

- The actual temperature is 5°F.
- At first, the wind made it feel 6° colder than the actual temperature.
- Later the wind made it feel 3° colder than when Alma first went outside.

PLAN

Use a number line. Record actual temperatures above 0°F as positive integers. Record temperature drops as negative integers.

SOLVE

Find the temperature after the first change.

$$5 + {}^-6 = {}^-1$$

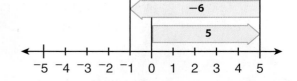

Find how cold Alma feels after the second change.

$$^-1 + {}^-3 = {}^-4$$

The temperature feels like ⁻4°F to Alma.

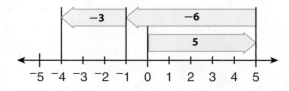

LOOK BACK

Can you check your answer by working through the problem in the opposite direction?

▶ **Guided Problem Solving**

Use the Ask Yourself questions to help you solve this problem.

1. One day the temperature went up 8° and then down 12°. If the final temperature is ⁻7°F, what was the temperature at first?

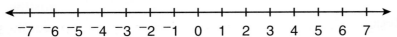

Ask Yourself
• Where do I start on the number line?
• Do I move right or left to record temperatures that increase?
• Do I move right or left to record temperatures that decrease?

 Math Talk Explain the difference between showing a temperature on a number line and showing how much the temperature increases or decreases using a number line.

▶ **Independent Problem Solving**

Use a number line to solve. Explain why your answer makes sense.

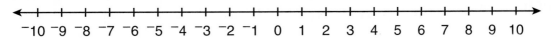

2. Bobi measured the temperature at Lake Tahoe. In the morning, the temperature was ⁻2°F. During the day, the temperature rose 4° and then dropped 10°. What was the temperature at the end of the day?

3. At 6:00 A.M., the temperature was ⁻5°F. By noon, the temperature was 6°F. The high temperature for the day was 10°F. By how many degrees did the temperature change?

4. At halftime, the temperature was 10° lower than at the start of the game. By the end of the game, the temperature was ⁻2°F, which was 3° higher than at halftime. Find the temperature at the start of the game.

5. On Monday it was 40°F. The temperature went down by 10° by the end of the day. On Tuesday the temperature went up 5°, but dropped 15° by evening. What was the temperature on Tuesday evening?

6. **Challenge** The record low temperature in Antarctica was about 70°F lower than the average daily temperature of ⁻58°F. Is ⁻130°F a reasonable estimate for the record low temperature? Explain.

7. **Create and Solve** Write a word problem that could be solved in 3 or more steps by working backward on a number line.

Reading & Writing Math

Vocabulary

Use the **Word Bank** to complete each sentence.
Write and solve an equation that fits the situation.

Word Bank

positive
negative
absolute value

1. The sum of two positive integers is _____.

2. The sum of two negative integers is _____.

3. The sum of a positive integer and a negative integer
will have the same sign as the integer with the
greater _____.

Writing
Deb said ⁻47 + ⁻23 = 70. Is she correct?
Tell why a number line is a good tool to use to
explain your thinking.

Reading
Check out this book in your library.
A Gebra Named Al, by Wendy Isdell

CA Standards
MR 2.3 Use a variety of
methods, such as words, numbers,
symbols, charts, graphs, tables,
diagrams, and models, to explain
mathematical reasoning.

Also KEY NS 2.1

Standards-Based Extra Practice

Set A ──────────────────────────────────── KEY **NS 2.1** page 564

Subtract.

1. 9 − ⁻9　　　　**2.** ⁻5 − 7　　　　**3.** ⁻8 − ⁻3　　　　**4.** 7 − 10

5. 5 − 5　　　　**6.** ⁻2 − 3　　　　**7.** 7 − 5　　　　**8.** 6 − ⁻4

9. 7 − 3　　　　**10.** ⁻4 − 5　　　　**11.** 10 − 12　　　　**12.** 8 − ⁻6

Complete each pair of number sentences.

13. 6 − ⁻6 = ■　　**14.** ⁻4 − ⁻7 = ■　　**15.** ⁻8 − ⁻8 = ■　　**16.** 12 − ⁻4 = ■
　　6 + 6 = ■　　　　⁻4 + 7 = ■　　　　⁻8 + 8 = ■　　　　12 + 4 = ■

17. A football team gained 10 yards on the first play of the game and lost 20 yards on the second play. What integer represents the team's total gain or loss for the first two plays of the game?

Set B ──────────────────────────────────── KEY **NS 2.1** page 568

Decide if each sum or difference is positive or negative. Explain how you decided. Then solve.

1. 8 + ⁻1　　　　**2.** 4 + ⁻6　　　　**3.** ⁻3 − 5　　　　**4.** ⁻8 + ⁻4

5. 6 − ⁻7　　　　**6.** ⁻4 + 9　　　　**7.** ⁻5 + ⁻3　　　　**8.** 2 − ⁻5

Use the equation to complete the function table.

9.

$y = x + 4$	
x	y
⁻6	■
⁻4	■
1	■
3	■

10.

$y = x - 3$	
x	y
5	■
2	■
⁻2	■
⁻4	■

11.

$y = x + 2$	
x	y
⁻7	■
⁻3	■
⁻1	■
4	■

Solve.

12. Helen set up two thermometers in her yard. One thermometer is in the sun. The other is in the shade. She checks the temperature on each thermometer at noon. The temperature in the sun is 3°F. The temperature in the shade is ⁻2°F. How much greater is the temperature in the sun?

Education Place
Visit www.eduplace.com/camap/
for more **Extra Practice**.

Chapter Review/Test

Vocabulary and Concepts ———————————— MR 2.3, KEY NS 2.1

Write the best word to complete each sentence.

1. The sum of two negative integers is a _____ number.

2. The sum of two positive integers is a _____ number.

Skills ———————————————————— KEY NS 1.5, KEY NS 2.1

Use the number line for Exercises 3–14.

```
←—+——+——+——+——+——+——+——+——+——+——+——+——+——+——+——+——+——+——+——→
  ⁻9  ⁻8  ⁻7  ⁻6  ⁻5  ⁻4  ⁻3  ⁻2  ⁻1  0   1   2   3   4   5   6   7   8   9
```

Solve.

3. $8 - {}^-3$ 4. ${}^-4 - 3$ 5. $1 - {}^-6$ 6. ${}^-9 - {}^-2$

7. $4 - {}^-2$ 8. ${}^-5 - 2$ 9. $3 - {}^-2$ 10. ${}^-2 - {}^-6$

Complete each pair of number sentences.

11. $2 - {}^-6 = \blacksquare$
    $2 + 6 = \blacksquare$

12. ${}^-6 - 3 = \blacksquare$
    ${}^-6 + {}^-3 = \blacksquare$

13. ${}^-5 - 3 = \blacksquare$
    ${}^-3 + {}^-5 = \blacksquare$

14. ${}^-2 - {}^-2 = \blacksquare$
    $2 + {}^-2 = \blacksquare$

Decide if each sum or difference is positive or negative. Then solve.

15. $12 - {}^-3$ 16. ${}^-7 - 14$ 17. $4 - 5$ 18. $8 - {}^-4$

Problem Solving and Reasoning ———————— KEY NS 2.1, MR 1.1, MR 2.3

Write an equation to solve the problem.

19. Bob owes his cousin Jeremy $12. After he gets his allowance Bob pays his cousin $5. How much does Bob still owe his cousin?

20. At daybreak, the temperature was 75°F. During the day, the temperature dropped 4 degrees, and then rose 15 degrees. What was the temperature at the end of the day?

Writing Math When subtracting positive and negative integers, how do you know if the answer will be positive or negative?

Spiral Review and Test Practice

1. Ryan is putting 59 vacation photos in 4 photo albums. If he puts an equal number of photos in each album, how many photos will be left over?

   A 0

   B 2

   C 3

   D 14

   Test Tip
   Read the problem carefully and make sure you understand the question.

   KEY **NS 2.2** page 328

2. Which number sentence is true?

   A $9 < {}^-10$

   C ${}^-8 > {}^-10$

   B ${}^-10 > {}^-6$

   D ${}^-2 < {}^-5$

   NS **1.0** page 544

3. Which letter shows the ordered pair (3, 0)?

   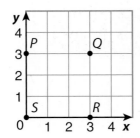

   A *P*

   C *R*

   B *Q*

   D *S*

   KEY **SDAP 1.5** page 364

4. What is $\frac{3}{5}$ written as a percent?

   A 6%

   B 20%

   C 35%

   D 60%

   Test Tip
   Remember, percent is part of 100.

   KEY **NS 1.2** page 502

5. Which point on the number line *best* represents ${}^-1.75$?

   A

   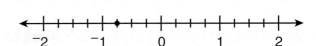

   B

   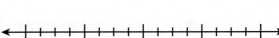

   C

   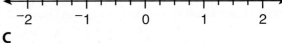

   D

   KEY **NS 1.5** page 550

6. ${}^-4 - 3$

   A 7

   C ${}^-1$

   B 1

   D ${}^-7$

   KEY **NS 2.1** page 564

Education Place
Visit www.eduplace.com/camap/ for
Test-Taking Tips and **Extra Practice**.

Chapter 26 Spiral Review and Test Practice   **577**

Unit 11 Review/Test

Vocabulary and Concepts —————————— KEY **NS 1.5**, KEY **NS 2.1**, MR 2.3 Chapters 25–26

Choose the best term to complete each sentence.

1. Negative integers are always less than _____ integers.

2. Whole numbers less than zero are _____.

3. Two numbers that are the same distance, but in opposite directions, from zero on a number line are _____.

Skills ———————————————————— KEY **NS 2.1**, KEY **NS 1.5** Chapter 25, Lesson 2

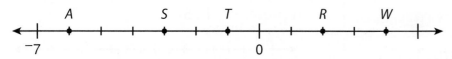

Write the integer that belongs at each point.

4. Point A   5. Point R   6. Point S   7. Point T   8. Point W

Write the integers in order from least to greatest.

9. $7, {}^-5, 0, 2$ 10. ${}^-3, 9, 1, 0$ 11. $0, {}^-4, 4, 2, {}^-1$

Write the addition expression shown by the counters and then find the sum. Chapter 25, Lesson 3

12. ●●●●◐○○   13. ○●●●●○

Use the number line to add or subtract. Chapters 25–26

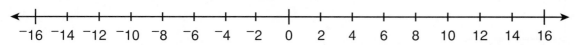

14. ${}^-6 + 3$ 15. $4 + {}^-9$ 16. ${}^-10 + 3$ 17. $12 + 6$

18. $8 - 8$ 19. $5 - 7$ 20. $2 - {}^-4$ 21. $3 - 0$

Problem Solving and Reasoning

KEY **NS 2.1**, MR 2.3 Chapters 25–26

Solve.

22. Sarah made up a card game. Each card had a number from ⁻10 to 10. Your score is the sum of the cards you draw. Sarah drew a 7 and a ⁻8. Josh drew a ⁻5 and a 6. Who won?

23. Roxanne borrowed $12 from Dominique. Last week Dominique borrowed $35 from Roxanne. Who owes whom money, and how much?

24. One day in Alaska the temperature was ⁻12°F. It went up 5°. What was the temperature then?

25. In a game Karl gained 3 points, then lost 5 points, then lost 8 points, and finally gained 6 points. What is his score?

Writing Math What is the difference between an integer and the absolute value of an integer?

Performance Assessment

What's the Score?

KEY **NS 2.1**, MR 1.1, MR 2.4

Five students are playing an integer game. They finished the game in order of their names. Amelia won, Ben came in second, Ciara was third, Dante was fourth, and Eduardo came in last.

Task	Information You Need
Use the information above and to the right to find the scores for the players. Write addition number sentences. Who gets each score? Which numbers did they draw to get the scores? Find two different solutions.	A score is the sum of any two of the integer cards.
	No player made a score that was greater than 5.
	No player made a score that was less than ⁻5.

Divide by 10

It's easy to divide by 10, just drop the zero at the end!

I have a fast way to do 50 ÷ 10. The answer is 50 without the zero, or 5. The problem is really just to figure out how many tens there are. Since 50 is 5 tens, simply drop the zero to get the answer!

1. 50 ÷ 10 = ☐ 5
   Number of Tens

2. 80 ÷ 10 = ☐
   Number of Tens

3. 160 ÷ 10 = ☐
   Number of Tens

4. 340 ÷ 10 = ☐
   Number of Tens

You are doing great!

5. 40 ÷ 10 = ☐

6. 150 ÷ 10 = ☐

7. 70 ÷ 10 = ☐

8. 230 ÷ 10 = ☐

9. 90 ÷ 10 = ☐

10. 360 ÷ 10 = ☐

11. 100 ÷ 10 = ☐

12. 410 ÷ 10 = ☐

13. 590 ÷ 10 = ☐

14. 890 ÷ 10 = ☐

Doing Great!

Take It Further!
Now try doing all the steps in your head!

15. 60 ÷ 10   **16.** 520 ÷ 10   **17.** 750 ÷ 10   **18.** 620 ÷ 10

Coordinate Plane

BIG IDEAS!

- Using integers, you can plot points in the coordinate plane.

- Rules about sets of numbers can be written as equations, used to complete function tables, and plotted on graphs as lines.

Chapter 27
Plot Points

Chapter 28
Graph Linear Equations

Songs and Games

Math Music Track 12:
A Coordinate Plane

eGames at
www.eduplace.com/camap/

Math Readers

A young western skink sips dew from a metal garden grid.

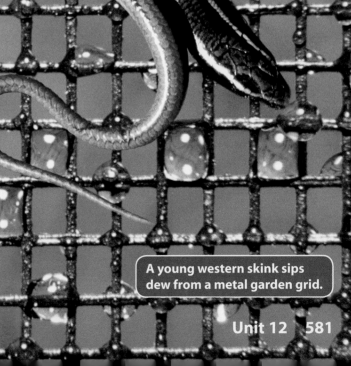

Game

Treasure Hunt

Object of the Game Find and dig up all of the buried treasure on your partner's map.

Materials
- Counters
- Learning Tool 30: Coordinate Grid (2 per player)

Set Up
Each player has 2 copies of the coordinate grid and 4 counters.

Number of Players 2

How to Play

1 Each player places four counters anywhere on the map. The counters are their "treasures." The treasures must be placed on an ordered pair.

2 Players take turns naming points on the map using an ordered pair. By naming a point, the player is "digging up" that area.

3 After each attempt, the player is told whether or not the dug-up point contained a treasure and records the result on the second treasure map.

4 A player must name the point covered by a treasure to dig up that treasure. If they are correct, their partner must remove the counter and give it to them.

5 Play continues until one player digs up and receives all four treasures.

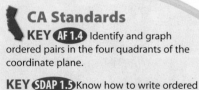
CA Standards
KEY AF 1.4 Identify and graph ordered pairs in the four quadrants of the coordinate plane.

KEY SDAP 1.5 Know how to write ordered pairs correctly; for example, (x, y).

Also MR 1.0

Education Place
Visit www.eduplace.com/camap/ for **Brain Teasers** and **eGames** to play.

Reading Vocabulary is important in everyday language. Mathematics also has its own set of words that you need to learn.

1. **Math words have specific meanings.** Many words have one meaning in everyday language and a different meaning in mathematics For example, in everyday language, an *axis* is an imaginary line through the center of the Earth, around which it rotates. In mathematics, an axis is a number line.

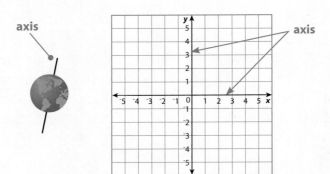

axis   axis

I keep a log of all the math words I learn.

2. **You need to know the language of math in order to keep learning.** In mathematics, you learn something new in every grade. You learn something new in every chapter and lesson. In mathematics, you build on what you know.

Writing Preview Chapter 27. Make a list of words that are highlighted or in boldface type. Write "Yes" next to each word you know. Write "No" next to those that are new. Keep the list handy as you work on the lessons. Turn every "No" into a "Yes"!

WORD LOG—Chapter 27

	Word	Already Know	Meaning
Lesson 1	coordinate plane	No	

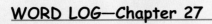

Plot Points

The constellation Orion as it appears over Death Valley, CA

Vocabulary and Concepts GRADE 4 KEY MG 2.0, KEY MG 2.1

Match each term with a definition.

1. ordered pair
2. origin
3. function

   a. the point where the *x*- and *y*-axis intersect in a coordinate grid
   b. a pair of numbers indicating the *x*-coordinate and *y*-coordinate of a point on a coordinate grid
   c. a set of ordered pairs of numbers

Skills GRADE 4 KEY AF 1.5

Copy and complete each function table.

4.

$y = x + 3$	
x	*y*
5	
7	
9	
12	

5.

$y = 2x - 4$	
x	*y*
3	
4	
5	
6	

6.

$y = 10 - 3x$	
x	*y*
0	
1	
2	
3	

Problem Solving and Reasoning GRADE 4 KEY MG 2.0

7. Ana plotted points on a coordinate grid at (4, 6) and (5, 4). Which point is closest to the *x*-axis?

Vocabulary

Visualize It!

y-axis
the vertical number line

coordinate plane
formed by two perpendicular number lines in which every point is assigned an ordered pair of numbers

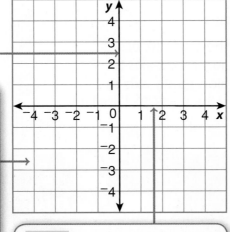

x-axis
the horizontal number line

Language Tips

In everyday language, *coordinate* descr the process of organizing or leading an activity. In mathematics, *coordinate* des the location of a point on a coordinate in relation to the *x*- and *y*-axis.

Math words that look alike in English ar Spanish often have the same meaning.

English	Spanish
coordinate	coordenada
origin	origen
function	función

See **English-Spanish Glossary** pages 628–6

 Education Place Visit www.eduplace.com/camap/ for the **eGlossary** and **eGames**.

CA Standards MR 2.3 Use a variety of methods, such as words, numbers, symbols, charts, graphs, tables, diagrams, and models, to explain mathematical reasoning. **Also KEY** AF 1.4

Chapter 27

CA Standards

KEY AF 1.4 Identify and graph ordered pairs in the four quadrants of the coordinate plane.

KEY SDAP 1.5 Know how to write ordered pairs correctly; for example, (x, y).

Also MR 2.3

Vocabulary

coordinate plane

x-axis

y-axis

Materials
- Workmat 8
- Learning Tool 10 (Centimeter Grid)

Vocabulary Tip

A **constellation** is a group of stars that appear together in the sky.

Hands On
Plot Points in the Coordinate Plane

Objective Graph ordered pairs in the coordinate plane.

▶ **Explore**

Coordinate grids, like the ones you worked with in Chapter 17, can be extended to include negative numbers. Sometimes this is referred to as a **coordinate plane** because a plane extends in all directions without end.

In a coordinate plane, all the points to the left of the **y-axis** have a negative number as the x-coordinate. The points below the **x-axis** have negative numbers as y-coordinates.

Question How do you plot points in the coordinate plane?

Graph the majors stars in the **constellation** Volans, or the Flying Fish. Use Workmat 8.

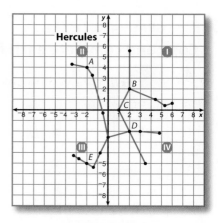

1 Plot the first star.

- Start at the origin (0, 0).
- Go left along the x-axis to ⁻8 and up along the y-axis to 3.
- Mark a point at (⁻8, 3). Label it V.

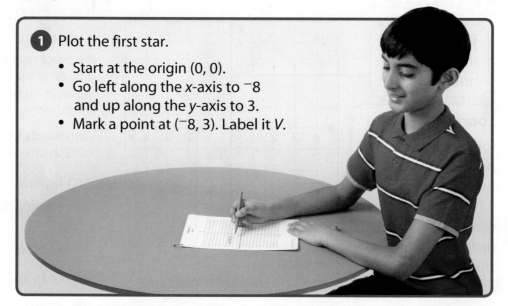

2 Plot the other stars.

Use these ordered pairs to graph the other stars in the coordinate plane. Label the point with the letter name shown.

A (3, ⁻3)   N (6, 3)

L (0, 2)   O (⁻3, 4)

S (7, ⁻1)

 Extend

Use the coordinate plane to write the ordered pair for each point.

1. B   2. D   3. F

4. I   5. K   6. L

7. P   8. M   9. N

Write the letter name of each point.

10. (⁻8, ⁻1)   11. (⁻3, ⁻4)   12. (⁻2, ⁻7)

13. (⁻6, 3)   14. (2, 7)   15. (3, ⁻6)

Find the distance between each pair of points.

16. G and H   17. Z and F   18. L and G

Use grid paper. Plot points using the coordinates for stars in the constellation called the Whale. Label the point with its letter.

19. A (⁻12, 5)   20. B (⁻11, 8)   21. C (⁻9, 8)

22. D (⁻9, 4)   23. E (⁻8, 2)   24. F (⁻4, 0)

25. G (0, ⁻4)   26. H (4, ⁻4)   27. I (10, ⁻5)

28. J (7, ⁻9)   29. K (⁻2, ⁻10) 30. L (⁻11, ⁻4)

31. M (1, ⁻7)   32. N (6, ⁻5)

 Writing Math

Is the location of (⁻2, 4) the same as (2, ⁻4)? Why or why not?

CA Standards
KEY **AF 1.4** Identify and graph ordered pairs in the four quadrants of the coordinate plane.

KEY **SDAP 1.4** Identify ordered pairs of data from a graph and interpret the meaning of the data in terms of the situation depicted in the graph.

Also KEY **SDAP 1.5**, AF 1.1, MR 3.1, MR 2.3

Read a Map

Objective Locate points on a map (coordinate plane) using ordered pairs.

▶ **Learn by Example**

You can use a coordinate plane and ordered pairs to create or read a map.

Noemi mapped her neighborhood on a coordinate plane. She set her home at the origin (0, 0).

Find Noemi's location after she goes 3 blocks west and 5 blocks north.

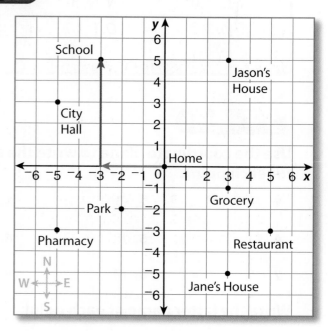

1 The red arrow shows that after walking 3 blocks west, Noemi is at point (⁻3, 0).

2 The blue arrow shows that walking 5 blocks north brings her to (⁻3, 5).

Solution: Noemi is at school.

▶ **Guided Practice**

Use the map above.

1. Write an ordered pair for the location of the park.

2. What is located at (3, 5)?

3. How far is it from School to Jason's House?

123 **Math Talk** How do the points of the compass correspond to Noemi's coordinate plane?

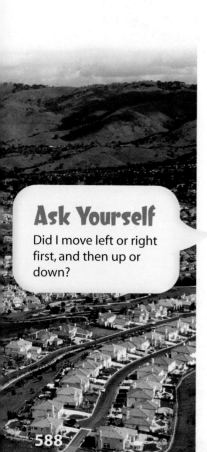

Ask Yourself

Did I move left or right first, and then up or down?

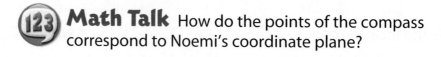

Use the map. Copy the location and write the name of the animals that you can see at each location.

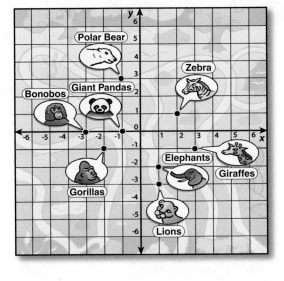

4. (⁻1, 0) **5.** (⁻1, 3)

6. (3, ⁻1) **7.** (1, ⁻3)

Write the location for the animals.

8. Gorillas **9.** Bonobos

10. Zebras **11.** Elephants

Solve.

12. Flamingos can be found 2 units west of the bonobos. At which ordered pair are the flamingos located? Write the animal name and location.

13. A Skyfari Aerial terminal is found at (0, 3). How far is the terminal from the polar bear exhibit?

14. What animals can be found west of the Skyfari Aerial terminal? Write the animal names and locations.

15. Look at the coordinates you wrote for Problem 14. What can you say about the coordinates for animals west, or to the left, of the y-axis? Why is this so?

16. Challenge Imagine there were animals located somewhere north and east of the lions. What do you know about the coordinates for all possible locations? Why?

 Spiral Review and Test Practice

Find the value of n. KEY NS 1.2 page 508

17. n = 15% of $300 **18.** n = 25% of $88

19. n = 50% of $350 **20.** n = 10% of 435

Write the letter of the correct answer. KEY AF 1.4

21. The map shows the location where four trees are to be planted. Which tree is to be planted at the point (⁻3, 2)?

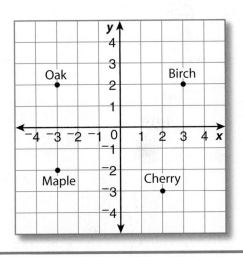

  A Oak **C** Maple

  B Birch **D** Cherry

LESSON 3

CA Standards

AF 1.0 Students use variables in simple expressions, compute the value of the expression for specific values of the variable, and plot and interpret the results.

KEY AF 1.5 Solve problems involving linear functions with integer values; write the equation; and graph the resulting ordered pairs of integers on a grid.

Also KEY SDAP 1.5, MR 1.1, MR 2.3, MR 3.0

Integers and Functions

Objective Complete a table of values for a given function, and choose an equation for a given function table.

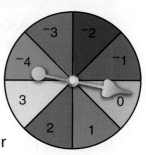

▶ **Learn by Example**

In previous lessons, you used function rules with positive integers. In this lesson, you will extend your work with functions to include negative integers.

Example 1

Latanya spins a number and adds 5 points to it to get her score. She can find all the possible scores by using the equation $y = x + 5$, where x is the number she spins and y is her total score.

1. Make a function table to find the ordered pairs. Use numbers on the spinner for x.

2. Use the equation to find the missing y-values. Then write the ordered pairs.

Rule: $y = x + 5$

x	y	Ordered Pairs
⁻4	1	(⁻4, 1)
⁻3	2	(⁻3, 2)
⁻2	▨	(⁻2, 3)
⁻1	▨	(⁻1, 4)
0	▨	(0, 5)
1	▨	(1, 6)
2	▨	(2, 7)
3	▨	(3, 8)

Solution: The function table and list of ordered pairs show the score (y) for every possible spin (x).

Example 2

Cynthia made the following function table.

Which equation shows the relationship of all the values in the table?

A $y = \dfrac{x}{2}$ **C** $y = 2x$

B $y = \dfrac{x}{3}$ **D** $y = 3x$

Rule:	x	1	3	4	5
?	y	2	6	8	10

Test each equation by substituting ordered pairs from the table into the equation. Remember that the equation must work for all of the ordered pairs.

Since the equation in choice C works for all of the ordered pairs, it is not necessary to test the equation in choice D.

Solution: The equation is $y = 2x$, choice C.

Copy and complete each function table.

1.

$y = x + 4$	
x	y
⁻2	▢
⁻1	▢
0	▢
1	▢

2.

$y = x - 3$	
x	y
⁻3	▢
⁻1	▢
0	▢
▢	⁻1

3.

$y = x - 5$	
x	y
12	▢
9	▢
▢	1
0	▢

Choose the equation that shows the relationship of all the values in the table. Then find the value of y for the given value of x.

4.

Rule: ?	
x	y
1	3
2	6
3	9
4	▢

A $y = 3x$
B $y = x - 3$
C $y = x + 8$
D $y = \frac{x}{8}$

5.

Rule: ?	
x	y
2	⁻13
4	⁻11
6	⁻9
7	▢

A $y = x - 17$
B $y = x + 11$
C $y = x - 15$
D $y = x - 21$

6.

Rule: ?	
x	y
⁻1	4
⁻2	5
⁻3	6
⁻5	▢

A $y = x + 5$
B $y = x + 3$
C $y = 5 - x$
D $y = 3 - x$

(123) Math Talk Did you test every equation in Exercise 4 to choose the correct equation?

Copy and complete each function table.

7.

$y = x + 7$	
x	y
⁻2	▢
⁻1	▢
▢	7
▢	8

8.

$y = x - 5$	
x	y
⁻4	▢
⁻2	▢
0	▢
1	▢

9.

$y = 4x$	
x	y
6	▢
4	▢
3	▢
▢	8

Choose the equation that shows the relationship of all the values in the table. Then find the value of y for the given value of x.

10.

Rule: ?	
x	**y**
1	⁻11
2	⁻10
3	⁻9
4	▪

A $y = x - 9$
B $y = x - 10$
C $y = x - 12$
D $y = -9 - x$

11.

Rule: ?	
x	**y**
⁻18	⁻15.5
⁻15	⁻12.5
⁻11	⁻8.5
⁻4	▪

A $y = x - 3.5$
B $y = x + 3.5$
C $y = x - 2.5$
D $y = x + 2.5$

12.

Rule: ?	
x	**y**
2	1
6	3
8	4
12	▪

A $y = x - 4$
B $y = \frac{x}{2}$
C $y = 2x$
D none of these

 Real World Data

Skydivers jump from a plane traveling at 1.6 miles per minute. The data table shows the distance the plane has traveled at different times during the jump.

13. Which equation describes the relationship between the time in minutes (*m*) and the distance (*d*)?

A $d = m + 1.6$ **B** $d = 1.6m$ **C** $d = \frac{m}{1.6}$

14. What happens to the distance as the time increases by 1 minute?

15. How far had the plane traveled 7 minutes into the jump?

Time (min)	0	1	2	3	4	5
Distance (mi)	0	1.6	3.2	4.8	6.4	8.0

 Spiral Review and Test Practice

Divide. KEY NS 2.1 pages 320 and 326

16. $78\overline{)4{,}914}$ **17.** $56\overline{)705.6}$ **18.** $9\overline{)40.5}$ **19.** $62\overline{)2{,}790}$

Write the letter of the correct answer. KEY AF 1.5

20. Which equation could have been used to create this function table?

A $y = x + 4$ **B** $y = x - 4$ **C** $y = x - 6$ **D** $y = x + 6$

x	**y**
⁻8	⁻2
⁻5	1
4	10

Extra Practice See page 599, Set B.

Key Standards Review

Need Help?
See Key Standards Handbook.

Name the location of the point on the number line. KEY NS 1.5

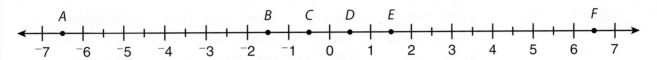

1. A

2. B

3. C

4. D

5. E

6. F

Use the number line to solve. KEY NS 2.1

7. $^-4 - 3$

8. $3 + {}^-5$

9. $^-6 + 5$

10. $3 - 3$

11. $^-6 - 5$

12. $^-6 - 0$

Challenge   Problem Solving

City Search

KEY AF 1.4, KEY SDAP 1.5, KEY NS 2.1, NS 1.3

The graph shows part of California's coastline. Use the clues to name the ordered pair for each city. Then find each city on the map.

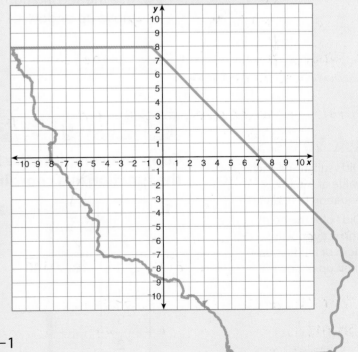

1. Los Angeles, CA
   x-coordinate: two to the
                second power
   y-coordinate: 8 less than $^-2$

2. Bakersfield, CA
   x-coordinate: an even prime
                number
   y-coordinate: four more than $^-8$

3. San Francisco, CA
   x-coordinate: ten less than $\left(\frac{1}{4} \div \frac{1}{4} \right) - 1$
   y-coordinate: a prime factor of 49

CA Standards
KEY **AF 1.5** Solve problems involving linear functions with integer values; write the equation; and graph the resulting ordered pairs of integers on a grid.
Also AF 1.0, MR 1.0, MR 2.3, MR 3.1

Materials
• Workmat 8
• Learning Tool 31 (Coordinate Plane)

Graph Functions and Integers

Objective Graph functions.

▶ **Learn by Example**

In the last lesson, you completed a function table showing all the possible scores Latanya could get in her spinner game. In this lesson, you will learn how to graph those results in a coordinate plane.

Rule: $y = x + 5$

x	⁻4	⁻3	⁻2	⁻1	0	1	2	3
y	1	2	3	4	5	6	7	8

Example

Plot the points in the coordinate plane.

1. Use the first number in each ordered pair to move right or left along the *x*-axis

2. Use the second number to move up or down.

Solution:

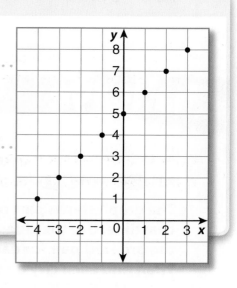

Ask Yourself
• Did I substitute each value of *x* in the equation to find *y*?
• Did I plot the point correctly, moving right or left first, and then up or down?

▶ **Guided Practice**

Copy and complete the function table. Then graph the function in a coordinate plane.

1.

$y = x + 3$	
x	y
⁻5	
⁻4	
⁻3	
⁻2	
⁻1	
0	

2.

$y = 1 - x$	
x	y
⁻3	
⁻2	
⁻1	
0	
1	
2	

3.

$y = \dfrac{x}{4}$	
x	y
0	
4	
8	
12	
16	
20	

Guided Problem Solving

Use the questions to solve this problem.

4. For an air show, 8 teams of sky divers will jump in formation. The equation $y = 15x$ shows the number of seconds (y) it will take the teams (x) to exit the plane. Make a graph showing the times the teams jump.

   a. **Understand** What values should you use for x? What is the greatest value you could use for x?

   b. **Plan/Solve** Make and complete a function table. Use grid paper and plot the points in a coordinate plane. Choose appropriate scales for the axes.

   c. **Look Back** Describe your graph.

 Math Talk Look at your graph for Problem 4. What happens to the time as x increases?

▶ **Practice and Problem Solving**

Copy and complete the function table. Then graph the function in a coordinate plane.

5.

$y = 2 - x$						
x	⁻6	⁻3	0	1	4	5
y						

6.

$y = 5x$						
x	0	1	2	3	4	5
y						

 Spiral Review and Test Practice

Solve. KEY **NS 1.2** page 508

7. Find 20% of 90   8. Find 16% of 80   9. Find 80% of 25   10. Find 25% of 60

Write the letter of the correct answer. KEY **AF 1.5**

11. Which equation could be used to create the graph?

   A $y = x - 4$ **C** $y = x + 1$

   B $y = x - 2$ **D** $y = 3 - x$

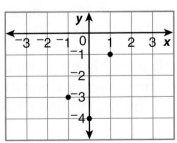

Extra Practice See page 599, Set C.

LESSON 5

Field Trip...

Palomar, CA

CA Standards
MR 1.0, MR 1.2,
MR 2.0, MR 2.3,
MR 2.6, KEY NS 1.2,
KEY NS 2.1, KEY AF 1.4,
MG 2.0

Problem Solving

Objective Use skills and strategies to solve word problems.

The observatory is open to the public for self-guided visits to the 200-inch Hale telescope.

The Palomar Observatory is home to five telescopes that are used to research the night sky.

Solve. Tell which strategy or method you used.

1. Sabia has $20.00. She wants to buy a T-shirt for $14.50, a key chain for $3.95, and a pen for $1.99. Does she have enough money? If not, how much more money will she need?

   Suppose the T-shirt was on sale for 10% off. Would Sabia have enough money to buy everything?

2. Reservations for tours are made well in advance. In one year, 4 tours are given per day for 11 days. If 33 tours have already filled up, what percent of the tours are left?

3. Use grid paper to plot the following coordinates in a constellation. What shape does the constellation make?
   $A(5, 4)$ $B(^-3, 4)$ $C(5, ^-3)$ $D(^-3, ^-3)$

4. Look at Problem 3. If the x-value in each ordered pair increased by 1, will the new figure be congruent to the original figure? Check by plotting the points.

Problem Solving On Tests

Select a Strategy
- Draw a Picture
- Write an Equation
- Guess and Check
- Choose the Operation
- Make a Table

1. As part of a town project, Owen will plant vegetables within a triangular-shaped garden. To prepare the garden, he needs to find the area of the garden. What is the area?

A 18 ft²

B 25.5 ft²

C 36 ft²

D 60 ft²

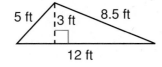
5 ft 3 ft 8.5 ft 12 ft

KEY **MG 1.1** page 460

2. Which point on the number line best represents the location of ⁻2?

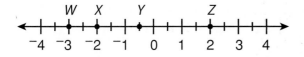
W X Y Z
⁻4 ⁻3 ⁻2 ⁻1 0 1 2 3 4

A W   **B** X   **C** Y   **D** Z

KEY **NS 1.5** page 544

3. Rene wrote the expression shown below to show how many hours she worked at the bakery.

Which situation *best* describes the expression $2h + 1$?

A Rene worked one hour more than twice the time she worked yesterday.

B Rene worked two hours yesterday and one hour today.

C Rene worked one hour today and two hours yesterday.

D Rene worked one hour more than she worked yesterday.

KEY **AF 1.2** page 104

4. The price of gasoline at a local gas station is $2.20 per gallon. If Larry puts 10.5 gallons into his car's gas tank, how much does he pay for gas?

A $2.31

B $13.70

C $23.10

D $231.00

Test Tip
Remember to add the symbols to show dollars and cents.

KEY **NS 2.1** page 278

5. The owner of the Davis Company has kept track of how the company has grown since it opened ten years ago. How old was the company when it first had 50 employees?

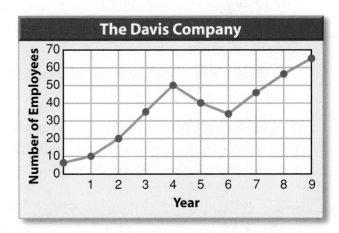
The Davis Company
Number of Employees / Year

A 3 years old   **C** 5 years old

B 4 years old   **D** 50 years old

SDAP 1.0, KEY **SDAP 1.4** page 346

Education Place
Visit www.eduplace.com/camap/ for
Test-Taking Tips and **Extra Practice**.

Vocabulary

Use the words in the Word Bank to label the coordinate plane.

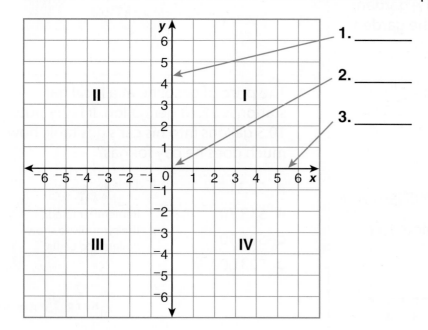

1. _____

2. _____

3. _____

Word Bank

x-axis

y-axis

quadrant

coordinate

origin

In which **quadrant** would you find these **coordinates**?

4. (4, 6) _____   **5.** (4, −6) _____   **6.** (−4, −6) _____   **7.** (−4, 6) _____

Use grid paper. Plot the following coordinates.

8. (0, 6)   **9.** (4, 6)

10. (2, 2)   **11.** (−2, 2)

12. What type of polygon did you make?

Writing Choose a polygon and plot it on a coordinate plane. Record the coordinates. Challenge a classmate to plot the points and identify the polygon.

Reading Look for this book in your library. *The Fly on the Ceiling* by Dr. Julie Glass

CA Standards

MR 2.3 Use a variety of methods, such as words, numbers, symbols, charts, graphs, tables, diagrams, and models, to explain mathematical reasoning.

Also KEY AF 1.4, **KEY** SDAP 1.4

Standards-Based Extra Practice

Set A ———————————————————————————— KEY **AF 1.4** page 588

Use the map. Write the name of the bird you can see at each location.

1. $(2, {}^-4)$ **2.** $({}^-3, {}^-1)$ **3.** $(4, {}^-3)$

4. $({}^-3, 4)$ **5.** $(4, 3)$ **6.** $({}^-3, 1)$

7. Which two birds are closest together? How far apart are they?

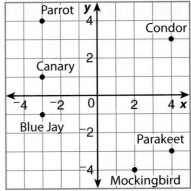

Set B ———————————————————————————— KEY **AF 1.5** page 590

Copy and complete each function table.

1.

$y = x - 4$	
x	y
0	■
1	■
2	■

2.

$y = x + 3$	
x	y
$^-4$	■
$^-3$	■
$^-2$	■

3.

$y = 2x - 5$	
x	y
0	■
2	■
3	■

Choose the equation that shows the relationship of all the values in the table. Then find the value of y for the given value of x.

4.

Rule: ?	
x	y
0	$^-3$
1	$^-2$
2	$^-1$
3	■

A $y = x - 5$
B $y = x - 3$
C $y = 2x + 1$
D $y = x + 4$

5.

Rule: ?	
x	y
$^-5$	$^-2$
$^-2$	$^-5$
$^-1$	$^-6$
4	■

A $y = x - 7$
B $y = x + 7$
C $y = -7 + x$
D $y = -7 - x$

Set C ———————————————————————————— KEY **AF 1.5** page 594

Copy and complete the function table. Then graph the function.

1.

$y = x - 2$	
x	y
0	■
1	■
2	■

2.

$y = 2x - 5$	
x	y
0	■
1	■
2	■

3.

$y = 4 - x$	
x	y
$^-3$	■
$^-2$	■
$^-1$	■

Education Place
Visit www.eduplace.com/camap/
for more **Extra Practice**.

Chapter Review/Test

Vocabulary and Concepts ———————— KEY AF 1.4 , KEY SDAP 1.4 , KEY SDAP 1.5 , MR 2.3

Choose the best term to complete the sentence.

1. A pair of numbers indicating the *x*-coordinate and the *y*-coordinate on a grid is called an _____.

2. The _____ is the point where the *x*-axis and the *y*-axis intersect on a coordinate plane. (0, 0).

Skills ——————————————————— KEY AF 1.4 , KEY SDAP 1.4 , KEY SDAP 1.5

Use the coordinate plane for Problems 3–10.

Write the ordered pair for each point.

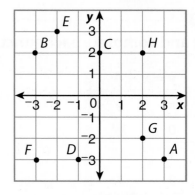

3. *A*   4. *B*   5. *C*   6. *D*

Write the letter name of each point.

7. (2, ⁻2)   8. (2, 2)   9. (⁻3, ⁻3)   10. (⁻2, 3)

Complete the ordered pairs for the function rule.

11. Rule: $y = 2x - 2$
    (0, ▢) (1, ▢) (2, ▢)

12. Rule: $y = x + 5$
    (⁻5, ▢) (⁻3, ▢) (⁻1, ▢)

13. Rule: $y = 3 - x$
    (0, ▢) (2, ▢) (4, ▢)

Problem Solving and Reasoning ———— KEY AF 1.4 , KEY SDAP 1.4 , KEY SDAP 1.5 , MR 1.1, MR 2.3, MR 1.0

Solve.

14. Zero represents ground level for an elevator. If it goes up 10 levels, down 6 levels, up 2 levels, and down 7 levels, at what level is it now?

15. The equation $y = x \times 11$ represents the elevations in feet of the levels above ground level. The letter *x* represents the level. Make a function table to show the heights of levels 3, 6, 10 and 12.

Writing Math When plotting points on a coordinate plane, how do you know which number to start with, the *x*, or the *y*?

Spiral Review and Test Practice

1. What value for *n* makes this equation true?

$$n - 26 = 17$$

A 9

B 17

C 26

D 43

> **Test Tip**
> Check your answer by substituting the number in the equation and solving.

KEY **AF 1.2** page 108

---

2. A store has a supply of 250 markers. If 20 of them are red, what percent of the markers are red?

A 2%   **C** 12.5%

B 8%   **D** 20%

SDAP 1.3 page 522

---

3. What is the length of the line segment shown on the grid?

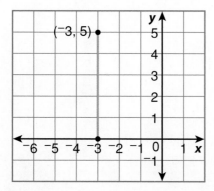

A 2 units   **C** 4 units

B 3 units   **D** 5 units

KEY **SDAP 1.5** page 366

---

4. $^-6 - 4 = s$

A $s = ^-10$

B $s = ^-2$

C $s = 2$

D $s = 10$

> **Test Tip**
> Use rules to check the sign of your answer.

KEY **NS 2.1** page 568

---

5. The map shows the location of 4 different buildings.

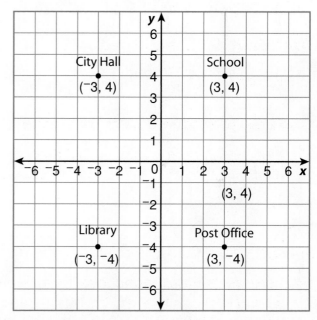

Which building is at point $(^-3, 4)$?

A Post Office

B School

C City Hall

D Library

KEY **AF 1.4** page 588

Education Place
Visit www.eduplace.com/camap/ for
Test-Taking Tips and **Extra Practice.**

Chapter 28

Graph Linear Equations

Photograph taken from Voyager 1 of Jupiter's bands, which are formed by clouds blown by high winds

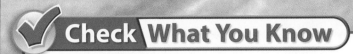
Vocabulary and Concepts KEY **AF 1.4**

Match each word with a definition. page 586

1. coordinates

2. equation

3. axis

   a. a horizontal or vertical number line in the coordinate plane

   b. a mathematical sentence that shows two expressions have the same value

   c. two numbers that give the location of a point in the coordinate plane

Skills KEY **AF 1.4**, KEY **SDAP 1.5**

Draw a coordinate grid on Workmat 8. Use the ordered pairs to plot points on the grid. page 586

4. ⁻5, 3   **5.** 3, 3   **6.** ⁻5, ⁻1   **7.** 3, ⁻1

8. What figure can you make by connecting the points in order?

Problem Solving and Reasoning KEY **AF 1.4**

9. Ana plotted points in the coordinate plane at (4, ⁻6) and (⁻6, 4). Which point is closest to the *y*-axis?

Vocabulary

Visualize It !

linear equation

an equation whose graph is in a line

$y = x + 1$	
x	*y*
2	3
1	2
0	1
⁻1	0
⁻2	⁻1

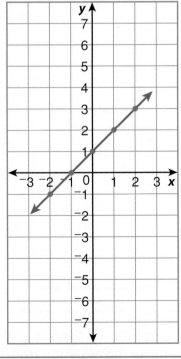

Language Tips

In everyday language, a *plane* refers to an airplane. In mathematics, a *plane*, or a coordinate plane, refers to a flat surface that extends without end in all directions.

Math words that look alike in English and Spanish often have the same meaning.

English	Spanish
equation	**ecuación**
graph	**gráfica**
point	**punta**

See **English-Spanish Glossary** pages 628–642.

Education Place Visit www.eduplace.com/camap/ for the **eGlossary** and **eGames**.

CA Standards MR 2.3 Use a variety of methods, such as words, numbers, symbols, charts, graphs, tables, diagrams, and models, to explain mathematical reasoning. **Also KEY AF 1.5**

CA Standards

KEY SDAP 1.5 Know how to write ordered pairs correctly, for example (x, y).

KEY AF 1.5 Solve problems involving linear functions with integer values; write the equation; and graph the resulting ordered pairs of integers on a grid.

Also KEY SDAP 1.4, AF 1.0, KEY AF 1.2, KEY AF 1.4, MR 2.3

Vocabulary

linear equations

Materials
- Workmat 8
- Learning Tool 31 (Coordinate Plane) or grid paper
- Straightedge

Vocabulary Tip

The word *linear* contains the word *line*.

Hands On
Linear Equations

Objective Explore graphing a linear equation in the coordinate plane.

▶ **Explore**

Question How can you graph a linear equation?

A **linear equation** is an equation whose graph is a line.

You can graph a linear equation by finding ordered pairs that make the equation true and drawing a line through the points.

Graph the equation $y = x - 4$.

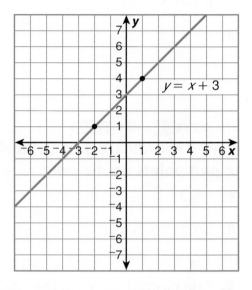

$y = x + 3$

---

1 Copy and complete the function table. Find the *y*-value for each *x*-value.

Write the ordered pairs.

$y = x - 4$	
x	**y**
$^-1$	
2	

---

2 Use Workmat 8. Plot the points in the coordinate plane. Then draw the line that passes through the points.

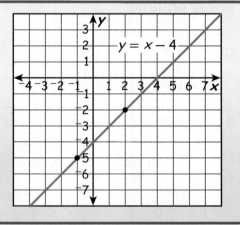

$y = x - 4$

---

3 Find two other points on the line and check to see if the coordinates make the equation true.

604

Graph a Two-Step Equation

Graph the equation $y = 2x - 5$.

1 Copy and complete the function table. Write the ordered pairs.

$y = 2x - 5$	
x	**y**
0	
4	

2 Use Workmat 8. Graph the line. Find two other points on the line and check to see if they work in the equation.

$y = 2x - 5$

▶ **Extend**

Use grid paper. Complete the steps to graph the linear equation and check your work.

1. $y = x + 5$
   a. Make a function table. Choose any values for x.
   b. Write the ordered pairs.
   c. Graph the equation.
   d. Find two other points on the line and check to see if the coordinates make the equation true.

2. $y = 2x - 3$
   a. Make a function table. Choose any values for x.
   b. Write the ordered pairs.
   c. Graph the equation.
   d. Find two other points on the line and check to see if the coordinates make the equation true.

3. Analyze Graph $y = x + 2$ and $y = 2x$ on the same coordinate plane. What do you notice about the point (2, 4)? What does this mean about the ordered pair?

Writing Math

Predict Look at the graph for $y = x - 4$ on page 604. If different points had been chosen to make the graph, would the graph have been the same? Explain your thinking.

Graphs of Formulas

Objective Graph formulas, and use the graphs to solve problems.

CA Standards

KEY AF 1.4 Identify and graph ordered pairs in the four quadrants of the coordinate plane.

KEY AF 1.5 Solve problems involving linear functions with integer values; write the equation; and graph the resulting ordered pairs of integers on a grid.

Also AF 1.0, AF 1.1, KEY AF 1.2 **, KEY** SDAP 1.4 **, KEY** SDAP 1.5 **, MR 2.3, MR 3.1**

Materials
• Grid paper
• Ruler

▶ **Learn by Example**

In the last lesson, you learned how to graph linear equations. Many formulas can be written as linear equations. In this lesson you will graph formulas.

Male crickets make chirping songs. Scientists have noticed a relationship between the number of chirps per minute (x) and the temperature in degrees Fahrenheit (F).

You can make a graph to represent this formula. $F = \frac{1}{4}x + 40$

1 Make a function table.

Write the ordered pairs.

$(0, 40), (8, 42)$

$\frac{1}{4} \times 0 + 40 = 40$

$\frac{1}{4} \times 8 + 40 = 2 + 40 = 42$

$F = \frac{1}{4}x + 40$	
x	F
0	40
8	42

Think

Since the number of chirps must be a whole number, do not connect the points. A point with x-value of $\frac{1}{2}$ has no meaning.

2 Plot the points on the coordinate plane.

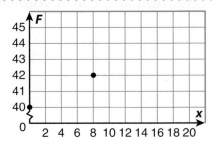

3 Find two other points that appear to be on the same line and check to see that the ordered pairs make the equation true.

Check

$(4, 41)$

$F = \frac{1}{4}x = 40$

$F = \frac{1}{4} \times 4 + 40$

$F = 1 + 40$

$F = 41$

Check

$(12, 43)$

$F = \frac{1}{4}x + 40$

$F = \frac{1}{4} \times 12 + 40$

$F = 3 + 40$

$F = 43$

Another Example

The formula $F = \frac{9}{5}C + 32$ converts Celsius (C) temperatures to Fahrenheit (F) temperatures. How can you use a graph to find the approximate Fahrenheit temperature equivalent of 25°C?

1 Make a function table.

$F = \frac{9}{5}C + 32$	
C	**F**
0	32
10	50

$\frac{9}{5} \times 0 + 32 = 32$

$\frac{9}{5} \times 10 + 32 = 18 + 32 = 50$

2 Write the ordered pairs.

(0, 32), (10, 50)

Plot the points on the coordinate plane. Then draw the line that passes through the points.

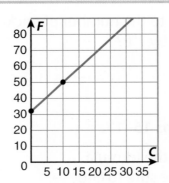

Think

You can connect the points. The temperatures are not always whole numbers.

3 Find 25°C on the horizontal axis. Draw a vertical line from this point to the graph. Mark the point on the graph. Then draw a horizontal line across to the vertical axis. The line crosses the vertical axis at about 78°F.

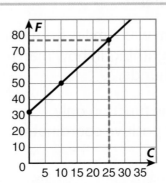

Solution: 25°C is about 78°F.

Guided Practice

Use the graph on page 606. Find *F* for each value of *x*. Use the formula to check your answer.

Ask Yourself
• Did I find the correct point on the graph?
• Did I name the correct coordinates?

1. $x = 16$ **2.** $x = 24$ **3.** $x = 20$

Find *x* (the number of chirps) for each value of *F*.

4. $F = 42°F$ **5.** $F = 41\frac{1}{2}°F$ **6.** $F = 44\frac{1}{2}°F$

123 Math Talk Why does the graph of the cricket formula show positive numbers only?

Use the graph on page 607. Find F for each value of C.
Use the formula to check your answer.

7. $C = 5°C$

8. $C = 20°C$

9. $C = 35°C$

Find C for each value of F.

10. $F = 59°F$

11. $F = 86°F$

12. $F = 104°F$

13. Mr. O'Reilly heard that the temperature was 2°C. What is the approximate equivalent Fahrenheit temperature?

14. Challenge What happens to the number of cricket chirps as the temperature increases by 1°F?

Science Link

Use the Fun Facts for Problems 15–17.

15. Create a function table for the formula. Then graph the function. Be sure to choose reasonable scales for your graph.

16. Courtney heard that a storm was 6 miles from her town. If she sees a bolt of lightning, in how many seconds will she hear the thunder?

17. Why should the graph of the function only contain points with zero or positive coordinates?

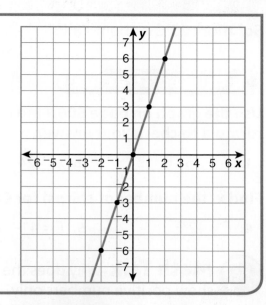

Fun Facts

You can use a formula to find out how far you are from a thunderstorm.

$$d = (0.2)t$$

distance (in miles) from the storm

time (in seconds) from seeing lightning to hearing thunder

Science **ES 4.C**

Spiral Review and Test Practice

Divide. **KEY** NS 2.2 page 326

18. $4,674 ÷ 82$

19. $19,849 ÷ 23$

20. $9,144 ÷ 36$

21. $8,946 ÷ 14$

Choose the correct answer. **KEY** AF 1.5

22. Which equation could have been used to create this graph?

A $y = 3x$ **B** $y = \frac{3}{x}$ **C** $y = x + 3$ **D** $y = \frac{x}{3}$

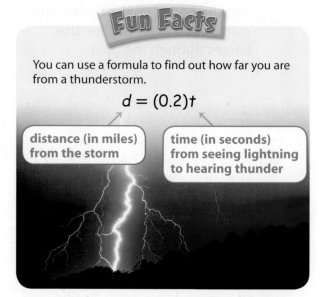

Extra Practice See page 619, Set A.

Key Standards Review

Need Help?
See Key Standards Handbook.

Use the graph on the right. Write the coordinates of each point. KEY **AF 1.4**

1. A   2. B

3. C   4. D

5. E   6. F

7. G   8. H

Use the graph on the right. Name the point for each ordered pair. KEY **AF 1.4**

9. (2, 5)   10. (⁻2, ⁻3)

11. (⁻4, 3)   12. (0, 4)

13. (4, ⁻1)   14. (⁻2, 3)

15. (5, 2)   16. (⁻1, 0)

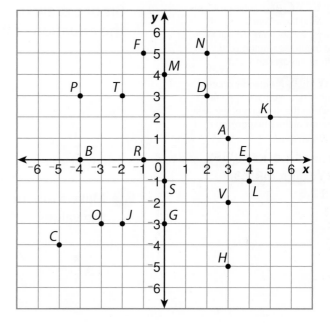

Challenge   Problem Solving

How Many Seats?   KEY **AF 1.4**, KEY **AF 1.5**, KEY **SDAP 1.4**

**A cafeteria has square tables that seat 4 people.
When 2 tables are side by side, 6 people can be seated.**

1. Make a function table to show how x (the number of tables) and y (the number of seats) are related. Use 1, 2, 3, and 4 for x.

Number of Tables (x)	1	2	3	4
Number of Seats (y)				

2. Graph the ordered pairs. Show the numbers 0–10 on the x-axis and 0–20 on the y-axis.

3. Use your graph to find how many people can be seated if 8 tables are side by side.

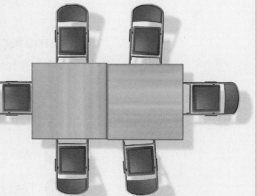

CA Standards

KEY AF 1.5 Solve problems involving linear functions with integer values; write the equation; and graph the resulting ordered pairs of integers on a grid.

KEY SDAP 1.4 Identify ordered pairs of data from a graph and interpret the meaning of the data in terms of the situation depicted by the graph.

Also AF 1.0, KEY AF 1.2, KEY AF 1.4, MR 2.3, MR 2.6

Write Equations For Lines

Objective Write equations for linear functions.

▶ **Learn by Example**

Brooke drew this graph. What is the equation of Brooke's line?

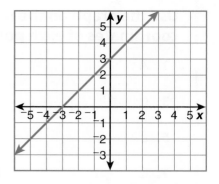

1. Make a function table. Write the values in the table.

x	y
0	3
2	5
−1	2

2. Look at each ordered pair. Find a rule that tells how you can find each y-value from the x-value.

   Each y-value is 3 more than the x-value.

3. Write an equation for your rule.

   $y = x + 3$

Check

Find two other points on the line and check to see if they work in the equation.

Another Example

Which is the equation of the line?

A $y = 2x + 5$ **C** $y = 4x - 1$

B $y = 5 - 2x$ **D** $y = 2 - 3x$

1. Make a function table.

2. Test the ordered pairs in each equation.

Solution: The equation of the line is $y = 5 - 2x$.

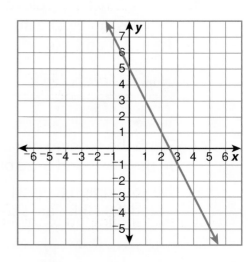

Write an equation for the function table or graph.

Ask Yourself
• Did I name the coordinates of the points correctly?
• Does each ordered pair make the equation true?

1.

Rule: _____

x	y
−3	−1
0	2
1	3

2.

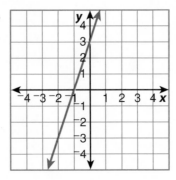

Choose the equation for the function table or graph.

3.

Rule: _____

x	y
−1	−1
0	1
1	3

A $y = x + 1$
B $y = 2x + 1$
C $y = 2x - 1$
D $y = x - 1$

4.

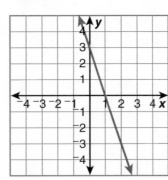

A $y = 4 - x$
B $y = 5 - 4x$
C $y = 3 - 3x$
D $y = 3x - 4$

Guided Problem Solving

Use the questions to solve the problem.

5. The graph shows the total number of inches of snowfall each hour. Write an equation to model the situation.

a. **Understand/Plan** Make a function table showing three points on the graph.

b. **Solve** Look for a pattern in the ordered pairs. Write your rule as an equation.

c. **Look Back** Check it by testing

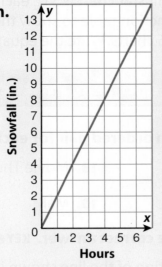

 Math Talk Why is the graph in Exercise 5 a line segment limited to the first quadrant?

Write an equation for the function table or graph.

6.

Rule: _____

x	y
0	⁻3
3	0
4	1

7.

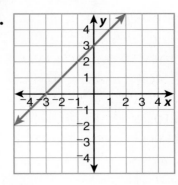

Choose the equation for the function table or graph.

8.

Rule: _____

x	y
⁻1	⁻4
0	⁻1
1	2

A $y = 2x - 3$
B $y = 4x - 2$
C $y = 3x - 1$
D $y = 4x$

9.

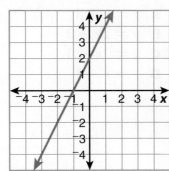

A $y = 6 - 2x$
B $y = 2x + 2$
C $y = 3 - \frac{1}{2}x$
D $y = 2x - 6$

10. Plot 3 or more points in a straight line on a coordinate plane. Write an equation for the line.

11. The cost for a souvenir star chart is $12 each plus $5 shipping per order. Make a function table to show the total cost for ordering 1, 2, 3, 4, or 5 charts. Write the equation for the function.

✓ **Spiral Review and Test Practice**

Use the map. Write an ordered pair for each location. KEY **SDAP 1.5** page 588

12. Pet Store

13. Movie Theater

14. Post Office

15. Mall

Write the letter of the correct answer. KEY **AF 1.5**

16. Which is the equation of the line shown in the graph?

A $y = x + 1$ **C** $y = 2x + 1$
B $y = 3x - 2$ **D** $y = 2x - 1$

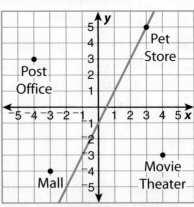

Extra Practice See page 619, Set B.

Photo Sale

Professional photographers make a living by selling copies of the photographs they take. Jenny would like to be a photographer so she took a photography class. She is starting to sell her photos at local craft fairs. At one fair, the cost to rent a small booth is $100. Jenny sells her photographs for $25 each.

Mount Williamson, CA.

1. Jenny uses the equation $y = 25x - 100$ to calculate her profits. What do x and y represent?

2. Make a function table for the equation. Use whole numbers from 1 to 16 as the x values.

3. Write the ordered pairs and then graph on a coordinate plane.

4. Does it make sense to connect the points with a line? Why or why not?

5. What is the smallest value of x that will represent a profit?

6. What value of x represents a profit of $300?

Twenty Lakes Basin in the
Sierra Nevada Mountains, CA

CA Standards
KEY **AF 1.5**, KEY **SDAP 1.4**,
MR 2.3, MR 3.1

CA Standards

KEY AF 1.4 Identify and graph ordered pairs in the four quadrants of the coordinate plane.

KEY AF 1.5 Solve problems involving linear functions with integer values; write the equation; and graph the resulting ordered pairs of integers on a grid.

Also KEY SDAP 1.4, MR 1.0, MR 2.3, MR 2.6

Materials

- Learning Tool 10 (Centimeter Grid)
- Straightedge

Think

All equations such as $y = 8$, $y = {}^-10$, and $y = 0.5$ will have graphs that are horizontal lines.

Equations of Horizontal and Vertical Lines

Objective Graph horizontal and vertical lines.

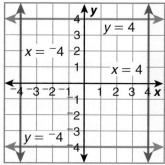

▶ **Learn by Example**

In this lesson, you will learn how to graph linear equations that contain one variable.

Example 1

Graph the line $y = 3$.

1 Make a function table. Find two points that lie on the line. There is no x. For any value of x, the value of y is 3.

y = 3	
x	**y**
${}^-2$	3
4	3

2 Plot the points, then draw the line that passes through the points.

The graph of $y = 3$ is a horizontal line.

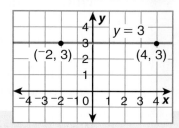

Example 2

Graph the line $x = {}^-4$.

Points that lie on the line $x = {}^-4$ will have x-coordinates of ${}^-4$.

x = ⁻4	
x	**y**
${}^-4$	1
${}^-4$	${}^-2$

← There is no y. For any value of y, the value of x is ${}^-4$.

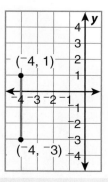

Example 3

Write the equation of a given line shown below.

The graph shows a horizontal line passing through points that have a y-coordinate of ${}^-2$, such as $(0, {}^-2)$ and $(3, {}^-2)$. The equation of the line is $y = {}^-2$.

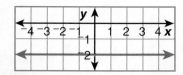

▶ **Guided Practice**

Graph the line with the given equation.

1. $y = 4$ **2.** $x = 4$ **3.** $y = {}^{-}6$ **4.** $x = {}^{-}1$

Write the equation of the line.

5.
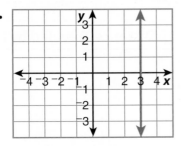

6.
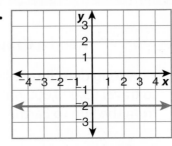

 Math Talk Explain why the graph of $y = 3$ is a horizontal line, even though the y-axis is a vertical line.

▶ **Practice and Problem Solving**

Graph the line with the given equation.

7. $x = 5$ **8.** $y = 5$ **9.** $x = {}^{-}3$ **10.** $y = {}^{-}1$

Write the equation of the line.

11.
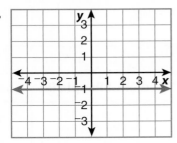

12.
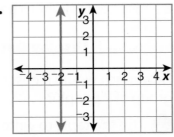

13. Challenge What equation represents the x-axis? What equation represents the y-axis?

✓ **Spiral Review and Test Practice**

Find the mean, median, and mode for each set of data. SDAP 1.1 page 344

14. 12, 12, 18, 14, 16, 12   **15.** 17, 4, 19, 17, 18

Line m is represented by the equation $y = 2$. KEY **AF 1.5**

16. Which ordered pair is located on line m?

    A (3, 2) **B** (0, 0) **C** (2, 3) **D** (2, 0)

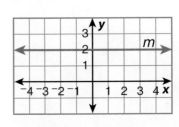

CA Standards

MR 2.3 Use a variety of methods, such as words, numbers, symbols, charts, graphs, tables, diagrams, and models, to explain mathematical reasoning.

KEY SDAP 1.4 Identify ordered pairs of data from a graph and interpret the meaning of the data in terms of the situation depicted by the graph.

Also SDAP 1.0, KEY SDAP 1.5, AF 1.1, KEY AF 1.2, KEY AF 1.4, KEY AF 1.5, MR 1.1, MR 2.0, MR 2.3, MR 3.0, MR 3.1, MR 3.2

Problem Solving Strategy
Use a Graph

Objective Interpret a graph to help solve problems.

▶ **Learn Through Reasoning**

Example 1 Read a Graph

How long does it take light to travel 93,000,000 miles from the Sun to Earth?

The original graph is shown in black. The graph was extended to reach 93,000,000 miles.

1 Draw a horizontal line from about 93,000,000 until it meets the graph.

2 Then draw a vertical line to find the time.

Solution: It takes about $8\frac{1}{2}$ minutes for light to travel 93,000,000 miles.

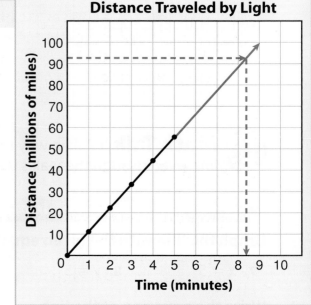

Distance Traveled by Light

Example 2 Display Data

How much would it cost for a group of 7 people?

1 Use the table to write ordered pairs. (2, 7) (3, 9) (4, 11)

2 Graph the given coordinates.

3 Extend the graph with coordinates for 5 through 8 people, as shown in red.

Solution: The cost for 7 people is $17.

Cost of Show	
Number of People (x)	**Cost (y)**
2	$7
3	$9
4	$11

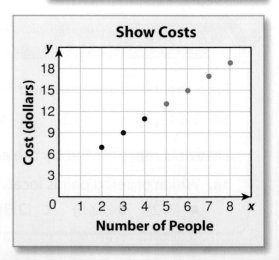

Show Costs

Think

Since you cannot have part of a person, the only points graphed are for counting numbers 2 through 8.

▶ Guided Problem Solving

Use the Ask Yourself questions and the graph on page 616 to help you solve this problem.

1. It takes light about 6 minutes to reach Venus from the Sun. About how far from the Sun is Venus?

(123) Math Talk Look at the graph in Example 2 on page 616. What do you think the equation is? How can you use the equation to check your answer?

Ask Yourself
- What do I need to find?
- What patterns do I see?

▶ Independent Problem Solving

Solve. Use a graph. Explain why your answer makes sense.

2. The graph at the left shows the relationship between an object's weight on Earth and its weight on Mars. Suppose a rock weighs 15 pounds on Mars. About how much would that same rock weigh on Earth?

3. On Earth an astronaut weighs 118 pounds. About how much would that astronaut weigh if she landed on Mars?

4. If an object weighs 50 pounds more on Earth than on Mars, what is its weight on Mars?

5. **Challenge** Martha says that the equation representing the data in the graph is $y = 4x$. If y is the weight on Earth and x is the weight on Mars, is Martha correct? Explain your reasoning.

6. **Create and Solve** Use one of the graphs in this lesson to write and solve your own word problem.

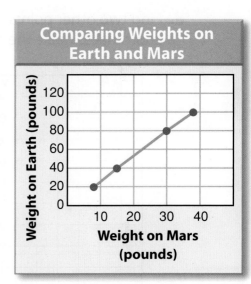

Comparing Weights on Earth and Mars

(Graph: Weight on Earth (pounds) vs. Weight on Mars (pounds))

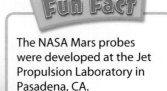

Fun Fact

The NASA Mars probes were developed at the Jet Propulsion Laboratory in Pasadena, CA.

Reading & Writing Math

Vocabulary

You can graph a **linear equation** by finding **ordered pairs** that make the equation true and drawing a line through the points.

Use grid paper. Complete the steps to graph the linear equation $y = x + 5$.

a. Make a function table.

b. Write the ordered pairs.

c. Graph the equation.

d. Find two other points on the line and check to see if the coordinates make the equation true.

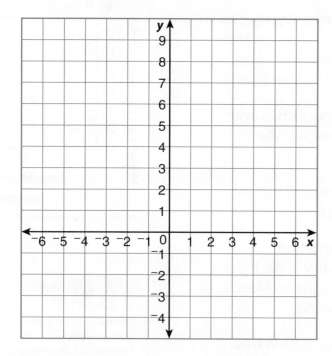

Writing Which is easier for you: generating a function from a line or generating a line from a function? Explain your answer.

Reading Look for this book in your library. *The Ancient Civilizations of Greece and Rome: Solving Algebraic Equations* by Kerri O'Donnell

CA Standards
MR 2.3 Use a variety of methods, such as words, numbers, symbols, charts, graphs, tables, diagrams, and models, to explain mathematical reasoning.

Also KEY AF 1.4, KEY AF 1.5

Standards-Based Extra Practice

Set A ———————————————————————————— **KEY AF 1.4** page 606

Copy and complete the function table. Then graph the function.

1.

y = 2x + 3	
x	**y**
0	■
1	■
2	■

2.

y = x − 5	
x	**y**
0	■
1	■
2	■

3.

y = x + 2	
x	**y**
⁻3	■
⁻2	■
⁻1	■

4.

y = 4x	
x	**y**
0	■
⁻1	■
⁻2	■

Set B ———————————————————————————— **KEY AF 1.5** page 610

Write an equation to show the rule of each function table.

1.

Rule:	?
x	**y**
3	9
4	12
5	15

2.

Rule:	?
x	**y**
0	⁻4
1	⁻3
2	⁻2

3.

Rule:	?
x	**y**
⁻1	2
0	3
1	4

4.

Rule:	?
x	**y**
4	⁻2
5	⁻3
6	⁻4

Which equation could have been used to create the function table?

5.

Rule:	?
x	**y**
0	⁻2
1	1
2	4

A $y = x - 2$
B $y = 3x - 2$
C $y = 2x$

6.

Rule:	?
x	**y**
0	⁻2
2	2
4	6

A $y = 2 - x$
B $y = x - 2$
C $y = 2x - 2$

Education Place
Visit www.eduplace.com/camap/
for more **Extra Practice**.

Chapter 28 Extra Practice **619**

Chapter Review/Test

Vocabulary and Concepts ———————————————— MR 2.3, KEY SDAP 1.5

Write the best term to complete the sentence.

1. A _____ equation is an equation whose graph is a line.

2. A mathematical sentence with an equals sign is an _____.

3. A pair of numbers indicating the *x*-coordinate and the *y*-coordinate on a grid is an _____.

Skills ———————————————————————————— KEY AF 1.5

Copy and complete the function tables.

4.

$y = x + 7$	
x	y
0	▩
1	▩
2	▩

5.

$y = 2x - 5$	
x	y
3	▩
4	▩
5	▩

6.

$y = x - 5$	
x	y
0	▩
2	▩
4	▩

7.

$y = x - 7$	
x	y
0	▩
⁻1	▩
⁻3	▩

Problem Solving and Reasoning —— KEY AF 1.2, KEY AF 1.5, KEY SDAP 1.4, KEY SDAP 1.5, MR 2.3

Use the graph for Problems 8–10.

8. Choose the equation for the graph.

   A $y = 2x - 3$ **C** $y = 2x + 1$

   B $y = 2x - 1$ **D** $y = 2x$

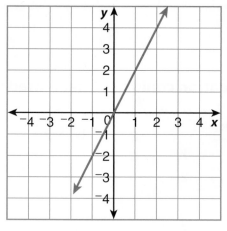

9. Make and complete a function table for 5 points on the line. At least one of the values should be a negative number.

10. Suppose the 2 in the equation for the graph was a 3. How would that change the graph?

Writing Math Look at the equation $y = 4$. Can you determine some of the coordinates without seeing the graph?

Spiral Review and Test Practice

1. How many feet did the tree grow between year 2 and year 6?

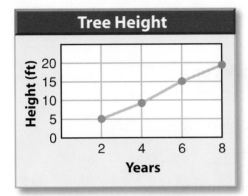

Tree Height

A 4

B 5

C 10

D 15

> **Test Tip**
> Familiarize yourself with the graph by reading the title and labels before you read the question.

KEY **SDAP 1.4** page 366

2. Monica's tarp is 6 meters long and 3 meters wide. Which formula shows the area of the rectangle in square meters?

A $18 = A \times 6$

B $A = 6 \times 3$

C $A = 6 + 3$

D $A = (2 \times 6) + (2 \times 3)$

6 m

3 m

KEY **AF 1.2** page 454

3. Which equation could have been used to create this function table?

x	y
0	⁻3
1	1
2	5
3	9

A $y = 4x - 3$ **C** $y = x - 3$

B $y = 5x - 3$ **D** $y = 2x - 1$

KEY **AF 1.5** page 610

4. Which point represents (2, 4) on this graph?

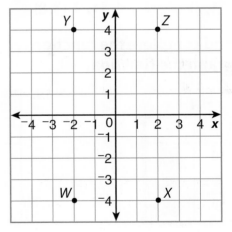

A W

B X

C Y

D Z

KEY **AF 1.4** page 588

Education Place
Visit www.eduplace.com/camap/ for
Test-Taking Tips and **Extra Practice**.

Chapter 28 Spiral Review and Test Practice   **621**

Unit 12 Review/Test

Vocabulary and Concepts
MR 2.3, KEY SDAP 1.5 Chapters 27–28

Complete each sentence with a vocabulary word from this unit.

1. A mathematical sentence built from expressions using one or more equal signs is called an _____.

2. A(n) _____ is a pair of numbers used to locate a point on a coordinate grid.

3. The vertical number line on a coordinate plane is called the _____.

4. The four regions of the coordinate plane are called _____.

5. The point where the x-axis and the y-axis in the coordinate plane intersect, (0, 0), is known as the _____.

Skills
KEY AF 1.4, KEY SDAP 1.4 Chapter 27, Lesson 2

Use grid paper to plot points for the following coordinates.

6. A (1, 4)
7. B (0, ⁻5)
8. C (2, 6)
9. D (5, ⁻2)

10. E (⁻1, 7)
11. F (3, 8)
12. G (⁻6, 3)
13. H (0, ⁻4)

Copy and complete the function table. Then graph the function.
KEY AF 1.5, KEY SDAP 1.4 Chapter 27, Lesson 3; Chapter 28, Lesson 2

14.

$y = 4 - x$	
x	y
10	▧
8	▧
6	▧

15.

$y = 4x - 3$	
x	y
0	▧
1	▧
2	▧

16.

$y = x - 8$	
x	y
8	▧
6	▧
4	▧

Problem Solving and Reasoning
KEY NS 2.1, KEY SDAP 1.4, KEY SDAP 1.5 Chapter 27, Lesson 4; Chapter 28, Lesson 4

Solve.

17. The cost of an animal poster is $4 plus an additional $1 shipping for an order. Make a function table to show the cost of 1, 2, 3, 4, and 5 posters in one order.

18. The points on the map show the location along the same road of some students' houses. Santo's house is 4 units west and 1 unit North of Dawn's house. Name the ordered pair for Santo's house. Does he live on the same road as the others? Explain.

19. Miguel's house is between Emily's house and Steve's house on the same road. Where could Miguel live?

20. Elaine lives more than 4 units to the East and South of the others. Extend the line. Where is the closest to the others that Elaine could live?

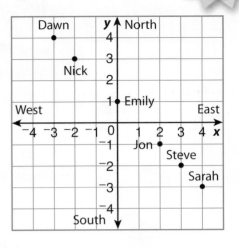

Writing Math If you are given a function table with a missing rule, how do you determine the equation for the rule?

Performance Assessment

X Marks the Spot

KEY **AF 1.4**, KEY **SDAP 1.5**, MR 2.3

There is an old legend that there are hidden treasures on the moon.

Task	Information You Need
Use the information to the right to find the hidden treasure. Plot the points on a coordinate grid. The treasure is said to be at the intersection of lines A and B. Explain what you do.	These ordered pairs describe line A: $(10, 8)$, $(8, 6)$, $(6, 4)$, $(4, 2)$, $(2, 0)$, $(0, -2)$, $(-2, -4)$
	These ordered pairs describe line B: $(-2, 8)$, $(0, 6)$, $(2, 4)$, $(4, 2)$, $(6, 0)$, $(8, -2)$, $(10, -4)$
	While exploring on the moon, you discover another treasure. Name a point where you find the treasure. Using the terms *east*, *west*, *north*, and *south*, give directions to your discovered treasure.

Greg Tang's Go Fast, Go Far

Unit 12 Mental Math Strategies

Divide and Conquer

First, do a piece that's fast for you, divide what's left and add the two!

I have a fast way to do $91 \div 7$. I think of 91 as $70 + 21$. I know $70 \div 7 = 10$ and $21 \div 7 = 3$. I add $10 + 3$ to get 13.

Divide.

1. $91 \div 7 = 70 \div 7 + 21 \div 7$
$\quad\quad = 10 + 3$
$\quad\quad = 13$

2. $85 \div 5 = 50 \div 5 + 35 \div 5$
$\quad\quad = \blacksquare + \blacksquare$
$\quad\quad = \blacksquare$

3. $176 \div 4 = 160 \div 4 + 16 \div 4$
$\quad\quad = \blacksquare + \blacksquare$
$\quad\quad = \blacksquare$

4. $208 \div 4 = 200 \div 4 + 8 \div 4$
$\quad\quad = \blacksquare + \blacksquare$
$\quad\quad = \blacksquare$

Nice work! Try some more practice!

Doing Great!

5. $64 \div 4$

6. $126 \div 7$

7. $184 \div 8$

8. $51 \div 3$

9. $196 \div 4$

10. $240 \div 5$

Try them again. Did you go faster?

Go Faster!

Take It Further!

You can use a strategy like this one for greater numbers.

11. $310 \div 5$

12. $432 \div 4$

13. $832 \div 8$

14. $580 \div 5$

Looking Ahead

THIS YEAR I learned to ...

Number Sense

- interpret percents as part of a hundred;
- find decimal and percent equivalent for common fractions;
- determine prime factors of numbers through 50;
- identify and represent fractions, mixed numbers, decimals, and positive and negative integers on a number line;
- add and subtract integers; and
- solve problems involving fractions and mixed numbers and express answers in simplest form.

Which letter best represents the quantity on the number line? KEY NS 1.5

1. 1.7

2. $2\frac{75}{100}$

3. $^-1$

4. 0.6

Algebra and Functions

- use a letter to represent an unknown number;
- write and evaluate simple algebraic expressions in one variable by substitution;
- identify and graph ordered pairs in the coordinate plane; and
- solve problems involving linear functions with integer values.

If $n = 3$, what is the value of each expression? KEY AF 1.2

5. $14 - n - 2$

6. $(n \times 2) + (n \times 3)$

7. $18 \div (9 - n)$

- use a formula to find the area of a triangle and parallelogram by comparing it to the formula for the area of a rectangle;
- construct a rectangular box and a cube from two-dimensional patterns and use the patterns to find their surface areas;
- compute the volume of rectangular solids;
- measure, identify, and draw angles, perpendicular and parallel lines, rectangles, and triangles using appropriate tools;
- use the knowledge of the sum of the angles of triangles (180°) and quadrilaterals (360°) to solve problems.

What is the measure of angle *p* in each figure? KEY MG 2.2

8.

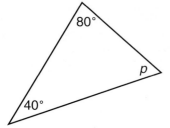

9.

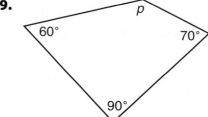

NEXT YEAR I will learn more about...

- statistics and probability;
- mean, median, and mode of data sets;
- probability of compound events;
- ratios, proportions and percents;
- the formulas for the circumference and area of a circle; and
- solving one-step linear equations.

I can use the Review/Preview worksheets to get ready for next year.

Looking Ahead

Looking Ahead Activities

Next year, you will learn more about problem solving with whole numbers and fractions, geometry, and data. The Looking Ahead activities will help you get ready.

Table of Measures

Customary Units of Measure

Metric Units of Measure

Length

1 foot (ft)	=	12 inches (in.)
1 yard (yd)	=	36 inches
1 yard	=	3 feet
1 mile (mi)	=	5,280 feet
1 mile	=	1,760 yards

1 centimeter (cm)	=	10 millimeters (mm)
1 decimeter (dm)	=	10 centimeters
1 meter (m)	=	1,000 millimeters
1 meter	=	100 centimeters
1 meter	=	10 decimeters
1 kilometer (km)	=	1,000 meters

Area

144 square inches (in.^{2})	=	1 square foot (ft^2)
9 square feet	=	1 square yard (yd^2)

1 square centimeter (cm^2)	=	100 square millimeters (mm^2)
1 square decimeter (dm^2)	=	100 square centimenters
1 square meter (m^2)	=	100 square decimeters

Volume

1,728 cubic inches (in.^{3})	=	1 cubic foot (ft^3)
27 cubic feet	=	1 cubic yard (yd^3)

1 cubic centimeter (cm^3)	=	1,000 cubic millimeters (cm^3)
1 cubic decimeter (dm^3)	=	1,000 cubic centimeters
1 cubic meter (m^3)	=	1,000 cubic decimeters

Capacity

1 tablespoon (tbsp)	=	3 teaspoons (tsp)
1 fluid ounce (fl oz)	=	2 tablespoons
1 cup (c)	=	8 fluid ounces
1 pint (pt)	=	2 cups
1 quart (qt)	=	2 pints
1 quart	=	4 cups
1 gallon (gal)	=	4 quarts
1 gallon	=	8 pints
1 gallon	=	16 cups

1 liter (L)	=	1,000 milliliters (mL)
1 liter	=	10 deciliters (dL)
1 liter	=	1 cubic decimeter (dm^3)
1,000 liters	=	1 cubic meter (m^3)
1 milliliter (mL)	=	1 cubic centimeter (cm^3)

Weight/Mass

1 pound (lb)	=	16 ounces (oz)
1 ton (T)	=	2,000 pounds (lb)

1 gram (g)	=	1,000 milligrams (mg)
1 kilogram (kg)	=	1,000 grams
1 metric ton (t)	=	1,000 kilograms

Units of Time

1 minute (min)	=	60 seconds (s)
1 hour (hr)	=	60 minutes
1 day	=	24 hours
1 week (wk)	=	7 days
1 year (yr)	=	12 months (mo)

1 year	=	365 days
1 leap year	=	366 days
1 decade	=	10 years
1 century	=	100 years
1 millennium	=	1,000 years

California English-Spanish

 Glossary

absolute value The distance a number is from zero on a number line.

valor absoluto Distancia entre un número y cero en una recta numérica.

acute angle An angle with a measure less than that of a right angle.

ángulo agudo Ángulo que mide menos que un ángulo recto.

acute triangle A triangle that has three acute angles.

triángulo acutángulo Triángulo que tiene tres ángulos agudos.

algebraic expression An expression that contains one or more variables.

expresión algebraica Expresión que tiene una o más variables.

angle An angle is formed by two rays with the same endpoint.

ángulo Un ángulo está formado por dos semirrectas que tienen el mismo extremo.

area The number of square units needed to cover a region.

área Número de unidades cuadradas en una región.

Associative Property of Addition The property that states that the way in which addends are grouped does not change the sum. It is also called the Grouping Property of Addition.

Propiedad asociativa de la suma Propiedad que establece que la manera en que se agrupan los sumandos no cambia la suma. Es también llamada Propiedad de agrupación en la suma.

Associative Property of Multiplication The property that states that the way in which factors are grouped does not change the product. It is also called the Grouping Property of Multiplication.

Propiedad asociativa de la multiplicación Propiedad que establece que la manera en que se agrupan los factores no cambia el producto. Es también llamada Propiedad de agrupación en la multiplicación.

average The number found by dividing the sum of a group of numbers by the number of addends.

promedio Número que resulta de dividir la suma de un grupo de números entre el número de sumandos.

base **(of a geometric figure)** A bottom side or face of a geometric figure.

base (de una figura geométrica) Lado o cara inferior de una figura geométrica.

base of a power The factor that is multiplied repeatedly to obtain a power. $5^3 = 5 \times 5 \times 5 = 125$. 5 is the base of 5^3.

base de una potencia Factor que se multiplica varias veces para obtener una potencia. $5^3 = 5 \times 5 \times 5 = 125$. 5 es la base de 5^3.

billon The number 1,000,000,000 or 10^9. It is one thousand million.

mil millones El número 1,000,000,000 ó 10^9.

circle graph A graph used for data that are parts of a whole.

gráfica circular Gráfica que representa datos que son partes de un entero.

common denominator Any common multiple of the denominators of two or more fractions.

denominador común Cualquier múltiplo común de los denominadores de dos o más fracciones.

common factor A number that is a factor of two or more given numbers.

factor común Número que es factor de dos o más números dados.

common multiple A whole number that is a multiple of two or more given whole numbers.

múltiplo común Número entero que es múltiplo de dos o más números enteros dados.

Commutative Property of Addition The property which states that the order of addends does not change the sum. It is also called the Order Property of Addition.

Propiedad conmutativa de la suma Propiedad que establece que el orden de los sumandos no cambia la suma. También es llamada Propiedad del orden de la suma.

Commutative Property of Multiplication The property which states that the order of factors does not change the product. It is also called the Order Property of Multiplication.

Propiedad conmutativa de la multiplicación Propiedad que establece que el orden de los factores no cambia el producto. También es llamada Propiedad del orden de la multiplicación.

compass An instrument used for drawing circles and for transferring the distance between two points from one place to another.

compás Instrumento usado para dibujar círculos y para transferir de un lugar a otro la distancia entre dos puntos.

compatible numbers Numbers or number pairs that are easy to use with mental computation.

números compatibles Números o pares de números que son fáciles de usar para hacer cálculos mentales.

composite number A whole number, greater than 1, that has more than two factors.

número compuesto Número entero mayor que 1, que tiene más de dos factores.

congruent figures Plane figures that have the same size and the same shape are congruent.

figuras congruentes Las figuras planas que tienen el mismo tamaño y la misma forma son congruentes.

coordinate grid (See coordinate plane.)

cuadrícula de coordenadas (Ver plano de coordenadas.)

coordinate plane A plane formed by two perpendicular number lines used to assign an ordered pair of numbers to each point of the plane.

plano de coordenadas Plano formado por dos rectas numéricas perpendiculares usado para asignar un par ordenado de números a cada punto del plano.

coordinates An ordered pair of numbers that locates a point in the coordinate plane with reference to the *x*- and *y*-axes.

coordenadas Par ordenado de números que representa un punto en el plano de coordenadas con referencia a los ejes *x* e *y*.

counting number Any of the positive whole numbers. Counting numbers do not include 0.

número positivo Cualquier número entero positivo. Los números positivos no incluyen el 0.

cube A solid figure that has six square faces of equal size.

cubo Cuerpo geométrico que tiene seis caras cuadradas de igual tamaño.

cubic units Units for measuring volume. A cubic unit is the volume of a cube with each side 1 unit long.

unidades cúbicas Unidades para medir volumen. Es el volumen de un cubo con lados de 1 unidad de largo.

D

decimal A number with one or more digits to the right of a decimal point.

número decimal Número con uno o más dígitos a la derecha de un punto decimal.

decimal equivalent A decimal that is equal to a given fraction. 0.25 is a decimal equivalent of $\frac{1}{4}$.

decimal equivalente Decimal que es igual a una fracción dada. 0.25 es un decimal equivalente de $\frac{1}{4}$.

decimal point A symbol used to separate the ones and tenths place in a decimal.

punto decimal Símbolo que separa las unidades y las décimas en un número decimal.

degrees Units used to describe angle measures and units used to describe temperature. Its symbol is °.

grados Unidades usadas para describir medidas de ángulos y unidades que se usan para describir temperatura. Su símbolo es °.

denominator The number below the bar in a fraction.

denominador Número debajo de la barra en una fracción.

digit Any one of the numerals: 0, 1, 2, 3, 4, 5, 6, 7, 8, 9.

dígito Cualquiera de los números: 0, 1, 2, 3, 4, 5, 6, 7, 8, 9.

Distributive Property The property which states that when two addends are multiplied by a factor, the product is the same as when each addend is multiplied by the factor and those products are added.

Propiedad distributiva Propiedad que establece que cuando se multiplican dos sumandos por un factor, el producto es el mismo que cuando cada sumando se multiplica por el factor y se suman esos productos.

divisible One number is divisible by another if the quotient is a whole number and the remainder is 0. For example, 10 is divisible by 2, since $10 \div 2 = 5 \text{ R } 0$.

divisible Un número es divisible entre otro si el cociente es un número entero y el residuo es 0. Por ejemplo, 10 es divisible entre 2, porque $10 \div 2 = 5 \text{ R } 0$.

divisor The number by which a number is being divided. In $6 \div 3 = 2$, the divisor is 3.

divisor Número entre el que se divide otro número. En $6 \div 3 = 2$, el divisor es 3.

double bar graph A graph in which data are compared using pairs of rectangular bars drawn next to each other.

gráfica de doble barra Gráfica en la que se comparan datos usando pares de barras rectangulares dibujadas una al lado de la otra.

double line graph A graph that is used to show data using two broken lines.

gráfica de doble línea Gráfica en la que se representan datos con dos líneas quebradas.

edge The segment where two faces of a solid figure meet.

arista Segmento donde se encuentran dos caras de un cuerpo geométrico.

endpoint The point at either end of a line segment. The beginning point of a ray.

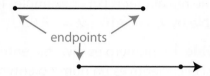

endpoints

extremo Punto que se encuentra al inicio o final de un segmento de recta. El punto inicial de una semirrecta.

Equality Property of Addition If the same number is added to both sides of an equation, then the two sides remain equal. If $a = b$, then $a + c = b + c$.

Propiedad de igualdad de la suma Si se suma el mismo número a ambos lados de una ecuación, los dos lados permanecen iguales. Si $a = b$, entonces $a + c = b + c$.

Equality Property of Multiplication If both sides of an equation are multiplied by the same number, then the two sides remain equal. If $a = b$, then $a \times c = b \times c$.

Propiedad de igualdad de la multiplicación Si se multiplican ambos lados de una ecuación por el mismo número, los dos lados permanecen iguales. Si $a = b$, entonces $a \times c = b \times c$.

equation A mathematical sentence with an equals sign.
Examples: $3 + 1 = 4$ and $2x + 5 = 9$ are equations.

ecuación Enunciado matemático que tiene un signo de igual.
Ejemplos: $3 + 1 = 4$ y $2x + 5 = 9$ son ecuaciones.

equilateral triangle A triangle that has three congruent sides.

triángulo equilátero Triángulo que tiene tres lados congruentes.

equivalent fractions Different fractions that name the same number.
Example: $\frac{1}{2}$ and $\frac{4}{8}$ are equivalent.

fracciones equivalentes Fracciones diferentes que representan el mismo número.
Ejemplo: $\frac{1}{2}$ y $\frac{4}{8}$ son equivalentes.

estimate A number close to an exact amount. An estimate tells *about* how much or *about* how many.

estimación Número cercano a una cantidad exacta. Una estimación indica *aproximadamente* cuánto o cuántos.

evaluate (an expression) Substitute given values for the variables and perform the operations to find the value of the expression.

hallar el valor (de una expresión) Sustituir variables con valores específicos y realizar las operaciones para despejar la expresión.

expanded form *(Also called expanded notation)* A way of writing a number as the sum of the values of its digits.

forma extendida *(También llamada notación extendida)* Manera de escribir un número como la suma de los valores de sus dígitos.

exponent The number in a power that tells how many times a factor is repeated.

$$\text{base} \longrightarrow 5^3 \longleftarrow \text{exponent}$$

exponente Número en una potencia que dice cuántas veces se repite un factor.

expression A number, variable, or any combination of numbers, variables, and operations.

expresión Número, variable o cualquier combinación de números, variables y operaciones.

face One of the flat surfaces of a solid figure.

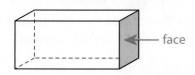

cara Una de las superficies planas de un cuerpo geométrico.

factor One of two or more numbers that are multiplied to give a product.

factor Uno de dos o más números que se multiplican para obtener un producto.

factor tree A diagram that is used to find the prime factorization of a number.

árbol de factores Diagrama que se usa para hallar la descomposición en factores primos de un número.

foot **(ft)** A customary unit used to measure length. 12 inches = 1 foot.

pie Unidad del sistema usual para medir longitud. 12 pulgadas = 1 pie.

formula An equation that shows a mathematical relationship. For example, The formula for the perimeter of a square is $p = 4s$, where s is the length of each side of the square.

fórmula Ecuación que muestra una relación matemática. Por ejemplo, la fórmula del perímetro de un cuadrado es $p = 4s$, donde s es la longitud de cada lado del cuadrado.

fraction A way of writing a number to show parts of a whole, parts of a collection, and division of whole numbers by whole numbers.
Examples: $\frac{1}{2}$, $\frac{2}{3}$, and $\frac{3}{4}$ are fractions.

fracción Manera de escribir un número para mostrar partes de un entero o de un grupo y la división de números enteros entre números enteros.
Ejemplos: $\frac{1}{2}$, $\frac{2}{3}$ y $\frac{3}{4}$ son fracciones.

frequency table A table used to record the number of times an event occurs.

tabla de frecuencia Tabla que se usa para registrar el número de veces que ocurre un suceso.

function rule A rule that gives exactly one value of y for every value of x.

regla de función Regla que da exactamente un valor de y para cada valor de x.

function table A table that matches each input value in a function with one output value.

tabla de función Tabla en la que cada valor de entrada en una función tiene un valor de salida.

greatest common factor The greatest whole number that is a common factor of two or more numbers. It is also called the greatest common divisor.

máximo común divisor El número entero más grande que es divisor de dos o más números dados.

height (*h*) (of a parallelogram) The perpendicular distance from the base of a parallelogram to the opposite vertex.

altura (*h*) (de un paralelogramo) Distancia perpendicular desde la base de un paralelogramo al vértice opuesto.

height (*h*) (of a triangle) The perpendicular distance from the base of the triangle to the opposite vertex.

altura (*h*) (de un triángulo) Distancia perpendicular de la base del triángulo al vértice opuesto.

histogram A graph in which bars are used to display how frequently data occurs within equal intervals.

histograma Gráfica en la que se usan barras para mostrar con qué frecuencia ocurren los datos, dentro de intervalos iguales.

horizontal axis The *x*-axis in a coordinate system. It is a number line that locates points to the left or to the right of the origin.

eje horizontal Eje de las *x* en un sistema de coordenadas. Es una recta numérica que representa puntos a la izquierda o a la derecha del origen.

Identity Property of Addition The property that states that the sum of any number and 0 is that number.

Propiedad de identidad en la suma Propiedad que establece que la suma de cualquier número y 0 es ese mismo número.

Identity Property of Multiplication The property that states that the product of any number and 1 is that number.

Propiedad de identidad en la multiplicación Propiedad que establece que el producto de cualquier número y 1 es ese mismo número.

improper fraction A fraction greater than or equal to 1. The numerator in an improper fraction is greater than or equal to the denominator.

fracción impropia Fracción mayor o igual a 1. El numerador de una fracción impropia es mayor o igual al denominador.

inequality A sentence that contains > (is greater than) or < (is less than).
Examples: 8 > 2, 5 < 6

desigualdad Enunciado que tiene > (mayor que) o < (menor que).
Ejemplos: 8 > 2, 5 < 6

integer Any one of the set of whole numbers and their opposites (negative numbers) or 0.
..., -3, -2, -1, 0, +1, +2, +3, ...

números enteros positivos y negativos Números enteros, sus opuestos (números negativos) y 0.
..., -3, -2, -1, 0, +1, +2, +3, ...

intersecting lines Lines that meet or cross at a common point.

rectas secantes Líneas que se encuentran o cruzan en un punto en común.

inverse operations Operations that have opposite effects. Subtraction is the inverse operation of addition. Division is the inverse operation of multiplication.

operaciones inversas Operaciones que tienen efectos opuestos. La resta es la operación inversa de la suma. La división es la operación inversa de la multiplicación.

isosceles triangle A triangle that has at least two congruent sides.

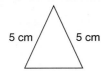

5 cm   5 cm

triángulo isósceles Triángulo que tiene por lo menos dos lados congruentes.

line A straight, continuous, and unending set of points in a plane.

recta Conjunto continuo, recto e infinito de puntos en un plano.

line graph A graph that uses a broken line to show changes in data.

gráfica lineal Gráfica en la que una línea quebrada representa cambios en los datos.

line segment A part of a line that has two endpoints.

segmento de recta Parte de una recta que tiene dos extremos.

mean The number found by dividing the sum of a group of numbers by the number of addends. In arithmetic, the mean is also called the average.

media Número que se obtiene al dividir la suma de un grupo de números entre el número de sumandos. En aritmética, la media es llamada promedio también.

median The middle number when a set of numbers is arranged in order from least to greatest.
Examples: The median of 2, 5, 7, 9, and 10 is 7. For an even number of numbers, it is the average of the two middle numbers. The median of 2, 5, 7, and 12 is $(5 + 7) \div 2$ or 6.

mediana Número del medio cuando un conjunto de números está ordenado de menor a mayor.
Ejemplos: La mediana de 2, 5, 7, 9 y 10 es 7. Para un número par de números, es el promedio de los dos números del medio. La mediana de 2, 5, 7 y 12 es $(5 + 7) \div 2$ ó 6.

mixed number A number made up of a whole number and a fraction.

whole number ⟶ $5\frac{2}{3}$ ⟵ fraction
↑
mixed number

número mixto Número formado por un número entero y una fracción.

mode The number or numbers that occur most often in a set of data.

moda Número o números que aparecen con más frecuencia en un conjunto de datos.

multiple A number that is the product of the given whole number and another whole number.

múltiplo Número que es el producto de un número entero dado y otro número entero.

negative integer An integer less than 0.
Examples: -4, -7, -100

número entero negativo Número entero menor que 0.
Ejemplos: -4, -7, -100

negative number A number that is less than 0.
Examples: $-\frac{7}{8}$, -5, and −2.8 are negative numbers.

número negativo Número que es menor que 0.
Ejemplos: $-\frac{7}{8}$, -5 y −2.8 son números negativos

net *(Also called a pattern)* A 2-dimensional pattern that can be folded to make a solid.

red *(También llamada patrón).* Patrón de 2 dimensiones que puede doblarse para formar un cuerpo geométrico.

obtuse angle An angle with a measure greater than that of a right angle and less than 180°.

ángulo obtuso Ángulo mayor que un ángulo recto y menor que 180°.

obtuse triangle A triangle that has one obtuse angle.

triángulo obtusángulo Triángulo que tiene un ángulo obtuso.

opposites Two numbers whose sum is 0. *Examples:* +2 and –2 and –12 and +12. Zero is its own opposite.

opuestos Dos números cuya suma es 0. *Ejemplos:* +2 y –2, y –12 y +12. El opuesto de cero es cero.

ordered pair A pair of numbers in which one number is considered to be first and the other number second.

par ordenado Par de números en el que un número es considerado el primero y el otro número, el segundo.

order of operations Rules for performing operations in order to simplify expressions.

orden de las operaciones Reglas para realizar operaciones con el objeto de simplificar expresiones.

origin A point assigned to zero on the number line or the point where the *x*- and *y*-axes intersect in a coordinate plane.

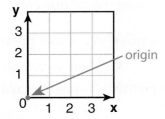

origen Punto asignado a cero en una recta numérica, o el punto donde los ejes *x* e *y* se intersecan en un plano de coordenadas.

parallel lines Lines that lie in the same plane and do not intersect. They are the same distance apart everywhere.

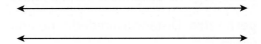

rectas paralelas Líneas que están en el mismo plano y que no se intersecan. Están separadas por la misma distancia en todos sus puntos.

parallelogram A quadrilateral in which both pairs of opposite sides are parallel.

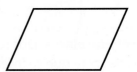

percent (%) Per hundred.
Example: 7% means 7 out of 100 or 7/100.

por ciento (%) Por cada cien.
Ejemplo: 7% significa 7 de 100 ó 7/100.

perimeter The distance around a figure.

perímetro Distancia alrededor de una figura.

perpendicular lines Two lines or line segments that intersect to form right angles.

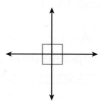

rectas perpendiculares Dos rectas o segmentos de recta que se intersecan y forman ángulos rectos.

place value The value of a digit determined by its place in a number.

valor de posición Valor de un dígito que se deterrmina por su lugar en un número.

plane A flat surface made up of a continuous and unending collection of points.

plano Superficie llana formada por una colección continua e infinita de puntos.

plane figure A geometric figure that lies entirely in one plane.

figura plana Figura geométrica que se extiende completamente en un plano.

plot To locate points in a coordinate system. To plot (-3, 2) in a coordinate system, go 3 units to the left from the origin and up 2 units.

trazar Ubicar puntos en un sistema de coordenadas. Para trazar (-3, 2) en un sistema de coordenadas, avanza 3 unidades hacia la izquierda desde el origen y 2 hacia arriba.

point An exact location in space, represented by a dot.

punto Ubicación exacta en el espacio, representada por un punto.

polygon A simple, closed plane figure made up of three or more line segments.

polígono Figura plana simple cerrada formada por tres o más segmentos de recta.

positive integer Any whole number greater than zero.

número entero positivo Cualquier número entero mayor que cero.

positive number A number greater than zero.

número positivo Número mayor que cero.

power A product obtained by multiplying a given factor repeatedly.

potencia Producto que se obtiene al multiplicar un factor dado varias veces.

power of 10 A product obtained by multiplying 10 repeatedly.

potencia de 10 Producto que se obtiene al multiplicar 10 varias veces.

prime factorization Factoring a number into its prime factors only.
Example: the prime factorization of 30 is 2 x 3 x 5.

descomposición en factores primos Descomponer un número en sus factores primos solamente.
Ejemplo: la descomposición en factores primos de 30 es 2 x 3 x 5.

prime number A whole number, greater than 1, that has exactly two factors, 1 and the number itself.

número primo Número entero mayor que 1, que tiene exactamente dos factores, 1 y el mismo número.

Property of Zero for Multiplication The property that states that if 0 is a factor, the product is 0.

Propiedad del cero en la multiplicación Propiedad que establece que si 0 es un factor, el producto es 0.

protractor A tool for measuring angles in degrees.

transportador Instrumento para medir ángulos en grados.

Q

quadrilateral A polygon with four sides.

cuadrilátero Polígono de cuatro lados.

R

ray Part of a line that starts at an endpoint and goes on forever in one direction.

semirrecta Parte de una recta que empieza en un extremo y se extiende de manera infinita en una dirección.

reciprocal The product of a number and its reciprocal is 1.
Example: $\frac{2}{3} \times \frac{3}{2} = 1$, so $\frac{2}{3}$ and $\frac{3}{2}$ are reciprocals of each other.

número recíproco El producto de un número y su número recíproco es 1.
Ejemplo: $\frac{2}{3} \times \frac{3}{2} = 1$, entonces $\frac{2}{3}$ y $\frac{3}{2}$ son números recíprocos.

rectangular prism A solid with six faces that are rectangles.

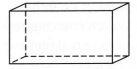

prisma rectangular Cuerpo geométrico con seis caras que son rectángulos.

rhombus A parallelogram with all four sides the same length.

rombo Paralelogramo cuyos cuatro lados tienen la misma longitud.

right angle An angle that measures 90°.

ángulo recto Ángulo que mide 90°.

right triangle A triangle that has one right angle.

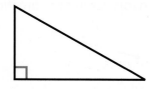

triángulo rectángulo Triángulo que tiene un ángulo recto.

scalene triangle A triangle with all sides of different lengths.

triángulo escaleno Triángulo con todos los lados de longitudes diferentes.

simplest form of a fraction A fraction whose numerator and denominator have the number 1 as the only common factor.

mínima expresión de una fracción Fracción cuyo numerador y denominador tienen al número 1 como el único factor común.

standard form A way of writing a number using only digits.

forma normal Manera de escribir un número usando solamente dígitos.

straight angle An angle that measures 180°.

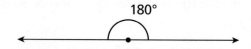

ángulo llano Ángulo que mide 180°.

surface area The total area of the surface of a solid.

área de la superficie Área total de la superficie de un cuerpo geométrico.

thousandth One of 1,000 equal parts of a region or set.

milésima Una de las 1,000 partes iguales de una región o conjunto.

trapezoid A quadrilateral with exactly one pair of parallel sides.

trapecio Cuadrilátero que tiene exactamente un par de lados paralelos.

unit fraction A fraction in which the numerator is 1.
Example: $\frac{1}{5}$

fracción unitaria Fracción en la que el numerador es 1.
Ejemplo: $\frac{1}{5}$

unlike denominators When the denominators of two or more fractions are not the same.

denominadores no comunes Cuando los denominadores de dos o más fracciones no son iguales.

variable A letter or a symbol that represents a number in an algebraic expression.

variable Letra o símbolo que representa un número en una expresión algebraica.

vertex A point common to two sides of an angle, polygon, or prism.

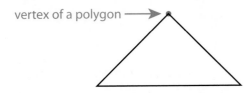

vertex of a polygon

vértice Punto común de dos lados de un ángulo, polígono o prisma.

vertical axis The *y*-axis in the coordinate system. It is a number line that locates points up or down from the origin.

eje vertical El eje de las *y* en el sistema de coordenadas. Es una recta numérica que representa puntos hacia arriba o hacia abajo del origen.

volume The number of cubic units that make up a solid figure.

volumen Número de unidades cúbicas que forman un cuerpo geométrico.

whole number A number that belongs to the set {0, 1, 2, 3, 4...} There is no largest whole number.

número entero Número que pertenece al conjunto {0, 1, 2, 3, 4...} No existe un número entero más grande que todos los demás.

word form A number named by words, such as fifty-six.

forma verbal Número escrito con palabras, como cincuenta y seis.

x-axis The horizontal number line in a coordinate system.

eje de las *x* Recta numérica horizontal en un sistema de coordenadas.

x-coordinate The first number of an ordered pair of numbers that names a point in a coordinate system.

coordenada *x* Primer número de un par ordenado de números que representa un punto en un sistema de coordenadas.

y-axis The vertical number line in a coordinate system.

eje de las *y* Recta numérica vertical en un sistema de coordenadas.

y-coordinate The second number of an ordered pair of numbers that names a point in a coordinate system.

coordenada *y* Segundo número de un par ordenado de números que representa un punto en un sistema de coordenadas.

Zero Property of Addition The property that states that the sum of any number and 0 is that number.

Propiedad del cero en la suma Propiedad que establece que la suma de cualquier número y 0 es ese número.

Zero Property of Multiplication The property that states that the product of any number and 0 is 0.

Propiedad del cero en la multiplicación Propiedad que establece que el producto de cualquier número y 0 es 0.

Index

Index

apply simpler problems to more complex problems, 314–315, 316–318, 390–393

break problems into simpler parts, 40–41, 438–439

develop generalizations, 84–85

distinguish relevant from irrelevant information, 38–39, 100–101, 108–110, 124–125, 126–127, 128–130, 148–150

express the solution clearly and logically, 8–9, 16–18, 114–115, 170–172, 174–176, 486–487, 506–507

indicate the advantages of exact and approximate solutions, 68–69

make precise calculations to check results, 158–159, 240–241, 328–329, 512–513

note the method by deriving the solution, 146–147, 152–153, 508–510

observe patterns, 38–39, 100–101, 108–110, 124–125, 126–127, 128–130, 148–150

sequence and prioritize information, 38–39, 100–101, 108–110, 124–125, 126–127, 128–130, 148–150

support solutions with evidence, 8–9, 114–115, 170–172, 174–176, 486–487, 506–507

use a variety of methods, 12–13, 28–29, 76–77, 78–80, 122–123, 168–169, 196–197, 254–255, 346–348, 356–357, 398–400, 422–423, 500–501, 502–504, 572–573, 614–615, 616–617

use strategies/skills/concepts to find solutions, 62–64

Math Journal, 7, 29, 55, 77, 123, 147, 153, 169, 187, 211, 231, 255, 271, 295, 315, 343, 365, 393, 411, 431, 453, 459, 473, 476, 501, 521, 543, 549, 563, 587, 605

Math Talk, 9, 13, 15, 17, 31, 35, 39, 41, 57, 60, 63, 67, 69, 79, 83, 85, 103, 105, 109, 113, 115, 125, 127, 129, 149, 155, 159, 171, 175, 189, 190, 193, 213, 217, 231, 235, 237, 241, 257, 259, 273, 277, 279, 283, 287, 297, 299, 301, 305, 307, 317, 321, 323, 327, 329, 348, 351, 353, 357, 367, 371, 375, 395, 399, 413, 417, 421, 437, 439, 455, 461, 479, 483, 487, 503, 507, 509, 513, 523, 527, 545, 551, 565, 569, 589, 591, 595, 607, 611, 615, 617

MathWorks!, 19, 37, 59, 111, 157, 177, 219, 239, 281, 325, 349, 373, 401, 419, 463, 511, 553, 571, 613

Mean, 342

Measure and draw angles, 390–393

Measurement
area
of complex figures, 436–437
of parallelograms, 452–453, 454–456
of triangles, 458–459, 460–462
units appropriate for, 486–487
perimeter, 436–437, 486–487
surface area, 472–473, 474–476, 478–481
units for three-dimensional objects, 482–484
units for two-dimensional objects, 486–487
volume, 482–484, 486–487

Measurement and Geometry
construct a cube and rectangle box and use these patterns to compute the surface area, 472–473, 478–481
derive and use the formula for the area of a triangle and a parallelogram, 452–453, 454–456, 458–459
differentiate between and use appropriate units of measures for 2-and 3-dimensional objects, 482–484, 486–487

identify the relationships between plane and solid geometric figures, 418, 430–430, 472–473

know the sum of angles of any triangle and of any quadrilateral, 410–411, 412–414, 416–418, 422–423

measure, and draw angles, perpendicular and parallel lines, rectangles and triangles, 398–400, 420–421, 430–431, 432–434

understand and compute volume, 436–437, 438–439, 452–453, 454–456, 458–459, 478–481

understand the concept of volume, 482–484

visualize and draw two-dimensional views of three-dimensional objects, 474–476

Median, 344–345

Mental Math, *See also* Computation and Mental Math Challenge, 195, 303
division and, 315
Go Fast, Go Far, 48, 94, 140, 204, 248, 336, 384, 446, 494, 536, 624

Missing angle problems, 422–423

Mixed numbers
addition with fractions, 170–172
compare and order, 82–83, 84–85
decimals equivalent to, 79, 80
division with, 236–238
express in simplest form, 146–147, 157, 158–159, 169, 170–172, 174–176, 186–187, 188–189, 190–191, 192–194, 196–197, 211, 212–214, 216–217
fractions and, 30–32
fraction part of, 168–169
fractions equivalent to, 78–80
hands on, 168–169
multiplication of, 216–218
on a number line, 30, 31, 32, 34, 78, 80, 82, 83, 84, 85, 87, 133, 178, 193, 597

Multistep Problems, 438–439
Patterns in Tables, 196–197
Percent Problems, 512–513
Perimeter, Area, or Volume?,
  486–487
Reasonable Answers, 240–241
Use a Graph, 616–617
Use a Number Line, 572–573
Use a Simpler Problem, 306–307
Use the Remainder, 328–329
Work Backward, 158–159
Write an Expression, 114–115

Problem Solving on Tests, *See*
Assessment

Product, *See also* Multiplication
estimate, 276–277
of fractions and mixed numbers,
  216–218
of two fractions, 210–211
partial, 122–122
zeros in, 282–284

Properties
associative
  of addition, 126–127
  of multiplication, 128–130
commutative
  of addition, 126–127
  of multiplication, 128–130
distributive property of
  multiplication, 122–123,
  124–125
identity
  of addition, 126–127
  of multiplication, 128–130
of addition
  associative, 126–127
  commutative, 126–127
  identity, 126–127
of multiplication
  associative, 128–130
  commutative, 128–130
  identity, 128–130
use to evaluate expressions
  and solve problems, 122–123,
  124–125, 128–130
zero property of multiplication,
  128–130

Protractor, 351, 390–393,
  395–396, 398, 412, 414, 417,
  420–421, 423, 430, 432,
  520–521, 522, 528, 555

Quadrilaterals
classify, 415, 416–417
missing angle measures, 415,
  416–417, 422–423
parallelograms, 452–453,
  454–456
sum of angles, 410–411

Quotients, *See also* Division
division with decimal quotients,
  298–299
estimate, 316–318
too large or too small when
  estimated, 322–324

Ray, *See also* Angles
390–391

Reading and Writing Math,
3, 51, 97, 143, 207, 251, 339,
387, 449, 497, 539, 583

Reading Strategy, 3, 51, 97,
143, 207, 251, 339, 387, 449,
497, 539, 583

Real World Data, 10, 13, 61,
106, 125, 156, 192, 218, 238,
257, 284, 297, 318, 400, 437,
481, 504, 527, 552, 570, 592

Reasonable answers, 240–241,
256–257, 276–277, 282–284,
299, 324, 437, 548–549,
568–570

Reasoning
learn through, 68, 286, 357, 486,
  512, 616
problem solving and, 46, 47, 92,
  93, 138, 139, 202, 203, 246,
  247, 334, 335, 382, 383, 444,
  445, 492, 493, 534, 535, 578,
  579, 622, 623

Reciprocals
fractions by counting numbers,
  231–232
use to divide by a fraction,
  234–235
with mixed numbers, 236–238

Rectangles, *See also* Surface
area
construct, 432–434
identify, describe, and classify
  the properties of, 416–418

Rectangular prism
compute volume of, 482–484
construct from two-dimensional
  patterns, 478–481
surface area, 472–473, 478–481

Rectangular solid, *See*
Rectangular Prism

**Regrouping, addition of mixed
numbers,** 174–176

Relative magnitude, 59

**Remainder, using in division
word problems,** 328–329

Rename to Subtract, 186–187,
188–189

Represent Fractions, 28–29

**Represent Whole Numbers
and Decimals,** 54–55

Results, *See also* Reasonable
answers
validate using calculations,
  146–147, 153, 158–159,
  240–241, 328–329, 512–513
verify reasonableness of the
  results, 256–257, 299, 305,
  306–307, 324, 437, 548–549,
  568–570

Rhombus, 416–418

Right angle, 394–396

Right triangle, 412–414

Rounding
decimals and whole numbers,
  66–67
very large and very small
  numbers, 54–55, 66–67

Rules, *See also* Properties
for addition of integers, 568–570
function rules, 100–101,
  112–113, 172, 196–196, 217,
  218, 232, 324, 368, 371, 372,
  594–595

Scalene triangle, 412–414

Credits

PHOTOGRAPHY

1 ©Burke/Triolo Productions/BrandX/Corbis bckgd 4-5 ©Richard Broadwell/Alamy spread 9 ©Jeff Greenberg/Index Stock Imagery cr 10 © Wolfgang Kaehler / Alamy cr 13 Leo/Shutterstock cr 13 ©2000 N.Carter/North Wind Picture Archives cr 16 ©PEPE / Alamy bc 20 ©Bill Freeman/PhotoEdit tr 20 ©Courtesy of Agua Caliente Cultural Museum br 26-7 ©Michael Grant/Alamy spread 30 © WaterFrame / Alamy bl 31 © Stuart Westmorland/CORBIS cr 32 © Kennan Ward/ CORBIS cr 34 ©Ken Bohn/San Diego Zoo via Getty Images/ Newscom.com bl 35 © Darryl Leniuk / Masterfile cr 36 ©Georgette Douwma/The Image Bank/Getty Images cr 37 © Mark Karrass/Corbis b 37 ©Cathy Melloan / Photo Edit bckgd 38 ©Gilbert S. Grant / Photo Researchers, Inc. tr 39 © Sea World of California/Corbis cr 40 © Michael S. Lewis/CORBIS r 41 © David A. Northcott/CORBIS br 47 © Paul A. Souders/CORBIS cr 49 ©Keren Su/China Span/Alamy bckgd 52-3 ©Jeff Greenberg/age fotostock spread 52-3 ©Jason Cheever/ Shutterstock 57 © Denis Scott/Corbis cr 58 Lewis and Clark with Sacagawea (colour litho) (detail) by Paxson, Edgar Samuel (1852-1915) ©Private Collection/ Peter Newark American Pictures/ The Bridgeman Art Library cr 59 © Richard Cummins/CORBIS tr 59 © Dennis Cox / Alamy bckgd 62 © Frank Chmura / Alamy bl 66 ©Royalty-Free/Corbis bl 68 © Michael Maloney/San Francisco Chronicle/Corbis bl 69 ©Zia Soleil/Iconica/Getty Images br 74-5 ©Emilio Ereza/Alamy 74-5 ©Aaron Warkov/Iconica/Getty Images spread 76 ©John Pyle/Icon SMI/Corbis bl 76 ©John Pyle/Icon SMI/ Corbis cr 78 ©Visions of America, LLC / Alamy tr 79 © Joseph Sohm/ Visions of America/Corbis cr 79 ©Visions of America, LLC / Alamy cr 80 NASA Kennedy Space Center (NASA-KSC) cr 81 ©Tomasso DeRosa/Corbis News Agency/Corbis br 83 ©Pixland/Corbis cr 85 ©Gareth Brown/CORBIS cr 86 ©ABN Stock Images/Alamy tc 86 ©Horizon International Images Limited/Alamy br 93 ©Rob Walls/ Alamy 95 ©R H Productions/Robert Harding World Imagery/Corbis bckgd 97 ©Mika/zefa/Corbis br 98-9 ©Neil Rabinowitz/Corbis spread 102 ©Jim Graham/Getty Images bl 105 ©Michael Newman/ PhotoEdit cr 108 © Charles Uhlhorn / SuperStock bl 109 ©Justin Sullivan/Getty Images News/Getty Images cr 110 ©PhotoDisc/Getty Images cr 114 © Jeff Greenberg / Alamy tr 115 © Steve Skjold / Alamy br 120-1 ©Alan Kearney/Botanica/Jupiter Images spread 124 © GeoTrac / Alamy bl 125 ©A. B. Joyce / Photo Researchers, Inc. cr 125 ©Andrew J. Martinez / Photo Researchers, Inc. cr 130 ©Kanwarijit Singh Boparai/Shutterstock, Inc. cr 132 ©2007 The Fresno Metropolitan Museum of Art and Science br 132 ©2007 The Fresno Metropolitan Museum of Art and Science tc 139 ©Martin Plsek/Shutterstock Inc. 139 ©Royalty-free/David De Lossy/Photodisc Green/Getty Images 141 ©Uwe Wieczorek/Botanica/Jupiterimages bckgd 144-5 ©Douglas Johns Studio Inc./StockFood spread 147 © David Cantrille / Alamy tr 148 © foodfolio / Alamy bl 149 © foodfolio / Alamy cr 150 © Visuals Unlimited/Corbis cr 153 ©Thinkstock/ Alamy br 154 © Vic Pigula / Alamy cr 156 ©Volkov Ilya/Shutterstock cr 157 © Kelly-Mooney Photography/Corbis bckgd 157 ©Jamie Rector/Getty Images News/Getty Images tr 158 © Zach Holmes /

Alamy bckgd 159 © John-Francis Bourke/zefa/Corbis br 166-7 ©mcx images/Alamy spread 170 ©Reed Kaestner/CORBIS bl 171 ©Liz Van Steenburgh/Shutterstock cr 172 ©Gibson Stock Photography cr 174 ©Phil Schermeister/CORBIS bl 176 © Corbis cr 178 © Stockbyte Platinum / Alamy br 178 © JLP/Jose Luis Pelaez/zefa/Corbis tr 178 ©Karen Struthers/Shutterstock cr 184-5 ©David Sailors/Corbis bckgd 187 ©DLILLC/Corbis cr 188 © Steve Hamblin / Alamy bl 190 ©Hemera Technologies/Jupiter Images tr 192 © marilyn barbone/ Shutterstock bl 193 © Nina Buesing / Alamy cr 194 © Scott Gibson/ Corbis cr 196 ©Royalty Free/Photodisc Green/Getty Images bl 203 © O'Brien Productions/CORBIS 205 ©Glowimages/Getty Images bckgd 208-9 ©Greg Kuchik/Photodisc/Getty Images spread 212 ©Randy Faris/Corbis bl 216 ©Roger Ressmeyer/CORBIS bl 218 © Richard Cummins/CORBIS cr 219 ©Masterfile (Royalty-Free Div.) bckgd 219 ©Zoomstock/Masterfile tr 220 © Muntz/Taxi/Getty Images br 226-7 ©Steven S. Miric/SuperStock spread 226-7 ©Photosindia/ Getty Images 230 ©Burke/Triolo Productions/Brand X/Corbis c 231 ©Mika/zefa/Corbis cr 235 ©Tom Stewart/CORBIS cr 236 ©Ben Blankenburg/Corbis bl 238 ©Reven T.C. Wurman/Alamy bl 240 ©Profimedia International s.r.o./Alamy bl 241 © BananaStock / Alamy br 249 ©Richard Hamilton Smith/Corbis bckgd 252-3 ©Tony Freeman/PhotoEdit spread 257 © LHB Photo / Alamy bl 260 © IAU/ Martin Kommesser/Handout/epa/Corbis cr 262 © Gary Crabbe / Alamy tc 262 © Mark Downey / Lucid Images/Corbis br 268-9 ©Mark Moffett/Minden Pictures spread 272 ©Royalty-Free/Hola Images/Getty Images br 276 ©Chris Gordon/Getty Images Entertainment/Getty Images bl 277 ©Comstock Premium / Alamy bl 278 ©M Stock / Alamy tr 280 © James L. Amos/CORBIS c 281 ©SHOTFILE/Alamy bckgd 281 ©Robert Michael/Corbis tr 286 © Thinkstock/Corbis bl 287 © Michael Pole/CORBIS cr 292-3 ©Mark Gibson Photography spread 294 © Blend Images / Alamy bl 296 ©David Madison/CORBIS bl 297 © Carol Buchanan / Alamy cr 298 ©Jose Carillo / Photo Edit -- All rights reserved. bl 299 ©James Shaffer / Photo Edit -- All rights reserved. cr 300 © imagebroker / Alamy bl 301 © image100/Corbis cr 302 © David Ashley/Corbis cr 305 © Stefan Schuetz/zefa/Corbis c 306 ©David Young-Wolff/Alamy tr 307 ©Jim Ruymen/REUTERS/Newscom.com br 307 ©Geoff Hardy/ Shutterstock Inc. cr 312-3 ©MIXA/age fotostock spread 316 © Mary Evans Picture Library / Alamy cr 322 © Car Culture/Corbis bl 323 © Rykoff Collection/CORBIS br 326 ©Bettmann/CORBIS tr 328 © Jose Luis Pelaez Inc/Blend Images/Corbis bl 329 © Colorblind/Corbis br 335 Photos courtesy The President's Challenge 337 ©David South/ Alamy bckgd 340-1 ©Buzz Pictures/Alamy spread 343 © Brand X Pictures / Alamy cr 344 © Image Source 7 / Alamy bl 345 © Galen Rowell/CORBIS cr 346 © Image Source/Corbis bl 348 ©Private Collection, Archives Charmet/The Bridgeman Art Library International cl 350 © Dennis O'Clair/Photographer's Choice/Getty Images bl 352 © Stefan Sollfors / Alamy bl 354 ©LOOK Die Bildagentur der Fotografen GmbH / Alamy cr 357 © Design Pics Inc. / Alamy br 362-3 ©MasPix/Alamy spread 367 ©Mike Norton/ Shutterstock cr 368 ©fenix rising/Alamy cr 369 ©Jose Luis Pelaez, Inc./Blend Images/Corbis cr 370 ©Lake County Museum/CORBIS bl 370 ©Lake County Museum/CORBIS bl 370 ©Lake County Museum/ CORBIS cl 371 © Lake County Museum/CORBIS br 372 © Robert

Shantz / Alamy cr **373** © Brand X Pictures / Alamy tr **373** © Design Pics Inc. / Alamy bckgd **373** © Guy Edwardes Photography / Alamy bckgd **376** © Americana Images / SuperStock tc **376** ©Jim Sugar/ CORBIS br **385** ©Miguel Fonseca da Costa/StockFood Muni/ StockFood bckgd **388-9** ©Larry Brownstein/California Stock Photo spread **392** © Craig Steven Thrasher / Alamy br **392** © TongRo Image Stock / Alamy bl **392** © Stuart Westmorland/Corbis cl **394** © Dewitt Jones/CORBIS bl **395** © Pete Saloutos/zefa/Corbis cl **396** ©Stocktrek/ Corbis b **398** © John and Lisa Merrill/Corbis b **399** © Bob Rowan; Progressive Image/CORBIS br **400** © aerialarchives.com / Alamy b **402** ©Bonnie Kamin/PhotoEdit Inc. tc **402** ©xela/Alamy br **408-9** ©Andre Jenny/Alamy spread **410** ©B.S.P.I./Corbis tr **412** © Alex Maclean/Photonica/Getty Images **413** © Rudy Sulgan/Corbis l **413** ©Lawrence Manning/Corbis r **414** © wherrett.com / Alamy tr **416** © Rodolfo Arpia / Alamy **419** © Ei Katsumata / Alamy bckgd **420** ©Tom Shaw/Reportage/Getty Images **423** © Helene Rogers / Alamy cr **428-9** ©Alan Schein/Alamy spread **432** ©Dennis Hallinan / Alamy **436** © Stock Connection Distribution / Alamy **439** © Dennis MacDonald / Alamy b **445** ©Ken Cedeno/Corbis b **446** © Ken Cedeno/Corbis **447** ©Gavin Hellier/Photographer's Choice/Getty Images bckgd **450-1** ©Tom Myers/Corbis spread **453** ©Thomas A. Heinz/CORBIS **454** ©Image Source/Alamy **456** ©Atmoosh/Alamy r **460** ©2006 GlobeXplorer **463** ©Ariel Skelley/Blend Images/Getty Images bckgd **464** ©david sanger photography / Alamy br **470-1** ©Robert Harding Picture Library Ltd/Alamy spread **481** ©White Packert/Photonica/Getty Images **482** ©Tony Freeman/PhotoEdit Inc. **484** © Galen Rowell/CORBIS **485** © Trains and Planes / Alamy **487** © Brand X Pictures / Alamy br **495** ©Bob Elsdale/The Image Bank/ Getty Images bckgd **498-9** ©Alan Thornton/Stone/Getty Images spread **506** ©Ryan McVay/Stone/Getty Images **508** Steve Albano/ Shutterstock **509** ©Martin Poole/The Image Bank/Getty Images **510** © David Fleetham / Alamy **511** ©Ted Pink / Alamy bckgd **512** © Stephen Mallon/The Image Bank/Getty Images bl **513** © Ed Murray/ Star Ledger/Corbis br **518-9** ©WoodyStock/Alamy spread **521** ©Thinkstock/Corbis br **523** Katrina Leigh, 2007 used under license from Shutterstock Inc. c **523** ©Chee-Onn Leong/Shutterstock b **524** ©Royalty Free/Dave Thompson/Life File/Photodisc Green/Getty Images **526** ©Mike McGill/CORBIS **528** ©Joseph Sohm; Visions of America/CORBIS tc **528** ©Ed Young/Corbis br **537** ©David Young-Wolff/Photo Edit bckgd **537** ©BananaStock/SuperStock bckgd **540-1** ©Mark Keller/SuperStock spread **544** ©Visuals Unlimited/ Corbis l **544** © George D. Lepp/CORBIS bckgd **546** © James Marshall/ CORBIS **547** © Steve Bloom Images / Alamy br **552** ©Johanna Goodyear/Shutterstock **553** ©Graham Neden; Ecoscene/CORBIS bckgd **553** ©Graham Neden; Ecoscene/CORBIS cr **554** ©Discovery Science Center tc **554** © Visuals Unlimited/Corbis r **554** ©Discovery Science Center br **560-1** ©Bill Lies/California Stock Photo spread **565** © Chuck Savage/CORBIS cr **566** © Paul Seheult; Eye Ubiquitous/ CORBIS cr **569** © John Block/Brand X/Corbis cr **570** © Len Wilcox / Alamy cr **572** ©Mary-Ella Keith/Alamy bl **573** ©Kevin Schafer/CORBIS b **581** ©Robert Clay/California Stock Photo bckgd **584-5** ©Jerry Schad/Photo Researchers, Inc spread **588** © Macduff Everton/ CORBIS **592** ©G. Savage/Vandistadt/Photo Researchers Inc. cr **595** © Terrance Klassen / Alamy tr **596** ©Phil Schermeister/CORBIS br **596** ©Roger Ressmeyer/CORBIS tc **602-3** ©NASA/Photo Researchers, Inc spread **606** © Worldwide Picture Library / Alamy **608** © David Currier/Shutterstock **613** © Joe McDonald/CORBIS b **613** © Stock Connection / Alamy tr **613** © Ambient Images Inc. / Alamy bckgd

616-7 ©NASA spread **623** ©ImageState/Alamy

ASSIGNMENT PHOTOGRAPHY

i, vi, 4-5 HMCo./ Sharon Hoogstraten Photography. **KSH1** (t) and (tr)Sharon Hoogstraten Photography.

152 cr **502** ©Dave Starrett Photography bl

217 br **239** ©HMCo./Angela Coppola bl

550 ©HMCo./Richard Hutchings br

3 br **28** bl **76** c **111** bl **146** b **168** bl **250** br **254** bl **325** bl **325** tr **325** cl **338** br **339** br **364** br **520** br **571** bl **582** Allan Landau Photography, Chicago Illinois br

2 br **6** bl **18** cr **50** b **51** b **54** cr **96** br **97** br **100** bl **122** bl **129** cr **142** br **143** br **186** bl **206** br **207** br **210** br **228** bl **232** cr **239** bl **251** br **254** tc **254** bc **255** tl **255** cl **270** br **295** br **314** bl **342** br **364** cr **364** bl **386** br **387** br **390** tr **390** cr **390** br **391** tr **391** cl **391** cr **391** tl **401** bl **410** c **410** cr **410** br **430** bl **448** br **449** br **452** br **458** bl **472** b **474** c **496** br **497** br **500** br **522** bl **538** br **539** br **542** bl **562** br **583** br **586** Ray Boudreau Photography b

STOCK PHOTOGRAPHY

KSH1 (tl) ©ThinkStock/SuperStock; (br) Alamy Images.

ILLUSTRATION

60 Joe LeMonnier tr **106** Bart Vallecoccia cr **156** Chris Reed cr **214** Karen Minot cr **220** Malcolm Cullen tr **274** Theresa Sakno cr **280** Marek Jagucki tr **284** Ken Batelman cr **303** Rob Schuster br **324** Bart Vallecoccia c **366** Theresa Sakno cr **400** Joe LeMonnier cr **414** Theresa Sakno cr **422** Ken Batelman tr **437** Karen Minot cr **456** Theresa Sakno c **456** Theresa Sakno cr **462** Bart Vallecoccia cr **563** Bart Vallecoccia bl **589** Andy Levine tr **609** Ken Hansen br